PHILIP'S

COMPACT ATLAS
Britain

Contents

II **Route planning maps** with key to map pages

VIII **Key to road map symbols**

2 **Road maps at 3.3 miles to 1 inch**

289 **Town plans**

289 Aberdeen
Bath

290 Birmingham

291 Bristol

292 Cardiff

293 Cambridge
Coventry

294 Edinburgh

295 Glasgow

296 Gloucester
Leicester

297 Leeds

298 Liverpool

299 London

300 Manchester

301 Newcastle

302 Nottingham
Oxford

303 Sheffield

304 Swansea
York

305 **Index** to road maps of Great Britain

First published in 2006 by
Philip's a division of
Octopus Publishing Group Ltd
2–4 Heron Quays, London E14 4JP

www.philips-maps.co.uk

First edition 2006
First impression 2006

Cartography by Philip's
Copyright © 2006 Philip's

Ordnance Survey®

This product includes mapping data licensed from
Ordnance Survey®, with the permission of the Controller of
Her Majesty's Stationery Office. © Crown copyright 2006.
All rights reserved. Licence number 100011710

Data for the speed cameras provided by PocketGPSWorld.
com Ltd.

Information for Tourist Attractions in England supplied by
the British Tourist Authority / English Tourist Board.

Information for National Parks, Areas of Outstanding
Natural Beauty, National Trails and Country Parks in Wales
supplied by the Countryside Council for Wales.

Information for National Parks, Areas of Outstanding
Natural Beauty, National Trails and Country Parks in
England supplied by the Countryside Agency.

Data for Regional Parks, Long Distance Footpaths and
Country Parks in Scotland provided by Scottish Natural
Heritage.

Gaelic name forms used in the Western Isles provided by
Comhairle nan Eilean.

Data for the National Nature Reserves in England provided
by English Nature.

Data for the National Nature Reserves in Wales provided by
Countryside Council for Wales. Darparwyd data'n ymwneud
â Gwarchodfeydd Natur Cenedlaethol Cymru gan Gyngor
Cefn Gwlad Cymru.

Information on the location of National Nature Reserves in
Scotland was provided by Scottish Natural Heritage.

Data for National Scenic Areas in Scotland provided by
the Scottish Executive Office. Crown copyright material is
reproduced with the permission of the Controller of HMSO
and the Queen's Printer for Scotland. Licence number
C02W0003960.

Cover photograph:
The Malvern Hills from Herefordshire Beacon 79 C5
James Osmond / Alamy

Printed by Toppan, China

About Philip's maps

This atlas contains maps at different scales to get you to your destination as easily and as quickly as possible.

Route planning maps show the whole country at a glance, so you can choose the most direct route, whether on motorways or A-roads. Major road numbers and dual carriageways are all clearly marked.

Road maps at 3.3 miles to 1 inch (Scottish Islands at 6.7 miles to 1 inch) show the road network in detail and mark hundreds of places of interest. The roads are colour coded according to importance. Scenic routes are highlighted and in country areas lanes over 4 metres wide are coloured yellow.

Town plans show the streets in the central area and mark one ways, car parks, stations and important buildings.

Philip's road maps were voted the clearest and most detailed in an independent consumer survey with 442 respondents.

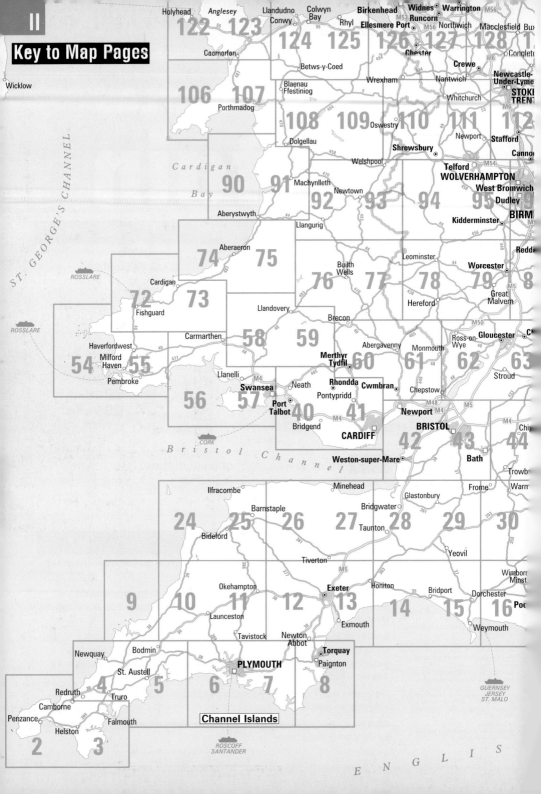

Key to Map Pages

Channel Islands

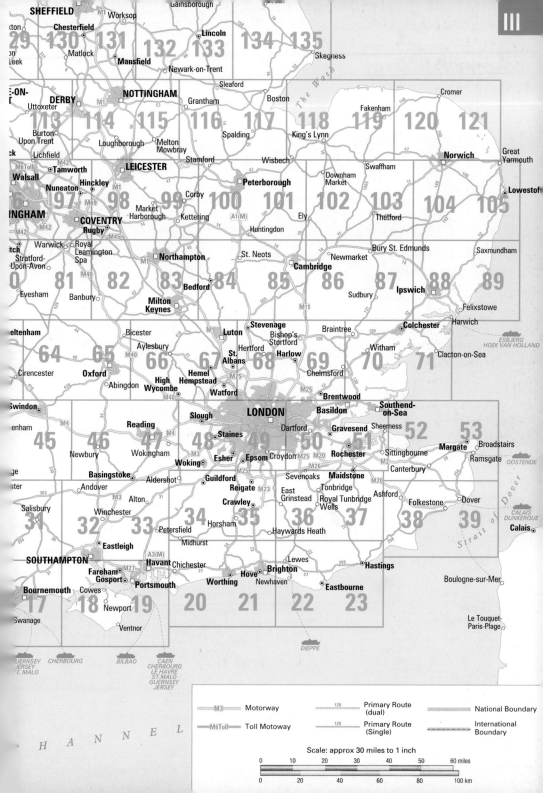

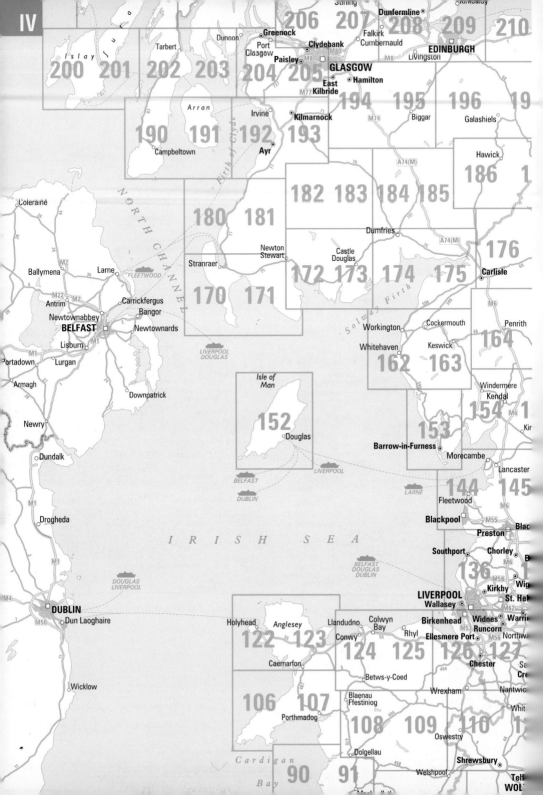

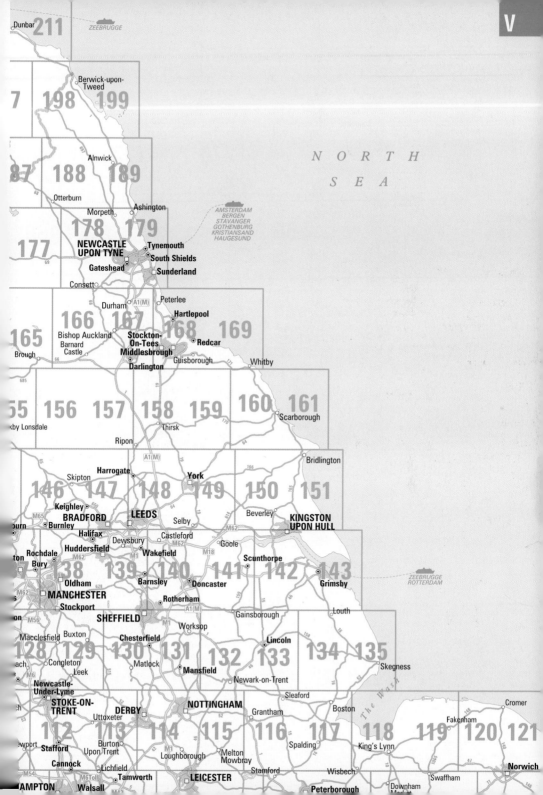

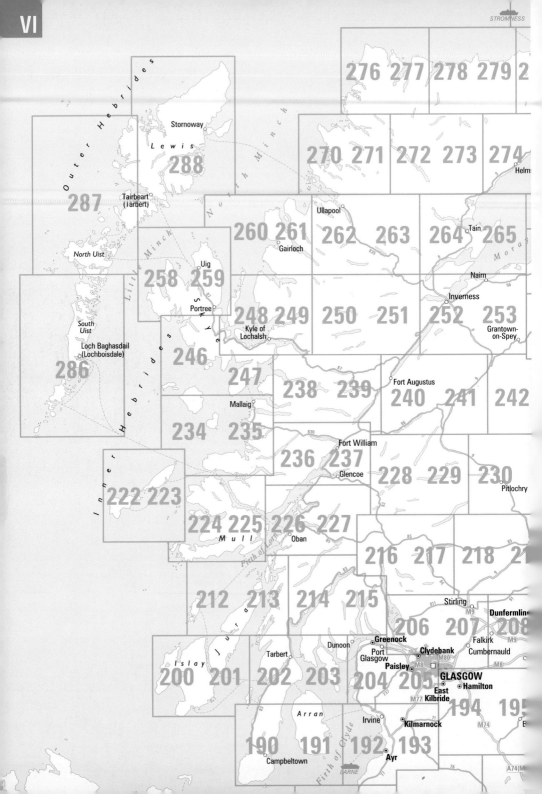

Road map symbols

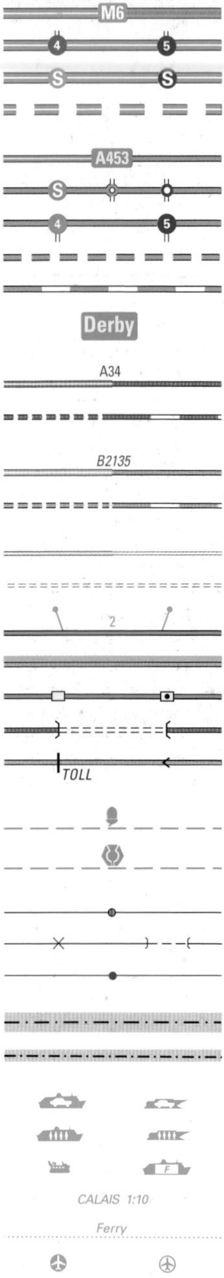

Motorway, toll motorway

Motorway junction – full, restricted access

Motorway service area – full, restricted access

Motorway under construction

Primary route – dual, single carriageway

Service area, roundabout, multi-level junction

Numbered junction – full, restricted access

Primary route under construction

Narrow primary route

Primary destination

Derby

A34

A road – dual, single carriageway

A road under construction, narrow A road

B2135

B road – dual, single carriageway

B road under construction, narrow B road

Minor road – over 4 metres, under 4 metres wide

Minor road with restricted access

Distance in miles

Scenic route

Speed camera – single, multiple

Tunnel

Toll, steep gradient – arrow points downhill

TOLL

National trail – England and Wales

Long distance footpath – Scotland

Railway with station

Level crossing, tunnel

Preserved railway with station

National boundary

County / unitary authority boundary

Car ferry, catamaran

Passenger ferry, catamaran

Hovercraft, freight ferry

CALAIS 1:10

Ferry

Ferry destination, journey time – hrs : mins

Car ferry – river crossing

Principal airport, other airport

Relief

	Feet	metres
	3000	914
	2600	792
	2200	671
	1800	549
	1400	427
	1000	305
	0	0

Speed Cameras

Fixed camera locations are shown using the ▢ symbol.

In congested areas the ▣ symbol is used to show that there are two or more cameras on the road indicated.

Due to the restrictions of scale the camera locations are only approximate and cannot indicate the operating direction of the camera. Mobile camera sites, and cameras located on roads not included on the mapping are not shown. Where two or more cameras are shown on the same road, drivers are warned that this may indicate that a SPEC system is in operation. These cameras use the time taken to drive between the two camera positions to calculate the speed of the vehicle.

Road map symbols

National park

Area of Outstanding Natural Beauty – England and Wales **National Scenic Area** – Scotland
forest park / regional park / national forest

Woodland

Beach

Linear antiquity

Roman road

⚔ 1066   Hillfort, battlefield – with date

▲ 795   Viewpoint, nature reserve, spot height – in metres

Golf course, youth hostel, sporting venue

Camp site, caravan site, camping and caravan site

P&R   Shopping village, park and ride

29 Adjoining page number – road maps

Road map scale 1 : 212 857 or 3·36 miles to 1 inch

| 0 | 1 | 2 | 3 | 4 | 5 | 6 | 7 | 8 | 9 | 10 miles |

| 0 | 1 | 2 | 3 | 4 | 5 | 6 | 7 | 8 | 9 | 10 | 11 | 12 | 13 | 14 | 15 | 16km |

Town plan symbols

Motorway

Primary route – dual, single carriageway

A road – dual, single carriageway

B road – dual, single carriageway

Minor through road

one-way street

Pedestrian roads

Shopping streets

Railway with station

City Hall Tramway with station

Bus or railway station building

Shopping precinct or retail park

Park

Building of public interest

Theatre, cinema

Parking, shopmobility

Bank Underground station

West St Metro station

H Hospital, Police station

PO Post office

Tourist information

✝ Abbey, cathedral or priory

🏛 Ancient monument

🐟 Aquarium

🖼 Art gallery

🐦 Bird collection or aviary

🏰 Castle

⛪ Church

Country park
England and Wales
Scotland

🐎 Farm park

❀ Garden

⚓ Historic ship

🏠 House

🏡 House and garden

Motor racing circuit

🏛 Museum

Ⓐ Picnic area

🚂 Preserved railway

🏇 Race course

🐎 Roman antiquity

Ⓥ Safari park

🌳 Theme park

Tourist information
i centre open all year
i open seasonally

🐘 Zoo

✦ Other place of interest

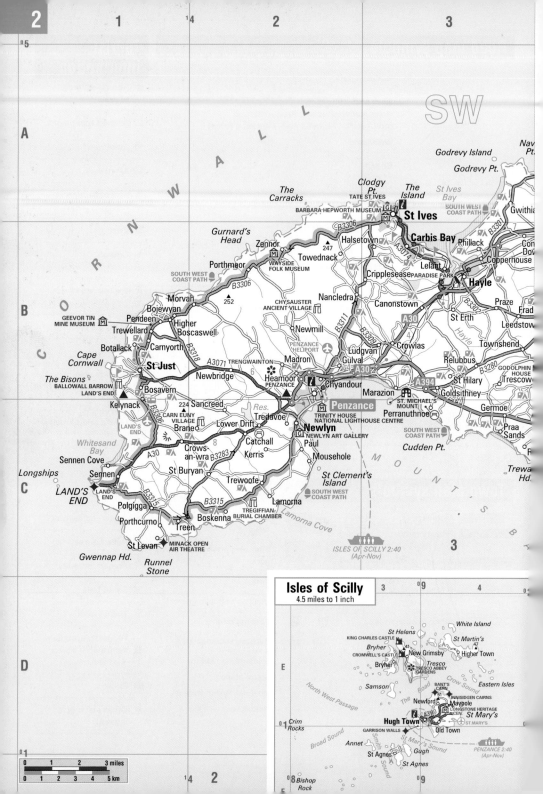

SW

CORNWALL

A

Nav
Pt.

Godrevy Island

Godrevy Pt.

The Carracks

Clodgy Pt.

The Island

St Ives Bay

SOUTH WEST COAST PATH

Gwithia

TATE ST IVES

BARBARA HEPWORTH MUSEUM

St Ives

Carbis Bay

Phillack

Con Dov

B3301

Gurnard's Head

Zennor

247

Halsetown

Towednack

Copperhouse

WAYSIDE FOLK MUSEUM

Cripplesease

Lelant

Hayle

Porthmeor

SOUTH WEST COAST PATH

B3306

PARADISE PARK

Praze

Frad

252

CHYSAUSTER ANCIENT VILLAGE

Nancledra

Canonstown

St Erth

B

Morvah

Bojewyan

Leedstow

GEEVOR TIN MINE MUSEUM

Pendeen

Higher Boscaswell

Newmill

B3311

A30

Townshend

Trewellard

PENZANCE HELIPORT

Crowlas

Carnyorth

TRENGWAINTON

Ludgvan

Gulval

Relubbus

Cape Cornwall

St Just

A3071

Madron

GODOLPHIN HOUSE

Trescow

Botallack

Newbridge

Heamoor PENZANCE

St Hilary

The Bisons

BALLOWALL BARROW LAND'S END

Bosavern

Chyandour

Marazion

Goldsithney

Germoe

Kelynack

224 Sancreed

CARN EUNY VILLAGE

Brane

Tredavoe

Lower Drift

Penzance

TRINITY HOUSE NATIONAL LIGHTHOUSE CENTRE

ST. MICHAEL'S MOUNT

Perranuthnoe

Praa Sands

LAND'S END

Whitesand Bay

Catchall

Kerris

Newlyn

Paul

NEWLYN ART GALLERY

Mousehole

Cudden Pt.

Trewa Hd.

Sennen Cove

Crows-an-wra

B3283

St Clement's Island

Longships

Sennen

St Buryan

Trewoofe

SOUTH WEST COAST PATH

C

LAND'S END

Polgigga

B3315

Lamorna

MOUNT'S BA

Porthcurno

Treen

Boskenna

TREGIFFIAN BURIAL CHAMBER

Lamorna Cove

St Levan

MINACK OPEN AIR THEATRE

ISLES OF SCILLY 2:40 (Apr-Nov)

Gwennap Hd.

Runnel Stone

3

0 1 2 3 miles
0 1 2 3 4 5 km

Isles of Scilly
4.5 miles to 1 inch

3   9   4

White Island

St Helens

St Martin's

KING CHARLES CASTLE

Bryher

Higher Town

CROMWELL'S CASTLE

New Grimsby

Bryher

Tresco

TRESCO ABBEY GARDENS

Eastern Isles

E

Samson

BANT'S CARN

Crow Sound

North West Passage

The Road

Newford

INNISIDGEN CAIRNS

Maypole

LONGSTONE HERITAGE CEN

St Mary's

Crim Rocks

Hugh Town

GARRISON WALLS

Old Town

ST. MARY'S

Broad Sound

Annet

St Agnes

Gugh

St Agnes

St Mary's Sound

Smith Sound

PENZANCE 2:40 (Apr-Nov)

D

Bishop Rock

4 **5** 20 **6**

A

SR SS

10

SW SX

B

Fire Beacon
Pt. B

BOSCASTLE
HARBOUR

Bos

Trevalga

CASTLE
Tintagel Hd.
OLD POST OFFICE   Bossiney
TINTAGEL   Tintagel
Treknow   308
Trewarmett
B3263
Start Pt.   Trebarwith

CORNWALL

B3314   B3

C

SOUTH WEST
COAST PATH   Treligga   Delabole
C   Valley Truckle

Port Isaac
Bay   Helstone

Port
Isaac   B3267
Port Quin   Port Gaverne   St Teath
Bay   Port Quin   B3267   Treveighan
Pentire Pt.   Pendoggett
New Polzeath   LONG CROSS   A39
Padstow   Trelights   St Endellion   Michaelstow
Gulland Rock   Bay   Polzeath   St Br
Trebetherick   Trelill   10   Row
Gunver Hd.   St Minver   Trewethern   St Tudy   St Br
Crugmeer   Pityme   St Kew   10
TREVOSE HEAD   PRIDEAUX   Chapel   St Kew
Constantine   PLACE   Rock   Amble   Highway   We Dordbrid
TREYARNON BAY   Trevone   B3314
D   Bay   Constantine   St   Camel   St Mabyn   Blis
Treyarnon   Bay   Merryn   Padstow   Bodieve   PENCARROW   Helland
SOUTH WEST   Shop   Trevanson   HOUSE
COAST PATH   Little   Wadebridge   Camel
Porthcothan   Petherick   Whitecross   St   Egloshayle   A389
B3276   Breock   Burlawn
Park Hd.   Penrose   St   A389   6
Ervan   Rumford   Tredinnick   A39   Washaway   Bodmin
4   St Jidgey   Forest   A30
RARE BREEDS   CREALY GREAT   5 REOCK DOWNS   5   Care
CENTRE   ADVENTURE   MONOLITH   20
St Eval   PARK

A

Woodbridge

King's Stag
Fifehead N'ville
Okeford Fitzpaine
Shillingstone
Hambledon Hill
Gunville
Tarrant Hinton
Gussage St Michael

Kingston
Hazelbury Bryan
Ibberton
Okeford
Turnworth
Stourpaine
Pimperne
Tarrant Launooton
Tarrant Monkton
ROYAL SIGNALS MUSEUM
Long Crichel
Moor Crichel
Manswood

Pulham
Woolland
Durweston
Bryanston
Blandford Forum
Tarrant Rushton
Tarrant Keyneston
Witchampton

Duntish
Westfields
Stoke Wake
274
Blandford St Mary
Tarrant Crawford
Shapwick
Kingston Lacy
Pamphill

Mappowder
Higher Ansty
Winterborne Houghton
Winterborne Stickland
Charlton Marshall
Spetisbury
B3082
Honeybrook Victor

Melcombe Bingham
261
Hilton
Winterborne Clenston
Thorncombe
Charlton Down
Sturminster Marshall

D o r s e t

Plush
MILTON ABBEY
Whatcombe
Milton Abbas
Almer
A31
Corfe Mullen
Eas

Piddletrenthide
Cheselbourne
Winterborne Whitechurch
Winterborne Zelston
B3075
Hill View

White Lackington
Dewlish
Winterborne Kingston
Anderson
Morden
Lytchett Matravers
Upton

Piddlehinton
Milborne St Andrew
Bloxworth
East Morden
Slepe
Lytchett Minster

B

B3142
MARTYRS MUSEUM
A35
109
Turners Puddle
FARMER PALMER'S FARM PARK
Holton Heath
Hamworthy

Puddletown
Tolpuddle
Bere Regis
Wareham Forest
MORDEN BOG
Sandford

Athelhampton
Burleston
Affpuddle
Briants Puddle
Lane End
Trigon Hill

HARDY'S COTTAGE GARDEN
Tincleton
Woodsford
88
Moreton
Bovington Camp
Northport
Wareham
Arne

Stinsford
Kingston Maurward
CLOUD'S HILL
TANK MUSEUM
MONKEY WORLD
Stokeford
Stoborough
Ridge
PURBECK TOY MUS.

THE DINOSAUR MUSEUM
West Stafford
East Burton
Wool
Stoborough Green
STOBOROUGH HEATH
HARTLAND MOOR

Whitcombe
Crossways
MILL HOUSE CIDER MUSEUM
East Stoke
West Holme
Grange Heath
Middlebere Heath
Wytch Heath

C

Winterborne Herringston
West Knighton
Warmwell
Coombe Keynes
THE BLUE POOL
Norden Heath

Broadmayne
Owermoigne
Winfrith Newburgh
LULWORTH CASTLE
East Creech
CASTLE
Church Knowle

Poxwell
Holworth
Chaldon Herring or East Chaldon
East Lulworth
Steeple
PURBECK HILLS
Corfe Castle
MODEL VILLAGE & GARDENS

Preston
Upton
Chaldon Down
SOUTH WEST COAST PATH
West Lulworth
199
Kingston
Harr Cross

Osmington
Osmington Mills
Ringstead Bay
LULWORTH COVE
Tyneham
Kimmeridge
LANGTON MATRAVERS MUS.

Weymouth
Durdle Door
Lulworth Cove
Worbarrow Bay
Kimmeridge Bay
203
Acton
Worth Matraver

D

WEYMOUTH BAY

ortuneswell
Grove
130
GUERNSEY 2:00
JERSEY 3:15
ST. MALO 5:00

Easton
ISLE OF
PORTLAND
MUSEUM

SY

St Alban's Head

0   1   2   3 miles
0   1   2   3   4   5 km

2   3

St Giles

Cripplestyle
EDMONDSHAM HO.
Edmondsham

Charing
Cross

Hungerford

Broomy
Lodge

Stoney Cross

Minstead

N 6 E W

North Gorley

KNOWLTON
CHURCH

Gussage
All Saints

HEAVY HORSE
CENTRE

South Gorley

Newtown

31

Ibsley

Mockbeggar

F O R E S T

Knowlton

Verwood

Woodlands

A338

Linwood

10

Emery Down

Horton

Ringwood

Moyles Court

A31

Chalbury

B3081

Forest

Rockford

REPTILIARY

Ly

Chalbury Common

Mannington

Blashford

Linford

Burley
Lodge

Bank

Hinton
Martell

Three Legged
Cross

MOORS
VALLEY

Ashley

Picket
Post

Burley Street

New Park

Gaunt's
Common

Ashley
Heath

Ringwood

Moortown

BURLEY

A

Stanbridge

Holt

St Ives

Burley

Bisterne
Close

Stabridge

HOLT
HEATH

St Leonards
ST LEONARDS
SERVICES

B3347

RAPTOR AND
REPTILE CENTRE

Broom Hill

West
Moors

Kingston

KINGSTON
GREAT COMMON

12

Brockenhurst

Clapgate

6

Colehill

Canford
Bottom

A31

St
Leonards

St HEATH

18

butts

WALFORD MILL

Stapehill

Trickett's Cross

THE MATCHAMS
EXPERIENCE

A338

Sway

Wimborne
Minster

KNOLL GDNS.

Ferndown

BOURNEMOUTH
INTERNATIONAL

Avon

Thorney
Hill

Wootton

Hampreston

West
Parley

Ripley

B3058

Longham

B3073

Bransgore

Marley
Mount

Mount
Pleasant

Oakley

Canford
Magna

A348

Parley
Cross

Hurn

Sopley

A35

Bashley

B3055

Buckla

End

Merley

A341

Bearwood

Ensbury

ALICE IN
WONDERLAND
MAZE

Neacroft

Winton

Godwinscroft

Golden
Hill

Hordle

LYMINGT

Broadstone

Bear
Cross

Kinson

Holdenhurst

Jumpers
Green

Burton

Hinton

New
Milton

Ashley

Everton

A337

Lym

Canford
Heath

B o u r n e m o u t h

A3049

Moordown

A35

Walkford

SAMMY MILLER'S
MOTORCYCLE MUS

Old Milton

Downton

Waterloo

A341

Talbot
Village

Winton

THE RED HOUSE
MUSEUM

Somerford

Highcliffe

Poole

A35

Newtown

Branksome

A338

Pokesdown

CHRISTCHURCH

Barton
on Sea

Milford
on Sea

Parkstone

Westbourne

Branksome
Park

Boscombe

ART GALL. AND MUS.

B3059

Wick

PRIORY
CHURCH

Mudeford

Purewell

Poole

Lilliput

Bournemouth

Southbourne

Christchurch Bay

Poole Harbour

COMPTON ACRES

Canford Cliffs

Hengistbury
Head

BROWNSEA
ISLAND

rownsea

Sandbanks

P O O L E   B A Y

Totland B
TOTLAND

Ferry
TOLL

SZ

Alum Bay

The Needles

Newton
Heath

STUDLAND BEACH
AND NATURE RESERVE

Studland

Bay

Studland

STUDLAND AND
GODLINGSTON HEATH

The Foreland
SOUTH WEST
COAST PATH

199

Ulwell

New Swanage

Swanage
SWANAGE RAILWAY

Swanage Bay

ngton
ravers

M

Peveril Pt.
SWANAGE

18

125
DURLSTON

Durlston Head

Tilly Whim
Caves

GUERNSEY 2:30
JERSEY 3:45   (Apr-Oct)
ST. MALO 5:25
CHERBOURG 2:15 (May-Sept)

CHERBOURG 4:15

D

0 7

4   5   2   6

North West Point
North East Point

LUNDY MARINE
NATURE RESERVE

LUNDY

142

ILFRACOMBE 2:15
BIDEFORD 2:15
CLOVELLY 1:30

South West Point

Surf Point

LUNDY 1:30

BIDEFO

N O R T H

HARTLAND POINT

Windbury Pt.

Titchberry

SS

Hartland Quay

Stoke

B3248

CLOVELLY VILLAGE

Clovelly

Hartland

Higher Clovelly

Philham

SOUTH WEST
COAST PATH

Milford

THE MILKY WAY AND
NORTH DEVON
BIRD OF PREY CENTR

ELMSCOTT

Eddistone

Elmscott

Tosberry

Woolfardisworthy

South Hole

Hartland Forest

Alm

Knaps Longpeak

Welcombe

235

Meddon

Wes

Woolley

Gooseham

156

Eastcott

Youlstone

Dinworthy

Higher Sharpnose Pt.

Morwenstow

Shop

A39

KILLARNEY SPRINGS
FAMILY LEISURE PARK

Lower Sharpnose Pt.

Woodford

BROCKLANDS
ADVENTURE
PARK

14

Bradworthy Cross

Bradwo

Coombe

Kilkhampton

Alfardisworthy

Soldon Cross

Stibb

10

DUNSDON

Hols

0   1   2   3 miles
0 1 2 3 4 5 km

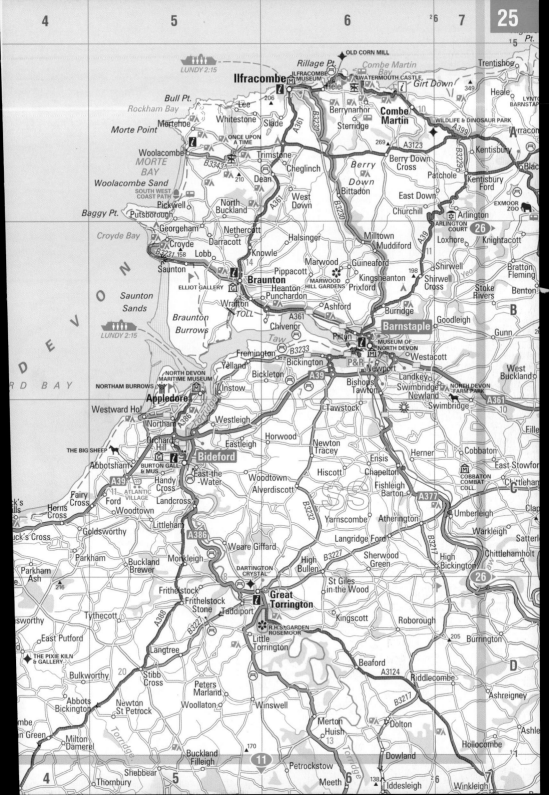

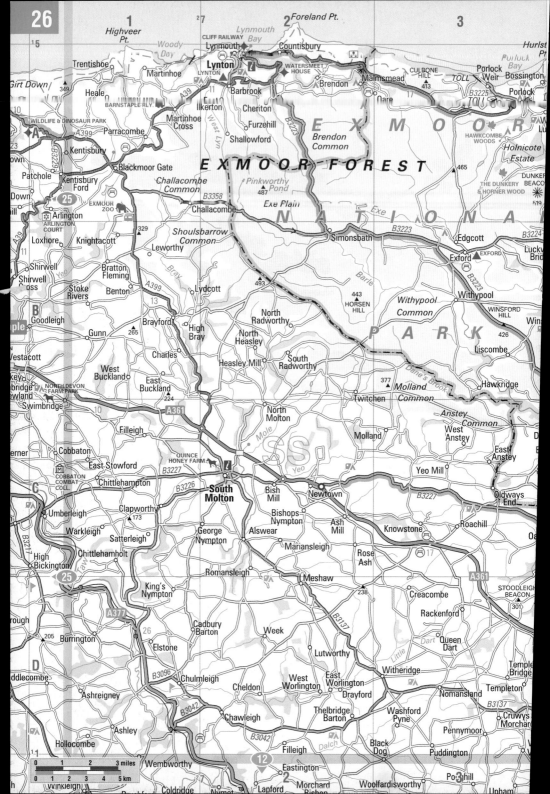

71

A

TR

B

THE SHELL GROTTO

Foreness Pt.

Cliftonville   Kingsgate

Margate   DREAMLAND   B2052   **NORTH**

Westgate on Sea   MARGATE   Northdown   **FORELAND**

RECULVER TOWERS
AND ROMAN FORT   *Minnis Bay*   LIGHTHOUSE

Reculver   Birchington   **St Peter's**

Hillborough   QUEX PARK   *Isle of Thanet*   **BROADSTAIRS**

A299   A28   Acol   SPITFIRE AND   Northwood   BLEAK HOUSE

omfield   St Nicholas   HURRICANE MEM.   DICKENS HOUSE MUSEUM

at Wade   A299   B2190   Manston   Dumpton

Boyden   Sarre   WINDMILL   A253   KENT   Newington   RAMSGATE BOULEVARD

Gate   Monkton   INTERNATIONAL   Way   **Ramsgate**

oath   Chislet   **Minster**   Cliffsend   Pegwell   MARITIME MUSEUM

pstreet   *Stour*   PEGWELL   MOTOR   MUSEUM

A28   West Stourmouth   BAY   SANDWICH &   *OOSTENDE 4:00*

re   Grove   East Stourmouth   ST. AUGUSTINE'S   PEGWELL BAY

STODMARSH   Westmarsh   CROSS   *Pegwell*

Preston   Ware   RICHBOROUGH   A256   *Bay*

Stodmarsh   Elmstone   Hoaden   CASTLE

mbreux   AMPHITHEATRE   Great Stonar   *Sandwich*

WINGHAM   A257   *Bay*

Ickham   BIRD PARK   **Sandwich**

ourne   Littlebourne   Wingham   Guilton   **Ash**   TOLL   ROYAL ST. GEORGE'S

Bramling   Staple   Marshborough   Stone Cross

Goodnestone   Gore   Woodnesborough   Worth

disham   GOODNESTONE PARK   **Eastry**   Ham   Finglesham

Aylesham   Knowlton   MARITIME AND

Chillenden   Betteshanger   Sholden   LOCAL HISTORY MUSEUM

Nonington   Easole Street   Northbourne   **DEAL**

Snowdown   Tilmanstone   DEAL CASTLE   *THE*

Womenswold   Elvington   Great   *DOWNS*

Barfreston   Mongeham   **Walmer**

EAST KENT   WALMER CASTLE

Woolage   RLY   East   Sutton   AND GARDENS

Green   **Eythorne**   Studdal   West   Ringwould   **Kingsdown**

C

D

1 ¹6 2 3 4

A

PEMBROKESHIRE
COAST
ARFORDIR PENFRO

Ynysduellyn

Penclegyr
Porthgain
Trefi

Abereiddy
Llanrhian
Croes-goch

²3

ST. DAVID'S
HEAD
PENMAEN DEWI

Tretio
Carnhedryn
Treffynnon
Treglemais

181 Treleddyd-
fawr

ST. DAVID'S
Rhodiad
Caerfarchell

BISHOP'S PALACE
A487

Whitchurch
Middle Mill

B

Rhosson

CATHEDRAL
St David's
(Tyddewi)
Nine
Wells

PENYC

Ramsey
Island
Ynys Dewi

RAMSEY
ISLAND

Ramsey Sound

Solva

4.

ST. BRIDES

C

SM

BAY

BAE SAIN FFRAID

PEMBROKES
COAST
LLWYBR ARFO
PE

BRO

Broa

Little H

Talbenny

Tower Point
Trwyn Twr

St Bride's

Wooltack Point
Trwyn Wooltack

GRASSHOLM
ISLAND

NATIONAL
NATURE RESERVE
79

Marloes

B4327
Hasgu

Skomer
Island
Ynys Skomer

SKOMER
ISLAND

MARLOES
SANDS

St
Ishmael's
Sa
Ha

Broad Sound

D

Gateholm
Island
Ynys Gateholm

Dale

MILFOR
ABERDA

Skokholm
Island
Ynys Skokholm

71

PEMBROKESHIRE

St Ann's Hd.
Pentir St. Ann

Sheep
Island
Ynys y Defaid

ROSSLARE 3:45

²0

PEN

E

| 0 | 1 | 2 | 3 miles |
| 0 | 1 | 2 | 3 | 4 | 5 km |

2 ¹7 3 4

Llandissilio
Hiraeth
Henllan Amgoed
Llanfallteg
Clunderwen
Bethesda
A40
Llanddewi Velfrey
145
Crinow
Lampeter Velfrey
Cold Blow
Princes Gate
Tavernspite
Ludchurch
Llanteg
Stepaside
Colby Woodland Garden
Amroth
Saundersfoot
Broadfield
New Hedges
Tudor Merchant's House
Tenby
(Dinbych-y-Pysgod)
Penally
Gumfreston
Giltar Pt.
Caldey Sound
Caldey Island
Ynys Bŷr
Chapel Pt.
Trwyn Capel

Cwmfelin Boeth
Whitland
Trevaughan
Llwyn-y-brain
Llanddowror
Red Roses
Marros
152
Pendine
Llangynin
Grovelands
10
Backe
Afon Taf
Halfpenny Furze
178
Llandawko
Llansadurnen
Brook
Museum of Speed
Pendine Sands
Traeth Pentywyn

Meidrim
B4298
Sarnau
Bancyfelin
St Clears
(Sanclêr)
A40
A4066
Afon Cywyn
Dylan Thomas Boathouse
Laugharne
Broadway
East Marsh
9

Dyffryn
Tre-vaughan
LOVESPOON GALLERY
Merthyr
Carmarthen
(Caerfyrddin)
CORS GOCH, LLANLLWCH
Llanllwch
Johns
Llangynog
153
Llangain
Morfa Bach
Afon Tywi
Llanybri
Llansteffan
CASTLE
Ferryside
Broadlay
Llansaint
Llanddо

Pembrey Forest
PEMBI

PEMBROKESHIRE COAST ARFORDIR PENFRO

CARMARTHEN

SN

BAY
BAE CAERFYRDDIN

SS

Burn
Holm

Rhos
B
Bae Rhos

Worms Head
Penrhyn-Gŵyr

Bosherston
Williamston
Hill
Kilgetty
Begelly
Thomas Chapel
Reynalton
Folly Farm
Loveston
New Moat

C

D

0   1   2   3 miles
0 1 2 3 4 5 km

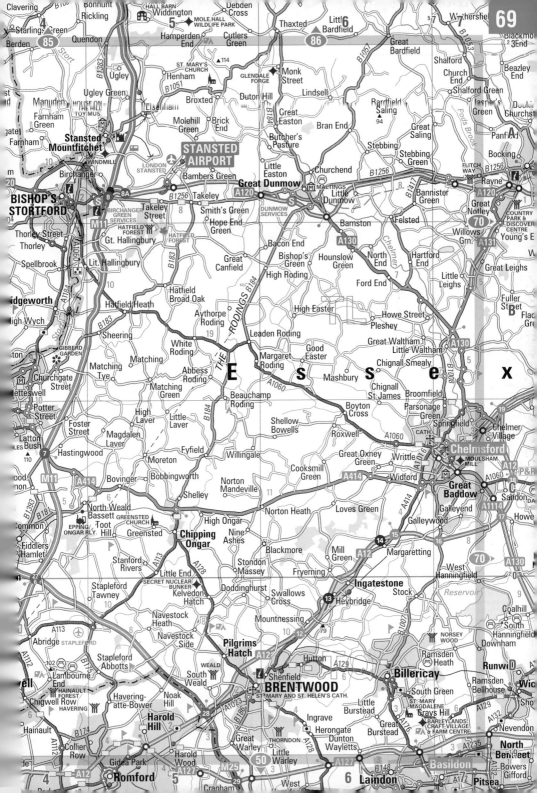

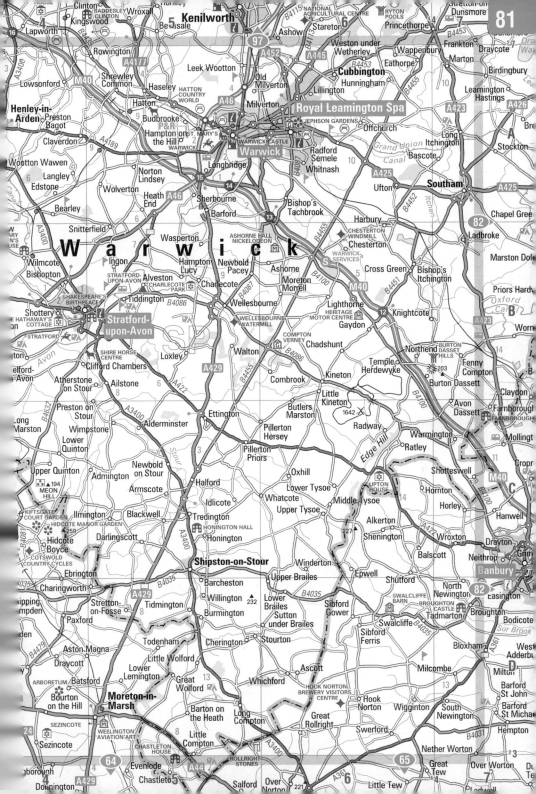

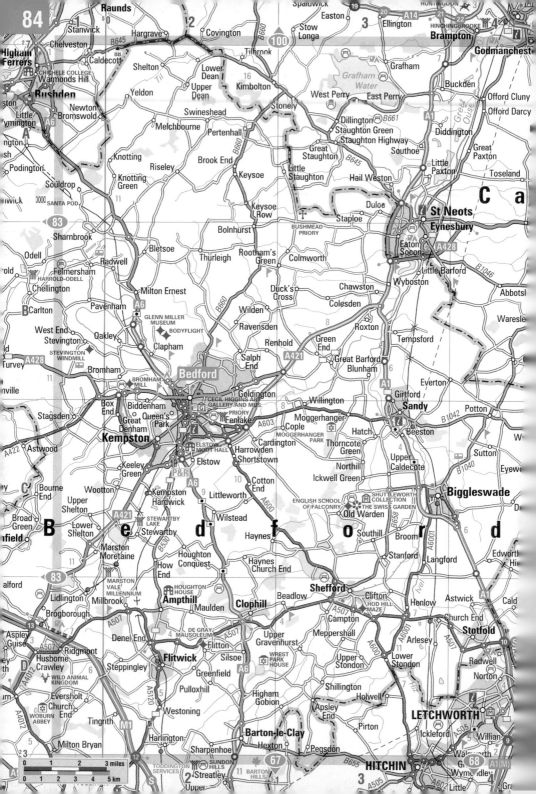

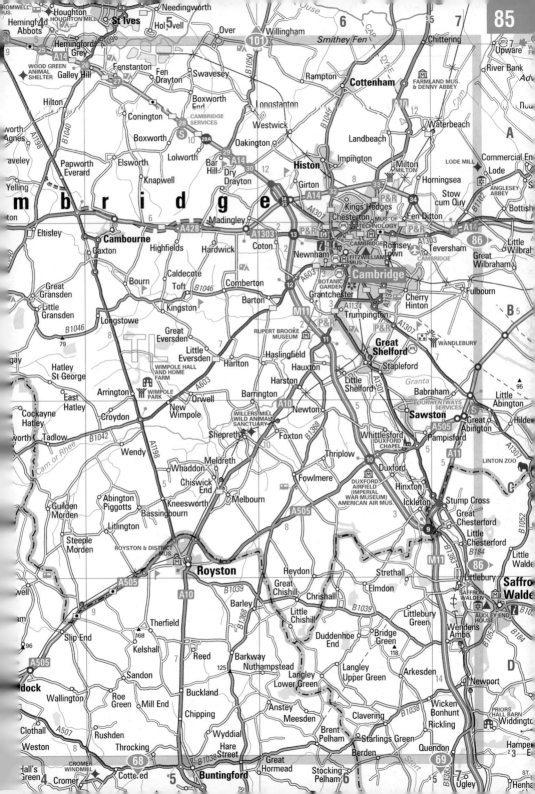

ham
Sibton
Green
High Street
Hemp
Green
Sibton
Yoxford
Rotten End
A12
Curlew
Green
ndham
Kelsale
ffling
Saxmundham
Benhall
Street
Sternfield
Benhall Green
Friston
Farnham
Gromford
Darsham
Middleton
Moor
North Green
Theberton
B1122
B1121
Carlton
B1119
Knodishall
Coldfair
Green
B1121
A1094
Middleton
Westleton
Dunwich
Forest
**DUNWICH UNDERWATER
EXPLORATION EXHIBITION**
Dunwich (105)
WESTLETON
HEATH

MINSMERE RSPB
NATURE RESERVE

Eastbridge
**LEISTON
ABBEY**
B1121
Leiston
Sizewell
Aldringham
B1069
B1353
Thorpeness
B1122
Snape
**SNAPE MALTINGS
RIVERSIDE CENTRE**
Blaxhall
B1069
Tunstall
*Tunstall
Forest*
Chillesford
utley
B1078
Sudbourne
High
Street
Iken
Alde
Aldeburgh
Aldeburgh Bay

NORTH WARREN RSPB
NATURE RESERVE

Sizewell

Butley High
Corner
B1084
**ORFORD
CASTLE**
Orford
Orford Ness
ORFORDNESS-
HAVERGATE
Andrew
Boyton
Stores
Corner
*Hollesley
Bay*
lesley
Shingle Street
sey

TM

A

B

C

D

ESBJERG 20:00
HOEK VAN HOLLAND 6:00

HOEK VAN HOLLAND 3:40

GOTHENBURG 38:30
ROTTERDAM 8:00

²3

SH

A

Llandanwg
Tal-y-bont
Llanbedr
Caerdeon
Llanaber
Cutiau

Barmouth
(Abermaw)
RNLI LIFEBOAT MUSEUM
Arthog
BARMOUTH BAY   The Bar
Yoysga
FAIRBOURNE & BARMOUTH
STEAM RAILWAY
BAE BERMO   Fairbourne
Friog
20

SNOWD
NATIO
PAR
Llwyngwril

B

Llangelynin
Rhoslefain   Llanegryn   Peniarth
Llanfendigaid
309
Tonfanau
Bryncrug   Pandy
Rhyd-yr-onen
TALYLLYN RAILWAY
Tywyn

Caethle

C A R D I G A N

276
Aberdovey   A493

C

B A Y   Aberdovey Bar
Bae Aberdyfi
DYFI
Ynyslas   B4353
Llancynfelyn
B A E   BORTH

Borth
C E R E D I G I O N   Upper Borth   Tal-
Dôl-y-Bo

Llandre
Pen-y-garn

D   SN   ARTS CENTRE   Bow
NATIONAL   Stree
LIBRARY   Clarach
CLIFF RAILWAY   148   Plas
Aberystwyth   A4
Comins
P&R   Coch
Llanbadarn-Fawr
CASTLE
Trefechan   Glanrafon
Southgate   Moriah
Penparcau
Rhydyfelin   Capel
Seion

0   1   2   3 miles
0   1   2   3   4   5 km

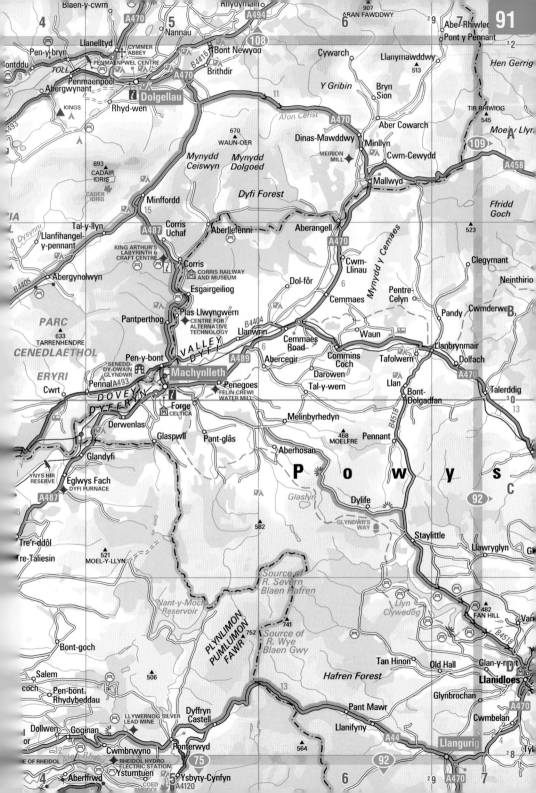

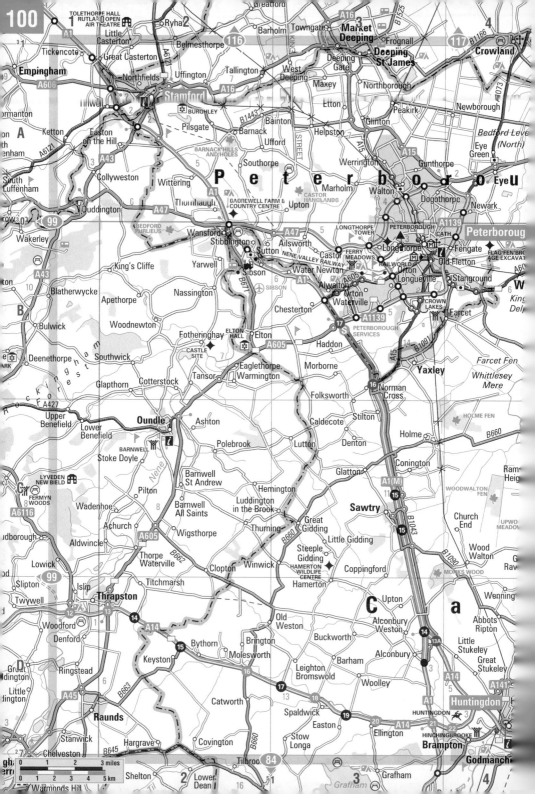

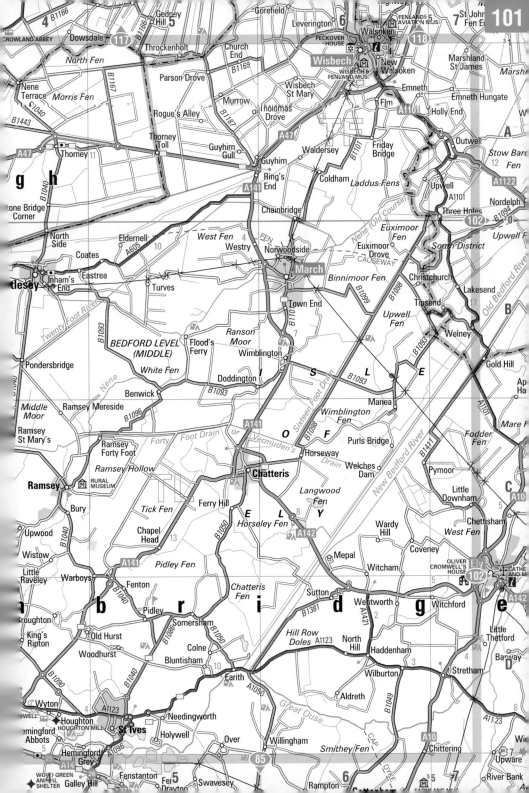

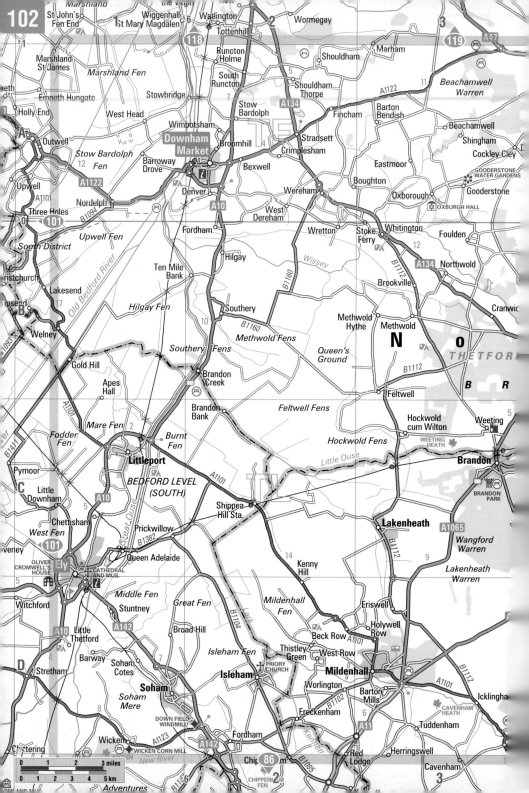

1 ²2 **2** **3**

³6

A

C A E R N A R F O N

B A Y

B A E

C A E R N A R F O N

Clyr

Gyrn-g

Bryn-yr-eryr

Ynys Llanddwyn

Ta

B

SH

564
YR EIFL

Trefor

Lla

B4417

6

Llithfaen

Llwyndyrys

Carreg Ddu

Porth
Dinllaen

Pistyll

Fron

Rhos-fawr

B435

A499

Morfa Nefyn

Nefyn

LLEYN HISTORICAL
MARITIME MUSEUM

Edern

Tan-y-
graig

Porth Ysgadan

B4417

Glanrhyd

CORS
GEIRCH

Boduan

A497

BODVEL HALL
ADVENTURE PARK

Llannor

Efailnewydd

Rhos-y-llan

Tudweiliog

Dinas

LLŶN

Rhyd-y-
clafdy

Denio

Pwllh

C

Porth Golmon

14

Bryn-mawr

Garnfadryn

Llaniestyn

B4415

Penrhos

7

South Be

Pen-y-graig

PENRHYN

Llangwnnadl

Sarn
Meyllteyrn

Rhedyn

Llanbedrog

Penrhyn Mawr

Ty-hen

Pen-y-
groeslon

Bryncroes

Botwnnog

Nanhoron

B4413

Mynytho

Trwyn Llanbedrog

Methlem

Rhydlios

Llandegwning

Llawr
Dref

A499

St Tudwal's
Road

Angorfa St Tudwal

Capel Carmel

Rhoshirwaun

B4413

304
MYNYDD
RHIW

PLAS-YN-
RHIW

Llangian

Abersoch

St Tudwal's Island Ea
Ynys St Tudwal Dwyra

191

Rhiw

Llanengan

Sarn
Bach

Marchroes

St Tudwal's Island West
Ynys St Tudwal Gorllew

Uwchmynydd

Aberdaron

Llanfaelrhys

Porth Neigwl or
Hell's Mouth

Bwlchtocyn

D

Bodermid

Pen-y-cil

Cilan Uchaf

Trwyn Cilan

N

Bardsey Sound
Swnt Enlli

³2

YNYS ENLLI

167

Bardsey
Island
Ynys Enlli

L L Ê Y N

L L E Y N

0   1   2   3 miles
0 1 2 3 4 5 km

²2 **2** **3**

122

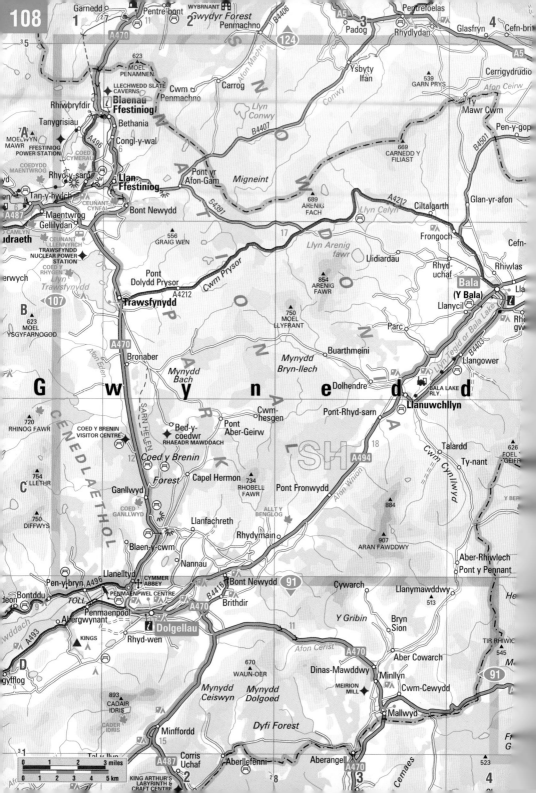

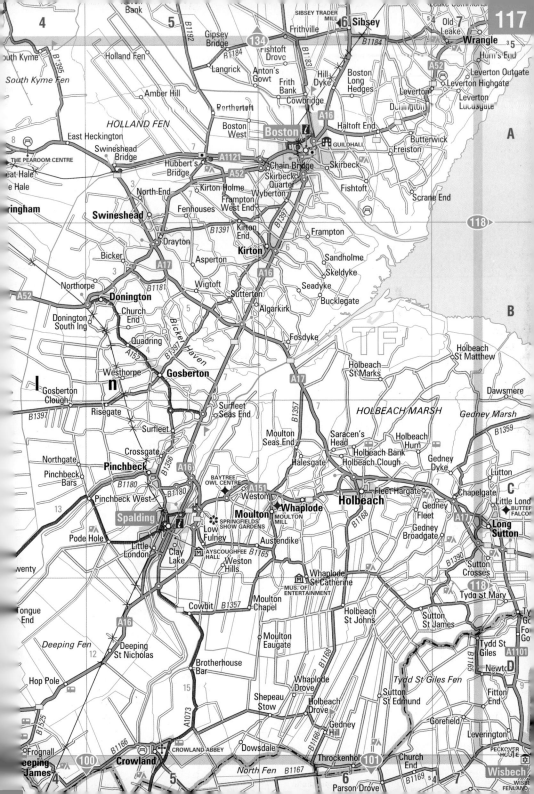

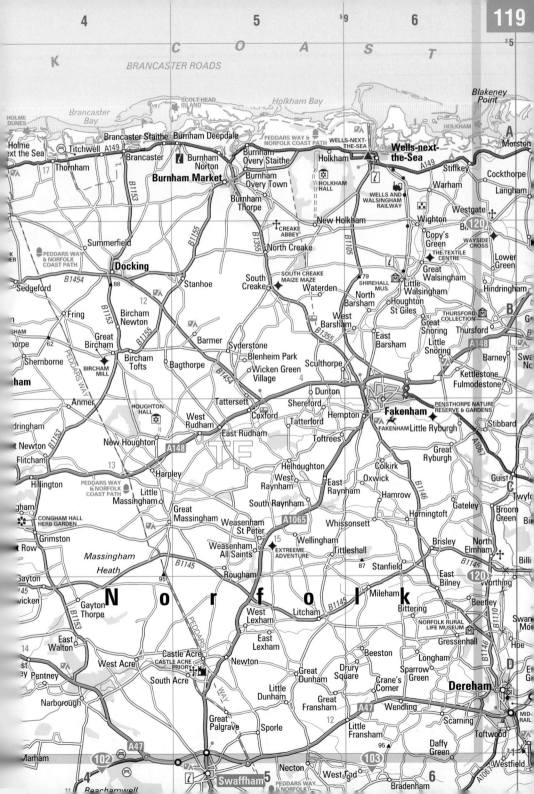

K C O A S T

BRANCASTER ROADS

Blakeney
Point

Brancaster
Bay

SCOLT HEAD
ISLAND

Holkham Bay

HOLME
DUNES

HOLKHAM

Morston

Holme
next the Sea

Titchwell A149

Brancaster Staithe

Burnham Deepdale

PEDDARS WAY &
NORFOLK COAST PATH

WELLS-NEXT-
THE-SEA

Wells-next-
the-Sea

Stiffkey

Cockthorpe

Thornham

Brancaster

Burnham
Norton

Burnham
Overy Staithe

Holkham

A149

Warham

Langham

Burnham Market

Burnham
Overy Town

HOLKHAM
HALL

Westgate

Burnham
Thorpe

WELLS AND
WALSINGHAM
RAILWAY

Wighton

120

Summerfield

CREAKE
ABBEY

New Holkham

Copy's
Green

WAYSIDE
CROSS

Lower
Green

Sedgeford

Docking

Stanhoe

North Creake

THE TEXTILE
CENTRE

SOUTH CREAKE
MAIZE MAZE

South
Creake

Waterden

Great
Walsingham

Hindringham

Fring

Bircham
Newton

12

Barmer

West
Barsham

North
Barsham

SHIREHALL
MUS.

Little
Walsingham

Houghton
St Giles

Great
Snoring

THURSFORD
COLLECTION

Thursford

Barney

Shernborne

Great
Bircham

BIRCHAM
MILL

Bircham
Tofts

Bagthorpe

Syderstone

Blenheim Park

Wicken Green
Village

Sculthorpe

East
Barsham

Little
Snoring

A148

Kettlestone

Fulmodestone

Anmer

HOUGHTON
HALL

West
Rudham

Coxford

Tattersett

Dunton

Shereford

Tatterford

Hempton

Fakenham

PENSTHORPE NATURE
RESERVE & GARDENS

Stibbard

New Houghton

A148

East Rudham

Toftrees

FAKENHAM

Little Ryburgh

Great
Ryburgh

Guist

Harpley

13

Helhoughton

West
Raynham

East
Raynham

Colkirk

Oxwick

Hamrow

Horningtoft

Gateley

Broom
Green

Hillington

PEDDARS WAY
& NORFOLK
COAST PATH

Little
Massingham

Great
Massingham

Weasenham
St Peter

South Raynham

A1065

Wellingham

Whissonsett

Tittleshall

Brisley

North
Elmham

CONGHAM HALL
HERB GARDEN

Weasenham
All Saints

15

EXTREEME
ADVENTURE

120

Worthing

Grimston

Massingham
Heath

B1145

Rougham

87

Stanfield

East
Bilney

Beetley

Gayton
Thorpe

95

Litcham

Mileham

Bittering

NORFOLK RURAL
LIFE MUSEUM

Gressenhall

Longham

Hoe

East
Walton

West
Lexham

East
Lexham

Beeston

Sparrow
Green

Dereham

West Acre

CASTLE ACRE
PRIORY

Castle Acre

Newton

Great
Dunham

Drury
Square

Crane's
Corner

MID-
RAIL

South Acre

Little
Dunham

Great
Fransham

Wendling

Scarning

Narborough

Great
Palgrave

Sporle

A47

12

Little
Fransham

Toftwood

A47

102

Swaffham

103

PEDDARS WAY
& NORFOLK

Necton

West End

95

Daffy
Green

Westfield

Bradenham

A1067

Norfolk

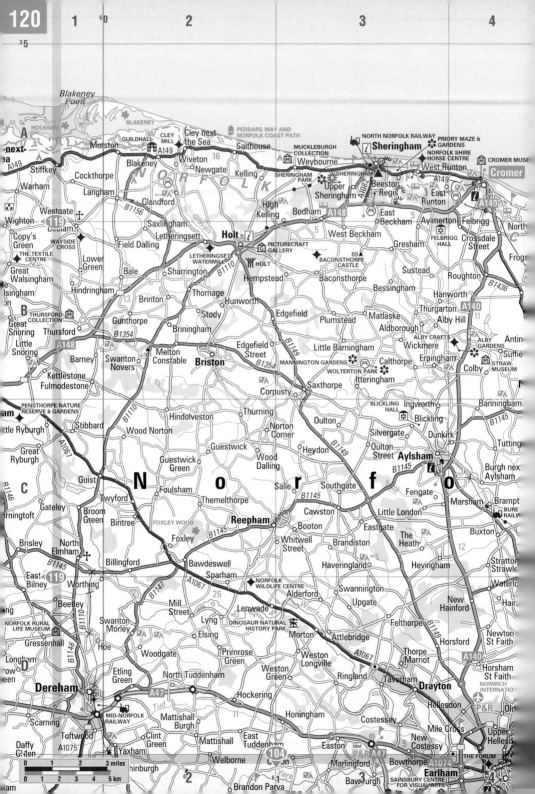

A

B

TG

C

D

rerstrand
Sidestrand
Trimingham
Southrepps
Gimingham
Mundesley
STOW MILL
Lower Street
Trunch
Paston
Knapton
Bacton
Bradfield
Broomholm
Keswick
Swafield
Edingthorpe
Walcott
Walsham
Edingthorpe Green
Spa Common
Witton Bridge
Ridlington
Happisburgh
Crostwight
Whimpwell Green
imingham
Happisburgh Common
Eccles on Sea
EAST RUSTON GARDEN
Lessingham
Hempstead
stwick
Bengate
Honing
East Ruston
Ingham Corner
Sea Palling
Worstead
WAXHAM BARN
Waxham
ton
A149
Dilham
Ingham
Sloley
Smallburgh
Stalham
Stalham Green
K
Scottow
Pennygate
MUSEUM OF THE BROADS
Hickling
utbois
Tunstead
Barton Turf
Wood Street
Sutton
Hickling Green
Sco Ruston
Neatishead
ANT BROADS AND MARSHES
Catfield
Hickling Heath
Horsey
Coltishall
WROXHAM BARNS
Ashmanhaugh
RA, BOAT TRIP
Barton Broad
Irstead
Hickling Broad
HORSEY WINDMILL
WINTERTON DUNES
HICKLING BROAD
MARTHAM BROAD
East Somerton
Belaugh
Threehammer Common
Sharp Street
Potter Heigham
West Somerton
Winterton-on-Sea
rostwick
Hoveton
Wroxham
OWINGS HORSE NCTUARY
Upper Street
Lower Street
Ludham
Bastwick
Martham
th kheath
Horning
Upper Street
Thurne
Repps
Rollesby
Hemsby
Newport
Wroxham Broad
Woodbastwick
BURE MARSHES
Ranworth
Clippesby
Ormesby St Michael
Scratby
California
wston pe End
Salhouse
B1140
Panxworth
South Walsham
FAIRHAVEN GARDEN TRUST
Billockby
Filby Broad
Ormesby St Margaret
A1064
CAISTER ROMAN TOWN
New Rackheath
Thorpe St Andrew
Little Plumstead
Hemblington
North Burlingham
Upton
THE CANDLEMAKER WORKSHOP
Burgh St Margaret
Thrigby
THRIGBY HALL WILDLIFE GARDENS
Filby
Mautby
West Caister
Caister-on-Sea
Great Plumstead
Blofield Heath
Acle
Runham
Stokesby
West End
NORTH DENES
YARMOUTH
Brundall
Lingwood
Beighton
Tunstall
Damgate
Bure
Great Yarmouth
Blofield
105
A47
A47
6
Runham
VICH
P&R

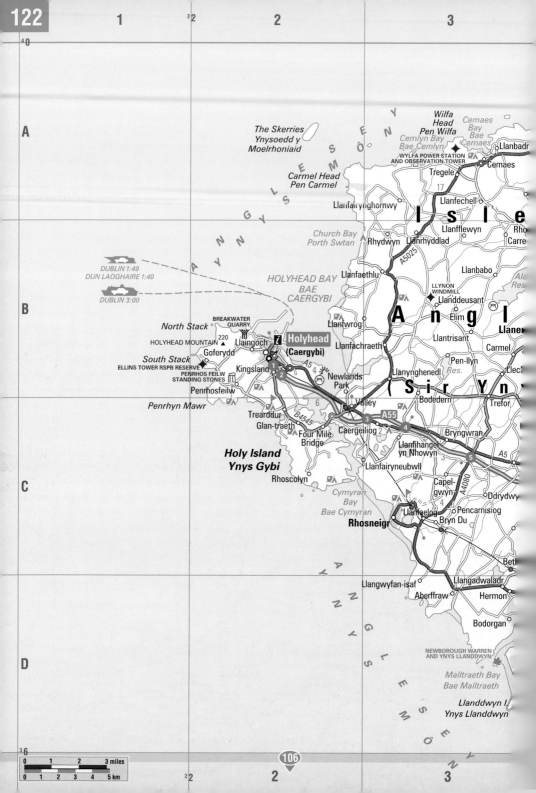

A

The Skerries
Ynysoedd y
Moelrhoniaid

Carmel Head
Pen Carmel

Wilfa
Head
Pen Wilfa

Cemaes
Bay
Bae
Cemaes

Cemlyn Bay
Bae Cemlyn

Llanbad

WYLFA POWER STATION
AND OBSERVATION TOWER

Cemaes

Tregele

17

Llanfechell

Llanfflewyn

Rho
Carre

Llanfairynghornwy

B

A N G L E S E Y   M Ô N

Church Bay
Porth Swtan

Rhydwyn

Llanrhyddlad

DUBLIN 1:49
DUN LAOGHAIRE 1:40

DUBLIN 3:00

A5025

HOLYHEAD BAY
BAE
CAERGYBI

Llanfaethlu

Llanbabo

LLYNON
WINDMILL

Al
Res

BREAKWATER
QUARRY

North Stack

220

Llaingoch

Holyhead
(Caergybi)

Llanfwrog

Llanddeusant

Elim

Isle

A n g l

Llane

HOLYHEAD MOUNTAIN

Goferydd

Llanfachraeth

Llantrisant

Carmel

South Stack

Kingsland

A5

Newlands
Park

Llanynghenedl

Pen-llyn
Res.

Llec

ELLINS TOWER RSPB RESERVE
PENRHOS FEILW
STANDING STONES

Penrhosfeilw

6

Valley

Bodedern

(S i r   Y n

Penrhyn Mawr

Trearddur

B4545

Glan-traeth

Four Mile
Bridge

3

A55

Caergeiliog

2

4

Bryngwran

Trefor

A5

Holy Island
Ynys Gybi

Rhoscolyn

Cymyran
Bay
Bae Cymyran

Llanfihangel
yn Nhowyn

Llanfairyneubwll

3

Capel-
gwyn

5

A4080

Ddrydwy

C

Llanfaelog

4

Pencarnisiog

Rhosneigr

Bryn Du

Bet

Llangwyfan-isaf

Aberffraw

Llangadwaladr

Hermon

Bodorgan

NEWBOROUGH WARREN
AND YNYS LLANDDWYN

D

Malltraeth Bay
Bae Malltraeth

Llanddwyn I.
Ynys Llanddwyn

0   1   2   3 miles
0 1 2 3 4 5 km

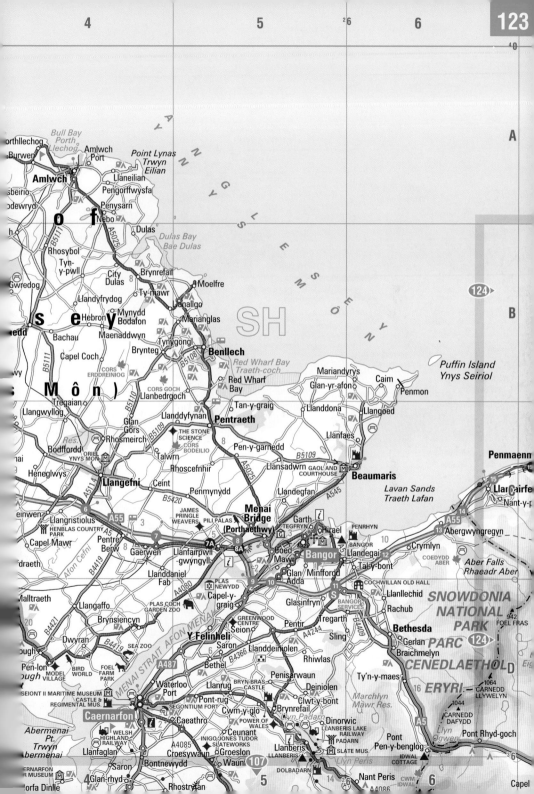

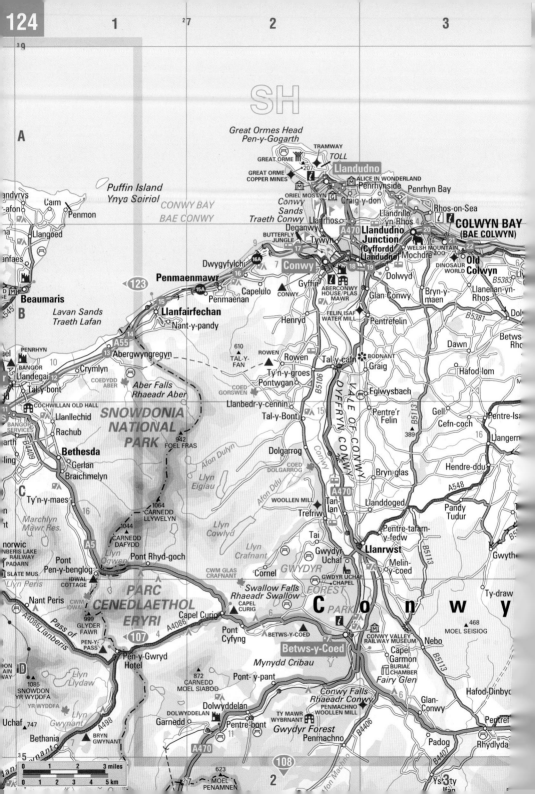

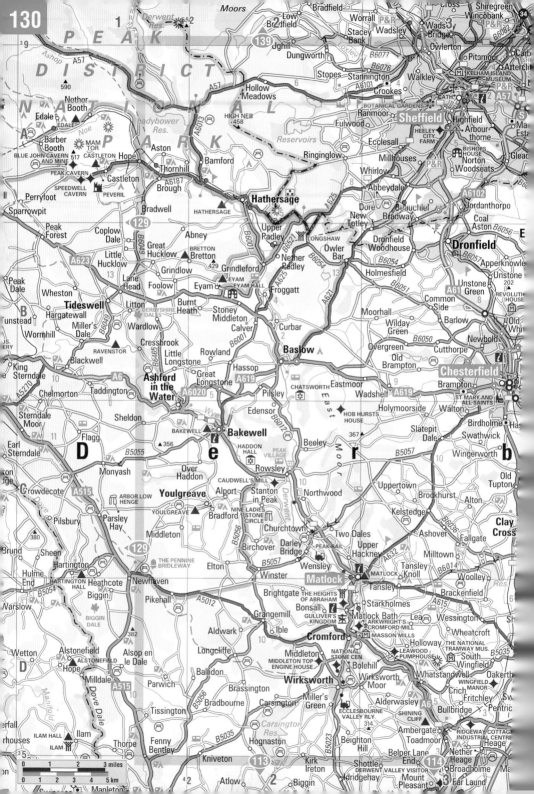

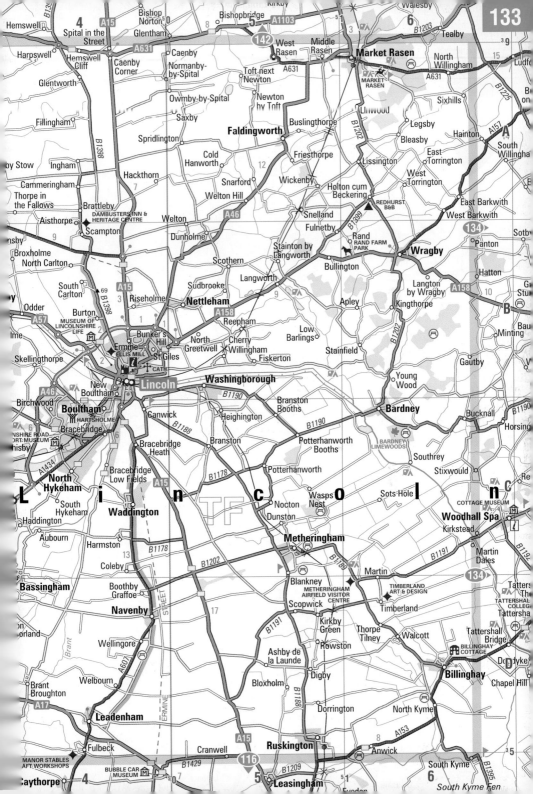

4 Elstronwick
Burton Pidsea
Tunstall
5 5 4 **6** 3

North End
Roos 151
Waxholme
B1242
Rimswell
Owthorne
Withernsea

Burstwick
B1362
Halsham
East End

Keyingham
Ottringham
Hollym

Winestead A1033
5

Welwick
6
Weeton

Patrington
B1445

Holmpton

Out Newton

Sunk Island
Skeffling
Easington

TA
B

Kilnsea

ROTTERDAM 12:30
ZEEBRUGGE 12:45

SPURN

ROTTERDAM
ZEEBRUGGE

SPURN HEAD

F
HOEK VAN HOLLAND 13:00
OOSTENDE 15:00

ingham
A180
Healing
Pyewipe

Grimsby

West Marsh
A180

MOUTH OF THE HUMBER

Great Coates

Old Clee
CLEETHORPES

F
BREVIK 33:00
CUXHAVEN 22:00
ESBJERG 22:00
GOTHENBURG 26:00
KRISTIANSAND 30:00
ROTTERDAM 11:45
ZEEBRUGGE 14:00

C

NATIONAL FISHING HERITAGE CENTRE

Freshney
Nunsthorpe
A46

CLEETHORPES COAST LIGHT RAILWAY

PLEASURE ISLAND THEME PARK
CLEETHORPES

Bradley
Scartho A1098

Humberston

rth East
B1219

New Waltham

Waltham
WALTHAM WINDMILL
Barnoldby le Beck

A16

Holton le Clay

A18
ncolnshire
B1203
Brigsley
Ashby cum Fenby
Waithe

A1031
Tetney Lock
North Cotes

Beelsby
Hatcliffe

Grainsby
Tetney

4

East Ravendale
10
B1201
Marshchapel
Donna Nook
TF

Eskham
Wragholme

North Thoresby
Fulstow
Grainthorpe

25
North Somercotes
DONNA NOOK

Wold Newton
A16
LINCOLNSHIRE WOLDS RLY
Covenham St Bartholomew
Conisholme
Skidbrooke North End
A1031
D

Ludborough
Covenham St Mary
South Somercotes
Skidbrooke
Saltfleet

Binbrook
C
North Ormsby
o
Utterby
Yarburgh
l
n

5
Fotherby
Little Grimsby
ALVINGHAM POTTERY AND CRAFTS
Alvingham
North Cockerington
Saltfleetby St Clements
SALTFLEET THEDDLET

Great Tows
Kelstern
North Elkington
RUSHMOOR
Saltfleetby All Saints
Theddlethorpe St Helen

DS
A631
134
South Elkington
A16
5
South Cockerington
Keddington
135
Saltfleetby St Peter
6
3

4
Welton
Grimoldby
B1200

1 | **2** | **3** | **4**

A590 | Bow Bridge | Baycliff
Hawcoat | Gleaston Watermill
Roosgill | Newto Furness Abbey | 87
Barrow-in-Furness | Dendron | Newbarns | aston | Aldingham
North Scalo | Yarlside | Newbiggin
THE DOCK MUSEUM | CUSTOM HO.
Vickerstown | Barrow Island | Leece
Roosebeck

A590
A5087
A5087

MORECAMBE

154

He

A

153 | Biggar
Roa Island | Rampside
South End | Piel Island
Isle of Walney | Foulney Island

BAY

Morecambe

Sandylands
White Lund
Heysham | La

A589
A683

South End Point
South Channel

B

DOUGLAS 3:30

DOUGLAS 2:00
(Summer Only)

BELFAST 9:00
DUBLIN 9:00
Shoulder of Lune

Sunderland Pt.
Lune
Middleto
Ov
Glasson
Th

LARNE 8:00

Cockerham Sands

Braides

19

Dam Side
Pilling Lane | Pilling
Stake Pool

Knott End-on-Sea
Fleetwood
Rossall Point | B5270
Preesall
FREEPORT FLEETWOOD
A588

Eagland Hill

C

Wyre
Stalmine
MARSH MILL-IN-WYRE | Staynall
Cleveleys | Trunnah | WYRE ESTUARY
Anchorsholme | **Thornton** | **Hambleton**
Norbreck
A584 | A587 | Out Rawcliffe | Moss E
Bispham | Skippool | Ratt
Warbreck | Carleton | Little Singleton | Little Eccleston | TOLL
A586 | Great Eccles
Blackpool | **Poulton-le-Fylde** | Singleton | Elswick
North Shore | Normoss | B52
Queenstown | B5266 | Thistleton
Blackpool | Layton | Staining | B5260 | Esprick
BLACKPOOL TOWER | ZOO PARK | **L** | Corner Row
SEA LIFE CENTRE | Great Marton | Weeton | **a**
LOUIS TUSSAUD'S WAXWORKS | A585 | **M55**
CYBERDOME CRYSTAL MAZE | Mereside | Great Plumpton | 3 | Wesham
Hawes Side | Little Plumpton | A583 | **Kirkh**
South Shore | Common Edge | Westby
BLACKPOOL PLEASURE BEACH | Squires Gate | Moss Side | **Wrea Green** | New
Higher Ballam | B5259

D

Blackpool

TOY AND TEDDY BEAR MUSEUM | 136
ROYAL LYTHAM | HAM
B ST ANNE'S | sdell Hall | Fl
Annes | 3 | A584 | Warton
Lytham St Anne's

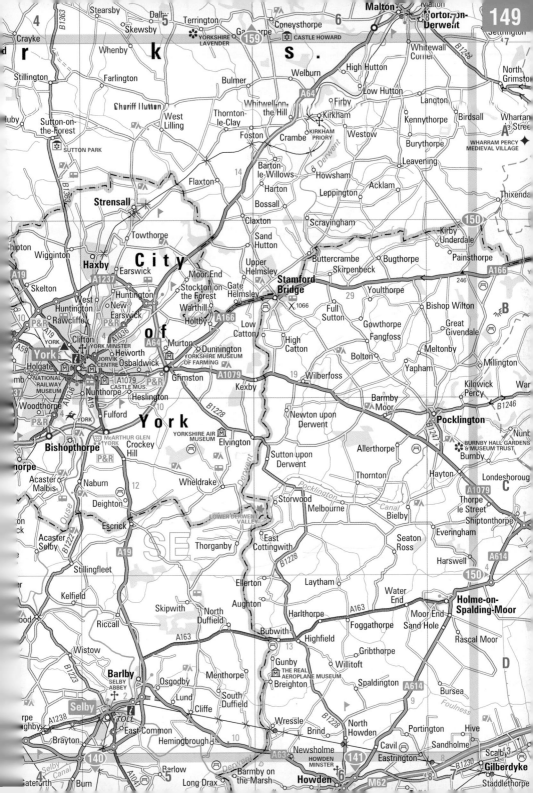

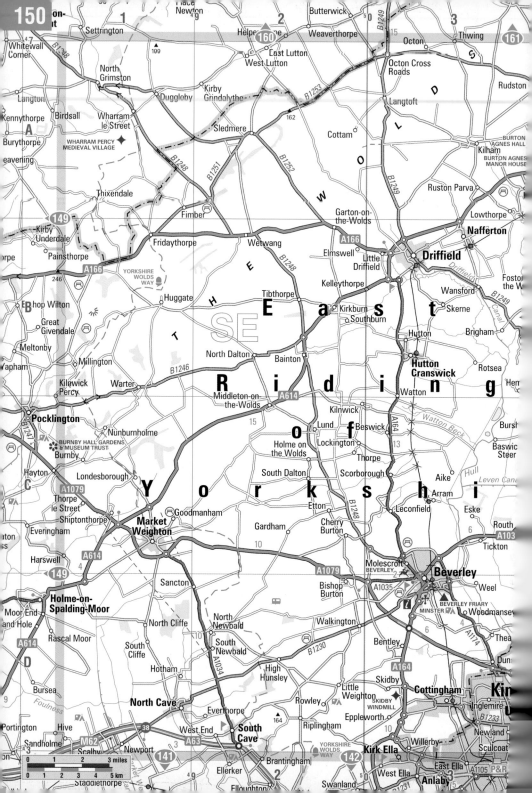

Grindale
A165
4
Flamborough
5
B1255
B1259
FLAMBOROUGH HEAD
161
6

Boynton
PRIORY
BAYLE MUSEUM
SEWERBY HALL AND GARDENS
Sewerby
BONDVILLE MODEL VILLAGE

1253
Bessingby
Carnaby
Bridlington
West Hill
OLD PENNY MEMORIES
A

Haisthorpe
holme
A614
Hilderthorpe
BRIDLINGTON BAY

Burton Agnes
PARK ROSE POTTERY AND LEISURE PARK

Fraisthorpe

Gransmoor
Barmston

reat Kelk
Lissett
14
Ulrome
A165
TA
B

Gembling
16
SKIPSEA CASTLE
EY
FARM
B1249
Skipsea
Beeford
Skipsea Brough

dingham
Dunnington
B1242
Atwick

Bewholme
North Cliff

Brandesburton
Hornsea
HORNSEA MUSEUM
FREEPORT HORNSEA
Seaton
Hornsea Bridge
B1244
Hornsea Mere
Rolston
C

Catwick
e
Sigglesthorne
Goxhill
Mappleton
Little Hatfield
A165
Rise
Great Hatfield
Great Cowden

Riston
B1243
Arnold
Withernwick

ux
New Ellerby
Skirlaugh
Marton
West Newton
Aldbrough
B1242
East Newton
17

Old Ellerby
BURTON CONSTABLE HALL
Flinton
Garton
Grimston
D
13
Swine
Coniston
Hilston

ransholme
Sutton on Hull
Thirtleby
Sproatley
Humbleton
Fitling
Sutton Ings
Ganstead
neferry
B1238
Lelley
Owstwick
Tunstall
A165
Bilton
B1240
Elstronwick
WILBERFORCE HOUSE
B1239
Preston
Burton Pidsea
Roos
North End
Summergangs
West End
142
P&R
143
Waxholme
Marfleet
A1033
Saltend
Owthorne
STREETLIFE
4
Hedon
5
B1362
Rimswell
6
Withernsea

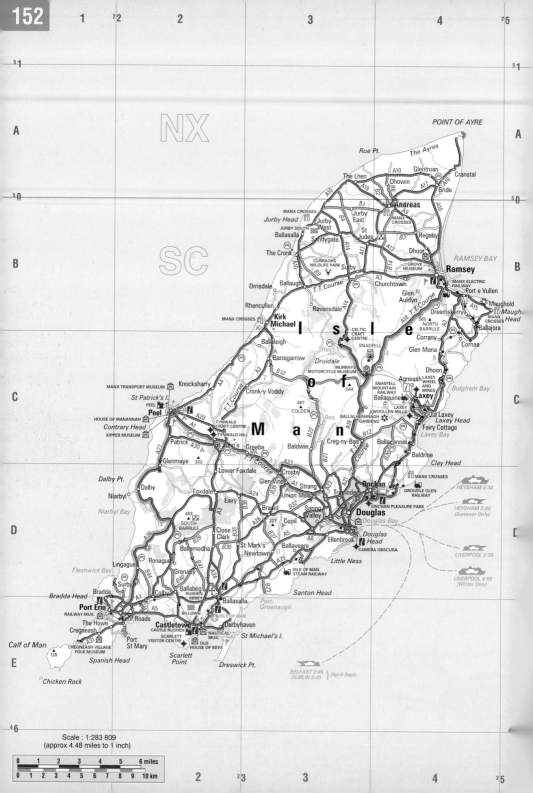

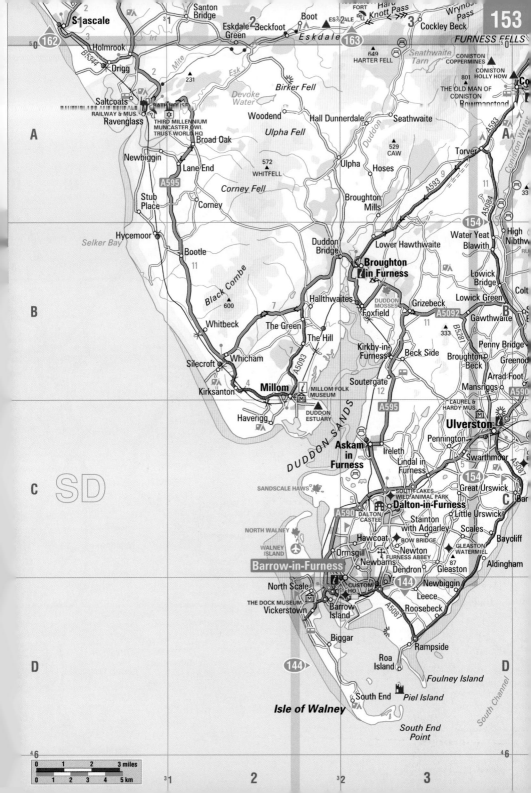

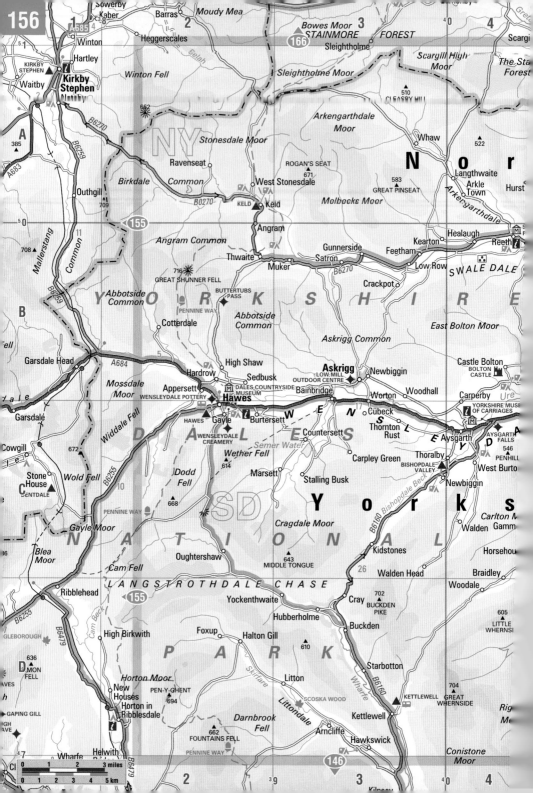

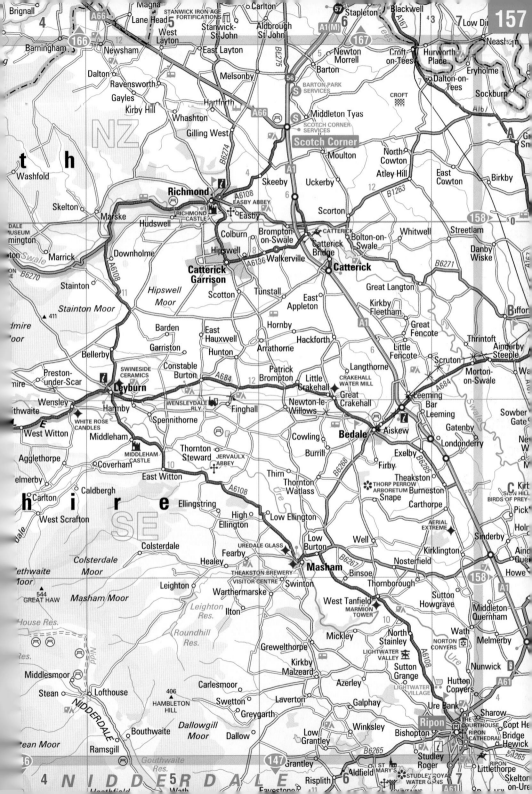

Brignall
4
Lane Head
5
Magna
Carlton
Stapleton
57
Blackwell
Low Di
7
A66
West Layton
166
Stanwick Iron Age Fortifications
Stanwick-St-John
Aldbrough St John
A1(M)
6
167
Neast
Barningham
12
Newsham
East Layton
5
Newton Morrell
Croft-on-Tees
Hurworth Place
Dalton
Ravensworth
Melsonby
56
Barton
S BARTON PARK SERVICES
Dalton-on-Tees
Eryholme
Gayles
Hartforth
CROFT
Sockburn
Kirby Hill
Whashton
A66
Middleton Tyas
SCOTCH CORNER SERVICES
NZ
Gilling West
S Scotch Corner
A
Sn
t
h
Moulton
North Cowton
East Cowton
Birkby
Washfold
A1
Skeeby
Uckerby
Atley Hill
12
B1263
Skelton
Richmond
A6108
EASBY ABBEY
Easby
Scorton
158
5
Marske
RICHMOND CASTLE
Easby
Whitwell
Streetlam
DALE MUSEUM
Hudswell
Colburn
Brompton-on-Swale
CATTERICK
Bolton-on-Swale
Danby Wiske
mington
Marrick
Downholme
Hipswell
Catterick Bridge
Catterick
B6271
Biffor
Swale
B6270
A6108
Walkerville
Great Langton
B
Stainton
Catterick Garrison
Scotton
Tunstall
East Appleton
Kirkby Fleetham
Great Fencote
Thrintoft
Ainderby Steeple
Stainton Moor
Hipswell Moor
A1
Little Fencote
Scruton
411
Barden
East Hauxwell
Hornby
Hackforth
Langthorne
Morton-on-Swale
dmire oor
Garriston
Hunton
Arrathorne
6
CRAKEHALL WATER MILL
A684
Wa
Bellerby
Constable Burton
Patrick Brompton
Little Crakehall
Leeming Bar
Preston-under-Scar
SWINESIDE CERAMICS
Leyburn
A684
12
Newton-le-Willows
Great Crakehall
Leeming
Sowber Gate
mire
Wensley
Harmby
WENSLEYDALE RLY.
Finghall
Aiskew
Gatenby
Ne W
thwaite
E
WHITE ROSE CANDLES
Spennithorne
Bedale
Londonderry
West Witton
Middleham
Cowling
Firby
Exelby
B6285
Agglethorpe
MIDDLEHAM CASTLE
Thornton Steward
Burrill
THORP PERROW ARBORETUM
Theakston
Burneston
Carthorpe
C Kirt
elmerby
Coverham
10
East Witton
JERVAULX ABBEY
Thirn
Snape
SIGH HILL BIRDS OF PREY
Carlton
Caldbergh
A6108
Ellingstring
Thornton Watlass
AERIAL EXTREME
Sinderby
Pick
h
i
r
e
West Scrafton
SE
High Ellington
Low Ellington
Well
Kirklington
Ainc
Quer
dale
Colsterdale
Fearby
Low Burton
Nosterfield
Howe
ethwaite Moor
Colsterdale Moor
Healey
UREDALE GLASS
Masham
Binsoe
158
A1
Moor
544 GREAT HAW
Leighton
THEAKSTON BREWERY VISITOR CENTRE
Swinton
Thornborough
Sutton Howgrave
A61
Masham Moor
Warthermarske
West Tanfield
MARMION TOWER
Middleton Quernham
House Res.
Leighton Res.
Ilton
Mickley
North Stainley
10
Wath
Melmerby
Middlesmoor
Roundhill Res.
Grewelthorpe
Kirkby Malzeard
Azerley
NORTON CONYERS
Sutton Grange
LIGHTWATER VALLEY
Nunwick
D
Stean
Lofthouse
406 HAMBLETON HILL
Carlesmoor
Laverton
Galphay
LIGHTWATER VILLAGE
Hutton Conyers
A61
4
NIDDERDALE
Swetton
Greygarth
Winksley
Ure Bank
Sharow
Copt H
ean Moor
Bouthwaite
Dallowgill Moor
Dallow
Low Grantley
THE COURTHOUSE
Ripon
RIPON CATHEDRAL
Bridge
Hewick
Ramsgill
Gouthwaite Res.
147
Grantley
Risplith
Studley Roger
STUDLEY ROYAL WATER GDNS
Littlethorpe
Skelton on-Ure
16
NIDDERDALE
4
Heathfield
Wath
5
Faveston
Risplith
6
Aldfield
ST MARY'S
FOUNTAINS
7
Bishopton

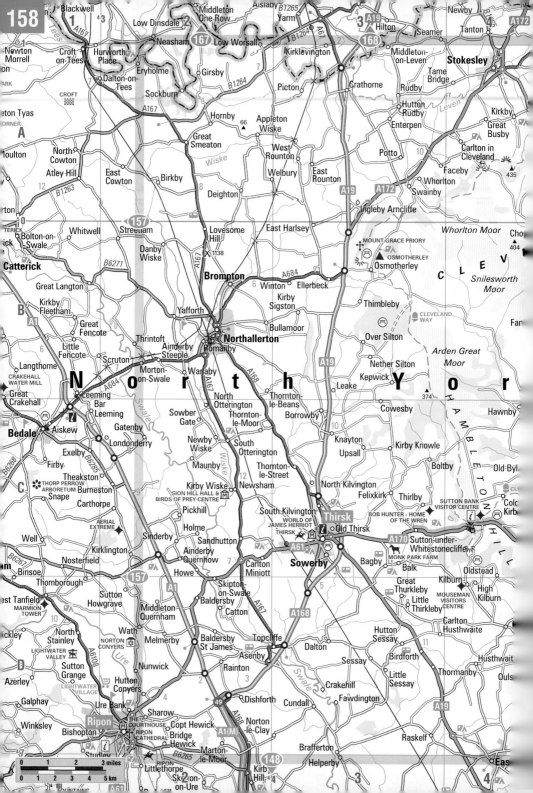

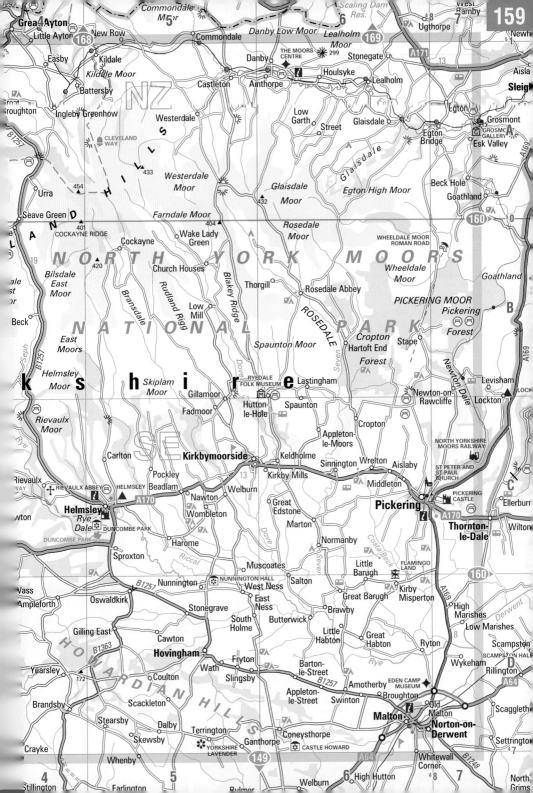

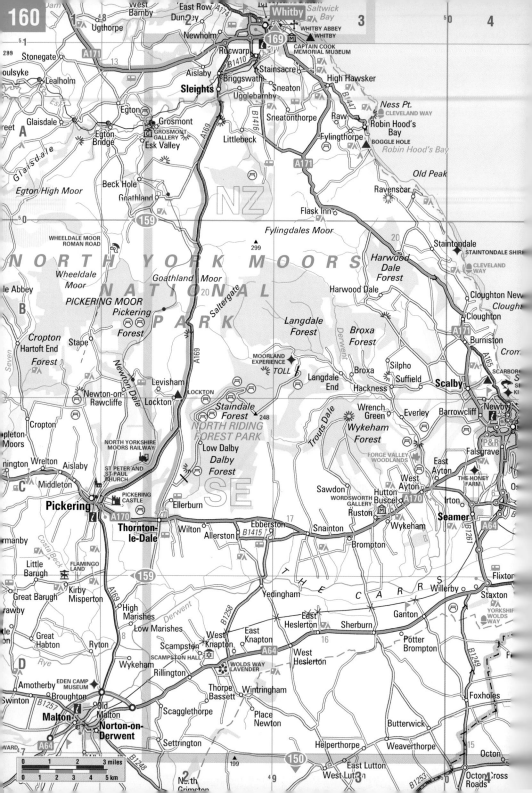

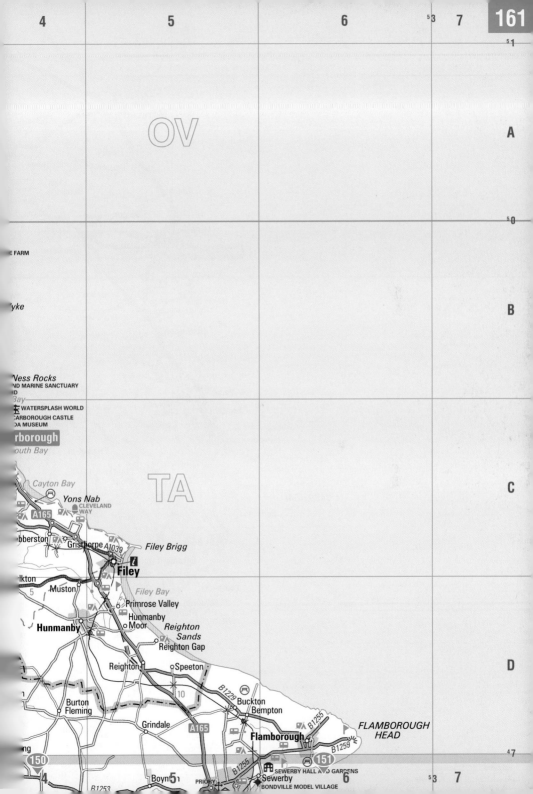

⁵1

A

⁵0

B

E FARM

'yke

'Ness Rocks
AND MARINE SANCTUARY
D
'Bay
WATERSPLASH WORLD
CARBOROUGH CASTLE
A MUSEUM

rborough
outh Bay

C

Cayton Bay

Yons Nab
CLEVELAND
WAY

TA

bberston   Gristhorpe *A1039*   *Filey Brigg*
A165

kton   Muston
5

Filey Bay

Filey

Hunmanby   *Primrose Valley*
   Hunmanby
   Moor   *Reighton
     Sands*
  Reighton Gap

Reighton   Speeton

D

B1229

10   Buckton
Burton   Bempton
Fleming

B1255

Grindale   **A165**

*FLAMBOROUGH
HEAD*

Flamborough

B1259

⁴7

ng   **150**

SEWERBY HALL AND GARDENS
Sewerby
BONDVILLE MODEL VILLAGE

Boyn   5₁   PRIORY   6   ⁵3   7

B1253

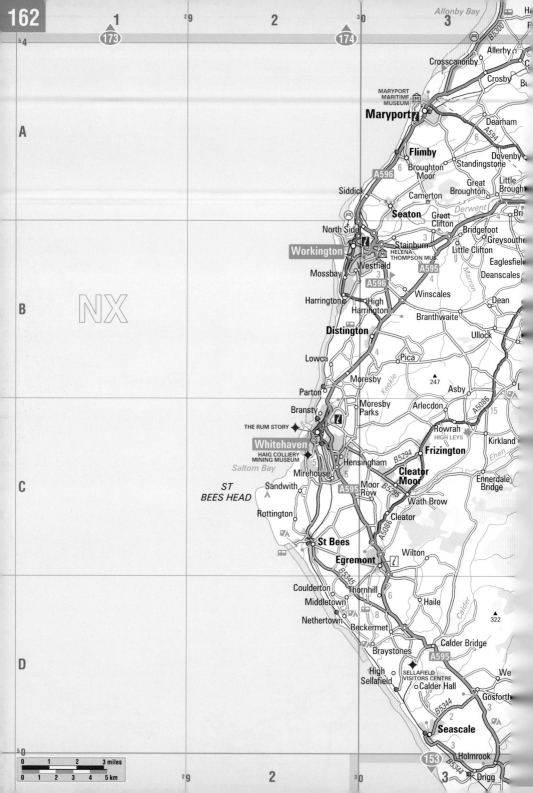

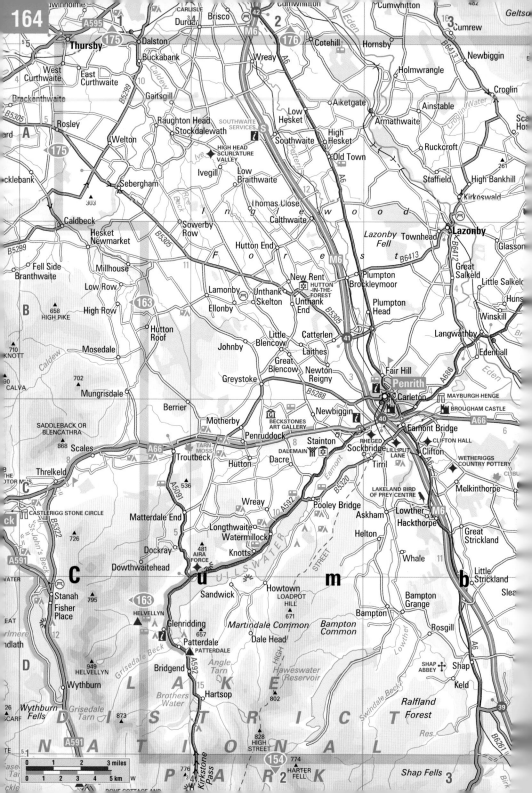

Map grid references (top)

4 5 6 ⁴9 7

⁵5

Grid labels (right margin)

A

B

C

D

Map labels

NZ

MINIATURE RAILWAY

Saltburn-by-the-Sea

CHRIS BIRKBECK INTERNATIONAL RALLY SCHOOL

166

Brotton

Skinningrove

Boulby

Carlin How

Loftus

A174

Staithes

North Skelton

Kilton Thorpe

Easington

Port Mulgrave

Lingdale

Hinderwell

Runswick Bay

Stanghow

Roxby

Newton Mulgrave

Runswick Bay

Kettleness

argrove

Liverton

5

Goldsborough

9

Moorsholm

B1366

Ellerby

149

Scaling

A174

Lythe

Sandsend

THE DRACULA EXPERIENCE

es.

A171

B1266

Mickleby

East Barnby

Sandsend Wyke

SUTCLIFFE GALLERY

West Barnby

East Row

Saltwick Bay

Scaling Dam Res.

Ugthorpe

Dunsley

Whitby

WHITBY

Danby Low Moor

Lealholm

Newholm

WHITBY ABBEY WHITBY

Commondale

Moor

299

Stonegate

159

THE MOORS CENTRE

13

160

Ruswarp

CAPTAIN COOK MEMORIAL MUSEUM

Danby

Houlsyke

A171

Aislaby

Briggswath

B1410

Sta..acre

High Hawsker

4 5 6 7

1 **2** **3**

Barnhills
Portencalzie
North Cairn
257
South Cairn
180
Main Water of Luce
Cross Water of Lu
Dounan Bay
D738
Corsewall
Penwhirn
Loch
Connell
Kirkcolm
Cairnryan
Res.
Mains of Airies
Ervie
Braid Fell
B798
Low
Salchrie
The Wig
A77
New Luce
Knocknain
A
B738
Leswalt
LOCH RYAN
Slouchnawen
Bay
Innermessan
Auchmantle
Craigencross
B7043
A718
A751
CASTLE KENNEDY
GARDENS
Broadsea Bay
Glenstockadale
Black Loch
Water of Luce
Wh
Stranraer
Aird
Castle Kennedy
T **H** **E** CASTLE OF
ST JOHN
VISITOR
CENTRE
R **H** **I** **N**
Knockglass
WIGTOWN
DISTRICT
MUSEUM
Soulseat
Loch
A75
GLENWHAN
GARDENS
Dunragit
CASTLE
OF PARK
Lochans
Mark
Black Hd.
B738
182
NW
Dunskey Ho.
A77
B7077
5
6
Torrs Warren
B
LITTLE
WHEELS
Awhirk
5
B7084
6
Luce Sands
Portpatrick
Stoneykirk
A716
8
Sta
Port of Spittal Bay
B7042
Cairngarroch
Sandhead
KIRKMADRINE
STONES
Sandhead Bay
Cairngarroch Bay
Money Hd.
Clachanmore
Hole Stone Bay
Ardwell
Chapel Rossan Bay
C
Ardwell
Mains
Ardwell Pt.
Logan
Mains
10
LOGAN
BOTANIC
GARDEN
Balgowan Pt.
L
Mull of Logan
LOGAN FISH POND
MARINE LIFE CENTRE
Port Nessock or Port Logan Bay
Port Logan
Cairnywellan Hd.
B7065
A716
Clanyard Bay
Low Clanyard
Laggantalluch Hd.
Kirkmaiden
Drummore
Cailliness Pt.
164
D
Damnaglaur
B7041
Crammag Hd.
Maryport
Cairngaan
Port Kemin
MULL OF

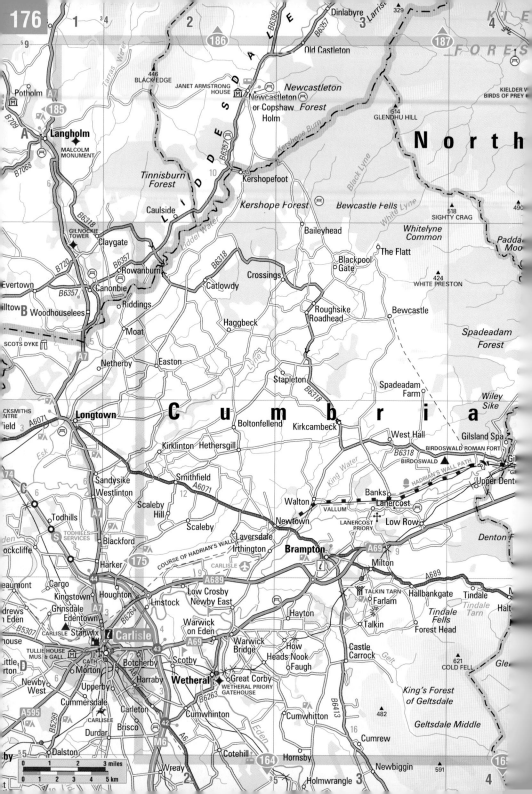

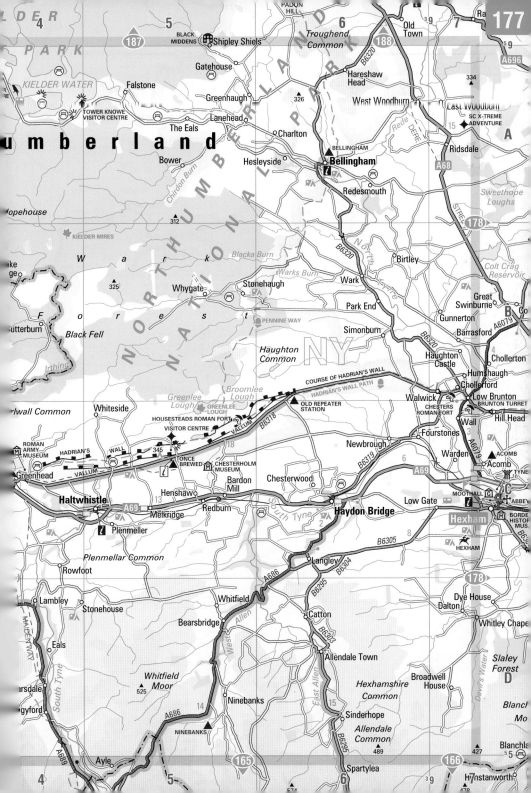

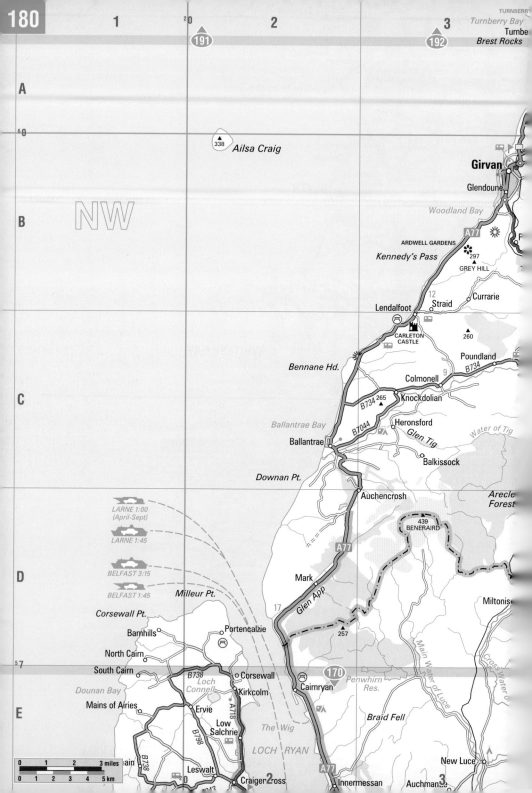

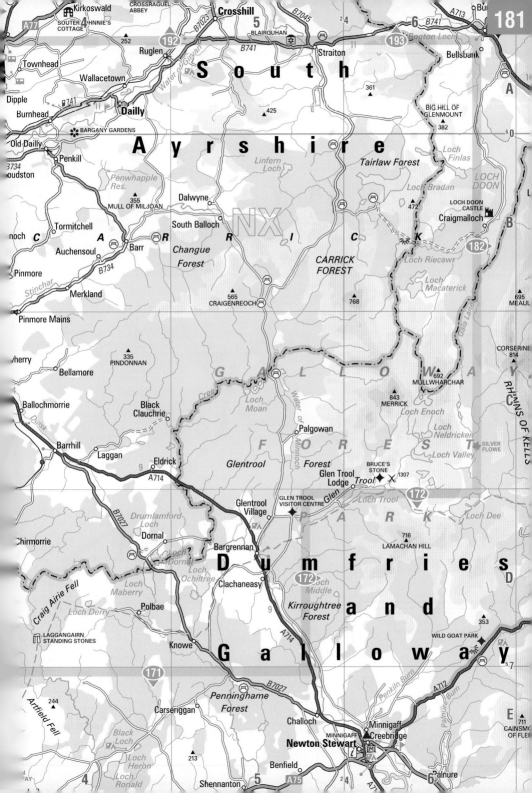

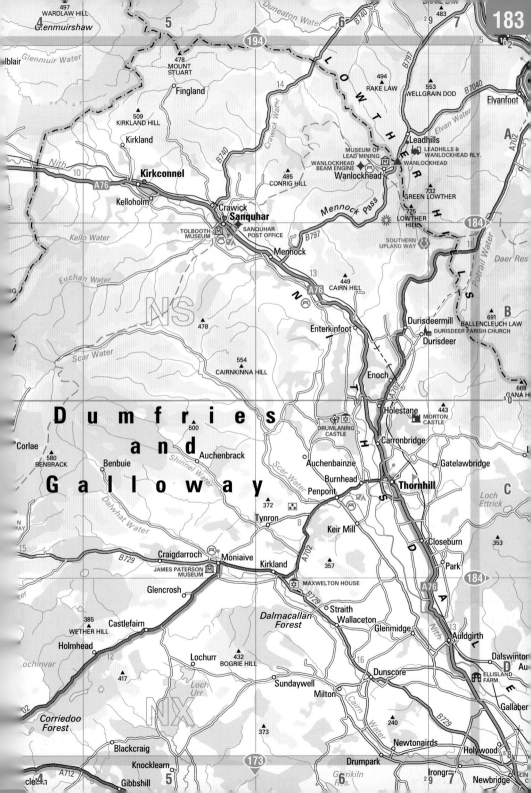

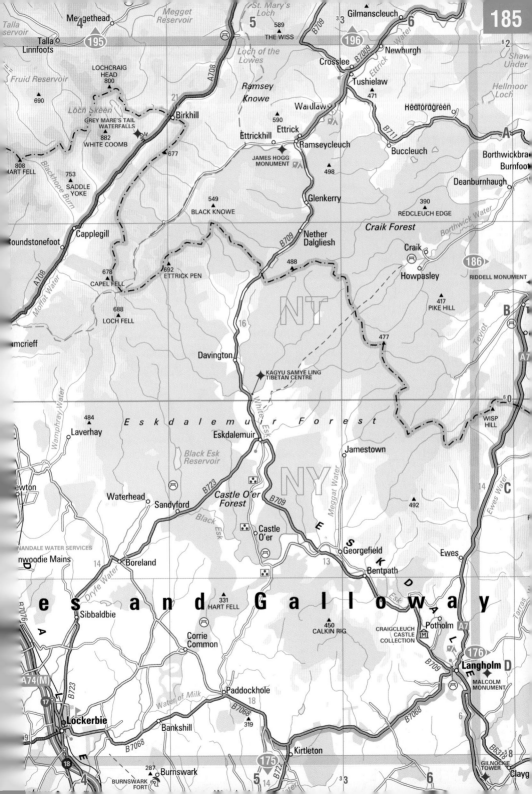

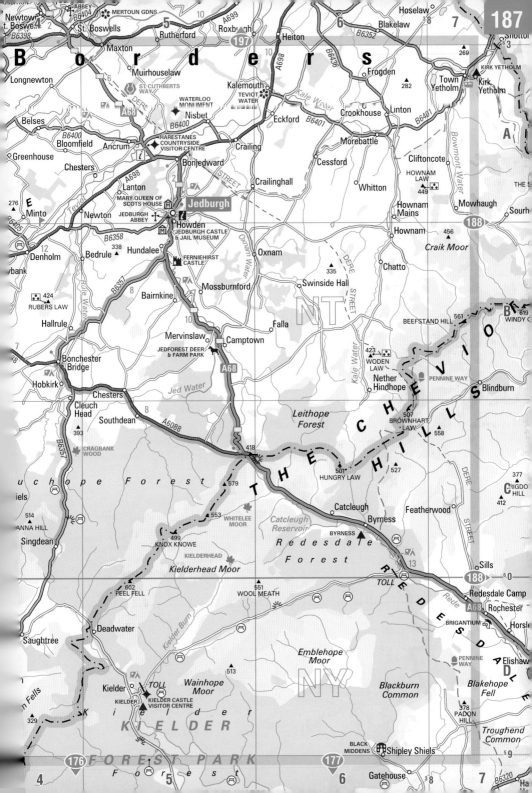

Map labels

NORTH

Thundergay
MEALL NAN DAMH 570
Pirnmill
...land
573
5
859
Loch Tanna
798
CIR MHÔR
721
BEINN BHARRAIN
BEINN TARSUINN
825
874
GOAT FELL
Imachar
202
I S L E

NORTH SANNOX FARM PARK
A841 20
14
Sannox
Sannox Bay
Glen Sannox
Corrie
203
ARDROSSAN 0:55

A R R A N

Dougarie
228
Glen Iorsa
Machrie Water
Glen Rosa
BRODICK
BRODICK CASTLE
ARRAN AROMATICS VISITOR CENTRE
Brodick Bay
ISLE OF ARRAN HERITAGE MUSEUM
Brodick
Strathwhillan

O F

192

Auchagallon
Glenloig
A'CHRUACH
512
Glen Cloy
A841
Clauchlands Pt.
Machrie Bay
18
B880
10

A R R A N

Tormore
MACHRIE MOOR STANDING STONES
503
Blairbeg
Margnaheglish
Lamlash
Lamlash Bay
KING'S CAVE
BALMICHAEL VISITOR CENTRE
Balmichael
Cordon
Holy Island
Torbeg
Shiskine
11
314
...adoon Pt.
Blackwaterfoot
Kilpatrick
KILPATRICK DUN
Kingscross Pt.
Drumadoon Bay
Auchencairn
Kingscross
Knockenkelly
Whiting Bay
Glenree
458
TIGHVEIN
North Kiscadale
Whiting Bay
South Kiscadale
Brown Hd.
CARN BAN
Corriecravie
Sliddery Water
GLENASHDALE FALLS
WHITING BAY
Largymore
Kilmory Water
Largybeg
Sliddery
13
Lagg
Dippen
Kilmory
Levencorroch
Dippin Head
A841
Bennan
SOUTH BANK FARM PARK
Kildonan
TORRYLINN CAIRN
Bennan Hd.
Sound of Pladda
Pladda

NR
NS
192

180

Map labels

Seamill
Auchentiber
A737
DALGARVEN MILL
B714
B780
2
B714
3
B77
204
B778
Dalgarven
12
B780
4
Abbey
Torranyard
Chapelhill
Dykesmains
Kilwinning
A736
Horse Isle
6
EGLINTON
Benslie
Cunninghamhead
Ardrossan
A78
B7080
Kil
BRODICK 0:55
A738
Stevenston
NORTH AYRSHIRE MUSEUM
Saltcoats
2
Girdle
Toll
Perceton
Knockentibe

A

B
NS
THE BIG IDEA
Irvine
Glasgow
Springside
VENNEL MUS
SCOTTISH MARITIME MUSEUM
Fullarton
B7081
A737
Dreghorn
Drybridge
Gatehead
Irvine Bay
A759
A71
B730
191
A78
Dundonald
DUNDONALD
CASTLE
Barassie
6
Bogen
North Bay
Muirhead
A759
Loans
Symington
Lady Isle
Troon
Har
Vill
South Bay
LARNE 1:49
ROYAL TROON
(March-Sept)
A749
Monkton
A77
C
GLASGOW
PRESTWICK
LARNE 4:30
INTERNATIONAL
Prestwick
Woodfield
5
St
Quivo
Newton on Ayr
B743
Wallacetown
Whitletts
Ayr
AYR
Belston
Seafield
2
Masonhill
A70
BURNS COTTAGE
Belmont
Heads of Ayr
Doonfoot
MACLAURIN GALLER
HEADS OF AYR FARM PARK
A719
Alloway
& ROZELLE HOUSE
BURNS
TAM O'SHANTER
NATIONAL
EXPERIENCE
Fisherton
HERITAGE PARK
A77
B7
Dunure
287
A77
Laigh Glengall
A713
Culroy
B7024
Dalrymple
ELECTRIC BRAE
Minishant
17
B742
182
Culzean Bay
196
6 1
CULZEAN CASTLE
B7023
270
Whitefaulds
B7045
CULZEAN
Maybole
Kirkmichael
Maidenhead Bay
COLLEGIATE
CHURCH
Aitkenhead
Maidens
A719
7
A77
CROSSRAGUEL
4
B7045
TURNBERRY
ABBEY
Crosshill
Kirkoswald
B7023
Turnberry Bay
SOUTER JOHNNIE'S
COTTAGE
BLAIRQUHAN
Turnberry
252
**Brest
Rocks**
180
Ruglen
181
B741
Townhead
3
Wallacetown

D

E

0   1   2   3 miles
0   1   2   3   4   5 km

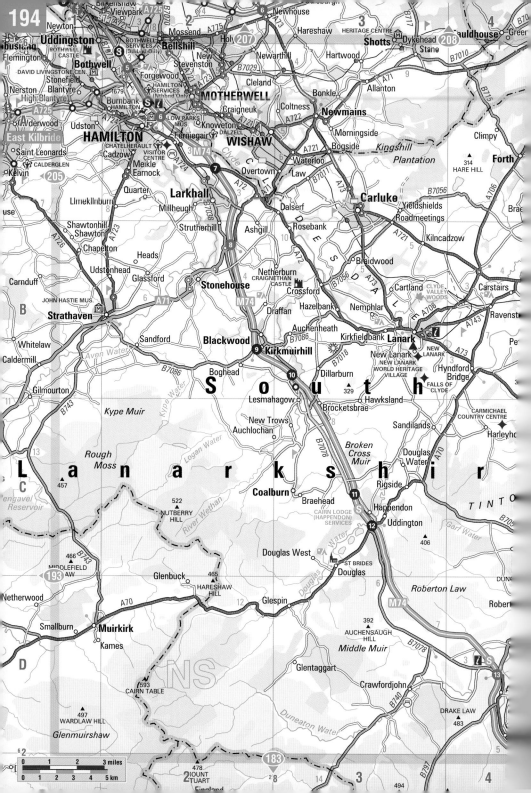

⁶6

A

ed

H
U
M
B
E
R
L
A
N
D

Goswick

ston

Low

Beal

NU

B

LINDISFARNE

Emmanuel Hd.

**Holy Island
(Lindisfarne)**

Causeway
Holy
Island
Sands

Holy
Island

LINDISFARNE CASTLE
Castle Pt.

LINDISFARNE
PRIORY

HERITAGE
CENTRE

Fenwick

Guile
Pt.

Fenham

East
Kyloe

Buckton

Elwick

Ross

Budle
Bay

Farne
Islands

Staple Sound

FARNE ISLANDS

C

Detchant

Middleton

Budle

BAMBURGH
CASTLE

Inner Sound

211

h Hazelrigg

Belford

Easington

B1342

Waren Mill

Glororum

Bamburgh

Burton

B1340

C
O
A
S
T

B6349

Spindlestone

Mousen

Bradford

B1341

Elford

North
Sunderland

Seahouses

i

Bellshill

Warenton

Adderstone

Lucker

189

Beadnell

Benthall

Greendikes

B6348

Warenford

Newham
Hall

Swinhoe

Beadnell
Bay

Newham

Fleetham

A1

Newstead

Chathill

hillingham

CHILLINGHAM
WILD CATTLE

Rosebrough

Ellingham

Preston

High Newton-
by-the-Sea

D

315

15

Brockdam

PRESTON TOWER

Brunton

Low Newton-
by-the-Sea

Hepburn

Brownyside

North Charlton

Doxford

Christon
Bank

Embleton Bay

Embleton

Dunstan Steads

Castle Point

Old Bewick

West
Ditchburn

South
Charlton

Rock

DUNSTANBURGH
CASTLE

B6346

Harehope

Dunstan

Craster

ew

wick

Eglingham

B6347

B6341

Rennington

i

⁶2

169

101

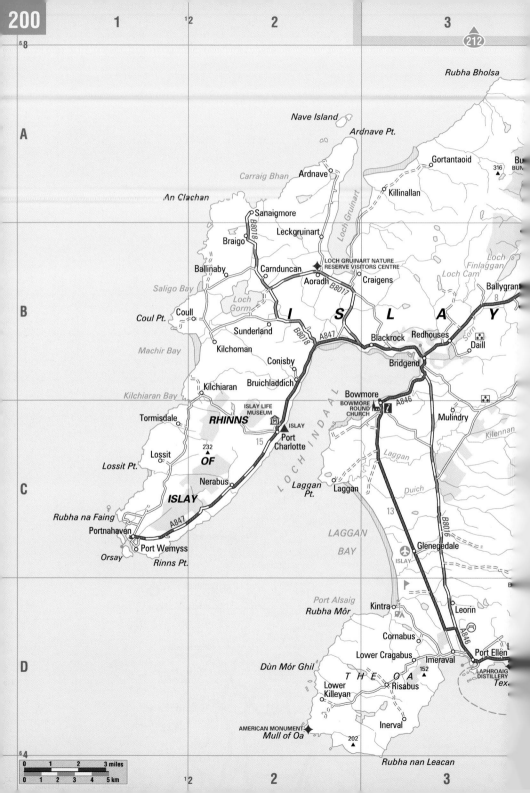

Rubha Bholsa

Nave Island

Ardnave Pt.

Carraig Bhan

An Clachan

Ardnave

Gortantaoid

316

Bu
BUN

Killinallan

Sanaigmore

Leckgruinart

B8018

Braigo

Loch Gruinart

Ballinaby

Carnduncan

LOCH GRUINART NATURE
RESERVE VISITORS CENTRE

Aoradh

Craigens

Loch
Finlaggan

Loch Cam

Saligo Bay

Ballygrant

Loch
Gorm

B8017

8

Coull

Coul Pt.

I S L A Y

Sunderland

B8018

A847

Blackrock

Redhouses

Sorn

Daill

Machir Bay

Kilchoman

Conisby

Bridgend

Kilchiaran Bay

Kilchiaran

Bruichladdich

Bowmore

RHINNS

ISLAY LIFE
MUSEUM

BOWMORE
ROUND
CHURCH

7

A846

Mulindry

Kilennan

Tormisdale

ISLAY

Port
Charlotte

15

232

OF

Lossit

Lossit Pt.

Nerabus

ISLAY

A847

Laggan
Pt.

Laggan

Duich

13

B8016

LOCH INDAAL

Laggan

Rubha na Faing

Portnahaven

Port Wemyss

Orsay

Rinns Pt.

**LAGGAN
BAY**

ISLAY

Glenegedale

B

Port Alsaig

Rubha Môr

Kintra

Leorin

Cornabus

Lower Cragabus

Imeraval

A846

Port Ellen

L

Dùn Mór Ghil

T H E   O A

152

LAPHROAIG
DISTILLERY

Tex

Lower
Killeyan

Risabus

Inerval

AMERICAN MONUMENT

Mull of Oa

202

Rubha nan Leacan

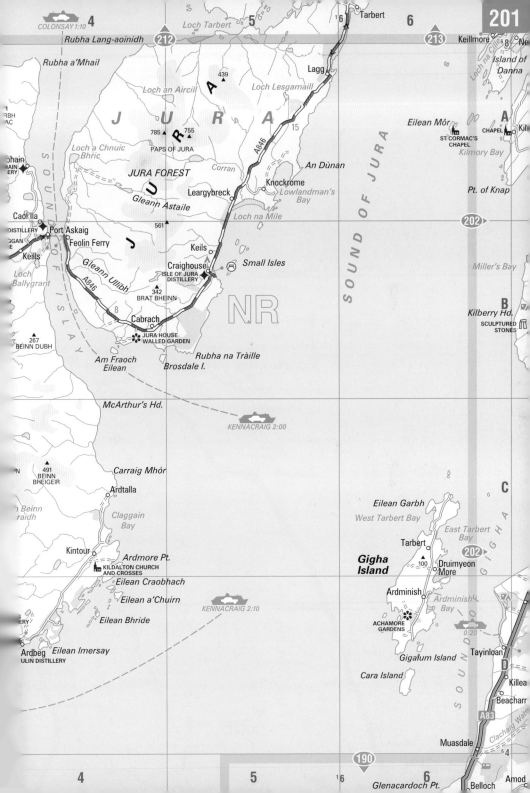

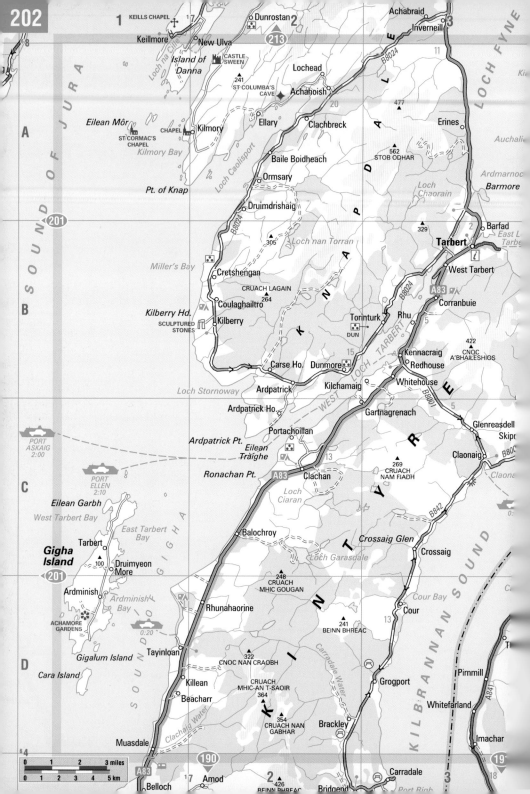

1 KEILLS CHAPEL **2** Dunrostan **3** Achabraid
Inverneill
Keillmore New Ulva **213**
B8024 11

Island of Danna CASTLE SWEEN
Lochead
241 ST COLUMBA'S CAVE
Achahoish Erines
20
A Eilean Môr CHAPEL
ST CORMAC'S CHAPEL Kilmory 477
Kilmory Bay Ellary Clachbreck Auchali
477
Pt. of Knap Baile Boidheach STOB ODHAR 562 Ardmarno
Ormsary Barmore
Druimdrishaig Loch Chaorain
201 B8024
305 329 Barfad
Loch nan Torran Tarbert East L
Miller's Bay Cretshengan 2
CRUACH LAGAIN West Tarbert
264
B Coulaghailtro A83 Corranbuie
Kilberry Hd. Kilberry B8024 5
SCULPTURED STONES Rhu
Torinturk 422 CNOC A'BHAILESHIOS
DUN
Carse Ho. Dunmore Kennacraig
15 Redhouse
Ardpatrick Kilchamaig Whitehouse
Loch Stornoway
Ardpatrick Ho. Gartnagrenach 5
Glenreasdell
Portachoillan Skipr
PORT ASKAIG 2:00 Ardpatrick Pt. Claonaig
Eilean Tràighe 269 CRUACH NAM FIADH
C PORT ELLEN 2:10 Ronachan Pt. 13 B842
Eilean Garbh **A83** Clachan
West Tarbert Bay Loch Ciaran
East Tarbert Bay
Gigha Island Tarbert Balochroy Crossaig Glen
100 Druimyeon More Loch Garasdale Crossaig
201 248 CRUACH MHIC GOUGAN
Ardminish Cour Bay
ACHAMORE GARDENS Rhunahaorine Cour
Ardminish Bay 241 BEINN BHREAC
Gigalum Island 0:20 13
D Cara Island Tayinloan 322 CNOC NAN CRAOBH Grogport Pirnmill
Killean CRUACH MHIC-AN T-SAOIR Whitefarland
Beacharr 364
354 CRUACH NAN GABHAR Brackley Imachar
Muasdale **190** **19**
A83 Amod **2** 426 Carradale **3**
Belloch BEINN BHREAC Bridgend Port Rig

0 1 2 3 miles
0 1 2 3 4 5 km

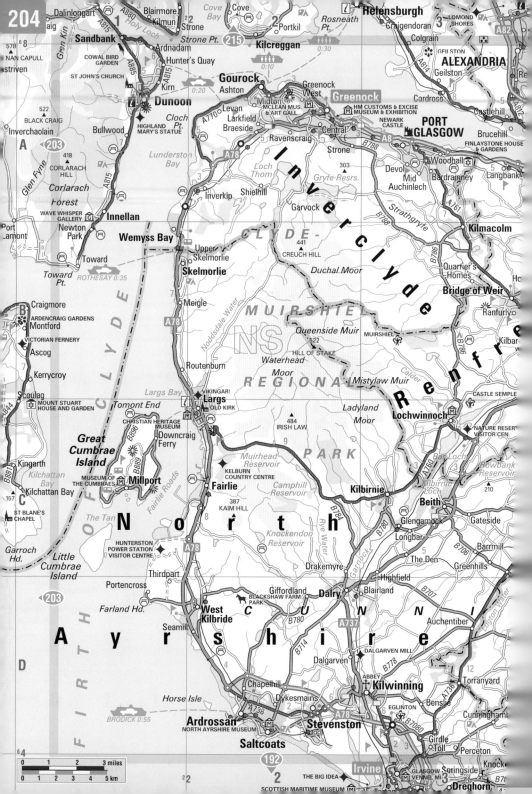

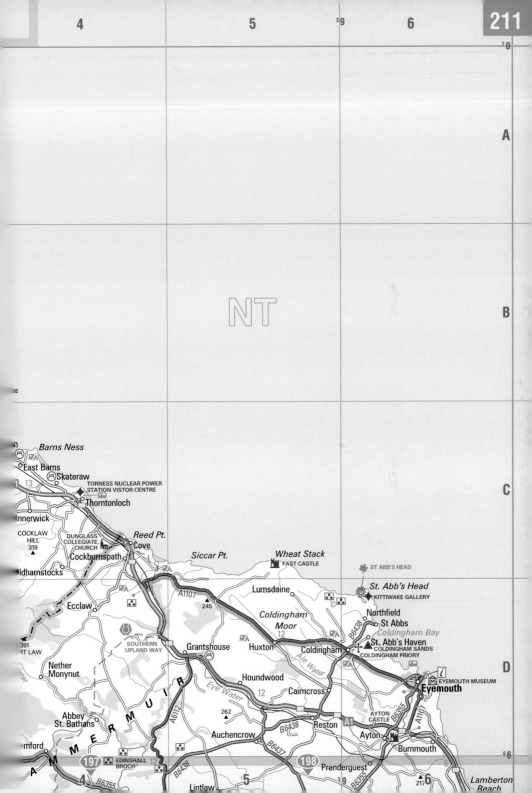

NT

A

B

C

D

4   5   ³9   6

Barns Ness

East Barns
Skateraw

TORNESS NUCLEAR POWER
STATION VISTOR CENTRE
Thorntonloch

13

Innerwick

COCKLAW
HILL
319

Reed Pt.
DUNGLASS
COLLEGIATE
CHURCH   Cove
Cockburnspath

Siccar Pt.

Wheat Stack
FAST CASTLE

St ABB'S HEAD

Oldhamstocks

A1107

Lumsdaine

St. Abb's Head
KITTIWAKE GALLERY

Ecclaw

245

Coldingham
Moor

Northfield
St Abbs

Coldingham Bay

391
RT LAW

SOUTHERN
UPLAND WAY

Grantshouse

Huxton

12

Coldingham

B6438

St. Abb's Haven
COLDINGHAM SANDS
COLDINGHAM PRIORY

Ale Water

Nether
Monynut

Eye Water

Houndwood

12

Cairncross

EYEMOUTH MUSEUM
Eyemouth

Abbey
St. Bathans

A6112

262

Reston

A1

AYTON
CASTLE

B6355

A1107

Auchencrow

B6438

Ayton

Burnmouth

HAMMERMUIR

197   EDINSHALL
BROCH

198

Prenderguest

Lamberton
Beach

mford   B6355

Lintlaw

4   5   ³9   217   6   ⁶6

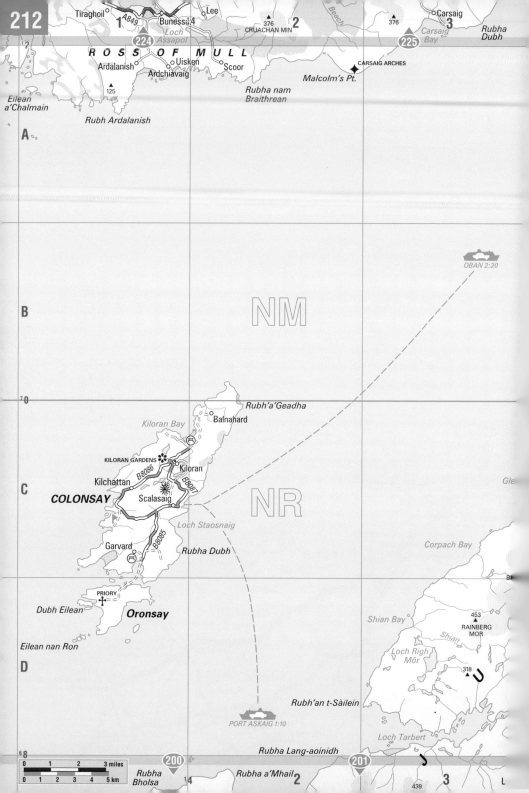

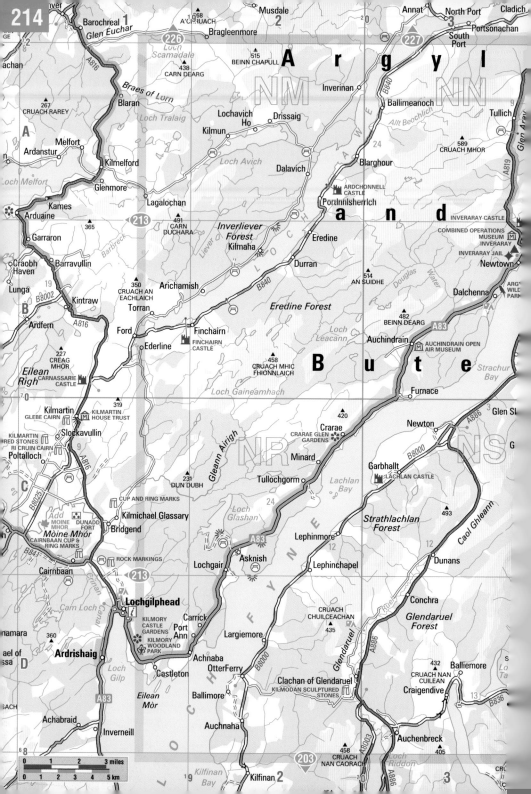

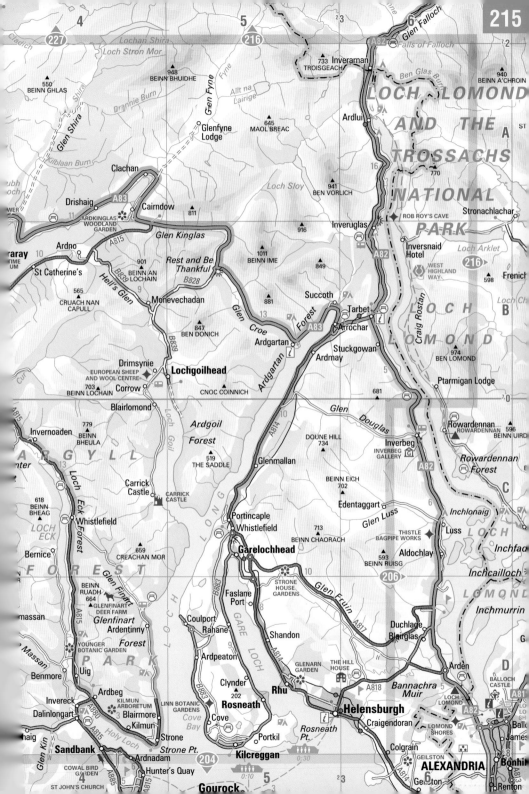

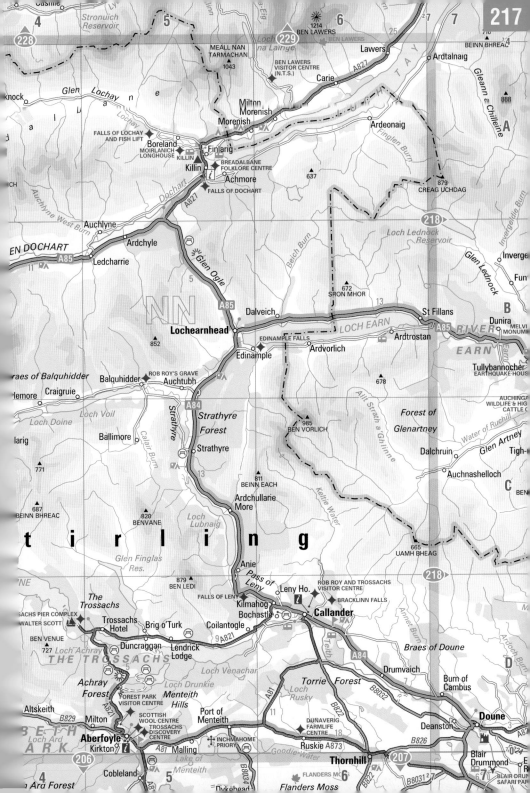

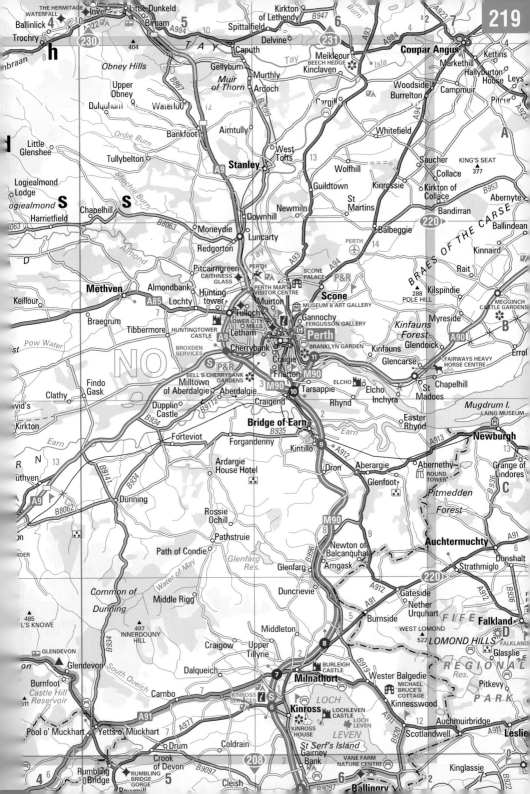

Map labels

4 5 6 7

Hayhillock
Carmyllie
Denhead of Arbilot
Hayshead
Cliffburn
The Deil's Heid
7

B961
B9127
CROMBIE
Crombie
259
Arbirlot
Arbroath
ABROATH ABBEY

232
233

Kirkton of Monikie
Balmirmer
Elliot
SIGNAL TOWER MUSEUM

Monikie
MONIKIE
Craigton
Muirdrum
Salmond's Muir
A92

B978
CARLUNGIE SOUTERRAIN
Monikie Burn
7 4

Wellbank
Newbigging
East Haven

Drumsturdy
Kellas

B961
SOUTERRAIN ARDESTIE
Barry
BARRY MILL
A930
Panbride

Mains of Ardestie
Carnoustie

baldovie
11
CARNOUSTIE

A

92
13
Barry Links

West Ferry
Monifieth

Barnhill
BROUGHTY CASTLE MUSEUM
Buddon Ness

Tayport
TENTSMUIR POINT

Tentsmuir
Forest
NO

B

uchars
EUCHARS NORMAN CHURCH
EARLSHALL CASTLE AND GARDENS
Eden Mouth

rdbridge
EN ESTIVANT CENTRE
ST ANDREWS BAY

St Andrews
ST ANDREWS AQUARIUM

TISH GOLF MUS.
St Andrews
CATH. & ST RULE'S TOWER
Buddo Ness

Newpark
Brownhills
Babbet Ness

B939
ST ANDREWS BOTANIC GARDEN
Boarhills

Balone
Prior Muir
Kingsbarns
Cambo Ness
Carr Brigs

CRAIGTOUN
B9131
CAMBO GARDENS
Tullybothy Craigs

C

Denhead
Stravithie
Balcomie
Craighead

Cameron Res.
Cameron Burn
Dunino
A917
Fife Ness

Inn
11
9
B940
Crail Tolbooth

dernie
Kingsmuir
SCOTLAND'S SECRET BUNKER
Crail
CRAIL MUSEUM AND HERITAGE CENTRE

Lathones
Lochty
B9171
Pitcorthie
West Ness

Largoward
Carnbee
Pitkierie
FIFE COASTAL PATH

B941
KELLIE CASTLE AND GARDEN
Kilrenny
D

Arncroach
B9171
B9131
Anstruther Easter
SCOTTISH FISHERIES MUSEUM

olinsburgh
B942
Abercrombie
Pittenweem
Anstruther Wester

stie
Kilconquhar
ST FILLAN'S CAVE
ST MONAN'S WINDMILL

Ardross
St Monans
ST MONAN'S CHURCH

A917
Isle of May

Ferry
Elie
Sauchar Pt.
210
ISLE OF MAY

4
Chapel Ness
5
6
7

7

⁷7

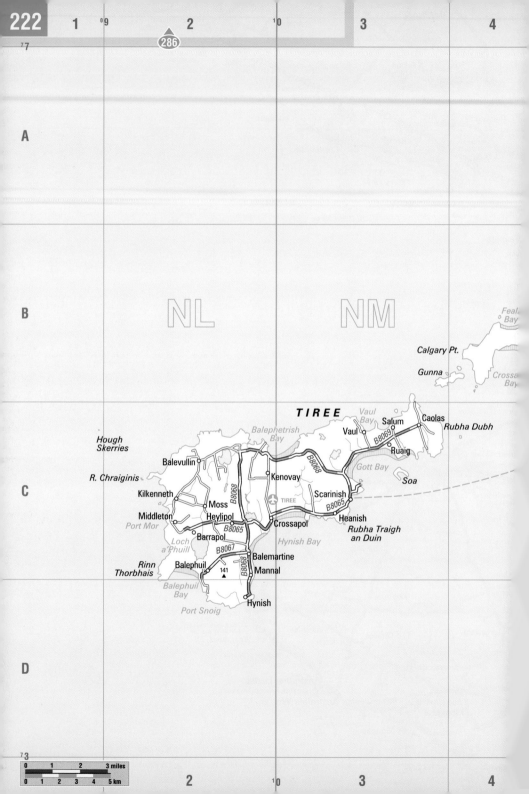

A

B

NL

NM

Feal Bay

Calgary Pt.

Gunna

Crossa Bay

T I R E E

Vaul Bay

Salum

Caolas

Vaul

Rubha Dubh

B8069

Ruaig

• *Hough Skerries*

Balephetrish Bay

Balevullin

R. Chraiginis

Kenovay

Gott Bay

Soa

B8068

C

Kilkenneth

Scarinish

B8068

TIREE

B8065

Moss

Middleton

Heylipol

Heanish

Port Mor

Crossapol

Rubha Traigh an Duin

B8065

Barrapol

Loch a'Phuill

Hynish Bay

B8067

Balemartine

Rinn Thorbhais

Balephuil

Mannal

141 ▲

B8068

Balephuil Bay

Hynish

Port Snoig

D

Sanna Point

Sanna Bay

San

Portuairk

Point of
Ardnamurchan
ARDNAMURCHAN LIGHTHOUSE

Achos

B80

A

Orms

Ormsai

An Acairseid

Cairns of Coll

234

Rubha Mor

Eilean Mor

Sorisdale

Bousd

Cliad Bay

B8072

Arnabost

Gallanach

Grishipoll

B8071

OBAN 2:40

Ardmore
Bay

yhaugh

B8071

104

Loch
Cliad

▲
73

C O L L

Totronald

B8070

Acha

Arinagour

Eilean
Ornsay

Loch Eatharna

Quinish Pt.

Glengo
Castle

Rubha
an Aird

M i s h n i s h

Quinish

B

Breachacha
Castle

Friesland

Caliach Pt.

Sunipol

M o r n i s h

Penmore
Mill

MULL LITTLE
THEATRE

Soa

Loch Breachacha

Calgary

Dervaig

Ac

THE OLD BYRE
HERITAGE CEN

0:55

Calgary Bay

Ensay

▲
342
CARN MOR

Bella

Treshnish Pt.

Haunn

B8073

Burg

Kilninian

Achna

Rubh a'Chaoil

224

Fladda

Achleck

Fanmore

▲
390

C

23

Ballygown

Treshnish Isles

Eilean Dioghlum

L O C H　　T U A T H

EAS FORS
WATERFALL

Lunga

Gometra

Bearnus

313

Laggan
Bay

Bac Mor

U l v a

Ulva House

Sound

Little
Colonsay

INCH KENNETH
CHAPEL

Staffa

STAFFA

**Inch
Kenneth**

D

FINGAL'S CAVE

MACKINNON'S CAVE

Erisgeir

51

IONA 0:45
(April-Oct)

BEIN3 NA S

224

A R D M E A N A C H

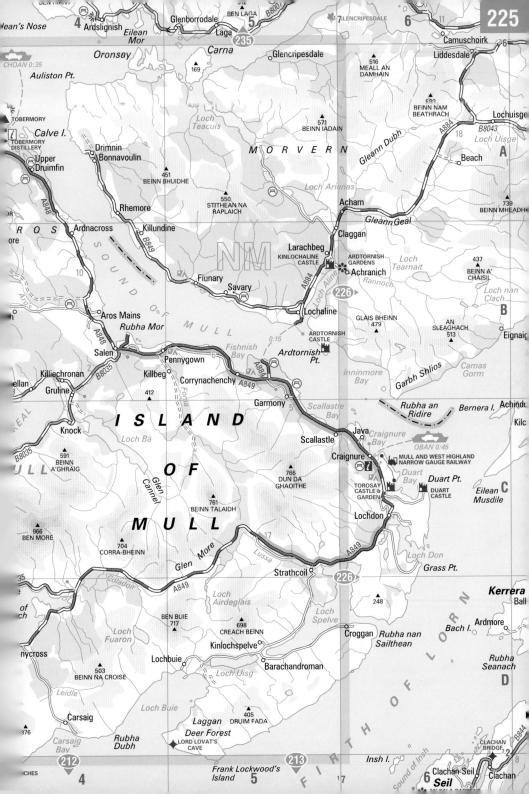

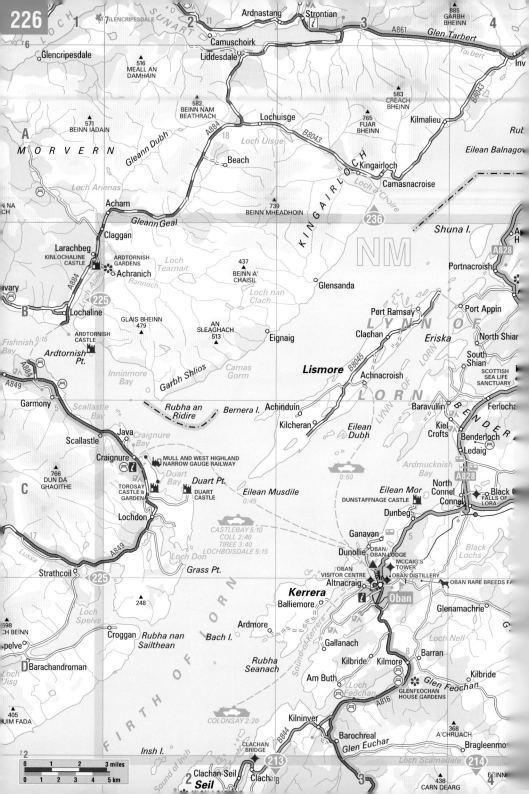

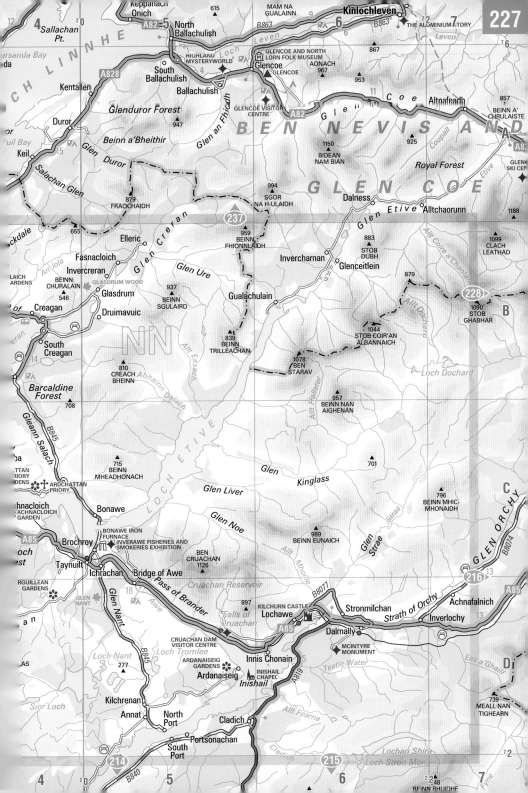

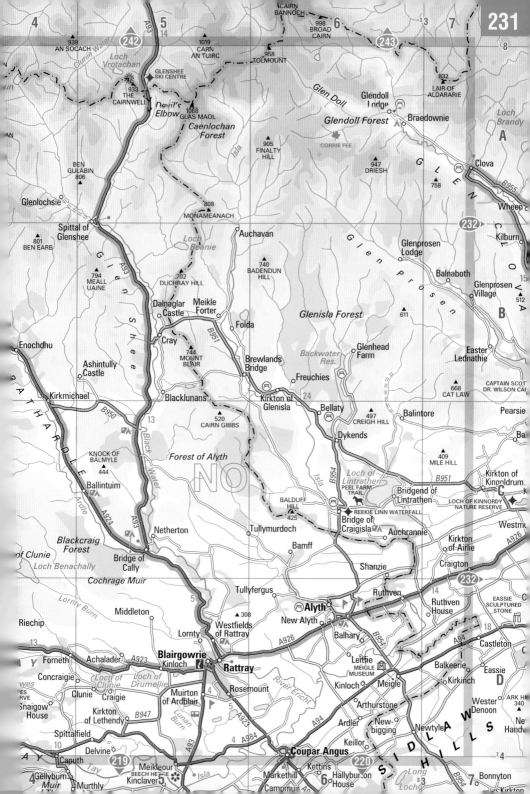

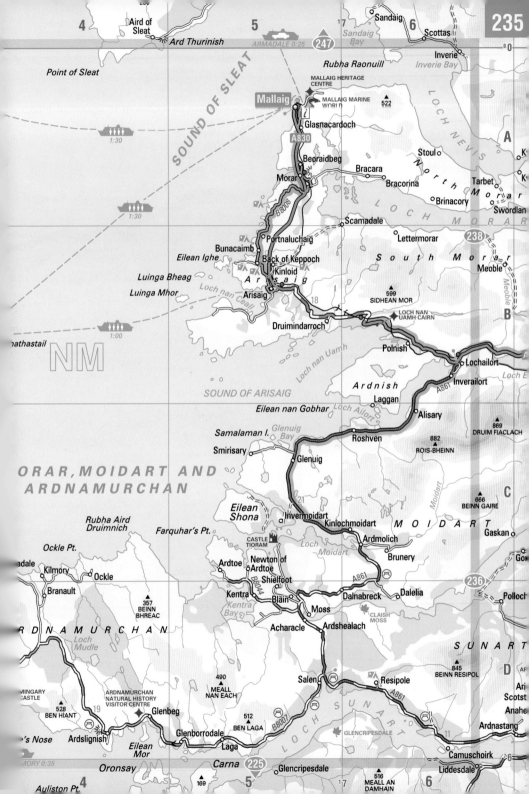

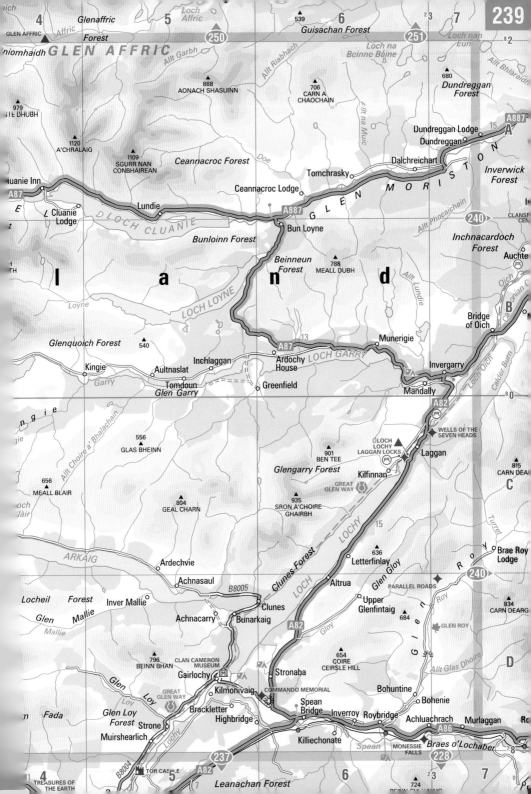

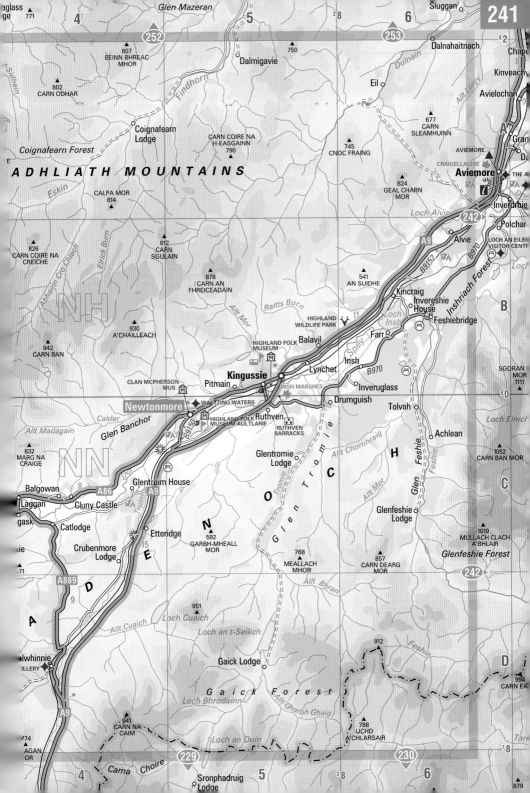

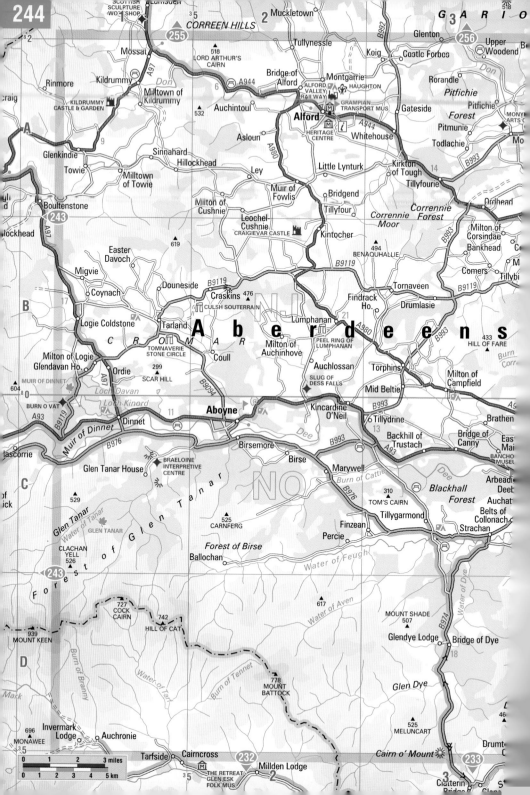

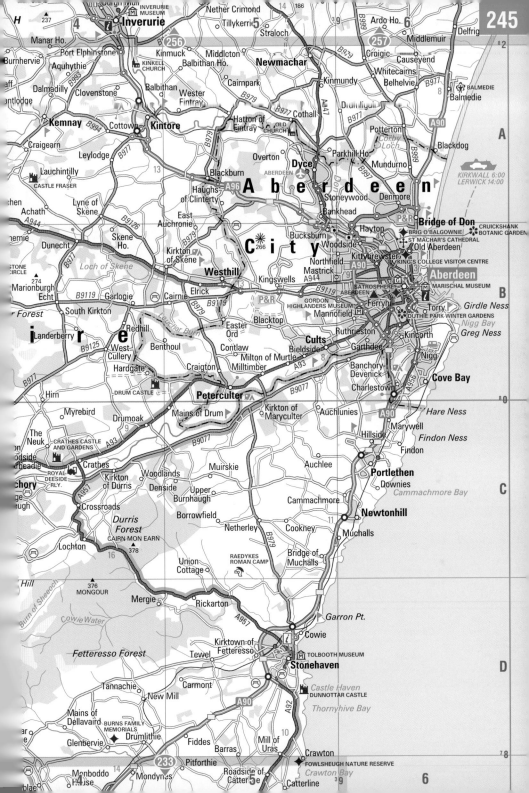

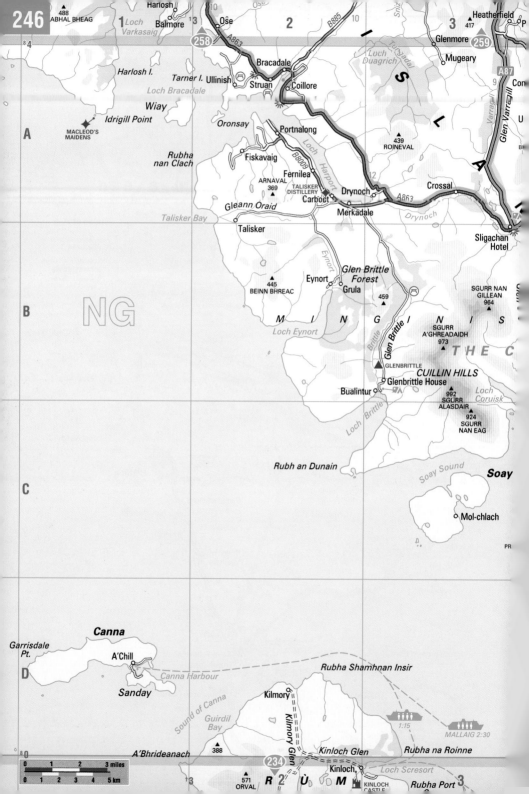

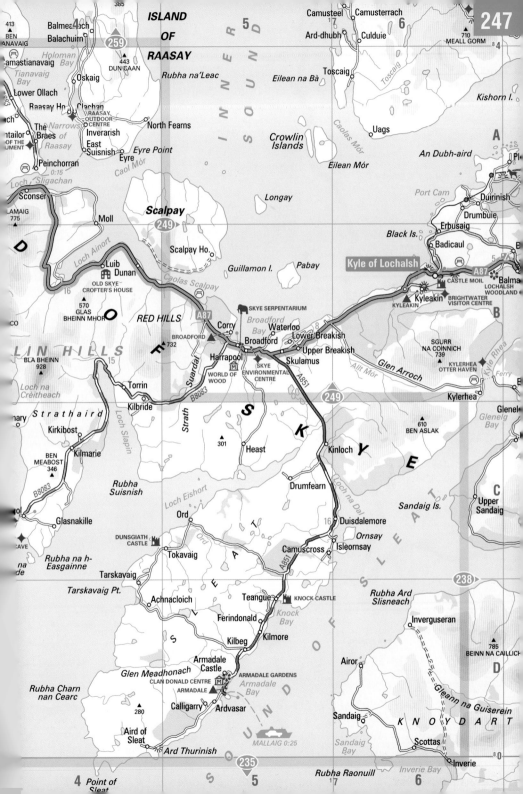

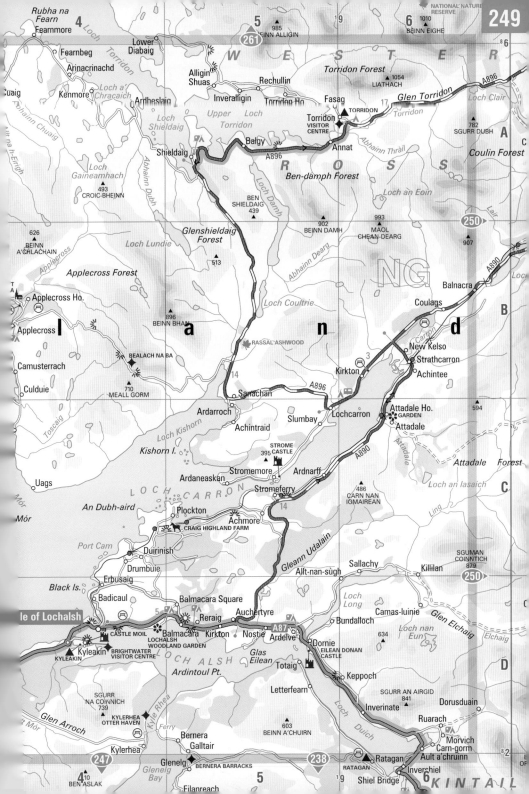

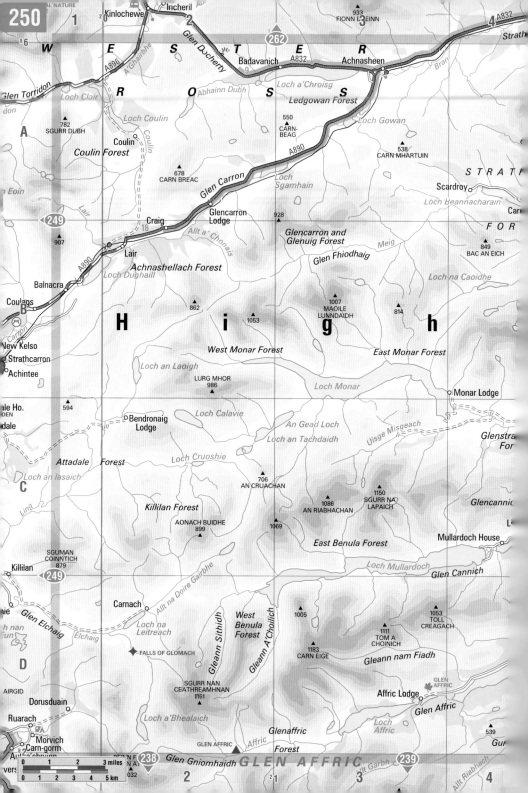

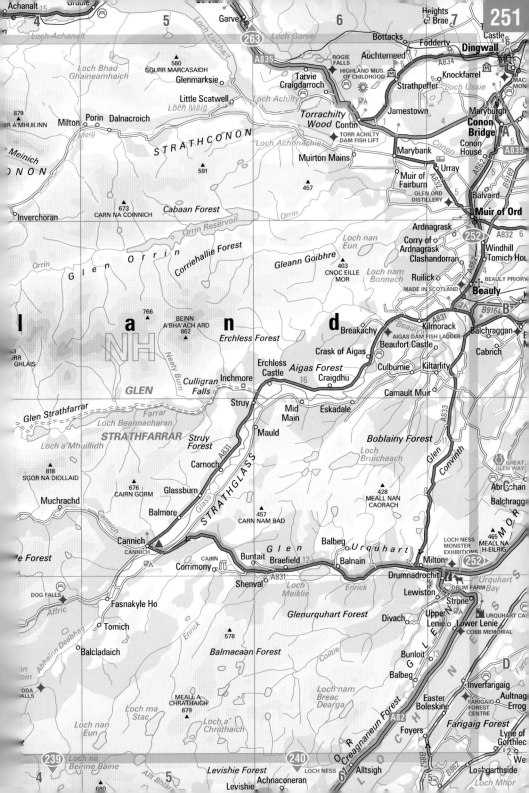

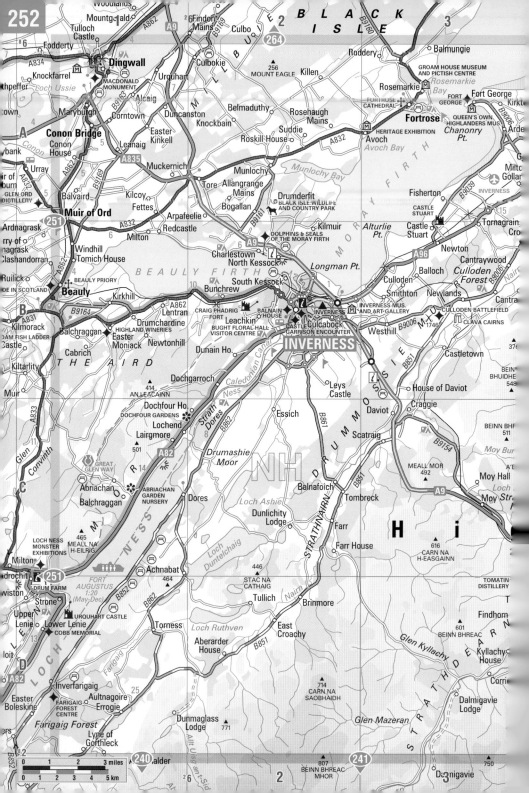

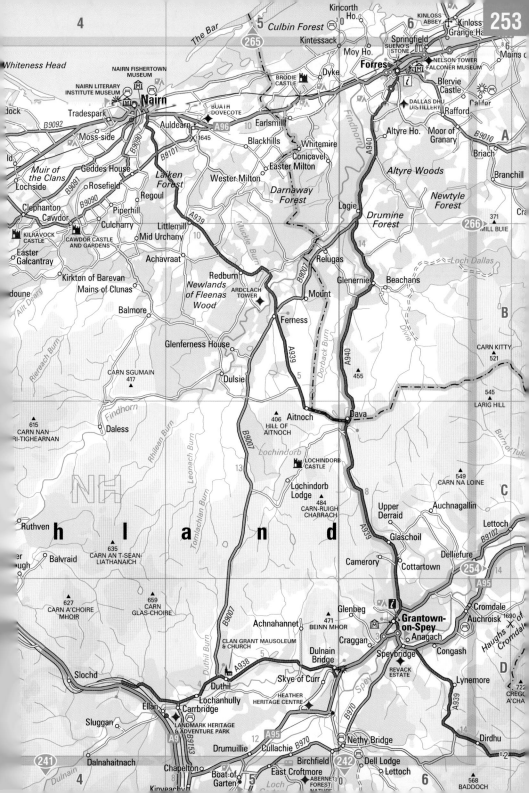

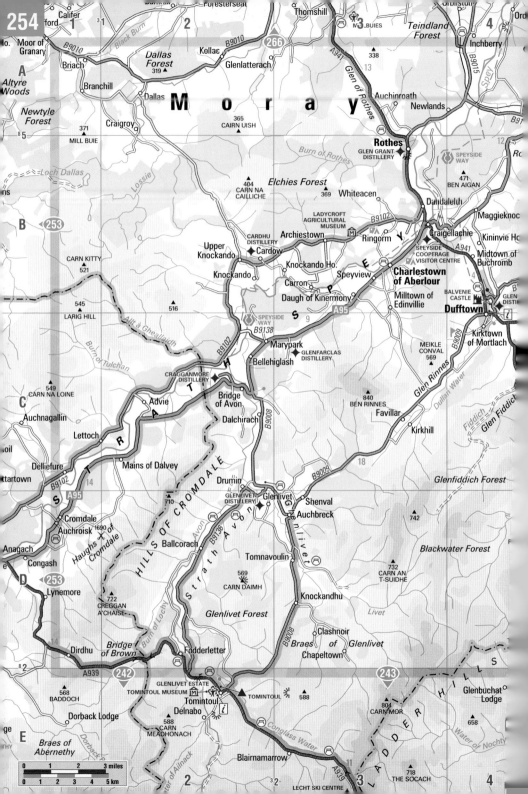

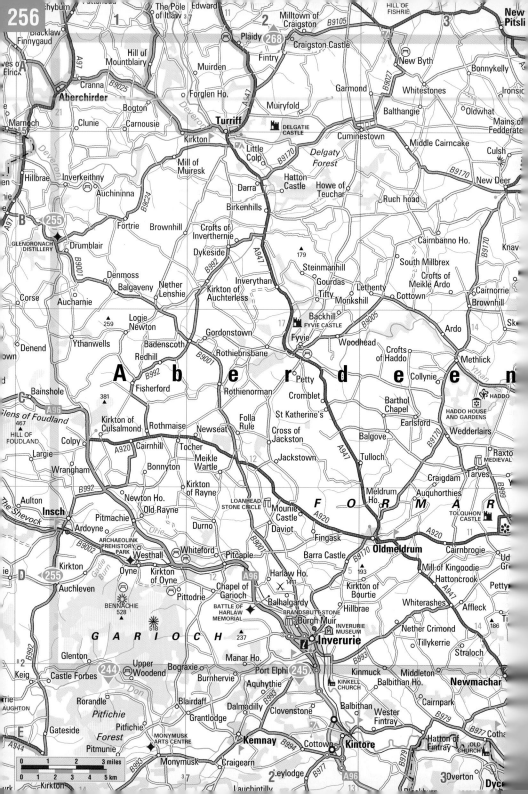

1 | 2 | 2 | 3

Fladda-chùain

Rubha H

A

TARBERT
1:45

LOCHMADDY
1:50

287

Lub
Score

Hungladder
Bornesketaly
Kilmuir
FLORA MACDONALD'S
MEMORIAL

B

Waternish Point

W
A
T
E
R
N
I
S
H

Ascrib
Islands

BEN
GEARY
284

Geary
Knockbreck
Gillen

Kilbride Point

Ru Chorachan

Totscore

Idrigill

Uig Bay

L   O   C   H

TRUMPAN CHURCH
Trumpan

Ard Beag

Ardmore Pt.

Lower
Halistra

Upper Halistra

Hallin

Stein

Lusta

S   N   I   Z   O   R   T

I   S   L   A

Lyndale Pt.

A

Dunvegan Head

Mingay

Isay

Loch
Bay

B886
Bay River

Greshornish
Pt.

Greshornish

Loch Greshornish

O   F

Lyndale Ho.

Loch Sn

C

L
O
C
H

D
U
N
V
E
G
A
N

Galtrigill

THE MACCRIMMON PIPING
HERITAGE CENTRE
Borreraig
BORRERAIG PARK
MUSEUM

Uig

Claigan

327
BEINN
BHREAC

18
Flashader

Treasla
Sulada

Edinbane

S   K   Y

Blackhill

Glen Ber

An Ceannaich

Loch Poolt

Husabost

Feriniquarrie

Lower Milovaig

Glasphein

Totaig

B884

Oisgill Bay

Upper
Milovaig

Lephin

Holmisdale

Glen Dale

Hamara

COLBOST FOLK
MUSEUM
Colbost

TOY MUSEUM

Skinidin

DUNVEGAN
CASTLE

A850

i

GIANT ANGUS
MACKASKILL MUSEUM

CRUACHAN BEINN
A'CHEARCAILL
266

Glen Ber

LIGHTHOUSE
Neist
Point

Moonen
Bay

Ramasaig

HEALABHAL
MHOR
468

Macleod's
Tables

488
HEALABHAL BHEAG

Dunvegan

Kilmuir
Lonmore

Roskhill

Roag

Vatten

Orbost

Harlosh

Loch
Varkasaig

Balmore

Loch Caroy

246

10

Ose

A863

Loch Connar

Loch

Ose

B88

Hoe Rape

Hoe Point

Geodha Mor

2

Harlosh I.

Tarner I. Ullinish

Bracadale

0   1   2   3 miles
0 1 2 3 4 5 km

260

261

A

B

Eilean Trodday

Rubha na h-Aiseig

Balmacqueen
20
Kilmaluag
SEUM OF
AND LIFE

Eilean Flodigarry
Flodigarry

MEALL NA
SUIRAMACH
543
Digg
Glashvin
THE QUIRAING
Brogaig
Stenscholl
Staffin
TROTTERNISH
466
BIOD BUIDHE

Staffin I.

Staffin Bay

Kilt Rock
KILT ROCK & MEALT FALLS

Elishader
Maligar
Marishader
Loch Mealt
Valtos
Garros
Breckrey
Lealt
LEALT FALLS
611
BEINN EDRA
Balnaknock

A855

Rubha nam Brathairean
Culnaknock

Lower Tote
Upper Tote

NG

Lealt

Hinnisdal
D
607
CREAG A'LAIN
Romesdal

719
THE STORR
OLD MAN OF STORR
13

TROTTERNISH
Haultin

Eyre
yre
sdale

A855

Borve
Carbost
eabost
hader
Drumuie
Glengrasco
392

Bearreraig Bay
Holm I.
Loch Leathan
Loch Fada
PRINCE CHARLES'S
CAVE
Rubha na h Airde Glaise

Achachork
AN TUIREANN ARTS
CENTRE
Torvaig
Shulishadermor
THE AROS
EXPERIENCE
Portree

Heatherfield
417
Penifiler
413
BEN
TIANAVAIG

Glenmore

Mugeary

125
Island of Rona

Eilean Garbh

Callakille
C
Lonbain

Eilean Tigh
Garbh Eilean

SOUND OF RAASAY

Caol Rona

An Caol
Loch a' Sguirr

Eilean Fladday

249
Torran
Arnish
Loch Arnish

BROCHEL CASTLE
Brochel

Glame
385
ISLAND OF RAASAY

Balmeanach
Balachuirn
248
443
DUN CAAN
Uskaig

INNER SOUND

Loch nan Eun

CHAPEL OF
MAELRUB

D
Applecross Bay

Camusteel
Ard-dhubh
Toscaig

Rubha na'Leac
Eilean na Bà

1 ¹5 **2** **3**

⁹0
*Garbh
Eilean*

Eilean Mhuire

Eilean an Tighe

◁288

*Na h-Eileanan Mòra
(Shiant Islands)*

A

288

B

NG

259

Eilean Trodday

*Rubha
Hunish*

Rubha na h-Aiseig

C
DUN CLM
CASTLE
Duntulm   20   ◦ Balmacqueen

Kilmaluag

MUSEUM OF
ISLAND LIFE

*Eilean
Flodigarry*

Flodigarry

MEALL NA
SUIRAMACH
543
▲

259◁

Kilvaxter

Staffin I.

Digg   *Staffin
Bay*

THE QUIRAING   Glashvin

Linicro   Brogaig

Stenscholl   ◦ Staffin

TROTTERNISH   **Kilt Rock**
466   KILT ROCK & MEALT FALLS
▲
BIOD BUIDHE

D   Elishader
Maligar
Loch Mealt
Marishader   Valtos

Uig   Garros
UIG
Balnaknock   *Rubha nam
611   Breckrey   Brathairean*
BEINN EDRA
Culnaknock   **Island of Rona**
Earlish
Lealt
LEALT FALLS

⁸6   Lower Tote
0   1   2   3 miles
0 1 2 3 4 5 km   Upper Tote
¹5   **2**   **3**

Bottle I.

270

Cailleach Hd.

Greenstone Point

Rubha Beag

Stattic Pt.

Opinan

Rubha Mor

Gruinard I.

Badluarach

Mellon Udrigle

A

Mungasdale

A832

Achgarve

Gruinard Bay

Gruinard House

155

Mellon Charles

Laide

First Coast

Inchina

Ormiscaig

Sand

262

Second Coast

Tighnafiline

Little Gruinard

302

Aultbea

Drumchork

Loch a'Bhaid-luachraich

Isle of Ewe

Cove

Loch an Draing

B8057

Loch Sguod

Inverasdale

Midtown

L O C H

E W E

14

Loch Fada

Aird Dubh

B

Brae

Rubha 'Ard na Bà

Tournaig

680

BEINN A'CHAISGEIN BEAG

Fisherfield Forest

Sròn a' Gheodha Dhuibh

Rubha Reidh

Camas Mór

Eilean Furadh Mór

296

AN CUAIDH

Seana Chamas

Melvaig

Aultgrishan

Peterburn

Naast

INVEREWE GARDEN

Loch Bad a'Chreamh

A832

Londubh

Loch Kernsary

FIONN LOCH

Dubh Loch

rt Erradale

North Erradale

B8021

Poolewe

Loch Ewe

Loch Tollaidh

Loch

bha Bàn

Big Sand

CARN DEARG

Caolas Beag

Smithstown

Strath

GAIRLOCH HERITAGE MUSEUM

Gairloch

791

BEINN AIRIGH CHARR

onga nd

MEALL AN DOIREAN 420

LOCH GAIRLOCH

Charlestown

A832

Eilean Subhainn

LOCH MAREE ISLANDS

L e t t e r e w e   F o r e s t

BEINN LAIR 860

C

Port Henderson

Aird

B8056

Badachro

Kerrysdale

Letterewe

262

Opinan

Shieldaig

Kerry

Loch Bad an Sgalaig

VICTORIA FALLS

Talladale

980 SLIOC

Loch Clàir

South Erradale

Redpoint

Erradale

Dubh Loch

Abhainn a' Gharbh Choire

19

A832

Glen Grudie

878

D

Rubha na Fearn

Loch Gaineamhach

Flowerdale   Forest

Loch na h-Oidhche

W E S T E R

Kinlochewe Forest

Kinl

Abhainn Braigh-horrisdale

875

BAOSBHEINN

Shieldaig   Forest

R O S S

BEINN EIGHE NATIONAL NATURE RESERVE

1010

BEINN EIGHE

A89

624

BEINN BHREAC

Loch a'Bhealaich

Craig

W

E

985

BEINN ALLIGIN

S

T

E

R

O

S

S

Fearnmore

Fearnbeg

Ari acrinachd

Loch Torridon

Lower Diabaig

249

Allig

Rochullin

To don Forest

1054

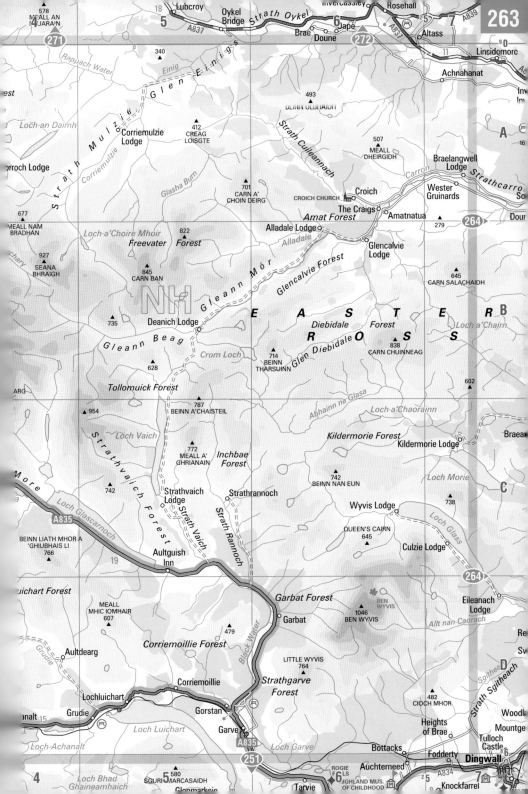

Lubcroy
Oykel Bridge Strath Oykel Invercassley Rosehall
A837 Cape Altass
Brae Doune 272 A839 Lincidomorc
271 Rappach Water
578 MEALL AN FÙJARA'N 18 5 6 7 9 0
11
340 Einig Glen Einig Achnahanat
493 BEINN OLDHAIDH A
Loch-an Daimh Corriemulzie Lodge Strath Cuileannach Inv
412 CREAG LOISGTE 507 MEALL DHEIRGIDH 16
orroch Lodge Corriemulzie Glasha Burn Carron Braelangwell Lodge Strathcarro
701 CARN A' CHOIN DEIRG CROICH CHURCH Croich Wester Gruinards So
677 The Craigs Amatnatua Dour
MEALL NAM BRADHAN Amat Forest 279 264
Loch-a'Choire Mhoir Alladale Lodge Alladale Glencalvie Lodge
822 Freevater Forest Glencalvie Forest 645 CARN SALACHAIDH
927 SEANA BHRAIGH 845 CARN BAN NH B
Gleann Mòr Loch a'Chairn
uchary 735 E A S T 602
Deanich Lodge R O S S
Gleann Beag Crom Loch Diebidale Forest
628 714 BEINN THARSUINN Glen Diebidale 838 CARN CHUINNEAG
ARG Tollomuick Forest Abhainn na Glasa Loch-a'Chaorainn
954 787 BEINN A'CHAISTEIL Kildermorie Forest Braea
Loch Vaich Kildermorie Lodge
772 MEALL A' GHRIANAIN Inchbae Forest Loch Morie C
742 742 BEINN NAN EUN 738
More Strathvaich Lodge Strathrannoch Wyvis Lodge
Loch Glascarnoch QUEEN'S CAIRN 645 Culzie Lodge Loch Glass
A835 19 Strathvaich Forest Strath Vaich Strath Rannoch 264
Aultguish Inn Eileanach Lodge
uichart Forest Garbat Forest BEN WYVIS Allt nan Caorach D
BEINN LIATH MHOR A 'GHIUBHAIS LI 766 MEALL MHIC IOMHAIR 607 479 Garbat 1046 BEN WYVIS Strath Sgitheach
Aultdearg Corriemoillie Forest Black Water LITTLE WYVIS 764 482 CIOCH MHOR Woodla
Grudie Corriemoillie Strathgarve Forest Heights of Brae Mountge
Lochluichart Gorstan Tulloch Castle
analt 15 Grudie Garve Bottacks Fodderty Dingwall
Loch Luichart A835 Loch Garve 251 Auchterneed A834 6
4 Loch Achanalt ROGIE FLS HIGHLAND MUS. OF CHILDHOOD Knockfarrel
Loch Bhad Ghaineamhaich 580 SGURI MARCASAIDH Glenmarksie Tarvie 5 7

A

B

◄ 265

C

D

E

Lossiemouth
Branderburgh
Halliman Skerries
Stotfield
LOSSIEMOUTH FISHERIES & COMMUNITY MUSEUM
Covesea Skerries
Covesea
Hopeman
B9040
Duffus
Gordonstoun
Burghead
BURGHEAD MUSEUM
Cummingston
Roseisle
DUFFUS CASTLE
PALACE OF SPYNIE
Loch Spynie
Lossie Forest
S P
Kingston
Roseisle Forest
B9089
B9013
Quarrywood
B9012
Spynie
Bishopmill
Leuchars Ho.
Lochhill
Garmouth
BURGHEAD BAY
Lower Hempriggs
Newton
Coltfield
Miltonhill
Alves
Elgin
ELGIN MUSEUM
CATHEDRAL
OLD MILLS
CASHMERE VISITOR CENTRE
Urquhart
Lhanbryde
Lochs Crofts
B9015
B9011
KINLOSS ABBEY
Kinloss
Grange Hall
A96
12
Pittendreich
MORAY MOTOR MUSEUM
New Elgin
A96
Moss of Barmuckity
COXTON TOWER
Mosstodloch
BA HIG VIL
SP
gfield
NELSON TOWER
FALCONER MUSEUM
Mains of Burgie
Miltonduff
Paddockhaugh
Longmorn
Blackhills
B9103
Dipple
Orbliston
Blervie Castle
Califer
PLUSCARDEN ABBEY
Monaughty Forest
Auchtertyre
BIRNIE CHURCH
Thomshill
MILLBUIES
Teindland Forest
Inchberry
DALLAS DHU DISTILLERY
Rafford
Barnhill
Foresterseat
Ho.
Moor of Granary
B9010
Black Burn
Kellas
B9010
Glenlatterach
338
13
B9015
Spey
Briach
Dallas Forest
319 ▲
Altyre Woods
Branchill
Dallas
M o r a y
Glen of Rothes
A941
Auchinroath
Newlands
Newtyle Forest
253
Craigroy
371
MILL BUIE
365
CAIRN UISH
Rothes
GLEN GRANT DISTILLERY
SPEYSIDE WAY
471
BEN AIGAN
Loch Dallas
Lossie
Burn of Rothes
ans
404
CARN NA CAILLICHE
Elchies Forest
369
Whiteacen
Dandaleith
Maggie
LADYCROFT AGRICULTURAL MUSEUM
B9102
Craigellachie
SPEYSIDE COOPERAGE
A941
Kinin
Midtov
254
Archiestown
CARDHU DISTILLE
Cardi v
Ringorm
Upper Knockando
CARN KITTY

0   1   2   3 miles
0 1 2 3 4 5 km

A

8

NJ NK

B

C

D

8 5

E

Fraserburgh

SANDHAVEN MEAL MILL
ehearty
B9031
Pittulie
FRASERBURGH HERITAGE MUSEUM
Broadsea
ITSLIGO CASTLE
Sandhaven
Kinnaird Head
Peathill
KINNAIRD CASTLE LIGHTHOUSE & SCOTLAND'S LIGHTHOUSE MUSEUM
Percyhorner
Pitblae
Fraserburgh Bay
Cairnbulg Pt.
per yndlie
Coburty
A981
B9107
Inverallochy
Mid Ardlaw
B9032
Cairnbulg Castle
A90
B9033
MAGGIE'S HOOSIE
Tyrie
Memsie
Gowanhill
St Combs
Whitewell
MEMSIE BURIAL CAIRN
Rathen
Inzie Head
Strathellie
B9033
A98
10
Cairness
Loch of Strathbeg
Hillhead of Auchentumb
Newburgh
Crimonmogate
LOCH OF STRATHBEG NATURE RESERVE VISITOR CENTRE
230
Lonmay
Rattray Head
16
MORMOND HILL
Crimond
Old Rattray
Knowhead
093
Strichen
A952
Nether Park
Blackhill
A90
New Leeds
Longhill
B9093
Balearn
Adziel
Leys
St Fergus Moss
Kirktown
St Fergus
Scotstown Hd.
Little Skillymarno
North Kirkton
11
Denhead
Backfolds
Kirkton Hd.
Fetterangus
Hythie
Rora Moss
A981
Toux
Rora
Lunderton
Ugie
Forest of Deer
DEER ABBEY
Woodside
Inverugie
UGIE SALMON FISH HOUSE
U C H A N
Dunshillock
INVERUGIE CASTLE
Buchanhaven
aud
B9029
Newseat
Torterston
Peterhead
Old Deer
Mintlaw
Longside
Water
Keith Inch
ARBUTHNOT MUSEUM & ART GALLERY
ABERDEENSHIRE FARMING MUSEUM
Flushing
A982
Stuartfield
South Ugie
Inverquhomery
A950
PETERHEAD MARITIME
Bulwark
Millbreck
Net
Hillhead of Cocklaw
Peterhead Bay
ymuir
Mains of Crichie
257
Invernettie
ethermuir
Crichie
B9030
Kinmundy
Little Dens
Sandford Bay

4
40
5
41
6

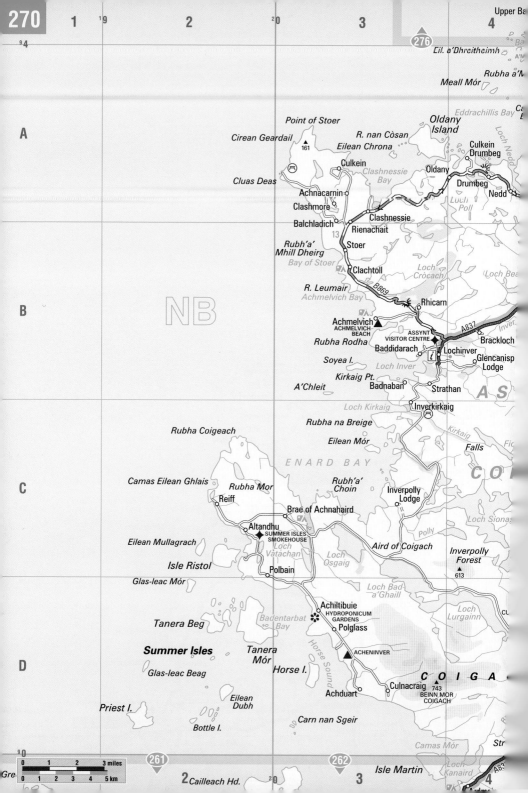

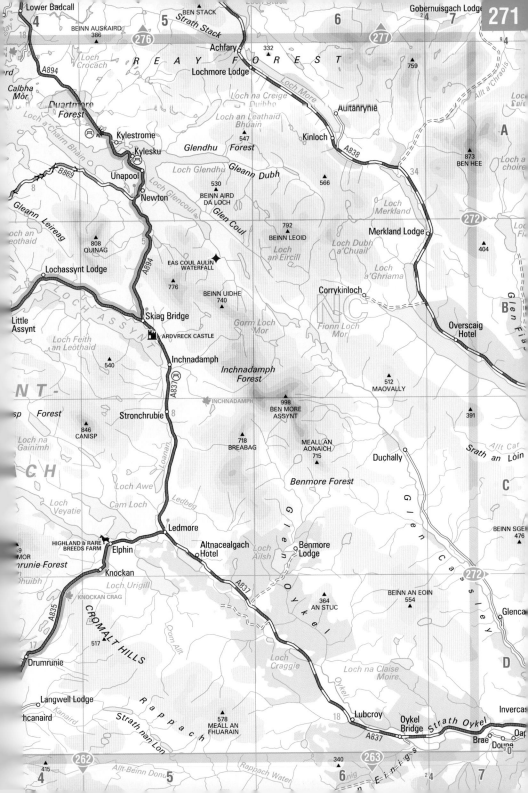

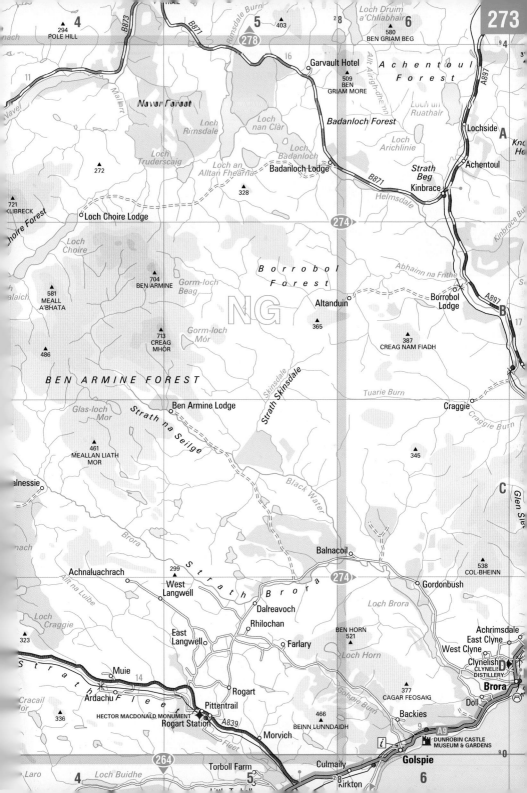

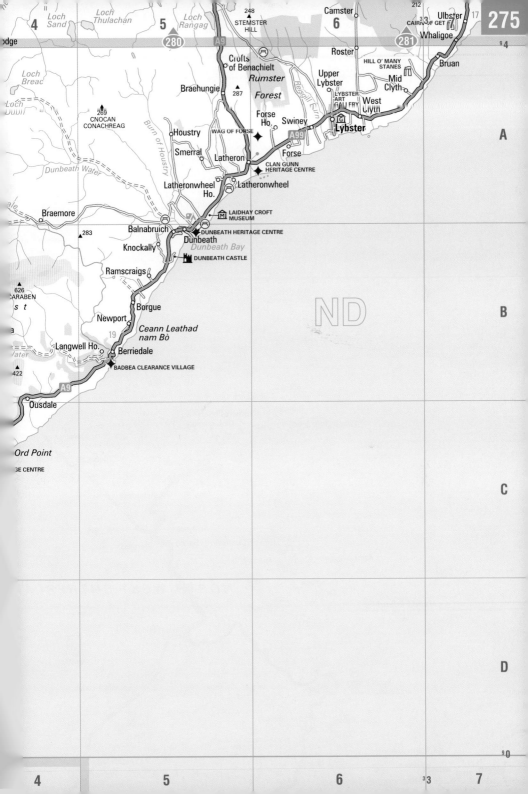

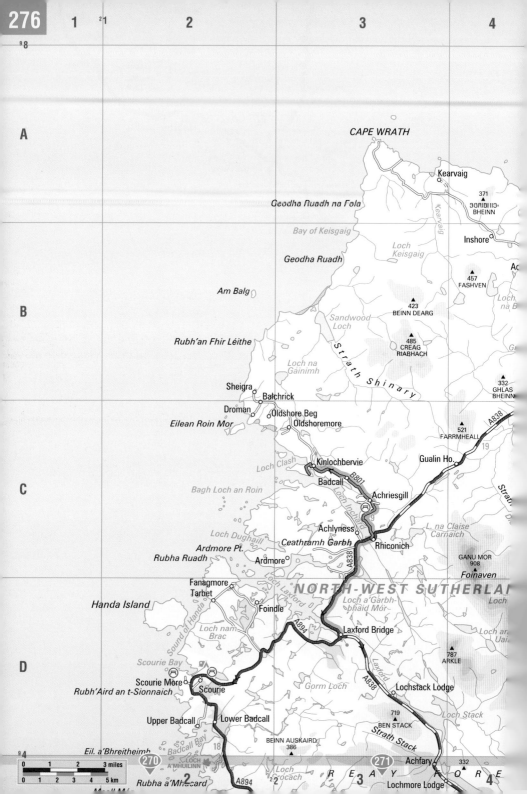

98

A

277

Whiten
Head

Rubha Thormaid

Port Vasgo

Eilean nan Ron

Ardmore Pt.

Kirtomy Pt.

B
408
BEN
HUTIG
Strathan
Midfield
West Strathan
Talmine
Skinnet
Midtown
A'Mhoine
A838

Rabbit
Is.
Tongue
Bay

Skerray

Caol Raineach

Neave I. or
Coombe I.

Farr Pt.

Torrisdale
Bay

Achtoty
Airdtorrisdale
Torrisdale

Skullomie
Coldbackie

STRATHNAVER
MUSEUM

Farr

Kirtomy

Swordly

Armadale

A836
17

Achuvoldrach

Tongue
Kirkiboll
Tongue
CASTLE
VARRICH

KYLE OF TONGUE

Ribigill

Borgie

Borgie Forest

Bettyhill
Achina
Invernaver
Leckfurin

A836

ACHANLOCHY
CLEARANCE VILLAGE
Skelpick

Loch Meadie

Loch
Buidhe Mor

229

C
Cuim nan Cliar
310

Loch Mor
Caorac

Loch na
Clach

Achagary

STRATHNAVER

Skelpick Burn

KYLE OF TONGUE
Loch na Seilg
Kinloch Lodge
Kinloch
Loch
Craggie

B871

Clachan Burn

Carnachy
Rhifail
9

Loch a'
Ghobha-
Dhuibh
277
16
Loch
Loyal
764
BEN LOYAL
527
BEINN
STUMANADH

Skail

293
BEINN
RIFA-GIL

Loch
Strathy

D
Loch an
Dherue
Loch Loyal Lodge
557
CNOC NAN
CULLEAN
Loch Haluim
Langdale
Naver
Loch
Syre
Syre
Dalvina Lo.
B873
ROSAL CLEARANCE
TRAIL

416
Inchkinloch
Loch Coulside
Loch Eileanach
294
POLE HILL
273
B871
403
16

Loch
Meadie

94
0   1   2   3 miles
0 1 2 3 4 5 km
A836
26
11
2
3

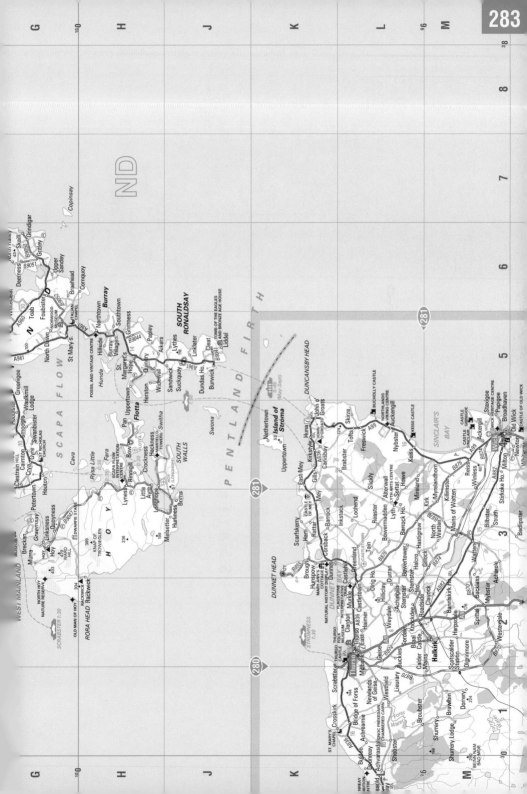

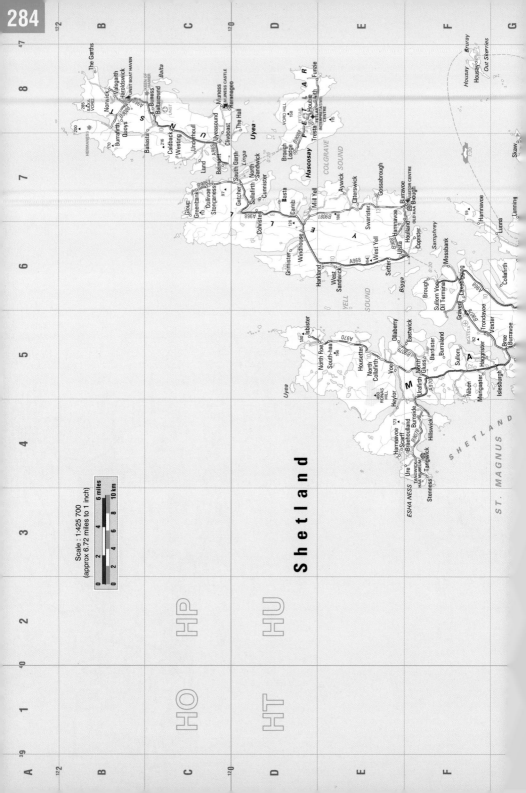

Shetland

Scale : 1:425 700
(approx 6.72 miles to 1 inch)

0   2   4   6 miles

0   2   4   6   8   10 km

HO
HP
HU
HT

ST. MAGNUS

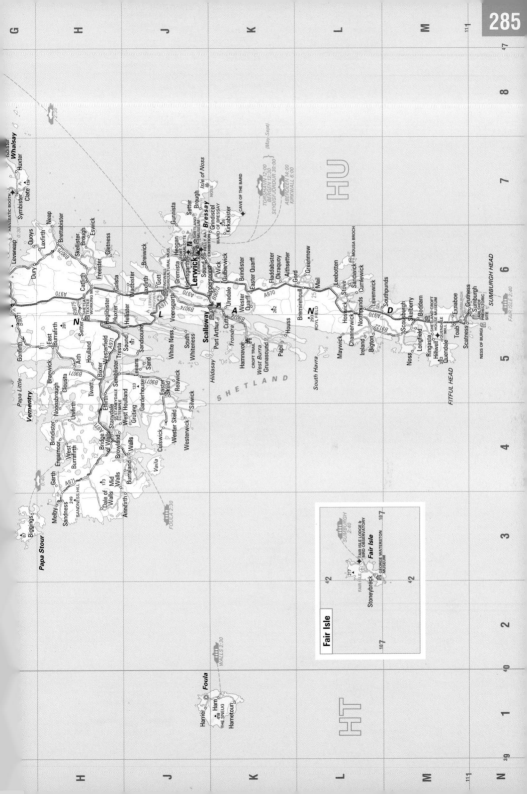

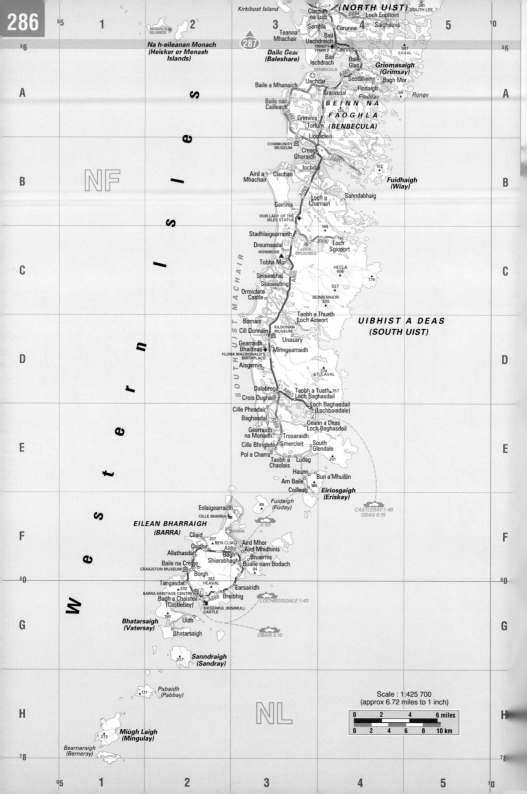

Aberdeen

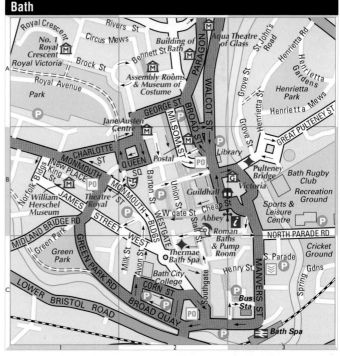

Aberdeen

Bath

Bath

Birmingham

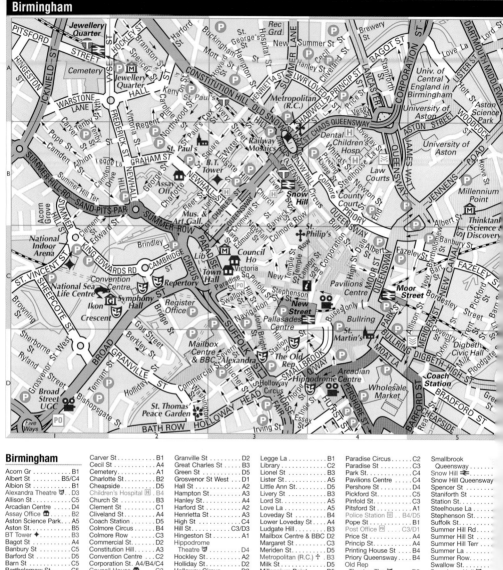

Birmingham

Acorn Gr B1
Albert St B5/C4
Albion St B1
Alexandra Theatre 🎭 . D3
Allison St C5
Arcadian Centre D4
Assay Office 🏛 B2
Aston Science Park . . . A5
Aston St B5
BT Tower ✦ B3
Bagot St A4
Banbury St C5
Barford St D5
Barn St C5
Bartholomew St. C5
Barwick St B3
Bath Row D2
Berkley St D2
Bishopsgate St D1
Blucher St D3
Bordesley St C5
Bradford St D5
Branston St A2
Brewery St A4
Bridge St C2
Brindley Dr. C2
Broad St C2/D1
Broad Street UGC . . . D1
Browning St. C1
Buckingham St A3
Bull Ring C4
Bull St C4
Cambridge St C2
Camden Dr B1
Camden St B1
Cannon St C3
Caroline St A2

Carver St B1
Cecil St A4
Cemetery A1
Charlotte St B2
Cheapside D5
Church St B3
Clement St C1
Cleveland St D3
Coach Station D5
Colmore Circus B4
Colmore Row C3
Commercial St D2
Constitution Hill. A3
Convention Centre . . . C2
Corporation St . . . A4/B4/C4
Council House 🏛 C3
County Court. B4
Coventry St D5
Cox St A2
Crescent Theatre 🎭 . . C1
Cromwell St B3
Dale End C4
Dartmouth Middleway . A5
Dental Hospital 🇭 . . . B4
Digbeth Civic Hall . . . D5
Digbeth High St D5
Edmund St C3
Edward St C1
Ellis St D3
Essex St D3
Fazeley St C5
Five Ways D1
Fleet St B2
Floodgate St D5
Fore St C4
Frederick St B2
Gas St C2
George St B2
Graham St B2

Granville St D2
Great Charles St B3
Green St D5
Grosvenor St West . . . D1
Hall St B2
Hampton St A3
Hanley St A4
Harford St A2
Henrietta St A3
High St C4
Hill St C3/D3
Hingeston St A1
Hippodrome
    Theatre 🎭 D4
Hockley St A2
Holliday St D2
Holloway Circus D3
Holloway Head D3
Holt St A5
Horse Fair D3
Hospital St A3
Howard St A3
Howe St B5
Hurst St D4
Icknield St A1
Ikon Gallery 🏛 C2
Information Ctr 🅸 C3
Inge St D3
Irving St D3
James Watt
    Queensway B4
Jennens Rd B4
Jewellery Quarter 🚉 . A1
Jewellery Quarter
    Museum 🏛 A2
John Bright St D3
Kenyon St A2
King Edwards Rd C1
Lancaster St B4
Law Courts B4

Legge La B1
Library C2
Lionel St B3
Lister St B5
Little Ann St D5
Livery St A3
Lord St. A5
Love La A5
Loveday St B4
Lower Loveday St A4
Ludgate Hill B3
Mailbox Centre & BBC D2
Margaret St C3
Meriden St D5
Metropolitan (R.C.) ✝ . B3
Milk St. D5
Millennium Point B5
Moat La D4
Moor St C4
Moor St Queensway . . C4
Mott St A3
Museum & Art
    Gallery 🏛 C3
National Indoor
    Arena ✦ C1
National Sea Life
    Centre ★ C1
Navigation St C3
New Bartholomew St . . C5
New Canal St C5
New St C3
New Street 🚉 C3
New Summer St A3
Newhall Hill B2
Newhall St B2/C3
Newton St B4
Northwood St A2
Old Snow Hill A3
Oxford St D5
Pallasades Centre C3

Paradise Circus C2
Paradise St C3
Park St. C4
Pavilions Centre C4
Pershore St D4
Pickford St C5
Pinfold St C3
Pitsford St A1
Police Station 🅿 . . B4/D5
Pope St B1
Post Office 🄿 C3/D1
Price St A4
Princip St A4
Printing House St B4
Priory Queensway . . . B4
Old Rep
    Theatre, The 🎭 . . . D3
Queensway B3
Railway Mosaics ✦ . . . B3
Rea St D5
Regent Pl. B2
Register Office C2
Repertory Theatre 🎭 . C2
Ryland St D1
St Chads Circus B3
St Chads Queensway . . A4
St George's St A3
St Martin's 🛐 D4
St Paul's 🚉 B3
St Paul's Metro station A3
St Paul's Sq. B2
St Philip's ✝ C3
St Thomas' Peace
    Garden ✿ D2
St Vincent St C1
Sand Pits Pde B1
Severn St. D3
Shadwell St A4
Sheepcote St D1
Sherborne St D1

Smallbrook
    Queensway C3
Snow Hill 🚉 B3
Snow Hill Queensway . B4
Spencer St B2
Staniforth St A4
Station St C3
Steelhouse La B4
Stephenson St. C3
Suffolk St C3
Summer Hill Rd B1
Summer Hill St B1
Summer Hill Terr B1
Summer La A4
Summer Row. B2
Swallow St. C3
Symphony Hall 🎭 . . . C2
Temple Row. C3
Temple St. C3
Tenby St B1
Tenby St North B1
Tennant St C1
Thinktank (Science
    & Discovery) 🏛 . . . B5
Thorpe St. D3
Town Hall 🏛 C2
Trent St C5
University of Central
    England B4
University of Aston . . . B5
Vesey St B4
Victoria Sq. C3
Vittoria St B1
Vyse St B1
Warstone La B1
Washington St. D2
Water St B3
Whittall St B4
Wholesale Market . . . D4
Woodcock St A5

Bristol

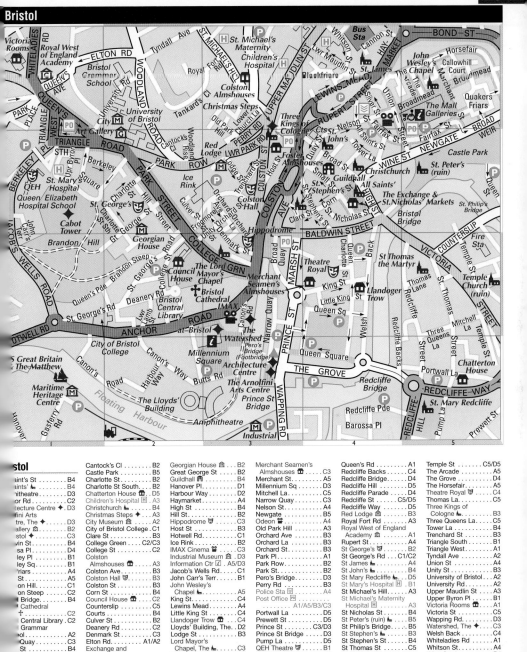

Cantock's Cl B2
Castle Park B5
Charlotte St B2
Charlotte St South. . . . B2
Chatterton House 🏛 . D5
Children's Hospital Ⓗ . A3
Christchurch ⛪ B4
Christmas Steps ✦ . A3
City Museum 🏛 A2
City of Bristol College . C1
Clare St B3
College Green C2/C3
College St C2
Colston
  Almshouses 🏛 . . . A3
Colston Ave. B3
Colston Hall 🎭 B3
Colston St B3
Corn St B4
Council House 🏛 . . . C2
Counterslip C4
Courts B4
Culver St B3
Deanery Rd C2
Denmark St C3
Elton Rd A1/A2
Exchange and
  St Nicholas'
  Mkts, The 🏛 B4
Fairfax St B4/B5
Fire Station C5
Floating Harbour D2
Foster
  Almshouses 🏛 . . B3
Frogmore St B2
Gasferry Rd D1

Georgian House 🏛 . . B2
Great George St . . . B2
Guildhall 🏛 B4
Hanover Pl. D1
Harbour Way D2
Haymarket B4
High St B4
Hill St. B2
Hippodrome 🎭 C3
Host St B3
Hotwell Rd. C1
Ice Rink B2
IMAX Cinema 🎬 . . . C3
Industrial Museum 🏛 . D3
Information Ctr 🛈 . A5/D3
Jacob's Wells Rd C1
John Carr's Terr B1
John Wesley's
  Chapel A5
King St. C4
Lewins Mead A4
Little King St C4
Llandoger Trow 🏛 . . C4
Lloyds' Building, The . . B4
Lodge St B3
Lord Mayor's
  Chapel, The ⛪ . . C3
Lower Church La A3
Lower Lamb St C2
Lower Maudlin St . . . A4
Lower Park Rd B3
Mall Galleries
  Shopping Ctr, The . . A5
Maritime Heritage
  Centre D1
Marsh St C3

Merchant Seamen's
  Almshouses 🏛 . . . C3
Merchant St. A5
Millennium Sq D3
Mitchell La. C5
Narrow Quay C3
Nelson St A4
Newgate B5
Odeon 🎭 A4
Old Park Hill A3
Orchard Ave B3
Orchard La B3
Orchard St B3
Park Pl A1
Park Row B2
Park St. B2
Pero's Bridge D3
Perry Rd B3
Police Sta 🚓 A4
Post Office 🏤
  . . . . A1/A5/B3/C3
Portwall La D5
Prewett St D5
Prince St C3/D3
Prince St Bridge D3
Pump La D5
QEH Theatre 🎭 B1
Quakers Friars A5
Quay St B4
Queen Charlotte St . . C4
Queen Elizabeth
  Hospital School. . . B1
Queen Sq C4/D4
Queen St B5
Queen's Ave A1
Queen's Parade C1

Queen's Rd A1
Redcliffe Backs C4
Redcliffe Bridge D4
Redcliffe Hill D5
Redcliffe Parade D4
Redcliffe St C5/D5
Redcliffe Way D5
Red Lodge 🏛 B3
Royal Fort Rd A3
Royal West of England
  Academy 🏛 A1
Rupert St B2
St George's 🎭 B2
St George's Rd . . . C1/C2
St James ⛪ A4
St John's ⛪ B4
St Mary Redcliffe ⛪ . D5
St Michael's Hill A3
St Michael's Maternity
  Hospital Ⓗ A3
St Nicholas St B4
St Peter's (ruin) ⛪ . . B5
St Philip's Bridge B5
St Stephen's ⛪ B3
St Stephen's St B4
St Thomas St C5
St Thomas the
  Martyr ⛪ C5
Silver St A4
Small St. B4
SS Great Britain and
  The Matthew ⚓ . . D1
Tankard's St. A2
Temple Church
  (ruin) ⛪ C5

Temple St C5/D5
The Arcade A5
The Grove D4
The Horsefair. A5
Theatre Royal 🎭 . . . C4
Thomas La. C5
Three Kings of
  Cologne ⛪ B3
Three Queens La. . . . C5
Tower La B4
Trenchard St B3
Triangle South B1
Triangle West A1
Tyndall Ave A2
Union St A4
Unity St B3
University of Bristol. . . A2
University Rd A2
Upper Maudlin St . . . A3
Upper Byron Pl B1
Victoria Rooms 🏛 . . . A1
Victoria St C5
Wapping Rd. D3
Watershed, The ✦ . . C4
Welsh Back C4
Whiteladies Rd A1
Whitson St A4
Wine St B4
Woodland Rise B2
Woodland Rd. A2
YHA ▲ D3

stol
──────────
aint's St B4
aint's ⛪ B4
hitheatre. D3
or Rd C2
tecture Centre ✦ . D3
fini Arts
tre, The ✦. D3
allery 🏛 B2
stol ✦ B4
win St. B4
sa Pl B1
ley Pl B1
ley Sq. B1
Friars A4
St A5
on Hill. C1
on Steep C2
Bridge. B4
Cathedral
✦ C2
Central Library . C2
Grammar
ol A2
Quay C3
St A5
Weir A5
mead A5
ation A4
Rd B3
Tower ✦ B1
hill Ct A5
n St. B4
's Rd C3/D1
's Way D2

Cardiff / Caerdydd

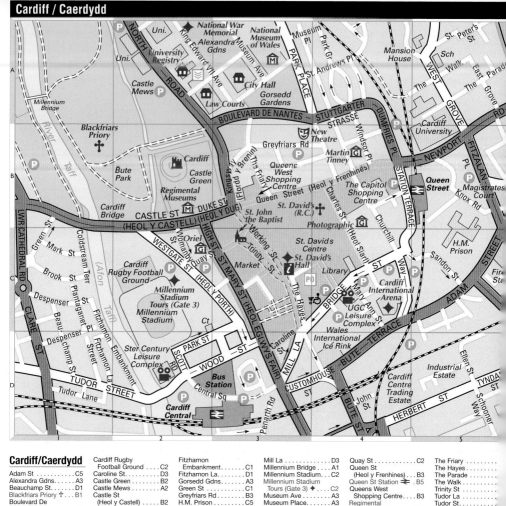

Cardiff/Caerdydd

Adam St C5
Alexandra Gdns A3
Beauchamp St D1
Blackfriars Priory ✝ . . B1
Boulevard De
Nantes A3
Bridge St C4
Brook St C1
Bus Station D3
Bute Park B2
Bute St D4
Bute Terr D4
Capitol Shopping
Centre, The B4
Cardiff Bridge B1
Cardiff Castle 🏰 . . B2
Cardiff Central
Station ⇌ D3
Cardiff Centre
Trading Estate D4
Cardiff International
Arena ✦ C4

Cardiff Rugby
Football Ground C2
Caroline St. D3
Castle Green B2
Castle Mews A2
Castle St
(Heol y Castell) B2
Central Sq D2
Charles St
(Heol Siarl) B4
Churchill Way C4
City Hall 🏛 A3
Clare St D1
Coldstream Terr C1
Court C2
Customhouse St D3
Despenser Place D1
Despenser St. C1
Duke St (Heol y Dug) . . B3
Dumfries Pl B2
East Grove A5
Ellen St D5
Fire Station C5
Fitzalan Place B5

Fitzhamon
Embankment C1
Fitzhamon La. D1
Gorsedd Gdns A3
Green St C1
Greyfriars Rd B3
H.M. Prison C5
Herbert St D5
High St C2
Information Ctr 🅸 . . . C3
John St D4
King Edward VII Ave . . A2
Kingsway
(Ffordd y Brenin) . . . B3
Knox Rd B5
Law Courts 🏛 A2
Library C4
Lower Cathedral Rd . . . C1
Magistrates Court B5
Mansion House A5
Mark St C1
Market C3
Martin Tinney 🏛 B4
Mary Ann St C4

Mill La D3
Millennium Bridge A1
Millennium Stadium . . . C2
Millennium Stadium
Tours (Gate 3) ✦ . . . C2
Museum Ave A3
Museum Place A3
National Museum
of Wales 🏛 A3
National War
Memorial ✦ A2
New Theatre 🎭 B3
Newport Rd B5
North Rd A2
Oriel 🏛 C2
Park Grove A4
Park Place A3
Park St. D3
Penarth Rd D2
Photographic
Library B4
Plantaganet St. C1
Police Station 🅿 A2
Post Office 🖃 C3

Quay St C2
Queen St
(Heol y Frenhines) . . B3
Queen St Station ⇌ . . B5
Queens West
Shopping Centre . . . B3
Regimental
Museums 🏛 B2
St Andrews Place A4
St David's ✝ B4
St David's Centre C3
St David's Hall ✦ C3
St John The
Baptist ⛪ C3
St Mary St
(Heol Eglwys Fair) . . C3
St Peter's St A5
Sandon St C5
Schooner Way D5
Scott Rd D2
Station Terr B4
Ster Century Leisure
Complex 🎥 D2
Stuttgarter Strasse . . . A4

The Friary . . . .
The Hayes . . . .
The Parade . . . .
The Walk . . . .
Trinity St . . . .
Tudor La . . . .
Tudor St . . . .
Tyndall St . . . .
Tyndall Street
Industrial Estate . . . .
UGC Leisure
Complex 🎥 . . . . . .
Cardiff University . . A
University Registry 🏛
Wales International
Ice Rink . . . .
West Gr . . . .
Westgate St
(Heol y Porth) . . . . .
Windsor Place . . . . . .
Womanby St . . . .
Wood St. . . . .
Working St. . . . .

Cambridge

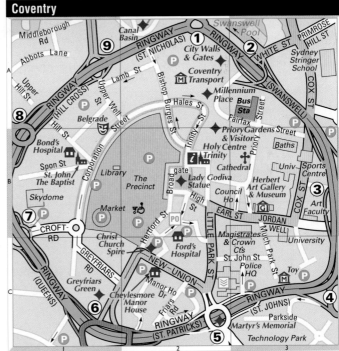

Coventry

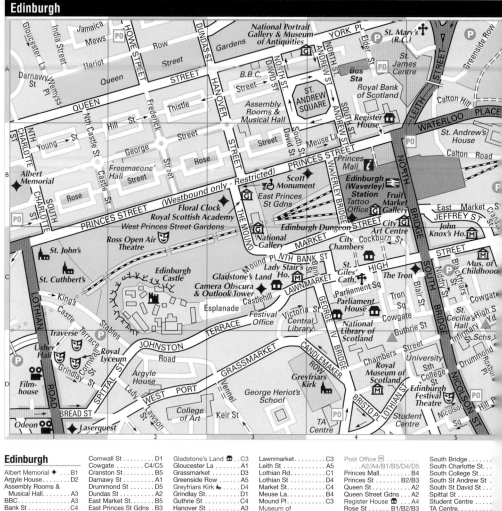

Edinburgh

Albert Memorial ✦ . . B1	Cornwall St D1	Gladstone's Land 🏛 . . C3	Lawnmarket C3	Post Office 🅿	South Bridge . . . .
Argyle House D2	Cowgate C4/C5	Gloucester La A1	Leith St A5	. . . A2/A4/B1/B5/D4/D5	South Charlotte St . . .
Assembly Rooms &	Cranston St B5	Grassmarket D3	Lothian Rd C1	Princes Mall B4	South College St . . .
Musical Hall A3	Darnaway St A1	Greenside Row A5	Lothian St D4	Princes St B2/B3	South St Andrew St .
BBC A3	Drummond St D5	Greyfriars Kirk ▙ . . . D4	Market St C4	Queen St A2	South St David St . .
Bank St C4	Dundas St A2	Grindlay St. D1	Meuse La B4	Queen Street Gdns . . A2	Spittal St . . . .
Blackfriars St. C5	East Market St. B5	Guthrie St C4	Mound Pl C3	Register House 🏛 . . A4	Student Centre . . .
Blair St C5	East Princes St Gdns B3	Hanover St A3	Museum of	Rose St B1/B2/B3	TA Centre. . . . . . .
Bread St D1	Edinburgh	Heriot Row A1/A2	Childhood 🏛 C5	Ross Open	Tattoo Office . . . . .
Bristo Pl. D4	(Waverley) 🚈 B4	High School Yard . . . C5	National Gallery 🏛 . . C4	Air Theatre 🎭 C2	The Mound . . . . . .
Bus Station A4	Edinburgh Castle 🏰 . . C2	High St C4	National Library of	Roxburgh Pl. D5	Thistle St . . . . A
Calton Hill A5	Edinburgh	Hill Pl D5	Scotland C4	Royal Bank	Traverse Theatre 🎭 .
Calton Rd B5	Dungeon ✦ B4	Hill St. B2	National Portrait	of Scotland A4	Tron Sq . . . .
Camera Obscura &	Edinburgh Festival	Howe St. A2	Gallery & Museum	Royal Lyceum 🎭 . . . D1	Tron, The ✦ . . . . . .
Outlook Tower ✦ . . C3	Theatre 🎭 D5	India St A1	of Antiquities 🏛 . . A3	Royal Museum	University. . . . . . .
Candlemaker Row. . . D4	Elder St A4	Infirmary St D5	Nicolson Sq. D5	of Scotland 🏛 . . . D4	Usher Hall 🎭 . . . . .
Castle St B1	Esplanade C3	Information Ctr 🅸 . . B4	Nicolson St D5	Royal Scottish	Vennel . . . .
Castle Terr. C1	Festival Office C3	Jamaica Mews A1	Niddry St C5	Academy 🏛 B3	Victoria St . . . . . .
Castlehill C3	Filmhouse 🎬 D1	Jeffrey St B5	North Bridge B4	St Andrew Sq A4	Waterloo Pl . . . . . .
Central Library. C4	Floral Clock ✦ B3	John Knox's	North Bank St C4	St Andrew's House . . A4	Waverley Bridge . . .
Chambers St D4	Frederick St. A2	House ▙ B4	North Castle St B1	St Cecilia's Hall C5	Wemyss Pl. . . . . . .
City Art Centre 🏛 . . B4	Freemasons' Hall . . . B2	Johnston Terr D2	North Charlotte St . . B1	St Cuthbert's ▙ C1	West Port. . . . .
City Chambers 🏛 . . C4	Fruit Market ✦ B4	Keir St D3	North St Andrew St . . A4	St Giles' ✝ C4	West Princes
Cockburn St C4	George Heriot's	King's Stables Rd . C1/D2	North St David St . . . A3	St James Centre . . . A4	Street Gdns. . . . .
College of Art D2	School. D3	Lady Lawson St D2	Odeon ✦ D1	St John's ▙ C1	York Pl . . . .
	George IV Bridge . . . C4	Lady Stair's House ✦ . C3	Parliament House 🏛 . C4	St Mary's ✝ (R.C.) . . A5	Young St . . . .
	George St B2	Laserquest ✦ D1	Parliament Sq C4	Scott Monument ✦ . . B4	Youth Hostel ▲ . . . .

Glasgow

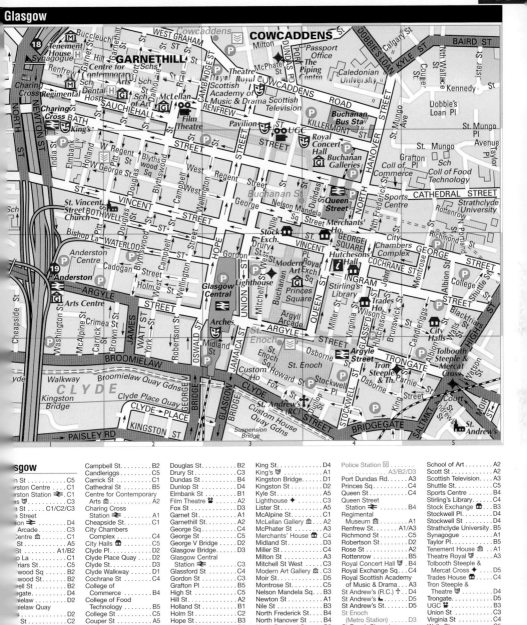

sgow

n St C5
rston Centre C1
rston Station C1
s ☉ C3
e St . . . C1/C2/C3
e Street
tion ☉ D4
Arcade C3
Centre ▥ A5
St A5
. . . . A1/B2
p La C1
riars St C5
wood Sq B2
wood St. B2
ell St B2
egate. D2
mielaw D2
mielaw Quay
. . . . D2
St C2
wick St B2
euch St A4
nan Galleries ▥ . . B4
nan Bus Station . A4
nan St B3
nan St. B3
o Station) B3
St C2
nian University . . . A4
y St A4
dge St A3

Campbell St. B2
Candleriggs C5
Carrick St C1
Cathedral St B5
Centre for Contemporary
    Arts ▥ A2
Charing Cross
    Station ≋ A1
Cheapside St. C1
City Chambers
    Complex C4
City Halls ▥ C5
Clyde Pl. D2
Clyde Place Quay . . . D2
Clyde Walkway D1
Cochrane St C4
College of
    Commerce B4
College of Food
    Technology B5
College St C5
Couper St A5
Cowcaddens
    (Metro Station) . . . A3
Cowcaddens Rd A3
Crimea St C1
Custom House D3
Custom House
    Quay Gdns D3
Dalhousie St A2
Dobbie's Loan A4
Dobbie's Loan Pl . . . A5

Douglas St B2
Drury St. C3
Dundas St B4
Dunlop St D4
Elmbank St B1
Film Theatre ⌕ A2
Fox St D3
Garnet St A1
Garnethill St. A2
George Sq C4
George St C5
George V Bridge . . . D2
Glasgow Bridge. D3
Glasgow Central
    Station ≋ C3
Glassford St. C4
Gordon St C3
Grafton Pl B5
High St C5
Hill St A2
Holland St B1
Holm St. C2
Hope St. B3
Howard St D3
Hutcheson St C4
India St B1
Information Ctr ⌕ . . . C4
Ingram St. C4/C5
Jamaica St D3
James Watt St. C2
John St C4
Kennedy St A5
Killermont St B4

King St D4
King's ☉ A1
Kingston Bridge. D1
Kingston St D2
Kyle St A5
Lighthouse ◆ C3
Lister St A5
McAlpine St C1
McLellan Gallery ▥ . . A2
McPhater St. A3
Merchants' House ▥ . . C4
Midland St D3
Miller St C4
Milton St A3
Mitchell St West C3
Modern Art Gallery ▥ . C3
Moir St. D5
Montrose St. C5
Nelson Mandela Sq. . . B3
Newton St. A1
Nile St B3
North Frederick St . . B4
North Hanover St . . . B4
North Portland St . . . C5
North St. A1
North Wallace St . . . A5
Osborne St D4/D5
Oswald St D2
Paisley Rd D1
Parnie St D5
Passport Office A4
Pavilion Theatre ☉ . . A3
Piping Centre, The ◆ . A3
Pitt St. B2

Police Station ⌕ . . . . . .
    . . . . A3/B2/D3
Port Dundas Rd. A3
Princes Sq. C4
Queen St C4
Queen Street
    Station ≋ B4
Regimental
    Museum ▥ A3
Renfrew St A1/A3
Richmond St C5
Robertson St D2
Rose St A2
Rottenrow B5
Royal Concert Hall ☉ . B4
Royal Exchange Sq. . . C4
Royal Scottish Academy
    of Music & Drama. . A3
St Andrew's (R.C.) ✝ . D4
St Andrew's D5
St Andrew's St D5
St Enoch
    (Metro Station) . . . D3
St Enoch Shopping
    Centre. D3
St Enoch Sq D3
St Mungo Ave B5
St Mungo Pl A5
St Vincent Pl C4
St Vincent St B2
St Vincent Street
    Church B2
Saltmarket D5
Sauchiehall St A2/B3

School of Art A2
Scott St A2
Scottish Television. . . A3
Shuttle St. C5
Sports Centre B4
Stirling's Library. C4
Stock Exchange ▥ . . B3
Stockwell Pl. D4
Stockwell St D4
Strathclyde University. B5
Synagogue A1
Taylor Pl. B5
Tenement House ▥ . . A1
Theatre Royal ☉ A3
Tolbooth Steeple &
    Mercat Cross ◆ . . D5
Trades House ▥ C4
Tron Steeple &
    Theatre ☉ D4
Trongate. D5
UGC ☉ B3
Union St C3
Virginia St C4
Walls St C5
Washington St C1
Waterloo St C2
Watson St D5
Wellington St B3/C2
West George St . . . B2/B3
West George St . . . B2/B3
West Graham St A2
West Regent St . . . B2/B3
Wilson St C4
York St West C2

Gloucester

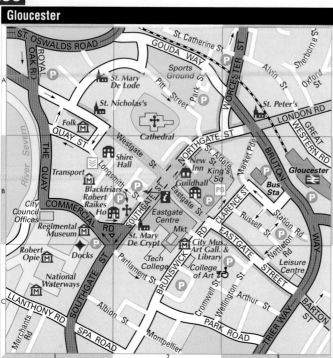

Leicester

Leeds

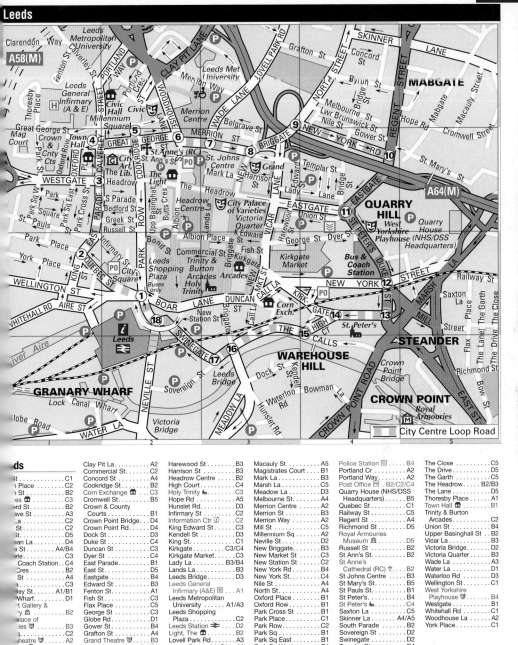

City Centre Loop Road

...ds	
...n Place C2	
...n St B2	
...es 🎭 B2	
...rd St A3	
...ave St A3	
...La C2	
...St C2	
...t. D5	
...ean La D4	
...s St A4/B4	
...te B4	
...Coach Station .. C4	
...Cres C4	
...t St B3	
...ge C3	
...ley St A1/B1	
...Wharf D1	
...t Gallery &	
...ry B2	
...alace of	
...es 🎭 B3	
...l. C2	
...heatre 🎭 C2	
...all 🎭 A2	
...don Way A1	

Clay Pit La A2	Harewood St B3	Macauly St A5	Police Station 🚓 B4	The Close C5
Commercial St C2	Harrison St B3	Magistrates Court .. B1	Portland Cr A2	The Drive D5
Concord St A4	Headrow Centre B2	Mark La B3	Portland Way A2	The Garth C5
Cookridge St B2	High Court C4	Marsh La C5	Post Office 🏤 . B2/C2/C4	The Headrow B2/B3
Corn Exchange 🎭 .. C3	Holy Trinity ⚓ C3	Meadow La D3	Quarry House (NHS/DSS	The Lane D5
Cromwell St B5	Hope Rd A5	Melbourne St A4	Headquarters) ... B5	Thoresby Place A1
Crown & County	Hunslet Rd D3	Merrion Centre A2	Quebec St C1	Town Hall 🎭 B1
Courts B1	Infirmary St C2	Merrion St B3	Railway St C5	Trinity & Burton
Crown Point Bridge .. D4	King Edward St C3	Merrion Way A2	Regent St A4	Arcades C2
Crown Point Rd D4	Kendell St D3	Mill St C5	Richmond St D5	Union St B4
Dock St D3	King St. C1	Millennium Sq A2	Royal Armouries	Upper Basinghall St . B3
Duke St C3	Kirkgate C3/C4	Neville St D2	Museum D5	Vicar La B3
Duncan St C3	Kirkgate Market C3	New Briggate B3	Russell St B2	Victoria Bridge D2
Dyer St B3	Lady La B3/B4	New Market St C3	St Ann's St. B2	Victoria Quarter B3
East Parade B2	Lands La B3	New Station St C2	St Anne's	Wade La A3
East St. D5	Leeds Bridge D3	New York Rd B4	Cathedral (RC) ✝ .. B2	Water La D1
Eastgate B3	Leeds General	New York St. C4	St Johns Centre B3	Waterloo Rd D3
Edward St B3	Infirmary (A&E) 🏥 .. A1	Nile St A4	St Mary's St. B5	Wellington St C1
Fenton St. A1	Leeds Metropolitan	North St. A4	St Pauls St. B1	West Yorkshire
Fish St. C3	University A1/A3	Oxford Place B1	St Peter's. B4	Playhouse B4
Flax Place C5	Leeds Shopping	Oxford Row B1	St Peter's. C4	Westgate B1
George St C3	Plaza C2	Park Cross St B1	Saxton La A4/A5	Whitehall Rd C1
Globe Rd D1	Leeds Station 🚉 D2	Park Place C1	Skinner La A4/A5	Woodhouse La A2
Grafton St A4	Light, The B2	Park Row B2	South Parade B2	York Place C1
Grand Theatre 🎭 ... B3	Lovell Park Rd A3	Park Sq East B1	Sovereign St D2	
Great George St .. B1/B2	Lower Brunswick St .. A4	Park Sq West. B1	Swinegate D2	
Greek St B2	Mabgate A5	Park St. B1	Templar St B4	
			The Calls D4	

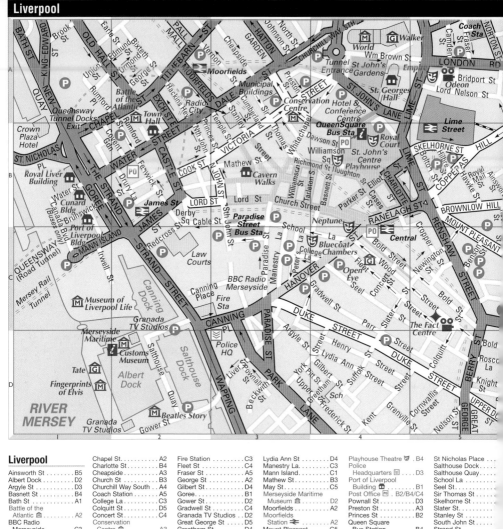

Liverpool

Ainsworth St B5
Albert Dock D2
Argyle St D3
Basnett St B4
Bath St A1
Battle of the
  Atlantic 🏛 A2
BBC Radio
  Merseyside C3
Beatles Story 🏛 D2
Beckwith St D3
Benson St C5
Berry St D5
Bixteth St. A2
Bluecoat
  Chambers 🎭 C4
Bold Place D5
Bold St C4/C5
Bolton St B5
Bridport St A5
Brook St A1
Brownlow Hill B5
Brunswick St B1
Cable St B2
Camden St A5
Canada Blvd B1
Canning Dock C2
Canning Place C3
Cases St B4
Castle St B2
Cavern Walks 🏛 B3
Central Station ⟶ . . . C4

Chapel St A2
Charlotte St B4
Cheapside A3
Church St B3
Churchill Way South . . A4
Coach Station A5
College La C3
Colquitt St D5
Concert St C4
Conservation
  Centre 🏛 A3
Cook St B2
Copperas Hill. B5
Cornwallis St D5
Covent Garden B2
Cropper St C5
Crown Plaza Hotel. . . . B1
Cumberland St A3
Cunard Building 🏛 . . . B1
Customs Museum 🏛 . D2
Dale St. A3
Dawson St B4
Derby Sq B2
Duke St C3/D4/D5
Earle St A2
Edmund St A2
Elliot St B4
Empire Theatre 🎭 . . . A5
Exchange St East A2
Fact Centre, The ♦ . . . C5
Fenwick St B2
Fingerprints
  of Elvis 🏛 D1

Fire Station C3
Fleet St C4
Fraser St A5
George St A2
Gilbert St D4
Goree. B1
Gower St D2
Gradwell St C4
Granada TV Studios . . D2
Great George St D5
Greetham St B5
Grenville St D4
Hackins Hey A2
Hanover St C3
Hatton Garden. A3
Hawke St B5
Henry St D4
Hilbre St. B5
Houghton St B4
Information Ctr 🅹 . B4/D2
Irwell St C1
James St B2
James St Station ⟶ . B2
Johnson St A3
Kent St D4
King Edward St A1
Knight St D5
Law Courts C2
Lime St A5/B5
Lime St Station ⟶. . B5
Liver St D3
London Rd. A5
Lord Nelson St A5
Lord St B2/B3

Lydia Ann St D4
Manesty La. C3
Mann Island C1
Mathew St B3
May St C5
Merseyside Maritime
  Museum 🏛 D2
Moorfields A2
Moorfields
  Station ⟶ A2
Mount Pleasant C5
Municipal Buildings. . . A3
Museum of
  Liverpool Life 🏛 . . . C1
Nelson St D5
Neptune Theatre 🎭 . . C4
New Quay A1
Newington St. C5
North John St B2/B3
North St A3
Norton St A5
Odeon A5
Old Hall St A1
Open Eye Gallery 🏛 . C4
Ormond St. A2
Pall Mall A2
Paradise St
  Bus Station C3
Park La D3
Parker St B4
Parr St D4
Peter's La C3
Pitt St. D4

Playhouse Theatre 🎭 . B4
Police
  Headquarters 🏢 . . . D3
Port of Liverpool
  Building 🏛 B1
Post Office 🄿 . B2/B4/C4
Pownall St D3
Preston St A3
Princes St B2
Queen Square
  Bus Station B4
Queensway Tunnel
  (Docks exit) A1
Queensway Tunnel
  (Entrance) A4
Radio City A4
Ranelagh St. B4
Redcross St. C5
Renshaw St C5
Richmond St B4
Rock St B5
Roscoe La C5
Roscoe St D5
Royal Court
  Theatre 🎭 B4
Royal Liver
  Building 🏛 B1
Royal Mail St B5
Rumford Place. A1
Rumford St B2
St Georges Hall 🏛 . . . A4
St John's Centre A4
St John's Gdns A4
St John's La A4

St Nicholas Place . . .
Salthouse Dock. . . . .
Salthouse Quay . . . .
School La . . . .
Seel St. . . . .
Sir Thomas St . . . . .
Skelhorne St . . . . . .
Slater St . . . .
Stanley St . . . .
South John St . . . . .
Strand St . . . .
Suffolk St. . . . .
Tarleton St . . . .
Tate Gallery 🏛 . . . .
Temple St . . . .
The Strand. . . . .
Tithebarn St. . . . . . .
Town Hall 🏛 . . . . . .
Union St . . . .
Upper Duke St. . . . .
Upper Frederick St .
Vernon St. . . . .
Victoria St . . . .
Walker Art Gallery 🏛
Wapping . . . .
Water St . . . .
Whitechapel. . . . . . .
Williamson Sq . . . . .
William Brown St. . .
Wood St. . . . .
World Museum 🏛 . .
York St. . . . .

London

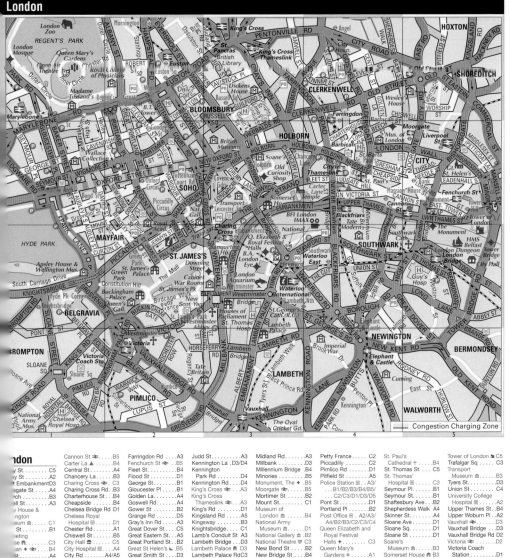

Manchester

Manchester

Air & Space
  Gallery 🏛 C1
Albert Sq C3
AMC 🎬 C2
Arndale Centre A3
Artillery St C1
Atherton St C1
Atkinson St C2
Aytoun St C5
Back Piccadilly B4
Blackfriars St A2
Bloom St C4/D4
Bombay St D4
Booth St A2
Booth St B3
Bootle St C2
Brazennose St B2
Brewer St B5
Bridge St B1
Bridgewater Hall D3
Bridgewater Pl B4
Bridgewater St D1
Brown St A1
Brown St B3
Buddhist Centre A4
Bury St A1
Bus & Coach Station . . B4
Bus Station B4
Byrom St C1
Cable St A5
Camp St C1
Canal St C4
Cannon St A3

Castle St D1
Cateaton St A3
Cathedral ✝ A3
Cathedral St A3
Chapel St A2
Charlotte St C4
Chatham St C5
Cheapside B3
Chepstow St D3
China La B5
Chorlton St C4
Church St A4
Clowes St A2
College Land B2
Collier St D1
Conference Centre D5
Cooper St C3
Copperas St A4
Cornerhouse 🎬 D3
Cross St B3
Crown Court C5
Dale St B5
Dantzic St A4
Deansgate B2/D2
Deansgate
  Station 🚆 D2
Duke Pl D1
Duke St D1
Edge St A4
Fairfield St D5
Faulkner St C3
Fennel St A3
Fountain St B3
Gartside St C1
George St C3

G-Mex (Metro Station). D2
Goadsby St A5
Gore St B1
Granada TV Studios . . . C1
Granby Row C4
Great Bridgewater St . . D2
Greater Manchester
  Exhibition Centre
  (G-Mex) D2
Green Room, The 🎭 . . D3
Hall St D3
Hardman St C2
Hart St C4
High St A4/A3
Hilton St A4/B5
Hope St B5
Houldsworth St A5
Information Ctr 🅸 C3
Jackson's Row C2
John Dalton St B2
John Ryland's
  Library B2
John St A1
Kennedy St B3
King St B3
King St West B2
Law Courts C2
Lever St B5
Library C3
Library Theatre 🎭 C3
Little Lever St A5
Liverpool Rd D1
Lloyd St C2
London Rd. C5
Lower Byrom St C1

Lower Mosley St D2
Luna St A5
Major St C4
Manchester Art
  Gallery 🏛 C3
Manchester Metropolitan
  University C5
Marble St B4
Market St B3
Market St
  (Metro Station) B4
Marsden St B3
Minshull St C4
Mosley St C3
Mosley St
  (Metro Station) B4
Mount St C3
Mulberry St B2
Museum of Science
  & Technology 🏛 C1
New Bailey St B1
New Quay St B1
Newgate St A4
Newton St B5
Nicholas St C3
Oak St A4
Odeon 🎬 A3
Oldham Rd A5
Oldham St B5
Opera House 🎭 C1
Oxford Road 🚆 D3
Oxford St D3
Palace Theatre 🎭 C4
Pall Mall B3
Parker St B4

Peoples' History
  Museum 🏛 B1
Peter St C2
Piccadilly B4
Piccadilly
  (Metro Station) C5
Piccadilly Gdns B4
Piccadilly
  (Metro Station) B4
Piccadilly Station 🚆 . . C5
Police Station 🚔 . . C2/C5
Port St B5
Portland St C4
Post Office 🖃 . B3/B5/D4
Princess St C3/D4
Quay St A1
Quay St B1
Queen St C2
Renold Theatre 🎭 A1
Rice St D1
Richmond St C4
Roby St C5
Roman Fort 🏛 D1
Royal Exchange 🎭 . . . B3
Sackville St C4/D5
St Ann St B3
St Ann's ⛪ B3
St James St C3
St John St C1
St Mary's ⛪ B2
St Mary's Gate. A3
St Mary's Parsonage. . B2
St Peter's Sq
  (Metro Station) C3
Salford Approach A2
Salford Central 🚆 B1

Shepley St C4
Shudehill A4
Shudehill
  (Metro Station) . . . .
Silver St B5
South King St B2
Spear St B5
Spring Gdns B3
Stanley St B1
Station Approach C5
Swan St A4
Tariff St B5
Thomas St A4
Tib La C3
Tib St . . . . A
Town Hall C3
Trafford St D2
Triangle, The . . . .
Trinity Way A1
Turner St A4
UMIST Manchester
  Conference Centre . . D5
Urbis Museum 🏛 . . . .
Victoria St A3
Watson St C1
West Mosley St C3
Whitworth St D3
Whitworth St West . . . .
William St A1
Windmill St C2
Withy Gr A4
Wood St B2
York St B3
York St C4

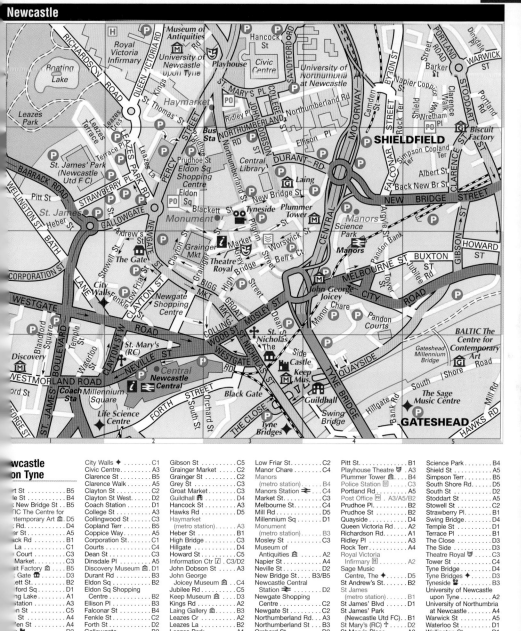

Nottingham

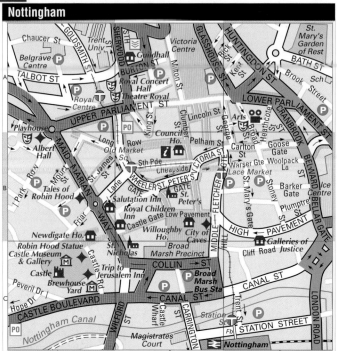

Oxford

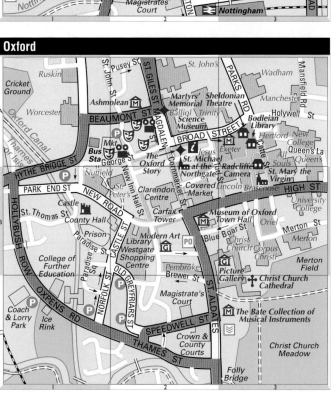

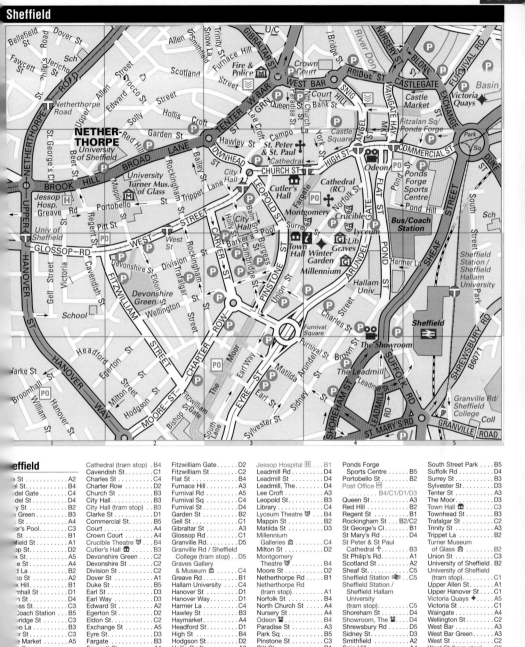

effield

...St A2	Cathedral (tram stop) . B4	Fitzwilliam Gate D2
...el St B4	Cavendish St C1	Fitzwilliam St C2
...del Gate C4	Charles St C4	Flat St B4
...del St D4	Charter Row D2	Furnace Hill A3
...y St B2	Church St B3	Furnival Rd A5
... Green B3	City Hall B3	Furnival Sq C4
... St A4	City Hall (tram stop) . B3	Furnival St D4
...er's Pool C3	Clarke St D1	Garden St B2
... St B1	Commercial St B5	Gell St C1
...field St D2	Court A4	Gibraltar St A3
...op St. D2	Crown Court A4	Glossop Rd C1
...k St. A5	Crucible Theatre B4	Granville Rd. D5
...e St. A4	Cutler's Hall B3	Granville Rd / Sheffield
...d La B2	Devonshire Green C2	College (tram stop) . . D5
...co St. A2	Devonshire St C2	Graves Gallery
...k Hill. B1	Division St C2	& Museum C4
...nhall St D1	Dover St A1	Greave Rd. B1
...n St D4	Duke St B5	Hallam University C4
...ess St. C3	Earl St D3	Hanover St D1
...Coach Station ... B5	Earl Way D3	Hanover Way D1
...bridge St C3	Edward St A2	Harmer La C4
...o La B3	Egerton St D2	Hawley St B3
...rt St. C3	Eldon St. C2	Haymarket A4
...e Market A5	Exchange St. A5	Headford St D1
...e Square	Eyre St. D3	High St B4
...n stop). B4	Fargate B3	Hodgson St D2
...gate A5	Fawcett St. A1	Hollis Croft. A2
...dral (RC) † B4	Fire & Police A3	Holly St B3
	Fitzalan Sq / Ponds	Information Ctr C4
	Forge (tram stop) . . B4	Jericho St A1

Jessop Hospital ... B1	Ponds Forge	South Street Park B5
Leadmill Rd D4	Sports Centre B5	Suffolk Rd D4
Leadmill St D4	Portobello St B2	Surrey St B3
Leadmill, The D4	Post Office	Sylvester St D3
Lee Croft A3	.... B4/C1/D1/D3	Tenter St A3
Leopold St B3	Queen St A3	The Moor. D3
Library C4	Red Hill B2	Town Hall C3
Lyceum Theatre B4	Regent St B1	Townhead St B3
Mappin St B2	Rockingham St .. B2/C2	Trafalgar St C2
Matilda St D3	St George's Cl. B1	Trinity St A3
Millennium	St Mary's Rd D4	Trippet La B2
Galleries C4	St Peter & St Paul	Turner Museum
Milton St D2	Cathedral †. B3	of Glass B2
Montgomery	St Philip's Rd. A1	Union St C3
Theatre B4	Scotland St A2	University of Sheffield . B2
Moore St D2	Sheaf St. C5	University of Sheffield
Netherthorpe Rd ... B1	Sheffield Station . C5	(tram stop). C1
Netherthorpe Rd	Sheffield Station /	Upper Allen St. A1
(tram stop). A1	Sheffield Hallam	Upper Hanover St. ... C1
Norfolk St B4	University	Victoria Quays A5
North Church St A4	(tram stop). C5	Victoria St C1
Nursery St A4	Shoreham St D4	Waingate A4
Odeon B4	Showroom, The D4	Wellington St C2
Paradise Sq A3	Shrewsbury Rd D5	West Bar A3
Park Sq B5	Sidney St. D3	West Bar Green. A3
Pinstone St C3	Smithfield A2	West St C2
Pitt St C1	Snig Hill. A4	West St (tram stop) .. C2
Police Station A3/A4	Snow La A3	William St D1
Pond Hill B5	Solly St A2	Winter Garden C4
Pond St. B4/C4	South La. D3	York St. B4

Swansea / Abertawe

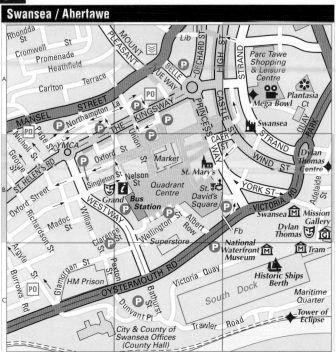

Swansea/Abertawe

York

York

Abbreviations used in the index

Aberdeen	**Aberdeen City**	Invclyd	**Inverclyde**
Aberds	**Aberdeenshire**	Jersey	**Jersey**
Ald	**Alderney**	Kent	**Kent**
Anglesey	**Isle of Anglesey**	Lancs	**Lancashire**
Angus	**Angus**	Leicester	**City of Leicester**
Argyll	**Argyll and Bute**	Leics	**Leicestershire**
Bath	**Bath and North East**	Lincs	**Lincolnshire**
	Somerset	London	**Greater London**
Beds	**Bedfordshire**	Luton	**Luton**
Bl Gwent	**Blaenau Gwent**	M Keynes	**Milton Keynes**
Blkburn	**Blackburn with**	M Tydf	**Merthyr Tydfil**
	Darwen	M'bro	**Middlesbrough**
Blkpool	**Blackpool**	Medway	**Medway**
Bmouth	**Bournemouth**	Mers	**Merseyside**
Borders	**Scottish Borders**	Midloth	**Midlothian**
Brack	**Bracknell**	Mon	**Monmouthshire**
Bridgend	**Bridgend**	Moray	**Moray**
Brighton	**City of Brighton and**	N Ayrs	**North Ayrshire**
	Hove	N Lincs	**North Lincolnshire**
Bristol	**City and County of**	N Lnrk	**North Lanarkshire**
	Bristol	N Som	**North Somerset**
Bucks	**Buckinghamshire**	N Yorks	**North Yorkshire**
Caerph	**Caerphilly**	NE Lincs	**North East**
Cambs	**Cambridgeshire**		**Lincolnshire**
Cardiff	**Cardiff**	Neath	**Neath Port Talbot**
Carms	**Carmarthenshire**	Newport	**City and County of**
Ceredig	**Ceredigion**		**Newport**
Ches	**Cheshire**	Norf	**Norfolk**
Clack	**Clackmannanshire**	Northants	**Northamptonshire**
Conwy	**Conwy**	Northumb	**Northumberland**
Corn	**Cornwall**	Nottingham	**City of Nottingham**
Cumb	**Cumbria**	Notts	**Nottinghamshire**
Darl	**Darlington**	Orkney	**Orkney**
Denb	**Denbighshire**	Oxon	**Oxfordshire**
Derby	**City of Derby**	P'boro	**Peterborough**
Derbys	**Derbyshire**	Pembs	**Pembrokeshire**
Devon	**Devon**	Perth	**Perth and Kinross**
Dorset	**Dorset**	Plym	**Plymouth**
Dumfries	**Dumfries and**	Poole	**Poole**
	Galloway	Powys	**Powys**
Dundee	**Dundee City**	Ptsmth	**Portsmouth**
Durham	**Durham**	Reading	**Reading**
E Ayrs	**East Ayrshire**	Redcar	**Redcar and**
E Dunb	**East Dunbartonshire**		**Cleveland**
E Loth	**East Lothian**	Renfs	**Renfrewshire**
E Renf	**East Renfrewshire**	Rhondda	**Rhondda Cynon Taff**
E Sus	**East Sussex**	Rutland	**Rutland**
E Yorks	**East Riding of**	S Ayrs	**South Ayrshire**
	Yorkshire	S Glos	**South**
Edin	**City of Edinburgh**		**Gloucestershire**
Essex	**Essex**	S Lnrk	**South Lanarkshire**
Falk	**Falkirk**	S Yorks	**South Yorkshire**
Fife	**Fife**	Scilly	**Scilly**
Flint	**Flintshire**	Shetland	**Shetland**
Glasgow	**City of Glasgow**	Shrops	**Shropshire**
Glos	**Gloucesterhire**	Slough	**Slough**
Gtr Man	**Greater Manchester**	Som	**Somerset**
Guern	**Guernsey**	Soton	**Southampton**
Gwyn	**Gwynedd**	Staffs	**Staffordshire**
Halton	**Halton**	Sthend	**Southend-on-Sea**
Hants	**Hampshire**	Stirl	**Stirling**
Hereford	**Herefordshire**	Stockton	**Stockton-on-Tees**
Herts	**Hertfordshire**	Stoke	**Stoke-on-Trent**
Highld	**Highland**	Suff	**Suffolk**
Hrtlpl	**Hartlepool**	Sur	**Surrey**
Hull	**Hull**	Swansea	**Swansea**
I o M	**Isle of Man**	T & W	**Tyne and Wear**
I o W	**Isle of Wight**	Telford	**Telford and Wrekin**

Index to road maps

How to use the index

Example

Adlestrop Glos **64** A3

— grid square
— page number
— county or unitary authority

Places of special interest are highlighted in magenta

Thamesdown	**Thamesdown**	W Sus	**West Sussex**
Thurrock	**Thurrock**	W Yorks	**West Yorkshire**
Torbay	**Torbay**	Warks	**Warwickshire**
Torf	**Torfaen**	Warr	**Warrington**
V Glam	**The Vale of**	Wilts	**Wiltshire**
	Glamorgan	Windsor	**Windsor and**
W Berks	**West Berkshire**		**Maidenhead**
W Dunb	**West**	Wokingham	**Wokingham**
	Dunbartonshire	Worcs	**Worcestershire**
W Isles	**Western Isles**	Wrex	**Wrexham**
W Loth	**West Lothian**	York	**City of York**
W Mid	**West Midlands**		

A

Ab Kettleby Leics 115 C5
Ab Lench Worcs 80 B3
Abbas Combe Som 29 C7
Abberley Worcs 79 A5
Abberton Essex 71 B4
Abberton Worcs 80 B2
Abberwick Northumb 189 B4
Abbess Roding Essex 69 B5
Abbey Devon 27 D6
Abbey-cwm-hir Powys 93 D4
Abbey Dore Hereford 78 D1
Abbey Field Essex 70 A3
Abbey Hulton Stoke 112 A3
Abbey St Bathans Borders 211 D4
Abbey Town Cumb 175 C4
Abbey Village Lancs 137 A5
Abbey Wood London 50 B1
Abbeydale S Yorks 130 A3
Abbeystead Lancs 145 B5
Abbots Bickington Devon 25 D4
Abbots Bromley Staffs 113 C4
Abbots Langley Herts 67 C5
Abbots Leigh N Som 43 B4
Abbots Morton Worcs 80 B3
Abbots Ripton Cambs 100 D4
Abbots Salford Warks 80 B3
Abbotsbury Dorset 15 C5
Abbotsbury Sub Tropical Gardens Dorset 15 C5
Abbotsford House Borders 197 C4
Abbotsham Devon 25 C5
Abbotskerswell Devon 8 A2
Abbotsley Cambs 84 B4
Abbotswood Hants 32 C2
Abbotts Ann Hants 32 A2
Abcott Shrops 94 D1
Abdon Shrops 94 C3
Aber Ceredig 74 D3
Aber-Arad Carms 73 C6
Aber-banc Ceredig 73 B6
Aber Cowarch Gwyn 91 A6
Aber-Giâr Carms 58 A2
Aber-gwynfi Neath 40 B3
Aber-Hirnant Gwyn 109 B4
Aber-nant Rhondda 41 A5
Aber-Rhiwlech Gwyn 108 C4
Aber-Village Powys 60 A3
Aberaeron Ceredig 74 B3
Aberaman Rhondda 41 A5
Aberangell Gwyn 91 A6
Aberarder Highld 240 D2
Aberarder House Highld 252 D2
Aberarder Lodge Highld 240 D2
Aberargie Perth 219 C6
Aberarth Ceredig 74 B3
Aberavon Neath 40 B2
Aberbeeg Bl Gwent 41 A7
Abercanaid M Tydf 41 A5
Abercarn Caerph 41 B7
Abercastle Pembs 55 A4
Abercegir Powys 91 B6
Aberchirder Aberds 268 D1
Aberconwy House, Conwy Conwy 124 B2
Abercraf Powys 59 D5
Abercych Pembs 73 B5
Abercynafon Powys 60 B2
Abercynon Rhondda 41 B5
Aberdalgie Perth 219 B5
Aberdâr = Aberdare Rhondda 41 A4
Aberdare = Aberdâr Rhondda 41 A4
Aberdaron Gwyn 106 D1
Aberdaugleddau = Milford Haven Pembs 55 D5
Aberdeen Aberdeen 245 B6
Aberdeen Airport Aberdeen 245 A5
Aberdesach Gwyn 107 A4
Aberdour Fife 209 B4
Aberdovey Gwyn 90 C4
Aberdulais Neath 40 A2
Aberedw Powys 77 C4
Abereiddy Pembs 54 A3
Abererch Gwyn 106 C3
Aberfan M Tydf 41 A5
Aberfeldy Perth 230 D2
Aberffraw Anglesey 122 D3
Aberffrwd Ceredig 75 A5

Aberford W Yorks 148 D3
Aberfoyle Stirl 217 D5
Abergavenny = Y Fenni Mon 61 B4
Abergele Conwy 125 B4
Abergorlech Carms 58 B2
Abergwaun = Fishguard Pembs 72 C2
Abergwesyn Powys 76 B2
Abergwili Carms 58 C1
Abergwynant Gwyn 91 A4
Abergwyngregyn Gwyn 123 C6
Abergwynolwyn Gwyn 91 B4
Aberhonddu = Brecon Powys 60 A2
Aberhosan Powys 91 C6
Aberkenfig Bridgend 40 C3
Aberlady E Loth 210 B1
Aberlemno Angus 232 C3
Aberllefenni Gwyn 91 B5
Abermagwr Ceredig 75 A5
Abermaw = Barmouth Gwyn 90 A4
Abermeurig Ceredig 75 C4
Abermule Powys 93 B5
Abernaint Powys 109 C6
Abernant Carms 73 D6
Abernethy Perth 219 C6
Abernyte Perth 220 A2
Aberpennar = Mountain Ash Rhondda 41 B5
Aberporth Ceredig 73 A5
Abersoch Gwyn 106 D3
Abersychan Torf 61 C4
Abertawe = Swansea Swansea 57 C6
Aberteifi = Cardigan Ceredig 73 B4
Aberthin V Glam 41 D5
Abertillery = Abertyleri Bl Gwent 41 A7
Abertridwr Caerph 41 C6
Abertridwr Powys 109 D5
Abertyleri = Abertillery Bl Gwent 41 A7
Abertysswg Caerph 60 C3
Aberuthven Perth 219 C4
Aberyscir Powys 60 A1
Aberystwyth Ceredig 90 D3
Abhainn Suidhe W Isles 287 D5
Abingdon Oxon 65 D5
Abinger Common Sur 35 B4
Abinger Hammer Sur 34 B3
Abington S Lnrk 194 D4
Abington Piggotts Cambs 85 C5
Ablington Glos 64 C2
Ablington Wilts 31 A5
Abney Derbys 130 B1
Aboyne Aberds 244 C2
Abram Gtr Man 137 C5
Abriachan Highld 252 C1
Abridge Essex 69 D4
Abronhill N Lnrk 207 C5
Abson S Glos 43 B6
Abthorpe Northants 82 C3
Aby Lincs 135 B4
Acaster Malbis York 149 C4
Acaster Selby N Yorks 149 C4
Accrington Lancs 137 A6
Acha Argyll 223 B4
Acha Mor W Isles 288 E4
Achabraid Argyll 213 D6
Achachork Highld 259 D4
Achafolla Argyll 213 A5
Achagary Highld 278 C3
Achahoish Argyll 202 A2
Achalader Perth 231 D5
Achallader Argyll 228 D2
Ach'an Todhair Highld 237 B4
Achanalt Highld 263 D4
Achanamara Argyll 213 D5
Achandunie Highld 264 C2
Achany Highld 272 D3
Achaphubuil Highld 237 B4
Acharacle Highld 235 D5
Acharn Highld 236 D1
Acharn Perth 229 D6
Acharole Highld 280 C4
Achath Aberds 245 A4
Achavanich Highld 280 D3
Achavraat Highld 253 B5
Achddu Carms 57 B4
Achduart Highld 270 D3
Achentoul Highld 274 A2
Achfary Highld 271 A5
Achgarve Highld 261 A5
Achiemore Highld 277 B4

Achiemore Highld 279 C4
A'Chill Highld 246 D1
Achiltibuie Highld 270 D3
Achina Highld 278 B3
Achinduich Highld 272 D3
Achinduin Argyll 226 C3
Achingills Highld 280 B3
Achintee Highld 237 B5
Achintee Highld 249 B6
Achintraid Highld 249 C5
Achlean Highld 241 C6
Achleck Argyll 224 B3
Achluachrach Highld 239 D6
Achlyness Highld 276 C3
Achmelvich Highld 270 B3
Achmore Highld 249 C5
Achmore Stirl 217 A5
Achnaba Argyll 226 C4
Achnaba Argyll 214 D2
Achnabat Highld 252 C1
Achnacarnin Highld 270 A3
Achnacarry Highld 239 D5
Achnacloich Argyll 227 C4
Achnacloich Highld 247 D4
Achnaconeran Highld 240 A2
Achnacraig Argyll 224 B3
Achnacroish Argyll 226 B3
Achnadrish Argyll 224 A3
Achnafalnich Argyll 227 D7
Achnagarron Highld 264 D2
Achnaha Highld 234 D3
Achnahanat Highld 263 A7
Achnahannet Highld 253 D5
Achnairn Highld 272 C3
Achnaluachrach Highld 273 D4
Achnasaul Highld 239 D5
Achnasheen Highld 250 A3
Achosnich Highld 234 D3
Achranich Highld 226 B2
Achreamie Highld 279 B6
Achriabhach Highld 237 C5
Achriesgill Highld 276 C3
Achrimsdale Highld 274 D3
Achtoty Highld 278 B2
Achurch Northants 100 C2
Achuvoldrach Highld 277 C6
Achvaich Highld 264 A3
Achvarasdal Highld 279 B5
Ackergill Highld 281 C5
Acklam M'bro 168 D2
Acklam N Yorks 149 A6
Ackleton Shrops 95 B5
Acklington Northumb 189 C5
Ackton W Yorks 140 A2
Ackworth Moor Top W Yorks 140 B2
Acle Norf 121 D6
Acock's Green W Mid 96 C4
Acol Kent 53 C5
Acomb Northumb 178 C1
Acomb York 149 B4
Aconbury Hereford 78 D3
Acre Lancs 137 A6
Acre Street W Sus 19 B6
Acrefair Wrex 110 A1
Acton Ches 127 D6
Acton Dorset 16 D3
Acton London 49 A5
Acton Shrops 93 C7
Acton Suff 87 C4
Acton Wrex 126 D3
Acton Beauchamp Hereford 79 B4
Acton Bridge Ches 127 B5
Acton Burnell Shrops 94 A3
Acton Green Hereford 79 B4
Acton Pigott Shrops 94 A3
Acton Round Shrops 95 B4
Acton Scott Shrops 94 C2
Acton Trussell Staffs 112 D3
Acton Turville S Glos 44 A2
Adbaston Staffs 111 C6
Adber Dorset 29 C5
Adderley Shrops 111 A5
Adderstone Northumb 199 C5
Addiewell W Loth 208 D2
Addingham W Yorks 147 C4
Addington Bucks 66 A2
Addington London 49 C6
Addington Kent 37 A4
Addinston Borders 197 A4
Addiscombe London 49 C6
Addlestone Sur 48 C3
Addlethorpe Lincs 135 C5
Adel W Yorks 148 D1
Adeney Telford 111 D6
Adfa Powys 93 A4
Adforton Hereford 94 D2

Adisham Kent 53 D4
Adlestrop Glos 64 A3
Adlingfleet E Yorks 141 A6
Adlington Lancs 137 B5
Admaston Staffs 112 C4
Admaston Telford 111 D5
Admington Warks 81 C5
Adstock Bucks 83 D4
Adstone Northants 82 B2
Adversane W Sus 34 D3
Advie Highld 254 C2
Adwalton W Yorks 139 A5
Adwell Oxon 66 D1
Adwick le Street S Yorks 140 C3
Adwick upon Dearne S Yorks 140 C2
Adziel Aberds 269 D4
Ae Village Dumfries 184 D2
Affleck Aberds 256 D3
Affpuddle Dorset 16 B2
Affric Lodge Highld 250 D3
Afon-wen Flint 125 B6
Afton I o W 18 C2
Agglethorpe N Yorks 157 C4
Agneash I o M 152 C4
Aigburth Mers 126 A3
Aiginis W Isles 288 D5
Aike E Yorks 150 C3
Aikerness Orkney 282 B5
Aikers Orkney 283 H5
Aiketgate Cumb 164 A2
Aikton Cumb 175 C5
Ailey Hereford 78 C1
Ailstone Warks 81 B5
Ailsworth P'boro 100 B3
Ainderby Quernhow N Yorks 158 C2
Ainderby Steeple N Yorks 158 B2
Aingers Green Essex 71 A5
Ainsdale Mers 136 B2
Ainsdale-on-Sea Mers 136 B2
Ainstable Cumb 164 A3
Ainsworth Gtr Man 137 B6
Ainthorpe N Yorks 159 A6
Aintree Mers 136 D2
Aintree Racecourse Mers 136 D2
Aird Argyll 213 B5
Aird Dumfries 170 A2
Aird Highld 261 C4
Aird W Isles 288 D6
Aird a Mhachair W Isles 286 B3
Aird a'Mhulaidh W Isles 288 F2
Aird Asaig W Isles 288 A5
Aird Dhail W Isles 288 A5
Aird Mhidhinis W Isles 286 F3
Aird Mhighe W Isles 288 H2
Aird Mhighe W Isles 287 F5
Aird Mhor W Isles 286 F3
Aird of Sleat Highld 247 D4
Aird Thunga W Isles 288 D5
Aird Uig W Isles 287 A5
Airdens Highld 264 A2
Airdrie N Lnrk 207 D5
Airdtorrisdale Highld 278 B2
Airidh a Bhruaich W Isles 288 F3
Airieland Dumfries 173 C5
Airmyn E Yorks 141 A5
Airntully Perth 219 A5
Airor Highld 247 D6
Airth Falk 208 B1
Airton N Yorks 146 B3
Airyhassen Dumfries 171 C5
Aisby Lincs 141 D6
Aisby Lincs 116 B3
Aisgernis W Isles 286 D3
Aiskew N Yorks 157 C6
Aislaby N Yorks 159 C6
Aislaby N Yorks 160 A2
Aislaby Stockton 168 D2
Aisthorpe Lincs 133 A4
Aith Orkney 282 F3
Aith Shetland 285 H5
Aith Shetland 284 D8
Aithsetter Shetland 285 K6
Aitkenhead S Ayrs 192 E3
Aitnoch Highld 253 C5
Akeld Northumb 188 A2
Akeley Bucks 83 D4
Akenham Suff 88 C2
Albaston Corn 11 D5
Alberbury Shrops 110 D2
Albert Dock, Liverpool Mers 126 A3
Albourne W Sus 21 A5
Albrighton Shrops 110 D3
Albrighton Shrops 95 A6
Alburgh Norf 104 C3
Albury Herts 68 A4

Albury Sur 34 B3
Albury End Herts 68 A4
Alby Hill Norf 120 B3
Alcaig Highld 252 A1
Alcaston Shrops 94 C2
Alcester Warks 80 B3
Alciston E Sus 22 B3
Alcombe Som 27 A4
Alcombe Wilts 44 C2
Alconbury Cambs 100 D3
Alconbury Weston Cambs 100 D3
Aldbar Castle Angus 232 C3
Aldborough Norf 120 B3
Aldborough N Yorks 148 A3
Aldbourne Wilts 45 B6
Aldbrough E Yorks 151 D5
Aldbrough St John N Yorks 167 D5
Aldbury Herts 67 B4
Aldcliffe Lancs 145 A4
Aldclune Perth 230 B3
Aldeburgh Suff 89 B5
Aldeby Norf 105 B5
Aldenham Herts 67 D6
Alderbury Wilts 31 C5
Aldercar Derbys 114 A2
Alderford Norf 120 D3
Alderholt Dorset 31 D5
Alderley Glos 62 D3
Alderley Edge Ches 128 B3
Aldermaston W Berks 46 C3
Aldermaston Wharf W Berks 47 C4
Alderminster Warks 81 C5
Alderney Airport Ald 7
Alder's End Hereford 79 C4
Aldersey Green Ches 127 D4
Aldershot Hants 34 A1
Alderton Glos 80 D2
Alderton Northants 83 C4
Alderton Shrops 110 C3
Alderton Suff 88 C4
Alderton Wilts 44 A2
Alderwasley Derbys 130 D3
Aldfield N Yorks 147 A4
Aldford Ches 127 D4
Aldham Essex 70 A3
Aldham Suff 87 C5
Aldie Highld 264 B3
Aldingbourne W Sus 20 B2
Aldingham Cumb 154 D1
Aldington Kent 38 B2
Aldington Worcs 80 C3
Aldington Frith Kent 38 B2
Aldochlay Argyll 206 A1
Aldreth Cambs 101 D6
Aldridge W Mid 96 A3
Aldringham Suff 89 A5
Aldsworth Glos 64 B2
Aldunie Moray 255 D5
Aldwark Derbys 130 D2
Aldwark N Yorks 148 A3
Aldwick W Sus 20 C2
Aldwincle Northants 100 C2
Aldworth W Berks 46 B3
Alexandria W Dunb 206 C1
Alfardisworthy Devon 24 D3
Alfington Devon 13 B6
Alfold Sur 34 C3
Alfold Bars W Sus 34 C3
Alfold Crossways Sur 34 C3
Alford Aberds 244 A2
Alford Lincs 135 B4
Alford Som 29 B6
Alfreton Derbys 131 D4
Alfrick Worcs 79 B5
Alfrick Pound Worcs 79 B5
Alfriston E Sus 22 B3
Algaltraig Argyll 203 A5
Algarkirk Lincs 117 B5
Alhampton Som 29 B6
Aline Lodge W Isles 288 F3
Alisary Highld 235 C6
Alkborough N Lincs 141 A6
Alkerton Oxon 81 C6
Alkham Kent 39 A4
Alkington Shrops 111 B4
Alkmonton Derbys 113 B5
All Cannings Wilts 45 C5
All Saints Church, Langham Suff 10
All Saints South Elmham Suff 104 C4
All Stretton Shrops 94 B2
Alladale Lodge Highld 263 B6
Allaleigh Devon 8 B2
Allanaquoich Aberds 242 C4
Allangrange Mains Highld 252 A2

Allanton Borders 198 A2
Allanton N Lnrk 194 A3
Allathasdal W Isles 286 F2
Allendale Town Northumb 177 D6
Allenheads Northumb 165 A6
Allens Green Herts 69 B4
Allensford Durham 178 D2
Allensmore Hereford 78 D2
Allenton Derby 114 B1
Aller Som 28 C4
Allerby Cumb 102 A3
Allerchurch Worcs 96 D3
Allerford Som 27 A4
Allerston N Yorks 160 C2
Allerthorpe E Yorks 149 C6
Allerton Mers 127 A4
Allerton W Yorks 147 D5
Allerton Bywater W Yorks 140 A2
Allerton Mauleverer N Yorks 148 B3
Allesley W Mid 97 C6
Allestree Derby 114 B1
Allet Corn 4 C2
Allexton Leics 99 A5
Allgreave Ches 129 C4
Allhallows Medway 51 B5
Allhallows-on-Sea Medway 51 B5
Alligin Shuas Highld 249 A5
Allimore Green Staffs 112 D2
Allington Lincs 115 A6
Allington Wilts 31 B6
Allington Wilts 45 C4
Allithwaite Cumb 154 D2
Alloa Clack 208 A1
Allonby Cumb 174 D3
Alloway S Ayrs 192 D3
Allt Carms 57 B5
Allt na h-Airbhe Highld 262 A3
Allt-nan-sùgh Highld 249 D6
Alltchaorunn Highld 237 D5
Alltforgan Powys 109 C4
Alltmawr Powys 77 C4
Alltnacaillich Highld 277 D5
Alltsigh Highld 240 A2
Alltwalis Carms 58 B1
Alltwen Neath 40 A2
Alltyblaca Ceredig 75 D4
Allwood Green Suff 103 D6
Almeley Hereford 78 B1
Almer Dorset 16 B3
Almholme S Yorks 140 C3
Almington Staffs 111 B6
Alminstone Cross Devon 24 C4
Almondbank Perth 219 B5
Almondbury W Yorks 139 B4
Almondsbury S Glos 43 A5
Alne N Yorks 148 A3
Alness Highld 264 D2
Alnham Northumb 188 B2
Alnmouth Northumb 189 B5
Alnwick Northumb 189 B4
Alperton London 49 A4
Alphamstone Essex 87 D4
Alpheton Suff 87 B4
Alphington Devon 13 B4
Alport Derbys 130 C2
Alpraham Ches 127 D5
Alresford Essex 71 A4
Alrewas Staffs 113 D5
Alsager Ches 128 D2
Alsagers Bank Staffs 112 A2
Alsop en le Dale Derbys 129 D6
Alston Cumb 165 A5
Alston Devon 14 A3
Alstone Glos 80 D2
Alstonefield Staffs 129 D6
Alswear Devon 26 C2
Altandhu Highld 270 C2
Altanduin Highld 274 B2
Altarnun Corn 10 C3
Altass Highld 272 D2
Alterwall Highld 281 B4
Altham Lancs 146 D1
Althorne Essex 70 D3
Althorp House, Great Brington Northants 82 A3
Althorpe N Lincs 141 C6
Alticry Dumfries 171 B4
Altnabreac Station Highld 279 D6
Altnacealgach Hotel Highld 271 C5
Altnacraig Argyll 226 D3
Altnafeadh Highld 237 D6
Altnaharra Highld 272 A3
Altofts W Yorks 139 A6
Alton Derbys 130 C3
Alton Hants 33 B6
Alton Staffs 113 A4

Alton Pancras Dorset 15 A7
Alton Priors Wilts 45 C5
Alton Towers Staffs 113 A4
Altrincham Gtr Man 128 A2
Altrua Highld 239 D6
Altskeith Stirl 217 D4
Altyre Ho. Moray 253 A6
Alvanley Ches 127 B4
Alvaston Derby 114 B1
Alvechurch Worcs 96 D3
Alvecote Warks 97 A5
Alvediston Wilts 30 C3
Alveley Shrops 95 C5
Alverdiscott Devon 25 C6
Alverstoke Hants 19 B5
Alverstone I o W 19 C4
Alverton Notts 115 A5
Alves Moray 266 C2
Alvescot Oxon 64 C3
Alveston S Glos 43 A5
Alveston Warks 81 B5
Alvie Highld 241 B6
Alvingham Lincs 143 D5
Alvington Glos 62 C2
Alwalton Cambs 100 B3
Alweston Dorset 29 D6
Alwinton Northumb 188 C2
Alwoodley W Yorks 148 C1
Alyth Perth 231 D6
Am Baile W Isles 286 E3
Am Buth Argyll 226 D3
Amatnatua Highld 263 A6
Amber Hill Lincs 117 A5
Ambergate Derbys 130 D3
Amberley Glos 63 C4
Amberley W Sus 20 A3
Amble Northumb 189 C5
Amblecote W Mid 96 C1
Ambler Thorn W Yorks 138 A3
Ambleside Cumb 154 A2
Ambleston Pembs 55 B6
Ambrosden Oxon 65 B7
Amcotts N Lincs 141 B6
American Adventure, Ilkeston Derbys 114 A2
American Air Museum, Duxford Cambs 85 C6
Amersham Bucks 67 D4
Amerton Working Farm, Stowe-by-Chartley Staffs 112 C3
Amesbury Wilts 31 A5
Amington Staffs 97 A5
Amisfield Dumfries 184 D2
Amlwch Anglesey 123 A4
Amlwch Port Anglesey 123 A4
Ammanford = Rhydaman Carms 57 A6
Amod Argyll 190 B3
Amotherby N Yorks 159 D6
Ampfield Hants 32 C3
Ampleforth N Yorks 159 D4
Ampney Crucis Glos 63 C6
Ampney St Mary Glos 64 C1
Ampney St Peter Glos 64 C1
Amport Hants 32 A1
Ampthill Beds 84 D2
Ampton Suff 103 D4
Amroth Pembs 56 B1
Amulree Perth 218 A3
An Caol Highld 248 A3
An Cnoc W Isles 288 D5
An Gleann Ur W Isles 288 D5
An t-Ob = Leverburgh W Isles 287 F5
Anagach Highld 253 D6
Anaheilt Highld 236 C2
Anancaun Highld 262 D2
Ancaster Lincs 116 A2
Anchor Shrops 93 C5
Anchorsholme Blkpool 144 C3
Ancroft Northumb 198 B3
Ancrum Borders 187 A5
Anderby Lincs 135 B5
Anderson Dorset 16 B2
Anderton Ches 127 B6
Andover Hants 32 A2
Andover Down Hants 32 A2
Andoversford Glos 63 B6
Andreas I o M 152 B4
Anfield Mers 136 D2
Angersleigh Som 28 D1
Angle Pembs 55 D4
Angmering W Sus 20 B3
Angram N Yorks 148 C4
Angram N Yorks 156 B2
Anie Stirl 217 C5

Ankerville Highld 265 C4
Anlaby E Yorks 142 A2
Anmer Norf 119 C4
Anna Valley Hants 32 A2
Annan Dumfries 175 B4
Annat Argyll 227 D5
Annat Highld 249 A5
Annbank S Ayrs 193 C4
Anne Hathaway's Cottage, Stratford-upon-Avon Warks 81 B4
Annesley Notts 131 D5
Annesley Woodhouse Notts 131 D4
Annfield Plain Durham 178 D3
Annifirth Shetland 285 J3
Annitsford T & W 179 B4
Annscroft Shrops 94 A2
Ansdell Lancs 136 A2
Ansford Som 29 B6
Ansley Warks 97 B5
Anslow Staffs 113 C6
Anslow Gate Staffs 113 C5
Anstey Herts 85 D6
Anstey Leics 98 A2
Anstruther Easter Fife 221 D5
Anstruther Wester Fife 221 D5
Ansty Hants 33 A6
Ansty Warks 97 C6
Ansty Wilts 30 C3
Ansty W Sus 35 D5
Anthill Common Hants 33 D5
Anthorn Cumb 175 C4
Antingham Norf 121 B4
Anton's Gowt Lincs 117 A5
Antonshill Falk 208 B1
Antony Corn 6 B3
Anwick Lincs 133 D6
Anwoth Dumfries 172 C3
Aoradh Argyll 200 B2
Apes Hall Cambs 102 B1
Apethorpe Northants 100 B2
Apeton Staffs 112 D2
Apley Lincs 133 B6
Apperknowle Derbys 130 B3
Apperley Glos 63 A4
Apperley Bridge W Yorks 147 D5
Appersett N Yorks 156 B2
Appin Argyll 226 B4
Appin House Argyll 226 B4
Appleby N Lincs 142 B1
Appleby-in-Westmorland Cumb 165 C4
Appleby Magna Leics 97 A6
Appleby Parva Leics 97 A6
Applecross Highld 249 B4
Applecross Ho. Highld 249 B4
Appledore Devon 25 B5
Appledore Devon 27 D5
Appledore Kent 38 C1
Appledore Heath Kent 38 B1
Appleford Oxon 65 D6
Applegarthtown Dumfries 185 D4
Appleshaw Hants 32 A2
Applethwaite Cumb 163 B5
Appleton Halton 127 A5
Appleton Oxon 65 C5
Appleton-le-Moors N Yorks 159 C6
Appleton-le-Street N Yorks 159 D6
Appleton Roebuck N Yorks 149 C4
Appleton Thorn Warr 127 A6
Appleton Wiske N Yorks 158 A2
Appletreehall Borders 186 B4
Appletreewick N Yorks 147 A4
Appley Som 27 C5
Appley Bridge Lancs 136 C4
Apse Heath I o W 19 C4
Apsley End Beds 84 D3
Apuldram W Sus 20 B1
Aquhythie Aberds 245 A4
Arabella Highld 265 C4
Arbeadie Aberds 244 C3
Arbeia Roman Fort and Museum T & W 179 C5
Arberth = Narberth Pembs 55 C7
Arbirlot Angus 233 D4
Arboll Highld 265 B4
Arborfield Wokingham 47 C5
Arborfield Cross Wokingham 47 C5
Arborfield Garrison Wokingham 47 C5
Arbour-thorne S Yorks 130 A3
Arbroath Angus 233 D4
Arbuthnott Aberds 233 A5

Archiestown Moray 254 B3
Arclid Ches 128 C2
Ard-dhubh Highld 249 B4
Ardachu Highld 273 D4
Ardalanish Argyll 224 E2
Ardanaiseig Argyll 227 D5
Ardaneaskan Highld 249 C5
Ardanstur Argyll 213 A6
Ardargie House Hotel Perth 219 C5
Ardarroch Highld 249 C5
Ardbeg Argyll 201 D4
Ardbeg Argyll 215 D4
Ardbeg Distillery, Port Ellen Argyll 201 D4
Ardcharnich Highld 262 B3
Ardchiavaig Argyll 224 E2
Ardchullarie More Stirl 217 C5
Ardchyle Stirl 217 B5
Arddleen Powys 110 D1
Ardechive Highld 239 C5
Ardeley Herts 68 A3
Ardelve Highld 249 D5
Arden Argyll 206 B1
Ardens Grafton Warks 80 B4
Ardentinny Argyll 215 D4
Ardentraive Argyll 203 A5
Ardeonaig Stirl 217 A6
Ardersier Highld 252 A3
Ardessie Highld 262 B2
Ardfern Argyll 213 B6
Ardgartan Argyll 215 B5
Ardgay Highld 264 A1
Ardgour Highld 237 C4
Ardheslaig Highld 249 A4
Ardiecow Moray 267 C6
Ardindrean Highld 262 B3
Ardingly W Sus 35 D6
Ardington Oxon 46 A2
Ardlair Aberds 255 D6
Ardlamont Ho. Argyll 203 B4
Ardleigh Essex 71 A4
Ardler Perth 231 D6
Ardley Oxon 65 A6
Ardlui Argyll 215 A6
Ardlussa Argyll 213 D4
Ardmair Highld 262 A3
Ardmay Argyll 215 B5
Ardminish Argyll 202 D1
Ardmolich Highld 235 C6
Ardmore Argyll 226 D2
Ardmore Highld 264 B3
Ardmore Highld 276 C3
Ardnacross Argyll 225 B4
Ardnadam Argyll 203 A6
Ardnagrask Highld 251 B7
Ardnarff Highld 249 C5
Ardnastang Highld 236 C2
Ardnave Argyll 200 A2
Ardno Argyll 215 B4
Ardo Aberds 256 C3
Ardo Ho. Aberds 257 D4
Ardoch Perth 219 A5
Ardochy House Highld 239 B6
Ardoyne Aberds 256 D1
Ardpatrick Argyll 202 B2
Ardpatrick Ho. Argyll 202 C2
Ardpeaton Argyll 215 D5
Ardrishaig Argyll 213 D6
Ardross Fife 221 D5
Ardross Highld 264 C2
Ardross Castle Highld 264 C2
Ardrossan N Ayrs 204 D2
Ardshealach Highld 235 D5
Ardsley S Yorks 140 C1
Ardslignish Highld 235 D4
Ardtalla Argyll 201 C4
Ardtalnaig Perth 218 A2
Ardtoe Highld 235 C5
Ardtrostan Perth 217 B6
Arduaine Argyll 213 A5
Ardullie Highld 264 D1
Ardvasar Highld 247 D5
Ardvorlich Perth 217 B6
Ardwell Dumfries 170 C3
Ardwell Mains Dumfries 170 C3
Ardwick Gtr Man 138 D1
Areley Kings Worcs 95 D6
Arford Hants 34 C1
Argoed Caerph 41 B6
Argoed Mill Powys 76 A3
Argyll & Sutherland Highlanders Museum (See Stirling Castle) Stirl 207 A5
Arichamish Argyll 214 B2
Arichastlich Argyll 216 A2
Aridhglas Argyll 224 D2

Arileod Argyll 223 B4
Arinacrinachd Highld 249 A4
Arinagour Argyll 223 B5
Arion Orkney 282 F3
Arisaig Highld 235 B5
Ariundle Highld 236 C2
Arkendale N Yorks 148 A2
Arkesden Essex 85 D6
Arkholme Lancs 155 D4
Arkle Town N Yorks 156 A4
Arkley London 68 D2
Arksey S Yorks 140 C3
Arkwright Town Derbys 131 B4
Arle Glos 63 A5
Arlecdon Cumb 162 C3
Arlesey Beds 84 D3
Arleston Telford 111 D5
Arley Ches 128 A1
Arlingham Glos 62 B3
Arlington Devon 25 A7
Arlington E Sus 22 B3
Arlington Glos 64 C2
Arlington Court Devon 25 A7
Armadale Highld 278 B3
Armadale W Loth 208 D2
Armadale Castle Highld 247 D5
Armathwaite Cumb 164 A3
Arminghall Norf 104 A3
Armitage Staffs 113 D4
Armley W Yorks 148 D1
Armscote Warks 81 C5
Armthorpe S Yorks 140 C4
Arnabost Argyll 223 B5
Arncliffe N Yorks 156 D3
Arncroach Fife 221 D5
Arne Dorset 16 C3
Arnesby Leics 98 B3
Arngask Perth 219 C6
Arnisdale Highld 238 A2
Arnish Highld 248 B2
Arniston Engine Midloth 209 D6
Arnol W Isles 288 C4
Arnold E Yorks 151 C4
Arnold Notts 114 A3
Arnolfini Gallery Bristol 43 B4
Arnprior Stirl 207 A4
Arnside Cumb 154 D3
Aros Mains Argyll 225 B4
Arowry Wrex 110 B3
Arpafeelie Highld 252 A2
Arrad Foot Cumb 154 C2
Arram E Yorks 150 C3
Arrathorne N Yorks 157 B6
Arreton I o W 18 C4
Arrington Cambs 85 B5
Arrivain Argyll 216 A2
Arrochar Argyll 215 B5
Arrow Warks 80 B3
Arthington W Yorks 147 C6
Arthingworth Northants 99 C4
Arthog Gwyn 90 A4
Arthrath Aberds 257 C4
Arthurstone Perth 231 D6
Artrochie Aberds 257 C5
Arundel W Sus 20 B3
Arundel Castle W Sus 20 B3
Aryhoulan Highld 237 C4
Asby Cumb 162 B3
Ascog Argyll 203 B6
Ascot Windsor 48 C2
Ascot Racecourse Windsor 48 C2
Ascott Warks 81 D6
Ascott-under-Wychwood Oxon 64 B4
Asenby N Yorks 158 D2
Asfordby Leics 115 D5
Asfordby Hill Leics 115 D5
Asgarby Lincs 116 A4
Asgarby Lincs 134 C3
Ash Kent 50 C2
Ash Kent 53 D4
Ash Som 29 C4
Ash Sur 34 A1
Ash Bullayne Devon 12 A2
Ash Green Warks 97 C6
Ash Magna Shrops 111 B4
Ash Mill Devon 26 C2
Ash Priors Som 27 C6
Ash Street Suff 87 C6
Ash Thomas Devon 27 D5
Ash Vale Sur 34 A1
Ashampstead W Berks 46 B3
Ashbocking Suff 88 B2
Ashbourne Derbys 113 A5
Ashbrittle Som 27 C5

Ashburton Devon 7 A6
Ashbury Devon 11 B6
Ashbury Oxon 45 A6
Ashby N Lincs 141 C7
Ashby by Partney Lincs 135 C4
Ashby cum Fenby
NE Lincs 143 C4
Ashby de la Launde Lincs 133 D5
Ashby-de-la-Zouch Leics 114 D1
Ashby Folville Leics 115 C5
Ashby Magna Leics 98 B2
Ashby Parva Leics 98 C2
Ashby Puerorum Lincs 134 B3
Ashby St Ledgers
Northants 82 A2
Ashby St Mary Norf 104 A4
Ashchurch Glos 80 D2
Ashcombe Devon 13 D4
Ashcott Som 28 B4
Ashdon Essex 86 C1
Ashe Hants 32 A4
Asheldham Essex 70 C3
Ashen Essex 86 C3
Ashendon Bucks 66 B2
Ashfield Carms 58 C3
Ashfield Stirl 218 D2
Ashfield Suff 88 A3
Ashfield Green Suff 104 D3
Ashfold Crossways W Sus 35 D5
Ashford Devon 25 B6
Ashford Hants 31 D5
Ashford Kent 38 A2
Ashford Sur 48 B3
Ashford Bowdler Shrops 94 D3
Ashford Carbonell Shrops 94 D3
Ashford Hill Hants 46 C3
Ashford in the Water
Derbys 130 C1
Ashgill S Lnrk 194 B2
Ashill Devon 27 D5
Ashill Norf 103 A4
Ashill Som 28 D3
Ashingdon Essex 70 D2
Ashington Northumb 179 A4
Ashington Som 29 C5
Ashington W Sus 21 A4
Ashintully Castle Perth 231 B5
Ashkirk Borders 186 A3
Ashlett Hants 18 A3
Ashleworth Glos 63 A4
Ashley Cambs 86 A2
Ashley Ches 128 A2
Ashley Devon 26 D1
Ashley Dorset 17 A5
Ashley Glos 63 D5
Ashley Hants 17 B6
Ashley Hants 32 B2
Ashley Northants 99 B4
Ashley Staffs 111 B6
Ashley Green Bucks 67 C4
Ashley Heath Dorset 17 A5
Ashley Heath Staffs 111 B6
Ashmanhaugh Norf 121 C5
Ashmansworth Hants 46 D2
Ashmansworthy Devon 24 D3
Ashmore Dorset 30 D3
Ashorne Warks 81 B6
Ashover Derbys 130 C3
Ashow Warks 97 D6
Ashprington Devon 8 B2
Ashreigney Devon 26 D1
Ashtead Sur 35 A4
Ashton Ches 127 C5
Ashton Corn 3 C4
Ashton Hants 33 D4
Ashton Hereford 78 A3
Ashton Invclyd 204 A2
Ashton Northants 83 C4
Ashton Northants 100 C2
Ashton Common Wilts 44 D2
Ashton-In-Makerfield
Gtr Man 137 D4
Ashton Keynes Wilts 63 D6
Ashton under Hill Worcs 80 D2
Ashton-under-Lyne
Gtr Man 138 D2
Ashton upon Mersey
Gtr Man 137 D6
Ashurst Hants 32 D2
Ashurst Kent 36 C3
Ashurst W Sus 21 A4
Ashurstwood W Sus 36 C2
Ashwater Devon 11 B4
Ashwell Herts 85 D4
Ashwell Rutland 115 D6

Ashwell Som 28 D3
Ashwellthorpe Norf 104 B2
Ashwick Som 29 A6
Ashwicken Norf 119 D4
Ashybank Borders 186 B4
Askam in Furness Cumb 153 C3
Askern S Yorks 140 B3
Askerswell Dorset 15 B5
Askett Bucks 66 C3
Askham Cumb 164 C3
Askham Notts 132 B2
Askham Bryan York 149 C4
Askham Richard York 148 C4
Asknish Argyll 214 C2
Askrigg N Yorks 156 B3
Askwith N Yorks 147 C5
Aslackby Lincs 116 B3
Aslacton Norf 104 B2
Aslockton Notts 115 B5
Asloun Aberds 244 A2
Aspatria Cumb 174 D4
Aspenden Herts 68 A3
Asperton Lincs 117 B5
Aspley Guise Beds 83 D6
Aspley Heath Beds 83 D6
Aspull Gtr Man 137 C5
Asselby E Yorks 141 A5
Asserby Lincs 135 B4
Assington Suff 87 D5
Assynt Ho. Highld 264 D1
Astbury Ches 128 C3
Astcote Northants 82 B3
Asterley Shrops 94 A1
Asterton Shrops 94 B1
Asthall Oxon 64 B3
Asthall Leigh Oxon 64 B4
Astley Shrops 111 D4
Astley Warks 97 C6
Astley Worcs 79 A5
Astley Abbotts Shrops 95 B5
Astley Bridge Gtr Man 137 B6
Astley Cross Worcs 79 A6
Astley Green Gtr Man 137 D6
Aston Ches 111 A5
Aston Ches 127 B5
Aston Derbys 130 A1
Aston Hereford 94 D2
Aston Herts 68 A2
Aston Oxon 64 C4
Aston Shrops 111 C4
Aston Staffs 111 A6
Aston S Yorks 131 A4
Aston Telford 95 A4
Aston W Mid 96 C3
Aston Wokingham 47 A5
Aston Abbotts Bucks 66 A3
Aston Botterell Shrops 95 C4
Aston-By-Stone Staffs 112 B3
Aston Cantlow Warks 80 B4
Aston Clinton Bucks 66 B3
Aston Crews Hereford 62 A2
Aston Cross Glos 80 D2
Aston End Herts 68 A2
Aston Eyre Shrops 95 B4
Aston Fields Worcs 80 A2
Aston Flamville Leics 98 B1
Aston Ingham Hereford 62 A2
Aston juxta Mondrum
Ches 127 D6
Aston le Walls Northants 82 B1
Aston Magna Glos 81 D4
Aston Munslow Shrops 94 C3
Aston on Clun Shrops 94 C1
Aston-on-Trent Derbys 114 C2
Aston Rogers Shrops 94 A1
Aston Rowant Oxon 66 D2
Aston Sandford Bucks 66 C2
Aston Somerville Worcs 80 D3
Aston Subedge Glos 80 C4
Aston Tirrold Oxon 46 A3
Aston Upthorpe Oxon 46 A3
Astrop Northants 82 D2
Astwick Beds 84 D4
Astwood M Keynes 83 C6
Astwood Worcs 79 B6
Astwood Bank Worcs 80 A3
Aswarby Lincs 116 B3
Aswardby Lincs 134 B3
Atch Lench Worcs 80 B3
Atcham Shrops 94 A3
Athelhampton Dorset 16 B1
Athelington Suff 104 D3
Athelney Som 28 C3
Athelstaneford E Loth 210 C2
Atherington Devon 25 C6
Atherstone Warks 97 B6
Atherstone on Stour
Warks 81 B5

Atherton Gtr Man 137 C5
Atley Hill N Yorks 157 A6
Atlow Derbys 113 A6
Attadale Highld 249 C6
Attadale Ho. Highld 249 C6
Attenborough Notts 114 B3
Atterby Lincs 142 D1
Attercliffe S Yorks 130 A3
Attleborough Norf 103 B6
Attleborough Warks 97 B6
Attlebridge Norf 120 D3
Atwick E Yorks 151 B4
Atworth Wilts 44 C2
Auburn Lincs 133 C4
Auchagallon N Ayrs 191 B4
Auchallater Aberds 243 D4
Aucharnie Aberds 256 B1
Auchattie Aberds 244 C3
Auchavan Angus 231 B5
Auchbreck Moray 254 D3
Auchenback E Renf 205 C5
Auchenbainzie Dumfries 183 C6
Auchenblae Aberds 233 A5
Auchenbrack Dumfries 183 C5
Auchenbreck Argyll 214 D3
Auchencairn Dumfries 173 C5
Auchencairn Dumfries 184 D2
Auchencairn N Ayrs 191 C6
Auchencrosh S Ayrs 180 D3
Auchencrow Borders 211 D5
Auchendinny Midloth 209 D5
Auchengray S Lnrk 195 A4
Auchenhalrig Moray 267 C4
Auchenheath S Lnrk 194 B3
Auchenlochan Argyll 203 A4
Auchenmalg Dumfries 171 B4
Auchensoul S Ayrs 181 B4
Auchentiber N Ayrs 204 D3
Auchertyre Highld 249 D5
Auchgourish Highld 242 A2
Auchincarroch W Dunb 206 B2
Auchindrain Argyll 214 B3
Auchindrean Highld 262 B3
Auchininna Aberds 256 B1
Auchinleck E Ayrs 193 C5
Auchinloch N Lnrk 205 A6
Auchinroath Moray 266 D3
Auchintoul Aberds 244 A2
Auchiries Aberds 257 C5
Auchlee Aberds 245 C5
Auchleven Aberds 256 D1
Auchlochan S Lnrk 194 C3
Auchlossan Aberds 244 B2
Auchlunies Aberds 245 C5
Auchlyne Stirl 217 B5
Auchmacoy Aberds 257 C4
Auchmair Moray 255 D4
Auchmantle Dumfries 170 A3
Auchmillan E Ayrs 193 C5
Auchmithie Angus 233 D4
Auchmuirbridge Fife 220 D2
Auchmull Angus 232 A3
Auchnacree Angus 232 B2
Auchnagallin Highld 253 C6
Auchnagatt Aberds 257 B4
Auchnaha Argyll 214 D2
Auchnashelloch Perth 218 C2
Aucholzie Aberds 243 C6
Auchrannie Angus 231 C6
Auchroisk Highld 253 D6
Auchronie Angus 244 D1
Auchterarder Perth 218 C4
Auchteraw Highld 240 B1
Auchterderran Fife 209 A5
Auchterhouse Angus 220 A3
Auchtermuchty Fife 220 C2
Auchterneed Highld 251 A6
Auchtertool Fife 209 A5
Auchtertyre Moray 266 D2
Auchtubh Stirl 217 B5
Auckengill Highld 281 B5
Auckley S Yorks 140 C4
Audenshaw Gtr Man 138 D2
Audlem Ches 111 A5
Audley Staffs 128 D2
Audley End Essex 87 D4
Audley End House Essex 86 D1
Aughton E Yorks 149 D6
Aughton Lancs 136 C2
Aughton Lancs 145 A5
Aughton S Yorks 131 A4
Aughton Wilts 45 D6
Aughton Park Lancs 136 C3
Auldearn Highld 253 A5
Aulden Hereford 78 B2
Auldgirth Dumfries 183 D7
Auldhame E Loth 210 B2

Auldhouse S Lnrk 205 C6
Ault a'chruinn Highld 249 D6
Aultanrynie Highld 271 A6
Aultbea Highld 261 B5
Aultdearg Highld 263 D4
Aultgrishan Highld 261 B4
Aultguish Inn Highld 263 C5
Aultibea Highld 274 B4
Aultiphurst Highld 279 B4
Aultmore Moray 267 D5
Aultnagoire Highld 252 D1
Aultnamain Inn Highld 264 B2
Aultnaslat Highld 239 B5
Aulton Aberds 255 D7
Aundorach Highld 242 A2
Aunsby Lincs 116 B3
Auquhorthies Aberds 256 D3
Aust S Glos 43 A4
Austendike Lincs 117 C5
Austerfield S Yorks 141 D4
Austrey Warks 97 A5
Austwick N Yorks 146 A1
Authorpe Lincs 135 A4
Authorpe Row Lincs 135 B5
Avebury Wilts 45 C5
Aveley Thurrock 50 A2
Avening Glos 63 D4
Averham Notts 132 D2
Aveton Gifford Devon 7 C5
Avielochan Highld 242 A2
Aviemore Highld 242 A1
Avington Hants 32 B4
Avington W Berks 46 C1
Avoch Highld 252 A3
Avon Hants 17 B5
Avon Dassett Warks 81 C7
Avonbridge Falk 208 C2
Avonmouth Bristol 43 B4
Avonwick Devon 7 B6
Awbridge Hants 32 C2
Awhirk Dumfries 170 B2
Awkley S Glos 43 A4
Awliscombe Devon 13 A6
Awre Glos 62 C3
Awsworth Notts 114 A2
Axbridge Som 42 D3
Axford Hants 33 A5
Axford Wilts 45 C6
Axminster Devon 14 B2
Axmouth Devon 14 B2
Axton Flint 125 A6
Aycliff Kent 39 A5
Aycliffe Durham 167 C5
Aydon Northumb 178 C2
Aylburton Glos 62 C2
Ayle Northumb 165 A5
Aylesbeare Devon 13 B5
Aylesbury Bucks 66 B3
Aylesby NE Lincs 143 C4
Aylesford Kent 37 A5
Aylesham Kent 53 D4
Aylestone Leicester 98 A2
Aylmerton Norf 120 B3
Aylsham Norf 120 C3
Aylton Hereford 79 D4
Aymestrey Hereford 78 A2
Aynho Northants 82 D2
Ayot St Lawrence Herts 68 B1
Ayot St Peter Herts 68 B2
Ayr S Ayrs 192 C3
Ayr Racecourse S Ayrs 192 C3
Aysgarth N Yorks 156 C4
Ayside Cumb 154 C2
Ayston Rutland 99 A5
Aythorpe Roding Essex 69 B5
Ayton Borders 211 D6
Aywick Shetland 284 E7
Azerley N Yorks 157 D6

B

Babbacombe Torbay 8 A3
Babbinswood Shrops 110 B2
Babcary Som 29 C5
Babel Carms 59 B5
Babell Flint 125 B6
Babraham Cambs 85 B7
Babworth Notts 132 A1
Bac W Isles 288 C5
Bachau Anglesey 123 B4
Back of Keppoch Highld 235 B5
Back Rogerton E Ayrs 193 C5
Backaland Orkney 282 D6
Backaskaill Orkney 282 B5
Backbarrow Cumb 154 C2
Backe Carms 56 A2
Backfolds Aberds 269 D5
Backford Ches 127 B4

Backford Cross Ches 126 B3
Backhill Aberds 256 C2
Backhill Aberds 257 C5
Backhill of Clackriach
Aberds 257 B4
Backhill of Fortree
Aberds 257 B4
Backhill of Trustach
Aberds 244 C3
Backies Highld 274 D2
Backlass Highld 280 C4
Backwell N Som 42 C3
Backworth T & W 179 B5
Bacon End Essex 69 B6
Baconsthorpe Norf 120 B3
Bacton Hereford 78 D1
Bacton Norf 121 B5
Bacton Suff 87 A6
Bacton Green Suff 87 A6
Bacup Lancs 138 A1
Badachro Highld 261 C4
Badanloch Lodge Highld 273 A5
Badavanich Highld 250 A3
Badbury Thamesdown 45 A5
Badby Northants 82 B2
Badcall Highld 276 C3
Badcaul Highld 262 A2
Baddeley Green Stoke 129 D4
Baddesley Clinton Warks 97 D5
Baddesley Clinton Hall
Warks 97 D5
Baddesley Ensor Warks 97 B5
Baddidarach Highld 270 B3
Baddoch Aberds 242 D4
Baddock Highld 252 A3
Badenscoth Aberds 256 C2
Badenyon Aberds 243 A6
Badger Shrops 95 B5
Badger's Mount Kent 50 C3
Badgeworth Glos 63 B5
Badgworth Som 42 D2
Badicaul Highld 249 D4
Badingham Suff 88 A4
Badlesmere Kent 52 D2
Badlipster Highld 280 D4
Badluarach Highld 262 A2
Badminton S Glos 44 A2
Badnaban Highld 270 B3
Badninish Highld 264 A3
Badrallach Highld 262 A2
Badsey Worcs 80 C3
Badshot Lea Sur 34 B1
Badsworth W Yorks 140 B2
Badwell Ash Suff 87 A5
Bae Colwyn = Colwyn
Bay Conwy 124 B3
Bag Enderby Lincs 134 B3
Bagby N Yorks 158 C3
Bagendon Glos 63 C6
Bagh a Chaisteil =
Castlebay W Isles 286 G2
Bagh Mor W Isles 286 A4
Bagh Shiarabhagh
W Isles 286 E3
Baghasdal W Isles 286 E3
Bagillt Flint 126 B2
Baginton Warks 97 D6
Baglan Neath 40 B2
Bagley Shrops 110 C3
Bagnall Staffs 129 D4
Bagnor W Berks 46 C2
Bagshot Sur 48 C2
Bagshot Wilts 45 C7
Bagthorpe Norf 119 B5
Bagthorpe Notts 131 D4
Bagworth Leics 98 A1
Bagwy Llydiart Hereford 61 A6
Bail Ard Bhuirgh W Isles 288 B5
Bail Uachdraich W Isles 287 H3
Baildon W Yorks 147 D5
Baile W Isles 287 ...
Baile a Mhanaich W Isles 286 ...
Baile Ailein W Isles 288 ...
Baile an Truiseil W Isles 288 ...
Baile Boidheach Argyll 202 ...
Baile Glas W Isles 286 ...
Baile Mhartainn W Isles 287 ...
Baile Mhic Phail W Isles 287 ...
Baile Mor Argyll 224 ...
Baile Mor W Isles 287 ...
Baile na Creige W Isles 286 ...
Baile nan Cailleach
W Isles 286 ...
Baile Raghaill W Isles 287 ...
Bailebeag Highld 240 ...
Baileyhead Cumb 176 ...
Bailiesward Aberds 255 ...
Baillieston Glasgow 205 ...

Bail'lochdrach W Isles 286 A4
Bail'Ur Tholastaidh W Isles 288 C6
Bainbridge N Yorks 156 B3
Bainsford Falk 208 B1
Bainshole Aberds 255 C7
Bainton E Yorks 150 B2
Bainton P'boro 100 A2
Bairnkine Borders 187 B5
Baker Street Thurrock 50 A3
Baker's End Herts 68 B3
Bakewell Derbys 130 C2
Bala = Y Bala Gwyn 108 B4
Balachuirn Highld 248 B2
Balavil Highld 241 B5
Balbeg Highld 251 D6
Balbeg Highld 251 C6
Balbeggie Perth 219 B6
Balbithan Aberds 245 A4
Balbithan Ho. Aberds 245 A5
Balblair Highld 264 D3
Balblair Highld 264 A1
Balby S Yorks 140 C3
Balchladich Highld 270 A3
Balchraggan Highld 252 C1
Balchraggan Highld 252 B1
Balchrick Highld 276 C2
Balchrystie Fife 221 D4
Balcladaich Highld 251 D4
alcombe W Sus 35 C6
alcombe Lane W Sus 35 C6
alcomie Fife 221 C6
alcurvie Fife 220 D3
aldersby N Yorks 158 D2
aldersby St James N Yorks 158 D2
alderstone Lancs 145 D6
alderton Ches 126 C3
alderton Notts 132 D3
aldhu Corn 4 C2
aldinnie Fife 220 C4
aldock Herts 84 D4
aldovie Dundee 221 A4
aldrine I o M 152 C4
aldslow E Sus 23 A5
aldwin I o M 152 C3
aldwinholme Cumb 175 C6
aldwin's Gate Staffs 112 A1
ale Norf 120 B2
alearn Aberds 269 D5
alemartine Argyll 222 C2
alephuil Argyll 222 C2
alerno Edin 209 D4
levullin Argyll 222 C2
lfield Angus 232 B3
lfour Orkney 282 F5
lfron Stirl 206 B3
lfron Station Stirl 206 B3
lgaveny Aberds 256 B1
lgavies Angus 232 C3
lgonar Fife 208 A3
lgove Aberds 256 C3
lgowan Highld 241 C4
lgown Highld 258 B3
grochan E Dunb 205 A6
gy Highld 249 A5
haldie Stirl 218 D3
halgardy Aberds 256 D2
ham London 49 B5
hary Perth 231 D6
iasta Shetland 284 C8
igill Highld 279 B4
intore Angus 231 C6
intore Highld 265 C4
ntraid Highld 264 C3
N Yorks 158 C3
eerie Angus 232 D1
emback Angus 220 A3
holme E Yorks 141 A5
issock S Ayrs 180 C3
Shrops 110 C2
Haye Green Staffs 129 D4
Hill Hants 46 C2
abeg I o M 152 D2
acannel I o M 152 C4
achulish Highld 237 D4
ajora I o M 152 B4
aleigh I o M 152 C3
amodha I o M 152 D2
antrae S Ayrs 180 C2
aquine I o M 152 C4
ards Gore Essex 70 D3
asalla I o M 152 B3
asalla I o M 152 D2
ater Aberds 243 C6
augh I o M 152 B3
veare I o M 152 D3
orach Moray 254 D2
Ballechin Perth 230 C3
Balleigh Highld 264 B3
Ballencrieff E Loth 210 C1
Ballentoul Perth 230 B2
Ballidon Derbys 130 D2
Balliemore Argyll 214 D3
Balliemore Argyll 226 D3
Ballikinrain Stirl 206 B3
Ballimeanoch Argyll 214 A3
Ballimore Argyll 214 D2
Ballimore Stirl 217 C5
Ballinaby Argyll 200 B2
Ballindean Perth 220 B2
Ballingdon Suff 87 C4
Ballinger Common Bucks 67 C4
Ballingham Hereford 78 D3
Ballingry Fife 209 A4
Ballinlick Perth 230 D3
Ballinluig Perth 230 C3
Ballintuim Perth 231 C5
Balloch Angus 232 C1
Balloch Highld 252 B3
Balloch N Lnrk 207 C5
Balloch W Dunb 206 B1
Ballochan Aberds 244 C2
Ballochford Moray 255 C4
Ballochmorrie S Ayrs 181 C4
Balls Cross W Sus 34 D2
Balls Green Essex 71 A4
Ballygown Argyll 224 B3
Ballygrant Argyll 200 B3
Ballyhaugh Argyll 223 B4
Balmacara Highld 249 D5
Balmacara Square Highld 249 D5
Balmaclellan Dumfries 173 A4
Balmacneil Perth 230 C3
Balmacqueen Highld 259 A4
Balmae Dumfries 173 D4
Balmaha Stirl 206 A2
Balmalcolm Fife 220 D3
Balmeanach Highld 248 B2
Balmedie Aberds 245 A6
Balmer Heath Shrops 110 B3
Balmerino Fife 220 B3
Balmerlawn Hants 18 A2
Balmichael N Ayrs 191 B5
Balmirmer Angus 221 A5
Balmoral Castle and Gardens Aberds 243 C5
Balmore Highld 258 D2
Balmore Highld 251 C5
Balmore Highld 253 B4
Balmore Perth 230 C3
Balmule Fife 209 B5
Balmullo Fife 220 B4
Balmungie Highld 252 A3
Balnaboth Angus 231 B7
Balnabruaich Highld 264 D3
Balnabruich Highld 275 B5
Balnacoil Highld 274 C2
Balnacra Highld 250 B1
Balnafoich Highld 252 C2
Balnagall Highld 265 B4
Balnaguard Perth 230 C3
Balnahard Argyll 212 C2
Balnahard Argyll 224 C3
Balnain Highld 251 C6
Balnakeil Highld 277 B4
Balnaknock Highld 259 B4
Balnapaling Highld 264 D3
Balne N Yorks 140 B3
Balochroy Argyll 202 C2
Balone Fife 221 C4
Balornock Glasgow 205 B6
Balquharn Perth 219 A5
Balquhidder Stirl 217 B5
Balsall W Mid 97 D5
Balsall Common W Mid 97 D5
Balsall Heath W Mid 96 C3
Balscott Oxon 81 C6
Balsham Cambs 86 B1
Baltasound Shetland 284 C8
Balterley Staffs 128 D2
Baltersan Dumfries 171 A6
Balthangie Aberds 268 D3
Baltonsborough Som 29 B5
Balvaird Highld 252 A1
Balvicar Argyll 213 A5
Balvraid Highld 238 A2
Balvraid Highld 253 C4
Bamber Bridge Lancs 137 A4
Bambers Green Essex 69 A5
Bamburgh Northumb 199 C5
Bamburgh Castle Northumb 199 C5
Bamff Perth 231 C6
Bamford Derbys 130 A2
Bamford Gtr Man 138 B1
Bampton Cumb 164 D3
Bampton Devon 27 C4
Bampton Oxon 64 C4
Bampton Grange Cumb 164 D3
Banavie Highld 237 B5
Banbury Oxon 82 C1
Bancffosfelen Carms 57 A4
Banchory Aberds 244 C3
Banchory-Devenick Aberds 245 B6
Bancycapel Carms 57 A4
Bancyfelin Carms 56 A3
Bancyffordd Carms 73 C7
Bandirran Perth 220 A2
Banff Aberds 268 C1
Bangor Gwyn 123 C5
Bangor-is-y-coed Wrex 110 A2
Bangor on Dee Racecourse Wrex 110 A2
Banham Norf 103 C6
Banham Zoo, Diss Norf 103 C6
Bank Hants 18 A1
Bank Newton N Yorks 146 B3
Bank Street Worcs 79 A4
Bankend Dumfries 174 B3
Bankfoot Perth 219 A5
Bankglen E Ayrs 182 A4
Bankhead Aberdeen 245 A5
Bankhead Aberds 244 B3
Banknock Falk 207 C5
Banks Cumb 176 C3
Banks Lancs 136 A2
Bankshill Dumfries 185 D4
Banningham Norf 120 C4
Banniskirk Ho. Highld 280 C3
Bannister Green Essex 69 A6
Bannockburn Stirl 207 A6
Banstead Sur 35 A5
Bantham Devon 7 C5
Banton N Lnrk 207 C5
Banwell N Som 42 D2
Banyard's Green Suff 104 D3
Bapchild Kent 51 C6
Bar Hill Cambs 85 A5
Barabhas W Isles 288 C4
Barabhas Iarach W Isles 288 C4
Barabhas Uarach W Isles 288 B4
Barachandroman Argyll 225 D5
Barassie S Ayrs 192 B3
Baravullin Argyll 226 C3
Barbaraville Highld 264 C3
Barber Booth Derbys 129 A6
Barbieston S Ayrs 182 A2
Barbon Cumb 155 C5
Barbridge Ches 127 D6
Barbrook Devon 26 A2
Barby Northants 98 D2
Barcaldine Argyll 227 B4
Barcaldine Sea Life Centre Argyll 226 B4
Barcheston Warks 81 D5
Barcombe E Sus 22 A2
Barcombe Cross E Sus 22 A2
Barden N Yorks 157 B5
Barden Scale N Yorks 147 B4
Bardennoch Dumfries 182 C3
Bardfield Saling Essex 69 A6
Bardister Shetland 284 F5
Bardney Lincs 133 C6
Bardon Leics 114 D2
Bardon Mill Northumb 177 C5
Bardowie E Dunb 205 A5
Bardrainney Invclyd 204 A3
Bardsea Cumb 154 D2
Bardsey W Yorks 148 C2
Bardwell Suff 103 D5
Bare Lancs 145 A4
Barfad Argyll 202 B3
Barford Norf 104 A2
Barford Warks 81 A5
Barford St John Oxon 82 D1
Barford St Martin Wilts 31 B4
Barford St Michael Oxon 82 D1
Barfreston Kent 53 D4
Bargod = Bargoed Caerph 41 B6
Bargoed = Bargod Caerph 41 B6
Bargrennan Dumfries 181 D5
Barham Cambs 100 D3
Barham Kent 53 D4
Barham Suff 88 B2
Barharrow Dumfries 172 C4
Barhill Dumfries 173 B6
Barholm Lincs 116 D3
Barkby Leics 98 A3
Barkestone-le-Vale Leics 115 B5
Barkham Wokingham 47 C5
Barking London 50 A1
Barking Suff 87 B6
Barking Tye Suff 87 B6
Barkingside London 50 A1
Barkisland W Yorks 138 B3
Barkston Lincs 116 A2
Barkston N Yorks 148 D3
Barkway Herts 85 D5
Barlaston Staffs 112 B2
Barlavington W Sus 20 A2
Barlborough Derbys 131 B4
Barlby N Yorks 149 D5
Barlestone Leics 98 A1
Barley Herts 85 D5
Barley Lancs 146 C2
Barley Mow T & W 179 D4
Barleythorpe Rutland 99 A5
Barling Essex 51 A6
Barlow Derbys 130 B3
Barlow N Yorks 140 A4
Barlow T & W 178 C3
Barmby Moor E Yorks 149 C6
Barmby on the Marsh E Yorks 141 A4
Barmer Norf 119 B5
Barmoor Castle Northumb 198 C3
Barmoor Lane End Northumb 198 C4
Barmouth = Abermaw Gwyn 90 A4
Barmpton Darl 167 D6
Barmston E Yorks 151 B4
Barnack P'boro 100 A2
Barnacle Warks 97 C6
Barnard Castle Durham 166 D3
Barnard Gate Oxon 65 B5
Barnardiston Suff 86 C3
Barnbarroch Dumfries 173 C6
Barnburgh S Yorks 140 C2
Barnby Suff 105 C5
Barnby Dun S Yorks 140 C4
Barnby in the Willows Notts 132 D3
Barnby Moor Notts 131 A6
Barnes Street Kent 36 B4
Barnet London 68 D2
Barnetby le Wold N Lincs 142 C2
Barney Norf 120 B1
Barnham Suff 103 D4
Barnham W Sus 20 B2
Barnham Broom Norf 104 A1
Barnhead Angus 233 C4
Barnhill Ches 127 D4
Barnhill Dundee 221 A4
Barnhill Moray 266 D2
Barnhills Dumfries 180 D1
Barningham Durham 166 D3
Barningham Suff 103 D5
Barnoldby le Beck NE Lincs 143 C4
Barnoldswick Lancs 146 C2
Barns Green W Sus 35 D4
Barnsley Glos 64 C1
Barnsley S Yorks 139 C6
Barnstaple Devon 25 B6
Barnston Essex 69 B6
Barnston Mers 126 A2
Barnstone Notts 115 B5
Barnt Green Worcs 96 D3
Barnton Ches 127 B6
Barnton Edin 209 C4
Barnwell All Saints Northants 100 C2
Barnwell St Andrew Northants 100 C2
Barnwood Glos 63 B4
Barochreal Argyll 226 D3
Barons Cross Hereford 78 B2
Barr S Ayrs 181 B4
Barra Airport W Isles 286 F2
Barra Castle Aberds 256 D2
Barrachan Dumfries 171 C5
Barrack Aberds 256 B3
Barraglom W Isles 288 D2
Barrahormid Argyll 213 D5
Barran Argyll 226 D3
Barrapol Argyll 222 C2
Barras Aberds 245 D5
Barras Cumb 165 D6
Barrasford Northumb 177 B7
Barravullin Argyll 213 B6
Barregarrow I o M 152 C3
Barrhead E Renf 205 C4
Barrhill S Ayrs 181 C4
Barrington Cambs 85 C5
Barrington Som 28 D3
Barripper Corn 3 B4
Barmill N Ayrs 204 C3
Barrock Highld 281 A4
Barrock Ho. Highld 281 B4
Barrow Lancs 146 D1
Barrow Rutland 116 D1
Barrow Suff 86 A3
Barrow Green Kent 51 C6
Barrow Gurney N Som 43 C4
Barrow Haven N Lincs 142 A2
Barrow-in-Furness Cumb 153 D3
Barrow Island Cumb 153 D2
Barrow Nook Lancs 136 C3
Barrow Street Wilts 30 B2
Barrow upon Humber N Lincs 142 A2
Barrow upon Soar Leics 114 D3
Barrow upon Trent Derbys 114 C1
Barroway Drove Norf 102 A1
Barrowburn Northumb 188 B1
Barrowby Lincs 116 B1
Barrowcliff N Yorks 160 C4
Barrowden Rutland 99 A6
Barrowford Lancs 146 D2
Barrows Green Ches 128 D1
Barrows Green Cumb 154 C4
Barrow's Green Mers 127 A5
Barry Angus 221 A5
Barry = Y Barri V Glam 41 E6
Barry Island V Glam 41 E6
Barsby Leics 115 D4
Barsham Suff 105 C4
Barston W Mid 97 D5
Bartestree Hereford 78 C3
Barthol Chapel Aberds 256 C3
Barthomley Ches 128 D2
Bartley Hants 32 D2
Bartley Green W Mid 96 C3
Bartlow Cambs 86 C1
Barton Cambs 85 B6
Barton Ches 127 D4
Barton Glos 64 A2
Barton Lancs 136 C2
Barton Lancs 145 D5
Barton N Yorks 157 A6
Barton Oxon 65 C6
Barton Torbay 8 A3
Barton Warks 80 B4
Barton Bendish Norf 102 A3
Barton Hartshorn Bucks 82 D3
Barton in Fabis Notts 114 B3
Barton in the Beans Leics 97 A6
Barton-le-Clay Beds 84 D2
Barton-le-Street N Yorks 159 D6
Barton-le-Willows N Yorks 149 A6
Barton Mills Suff 102 D3
Barton on Sea Hants 17 B6
Barton on the Heath Warks 81 D5
Barton St David Som 29 B5
Barton Seagrave Northants 99 D5
Barton Stacey Hants 32 A3
Barton Turf Norf 121 C5
Barton-under-Needwood Staffs 113 D5
Barton-upon-Humber N Lincs 142 A2
Barton Waterside N Lincs 142 A2
Barugh S Yorks 139 C6
Barway Cambs 102 D1
Barwell Leics 98 B1
Barwick Herts 68 B3
Barwick Som 29 D5
Barwick in Elmet W Yorks 148 D2
Baschurch Shrops 110 C3
Bascote Warks 81 A7
Basford Green Staffs 129 D4
Bashall Eaves Lancs 145 C6
Bashley Hants 17 B6
Basildon Essex 51 A4
Basingstoke Hants 47 D4
Baslow Derbys 130 B2
Bason Bridge Som 28 A3
Bassaleg Newport 42 A1
Bassenthwaite Cumb 163 A5
Bassett Soton 32 D3
Bassingbourn Cambs 85 C5
Bassingfield Notts 115 B4
Bassingham Lincs 133 C4
Bassingthorpe Lincs 116 C2
Basta Shetland 284 D7
Baston Lincs 116 D4
Bastwick Norf 121 D6
Baswick Steer E Yorks 150 C3
Batchworth Heath Herts 67 D5
Batcombe Dorset 15 A6
Batcombe Som 29 B6

Bate Heath Ches 128 B1
Bateman's, Burwash E Sus 37 D4
Batford Herts 67 B6
Bath Bath 43 C6
Bath Abbey Bath 43 C6
Bath Racecourse Bath 43 C6
Bathampton Bath 44 C1
Bathealton Som 27 C5
Batheaston Bath 44 C1
Bathford Bath 44 C1
Bathgate W Loth 208 D2
Bathley Notts 132 D2
Bathpool Corn 10 D3
Bathpool Som 28 C2
Bathville W Loth 208 D2
Batley W Yorks 139 A5
Batsford Glos 81 D4
Battersby N Yorks 159 A4
Battersea London 49 B5
Battisborough Cross Devon 7 C4
Battisford Suff 87 B6
Battisford Tye Suff 87 B6
Battle E Sus 23 A5
Battle Powys 76 D4
Battle Abbey E Sus 23 A5
Battledown Glos 63 A5
Battlefield Shrops 111 D4
Battlesbridge Essex 70 D1
Battlesden Beds 67 A4
Battlesea Green Suff 104 D3
Battleton Som 27 C4
Battram Leics 98 A1
Battramsley Hants 18 B2
Baughton Worcs 80 C1
Baughurst Hants 46 D3
Baulking Oxon 64 D4
Baumber Lincs 134 B2
Baunton Glos 63 C6
Baverstock Wilts 31 B4
Bawburgh Norf 104 A2
Bawdeswell Norf 120 C2
Bawdrip Som 28 B3
Bawdsey Suff 88 C4
Bawtry S Yorks 141 D4
Baxenden Lancs 137 A6
Baxterley Warks 97 B5
Baybridge Hants 32 C4
Baycliff Cumb 154 D1
Baydon Wilts 45 B6
Bayford Herts 68 C3
Bayford Som 30 C1
Bayles Cumb 165 A5
Baylham Suff 88 B2
Baynard's Green Oxon 65 A6
Bayston Hill Shrops 94 A2
Baythorn End Essex 86 C3
Bayton Worcs 95 D4
Beach Highld 236 D1
Beachampton Bucks 83 D4
Beachamwell Norf 102 A3
Beachans Moray 253 B6
Beacharr Argyll 202 D1
Beachborough Kent 38 B3
Beachley Glos 62 D1
Beacon Devon 14 A1
Beacon End Essex 70 A3
Beacon Hill Sur 34 C1
Beacon's Bottom Bucks 66 D2
Beaconsfield Bucks 67 E4
Beacrabhaic W Isles 288 H2
Beadlam N Yorks 159 C5
Beadlow Beds 84 D3
Beadnell Northumb 189 A5
Beaford Devon 25 D6
Beal Northumb 199 B4
Beal N Yorks 140 A3
Beale Park, Goring W Berks 47 B4
Beamhurst Staffs 113 B4
Beaminster Dorset 15 A4
Beamish Durham 179 D4
Beamish Open Air Museum, Stanley Durham 179 D4
Beamsley N Yorks 147 B4
Bean Kent 50 B2
Beanacre Wilts 44 C3
Beanley Northumb 188 B3
Beaquoy Orkney 282 E4
Bear Cross Bmouth 17 B4
Beardwood Blkburn 137 A5
Beare Green Sur 35 B4
Bearley Warks 81 A4
Bearnus Argyll 224 B2
Bearpark Durham 167 A5

Bearsbridge Northumb 177 D5
Bearsden E Dunb 205 A5
Bearsted Kent 37 A5
Bearstone Shrops 111 B6
Bearwood Hereford 78 B1
Bearwood Poole 17 B4
Bearwood W Mid 96 C3
Beattock Dumfries 184 B3
Beauchamp Roding Essex 69 B5
Beauchief S Yorks 130 A3
Beaufort Bl Gwent 60 B3
Beaufort Castle Highld 251 B7
Beaulieu Hants 18 A2
Beauly Highld 252 B1
Beaumaris Anglesey 123 C6
Beaumaris Castle Anglesey 123 C6
Beaumont Cumb 175 C6
Beaumont Essex 71 A5
Beaumont Hill Darl 167 D5
Beausale Warks 97 D5
Beauworth Hants 33 C4
Beaworthy Devon 11 B5
Beazley End Essex 70 A1
Bebington Mers 126 A3
Bebside Northumb 179 A4
Beccles Suff 105 B5
Becconsall Lancs 136 A3
Beck Foot Cumb 155 B5
Beck Hole N Yorks 159 A7
Beck Row Suff 102 D2
Beck Side Cumb 153 B3
Beckbury Shrops 95 A5
Beckenham London 49 C6
Beckermet Cumb 162 D3
Beckfoot Cumb 163 D4
Beckfoot Cumb 174 D3
Beckford Worcs 80 D2
Beckhampton Wilts 45 C4
Beckingham Lincs 132 D3
Beckingham Notts 141 E5
Beckington Som 44 D2
Beckley E Sus 37 D6
Beckley Hants 17 B6
Beckley Oxon 65 B6
Beckton London 50 A1
Beckwithshaw N Yorks 147 B6
Becontree London 50 A1
Bed-y-coedwr Gwyn 108 C2
Bedale N Yorks 157 C6
Bedburn Durham 166 B4
Bedchester Dorset 30 D2
Beddau Rhondda 41 C5
Beddgelert Gwyn 107 B5
Beddingham E Sus 22 B2
Beddington London 49 C6
Bedfield Suff 88 A3
Bedford Beds 84 B2
Bedham W Sus 34 D3
Bedhampton Hants 19 A6
Bedingfield Suff 88 A2
Bedlam N Yorks 147 A6
Bedlington Northumb 179 A4
Bedlington Station Northumb 179 A4
Bedlinog M Tydf 41 A5
Bedminster Bristol 43 B4
Bedmond Herts 67 C5
Bednall Staffs 112 D3
Bedrule Borders 187 B5
Bedstone Shrops 94 D1
Bedwas Caerph 41 C6
Bedworth Warks 97 C6
Bedworth Heath Warks 97 C6
Beeby Leics 98 A3
Beech Hants 33 B5
Beech Staffs 112 B2
Beech Hill Gtr Man 137 C4
Beech Hill W Berks 47 C4
Beechingstoke Wilts 45 C4
Beedon W Berks 46 B2
Beeford E Yorks 151 B4
Beeley Derbys 130 C2
Beelsby NE Lincs 143 C4
Beenham W Berks 46 C3
Beeny Corn 10 B2
Beer Devon 14 C2
Beer Hackett Dorset 29 D6
Beercrocombe Som 28 C3
Beesands Devon 8 C2
Beesby Lincs 135 A4
Beeson Devon 8 C2
Beeston Beds 84 C3
Beeston Ches 127 D5
Beeston Norf 119 D6
Beeston Notts 114 B3
Beeston W Yorks 148 D1
Beeston Castle Ches 127 D5

Beeston Regis Norf 120 A3
Beeswing Dumfries 173 B6
Beetham Cumb 154 D3
Beetley Norf 119 D6
Begbroke Oxon 65 B5
Begelly Pembs 55 D7
Beggar's Bush Powys 77 A6
Beguildy Powys 93 D5
Beighton Norf 105 A4
Beighton S Yorks 131 A4
Beighton Hill Derbys 130 D2
Beith N Ayrs 204 C3
Bekesbourne Kent 52 D3
Bekonscot Model Village, Beaconsfield Bucks 67 D4
Belaugh Norf 121 D4
Belbroughton Worcs 96 D2
Belchamp Otten Essex 87 C4
Belchamp St Paul Essex 86 C3
Belchamp Walter Essex 87 C4
Belchford Lincs 134 B2
Belford Northumb 199 C5
Belhaven E Loth 210 C3
Belhelvie Aberds 245 A6
Belhinnie Aberds 255 D5
Bell Bar Herts 68 C2
Bell Busk N Yorks 146 B3
Bell End Worcs 96 D2
Bell o'th'Hill Ches 111 A4
Bellabeg Aberds 243 A6
Bellamore S Ayrs 181 C4
Bellanoch Argyll 213 C5
Bellaty Angus 231 C6
Belleau Lincs 135 B4
Bellehiglash Moray 254 C2
Bellerby N Yorks 157 B5
Bellever Devon 12 D1
Belliehill Angus 232 B3
Bellingdon Bucks 67 C4
Bellingham Northumb 177 A6
Belloch Argyll 190 B2
Bellochantuy Argyll 190 B2
Bells Yew Green E Sus 36 C4
Bellsbank E Ayrs 182 B2
Bellshill N Lnrk 207 D5
Bellshill Northumb 199 C5
Bellspool Borders 195 C6
Bellsquarry W Loth 208 D3
Belmaduthy Highld 252 A2
Belmesthorpe Rutland 116 D3
Belmont Blkburn 137 B5
Belmont London 49 C5
Belmont S Ayrs 192 C3
Belmont Shetland 284 C7
Belnacraig Aberds 243 A6
Belowda Corn 5 A4
Belper Derbys 114 A1
Belper Lane End Derbys 114 A1
Belsay Northumb 178 B3
Belsay Hall Northumb 178 B2
Belses Borders 187 A4
Belsford Devon 7 B6
Belstead Suff 88 C2
Belston S Ayrs 192 C3
Belstone Devon 11 B7
Belthorn Lancs 137 A6
Beltinge Kent 52 C3
Beltoft N Lincs 141 C6
Belton Leics 114 C2
Belton Lincs 116 B2
Belton N Lincs 141 C5
Belton Norf 105 A5
Belton House, Grantham Lincs 116 B2
Belton in Rutland Rutland 99 A5
Beltring Kent 37 B4
Belts of Collonach Aberds 244 C3
Belvedere London 50 B1
Belvoir Leics 115 B6
Belvoir Castle Leics 115 B6
Bembridge I o W 19 C5
Bemersyde Borders 197 C4
Bemerton Wilts 31 B5
Bempton E Yorks 161 D5
Ben Alder Lodge Highld 229 A4
Ben Armine Lodge Highld 273 C5
Ben Casgro W Isles 288 E5
Benacre Suff 105 C6
Benbecula Airport W Isles 286 A3
Benbuie Dumfries 183 C5
Benderloch Argyll 226 C4
Bendronaig Lodge Highld 250 C2
Benenden Kent 37 C6
Benfield Dumfries 171 A5
Bengate Norf 121 C5
Bengeworth Worcs 80 C3

Benhall Green Suff 89 A4
Benhall Street Suff 89 A4
Benholm Aberds 233 B6
Deningbrough N Yorks 148 B4
Beningbrough Hall N Yorks 148 B4
Benington Herts 68 A2
Benington Lincs 117 A6
Benllech Anglesey 123 B5
Benmore Argyll 215 D4
Benmore Stirl 216 B4
Benmore Lodge Highld 271 C6
Bennacott Corn 10 B3
Bennan N Ayrs 191 C5
Benniworth Lincs 134 A2
Benover Kent 37 B5
Bensham T & W 179 C4
Benslie N Ayrs 204 D3
Benson Oxon 65 D7
Bent Aberds 233 A4
Bent Gate Lancs 137 A6
Benthall Northumb 189 A5
Benthall Shrops 95 A4
Bentham Glos 63 B5
Benthoul Aberdeen 245 B5
Bentlawnt Shrops 94 A1
Bentley E Yorks 150 D3
Bentley Hants 33 A6
Bentley S Yorks 140 C3
Bentley Suff 88 D2
Bentley Warks 97 B5
Bentley Worcs 80 A2
Bentley Heath W Mid 97 D4
Benton Devon 26 B1
Bentpath Dumfries 185 C6
Bents W Loth 208 D2
Bentworth Hants 33 A5
Benvie Dundee 220 A3
Benwick Cambs 101 B5
Beoley Worcs 80 A3
Beoraidbeg Highld 235 A5
Bepton W Sus 20 A1
Berden Essex 69 A4
Bere Alston Devon 6 A3
Bere Ferrers Devon 6 A3
Bere Regis Dorset 16 B2
Berepper Corn 3 C4
Bergh Apton Norf 104 A4
Berinsfield Oxon 65 D6
Berkeley Glos 62 D2
Berkhamsted Herts 67 C4
Berkley Som 30 A2
Berkswell W Mid 97 D5
Bermondsey London 49 B6
Bernera Highld 249 D5
Bernice Argyll 215 C4
Bernisdale Highld 259 C4
Berrick Salome Oxon 65 D7
Berriedale Highld 275 B5
Berrier Cumb 164 C1
Berriew Powys 93 A5
Berrington Northumb 198 B4
Berrington Shrops 94 A3
Berrow Som 42 D2
Berrow Green Worcs 79 B5
Berry Down Cross Devon 25 A6
Berry Hill Glos 62 B1
Berry Hill Pembs 72 B3
Berry Pomeroy Devon 8 A2
Berryhillock Moray 267 C6
Berrynarbor Devon 25 A6
Bersham Wrex 110 A2
Berstane Orkney 282 F5
Berwick E Sus 22 B3
Berwick Bassett Wilts 45 B4
Berwick Hill Northumb 178 B3
Berwick St James Wilts 31 B4
Berwick St John Wilts 30 C3
Berwick St Leonard Wilts 30 B3
Berwick-upon-Tweed Northumb 198 A3
Bescar Lancs 136 B2
Besford Worcs 80 C2
Bessacarr S Yorks 140 C4
Bessels Leigh Oxon 65 C5
Bessingby E Yorks 151 A4
Bessingham Norf 120 B3
Bestbeech Hill E Sus 36 C4
Besthorpe Norf 103 B6
Besthorpe Notts 132 C3
Bestwood Nottingham 114 A3
Bestwood Village Notts 114 A3
Beswick E Yorks 150 C3
Betchworth Sur 35 B5
Beth Shalom Holocaust Centre, Laxton Notts 132 C2
Bethania Ceredig 75 B4
Bethania Gwyn 107 A6

Bethania Gwyn 108 A2
Bethel Anglesey 122 C3
Bethel Gwyn 123 D5
Bethel Gwyn 109 B4
Bethersden Kent 38 A1
Bethesda Gwyn 123 D6
Bethesda Pembs 55 C6
Bethlehem Carms 58 C3
Bethnal Green London 49 A6
Betley Staffs 111 A6
Betsham Kent 50 B3
Betteshanger Kent 53 D5
Bettiscombe Dorset 14 B3
Bettisfield Wrex 110 B3
Betton Shrops 93 A7
Betton Shrops 111 B5
Bettws Bridgend 40 C4
Bettws Newydd Mon 61 D4
Bettws Cedewain Powys 93 B5
Bettws Gwerfil Goch Denb 109 A5
Bettws Ifan Ceredig 73 B6
Bettws-y-crwyn Shrops 93 C6
Bettyhill Highld 278 B3
Betws Carms 57 A4
Betws Bledrws Ceredig 75 C
Betws-Garmon Gwyn 107 A4
Betws-y-Coed Conwy 124 D3
Betws-yn-Rhos Conwy 125 B4
Beulah Ceredig 73 B5
Beulah Powys 76 B3
Bevendean Brighton 21 B6
Bevercotes Notts 132 B1
Beverley E Yorks 150 D3
Beverley Minster E Yorks 150 D3
Beverley Racecourse E Yorks 150 C3
Beverston Glos 63 D4
Bevington Glos 62 D2
Bewaldeth Cumb 163 A4
Bewcastle Cumb 176 B3
Bewdley Worcs 95 D5
Bewerley N Yorks 147 A4
Bewholme E Yorks 151 B4
Bexhill E Sus 23 B5
Bexley London 50 B1
Bexleyheath London 50 B1
Bexwell Norf 102 A4
Beyton Suff 87 A5
Bhaltos W Isles 287 A5
Bhatarsaigh W Isles 286 G2
Bibury Glos 64 C1
Bicester Oxon 65 A6
Bickenhall Som 28 D2
Bickenhill W Mid 97 C4
Bicker Lincs 117 B5
Bickershaw Gtr Man 137 C5
Bickerstaffe Lancs 136 C3
Bickerton Ches 127 D5
Bickerton N Yorks 148 B3
Bickington Devon 12 D2
Bickington Devon 25 B6
Bickleigh Devon 13 D4
Bickleigh Devon 7 A4
Bickleton Devon 25 B6
Bickley London 49 C7
Bickley Moss Ches 111 A4
Bicknacre Essex 70 C1
Bicknoller Som 27 B6
Bicknor Kent 37 A6
Bickton Hants 31 D5
Bicton Shrops 110 D3
Bicton Shrops 93
Bicton Park Gardens Devon 13 C5
Bidborough Kent 36 B3
Biddenden Kent 37 C6
Biddenham Beds 84 B2
Biddestone Wilts 44 B2
Biddisham Som 42 D2
Biddlesden Bucks 82 C3
Biddlestone Northumb 188 C2
Biddulph Staffs 128 D3
Biddulph Moor Staffs 129 D4
Bideford Devon 25 C5
Bidford-on-Avon Warks 80 B4
Bidston Mers 126 A2
Bielby E Yorks 149 C6
Bieldside Aberdeen 245 B5
Bierley I o W 19 D4
Bierley W Yorks 147 D5
Bierton Bucks 66 B3
Big Pit National Mining Museum, Blaenavon Torf 61 C4
Big Sand Highld 261
Bigbury Devon 7 B5

Bigbury on Sea Devon 7 C5
Bigby Lincs 142 C2
Biggar Cumb 153 D2
Biggar S Lnrk 195 C5
Bggin Derbys 129 D6
Biggin Derbys 113 A6
Biggin N Yorks 148 D4
Biggin Hill London 36 A2
Biggings Shetland 285 G3
Biggleswade Beds 84 C3
Bighouse Highld 279 B4
Bighton Hants 33 B5
Bignor W Sus 20 A2
Bigton Shetland 285 L5
Bilberry Corn 5 A5
Bilborough Nottingham 114 A3
Bilbrook Som 27 A5
Bilbrough N Yorks 148 C4
Bilbster Highld 281 C4
Bildershaw Durham 167 C5
Bildeston Suff 87 C5
Billericay Essex 69 D6
Billesdon Leics 99 A4
Billesley Warks 80 B4
Billingborough Lincs 116 B4
Billinge Mers 136 C4
Billingford Norf 120 C2
Billingham Stockton 168 C2
Billinghay Lincs 133 D6
Billingley S Yorks 140 C2
Billingshurst W Sus 34 D3
Billingsley Shrops 95 C5
Billington Beds 67 A4
Billington Lancs 145 D7
Billockby Norf 121 D6
Billown Motor Racing Circuit I o M 152 E2
Billy Row Durham 167 B4
Bilsborrow Lancs 145 D5
Bilsby Lincs 135 B4
Bilsham W Sus 20 B2
Bilsington Kent 38 B2
Bilson Green Glos 62 B2
Bilsthorpe Notts 131 C6
Bilsthorpe Moor Notts 131 D6
Bilston Midloth 209 D5
Bilston W Mid 96 B2
Bilstone Leics 97 A6
Bilting Kent 38 A2
Bilton E Yorks 151 D4
Bilton Northumb 189 B5
Bilton Warks 98 D1
Bilton in Ainsty N Yorks 148 C3
Bimbister Orkney 282 F4
Binbrook Lincs 143 D4
Binchester Blocks Durham 167 B5
Bincombe Dorset 15 C6
Bindal Highld 265 B5
Binegar Som 29 A6
Binfield Brack 47 B6
Binfield Heath Oxon 47 B5
Bingfield Northumb 178 B1
Bingham Notts 115 B5
Bingley W Yorks 147 D5
Bings Heath Shrops 111 D4
Binham Norf 120 B1
Binley Hants 46 D2
Binley W Mid 97 D6
Binley Woods Warks 97 D6
Binniehill Falk 207 C6
Binsoe N Yorks 157 D6
Binstead I o W 19 B4
Binsted Hants 33 A6
Binton Warks 80 B4
Bintree Norf 120 C2
Binweston Shrops 93 A7
Birch Essex 70 B3
Birch Gtr Man 138 C1
Birch Green Essex 70 B3
Birch Heath Ches 127 C5
Birch Hill Ches 127 B5
Birch Vale Derbys 129 A5
Bircham Newton Norf 119 B4
Bircham Tofts Norf 119 B4
Birchanger Herts 69 A5
Birchencliffe W Yorks 139 B4
Bircher Hereford 78 A2
Birchfield Highld 253 D5
Birchgrove Cardiff 41 D6
Birchgrove Swansea 40 B2
Birchington Kent 53 C4
Birchmoor Warks 97 A5
Birchover Derbys 130 C2
Birchwood Lincs 133 C4
Birchwood Warr 137 D5
Bircotes Notts 140 D4
Birdbrook Essex 86 C3

Birdforth N Yorks 158 D3
Birdham W Sus 20 C1
Birdholme Derbys 130 C3
Birdingbury Warks 82 A1
Birdland Park, Bourton-on-the-Water Glos 64 A2
Birdlip Glos 63 B5
Birds Edge W Yorks 139 C5
Birdsall N Yorks 149 A7
Birdsgreen Shrops 95 C5
Birdsmoor Gate Dorset 14 A0
Birdston E Dunb 205 A6
Birdwell S Yorks 139 C6
Birdwood Glos 62 B3
Birdworld and Underwaterworld, Farnham Hants 33 A7
Birgham Borders 198 C1
Birkby N Yorks 158 A2
Birkdale Mers 136 B2
Birkenhead Mers 126 A3
Birkenhills Aberds 256 B2
Birkenshaw N Lnrk 207 D4
Birkenshaw W Yorks 139 A5
Birkhall Aberds 243 C6
Birkhill Angus 220 A3
Birkhill Dumfries 185 A5
Birkholme Lincs 116 C2
Birkin N Yorks 140 A3
Birley Hereford 78 B2
Birling Kent 50 C3
Birling Northumb 189 C5
Birling Gap E Sus 22 C3
Birlingham Worcs 80 C2
Birmingham W Mid 96 C3
Birmingham Botanical Gardens W Mid 96 C3
Birmingham International Airport W Mid 97 C4
Birmingham Museum and Art Gallery W Mid 96 C3
Birmingham Museum of Science and Technology W Mid 96 C3
Birnam Perth 230 D4
Birse Aberds 244 C2
Birsemore Aberds 244 C2
Birstall Leics 98 A2
Birstall W Yorks 139 A5
Birstwith N Yorks 147 B6
Birthorpe Lincs 116 B4
Birtley Hereford 78 A1
Birtley Northumb 177 B6
Birtley T & W 179 D4
Birts Street Worcs 79 D5
Bisbrooke Rutland 99 B5
Biscathorpe Lincs 134 A2
Biscot Luton 67 A5
Bish Mill Devon 26 C2
Bisham Windsor 47 A6
Bishampton Worcs 80 B2
Bishop Auckland Durham 167 C5
Bishop Burton E Yorks 150 D2
Bishop Middleham Durham 167 B6
Bishop Monkton N Yorks 148 A2
Bishop Norton Lincs 142 D1
Bishop Sutton Bath 43 D4
Bishop Thornton N Yorks 147 A6
Bishop Wilton E Yorks 149 B6
Bishopbridge Lincs 142 D2
Bishopbriggs E Dunb 205 B6
Bishopmill Moray 266 C3
Bishops Cannings Wilts 44 C4
Bishop's Castle Shrops 93 C7
Bishop's Caundle Dorset 29 D6
Bishop's Cleeve Glos 63 A5
Bishops Frome Hereford 79 C4
Bishop's Green Essex 69 B6
Bishop's Hull Som 28 C2
Bishop's Itchington Warks 81 B6
Bishops Lydeard Som 27 C6
Bishops Nympton Devon 26 C2
Bishop's Offley Staffs 112 C1
Bishop's Stortford Herts 69 A4
Bishop's Sutton Hants 33 B5
Bishop's Tachbrook Warks 81 A6
Bishops Tawton Devon 25 B6
Bishop's Waltham Hants 33 D4
Bishop's Wood Staffs 95 A6
Bishopsbourne Kent 52 D3
Bishopsteignton Devon 13 D4
Bishopstoke Hants 32 D3
Bishopston Swansea 57 D5
Bishopstone Bucks 66 B3
Bishopstone E Sus 22 B2
Bishopstone Hereford 78 C2

Bishopstone Thamesdown 45 A6
Bishopstone Wilts 31 C4
Bishopstrow Wilts 30 A2
Bishopswood Som 28 D2
Bishopsworth Bristol 43 C4
Bishopthorpe York 149 C4
Bishopton Darl 167 C6
Bishopton Dumfries 171 C6
Bishopton N Yorks 157 D7
Bishopton Renfs 205 A4
Bishopton Warks 81 B4
Bishton Newport 42 A2
Bisley Glos 63 C5
Bisley Sur 34 A2
Bispham Blkpool 144 C3
Bispham Green Lancs 136 B3
Bissoe Corn 4 C2
Bisterne Close Hants 17 A6
Bitchfield Lincs 116 C2
Bittadon Devon 25 A6
Bittaford Devon 7 B5
Bittering Norf 119 D6
Bitterley Shrops 94 D3
Bitterne Soton 32 D3
Bitteswell Leics 98 C2
Bitton S Glos 43 C5
Bix Oxon 47 A5
Bixter Shetland 285 H5
Blaby Leics 98 B2
Black Bourton Oxon 64 C3
Black Callerton T & W 178 C3
Black Clauchrie S Ayrs 181 C4
Black Corries Lodge Highld 228 C1
Black Crofts Argyll 226 C4
Black Dog Devon 12 A3
Black Heddon Northumb 178 B2
Black Lane Gtr Man 137 C6
Black Marsh Shrops 94 B1
Black Mount Argyll 228 D1
Black Notley Essex 70 A1
Black Pill Swansea 57 C6
Black Tar Pembs 55 D5
Black Torrington Devon 11 A5
Blackadder West Borders 198 A2
Blackawton Devon 8 B2
Blackborough Devon 13 A5
Blackborough End Norf 118 D3
Blackboys E Sus 36 D3
Blackbrook Derbys 114 A1
Blackbrook Mers 136 D4
Blackbrook Staffs 111 B6
Blackburn Aberds 255 C6
Blackburn Aberds 245 A5
Blackburn Blkburn 137 A5
Blackburn W Loth 208 D2
Blackcraig Dumfries 183 D5
Blackden Heath Ches 128 B2
Blackdog Aberds 245 A6
Blackfell T & W 179 D4
Blackfield Hants 18 A3
Blackford Cumb 175 B6
Blackford Perth 218 D3
Blackford Som 28 A4
Blackford Som 29 C6
Blackfordby Leics 114 D1
Blackgang I o W 18 D3
Blackgang Chine Fantasy I o W 18 D3
Blackhall Colliery Durham 168 B2
Blackhall Mill T & W 178 D3
Blackhall Rocks Durham 168 B2
Blackham E Sus 36 C2
Blackhaugh Borders 196 C3
Blackheath Essex 71 A4
Blackheath Suff 105 D5
Blackheath Sur 34 B3
Blackheath W Mid 96 C2
Blackhill Aberds 257 B5
Blackhill Aberds 269 D5
Blackhill Highld 258 C3
Blackhills Highld 253 A5
Blackhills Highld 266 D3
Blackhorse S Glos 43 B5
Blacko Lancs 146 C2

Blackpool Blkpool 144 D3
Blackpool Devon 8 C2
Blackpool Pembs 55 C6
Blackpool Airport Lancs 144 D3
Blackpool Gate Cumb 176 B3
Blackpool Pleasure Beach Blkpool 144 D3
Blackpool Sea Life Centre Blkpool 144 D3
Blackpool Tower Blkpool 144 D3
Blackpool Zoo Park Blkpool 144 D3
Blackridge W Loth 208 D1
Blackrock Argyll 200 B3
Blackrock Mon 60 B4
Blackrod Gtr Man 137 B5
Blackshaw Dumfries 174 B3
Blackshaw Head W Yorks 138 A2
Blacksmith's Green Suff 88 A2
Blackstone W Sus 21 A5
Blackthorn Oxon 65 B7
Blackthorpe Suff 87 A5
Blacktoft E Yorks 141 A6
Blacktop Aberdeen 245 B5
Blacktown Newport 42 A1
Blackwall Tunnel London 49 A6
Blackwater Corn 4 C2
Blackwater Hants 34 A1
Blackwater I o W 18 C4
Blackwaterfoot N Ayrs 191 C4
Blackwell Darl 167 D5
Blackwell Derbys 129 B6
Blackwell Derbys 131 D4
Blackwell Warks 81 C5
Blackwell Worcs 96 D2
Blackwell W Sus 36 C1
Blackwood S Lnrk 194 B2
Blackwood = Coed Duon Caerph 41 B6
Blackwood Hill Staffs 129 D4
Blacon Ches 126 C3
Bladnoch Dumfries 171 B6
Bladon Oxon 65 B5
Blaen-gwynfi Neath 40 B3
Blaen-y-coed Carms 73 C6
Blaen-y-Cwm Denb 109 B5
Blaen-y-cwm Gwyn 108 C2
Blaen-y-cwm Powys 109 C5
Blaenannerch Ceredig 73 B5
Blaenau Ffestiniog Gwyn 108 A2
Blaenavon Torf 61 C4
Blaenawon Torf 61 B4
Blaencelyn Ceredig 73 A6
Blaendyryn Powys 59 B6
Blaenffos Pembs 73 C4
Blaengarw Bridgend 40 B4
Blaengwrach Neath 59 E5
Blaenpennal Ceredig 75 B5
Blaenplwyf Ceredig 75 A4
Blaenporth Ceredig 73 B5
Blaenrhondda Rhondda 40 A4
Blaenycwm Ceredig 92 D2
Blagdon N Som 43 D4
Blagdon Torbay 8 A2
Blagdon Hill Som 28 D2
Blagill Cumb 165 A5
Blaguegate Lancs 136 C3
Blaich Highld 237 B4
Blain Highld 235 D5
Blaina Bl Gwent 60 C4
Blair Atholl Perth 230 B2
Blair Castle, Blair Atholl Perth 230 B2
Blair Drummond Stirl 207 A5
Blair Drummond Safari Park, Dunblane Stirl 207 A5
Blairbeg N Ayrs 191 B6
Blairdaff Aberds 244 A3
Blairglas Argyll 206 B1
Blairgowrie Perth 231 D5
Blairhall Fife 208 B3
Blairingone Perth 208 A2
Blairland N Ayrs 204 D3
Blairlogie Stirl 207 A6
Blairlomond Argyll 215 C4
Blairmore Argyll 215 D4
Blairnamarrow Moray 243 A5
Blairquhosh Stirl 206 B3
Blair's Ferry Argyll 203 B4
Blairskaith E Dunb 205 A5
Blaisdon Glos 62 B3
Blakebrook Worcs 95 D6
Blakedown Worcs 96 D1
Blakelaw Borders 197 C6
Blakeley Staffs 95 B6
Blakeley Lane Staffs 112 A3
Blakemere Hereford 78 C1

Blakeney Glos 62 C2
Blakeney Norf 120 A2
Blakeney Point NNR Norf 120 A2
Blakenhall Ches 111 A6
Blakenhall W Mid 96 B2
Blakeshall Worcs 95 C6
Blakesley Northants 82 B3
Blanchland Northumb 178 D1
Bland Hill N Yorks 147 B6
Blandford Forum Dorset 16 A2
Blandford St Mary Dorset 16 A2
Blanefield Stirl 205 A5
Blankney Lincs 133 C5
Blantyre S Lnrk 194 A1
Blar a'Chaorainn Highld 237 C5
Blaran Argyll 214 A1
Blarghour Argyll 214 A2
Blarmachfoldach Highld 237 C4
Blarnalearoch Highld 262 A3
Blashford Hants 17 A5
Blaston Leics 99 B5
Blatherwycke Northants 99 B6
Blawith Cumb 154 C1
Blaxhall Suff 89 A4
Blaxton S Yorks 141 C4
Blaydon T & W 178 C3
Bleadon N Som 42 D2
Bleak Hey Nook Gtr Man 138 C3
Blean Kent 52 C3
Bleasby Lincs 133 A6
Bleasby Notts 115 A5
Bleasdale Lancs 145 C5
Bleatarn Cumb 165 D5
Blebocraigs Fife 220 C4
Bleddfa Powys 77 A6
Bledington Glos 64 A3
Bledlow Bucks 66 C2
Bledlow Ridge Bucks 66 D2
Blegbie E Loth 210 D1
Blencarn Cumb 165 B4
Blencogo Cumb 175 D4
Blendworth Hants 33 D6
Blenheim Palace, Woodstock Oxon 65 B5
Blenheim Park Norf 119 B5
Blennerhasset Cumb 175 D4
Blervie Castle Moray 253 A6
Bletchingdon Oxon 65 B6
Bletchingley Sur 35 A6
Bletchley M Keynes 83 D5
Bletchley Shrops 111 B5
Bletherston Pembs 55 B6
Bletsoe Beds 84 B2
Blewbury Oxon 46 A3
Blickling Norf 120 C3
Blickling Hall, Aylsham Norf 120 C3
Blidworth Notts 131 D5
Blindburn Northumb 188 B1
Blindcrake Cumb 163 A4
Blindley Heath Sur 35 B6
Blisland Corn 10 D2
Bliss Gate Worcs 95 D5
Blissford Hants 31 D5
Blisworth Northants 83 B4
Blithbury Staffs 113 C4
Blitterlees Cumb 174 C4
Blockley Glos 81 D4
Blofield Norf 104 A4
Blofield Heath Norf 121 D5
Blo'Norton Norf 103 D6
Bloomfield Borders 187 A4
Blore Staffs 113 A5
Blount's Green Staffs 113 B4
Blowick Mers 136 B2
Bloxham Oxon 82 D1
Bloxholm Lincs 133 D5
Bloxwich W Mid 96 A2
Bloxworth Dorset 16 B2
Blubberhouses N Yorks 147 B5
Blue Anchor Som 27 A5
Blue Anchor Swansea 57 C5
Blue Planet Aquarium Ches 127 B4
Blue Row Essex 71 B4
Blundeston Suff 105 B6
Blunham Beds 84 B3
Blunsdon St Andrew Thamesdown 45 A5
Bluntington Worcs 96 D1
Bluntisham Cambs 101 D5
Blunts Corn 6 A2
Blyborough Lincs 142 D1
Blyford Suff 105 D5
Blymhill Staffs 112 D2

Blyth Notts 131 A6
Blyth Northumb 179 A5
Blyth Bridge Borders 195 B6
Blythburgh Suff 105 D5
Blythe Borders 197 B4
Blythe Bridge Staffs 112 A3
Blyton Lincs 141 D6
Boarhills Fife 221 C5
Boarhunt Hants 19 A5
Boars Head Gtr Man 137 C4
Boars Hill Oxon 65 C5
Boarshead E Sus 36 C3
Boarstall Bucks 66 B1
Boasley Cross Devon 11 B5
Boat of Garten Highld 242 A2
Boath Highld 264 C1
Bobbing Kent 51 C5
Bobbington Staffs 95 B6
Bobbingworth Essex 69 C5
Bocaddon Corn 5 B6
Bochastle Stirl 217 D6
Bocking Essex 70 A1
Bocking Churchstreet
  Essex 70 A1
Boddam Aberds 257 B6
Boddam Shetland 285 M5
Boddington Glos 63 A4
Bodedern Anglesey 122 B3
Bodelwyddan Denb 125 B5
Bodenham Hereford 78 B3
Bodenham Wilts 31 C5
Bodenham Arboretum
  and Earth Centre Worcs 95 C6
Bodenham Moor Hereford 78 B3
Bodermid Gwyn 106 D1
Bodewryd Anglesey 122 A3
Bodfari Denb 125 B5
Bodffordd Anglesey 123 C4
Bodham Norf 120 A3
Bodiam E Sus 37 D5
Bodiam Castle E Sus 37 D5
Bodicote Oxon 82 D1
Bodieve Corn 9 D5
Bodinnick Corn 5 B6
Bodle Street Green E Sus 23 A4
Bodmin Corn 5 A5
Bodnant Garden, Colwyn
  Bay Conwy 124 B3
Bodney Norf 103 B4
Bodorgan Anglesey 122 D3
Bodsham Kent 38 A3
Boduan Gwyn 106 C3
Bodymoor Heath Warks 97 B4
Bogallan Highld 252 A2
Bogbrae Aberds 257 C5
Bogend Borders 198 B1
Bogend S Ayrs 192 B3
Boghall W Loth 208 D2
Boghead S Lnrk 194 B2
Bogmoor Moray 267 C4
Bogniebrae Aberds 255 B6
Bognor Regis W Sus 20 C2
Bograxie Aberds 256 E2
Bogside N Lnrk 194 A3
Bogton Aberds 268 D1
Bogue Dumfries 182 D4
Bohenie Highld 239 D6
Bohortha Corn 4 D3
Bohuntine Highld 239 D6
Boirseam W Isles 287 F5
Bojewyan Corn 2 B1
Bolam Durham 167 C4
Bolam Northumb 178 A2
Bolberry Devon 7 D5
Bold Heath Mers 127 A5
Boldon T & W 179 C5
Boldon Colliery T & W 179 C5
Boldre Hants 18 B2
Boldron Durham 166 D3
Bole Notts 132 A2
Bolehill Derbys 130 D2
Boleside Borders 196 C3
Bolham Devon 27 D4
Bolham Water Devon 27 D6
Bolingey Corn 4 B2
Bollington Ches 129 B4
Bollington Cross Ches 129 B4
Bolney W Sus 35 D5
Bolnhurst Beds 84 B2
Bolshan Angus 233 C4
Bolsover Derbys 131 B4
Bolsterstone S Yorks 139 D5
Bolstone Hereford 78 D3
Boltby N Yorks 158 C3
Bolter End Bucks 66 D2

Bolton Cumb 165 C4
Bolton E Loth 210 C2
Bolton F Yorks 149 B6
Bolton Gtr Man 137 C6
Bolton Northumb 189 B4
Bolton Abbey N Yorks 147 B4
Bolton Abbey, Skipton
  N Yorks 147 B4
Bolton Bridge N Yorks 147 B4
Bolton-by-Bowland
  Lancs 146 C1
Bolton Castle, Leyburn
  N Yorks 156 B4
Bolton le Sands Lancs 145 A4
Bolton Low Houses Cumb 175 D5
Bolton-on-Swale N Yorks 157 B6
Bolton Percy N Yorks 148 C4
Bolton Town End Lancs 145 A4
Bolton upon Dearne
  S Yorks 140 C2
Boltonfellend Cumb 176 C2
Boltongate Cumb 175 D5
Bomere Heath Shrops 110 D3
Bon-y-maen Swansea 57 C6
Bonar Bridge Highld 264 A2
Bonawe Argyll 227 C5
Bonby N Lincs 142 B2
Boncath Pembs 73 C5
Bonchester Bridge
  Borders 187 B4
Bonchurch I o W 19 D4
Bondleigh Devon 12 A1
Bonehill Devon 12 D2
Bonehill Staffs 97 A4
Bo'ness Falk 208 B2
Bonhill W Dunb 206 C1
Boningale Shrops 95 A6
Bonjedward Borders 187 A5
Bonkle N Lnrk 194 A3
Bonnavoulin Highld 225 A4
Bonnington Edin 208 D4
Bonnington Kent 38 B2
Bonnybank Fife 220 D3
Bonnybridge Falk 207 B6
Bonnykelly Aberds 268 D3
Bonnyrigg and Lasswade
  Midloth 209 D6
Bonnyton Aberds 256 C1
Bonnyton Angus 220 A3
Bonnyton Angus 233 C4
Bonsall Derbys 130 D2
Bonskeid House Perth 230 B2
Bont Mon 61 B5
Bont-Dolgadfan Powys 91 B6
Bont-goch Ceredig 91 D4
Bont-newydd Conwy 125 B5
Bont Newydd Gwyn 108 A2
Bont Newydd Gwyn 108 C2
Bontddu Gwyn 91 A4
Bonthorpe Lincs 135 B4
Bontnewydd Ceredig 75 B5
Bontnewydd Gwyn 107 A4
Bontuchel Denb 125 D5
Bonvilston V Glam 41 D5
Booker Bucks 66 D3
Boon Borders 197 B4
Boosbeck Redcar 169 D4
Boot Cumb 163 D4
Boot Street Suff 88 C3
Booth W Yorks 138 A3
Booth Wood W Yorks 138 B3
Boothby Graffoe Lincs 133 D4
Boothby Pagnell Lincs 116 B2
Boothen Stoke 112 A2
Boothferry E Yorks 141 A5
Boothville Northants 83 A4
Bootle Cumb 153 B2
Bootle Mers 136 D2
Booton Norf 120 C3
Boquhan Stirl 206 B3
Boraston Shrops 95 D4
Borden Kent 51 C5
Borden W Sus 34 D1
Bordley N Yorks 146 A3
Bordon Hants 33 B7
Bordon Camp Hants 33 B6
Boreham Essex 70 C1
Boreham Wilts 30 A2
Boreham Street E Sus 23 A4
Borehamwood Herts 68 D1
Boreland Dumfries 185 C4
Boreland Stirl 217 A5
Borgh W Isles 286 F2
Borgh W Isles 287 F4
Borghastan W Isles 288 C3
Borgie Highld 278 C2
Borgue Dumfries 172 D4

Borgue Highld 275 B5
Borley Essex 87 C4
Bornais W Isles 286 D3
Bornesketaig Highld 258 A3
Borness Dumfries 172 D4
Borough Green Kent 36 A4
Boroughbridge N Yorks 148 A2
Borras Head Wrex 126 D3
Borreraig Highld 258 C1
Borrobol Lodge Highld 274 B2
Borrowash Derbys 114 B2
Borrowby N Yorks 158 C3
Borrowdale Cumb 163 C5
Borrowfield Aberds 245 C5
Borth Ceredig 90 C4
Borth-y-Gest Gwyn 107 C5
Borthertoft Lincs 117 A5
Borthwickbrae Borders 186 B3
Borthwickshiels Borders 186 B3
Borve Highld 259 D4
Borve Lodge W Isles 287 E5
Borwick Lancs 154 D4
Bosavern Corn 2 B1
Bosbury Hereford 79 C4
Boscastle Corn 10 B2
Boscombe Bmouth 17 B5
Boscombe Wilts 31 B6
Boscoppa Corn 5 B5
Bosham W Sus 19 A7
Bosherston Pembs 55 E5
Boskenna Corn 2 C2
Bosley Ches 129 C4
Bossall N Yorks 149 A6
Bossiney Corn 9 C6
Bossingham Kent 38 A3
Bossington Som 26 A3
Bostock Green Ches 127 C6
Boston Lincs 117 A6
Boston Long Hedges
  Lincs 117 A6
Boston Spa W Yorks 148 C3
Boston West Lincs 117 A5
Boswinger Corn 5 C4
Botallack Corn 2 B1
Botany Bay London 68 D2
Botcherby Cumb 175 C7
Botchton Leics 98 A1
Botesdale Suff 103 D6
Bothal Northumb 179 A4
Bothamsall Notts 131 B6
Bothel Cumb 163 A4
Bothenhampton Dorset 15 B4
Bothwell S Lnrk 194 A2
Botley Bucks 67 C4
Botley Hants 32 D4
Botley Oxon 65 C5
Botolph Claydon Bucks 66 A2
Botolphs W Sus 21 B4
Bottacks Highld 263 D6
Bottesford Leics 115 B6
Bottesford N Lincs 141 C6
Bottisham Cambs 86 A1
Bottlesford Wilts 45 D5
Bottom Boat W Yorks 139 A6
Bottom House Staffs 129 D5
Bottom of Hutton Lancs 136 A3
Bottom o'th'Moor
  Gtr Man 137 B5
Bottomcraig Fife 220 B3
Botusfleming Corn 6 A3
Botwnnog Gwyn 106 C2
Bough Beech Kent 36 B2
Boughrood Powys 77 D5
Boughspring Glos 62 D1
Boughton Norf 102 A2
Boughton Notts 131 C6
Boughton Northants 83 A4
Boughton Aluph Kent 38 A2
Boughton Lees Kent 38 A2
Boughton Malherbe Kent 37 B6
Boughton Monchelsea
  Kent 37 A5
Boughton Street Kent 52 D2
Boulby Redcar 169 D5
Boulden Shrops 94 C3
Boulmer Northumb 189 B5
Boulston Pembs 55 C5
Boultenstone Aberds 243 A7
Boultham Lincs 133 C4
Bourn Cambs 85 B5
Bourne Lincs 116 C3
Bourne End Beds 83 C6
Bourne End Bucks 48 A1
Bourne End Herts 67 C5
Bournemouth Bmouth 17 B4
Bournemouth
  International Airport
  Dorset 17 B5

Bournes Green Glos 63 C5
Bournes Green Sthend 51 A6
Bournheath Worcs 96 D2
Bournmoor Durham 179 D6
Bournville W Mid 96 C3
Bourton Dorset 30 B1
Bourton N Som 42 C2
Bourton Oxon 45 A6
Bourton Shrops 94 B3
Bourton on Dunsmore
  Warks 98 D1
Bourton on the Hill Glos 81 D4
Bourton-on-the-Water
  Glos 64 A2
Bousd Argyll 223 A5
Boustead Hill Cumb 175 C5
Bouth Cumb 154 C2
Bouthwaite N Yorks 157 D5
Boveney Bucks 48 B2
Boverton V Glam 41 E4
Bovey Tracey Devon 12 D3
Bovingdon Herts 67 C5
Bovingdon Green Bucks 47 A6
Bovingdon Green Herts 67 C5
Bovinger Essex 69 C5
Bovington Camp Dorset 16 C2
Bow Borders 196 B3
Bow Devon 12 A2
Bow Orkney 283 H4
Bow Brickhill M Keynes 83 D6
Bow of Fife Fife 220 C3
Bow Street Ceredig 90 D4
Bowbank Durham 166 C2
Bowburn Durham 167 B6
Bowcombe I o W 18 C3
Bowd Devon 13 B6
Bowden Borders 197 C4
Bowden Devon 8 C2
Bowden Hill Wilts 44 C3
Bowderdale Cumb 155 A5
Bowdon Gtr Man 128 A2
Bower Northumb 177 A5
Bower Hinton Som 29 D4
Bowerchalke Wilts 31 C4
Bowerhill Wilts 44 C3
Bowermadden Highld 280 B4
Bowers Gifford Essex 51 A4
Bowershall Fife 208 A3
Bowertower Highld 280 B4
Bowes Durham 166 D2
Bowgreave Lancs 145 C4
Bowgreen Gtr Man 128 A2
Bowhill Borders 186 A3
Bowhouse Dumfries 174 B3
Bowland Bridge Cumb 154 C3
Bowley Hereford 78 B3
Bowlhead Green Sur 34 C2
Bowling W Dunb 205 A4
Bowling W Yorks 147 D5
Bowling Bank Wrex 110 A2
Bowling Green Worcs 79 B6
Bowmanstead Cumb 154 B2
Bowmore Argyll 200 C3
Bowness-on-Solway
  Cumb 175 B5
Bowness-on-
  Windermere Cumb 154 B3
Bowood House and
  Gardens, Calne Wilts 44 C3
Bowsden Northumb 198 B3
Bowside Lodge Highld 279 B4
Bowston Cumb 154 B3
Bowthorpe Norf 104 A2
Box Glos 63 C4
Box Wilts 44 C2
Box End Beds 84 C2
Boxbush Glos 62 B3
Boxford Suff 87 C5
Boxford W Berks 46 B2
Boxgrove W Sus 20 B2
Boxley Kent 37 A5
Boxmoor Herts 67 C5
Boxted Essex 87 D6
Boxted Suff 87 B4
Boxted Cross Essex 87 D6
Boxted Heath Essex 87 D6
Boxworth Cambs 85 A5
Boxworth End Cambs 85 A5
Boyden Gate Kent 53 C4
Boylestone Derbys 113 B5
Boyndie Aberds 268 C1
Boynton E Yorks 151 A4
Boysack Angus 233 D4
Boyton Corn 10 B4
Boyton Suff 89 C4
Boyton Wilts 30 B3
Boyton Cross Essex 69 C6
Boyton End Suff 86 C3

Bozeat Northants 83 B6
Braaid I o M 152 D3
Braal Castle Highld 280 B3
Brabling Green Suff 88 A3
Brabourne Kent 38 A2
Brabourne Lees Kent 38 A2
Brabster Highld 281 B5
Bracadale Highld 246 A2
Bracara Highld 235 A6
Braceborough Lincs 116 D3
Bracebridge Lincs 133 C4
Bracebridge Heath Lincs 133 C4
Bracebridge Low Fields
  Lincs 133 C4
Braceby Lincs 116 B3
Bracewell Lancs 146 C2
Brackenfield Derbys 130 D3
Brackenthwaite Cumb 175 D5
Brackenthwaite N Yorks 148 B1
Bracklesham W Sus 19 B7
Brackletter Highld 239 D5
Brackley Argyll 202 D2
Brackley Northants 82 D2
Brackloch Highld 270 B4
Bracknell Brack 47 C6
Braco Perth 218 D3
Bracobrae Moray 267 D6
Bracon Ash Norf 104 B2
Bracorina Highld 235 A6
Bradbourne Derbys 130 D2
Bradbury Durham 167 C6
Bradda I o M 152 E1
Bradden Northants 82 C3
Braddock Corn 5 A6
Bradeley Stoke 128 D3
Bradenham Bucks 66 D3
Bradenham Norf 103 A4
Bradenstoke Wilts 44 B4
Bradfield Essex 88 D2
Bradfield Norf 121 B4
Bradfield W Berks 47 B4
Bradfield Combust Suff 87 B4
Bradfield Green Ches 128 D1
Bradfield Heath Essex 71 A5
Bradfield St Clare Suff 87 B5
Bradfield St George Suff 87 A5
Bradford Corn 10 D2
Bradford Derbys 130 C2
Bradford Devon 11 A4
Bradford Northumb 199 C5
Bradford W Yorks 147 D5
Bradford Abbas Dorset 29 D5
Bradford Cathedral
  W Yorks 147 D5
Bradford Industrial
  Museum W Yorks 147 D5
Bradford Leigh Wilts 44 C2
Bradford-on-Avon Wilts 44 C2
Bradford on Tone Som 28 C1
Bradford Peverell Dorset 15 B6
Brading I o W 19 C5
Bradley Derbys 113 A6
Bradley Hants 33 B5
Bradley NE Lincs 143 C4
Bradley Staffs 112 C2
Bradley W Mid 96 B2
Bradley W Yorks 139 B4
Bradley Green Worcs 80 A2
Bradley in the Moors
  Staffs 113 A4
Bradlow Hereford 79 D5
Bradmore Notts 114 B3
Bradmore W Mid 96 B1
Bradninch Devon 13 A5
Bradnop Staffs 129 D5
Bradpole Dorset 15 B4
Bradshaw Gtr Man 137 B6
Bradshaw W Yorks 138 B3
Bradstone Devon 11 C4
Bradwall Green Ches 128 C2
Bradway S Yorks 130 A3
Bradwell Derbys 129 A6
Bradwell Essex 70 A2
Bradwell M Keynes 83 C5
Bradwell Norf 105 A6
Bradwell Staffs 112 A2
Bradwell Grove Oxon 64 C3
Bradwell on Sea Essex 71 C4
Bradwell Waterside Essex 70 C3
Bradworthy Devon 24 D4
Bradworthy Cross Devon 24 D4
Brae Dumfries 173 A6
Brae Highld 277 D6
Brae Highld 272 D2
Brae Shetland 284 G5
Brae of Achnahaird
  Highld 270 C3
Brae Roy Lodge Highld 240 C2

Braeantra Highld 264 C1
Braedownie Angus 231 A6
Braefield Highld 251 C6
Braegrum Perth 219 B5
Braehead Dumfries 171 B6
Braehead Orkney 283 G6
Braehead Orkney 282 C5
Braehead S Lnrk 194 C3
Braehead S Lnrk 195 A4
Braehead of Lunan Angus 233 C4
Braehoulland Shetland 284 F4
Braehungie Highld 275 A5
Braelangwell Lodge
    Highld 263 A7
Braemar Aberds 243 C4
Braemore Highld 275 A4
Braemore Highld 262 C3
Braes of Enzie Moray 267 D4
Braeside Inyclyd 204 A2
Braeswick Orkney 282 D7
Braewick Shetland 285 H5
Brafferton Darl 167 C5
Brafferton N Yorks 158 D3
Brafield-on-the-Green
    Northants 83 B5
Bragar W Isles 288 C3
Bragbury End Herts 68 A2
Bragleenmore Argyll 226 D4
Braichmelyn Gwyn 123 D6
Braid Edin 209 D5
Braides Lancs 144 B4
Braidley N Yorks 156 C4
Braidwood S Lnrk 194 B3
Braigo Argyll 200 B2
Brailsford Derbys 113 A6
Brainshaugh Northumb 189 C5
Braintree Essex 70 A1
Braiseworth Suff 104 D2
Braishfield Hants 32 C2
Braithwaite Cumb 163 B5
Braithwaite S Yorks 140 B4
Braithwaite W Yorks 147 C4
Braithwell S Yorks 140 D3
Bramber W Sus 21 A4
Bramcote Notts 114 B3
Bramcote Warks 97 C7
Bramdean Hants 33 C5
Bramerton Norf 104 A3
Bramfield Herts 68 B2
Bramfield Suff 105 D4
Bramford Suff 88 C2
Bramhall Gtr Man 128 A3
Bramham W Yorks 148 C3
Bramhope W Yorks 147 C6
Bramley Hants 47 D4
Bramley Sur 34 B3
Bramley S Yorks 140 D2
Bramley W Yorks 147 D6
Bramling Kent 53 D4
Brampford Speke Devon 13 B4
Brampton Cambs 100 D4
Brampton Cumb 165 C4
Brampton Cumb 176 C3
Brampton Derbys 130 B3
Brampton Hereford 78 D2
Brampton Lincs 132 B3
Brampton Norf 120 C4
Brampton Suff 105 C5
Brampton S Yorks 140 C2
Brampton Abbotts
    Hereford 62 A2
Brampton Ash Northants 99 C4
Brampton Bryan Hereford 94 D1
Brampton en le Morthen
    S Yorks 131 A4
Bramshall Staffs 113 B4
Bramshaw Hants 31 D6
Bramshill Hants 47 C5
Bramshott Hants 34 C1
Bran End Essex 69 A6
Branault Highld 235 D4
Brancaster Norf 119 A4
Brancaster Staithe Norf 119 A4
Brancepeth Durham 167 B5
Branch End Northumb 178 C2
Branchill Moray 266 D1
Brand Green Glos 62 A3
Branderburgh Moray 266 B3
Brandesburton E Yorks 151 C4
Brandeston Suff 88 A3
Brand Hill Shrops 94 D2
Brandis Corner Devon 11 A5
Brandiston Suff 120 C3
Brandon Durham 167 B5
Brandon Lincs 116 A2
Brandon Northumb 188 B3
Brandon Suff 102 C3
Brandon Warks 97 D7

Brandon Bank Norf 102 C2
Brandon Creek Norf 102 B2
Brandon Parva Norf 104 A1
Brands Hatch Motor
    Racing Circuit Kent 50 C2
Brandsby N Yorks 159 D4
Brandy Wharf Lincs 142 D2
Brane Corn 2 C2
Branksome Poole 17 B4
Branksome Park Poole 17 B4
Bransby Lincs 132 B3
Branscombe Devon 14 C1
Bransford Worcs 79 B5
Bransgore Hants 17 B5
Branshill Clack 208 A1
Bransholme Hull 151 D4
Branson's Cross Worcs 96 D3
Branston Leics 115 C6
Branston Lincs 133 C5
Branston Staffs 113 C6
Branston Booths Lincs 133 C5
Branstone I o W 19 C4
Bransty Cumb 162 C2
Brant Broughton Lincs 133 D4
Brantham Suff 88 D2
Branthwaite Cumb 162 B3
Branthwaite Cumb 163 A5
Brantingham E Yorks 142 A1
Branton Northumb 188 B3
Branton S Yorks 140 C4
Branxholm Park Borders 186 B3
Branxholme Borders 186 B3
Branxton Northumb 198 C2
Brassey Green Ches 127 C5
Brassington Derbys 130 D2
Brasted Kent 36 A2
Brasted Chart Kent 36 A2
Brathens Aberds 244 C3
Bratoft Lincs 135 C4
Brattleby Lincs 133 A4
Bratton Telford 111 D5
Bratton Wilts 44 D3
Bratton Clovelly Devon 11 B5
Bratton Fleming Devon 26 B1
Bratton Seymour Som 29 C6
Braughing Herts 68 A3
Braunston Northants 82 A2
Braunston-in-Rutland
    Rutland 99 A5
Braunstone Town Leics 98 A2
Braunton Devon 25 B5
Brawby N Yorks 159 D6
Brawl Highld 279 B4
Brawlbin Highld 279 C6
Bray Windsor 48 B2
Bray Shop Corn 10 D4
Bray Wick Windsor 48 B1
Braybrooke Northants 99 C4
Braye Ald 7
Brayford Devon 26 B1
Braystones Cumb 162 D3
Braythorn N Yorks 147 C6
Brayton N Yorks 149 D5
Brazacott Corn 10 B3
Breach Kent 51 C5
Breachacha Castle Argyll 223 B4
Breachwood Green Herts 67 A6
Breacleit W Isles 288 D2
Breadsall Derbys 114 B1
Breadstone Glos 62 C3
Breage Corn 3 C4
Breakachy Highld 251 B6
Bream Glos 62 C2
Breamore Hants 31 D5
Brean Som 42 D1
Breanais W Isles 287 B4
Brearton N Yorks 148 A2
Breascleit W Isles 288 D3
Breaston Derbys 114 B2
Brechfa Carms 58 B2
Brechin Angus 232 B3
Breck of Cruan Orkney 282 F4
Breckan Orkney 283 G3
Breckrey Highld 259 B5
Brecon = Aberhonddu
    Powys 60 A2
Brecon Beacons
    Mountain Centre Powys 60 A1
Bredbury Gtr Man 138 D2
Brede E Sus 23 A6
Bredenbury Hereford 79 B4
Bredfield Suff 88 B3
Bredgar Kent 51 C5
Bredhurst Kent 51 C4
Bredicot Worcs 80 B2
Bredon Worcs 80 D2
Bredon's Norton Worcs 80 D2

Bredwardine Hereford 78 C1
Breedon on the Hill Leics 114 C2
Breibhig W Isles 286 G2
Breibhig W Isles 288 D5
Breich W Loth 208 D2
Breightmet Gtr Man 137 C6
Breighton E Yorks 149 D6
Breinton Hereford 78 D2
Breinton Common
    Hereford 78 C2
Breiwick Shetland 285 J6
Bremhill Wilts 44 B3
Bremirehoull Shetland 285 L6
Brenchley Kent 37 B4
Brendon Devon 26 A2
Brenkley T & W 179 B4
Brent Eleigh Suff 87 C5
Brent Knoll Som 42 D2
Brent Pelham Herts 85 D6
Brentford London 49 B4
Brentingby Leics 115 D5
Brentwood Essex 69 D5
Brenzett Kent 38 C2
Brereton Staffs 113 D4
Brereton Green Ches 128 C2
Brereton Heath Ches 128 C3
Bressingham Norf 104 C1
Bretby Derbys 113 C6
Bretford Warks 98 D1
Bretforton Worcs 80 C3
Bretherdale Head Cumb 155 A4
Bretherton Lancs 136 A3
Brettabister Shetland 285 H6
Brettenham Norf 103 C5
Brettenham Suff 87 B5
Bretton Derbys 130 B2
Bretton Flint 126 C3
Brewer Street Sur 35 A6
Brewlands Bridge Angus 231 B5
Brewood Staffs 96 A1
Briach Moray 266 D1
Briants Puddle Dorset 16 B2
Brick End Essex 69 A5
Brickendon Herts 68 C3
Bricket Wood Herts 67 C6
Bricklehampton Worcs 80 C2
Bride I o M 152 A4
Bridekirk Cumb 163 A4
Bridell Pembs 73 B4
Bridestowe Devon 11 C6
Brideswell Aberds 255 C6
Bridford Devon 12 C3
Bridfordmills Devon 12 C3
Bridge Kent 52 D3
Bridge End Lincs 116 B4
Bridge Green Essex 85 D6
Bridge Hewick N Yorks 158 D2
Bridge of Alford Aberds 244 A2
Bridge of Allan Stirl 207 A5
Bridge of Avon Moray 254 C2
Bridge of Awe Argyll 227 D5
Bridge of Balgie Perth 229 D4
Bridge of Cally Perth 231 C5
Bridge of Canny Aberds 244 C3
Bridge of Craigisla Angus 231 C6
Bridge of Dee Dumfries 173 C5
Bridge of Don Aberdeen 245 A6
Bridge of Dun Angus 233 C4
Bridge of Dye Aberds 244 D3
Bridge of Earn Perth 219 C6
Bridge of Ericht Perth 229 C4
Bridge of Feugh Aberds 245 C4
Bridge of Forss Highld 279 B6
Bridge of Gairn Aberds 243 C6
Bridge of Gaur Perth 229 C4
Bridge of Muchalls
    Aberds 245 C5
Bridge of Oich Highld 240 B1
Bridge of Orchy Argyll 216 A2
Bridge of Waith Orkney 282 F3
Bridge of Walls Shetland 285 H4
Bridge of Weir Renfs 204 B3
Bridge Sollers Hereford 78 C2
Bridge Street Suff 87 C4
Bridge Trafford Ches 127 B4
Bridge Yate S Glos 43 B5
Bridgefoot Angus 220 A3
Bridgefoot Cumb 162 B3
Bridgehampton Som 29 C5
Bridgehill Durham 178 D2
Bridgemary Hants 19 A4
Bridgemont Derbys 129 A5
Bridgend Aberds 255 C6
Bridgend Aberds 244 A2
Bridgend Angus 232 B3
Bridgend Argyll 214 C1
Bridgend Argyll 200 B3
Bridgend Argyll 190 B3

Bridgend Cumb 164 D1
Bridgend Fife 220 C3
Bridgend Moray 255 C4
Bridgend N Lnrk 207 C4
Bridgend Pembs 73 B4
Bridgend W Loth 208 C3
Bridgend = Pen-y-bont
    ar Ogwr Bridgend 40 D4
Bridgend of Lintrathen
    Angus 231 C6
Bridgerule Devon 10 A3
Bridges Shrops 94 B1
Bridgeton Glasgow 205 B6
Bridgetown Corn 10 C4
Bridgetown Som 27 B4
Bridgham Norf 103 C5
Bridgnorth Shrops 95 B5
Bridgnorth Cliff Railway
    Shrops 95 B5
Bridgtown Staffs 96 A2
Bridgwater Som 28 B3
Bridlington E Yorks 151 A4
Bridport Dorset 15 B4
Bridstow Hereford 62 A1
Brierfield Lancs 146 D2
Brierley Glos 62 B2
Brierley Hereford 78 B2
Brierley S Yorks 140 B2
Brierley Hill W Mid 96 C2
Briery Hill Bl Gwent 60 C3
Brig o'Turk Stirl 217 D5
Brigg N Lincs 142 C2
Briggswath N Yorks 160 A2
Brigham Cumb 162 A3
Brigham E Yorks 150 B3
Brighouse W Yorks 139 A4
Brighstone I o W 18 C3
Brightgate Derbys 130 D2
Brighthampton Oxon 65 C4
Brightling E Sus 37 D4
Brightlingsea Essex 71 B4
Brighton Brighton 21 B6
Brighton Corn 4 B4
Brighton Hill Hants 33 A5
Brighton Museum and
    Art Gallery Brighton 21 B6
Brighton Racecourse
    Brighton 21 B6
Brighton Sea Life Centre
    Brighton 21 B6
Brightons Falk 208 C2
Brightwalton W Berks 46 B2
Brightwell Suff 88 C3
Brightwell Baldwin Oxon 66 D1
Brightwell cum Sotwell
    Oxon 65 D6
Brignall Durham 166 D3
Brigsley NE Lincs 143 C4
Brigsteer Cumb 154 C3
Brigstock Northants 99 C6
Brill Bucks 66 B1
Brilley Hereford 77 C6
Brimaston Pembs 55 B5
Brimfield Hereford 78 A3
Brimington Derbys 131 B4
Brimley Devon 12 D2
Brimpsfield Glos 63 B5
Brimpton W Berks 46 C3
Brims Orkney 283 K3
Brimscombe Glos 63 C4
Brimstage Mers 126 A3
Brinacory Highld 235 A6
Brind E Yorks 149 D6
Brindister Shetland 285 H4
Brindister Shetland 285 K6
Brindle Lancs 137 A5
Brindley Ford Staffs 128 D3
Brineton Staffs 112 D2
Bringhurst Leics 99 B5
Brington Cambs 100 D2
Brinian Orkney 282 E5
Briningham Norf 120 B2
Brinkhill Lincs 134 B3
Brinkley Cambs 86 B2
Brinklow Warks 98 D1
Brinkworth Wilts 44 A4
Brinmore Highld 252 D2
Brinscall Lancs 137 A5
Brinsea N Som 42 C3
Brinsley Notts 114 A2
Brinsop Hereford 78 C2
Brinsworth S Yorks 131 A4
Brinton Norf 120 B2
Brisco Cumb 175 C7
Brisley Norf 119 C6
Brislington Bristol 43 B5
Bristol Bristol 43 B4

Bristol City Museum and
    Art Gallery Bristol 43 B4
Bristol International
    Airport N Som 43 C4
Bristol Zoo Bristol 43 B4
Briston Norf 120 B2
Britannia Lancs 138 A1
Britford Wilts 31 C5
Brithdir Gwyn 91 A5
British Legion Village Kent 37 A5
British Museum London 49 A5
Briton Ferry Neath 40 B2
Britwell Salome Oxon 66 D1
Brixham Torbay 8 B3
Brixton Devon 7 B4
Brixton London 49 B6
Brixton Deverill Wilts 30 B2
Brixworth Northants 99 D4
Brize Norton Oxon 64 C4
Broad Blunsdon
    Thamesdown 64 D2
Broad Campden Glos 81 D4
Broad Chalke Wilts 31 C4
Broad Green Beds 83 C6
Broad Green Essex 70 A2
Broad Green Worcs 79 B5
Broad Haven Pembs 55 C4
Broad Heath Worcs 79 A4
Broad Hill Cambs 102 D1
Broad Hinton Wilts 45 B5
Broad Laying Hants 46 C2
Broad Marston Worcs 80 C4
Broad Oak Carms 58 C2
Broad Oak Cumb 153 A2
Broad Oak Dorset 14 B4
Broad Oak Dorset 30 D1
Broad Oak E Sus 23 A6
Broad Oak E Sus 36 D4
Broad Oak Hereford 61 A6
Broad Oak Mers 136 D4
Broad Street Kent 37 A6
Broad Street Green Essex 70 C2
Broad Town Wilts 45 B4
Broadbottom Gtr Man 138 D2
Broadbridge W Sus 19 A7
Broadbridge Heath W Sus 35 C4
Broadclyst Devon 13 B4
Broadfield Gtr Man 138 B1
Broadfield Lancs 136 A4
Broadfield Pembs 56 B1
Broadfield W Sus 35 C5
Broadford Highld 247 B5
Broadford Bridge W Sus 34 D3
Broadhaugh Borders 186 C3
Broadhaven Highld 281 C5
Broadheath Gtr Man 128 A2
Broadhembury Devon 13 A6
Broadhempston Devon 8 A2
Broadholme Derbys 114 A1
Broadholme Lincs 132 B3
Broadland Row E Sus 23 A6
Broadlay Carms 56 B3
Broadley Lancs 138 B1
Broadley Moray 267 C4
Broadley Common Essex 68 C4
Broadmayne Dorset 16 C1
Broadmeadows Borders 196 C3
Broadmere Hants 33 A5
Broadmoor Pembs 55 D6
Broadoak Kent 52 C3
Broadrashes Moray 267 D5
Broadsea Aberds 269 C4
Broadstairs Kent 53 C5
Broadstone Poole 17 B4
Broadstone Shrops 94 C3
Broadtown Lane Wilts 45 B4
Broadview Gardens,
    Hadlow Kent 36 B4
Broadwas Worcs 79 B5
Broadwater Herts 68 A2
Broadwater W Sus 21 B4
Broadway Carms 56 B2
Broadway Pembs 55 C4
Broadway Som 28 D3
Broadway Suff 105 D4
Broadway Worcs 80 D3
Broadwell Glos 64 A3
Broadwell Glos 62 B1
Broadwell Oxon 64 C3
Broadwell Warks 82 A1
Broadwell House
    Northumb 177 D7
Broadwey Dorset 15 C6
Broadwindsor Dorset 14 A4
Broadwood Kelly Devon 11 A7

Broadwoodwidger Devon 11 C5
Brobury Hereford 78 C1
Brochel Highld 248 B2
Brochloch Dumfries 182 C3
Brochroy Argyll 227 C5
Brockamin Worcs 79 B5
Brockbridge Hants 33 D5
Brockdam Northumb 189 A4
Brockdish Norf 104 D3
Brockenhurst Hants 18 A2
Brocketsbrae S Lnrk 194 C3
Brockford Street Suff 88 A2
Brockhall Northants 82 A3
Brockham Sur 35 B4
Brockhampton Glos 63 A6
Brockhampton Hereford 78 D3
Brockhole -National Park Visitor Centre, Windermere Cumb 154 A2
Brockholes W Yorks 139 B4
Brockhurst Derbys 130 C3
Brockhurst Hants 19 A5
Brocklebank Cumb 175 D6
Brocklesby Lincs 142 B3
Brockley N Som 42 C3
Brockley Green Suff 87 B4
Brockleymoor Cumb 164 B2
Brockton Shrops 94 C1
Brockton Shrops 94 B3
Brockton Shrops 93 A7
Brockton Shrops 95 A5
Brockton Telford 111 D6
Brockweir Glos 62 C1
Brockwood Hants 33 C5
Brockworth Glos 63 B4
Brocton Staffs 112 D3
Brodick N Ayrs 191 B6
Brodick Castle N Ayrs 191 B6
Brodsworth S Yorks 140 C3
Brogaig Highld 259 B4
Brogborough Beds 83 D6
Broken Cross Ches 128 B1
Broken Cross Ches 128 B3
Brokenborough Wilts 44 A3
Bromborough Mers 126 A3
Brome Suff 104 D2
Brome Street Suff 104 D2
Bromeswell Suff 88 B4
Bromfield Cumb 175 D4
Bromfield Shrops 94 D2
Bromham Beds 84 B2
Bromham Wilts 44 C3
Bromley London 49 C7
Bromley W Mid 96 C2
Bromley Common London 49 C7
Bromley Green Kent 38 B1
Brompton Medway 51 C4
Brompton N Yorks 158 B2
Brompton N Yorks 160 C3
Brompton-on-Swale N Yorks 157 B6
Brompton Ralph Som 27 B5
Brompton Regis Som 27 B4
Bromsash Hereford 62 A2
Bromsberrow Heath Glos 79 D5
Bromsgrove Worcs 96 D2
Bromyard Hereford 79 B4
Bromyard Downs Hereford 79 B4
Bronaber Gwyn 108 B2
Brongest Ceredig 73 B6
Bronington Wrex 110 B3
Bronllys Powys 77 D5
Bronnant Ceredig 75 B5
Bronte Parsonage Museum, Keighley W Yorks 147 D4
Bronwydd Arms Carms 73 D7
Bronydd Powys 77 C6
Brongarth Shrops 110 B1
Brook Carms 56 B2
Brook Hants 32 D1
Brook Hants 32 C2
Brook I o W 18 C2
Brook Kent 38 A2
Brook Sur 34 C2
Brook Sur 34 B3
Brook End Beds 84 A2
Brook Hill Hants 31 D6
Brook Street Kent 36 B3
Brook Street Kent 38 A2
Brook Street W Sus 35 D6
Brooke Norf 104 B3
Brooke Rutland 99 A5
Brookenby Lincs 143 D4
Brookend Glos 62 D1

Brookfield Renfs 205 B4
Brookhouse Lancs 145 A5
Brookhouse Green Ches 128 C3
Brookland Kent 38 C1
Brooklands Dumfries 173 A6
Brooklands Gtr Man 137 D6
Brooklands Shrops 111 A4
Brookmans Park Herts 68 C2
Brooks Powys 93 B5
Brooks Green W Sus 35 U4
Brookthorpe Glos 63 B4
Brookville Norf 102 B3
Brookwood Sur 34 A2
Broom Beds 84 C3
Broom S Yorks 140 D2
Broom Warks 80 B3
Broom Worcs 96 D2
Broom Green Norf 120 C1
Broom Hill Dorset 17 A4
Broome Norf 105 B4
Broome Shrops 94 C2
Broome Park Northumb 189 B4
Broomedge Warr 128 A2
Broomer's Corner W Sus 35 D4
Broomfield Aberds 257 C4
Broomfield Essex 69 B7
Broomfield Kent 37 A6
Broomfield Kent 52 C3
Broomfield Som 28 B2
Broomfleet E Yorks 141 A6
Broomhall Ches 111 A5
Broomhall Windsor 48 C2
Broomhaugh Northumb 178 C2
Broomhill Norf 102 A2
Broomhill Northumb 189 C5
Broomhill S Yorks 140 C2
Broomholm Norf 121 B5
Broomley Northumb 178 C2
Broompark Durham 167 A5
Broom's Green Hereford 79 D5
Broomy Lodge Hants 31 D6
Brora Highld 274 D3
Broseley Shrops 95 A4
Brotherhouse Bar Lincs 117 D5
Brotherstone Borders 197 C5
Brotherton N Yorks 140 A2
Brotton Redcar 169 D4
Broubster Highld 279 B6
Brough Cumb 165 D5
Brough Derbys 130 A1
Brough E Yorks 142 A1
Brough Highld 280 A4
Brough Notts 132 D3
Brough Orkney 282 F4
Brough Shetland 284 F6
Brough Shetland 284 G7
Brough Shetland 284 F7
Brough Shetland 285 J7
Brough Shetland 285 H6
Brough Lodge Shetland 284 D7
Brough Sowerby Cumb 165 D5
Broughall Shrops 111 A4
Broughton Borders 195 C6
Broughton Cambs 101 D4
Broughton Flint 126 C3
Broughton Hants 32 B2
Broughton Lancs 145 D5
Broughton M Keynes 83 C5
Broughton N Lincs 142 C1
Broughton Northants 99 D5
Broughton N Yorks 146 B3
Broughton N Yorks 159 D6
Broughton Orkney 282 C5
Broughton Oxon 81 D7
Broughton V Glam 40 D4
Broughton Astley Leics 98 B2
Broughton Beck Cumb 154 C1
Broughton Common Wilts 44 C2
Broughton Gifford Wilts 44 C2
Broughton Hackett Worcs 80 B2
Broughton in Furness Cumb 153 B3
Broughton Mills Cumb 153 A3
Broughton Moor Cumb 162 A3
Broughton Park Gtr Man 138 C1
Broughton Poggs Oxon 64 C3
Broughtown Orkney 282 C7
Broughty Ferry Dundee 221 A4
Browhouses Dumfries 175 B5
Browland Shetland 285 H4
Brown Candover Hants 33 B4
Brown Edge Lancs 136 B2
Brown Edge Staffs 129 D4
Brown Heath Ches 127 C4
Brownhill Aberds 256 B3
Brownhill Aberds 256 B1
Brownhill Blkburn 145 D6
Brownhill Shrops 110 C3

Brownhills Fife 221 C5
Brownhills W Mid 96 A3
Brownlow Ches 128 C3
Brownlow Heath Ches 128 C3
Brownmuir Aberds 233 A5
Brown's End Glos 79 D5
Brownshill Glos 63 C4
Brownston Devon 7 B6
Brownyside Northumb 189 A4
Broxa N Yorks 160 D3
Broxbourne Herts 68 C3
Broxburn E Loth 210 C3
Broxburn W Loth 208 C3
Broxholme Lincs 133 B4
Broxted Essex 69 A5
Broxton Ches 127 D4
Broxwood Hereford 78 B1
Broyle Side E Sus 22 A2
Brù W Isles 288 C4
Bruairnis W Isles 286 F3
Bruan Highld 275 A7
Bruar Lodge Perth 230 A2
Brucehill W Dunb 206 C1
Bruera Ches 127 C4
Bruern Abbey Oxon 64 A3
Bruichladdich Argyll 200 B2
Bruisyard Suff 88 A4
Brumby N Lincs 141 C6
Brund Staffs 129 C6
Brundall Norf 104 A4
Brundish Suff 88 A3
Brundish Street Suff 104 D3
Brunery Highld 235 C6
Brunshaw Lancs 146 D2
Brunswick Village T & W 179 B4
Bruntcliffe W Yorks 139 A5
Bruntingthorpe Leics 98 B3
Brunton Fife 220 B3
Brunton Northumb 189 A5
Brunton Wilts 45 D6
Brushford Devon 12 A1
Brushford Som 27 C4
Bruton Som 29 B6
Bryanston Dorset 16 A2
Brydekirk Dumfries 175 A4
Bryher Scilly 2 E3
Brymbo Wrex 126 D2
Brympton Som 29 D5
Bryn Carms 57 B5
Bryn Gtr Man 137 C4
Bryn Neath 40 B3
Bryn Shrops 93 C6
Bryn-coch Neath 40 B2
Bryn Du Anglesey 122 C3
Bryn Gates Gtr Man 137 C4
Bryn-glas Conwy 124 C3
Bryn Golau Rhondda 41 C4
Bryn-Iwan Carms 73 C6
Bryn-mawr Gwyn 106 C2
Bryn-nantlech Conwy 125 C4
Bryn-penarth Powys 93 A5
Bryn Rhyd-yr-Arian Conwy 125 C4
Bryn Saith Marchog Denb 125 D5
Bryn Sion Gwyn 91 A6
Bryn-y-gwenin Mon 61 B5
Bryn-y-maen Conwy 124 B3
Bryn-yr-eryr Gwyn 106 B3
Brynamman Carms 59 D4
Brynberian Pembs 72 C4
Brynbryddan Neath 40 B2
Brynbuga = Usk Mon 61 C5
Bryncae Rhondda 41 C4
Bryncethin Bridgend 40 C4
Bryncir Gwyn 107 B4
Bryncroes Gwyn 106 C2
Bryncrug Gwyn 90 B4
Bryneglwys Denb 109 A6
Brynford Flint 126 B1
Bryngwran Anglesey 122 C3
Bryngwyn Ceredig 73 B5
Bryngwyn Mon 61 C5
Bryngwyn Powys 77 C5
Brynhenllan Pembs 72 C3
Brynhoffnant Ceredig 73 A6
Brynithel Bl Gwent 41 A7
Brynmawr Bl Gwent 60 B3
Brynmenyn Bridgend 40 C4
Brynmill Swansea 57 C6
Brynna Rhondda 41 C4
Brynrefail Anglesey 123 B4
Brynrefail Gwyn 123 D5
Brynsadler Rhondda 41 C5
Brynsiencyn Anglesey 123 D4
Brynteg Anglesey 123 B4
Brynteg Ceredig 58 A1

Buaile nam Bodach W Isles 286 F3
Bualintur Highld 246 B3
Buarthmeini Gwyn 108 B3
Bubbenhall Warks 97 D6
Bubwith E Yorks 149 D6
Buccleuch Borders 185 A6
Buchanhaven Aberds 257 B6
Buchanty Perth 218 B4
Buchlyvie Stirl 206 A3
Buckabank Cumb 164 A1
Buckden Cambs 84 A3
Buckden N Yorks 156 D3
Buckenham Norf 105 A4
Buckerell Devon 13 A6
Buckfast Devon 7 A6
Buckfast Abbey, Buckfastleigh Devon 7 A6
Buckfastleigh Devon 7 A6
Buckhaven Fife 209 A6
Buckholm Borders 196 C3
Buckholt Mon 61 B7
Buckhorn Weston Dorset 30 C1
Buckhurst Hill Essex 68 D4
Buckie Moray 267 C5
Buckies Highld 280 B3
Buckingham Bucks 82 D3
Buckingham Palace London 49 B5
Buckland Bucks 66 B3
Buckland Devon 7 C5
Buckland Glos 80 D3
Buckland Hants 18 B2
Buckland Herts 85 D5
Buckland Kent 39 A5
Buckland Oxon 64 D4
Buckland Sur 35 A5
Buckland Abbey Devon 6 A3
Buckland Brewer Devon 25 C5
Buckland Common Bucks 67 C4
Buckland Dinham Som 43 D6
Buckland Filleigh Devon 11 A5
Buckland in the Moor Devon 12 D2
Buckland Monachorum Devon 6 A3
Buckland Newton Dorset 15 A6
Buckland St Mary Som 28 D2
Bucklebury W Berks 46 B3
Bucklegate Lincs 117 B6
Bucklerheads Angus 221 A4
Bucklers Hard Hants 18 B3
Bucklesham Suff 88 C3
Buckley = Bwcle Flint 126 C2
Bucklow Hill Ches 128 A2
Buckminster Leics 116 C1
Bucknall Lincs 133 C6
Bucknall Stoke 112 A3
Bucknell Oxon 65 A6
Bucknell Shrops 94 D1
Buckpool Moray 267 C5
Buck's Cross Devon 24 C4
Bucks Green W Sus 34 C3
Bucks Horn Oak Hants 33 A7
Buck's Mills Devon 25 C4
Bucksburn Aberdeen 245 B5
Buckskin Hants 47 D4
Buckton E Yorks 161 D5
Buckton Hereford 94 D1
Buckton Northumb 199 C4
Buckworth Cambs 100 D3
Budbrooke Warks 81 A5
Budby Notts 131 C6
Budd's Titson Corn 10 A3
Bude Corn 10 A3
Budlake Devon 13 B4
Budle Northumb 199 C5
Budleigh Salterton Devon 13 C5
Budock Water Corn 4 D2
Buerton Ches 111 A5
Buffler's Holt Bucks 82 D3
Bugbrooke Northants 82 B3
Buglawton Ches 128 C3
Bugle Corn 5 B5
Bugley Wilts 30 A2
Bugthorpe E Yorks 149 B6
Buildwas Shrops 95 A4
Builth Road Powys 76 B4
Builth Wells = Llanfair-ym-Muallt Powys 76 B4
Buirgh W Isles 287 E5
Bulby Lincs 116 C3
Bulcote Notts 115 A4
Buldoo Highld 279 B5
Bulford Wilts 31 A5
Bulford Camp Wilts 31 A5
Bulkeley Ches 127 D5
Bulkington Warks 97 C6

Bulkington Wilts 44 D3
Bulkworthy Devon 25 D4
Bull Hill Hants 18 B2
Bullamoor N Yorks 158 B2
Bullbridge Derbys 130 D3
Bullbrook Brack 48 C1
Bulley Glos 62 B3
Bullgill Cumb 162 A3
Bullington Hants 32 A3
Bullington Lincs 133 B5
Bull's Green Herts 68 B2
Bullwood Argyll 203 A6
Bulmer Essex 87 C4
Bulmer N Yorks 149 A5
Bulmer Tye Essex 87 D4
Bulphan Thurrock 50 A3
Bulverhythe E Sus 23 B5
Bulwark Aberds 257 B4
Bulwell Nottingham 114 A3
Bulwick Northants 99 B6
Bumble's Green Essex 68 C4
Bun Abhainn Eadarra W Isles 288 G2
Bun a'Mhuillin W Isles 286 E3
Bun Loyne Highld 239 B6
Bunacaimb Highld 235 B5
Bunarkaig Highld 239 D5
Bunbury Ches 127 D5
Bunbury Heath Ches 127 D5
Bunchrew Highld 252 B2
Bundalloch Highld 249 D6
Buness Shetland 284 C8
Bunessan Argyll 224 D2
Bungay Suff 104 C4
Bunker's Hill Lincs 133 B6
Bunker's Hill Lincs 134 D2
Bunkers Hill Oxon 65 B6
Bunloit Highld 251 D7
Bunnahabhain Argyll 201 A4
Bunny Notts 114 C3
Buntait Highld 251 C5
Buntingford Herts 68 A3
Bunwell Norf 104 B2
Burbage Derbys 129 B5
Burbage Leics 98 B1
Burbage Wilts 45 C6
Burchett's Green Windsor 47 A6
Burcombe Wilts 31 B4
Burcot Oxon 65 D6
Burcott Bucks 66 A3
Burdon T & W 179 D5
Bures Suff 87 D5
Bures Green Suff 87 D5
Burford Ches 127 D5
Burford Oxon 64 B3
Burford Shrops 78 A3
Burg Argyll 224 B2
Burgar Orkney 282 E4
Burgate Hants 31 D5
Burgate Suff 104 D1
Burgess Hill W Sus 21 A6
Burgh Suff 88 B3
Burgh-by-Sands Cumb 175 C6
Burgh Castle Norf 105 A5
Burgh Heath Sur 35 A5
Burgh le Marsh Lincs 135 C5
Burgh Muir Aberds 256 A3
Burgh next Aylsham Norf 120 C4
Burgh on Bain Lincs 134 A2
Burgh St Margaret Norf 121 D6
Burgh St Peter Norf 105 B5
Burghclere Hants 46 C2
Burghead Moray 266 C2
Burghfield W Berks 47 C4
Burghfield Common W Berks 47 C4
Burghfield Hill W Berks 47 C4
Burghill Hereford 78 C2
Burghwallis S Yorks 140 B3
Burham Kent 51 C4
Buriton Hants 33 C6
Burland Ches 127 D6
Burlawn Corn 9 D5
Burleigh Brack 48 C1
Burlescombe Devon 27 D5
Burleston Dorset 16 B1
Burley Hants 18 A1
Burley Rutland 116 D2
Burley W Yorks 148 D1
Burley Gate Hereford 78 C3
Burley in Wharfedale W Yorks 147 C5
Burley Lodge Hants 18 A1
Burley Street Hants 18 A1
Burleydam Ches 111 A5
Burlingjobb Powys 77 B6
Burlow E Sus 22 A3
Burlton Shrops 110 C3

Burmarsh Kent 38 B2
Burmington Warks 81 D5
Burn N Yorks 140 A3
Burn of Cambus Stirl 218 D2
Burnaston Derbys 113 B6
Burnbank S Lnrk 194 A2
Burnby E Yorks 150 C1
Burncross S Yorks 139 D6
Burneside Cumb 154 B4
Burness Orkney 282 C7
Burneston N Yorks 157 C7
Burnett Bath 43 C5
Burnfoot Borders 186 B3
Burnfoot Borders 186 B4
Burnfoot E Ayrs 182 B2
Burnfoot Perth 219 D4
Burnham Bucks 48 A2
Burnham N Lincs 142 B2
Burnham Deepdale Norf 119 A5
Burnham Green Herts 68 B2
Burnham Market Norf 119 A5
Burnham Norton Norf 119 A5
Burnham-on-Crouch Essex 70 D3
Burnham-on-Sea Som 28 A3
Burnham Overy Staithe Norf 119 A5
Burnham Overy Town Norf 119 A5
Burnham Thorpe Norf 119 A5
urnhead Dumfries 183 C6
urnhead S Ayrs 181 A4
urnhervie Aberds 245 A4
urnhill Green Staffs 95 A5
urnhope Durham 167 A4
urnhouse N Ayrs 204 C3
urniston N Yorks 160 B4
urnlee W Yorks 139 C4
urnley Lancs 146 D2
urnley Lane Lancs 146 D2
urnmouth Borders 211 D6
urnopfield Durham 178 D3
urnsall N Yorks 147 A4
urnside Angus 232 C3
urnside E Ayrs 182 A3
urnside Fife 219 D6
urnside Shetland 284 F4
urnside S Lnrk 205 B6
urnside W Loth 208 C3
urnside of Duntrune Angus 220 A4
rnswark Dumfries 175 A4
rnt Heath Derbys 130 B2
rnt Houses Durham 166 C4
rnt Yates N Yorks 147 A6
rntcommon Sur 34 A3
rnthouse Corn 4 D2
rntisland Fife 209 B5
rnton E Ayrs 182 B2
rntwood Staffs 96 A3
rnwynd Edin 208 D4
rpham Sur 34 A3
rpham W Sus 20 B3
rradon Northumb 188 C2
rradon T & W 179 B4
rafirth Shetland 284 B8
raland Shetland 284 F5
raland Shetland 285 J4
rras Corn 3 B4
ravoe Shetland 284 G5
ravoe Shetland 284 F7
ray Village Orkney 283 H5
rells Cumb 165 D4
relton Perth 220 A2
ridge Devon 25 B6
ridge Hants 32 D4
rill N Yorks 157 C6
ringham N Lincs 141 C6
rington Devon 26 D1
rington Hereford 94 D2
ington N Som 42 D3
ough Green Cambs 86 B2
ough on the Hill ics 115 D5
ow-bridge Som 28 C3
owhill Sur 48 C2
y Swansea 57 C4
y Green Swansea 57 C4
y Port = Porth wyn Carms 57 B4
cough Lancs 136 B3
cough Bridge Lancs 136 B3
ea E Yorks 149 D7
hill E Yorks 150 C3
edon Hants 18 A3
em Stoke 112 A2
tall Suff 88 C1
tock Dorset 14 A4
Burston Norf 104 C2
Burston Staffs 112 B3
Burstow Sur 35 B6
Burstwick E Yorks 143 A4
Burtersett N Yorks 156 C2
Burtle Som 28 A3
Burton Ches 126 B3
Burton Ches 127 C5
Burton Dorset 17 B5
Burton Lincs 133 B4
Burton Northumb 199 C5
Burton Pembs 55 D5
Burton Som 28 A1
Burton Wilts 44 B2
Burton Agnes E Yorks 151 A4
Burton Bradstock Dorset 15 C4
Burton Dassett Warks 81 B6
Burton Fleming E Yorks 161 D4
Burton Green W Mid 97 D5
Burton Green Wrex 126 D3
Burton Hastings Warks 97 B7
Burton-in-Kendal Cumb 154 D4
Burton in Lonsdale N Yorks 155 D5
Burton Joyce Notts 115 A4
Burton Latimer Northants 99 D6
Burton Lazars Leics 115 D5
Burton-le-Coggles Lincs 116 C2
Burton Leonard N Yorks 148 A2
Burton on the Wolds Leics 114 C3
Burton Overy Leics 98 B3
Burton Pedwardine Lincs 116 A4
Burton Pidsea E Yorks 151 D5
Burton Salmon N Yorks 140 A2
Burton Stather N Lincs 141 B6
Burton upon Stather N Lincs 141 B6
Burton upon Trent Staffs 113 C6
Burtonwood Warr 137 D4
Burwardsley Ches 127 D5
Burwarton Shrops 95 C4
Burwash E Sus 37 D4
Burwash Common E Sus 36 D4
Burwash Weald E Sus 36 D4
Burwell Cambs 86 A1
Burwell Lincs 134 B3
Burwen Anglesey 123 A4
Burwick Orkney 283 K5
Bury Cambs 101 C4
Bury Gtr Man 137 B7
Bury Som 27 C4
Bury W Sus 20 A3
Bury Green Herts 68 A4
Bury St Edmunds Suff 87 A4
Burythorpe N Yorks 149 A6
Busby E Renf 205 C5
Buscot Oxon 64 D3
Bush Bank Hereford 78 B2
Bush Crathie Aberds 243 C5
Bush Green Norf 104 C3
Bushbury W Mid 96 A2
Bushby Leics 98 A3
Bushey Herts 67 D6
Bushey Heath Herts 67 D6
Bushley Worcs 80 D1
Bushton Wilts 45 B4
Buslingthorpe Lincs 133 A5
Busta Shetland 284 G5
Butcher's Cross E Sus 36 D3
Butcher's Pasture Essex 69 A6
Butcombe N Som 43 C4
Butetown Cardiff 41 D6
Butleigh Som 29 B5
Butleigh Wootton Som 29 B5
Butler's Cross Bucks 66 C3
Butler's End Warks 97 C5
Butlers Marston Warks 81 C6
Butley Suff 89 B4
Butley High Corner Suff 89 C4
Butt Green Ches 127 D6
Butterburn Cumb 177 B4
Buttercrambe N Yorks 149 B6
Butterknowle Durham 166 C4
Butterleigh Devon 13 A4
Buttermere Cumb 163 C4
Buttermere Wilts 46 C1
Buttershaw W Yorks 139 A4
Butterstone Perth 231 D4
Butterton Staffs 129 D5
Butterwick Durham 167 C6
Butterwick Lincs 117 A6
Butterwick N Yorks 159 D6
Butterwick N Yorks 160 D3
Buttington Powys 93 A6
Buttonoak Shrops 95 D5
Butt's Green Hants 32 C2
Buttsash Hants 18 A3
Buxhall Suff 87 B6
Buxhall Fen Street Suff 87 B6
Buxley Borders 198 A2
Buxted E Sus 36 D2
Buxton Derbys 129 B5
Buxton Norf 120 C4
Buxworth Derbys 129 A5
Bwcle = Buckley Flint 126 C2
Bwlch Powys 60 A3
Bwlch-Llan Ceredig 75 C4
Bwlch-y-cibau Powys 109 D6
Bwlch-y-fadfa Ceredig 74 D3
Bwlch-y-ffridd Powys 93 B4
Bwlch-y-sarnau Powys 92 D4
Bwlchgwyn Wrex 126 D2
Bwlchnewydd Carms 73 D6
Bwlchtocyn Gwyn 106 D3
Bwlchyddar Powys 109 C6
Bwlchygroes Pembs 73 C5
Byermoor T & W 178 D3
Byers Green Durham 167 B5
Byfield Northants 82 B2
Byfleet Sur 48 C3
Byford Hereford 78 C1
Bygrave Herts 85 D4
Byker T & W 179 C4
Bylchau Conwy 125 C4
Byley Ches 128 C2
Bynea Carms 57 C5
Byrness Northumb 187 C6
Bythorn Cambs 100 D2
Byton Hereford 78 A1
Byworth W Sus 34 D2

C

Cabharstadh W Isles 288 E4
Cablea Perth 218 A4
Cabourne Lincs 142 C3
Cabrach Argyll 201 B4
Cabrach Moray 255 D4
Cabrich Highld 252 B1
Cabus Lancs 145 C4
Cackle Street E Sus 36 D2
Cadbury Devon 13 A4
Cadbury Barton Devon 26 D1
Cadbury World, Bournville W Mid 96 C3
Cadder E Dunb 205 A6
Caddington Beds 67 B5
Caddonfoot Borders 196 C3
Cade Street E Sus 36 D4
Cadeby Leics 97 A7
Cadeby S Yorks 140 C3
Cadeleigh Devon 13 A4
Cadgwith Corn 3 D5
Cadham Fife 220 D2
Cadishead Gtr Man 137 D6
Cadle Swansea 57 C6
Cadley Lancs 145 D5
Cadley Wilts 45 D6
Cadley Wilts 45 C6
Cadmore End Bucks 66 D2
Cadnam Hants 32 D1
Cadney N Lincs 142 C2
Cadole Flint 126 C2
Cadoxton V Glam 41 E6
Cadoxton-Juxta-Neath Neath 40 B2
Cadshaw Blkburn 137 B6
Cadwell Park Motor Racing Circuit Lincs 134 A2
Cadzow S Lnrk 194 A2
Caeathro Gwyn 123 D4
Caehopkin Powys 59 D5
Caenby Lincs 133 A5
Caenby Corner Lincs 133 A4
Caer-bryn Carms 57 A5
Caer Llan Mon 61 C6
Caerau Bridgend 40 B3
Caerau Cardiff 41 D6
Caerdeon Gwyn 90 A4
Caerdydd = Cardiff Cardiff 41 D6
Caerfarchell Pembs 54 B3
Caerffili = Caerphilly Caerph 41 C6
Caerfyrddin = Carmarthen Carms 73 D7
Caergeiliog Anglesey 122 C3
Caergwrle Flint 126 D3
Caergybi = Holyhead Anglesey 122 B2
Caerleon = Caerllion Newport 61 D5
Caerllion = Caerleon Newport 61 D5
Caernarfon Gwyn 123 D4
Caernarfon Castle Gwyn 123 D4
Caerphilly = Caerffili Caerph 41 C6
Caersws Powys 92 B4
Caerwedros Ceredig 73 A6
Caerwent Mon 61 D6
Caerwych Gwyn 107 C6
Caerwys Flint 125 B6
Caethle Gwyn 90 C4
Caim Anglesey 123 B6
Caio Carms 58 B3
Cairinis W Isles 287 H3
Cairisiadar W Isles 287 A5
Cairminis W Isles 287 F5
Cairnbaan Argyll 213 C6
Cairnbanno Ho. Aberds 256 B3
Cairnborrow Aberds 255 B5
Cairnbrogie Aberds 256 D3
Cairnbulg Castle Aberds 269 C5
Cairncross Angus 232 A2
Cairncross Borders 211 D5
Cairndow Argyll 215 A4
Cairness Aberds 269 C5
Cairneyhill Fife 208 B3
Cairnfield Ho. Moray 267 C5
Cairngaan Dumfries 170 D3
Cairngarroch Dumfries 170 C2
Cairnhill Aberds 256 C1
Cairnie Aberds 255 B5
Cairnie Aberds 245 B5
Cairnorrie Aberds 256 B3
Cairnpark Aberds 245 A5
Cairnryan Dumfries 170 A2
Cairnton Orkney 283 G4
Caister-on-Sea Norf 121 D7
Caistor Lincs 142 C3
Caistor St Edmund Norf 104 A3
Caistron Northumb 188 C2
Caitha Bowland Borders 196 B3
Caithness Glass, Perth Perth 219 B5
Calais Street Suff 87 D5
Calanais W Isles 288 D3
Calbost W Isles 288 F5
Calbourne I o W 18 C3
Calceby Lincs 134 B3
Calcot Row W Berks 47 B4
Calcott Kent 52 C3
Caldback Shetland 284 C8
Caldbeck Cumb 163 A6
Caldbergh N Yorks 157 C4
Caldecote Cambs 85 B5
Caldecote Cambs 100 C3
Caldecote Herts 84 D4
Caldecote Northants 82 B3
Caldecott Northants 84 A1
Caldecott Oxon 65 D5
Caldecott Rutland 99 B5
Calder Bridge Cumb 162 D3
Calder Hall Cumb 162 D3
Calder Mains Highld 280 C2
Calder Vale Lancs 145 C5
Calderbank N Lnrk 207 D5
Calderbrook Gtr Man 138 B2
Caldercruix N Lnrk 207 D6
Caldermill S Lnrk 205 D6
Calderwood S Lnrk 205 C6
Caldhame Angus 232 D2
Caldicot Mon 42 A3
Caldwell Derbys 113 D6
Caldwell N Yorks 167 D4
Caldy Mers 126 A2
Caledrhydiau Ceredig 74 C3
Calfsound Orkney 282 D6
Calgary Argyll 224 A2
Califer Moray 266 D1
California Falk 208 C2
California Norf 121 D7
Calke Derbys 114 C1
Callakille Highld 248 A3
Callaly Northumb 188 C3
Callander Stirl 217 D6
Callaughton Shrops 95 B4
Callestick Corn 4 B2
Calligarry Highld 247 D5
Callington Corn 6 A2
Callow Hereford 78 D2
Callow End Worcs 79 C6
Callow Hill Wilts 44 A4
Callow Hill Worcs 95 D5
Callows Grave Worcs 78 A3
Calmore Hants 32 D2
Calmsden Glos 63 C6
Calne Wilts 44 B4
Calow Derbys 131 B4
Calshot Hants 18 A3
Calstock Corn 6 A3
Calstone Wellington Wilts 44 C4
Calthorpe Norf 120 B3
Calthwaite Cumb 164 A2
Calton N Yorks 146 B3
Calton Staffs 129 D6
Calveley Ches 127 D5
Calver Derbys 130 B2
Calver Hill Hereford 78 C1
Calverhall Shrops 111 B5
Calverleigh Devon 27 D4
Calverley W Yorks 147 D6
Calvert Bucks 66 A1
Calverton M Keynes 83 D4
Calverton Notts 115 A4
Calvine Perth 230 B2
Calvo Cumb 174 C4
Cam Glos 62 D3
Camas-luinie Highld 249 D6
Camasnacroise Highld 236 D2
Camastianavaig Highld 247 A4
Camasunary Highld 247 C4
Camault Muir Highld 251 B7
Camb Shetland 284 D7
Camber E Sus 38 D1
Camberley Sur 47 C6
Camberwell London 49 B6
Camblesforth N Yorks 141 A4
Cambo Northumb 178 A2
Cambois Northumb 179 A5
Camborne Corn 3 A4
Cambourne Cambs 85 B5
Cambridge Cambs 85 B6
Cambridge Glos 62 C3
Cambridge Airport Cambs 85 B6
Cambridge Town Sthend 51 A6
Cambus Clack 207 A6
Cambusavie Farm Highld 264 A3
Cambusbarron Stirl 207 A5
Cambuskenneth Stirl 207 A6
Cambuslang S Lnrk 205 B6
Cambusmore Lodge Highld 264 A3
Camden London 49 A5
Camelford Corn 10 C2
Camelot Theme Park, Chorley Lancs 136 B4
Camelsdale W Sus 34 C1
Camerory Highld 253 C6
Camer's Green Worcs 79 D5
Camerton Bath 43 D5
Camerton Cumb 162 A3
Camerton E Yorks 143 A4
Camghouran Perth 229 C4
Cammachmore Aberds 245 C6
Cammeringham Lincs 133 A4
Camore Highld 264 A3
Camp Hill Warks 97 B6
Campbeltown Argyll 190 C3
Campbeltown Airport Argyll 190 C2
Camperdown T & W 179 B4
Campmuir Perth 220 A2
Campsall S Yorks 140 B3
Campsey Ash Suff 88 B4
Campton Beds 84 D3
Camptown Borders 187 B5
Camrose Pembs 55 B5
Camserney Perth 230 D2
Camster Highld 281 D4
Camuschoirk Highld 235 D6
Camuscross Highld 247 C5
Camusnagaul Highld 237 B4
Camusnagaul Highld 262 B2
Camusrory Highld 238 C2
Camusteel Highld 249 B4
Camusterrach Highld 249 B4
Camusvrachan Perth 229 D5
Canada Hants 32 D1
Canadia E Sus 23 A5
Canal Side S Yorks 141 B4
Candacraig Ho. Aberds 243 A6
Candlesby Lincs 135 C4
Candy Mill S Lnrk 195 B5
Cane End Oxon 47 B4
Canewdon Essex 70 D2
Canford Bottom Dorset 17 A4
Canford Cliffs Poole 17 C4
Canford Magna Poole 17 B4
Canham's Green Suff 87 A6
Canholes Derbys 129 B5
Canisbay Highld 281 A5
Cann Dorset 30 C2
Cann Common Dorset 30 C2
Cannard's Grave Som 29 A6
Cannich Highld 251 C5
Cannington Som 28 B2
Cannock Staffs 96 A2

Cannock Wood Staffs 112 D4
Canon Bridge Hereford 78 C2
Canon Frome Hereford 79 C4
Canon Pyon Hereford 78 C2
Canonbie Dumfries 175 A6
Canons Ashby Northants 82 B2
Canonstown Corn 2 B3
Canterbury Kent 52 D3
Canterbury Cathedral Kent 52 D3
Canterbury Tales Kent 52 D3
Cantley Norf 105 A4
Cantley S Yorks 140 C4
Cantlop Shrops 94 A3
Canton Cardiff 41 D6
Cantraybruich Highld 252 B3
Cantraydoune Highld 252 B3
Cantraywood Highld 252 B3
Cantsfield Lancs 155 D5
Canvey Island Essex 51 A4
Canwick Lincs 133 C4
Canworthy Water Corn 10 B3
Caol Highld 237 B5
Caol Ila Argyll 201 A4
Caolas Argyll 222 C3
Caolas Scalpaigh W Isles 288 H3
Caolas Stocinis W Isles 288 H2
Capel Sur 35 B4
Capel Bangor Ceredig 91 D4
Capel Betws Lleucu
Ceredig 75 C5
Capel Carmel Gwyn 106 D1
Capel Coch Anglesey 123 B4
Capel Curig Conwy 124 D2
Capel Cynon Ceredig 73 B6
Capel Dewi Ceredig 58 A1
Capel Dewi Ceredig 90 D4
Capel Dewi Carms 58 C1
Capel Garmon Conwy 124 D3
Capel-gwyn Anglesey 122 C3
Capel Gwyn Carms 58 C1
Capel Gwynfe Carms 59 C4
Capel Hendre Carms 57 A5
Capel Hermon Gwyn 108 C2
Capel Isaac Carms 58 C2
Capel Iwan Carms 73 C5
Capel le Ferne Kent 39 B4
Capel Llanilltern Cardiff 41 C5
Capel Mawr Anglesey 123 C4
Capel St Andrew Suff 89 C4
Capel St Mary Suff 88 D1
Capel Seion Ceredig 75 A5
Capel Tygwydd Ceredig 73 B5
Capel Uchaf Gwyn 107 B4
Capel-y-graig Gwyn 123 D5
Capeluolo Conwy 124 B2
Capenhurst Ches 126 B3
Capernwray Lancs 154 D4
Capheaton Northumb 178 A2
Cappercleuch Borders 196 D1
Capplegill Dumfries 185 B4
Capton Devon 8 B2
Caputh Perth 219 A5
Car Colston Notts 115 A5
Carbis Bay Corn 2 B3
Carbost Highld 246 A2
Carbost Highld 259 D4
Carbrook S Yorks 130 A3
Carbrooke Norf 103 A5
Carburton Notts 131 B6
Carcant Borders 196 A2
Carcary Angus 233 C4
Carclaze Corn 5 B5
Carcroft S Yorks 140 B3
Cardenden Fife 209 A5
Cardeston Shrops 110 D2
Cardiff = Caerdydd Cardiff 41 D6
Cardiff Bay Barrage Cardiff 41 D6
Cardiff Castle Cardiff 41 D6
Cardiff International
Airport V Glam 41 E5
Cardigan = Aberteifi
Ceredig 73 B4
Cardington Beds 84 C2
Cardington Shrops 94 B3
Cardinham Corn 5 A6
Cardonald Glasgow 205 B5
Cardrona Borders 196 C2
Cardross Argyll 206 C1
Cardurnock Cumb 175 C4
Careby Lincs 116 D3
Careston Castle Angus 232 C3
Carew Pembs 55 D6
Carew Cheriton Pembs 55 D6
Carew Newton Pembs 55 D6

Carey Hereford 78 D3
Carfrae E Loth 210 D2
Cargenbridge Dumfries 174 A2
Cargill Perth 219 A6
Cargo Cumb 175 C6
Cargreen Corn 6 A3
Carham Northumb 198 C2
Carhampton Som 27 A5
Carharrack Corn 4 C2
Carie Perth 217 A6
Carie Perth 229 C5
Carines Corn 4 B2
Carisbrooke I o W 18 C3
Carisbrooke Castle I o W 18 C3
Cark Cumb 154 D2
Carlabhagh W Isles 288 C3
Carland Cross Corn 4 B3
Carlby Lincs 116 D3
Carlecotes S Yorks 139 C4
Carlesmoor N Yorks 157 D5
Carleton Cumb 164 C3
Carleton Cumb 176 D2
Carleton Lancs 144 D3
Carleton N Yorks 146 C3
Carleton Forehoe Norf 104 A1
Carleton Rode Norf 104 B2
Carlin How Redcar 169 D5
Carlingcott Bath 43 D5
Carlisle Cumb 175 C7
Carlisle Airport Cumb 176 C2
Carlisle Cathedral Cumb 175 C6
Carlisle Racecourse
Cumb 175 C6
Carlops Borders 195 A6
Carlton Beds 83 B6
Carlton Cambs 86 B2
Carlton Leics 97 A6
Carlton Notts 115 A4
Carlton N Yorks 159 C5
Carlton N Yorks 140 A4
Carlton N Yorks 157 C4
Carlton N Yorks 167 D4
Carlton Stockton 167 C6
Carlton Suff 89 A4
Carlton S Yorks 139 B6
Carlton W Yorks 139 A6
Carlton Colville Suff 105 C6
Carlton Curlieu Leics 98 B3
Carlton Husthwaite
N Yorks 158 D3
Carlton in Cleveland
N Yorks 158 A4
Carlton in Lindrick Notts 131 A5
Carlton le Moorland
Lincs 133 D4
Carlton Miniott N Yorks 158 C2
Carlton on Trent Notts 132 C2
Carlton Scroop Lincs 116 A2
Carluke S Lnrk 194 A3
Carmarthen =
Caerfyrddin Carms 73 D7
Carmel Anglesey 122 B3
Carmel Carms 57 A5
Carmel Flint 125 B6
Carmel Guern 6
Carmel Gwyn 107 A4
Carmont Aberds 245 D5
Carmunnock Glasgow 205 C6
Carmyle Glasgow 205 B6
Carmyllie Angus 232 D3
Carn-gorm Highld 249 D6
Carnaby E Yorks 151 A4
Carnach Highld 262 A2
Carnach Highld 250 D2
Carnach W Isles 288 H3
Carnachy Highld 278 C3
Càrnais W Isles 287 A5
Carnbee Fife 221 D5
Carnbo Perth 219 D5
Carnbrea Corn 3 A4
Carnduff S Lnrk 205 D6
Carnduncan Argyll 200 B2
Carne Corn 4 D4
Carnforth Lancs 154 D3
Carnhedryn Pembs 54 B4
Carnhell Green Corn 3 B4
Carnkie Corn 4 D2
Carnkie Corn 3 B4
Carno Powys 92 B3
Carnoch Highld 251 C5
Carnoch Highld 251 A4
Carnock Fife 208 B3
Carnon Downs Corn 4 C2
Carnousie Aberds 268 D1
Carnoustie Angus 221 A5
Carnwath S Lnrk 195 B4
Carnyorth Corn 2 B1
Carperby N Yorks 156 C4

Carpley Green N Yorks 156 C3
Carr S Yorks 140 D3
Carr Hill T & W 179 C4
Carradale Argyll 190 B4
Carragraich W Isles 288 H2
Carrbridge Highld 253 D5
Carrefour Selous Jersey 6
Carreg-wen Pembs 73 B5
Carreglefn Anglesey 122 B3
Carrick Argyll 214 D2
Carrick Fife 220 B4
Carrick Castle Argyll 215 C4
Carrick Ho. Orkney 282 C6
Carriden Falk 208 B3
Carrington Gtr Man 137 D6
Carrington Lincs 134 D3
Carrington Midloth 209 D6
Carrog Conwy 108 A2
Carrog Denb 109 A6
Carron Falk 208 B1
Carron Moray 254 B3
Carron Bridge N Lnrk 207 B5
Carronbridge Dumfries 183 C6
Carrshield Northumb 165 A6
Carrutherstown Dumfries 174 A4
Carrville Durham 167 A6
Carsaig Argyll 225 D4
Carsaig Argyll 213 D5
Carscreugh Dumfries 171 B4
Carse Gray Angus 232 C2
Carse Ho. Argyll 202 B2
Carsegowan Dumfries 171 B6
Carseriggan Dumfries 171 A5
Carsethorn Dumfries 174 C2
Carshalton London 49 C5
Carsington Derbys 130 D2
Carskiey Argyll 190 E2
Carsluith Dumfries 171 B6
Carsphairn Dumfries 182 C3
Carstairs S Lnrk 194 B4
Carstairs Junction S Lnrk 195 B4
Carswell Marsh Oxon 64 D4
Carter's Clay Hants 32 C2
Carterton Oxon 64 C3
Carterway Heads
Northumb 178 D2
Carthew Corn 5 B5
Carthorpe N Yorks 157 C7
Cartington Northumb 188 C3
Cartland S Lnrk 194 B3
Cartmel Cumb 154 D2
Cartmel Fell Cumb 154 C3
Cartmel Racecourse
Cumb 154 D2
Carway Carms 57 B4
Cary Fitzpaine Som 29 C5
Cas-gwent = Chepstow
Mon 62 D1
Cascob Powys 77 A6
Cashlie Perth 228 D3
Cashmere Visitor Centre,
Elgin Moray 266 C3
Cashmoor Dorset 30 D3
Casnewydd = Newport
Newport 42 A2
Cassey Compton Glos 63 B6
Cassington Oxon 65 B5
Cassop Durham 167 B6
Castell Denb 125 C6
Castell Coch Cardiff 41 C6
Castell-Howell Ceredig 74 D3
Castell-Nedd = Neath
Neath 40 B2
Castell Newydd Emlyn =
Newcastle Emlyn Carms 73 B6
Castell-y-bwch Torf 61 D4
Castellau Rhondda 41 C5
Casterton Cumb 155 D5
Castle Acre Norf 119 D5
Castle Ashby Northants 83 B5
Castle Bolton N Yorks 156 B4
Castle Bromwich W Mid 96 C4
Castle Bytham Lincs 116 D2
Castle Caereinion Powys 93 A5
Castle Camps Cambs 86 C2
Castle Carrock Cumb 176 D3
Castle Cary Som 29 B6
Castle Combe Wilts 44 B2
Castle Combe Motor
Racing Circuit Wilts 44 B2
Castle Donington Leics 114 C2
Castle Douglas Dumfries 173 B5
Castle Drogo, Exeter
Devon 12 B2
Castle Eaton Thamesdown 64 D2
Castle Eden Durham 168 B2
Castle Forbes Aberds 244 A3
Castle Frome Hereford 79 C4

Castle Green Sur 48 C2
Castle Gresley Derbys 113 D6
Castle Heaton Northumb 198 B3
Castle Hedingham Essex 86 D3
Castle Hill Kent 37 B4
Castle Howard, Malton
N Yorks 159 D6
Castle Huntly Perth 220 B3
Castle Kennedy Dumfries 170 B3
Castle O'er Dumfries 185 C5
Castle Pulverbatch Shrops 94 A2
Castle Rising Norf 118 C3
Castle Stuart Highld 252 B3
Castlebay = Bagh a
Chaisteil W Isles 286 G2
Castlebythe Pembs 55 B6
Castlecary N Lnrk 207 C5
Castlecraig Highld 265 D4
Castlefairn Dumfries 183 D5
Castleford W Yorks 140 A2
Castlehill Borders 195 C7
Castlehill Highld 280 B3
Castlehill W Dunb 206 C1
Castlemaddy Dumfries 182 D3
Castlemartin Pembs 55 E5
Castlemilk Dumfries 174 A4
Castlemilk Glasgow 205 C6
Castlemorris Pembs 55 A5
Castlemorton Worcs 79 D5
Castleside Durham 166 A3
Castlethorpe M Keynes 83 C5
Castleton Angus 232 D1
Castleton Argyll 214 D1
Castleton Derbys 129 A6
Castleton Gtr Man 138 B1
Castleton Newport 42 A1
Castleton N Yorks 159 A5
Castletown Ches 127 D4
Castletown Highld 280 B3
Castletown Highld 252 B3
Castletown I o M 152 E2
Castletown T & W 179 D5
Castleweary Borders 186 C3
Castley N Yorks 147 C6
Caston Norf 103 B5
Castor P'boro 100 B3
Catacol N Ayrs 203 D4
Catbrain S Glos 43 A4
Catbrook Mon 61 C7
Catchall Corn 2 C2
Catchems Corner W Mid 97 D5
Catchgate Durham 178 D3
Catcleugh Northumb 187 C6
Catcliffe S Yorks 131 A4
Catcott Som 28 B3
Caterham Sur 35 A6
Catfield Norf 121 C5
Catfirth Shetland 285 H6
Catford London 49 B6
Catforth Lancs 145 D4
Cathays Cardiff 41 D6
Cathcart Glasgow 205 B5
Cathedine Powys 60 A3
Catherington Hants 33 D5
Catherton Shrops 95 D4
Catlodge Highld 241 C4
Catlowdy Cumb 176 B2
Catmore W Berks 46 A2
Caton Lancs 145 A5
Caton Green Lancs 145 A5
Catrine E Ayrs 193 C5
Cat's Ash Newport 61 D5
Catsfield E Sus 23 A5
Catshill Worcs 96 D2
Cattal N Yorks 148 B3
Cattawade Suff 88 D2
Catterall Lancs 145 C4
Catterick N Yorks 157 B6
Catterick Bridge N Yorks 157 B6
Catterick Garrison
N Yorks 157 B5
Catterick Racecourse
N Yorks 157 B6
Catterlen Cumb 164 B2
Catterline Aberds 233 A6
Catterton N Yorks 148 C4
Catthorpe Leics 98 D2
Cattistock Dorset 15 B5
Catton Northumb 177 D6
Catton N Yorks 158 D2
Catwick E Yorks 151 C4
Catworth Cambs 100 D2
Caudlesprings Norf 103 A5
Caudwell's Mill, Matlock
Derbys 130 C2
Caulcott Oxon 65 A6
Cauldcots Angus 233 D4
Cauldhame Stirl 207 A4

Cauldmill Borders 186 B4
Cauldon Staffs 113 A4
Caulkerbush Dumfries 174 C2
Coulcido Dumfries 176 A2
Caunsall Worcs 95 C6
Caunton Notts 132 D2
Causeway End Dumfries 171 A6
Causeway Foot W Yorks 147 D4
Causeway-head Stirl 207 A5
Causewayend S Lnrk 195 C5
Causewayhead Cumb 174 C4
Causey Park Bridge
Northumb 189 D4
Causeyend Aberds 245 A6
Cautley N Yorks 155 B5
Cavendish Suff 87 C4
Cavendish Bridge Leics 114 C2
Cavenham Suff 86 A3
Caversfield Oxon 65 A6
Caversham Reading 47 B5
Caverswall Staffs 112 A3
Cavil E Yorks 149 D6
Cawdor Highld 253 B4
Cawdor Castle and
Gardens Highld 253 B4
Cawkwell Lincs 134 B2
Cawood N Yorks 149 D4
Cawsand Corn 6 B3
Cawston Norf 120 C3
Cawthorne S Yorks 139 C5
Cawthorpe Lincs 116 C3
Cawton N Yorks 159 D5
Caxton Cambs 85 B5
Caynham Shrops 94 D3
Caythorpe Lincs 116 A2
Caythorpe Notts 115 A4
Cayton N Yorks 161 C4
Ceann a Bhaigh W Isles 287 H2
Ceann a Deas Loch
Baghasdail W Isles 286 E3
Ceann Shiphoirt W Isles 288 F3
Ceann Tarabhaigh
W Isles 288 F3
Ceannacroc Lodge Highld 239 A5
Cearsiadair W Isles 288 F4
Cefn Berain Conwy 125 C4
Cefn-brith Conwy 125 D4
Cefn Canol Powys 110 B1
Cefn-coch Conwy 124 C3
Cefn Coch Powys 109 C6
Cefn-coed-y-cymmer
M Tydf 60 C2
Cefn Cribbwr Bridgend 40 C3
Cefn Cross Bridgend 40 C3
Cefn-ddwysarn Gwyn 109 B4
Cefn Einion Shrops 93 C6
Cefn-gorwydd Powys 76 C3
Cefn-mawr Wrex 110 A1
Cefn-y-bedd Flint 126 D3
Cefn-y-pant Carms 73 D4
Cefneithin Carms 57 A5
Cei-bach Ceredig 73 A7
Ceinewydd = New Quay
Ceredig 73 A6
Ceint Anglesey 123 C4
Cellan Ceredig 75 C5
Cellarhead Staffs 112 A3
Cemaes Anglesey 122 A3
Cemmaes Powys 91 B5
Cemmaes Road Powys 91 B5
Cenarth Carms 73 B5
Cenin Gwyn 107 B4
Central Invclyd 204 A2
Ceos W Isles 288 E4
Ceres Fife 220 C4
Cerne Abbas Dorset 15 B6
Cerney Wick Glos 63 D6
Cerrigceinwen Anglesey 123 C4
Cerrigydrudion Conwy 109 A4
Cessford Borders 187 A6
Ceunant Gwyn 123 D5
Chaceley Glos 79 D6
Chacewater Corn 4 C2
Chackmore Bucks 82 D3
Chacombe Northants 82 C1
Chad Valley W Mid 96 C3
Chadderton Gtr Man 138 C2
Chadderton Fold Gtr Man 138 C1
Chaddesden Derby 114 B1
Chaddesley Corbett Worcs 96 D2
Chaddleworth W Berks 46 B2
Chadlington Oxon 64 A4
Chadshunt Warks 81 B6
Chadwell Leics 115 C5
Chadwell St Mary Thurrock 50 B3
Chadwick End W Mid 97 D5
Chadwick Green Mers 136 D4
Chaffcombe Som 28 D3

Chagford Devon 12 C2
Chailey E Sus 22 A1
Chain Bridge Lincs 117 A6
Chainbridge Cambs 101 A6
Chainhurst Kent 37 B5
Chalbury Dorset 17 A4
Chalbury Common Dorset 17 A4
Chaldon Sur 35 A6
Chaldon Herring Dorset 16 C1
Chale I o W 18 D3
Chale Green I o W 18 D3
Chalfont Common Bucks 67 D5
Chalfont St Giles Bucks 67 D4
Chalfont St Peter Bucks 67 D5
Chalford Glos 63 C4
Chalgrove Oxon 66 D1
Chalk Kent 50 B3
Challacombe Devon 26 A1
Challoch Dumfries 171 A5
Challock Kent 52 D2
Chalton Beds 67 A5
Chalton Hants 33 D6
Chalvington E Sus 22 B3
Chancery Ceredig 75 A4
Chandler's Ford Hants 32 C3
Channel Tunnel Kent 38 B3
Channerwick Shetland 285 L6
Chantry Som 29 A7
Chantry Suff 88 C2
Chapel Fife 209 A5
Chapel Allerton Som 42 D3
Chapel Allerton W Yorks 148 D2
Chapel Amble Corn 9 D5
Chapel Brampton
  Northants 83 A4
Chapel Chorlton Staffs 112 B2
Chapel-en-le-Frith
  Derbys 129 A5
Chapel End Warks 97 B6
Chapel Green Warks 97 C5
Chapel Green Warks 82 A1
Chapel Haddlesey
  N Yorks 140 A3
Chapel Head Cambs 101 C5
Chapel Hill Aberds 257 C5
Chapel Hill Lincs 134 D2
Chapel Hill Mon 62 D1
Chapel Hill N Yorks 148 C2
Chapel Lawn Shrops 93 D7
Chapel-le-Dale N Yorks 155 D6
Chapel Milton Derbys 129 A5
Chapel Row W Berks 46 C3
Chapel St Leonards Lincs 135 B5
Chapel Stile Cumb 154 A2
Chapelgate Lincs 117 C7
Chapelhall N Lnrk 207 D5
Chapelhill Dumfries 184 C3
Chapelhill Highld 265 C4
Chapelhill N Ayrs 204 D2
Chapelhill Perth 220 B2
Chapelhill Perth 219 A5
Chapelknowe Dumfries 175 A6
Chapelton Angus 233 D4
Chapelton Devon 25 C6
Chapelton Highld 242 A2
Chapelton S Lnrk 194 B1
Chapeltown Blkburn 137 B6
Chapeltown Moray 254 D3
Chapeltown S Yorks 139 D6
Chapmans Well Devon 11 B4
Chapmanslade Wilts 30 A2
Chapmore End Herts 68 B3
Chappel Essex 70 A2
Charaton Som 14 A3
Chardstock Devon 14 A3
Charfield S Glos 62 D3
Charford Worcs 80 A2
Charing Kent 38 A1
Charing Cross Dorset 31 D5
Charing Heath Kent 38 A1
Charingworth Glos 81 D5
Charlbury Oxon 65 B4
Charlcombe Bath 43 C6
Charlecote Warks 81 B5
Charlecote Park,
  Wellesbourne Warks 81 B5
Charles Devon 26 B1
Charles Manning's
  Amusement Park,
  Felixstowe Suff 88 D3
Charles Tye Suff 87 B6
Charlesfield Dumfries 175 B4
Charleston Angus 232 D1
Charleston Renfs 205 B4
Charlestown Aberdeen 245 B6
Charlestown Corn 5 B5
Charlestown Derbys 138 D3

Charlestown Dorset 15 D6
Charlestown Fife 208 B3
Charlestown Gtr Man 137 C7
Charlestown Highld 252 B2
Charlestown Highld 261 C5
Charlestown W Yorks 138 A2
Charlestown of Aberlour
  Moray 254 B3
Charlesworth Derbys 138 D3
Charleton Devon 7 C6
Charlton London 49 B7
Charlton Hants 32 A2
Charlton Herts 68 A1
Charlton Northants 82 D2
Charlton Northumb 177 A6
Charlton Som 43 D5
Charlton Telford 111 D4
Charlton Wilts 30 C3
Charlton Wilts 45 D5
Charlton Wilts 44 A3
Charlton Worcs 80 C3
Charlton Abbots Glos 63 A6
Charlton Adam Som 29 C5
Charlton-All-Saints Wilts 31 C5
Charlton Down Dorset 15 B6
Charlton Horethorne Som 29 C6
Charlton Kings Glos 63 A5
Charlton Mackerell Som 29 C5
Charlton Marshall Dorset 16 A2
Charlton Musgrove Som 29 C7
Charlton on Otmoor Oxon 65 B6
Charltons Redcar 168 D4
Charlwood Sur 35 B5
Charlynch Som 28 B2
Charminster Dorset 15 B6
Charmouth Dorset 14 B3
Charndon Bucks 66 A1
Charney Bassett Oxon 65 D4
Charnock Richard Lancs 137 B4
Charsfield Suff 88 B3
Chart Corner Kent 37 A5
Chart Sutton Kent 37 B6
Charter Alley Hants 46 D3
Charterhouse Som 42 D3
Charterville Allotments
  Oxon 64 B4
Chartham Kent 52 D3
Chartham Hatch Kent 52 D3
Chartridge Bucks 67 C4
Chartwell, Westerham
  Kent 36 A2
Charvil Wokingham 47 B5
Charwelton Northants 82 B2
Chasetown Staffs 96 A3
Chastleton Oxon 64 A3
Chasty Devon 10 A4
Chatburn Lancs 146 C1
Chatcull Staffs 112 B1
Chatham Medway 51 C4
Chathill Northumb 189 A4
Chatsworth, Bakewell
  Derbys 130 B2
Chattenden Medway 51 B4
Chatteris Cambs 101 C5
Chattisham Suff 88 C1
Chatto Borders 187 B6
Chatton Northumb 188 A3
Chawleigh Devon 26 D2
Chawley Oxon 65 C5
Chawston Beds 84 B3
Chawton Hants 33 B6
Cheadle Gtr Man 128 A3
Cheadle Staffs 112 A4
Cheadle Heath Gtr Man 128 A3
Cheadle Hulme Gtr Man 128 A3
Cheam London 49 C5
Cheapside Sur 34 A3
Chearsley Bucks 66 B2
Chebsey Staffs 112 C2
Checkendon Oxon 47 A4
Checkley Ches 111 A6
Checkley Hereford 78 D3
Checkley Staffs 112 B4
Chedburgh Suff 86 B3
Cheddar Som 42 D3
Cheddar Showcaves and
  Gorge Som 42 D3
Cheddington Bucks 67 B4
Cheddleton Staffs 129 D4
Cheddon Fitzpaine Som 28 C2
Chedglow Wilts 63 D5
Chedgrave Norf 105 B4
Chedington Dorset 15 A4
Chediston Suff 105 D4
Chedworth Glos 63 B6
Chedworth Roman Villa
  Glos 63 B6

Chedzoy Som 28 B3
Cheeklaw Borders 198 A1
Cheeseman's Green Kent 38 B2
Cheglinch Devon 25 A6
Cheldon Devon 26 D2
Chelford Ches 128 B3
Chell Heath Stoke 128 D3
Chellaston Derby 114 B1
Chellington Beds 83 B6
Chelmarsh Shrops 95 C5
Chelmer Village Essex 70 C1
Chelmondiston Suff 88 D3
Chelmorton Derbys 129 C6
Chelmsford Essex 69 C7
Chelsea London 49 B5
Chelsfield London 50 C1
Chelsworth Suff 87 C5
Cheltenham Glos 63 A5
Cheltenham Racecourse
  Glos 63 A5
Chelveston Northants 84 A1
Chelvey N Som 42 C3
Chelwood Bath 43 C5
Chelwood Common E Sus 36 D2
Chelwood Gate E Sus 36 D2
Chelworth Wilts 63 D5
Chelworth Green Wilts 64 D1
Chemistry Shrops 111 A4
Chenies Bucks 67 D5
Cheny Longville Shrops 94 C2
Chepstow = Cas-gwent
  Mon 62 D1
Chepstow Racecourse
  Mon 62 D1
Chequerfield W Yorks 140 A1
Cherhill Wilts 44 B4
Cherington Glos 63 D5
Cherington Warks 81 D5
Cheriton Devon 26 A2
Cheriton Hants 33 C4
Cheriton Kent 38 B3
Cheriton Swansea 57 C4
Cheriton Bishop Devon 12 B2
Cheriton Fitzpaine Devon 12 A3
Cheriton or Stackpole
  Elidor Pembs 55 E5
Cherrington Telford 111 C5
Cherry Burton E Yorks 150 C2
Cherry Hinton Cambs 85 B6
Cherry Orchard Worcs 79 B6
Cherry Willingham Lincs 133 B5
Cherrybank Perth 219 B6
Chertsey Sur 48 C3
Cheselbourne Dorset 16 B1
Chesham Bucks 67 C4
Chesham Bois Bucks 67 D4
Cheshire Candle
  Workshops,
  Burwardsley Ches 127 D5
Cheshunt Herts 68 C3
Chesley Hay Staffs 96 A2
Chessington London 49 C4
Chessington World of
  Adventures London 49 C4
Chester Ches 127 C4
Chester Cathedral Ches 126 C3
Chester-Le-Street
  Durham 179 D4
Chester Moor Durham 167 A5
Chester Racecourse Ches 126 C3
Chester Zoo Ches 127 B4
Chesterblade Som 29 A6
Chesterfield Derbys 130 B3
Chesters Borders 187 B5
Chesters Borders 187 A5
Chesters Roman Fort
  Northumb 177 B7
Chesterton Cambs 100 B3
Chesterton Cambs 85 A6
Chesterton Oxon 63 C6
Chesterton Oxon 65 A6
Chesterton Shrops 95 B5
Chesterton Staffs 112 A2
Chesterton Warks 81 B6
Chesterwood Northumb 177 C6
Chestfield Kent 52 C3
Cheston Devon 7 B5
Cheswardine Shrops 111 C6
Cheswick Northumb 198 B4
Chetnole Dorset 15 A6
Chettiscombe Devon 27 D4
Chettisham Cambs 102 C1
Chettle Dorset 30 D3
Chetton Shrops 95 B4
Chetwode Bucks 66 A1
Chetwynd Aston Telford 111 D6
Cheveley Cambs 86 A2
Chevening Kent 36 A2

Chevington Suff 86 B3
Chevithorne Devon 27 D4
Chew Magna Bath 43 C4
Chew Stoke Bath 43 C4
Chewton Keynsham Bath 43 C5
Chewton Mendip Som 43 D4
Chicheley M Keynes 83 C6
Chichester W Sus 20 B1
Chichester Cathedral
  W Sus 20 B1
Chickering Suff 104 D3
Chickerell Dorset 15 C6
Chicklade Wilts 30 B3
Chicksgrove Wilts 30 B3
Chidden Hants 33 D5
Chiddingfold Sur 34 C2
Chiddingly E Sus 22 A3
Chiddingstone Kent 36 B2
Chiddingstone Causeway
  Kent 36 B3
Chiddingstone Hoath Kent 36 B2
Chideock Dorset 14 B4
Chidham W Sus 19 A6
Chidswell W Yorks 139 A5
Chieveley W Berks 46 B2
Chignall St James Essex 69 C6
Chignall Smealy Essex 69 B6
Chigwell Essex 68 D4
Chigwell Row Essex 69 D4
Chilbolton Hants 32 B2
Chilcomb Hants 32 C4
Chilcombe Dorset 15 B5
Chilcompton Som 43 D5
Chilcote Leics 113 D6
Child Okeford Dorset 30 D2
Childer Thornton Ches 126 B3
Childrey Oxon 46 A1
Child's Ercall Shrops 111 C5
Childswickham Worcs 80 D3
Childwall Mers 127 A4
Childwick Green Herts 67 B6
Chilfrome Dorset 15 B5
Chilgrove W Sus 20 A1
Chilham Kent 52 D2
Chilhampton Wilts 31 B4
Chilla Devon 11 A5
Chillaton Devon 11 C5
Chillenden Kent 53 D4
Chillerton I o W 18 C3
Chillesford Suff 89 B4
Chillingham Northumb 188 A3
Chillington Devon 8 C1
Chillington Som 28 D3
Chilmark Wilts 30 B3
Chilson Oxon 64 B4
Chilsworthy Corn 11 D5
Chilsworthy Devon 10 A4
Chilthorne Domer Som 29 D5
Chiltington E Sus 22 A1
Chilton Bucks 66 B1
Chilton Durham 167 C5
Chilton Oxon 46 A2
Chilton Cantelo Som 29 C5
Chilton Foliat Wilts 45 B7
Chilton Lane Durham 167 B6
Chilton Polden Som 28 B3
Chilton Street Suff 86 C3
Chilton Trinity Som 28 B2
Chilvers Coton Warks 97 B6
Chilwell Notts 114 B3
Chilworth Hants 32 D3
Chilworth Sur 34 B3
Chimney Oxon 65 C4
Chineham Hants 47 D4
Chingford London 68 D3
Chinley Derbys 129 A5
Chinley Head Derbys 129 A5
Chinnor Oxon 66 C2
Chipnall Shrops 111 B6
Chippenhall Green Suff 104 D3
Chippenham Cambs 86 A2
Chippenham Wilts 44 B3
Chipperfield Herts 67 C5
Chipping Herts 85 D5
Chipping Lancs 145 C6
Chipping Campden Glos 81 D4
Chipping Hill Essex 70 B2
Chipping Norton Oxon 64 A4
Chipping Ongar Essex 69 C5
Chipping Sodbury S Glos 43 A6
Chipping Warden
  Northants 82 C1
Chipstable Som 27 C5
Chipstead Kent 36 A2
Chipstead Sur 35 A5
Chirbury Shrops 93 B6
Chirk = Y Waun Wrex 110 B1
Chirk Bank Shrops 110 B1
Chirk Castle Wrex 110 B1

Chirmorrie S Ayrs 181 D4
Chirnside Borders 198 A2
Chirnsidebridge Borders 198 A2
Chirton Wilts 45 D4
Chisbury Wilts 45 C6
Chiselborough Som 29 D4
Chiseldon Thamesdown 45 B5
Chiserley W Yorks 138 A3
Chislehampton Oxon 65 D6
Chislehurst London 50 B1
Chislet Kent 53 C4
Chiswell Green Herts 67 C6
Chiswick London 49 B5
Chiswick End Cambs 85 C5
Chisworth Derbys 138 D2
Chithurst W Sus 34 D1
Chittering Cambs 101 D6
Chitterne Wilts 30 A3
Chittlehamholt Devon 26 C1
Chittlehampton Devon 26 C1
Chittoe Wilts 44 C3
Chivenor Devon 25 B6
Chobham Sur 48 C2
Choicelee Borders 197 A6
Cholderton Wilts 31 A6
Cholesbury Bucks 67 C4
Chollerford Northumb 177 B7
Chollerton Northumb 178 B1
Cholmondeston Ches 127 C6
Cholsey Oxon 46 A3
Cholstrey Hereford 78 B2
Chop Gate N Yorks 159 B4
Choppington Northumb 179 A4
Chopwell T & W 178 D3
Chorley Ches 127 D5
Chorley Lancs 137 B4
Chorley Shrops 95 C4
Chorley Staffs 113 D4
Chorleywood Herts 67 D5
Chorlton cum Hardy
  Gtr Man 137 D7
Chorlton Lane Ches 110 A3
Choulton Shrops 94 C1
Chowdene T & W 179 D4
Chowley Ches 127 D4
Chrishall Essex 85 D6
Christ Church Oxford Oxon 65 C6
Christchurch Cambs 101 B6
Christchurch Dorset 17 B5
Christchurch Glos 62 B1
Christchurch Newport 42 A2
Christchurch Priory Dorset 17 B5
Christian Malford Wilts 44 B3
Christleton Ches 127 C4
Christmas Common Oxon 66 D2
Christon N Som 42 D2
Christon Bank Northumb 189 A5
Christow Devon 12 C3
Chryston N Lnrk 207 C4
Chudleigh Devon 12 D3
Chudleigh Knighton Devon 12 D3
Chulmleigh Devon 26 D1
Chunal Derbys 138 D3
Church Lancs 137 A6
Church Aston Telford 111 D6
Church Brampton
  Northants 83 A4
Church Broughton
  Derbys 113 B6
Church Crookham Hants 47 D6
Church Eaton Staffs 112 D2
Church End Beds 67 A4
Church End Beds 84 D1
Church End Beds 84 D1
Church End Cambs 100 C4
Church End Cambs 101 A5
Church End E Yorks 150 B3
Church End Essex 86 C1
Church End Essex 69 A7
Church End Hants 47 D4
Church End Lincs 117 B5
Church End Warks 97 B5
Church End Warks 97 B5
Church End Wilts 44 B4
Church Enstone Oxon 65 A4
Church Fenton N Yorks 148 D4
Church Green Devon 14 B1
Church Green Norf 103 B6
Church Gresley Derbys 113 D6
Church Hanborough Oxon 65 B5
Church Hill Ches 127 C6
Church Houses N Yorks 159 B5
Church Knowle Dorset 16 C3
Church Laneham Notts 132 B3
Church Langton Leics 99 B4

Church Lawford Warks 98 B1
Church Lawton Ches 128 D3
Church Leigh Staffs 112 B4
Church Lench Worcs 80 B3
Church Mayfield Staffs 113 A5
Church Minshull Ches 127 C6
Church Norton W Sus 20 B3
Church Preen Shrops 94 B3
Church Pulverbatch
  Shrops 94 A2
Church Stoke Powys 93 B6
Church Stowe Northants 82 B3
Church Street Kent 51 B4
Church Stretton Shrops 94 B2
Church Town N Lincs 141 C5
Church Town Sur 35 A6
Church Village Rhondda 41 C5
Church Warsop Notts 131 C5
Churcham Glos 62 B3
Churchbank Shrops 93 D7
Churchbridge Staffs 96 A2
Churchdown Glos 63 B4
Churchend Essex 69 A6
Churchend Essex 71 D4
Churchend S Glos 62 D3
Churchfield W Mid 96 B3
Churchgate Street Essex 69 B4
Churchill Devon 25 B4
Churchill Devon 14 A3
Churchill N Som 42 D3
Churchill Oxon 64 A3
Churchill Worcs 96 D1
Churchill Worcs 80 B2
Churchinford Som 28 D2
Churchover Warks 98 C2
Churchstanton Som 28 D1
Churchstow Devon 7 C6
Churchtown Derbys 130 C2
Churchtown I o M 152 B4
Churchtown Lancs 145 C4
Churchtown Mers 136 B2
Churnsike Lodge
  Northumb 177 B4
Churston Ferrers Torbay 8 B3
Churt Sur 34 C1
Churton Ches 127 D4
Churwell W Yorks 139 A5
Chute Standen Wilts 45 D7
Chwilog Gwyn 107 C4
Chyandour Corn 2 B2
Cilan Uchaf Gwyn 106 D2
Cilcain Flint 126 C1
Cilcennin Ceredig 75 B4
Cifor Gwyn 107 C6
Cifrew Neath 40 A2
Cifynydd Rhondda 41 B5
Cilgerran Pembs 73 B4
Cilgwyn Carms 59 C4
Cilgwyn Gwyn 107 A4
Cilgwyn Pembs 72 C3
Ciliau Aeron Ceredig 74 C3
Cill Donnain W Isles 286 D3
Cille Bhrighde W Isles 286 E3
Cille Pheadair W Isles 286 E3
Cilmery Powys 76 B4
Cilsan Carms 58 C2
Ciltalgarth Gwyn 108 A3
Cilwendeg Pembs 73 C5
Cilybebyll Neath 40 A2
Cilycwm Carms 59 B4
Cimla Neath 40 B2
Cinderford Glos 62 B2
Cippyn Pembs 72 B4
Circebost W Isles 288 D2
Cirencester Glos 63 C6
Ciribhig W Isles 288 C2
City Powys 93 C6
City Dulas Anglesey 123 B4
City of London =
  London, City of London 49 A6
Clachaig Argyll 215 D4
Clachan Argyll 202 C2
Clachan Argyll 213 A5
Clachan Argyll 226 B3
Clachan Argyll 215 A4
Clachan Highld 248 C2
Clachan W Isles 286 B3
Clachan na Luib W Isles 287 H3
Clachan of Campsie
  E Dunb 205 A6
Clachan of Glendaruel
  Argyll 214 D2
Clachan-Seil Argyll 213 A5
Clachan Strachur Argyll 214 B3
Clachaneasy Dumfries 181 D5

Clachanmore Dumfries 170 C2
Clachbreck Argyll 202 A2
Clachnabrain Angus 232 B1
Clachtoll Highld 270 B3
Clackmannan Clack 208 A2
Clacton-on-Sea Essex 71 B5
Cladach Chireboist
  W Isles 287 H2
Claddach-knockline
  W Isles 287 H2
Cladich Argyll 227 D5
Claggan Highld 225 B5
Claggan Highld 237 B5
Claigan Highld 258 C2
Claines Worcs 79 B6
Clandown Bath 43 D5
Clanfield Hants 33 D5
Clanfield Oxon 64 C3
Clanville Hants 32 A2
Claonaig Argyll 202 C3
Claonel Highld 272 D3
Clap Hill Kent 38 B2
Clapgate Dorset 17 A4
Clapgate Herts 68 A4
Clapham Beds 84 B2
Clapham London 49 B5
Clapham N Yorks 146 A1
Clapham W Sus 20 B3
Clappers Borders 198 A3
Clappersgate Cumb 154 A2
Clapton Som 14 A4
Clapton-in-Gordano
  N Som 42 B3
Clapton-on-the-Hill Glos 64 B2
Clapworthy Devon 26 C1
Clarbeston Pembs 55 B6
Clarbeston Road Pembs 55 B6
Clarborough Notts 132 A2
Clardon Highld 280 B3
Clare Suff 86 C3
Clarebrand Dumfries 173 B5
Claremont Landscape
  Garden, Esher Sur 48 C4
Clarencefield Dumfries 174 B3
Clarilaw Borders 186 B4
Clark's Green Sur 35 C4
Clarkston E Renf 205 C5
Clashandorran Highld 251 B7
Clashcoig Highld 264 A2
Clashindarroch Aberds 255 C5
Clashmore Highld 270 A3
Clashmore Highld 264 A3
Clashnessie Highld 270 A3
Clashnoir Moray 254 D3
Clate Shetland 285 G7
Clathy Perth 219 C4
Clatt Aberds 255 D6
Clatter Powys 92 B3
Clatterford I o W 18 C3
Clatterin Bridge Aberds 233 A4
Clatworthy Som 27 B5
Claughton Lancs 145 C5
Claughton Lancs 145 A5
Claughton Mers 126 A3
Claverdon Warks 81 A4
Claverham N Som 42 C3
Clavering Essex 85 D6
Claverley Shrops 95 B5
Claverton Bath 44 C1
Clawdd-newydd Denb 125 D5
Clawthorpe Cumb 154 D4
Clawton Devon 11 B4
Claxby Lincs 142 D3
Claxby Lincs 135 B4
Claxton Norf 104 A4
Claxton N Yorks 149 A5
Clay Common Suff 105 C5
Clay Coton Northants 98 D2
Clay Cross Derbys 130 C3
Clay Hill W Berks 46 B3
Clay Lake Lincs 117 C5
Claybokie Aberds 242 D3
Claybrooke Magna Leics 98 C1
Claybrooke Parva Leics 98 C1
Claydon Oxon 82 B1
Claydon Suff 88 B2
Claygate Dumfries 175 A6
Claygate Kent 37 B5
Claygate Sur 49 C4
Claygate Cross Kent 36 A4
Clayhanger Devon 27 C5
Clayhanger W Mid 96 A3
Clayhidon Devon 27 D6
Clayhill E Sus 37 D6
Clayhill Hants 18 A2
Clayock Highld 280 C3

Claypole Lincs 115 A6
Clayton Staffs 112 A2
Clayton S Yorks 140 C2
Clayton W Sus 21 A5
Clayton W Yorks 147 D5
Clayton Green Lancs 137 A4
Clayton-le-Moors Lancs 146 D1
Clayton-le-Woods Lancs 137 A4
Clayton West W Yorks 139 B5
Clayworth Notts 132 A2
Cleadale Highld 234 B3
Cleadon T & W 179 C5
Clearbrook Devon 7 A4
Clearwell Glos 62 C1
Cleasby N Yorks 167 D5
Cleat Orkney 283 K5
Cleatlam Durham 166 D4
Cleator Cumb 162 C3
Cleator Moor Cumb 162 C3
Clebrig Highld 272 A3
Clee St Margaret Shrops 94 C3
Cleedownton Shrops 94 C3
Cleehill Shrops 94 D3
Cleethorpes NE Lincs 143 C5
Cleeton St Mary Shrops 95 D4
Cleeve N Som 42 C3
Cleeve Hill Glos 63 A5
Cleeve Prior Worcs 80 C3
Clegyrnant Powys 91 B7
Clehonger Hereford 78 D2
Cleish Perth 208 A3
Cleland N Lnrk 194 A3
Clench Common Wilts 45 C5
Clenchwarton Norf 118 C2
Clent Worcs 96 D2
Cleobury Mortimer Shrops 95 D4
Cleobury North Shrops 95 C4
Cleongart Argyll 190 B2
Clephanton Highld 253 A4
Clerklands Borders 186 A4
Clestrain Orkney 283 G4
Cleuch Head Borders 187 B4
Cleughbrae Dumfries 174 A3
Clevancy Wilts 45 B4
Clevedon N Som 42 B3
Cleveley Oxon 65 A4
Cleveleys Lancs 144 C3
Cleverton Wilts 44 A3
Clevis Bridgend 40 D3
Clewer Som 42 D3
Cley next the Sea Norf 120 A2
Cliaid W Isles 286 F2
Cliasmol W Isles 287 D5
Clibburn Cumb 164 C3
Click Mill Orkney 282 E4
Cliddesden Hants 33 A5
Cliff End E Sus 23 A6
Cliffburn Angus 233 D4
Cliffe Medway 51 B4
Cliffe N Yorks 149 D5
Cliffe Woods Medway 51 B4
Clifford Hereford 77 C6
Clifford W Yorks 148 C3
Clifford Chambers Warks 81 B4
Clifford's Mesne Glos 62 A3
Cliffsend Kent 53 C5
Clifton Beds 84 D3
Clifton Bristol 43 B4
Clifton Cumb 164 C3
Clifton Derbys 113 A5
Clifton Lancs 145 D4
Clifton Nottingham 114 B3
Clifton Northumb 179 A4
Clifton N Yorks 147 C5
Clifton Oxon 82 D1
Clifton Stirl 216 A3
Clifton S Yorks 140 D3
Clifton Worcs 79 C6
Clifton York 149 B4
Clifton Campville Staffs 113 D6
Clifton Green Gtr Man 137 C6
Clifton Hampden Oxon 65 D6
Clifton Reynes M Keynes 83 B6
Clifton upon Dunsmore
  Warks 98 D2
Clifton upon Teme Worcs 79 A5
Cliftoncote Borders 187 A7
Cliftonville Kent 53 B5
Climaen gwyn Neath 59 E4
Climping W Sus 20 B3
Climpy S Lnrk 194 A4
Clink Som 30 A1
Clint N Yorks 147 B6
Clint Green Norf 120 D2
Clintmains Borders 197 C5
Cliobh W Isles 287 A5
Clippesby Norf 121 D6

Clipsham Rutland 116 D2
Clipston Northants 99 C4
Clipstone Notts 131 C5
Clitheroe Lancs 146 C1
Cliuthar W Isles 288 H2
Clive Shrops 111 C4
Clivocast Shetland 284 C8
Clixby Lincs 142 C3
Clocaenog Denb 125 D5
Clochan Moray 267 C5
Clock Face Mers 136 D4
Clockmill Borders 197 A6
Cloddiau Powys 93 A6
Clodock Hereford 61 A5
Clola Aberds 257 B5
Clophill Beds 84 D2
Clopton Northants 100 C2
Clopton Suff 88 B3
Clopton Corner Suff 88 B3
Clopton Green Suff 86 B3
Close Clark I o M 152 D2
Closeburn Dumfries 183 C6
Closworth Som 29 D5
Clothall Herts 85 D4
Clotton Ches 127 C5
Clough Foot W Yorks 138 A2
Cloughton N Yorks 160 B4
Cloughton Newlands
  N Yorks 160 B4
Clousta Shetland 285 H5
Clouston Orkney 282 F3
Clova Aberds 255 D5
Clova Angus 232 A1
Clove Lodge Durham 166 D2
Clovelly Devon 24 C4
Clovelly Village Devon 24 C4
Clovenfords Borders 196 C3
Clovenstone Aberds 245 A4
Clovullin Highld 237 C4
Clow Bridge Lancs 137 A7
Clowne Derbys 131 B4
Clows Top Worcs 95 D5
Cloy Wrex 110 A2
Cluanie Inn Highld 239 A4
Cluanie Lodge Highld 239 A4
Clun Shrops 93 C7
Clunbury Shrops 94 C1
Clunderwen Carms 55 C7
Clune Highld 252 D3
Clunes Highld 239 D6
Clungunford Shrops 94 D1
Clunie Aberds 268 D1
Clunie Perth 231 D5
Clunton Shrops 94 C1
Cluny Fife 209 A5
Cluny Castle Highld 241 C4
Clutton Bath 43 D5
Clutton Ches 127 D4
Clwt-grugoer Conwy 125 C4
Clwt-y-bont Gwyn 123 D5
Clydach Mon 60 B4
Clydach Swansea 40 A1
Clydach Vale Rhondda 41 B4
Clydebank W Dunb 205 A4
Clydey Pembs 73 C5
Clyffe Pypard Wilts 45 B4
Clynder Argyll 215 D5
Clyne Neath 40 A3
Clynelish Highld 274 D2
Clynnog-fawr Gwyn 107 A4
Clyro Powys 77 C6
Clyst Honiton Devon 13 B4
Clyst Hydon Devon 13 A5
Clyst St George Devon 13 C4
Clyst St Lawrence Devon 13 A5
Clyst St Mary Devon 13 B4
Cnoc Amhlaigh W Isles 288 D6
Cnwch-coch Ceredig 75 A5
Coachford Aberds 255 B5
Coad's Green Corn 10 D3
Coal Aston Derbys 130 B3
Coalbrookdale Telford 95 A4
Coalbrookvale Bl Gwent 60 C3
Coalburn S Lnrk 194 C3
Coalburns T & W 178 C3
Coalcleugh Northumb 165 A6
Coaley Glos 62 C3
Coalhall E Ayrs 182 A2
Coalhill Essex 70 D1
Coalpit Heath S Glos 43 A5
Coalport Telford 95 A4
Coalsnaughton Clack 208 A2
Coaltown of Balgonie
  Fife 209 A5
Coaltown of Wemyss Fife 209 A6
Coalville Leics 114 D2
Coalway Glos 62 B1
Coat Som 29 C4

Coatbridge N Lnrk 207 D5
Coatdyke N Lnrk 207 D5
Coate Thamesdown 45 A5
Coate Wilts 44 C4
Coates Cambs 101 B5
Coates Glos 63 C5
Coates Lancs 146 C2
Coates Notts 132 A3
Coates W Sus 20 A2
Coatham Redcar 168 C3
Coatham Mundeville Darl 167 C5
Coatsgate Dumfries 184 B3
Cobbaton Devon 25 C7
Cobbler's Green Norf 104 B3
Coberley Glos 63 B5
Cobham Kent 50 C3
Cobham Sur 48 C4
Cobholm Island Norf 105 A6
Cobleland Stirl 206 A3
Cobnash Hereford 78 A2
Coburty Aberds 269 C4
Cock Bank Wrex 110 A2
Cock Bridge Aberds 243 B5
Cock Clarks Essex 70 C2
Cockayne N Yorks 159 B5
Cockayne Hatley Cambs 85 C4
Cockburnspath Borders 211 C4
Cockenzie and Port
  Seton E Loth 209 C7
Cockerham Lancs 145 B4
Cockermouth Cumb 163 A4
Cockernhoe Green Herts 67 A6
Cockfield Durham 166 C4
Cockfield Suff 87 B5
Cockfosters London 68 D2
Cocking W Sus 20 A1
Cockington Torbay 8 A2
Cocklake Som 28 A4
Cockley Beck Cumb 163 D5
Cockley Cley Norf 102 A3
Cockshutt Shrops 110 C3
Cockthorpe Norf 120 A4
Cockwood Devon 13 C4
Cockyard Hereford 78 D2
Codda Corn 10 D2
Coddenham Suff 88 B2
Coddington Ches 127 D4
Coddington Hereford 79 C5
Coddington Notts 132 D2
Codford St Mary Wilts 30 B3
Codford St Peter Wilts 30 B3
Codicote Herts 68 B2
Codmore Hill W Sus 34 D2
Codnor Derbys 114 A2
Codrington S Glos 43 B5
Codsall Staffs 95 A6
Codsall Wood Staffs 95 A6
Coed Duon = Blackwood
  Caerph 41
Coed Mawr Gwyn 123
Coed Morgan Mon 61
Coed-Talon Flint 126
Coed-y-bryn Ceredig 73
Coed-y-paen Mon 61
Coed-yr-ynys Powys 60
Coed Ystumgwern Gwyn 107
Coedely Rhondda 41
Coedkernew Newport 42
Coedpoeth Wrex 126
Coedway Powys 110
Coelbren Powys 59
Coffinswell Devon 8
Cofton Hackett Worcs 96
Cogan V Glam 41
Cogenhoe Northants 83
Cogges Oxon 65
Coggeshall Essex 70
Coggeshall Hamlet Essex 70
Coggins Mill E Sus 36
Coig Peighinnean W Isles 288
Coig Peighinnean
  Bhuirgh W Isles 288
Coignafearn Lodge
  Highld 24
Coilacriech Aberds 243
Coilantogle Stirl 217
Coilleag W Isles 286
Coillore Highld 246
Coity Bridgend 40
Col W Isles 288
Col Uarach W Isles 288
Colaboll Highld 272
Colan Corn
Colaton Raleigh Devon 1
Colbost Highld 25
Colburn N Yorks 15
Colby Cumb 16
Colby I o M 15

Colby Norf 120 B4
Colchester Essex 71 A4
Colchester Zoo Essex 70 A3
Colcot V Glam 41 E6
Cold Ash W Berks 46 C3
Cold Ashby Northants 98 D3
Cold Ashton S Glos 43 B6
Cold Aston Glos 64 B2
Cold Blow Pembs 55 C7
Cold Brayfield M Keynes 83 B6
Cold Hanworth Lincs 133 A5
Cold Harbour Lincs 116 B2
Cold Hatton Telford 111 C5
Cold Hesledon Durham 168 A2
Cold Higham Northants 82 B3
Cold Kirby N Yorks 158 C4
Cold Newton Leics 99 A4
Cold Northcott Corn 10 C3
Cold Norton Essex 70 C2
Cold Overton Leics 115 D6
Coldbackie Highld 277 C7
Coldbeck Cumb 155 A6
Coldblow London 50 B2
Coldean Brighton 21 B6
Coldeast Devon 12 D3
Colden W Yorks 138 A2
Colden Common Hants 32 C3
Coldfair Green Suff 89 A5
Coldham Cambs 101 A6
Coldharbour Glos 62 C1
Coldharbour Kent 36 A3
Coldharbour Sur 35 B4
Coldingham Borders 211 D6
Coldrain Perth 219 D5
Coldred Kent 39 A4
Coldridge Devon 12 A1
Coldstream Angus 220 A3
Coldstream Borders 198 C2
Coldwaltham W Sus 20 A3
Coldwells Aberds 257 B6
Coldwells Croft Aberds 255 D6
Coldyeld Shrops 94 B1
Cole Som 29 B6
Cole Green Herts 68 B2
Cole Henley Hants 46 D2
Colebatch Shrops 93 C7
Colebrook Devon 13 A5
Colebrooke Devon 12 B2
Coleby Lincs 133 C4
Coleby N Lincs 141 B6
Coleford Devon 12 A2
Coleford Glos 62 B1
Coleford Som 29 A6
Colehill Dorset 17 A4
Coleman's Hatch E Sus 36 C2
Colemere Shrops 110 B3
Colemore Hants 33 B6
Coleorton Leics 114 D2
Colerne Wilts 44 B2
Cole's Green Suff 88 A3
Coles Green Suff 88 C1
Colesbourne Glos 63 B5
Colesden Beds 84 B3
Coleshill Bucks 67 D4
Coleshill Oxon 64 D3
Coleshill Warks 97 C5
Colestocks Devon 13 A5
Colgate W Sus 35 C5
Colgrain Argyll 206 B1
Colinsburgh Fife 221 D4
Colinton Edin 209 D5
Colintraive Argyll 203 A5
Colkirk Norf 119 C6
Collace Perth 220 A2
Collafirth Shetland 284 G6
Collaton St Mary Torbay 8 B2
College Milton S Lnrk 205 B6
Collessie Fife 220 C2
Collier Row London 69 D5
Collier Street Kent 37 B5
Collier's End Herts 68 A3
Collier's Green Kent 37 C5
Colliery Row T & W 167 A6
Collieston Aberds 257 D5
Collin Dumfries 174 A3
Collingbourne Ducis Wilts 45 D6
Collingbourne Kingston Wilts 45 D6
Collingham Notts 132 C3
Collingham W Yorks 148 C2
Collington Hereford 79 A4
Collingtree Northants 83 B4
Collins Green Warr 137 D4
Colliston Angus 233 D4
Collycroft Warks 97 C6
Collynie Aberds 256 C3
Collyweston Northants 100 A1
Colmonell S Ayrs 180 C3

Colmworth Beds 84 B3
Coln Rogers Glos 64 C1
Coln St Aldwyn's Glos 64 C2
Coln St Dennis Glos 64 B1
Colnabaichin Aberds 243 B5
Colnbrook Slough 48 B3
Colne Cambs 101 D5
Colne Lancs 146 C2
Colne Edge Lancs 146 C2
Colne Engaine Essex 87 D4
Colney Norf 104 A2
Colney Heath Herts 68 C2
Colney Street Herts 67 C6
Colpy Aberds 256 C1
Colquhar Borders 196 B2
Colsterdale N Yorks 157 C5
Colsterworth Lincs 116 C2
Colston Bassett Notts 115 B4
Coltfield Moray 266 C2
Colthouse Cumb 154 B2
Coltishall Norf 121 D4
Coltness N Lnrk 194 A3
Colton Cumb 154 C2
Colton N Yorks 149 C4
Colton Norf 104 A2
Colton Staffs 113 C4
Colton W Yorks 148 D2
Colva Powys 77 B6
Colvend Dumfries 173 C6
Colvister Shetland 284 D7
Colwall Green Hereford 79 C5
Colwall Stone Hereford 79 C5
Colwell Northumb 178 B1
Colwich Staffs 112 C4
Colwick Notts 115 A4
Colwinston V Glam 40 D4
Colworth W Sus 20 B2
Colwyn Bay = Bae Colwyn Conwy 124 B3
Colyford Devon 14 B2
Colyton Devon 14 B2
Combe Hereford 78 A1
Combe Oxon 65 B5
Combe W Berks 46 C1
Combe Common Sur 34 C2
Combe Down Bath 43 C6
Combe Florey Som 27 B6
Combe Hay Bath 43 D6
Combe Martin Devon 25 A6
Combe Moor Hereford 78 A1
Combe Raleigh Devon 13 A6
Combe St Nicholas Som 28 D3
Combeinteignhead Devon 13 D4
Comberbach Ches 127 B6
Comberton Cambs 85 B5
Comberton Hereford 78 A2
Combpyne Devon 14 B2
Combridge Staffs 113 B4
Combrook Warks 81 B6
Combs Derbys 129 B5
Combs Suff 87 B6
Combs Ford Suff 87 B6
Combwich Som 28 A2
Comers Aberds 244 B3
Comins Coch Ceredig 90 D4
Commercial End Cambs 86 A1
Commins Capel Betws Ceredig 75 C5
Commins Coch Powys 91 B6
Common Edge Blkpool 144 D3
Common Side Derbys 130 B3
Commondale N Yorks 169 D4
Commonmoor Corn 6 A1
Commonside Ches 127 B5
Compstall Gtr Man 138 D2
Compton Devon 8 A2
Compton Hants 32 C3
Compton Sur 34 B1
Compton Sur 34 B2
Compton W Berks 46 B3
Compton Wilts 45 D5
Compton W Sus 33 D6
Compton Abbas Dorset 30 D2
Compton Abdale Glos 63 B6
Compton Acres Poole 17 C4
Compton Bassett Wilts 44 B4
Compton Beauchamp Oxon 45 A6
Compton Bishop Som 42 D2
Compton Chamberlayne Wilts 31 C4
Compton Dando Bath 43 C5
Compton Dundon Som 29 B4
Compton Martin Bath 43 D4
Compton Pauncefoot Som 29 C6
Compton Valence Dorset 15 B5
Comrie Fife 208 B3
Comrie Perth 218 B2

Conaglen House Highld 237 C4
Conchra Argyll 214 D3
Concraigie Perth 231 D5
Conder Green Lancs 145 B4
Conderton Worcs 80 D2
Condicote Glos 64 A2
Condorrat N Lnrk 207 C5
Condover Shrops 94 A2
Coney Weston Suff 103 D5
Coneysthorpe N Yorks 159 D6
Coneythorpe N Yorks 148 B2
Conford Hants 33 B7
Congash Highld 253 D6
Congdon's Shop Corn 10 D3
Congerstone Leics 97 A6
Congham Norf 119 C4
Congl-y-wal Gwyn 108 A2
Congleton Ches 128 C3
Congresbury N Som 42 C3
Congreve Staffs 112 D3
Conicavel Moray 253 A5
Coningsby Lincs 134 D2
Conington Cambs 100 C3
Conington Cambs 85 A5
Conisbrough S Yorks 140 D3
Conisby Argyll 200 B2
Conisholme Lincs 143 D6
Coniston Cumb 154 B2
Coniston E Yorks 151 D4
Coniston Cold N Yorks 146 B3
Conistone N Yorks 146 A3
Connah's Quay Flint 126 C2
Connel Argyll 226 C4
Connel Park E Ayrs 182 A4
Connor Downs Corn 2 B3
Conon Bridge Highld 252 A1
Conon House Highld 252 A1
Cononley N Yorks 146 C3
Conordan Highld 247 A4
Consall Staffs 112 A3
Consett Durham 178 D3
Constable Burton N Yorks 157 B5
Constantine Corn 3 C5
Constantine Bay Corn 9 D4
Contin Highld 251 A6
Contlaw Aberdeen 245 B5
Conwy Conwy 124 B2
Conwy Castle Conwy 124 B2
Conyer Kent 51 C6
Conyers Green Suff 87 A4
Cooden E Sus 23 B5
Cooil I o M 152 D3
Cookbury Devon 11 A5
Cookham Windsor 48 A1
Cookham Dean Windsor 47 A6
Cookham Rise Windsor 48 A1
Cookhill Worcs 80 B3
Cookley Suff 104 D4
Cookley Worcs 95 C6
Cookley Green Oxon 66 D1
Cookney Aberds 245 C5
Cookridge W Yorks 147 C6
Cooksbridge E Sus 22 A2
Cooksmill Green Essex 69 C6
Coolham W Sus 35 D4
Cooling Medway 51 B4
Coombe Corn 24 D3
Coombe Corn 4 B4
Coombe Hants 33 C5
Coombe Wilts 45 D5
Coombe Bissett Wilts 31 C5
Coombe Hill Glos 63 A4
Coombe Keynes Dorset 16 C2
Coombes W Sus 21 B4
Coopersale Common Essex 69 C4
Cootham W Sus 20 A3
Copdock Suff 88 C2
Copford Green Essex 70 A3
Copgrove N Yorks 148 A2
Copister Shetland 284 F6
Cople Beds 84 C3
Copley Durham 166 C3
Coplow Dale Derbys 129 B6
Copmanthorpe York 149 C4
Coppathorne Corn 10 A3
Coppenhall Staffs 112 D3
Coppenhall Moss Ches 128 D2
Copperhouse Corn 2 B3
Coppingford Cambs 100 C3
Copplestone Devon 12 A2
Coppull Lancs 137 B4
Coppull Moor Lancs 137 B4
Copsale W Sus 35 D4
Copshaw Holm = Newcastleton Borders 176 A2
Copster Green Lancs 145 D6

Copston Magna Warks 98 C1
Copt Heath W Mid 97 D4
Copt Hewick N Yorks 158 D2
Copt Oak Leics 114 D2
Copthorne Shrops 110 D3
Copthorne W Sus 35 C6
Copy's Green Norf 119 B6
Copythorne Hants 32 D2
Corbets Tey London 50 A2
Corbridge Northumb 179 C1
Corby Northants 99 C5
Corby Glen Lincs 116 C2
Cordon N Ayrs 191 B6
Coreley Shrops 95 D4
Cores End Bucks 48 A2
Corfe Som 28 D2
Corfe Castle Dorset 16 C3
Corfe Castle Dorset 16 C3
Corfe Mullen Dorset 16 B3
Corfton Shrops 94 C2
Corgarff Aberds 243 B5
Corhampton Hants 33 C5
Corlae Dumfries 183 C4
Corley Warks 97 C6
Corley Ash Warks 97 C5
Corley Moor Warks 97 C5
Cornaa I o M 152 C4
Cornabus Argyll 200 D3
Cornel Conwy 124 C2
Corner Row Lancs 144 D4
Corney Cumb 153 A2
Cornforth Durham 167 B6
Cornhill Aberds 267 D6
Cornhill-on-Tweed Northumb 198 C2
Cornholme W Yorks 138 A2
Cornish Cyder Farm, Truro Corn 4 B2
Cornish Hall End Essex 86 D2
Cornquoy Orkney 283 H6
Cornsay Durham 166 A4
Cornsay Colliery Durham 167 A4
Corntown Highld 252 A1
Corntown V Glam 40 D4
Cornwell Oxon 64 A3
Cornwood Devon 7 B5
Cornworthy Devon 8 B2
Corpach Highld 237 B4
Corpusty Norf 120 B3
Corran Highld 237 C4
Corran Highld 238 B2
Corranbuie Argyll 202 B3
Corrany I o M 152 C4
Corrie N Ayrs 203 D5
Corrie Common Dumfries 185 D5
Corriecravie N Ayrs 191 C5
Corriemoillie Highld 263 D5
Corriemulzie Lodge Highld 263 A5
Corrievarkie Lodge Perth 229 A4
Corrievorrie Highld 252 D3
Corrimony Highld 251 C5
Corringham Lincs 141 D6
Corringham Thurrock 51 A4
Corris Gwyn 91 B5
Corris Uchaf Gwyn 91 B5
Corrour Shooting Lodge Highld 228 B3
Corrow Argyll 215 B4
Corry Highld 247 B5
Corry of Ardnagrask Highld 251 B7
Corrykinloch Highld 271 B6
Corrymuckloch Perth 218 A3
Corrynachenchy Argyll 225 B5
Cors-y-Gedol Gwyn 107 D5
Corsback Highld 280 A4
Corscombe Dorset 15 A5
Corse Aberds 255 B7
Corse Glos 62 A3
Corse Lawn Worcs 79 D6
Corse of Kinnoir Aberds 255 B6
Corsewall Dumfries 170 A2
Corsham Wilts 44 B2
Corsindae Aberds 244 B3
Corsley Wilts 30 A2
Corsley Heath Wilts 30 A2
Corsock Dumfries 173 A5
Corston Bath 43 C5
Corston Wilts 44 A3
Corstorphine Edin 209 C4
Cortachy Angus 232 C1
Corton Suff 105 B6
Corton Wilts 30 A3
Corton Denham Som 29 C6
Coruanan Lodge Highld 237 C4
Corunna W Isles 287 H3
Corwen Denb 109 A5

Coryton Devon 11 C5
Coryton Thurrock 51 A4
Cosby Leics 98 B2
Coseley W Mid 96 B2
Cosgrove Northants 83 C4
Cosham Ptsmth 19 A5
Cosheston Pembs 55 D6
Cossall Notts 114 A2
Cossington Leics 115 D4
Cossington Som 28 A3
Costa Orkney 282 E4
Costessey Norf 120 D3
Costock Notts 114 C3
Coston Leics 115 C6
Cote Oxon 64 C4
Cotebrook Ches 127 C5
Cotehele House Corn 6 A3
Cotehill Cumb 176 D2
Cotes Cumb 154 C3
Cotes Leics 114 C3
Cotes Staffs 112 B2
Cotesbach Leics 98 C2
Cotgrave Notts 115 B4
Cothall Aberds 245 A5
Cotham Notts 115 A5
Cothelstone Som 28 B1
Cotherstone Durham 166 D3
Cothill Oxon 65 D5
Cotleigh Devon 14 A2
Cotmanhay Derbys 114 A2
Cotmaton Devon 13 C6
Coton Cambs 85 B6
Coton Northants 98 D3
Coton Staffs 112 C2
Coton Staffs 112 B3
Coton Clanford Staffs 112 C2
Coton Hill Shrops 110 D3
Coton Hill Staffs 112 B3
Coton in the Elms Derbys 113 D6
Cotswold Wild Life Park, Burford Oxon 64 C3
Cott Devon 8 A1
Cottam E Yorks 150 A2
Cottam Lancs 145 D5
Cottam Notts 132 B3
Cottartown Highld 253 C6
Cottenham Cambs 85 A6
Cotterdale N Yorks 156 B2
Cottered Herts 68 A3
Cotteridge W Mid 96 D3
Cotterstock Northants 100 B2
Cottesbrooke Northants 99 D4
Cottesmore Rutland 116 D2
Cotteylands Devon 27 D4
Cottingham E Yorks 150 D3
Cottingham Northants 99 B5
Cottingley W Yorks 147 D5
Cottisford Oxon 82 D2
Cotton Staffs 113 A4
Cotton Suff 87 A6
Cotton End Beds 84 C2
Cottown Aberds 255 D6
Cottown Aberds 245 A4
Cottown Aberds 256 B3
Cotwalton Staffs 112 B3
Couch's Mill Corn 5 B6
Coughton Hereford 62 A1
Coughton Warks 80 A3
Coulaghailtro Argyll 202 B2
Coulags Highld 249 B6
Coulby Newham M'bro 168 D3
Coulderton Cumb 162 D2
Coulin Highld 250 A2
Coull Aberds 244 B2
Coull Argyll 200 B2
Coulport Argyll 215 D5
Coulsdon London 35 A5
Coulston Wilts 44 D3
Coulter S Lnrk 195 C5
Coulton N Yorks 159 D5
Cound Shrops 94 A3
Coundon Durham 167 C5
Coundon W Mid 97 C6
Coundon Grange Durham 167 C5
Countersett N Yorks 156 C3
Countess Wilts 31 A5
Countess Wear Devon 13 C4
Countesthorpe Leics 98 B2
Countisbury Devon 26 A2
County Oak W Sus 35 C5
Coup Green Lancs 137 A4
Coupar Angus Perth 231 D6
Coupland Northumb 198 C3
Cour Argyll 202 D3
Courance Dumfries 184 C3

Court-at-Street Kent 38 B2
Court Henry Carms 58 C2
Courteenhall Northants 83 B4
Courtsend Essex 71 D4
Courtway Som 28 B2
Cousland Midloth 209 D6
Cousley Wood E Sus 37 C4
Cove Argyll 215 D5
Cove Borders 211 C4
Cove Devon 27 D4
Cove Hants 34 A1
Cove Highld 261 A5
Cove Bay Aberdeen 245 B6
Cove Bottom Suff 105 D5
Covehithe Suff 105 C6
Coven Staffs 96 A2
Coveney Cambs 101 C6
Covenham St Bartholomew Lincs 143 D5
Covenham St Mary Lincs 143 D5
Coventry W Mid 97 D6
Coventry Airport Warks 97 D6
Coventry Cathedral W Mid 97 D6
Coverack Corn 3 D5
Coverham N Yorks 157 C5
Covesea Moray 266 B2
Covington Cambs 100 D2
Covington S Lnrk 195 C4
Cow Ark Lancs 145 C6
Cowan Bridge Lancs 155 D5
Cowbeech E Sus 22 A4
Cowbit Lincs 117 D5
Cowbridge Lincs 117 A6
Cowbridge Som 27 A4
Cowbridge = Bont-Faen V Glam 41 D4
Cowdale Derbys 129 B5
Cowden Kent 36 B2
Cowdenbeath Fife 209 A4
Cowdenburn Borders 195 A7
Cowers Lane Derbys 113 A7
Cowes I o W 18 B3
Cowesby N Yorks 158 C3
Cowfold W Sus 35 D5
Cowgill Cumb 155 C6
Cowie Aberds 245 D5
Cowie Stirl 207 B6
Cowley Devon 13 B4
Cowley Glos 63 B5
Cowley London 48 A3
Cowley Oxon 65 C6
Cowleymoor Devon 27 D4
Cowling Lancs 137 B4
Cowling N Yorks 146 C3
Cowling N Yorks 157 C6
Cowlinge Suff 86 B3
Cowpe Lancs 138 A1
Cowpen Northumb 179 A4
Cowpen Bewley Stockton 168 C2
Cowplain Hants 33 D5
Cowshill Durham 165 A6
Cowstrandburn Fife 208 A3
Cowthorpe N Yorks 148 B3
Cox Common Suff 105 C4
Cox Green Windsor 48 B1
Cox Moor Notts 131 D5
Coxbank Ches 111 A5
Coxbench Derbys 114 A1
Coxford Norf 119 C5
Coxford Soton 32 D2
Coxheath Kent 37 A5
Coxhill Kent 39 A4
Coxhoe Durham 167 B6
Coxley Som 29 A5
Coxwold N Yorks 158 D4
Coychurch Bridgend 40 D4
Coylton S Ayrs 193 C4
Coylumbridge Highld 242 A2
Coynach Aberds 244 B1
Coynachie Aberds 255 C5
Coytrahen Bridgend 40 C3
Crabadon Devon 7 B6
Crabbs Cross Worcs 80 A3
Crabtree W Sus 35 D5
Crackenthorpe Cumb 165 C4
Crackington Haven Corn 10 B2
Crackley Warks 97 D5
Crackleybank Shrops 111 D6
Crackpot N Yorks 156 B3
Cracoe N Yorks 146 A3
Craddock Devon 27 D5
Cradhlastadh W Isles 287 A5
Cradley Hereford 79 C5
Cradley Heath W Mid 96 C2
Crafthole Corn 6 B2

Cragg Vale W Yorks 138 A3
Craggan Highld 253 D6
Craggie Highld 274 C2
Craggie Highld 252 C3
Craghead Durham 179 D4
Crai Powys 59 C5
Craibstone Moray 267 D5
Craichie Angus 232 D3
Craig Dumfries 173 A4
Craig Dumfries 173 B4
Craig Highld 250 B2
Craig Castle Aberds 255 D5
Craig-cefn-parc Swansea 40 A1
Craig Penllyn V Glam 41 D4
Craig-y-don Conwy 124 A2
Craig-y-nos Powys 59 D5
Craiganor Lodge Perth 229 C5
Craigdam Aberds 256 C3
Craigdarroch Dumfries 183 C5
Craigdarroch Highld 251 A6
Craigdhu Highld 251 B6
Craigearn Aberds 245 A4
Craigellachie Moray 254 B3
Craigencross Dumfries 170 A2
Craigend Perth 219 B6
Craigend Stirl 207 B5
Craigendoran Argyll 215 D6
Craigends Renfs 205 B4
Craigens Argyll 200 B2
Craigens E Ayrs 182 A3
Craighat Stirl 206 B2
Craighead Fife 221 D6
Craighlaw Mains Dumfries 171 A5
Craighouse Argyll 201 B5
Craigie Aberds 245 A6
Craigie Dundee 220 A4
Craigie Perth 219 B6
Craigie Perth 231 D5
Craigie S Ayrs 193 B4
Craigiefield Orkney 282 F5
Craigielaw E Loth 210 C1
Craiglockhart Edin 209 C5
Craigmalloch E Ayrs 182 C2
Craigmaud Aberds 268 D3
Craigmillar Edin 209 C5
Craigmore Argyll 203 B6
Craignant Shrops 110 B1
Craigneuk N Lnrk 194 A2
Craigneuk N Lnrk 207 D5
Craignure Argyll 225 C6
Craigo Angus 233 B4
Craigow Perth 219 D5
Craigrothie Fife 220 C3
Craigroy Moray 266 D2
Craigruie Stirl 217 B4
Craigston Castle Aberds 268 D2
Craigton Aberdeen 245 B5
Craigton Angus 232 C1
Craigton Angus 221 A5
Craigton Highld 264 A2
Craigtown Highld 279 C4
Craik Borders 185 B6
Crail Fife 221 D6
Crailing Borders 187 A5
Crailinghall Borders 187 A5
Craiselound N Lincs 141 D5
Crakehill N Yorks 158 D3
Crakemarsh Staffs 113 B4
Crambe N Yorks 149 A6
Cramlington Northumb 179 B4
Cramond Edin 209 C4
Cramond Bridge Edin 209 C4
Cranage Ches 128 C2
Cranberry Staffs 112 B2
Cranborne Dorset 31 D4
Cranbourne Brack 48 B2
Cranbrook Kent 37 C5
Cranbrook Common Kent 37 C5
Crane Moor S Yorks 139 C6
Crane's Corner Norf 119 D6
Cranfield Beds 83 C6
Cranford London 48 B4
Cranford St Andrew Northants 99 D6
Cranford St John Northants 99 D6
Cranham Glos 63 B4
Cranham London 50 A2
Crank Mers 136 D4
Crank Wood Gtr Man 137 C5
Cranleigh Sur 34 C3
Cranley Suff 104 D2
Cranmer Green Suff 103 D6
Cranmore I o W 18 C2
Cranna Aberds 268 D1
Crannich Argyll 225 B4

Crannoch Moray 267 D5
Cranoe Leics 99 B4
Cransford Suff 88 A4
Cranshaws Borders 210 D3
Cranstal I o M 152 A4
Crantock Corn 4 A2
Cranwell Lincs 116 A3
Cranwich Norf 102 B3
Cranworth Norf 103 A5
Craobh Haven Argyll 213 B5
Crapstone Devon 7 A4
Crarae Argyll 214 C2
Crask Inn Highld 272 B3
Crask of Aigas Highld 251 B6
Craskins Aberds 244 B2
Craster Northumb 189 B5
Craswall Hereford 77 D6
Cratfield Suff 104 D4
Crathes Aberds 245 C4
Crathes Castle and Gardens Aberds 245 C4
Crathie Aberds 243 C5
Crathie Highld 240 C3
Crathorne N Yorks 158 A3
Craven Arms Shrops 94 C2
Crawcrook T & W 178 C3
Crawford Lancs 136 C3
Crawford S Lnrk 195 D4
Crawfordjohn S Lnrk 194 D1
Crawick Dumfries 183 A5
Crawley Hants 32 B3
Crawley Oxon 64 B4
Crawley W Sus 35 C5
Crawley Down W Sus 35 C6
Crawleyside Durham 166 A2
Crawshawbooth Lancs 137 A7
Crawton Aberds 233 A6
Cray N Yorks 156 D3
Cray Perth 231 B5
Crayford London 50 B2
Crayke N Yorks 159 D4
Crays Hill Essex 69 D7
Cray's Pond Oxon 47 A4
Creacombe Devon 26 D3
Creag Ghoraidh W Isles 286 B3
Creagan Argyll 227 B4
Creaguaineach Lodge Highld 228 B2
Creaksea Essex 70 D3
Creaton Northants 99 D4
Creca Dumfries 175 A5
Credenhill Hereford 78 C2
Crediton Devon 12 A3
Creebridge Dumfries 171 A6
Creech Heathfield Som 28 C2
Creech St Michael Som 28 C2
Creed Corn 4 C4
Creekmouth London 50 A1
Creeting Bottoms Suff 88 B2
Creeting St Mary Suff 88 B1
Creeton Lincs 116 C3
Creetown Dumfries 171 B6
Creg-ny-Baa I o M 152 C3
Creggans Argyll 214 B3
Cregneash I o M 152 E1
Cregrina Powys 77 B5
Creich Fife 220 B3
Creigiau Cardiff 41 C5
Cremyll Corn 6 B3
Creslow Bucks 66 A3
Cressage Shrops 94 A3
Cressbrook Derbys 129 B6
Cresselly Pembs 55 D6
Cressing Essex 70 A1
Cresswell Northumb 189 D5
Cresswell Staffs 112 B3
Cresswell Quay Pembs 55 D6
Creswell Derbys 131 B5
Cretingham Suff 88 A3
Cretshengan Argyll 202 B2
Crewe Ches 127 D4
Crewe Ches 128 D2
Crewgreen Powys 110 D2
Crewkerne Som 14 A4
Crianlarich Stirl 216 B3
Cribyn Ceredig 75 C4
Criccieth Gwyn 107 C4
Crich Derbys 130 D3
Crichie Aberds 257 B4
Crichton Midloth 209 D6
Crick Mon 61 D6
Crick Northants 98 D2
Crickadarn Powys 77 C4
Cricket Malherbie Som 28 D3
Cricket St Thomas Som 14 A3
Crickheath Shrops 110 C1
Crickhowell Powys 60 B4
Cricklade Wilts 64 D2

Cricklewood London 49 A5
Cridling Stubbs N Yorks 140 A3
Crieff Perth 210 D3
Crieff Visitors' Centre Perth 218 B3
Criggion Powys 110 D1
Crigglestone W Yorks 139 B6
Crimond Aberds 269 D5
Crimonmogate Aberds 269 D5
Crimplesham Norf 102 A2
Crinan Argyll 213 C5
Cringleford Norf 104 A2
Cringles W Yorks 147 C4
Crinow Pembs 56 A1
Cripplesease Corn 2 B3
Cripplestyle Dorset 31 D4
Cripp's Corner E Sus 37 D5
Croasdale Cumb 162 C3
Crock Street Som 28 D3
Crockenhill Kent 50 C2
Crockernwell Devon 12 B2
Crockerton Wilts 30 A2
Crocketford or Ninemile Bar Dumfries 173 A6
Crockey Hill York 149 C5
Crockham Hill Kent 36 A2
Crockleford Heath Essex 71 A4
Crockness Orkney 283 H4
Croes-goch Pembs 54 A4
Croes-lan Ceredig 73 B6
Croes-y-mwyalch Torf 61 D5
Croeserw Neath 40 B3
Croesor Gwyn 107 B6
Croesyceiliog Carms 57 A4
Croesyceiliog Torf 61 D5
Croesywaun Gwyn 107 A5
Croft Leics 98 B2
Croft Lincs 135 C5
Croft Pembs 73 B4
Croft Warr 137 D5
Croft Motor Racing Circuit N Yorks 157 A6
Croft-on-Tees N Yorks 157 A6
Croftamie Stirl 206 B2
Croftmalloch W Loth 208 D2
Crofton Wilts 45 C6
Crofton W Yorks 140 B1
Crofts of Benachielt Highld 275 A5
Crofts of Haddo Aberds 256 C3
Crofts of Inverthernie Aberds 256 B2
Crofts of Meikle Ardo Aberds 256 B3
Crofty Swansea 57 C5
Croggan Argyll 225 D6
Croglin Cumb 164 A3
Croich Highld 263 A6
Crois Dughaill W Isles 286 D3
Cromarty Highld 264 D3
Cromblet Aberds 256 C2
Cromdale Highld 253 D6
Cromer Herts 68 A2
Cromer Norf 120 A4
Cromford Derbys 130 D2
Cromhall S Glos 62 D2
Cromhall Common S Glos 43 A5
Cromor W Isles 288 E5
Cromra Highld 240 C3
Cromwell Notts 132 C2
Cronberry E Ayrs 193 C6
Crondall Hants 33 A6
Cronk-y-Voddy I o M 152 C3
Cronton Mers 127 A4
Crook Cumb 154 B3
Crook Durham 167 B4
Crook of Devon Perth 219 D5
Crookedholm E Ayrs 193 B4
Crookes S Yorks 130 A3
Crookham Northumb 198 C3
Crookham W Berks 46 C3
Crookham Village Hants 47 D5
Crookhaugh Borders 195 D6
Crookhouse Borders 187 A6
Crooklands Cumb 154 C4
Croome Park, Pershore Worcs 80 C1
Cropredy Oxon 82 C1
Cropston Leics 114 D3
Cropthorne Worcs 80 C2
Cropton N Yorks 159 C6
Cropwell Bishop Notts 115 B4
Cropwell Butler Notts 115 B4
Cros W Isles 288 A6
Crosbost W Isles 288 E4
Crosby Cumb 162 A3
Crosby I o M 152 D3
Crosby N Lincs 141 B6

Crosby Garrett Cumb 155 A6
Crosby Ravensworth Cumb 165 D4
Crosby Villa Cumb 162 A3
Croscombe Som 29 A5
Cross Som 42 D3
Cross Ash Mon 61 B6
Cross-at-Hand Kent 37 B5
Cross Green Devon 11 C4
Cross Green Suff 87 B5
Cross Green Suff 87 B4
Cross Green Warks 81 B6
Cross Hands Carms 57 A5
Cross-hands Carms 73 D4
Cross Hands Pembs 55 C6
Cross Hill Derbys 114 A2
Cross Houses Shrops 94 A3
Cross in Hand E Sus 36 D3
Cross in Hand Leics 98 C2
Cross Inn Ceredig 73 A6
Cross Inn Ceredig 75 B4
Cross Inn Rhondda 41 C5
Cross Keys Kent 36 A3
Cross Lane Head Shrops 95 B5
Cross Lanes Corn 3 C4
Cross Lanes N Yorks 148 A4
Cross Lanes Wrex 110 A2
Cross Oak Powys 60 A3
Cross of Jackston Aberds 256 C2
Cross o'th'hands Derbys 113 A6
Cross Street Suff 104 D2
Crossaig Argyll 202 C3
Crossal Highld 246 A3
Crossapol Argyll 222 C2
Crossburn Falk 207 C6
Crossbush W Sus 20 B3
Crosscanonby Cumb 162 A3
Crossdale Street Norf 120 B4
Crossens Mers 136 B2
Crossflatts W Yorks 147 C5
Crossford Fife 208 B3
Crossford S Lnrk 194 B3
Crossgate Lincs 117 C5
Crossgatehall E Loth 209 D6
Crossgates Fife 208 B3
Crossgates Powys 77 A4
Crossgill Lancs 145 A5
Crosshill E Ayrs 193 C4
Crosshill Fife 209 A4
Crosshill S Ayrs 192 E3
Crosshouse E Ayrs 192 B3
Crossings Cumb 176 B3
Crosskeys Caerph 41 B7
Crosskirk Highld 279 A6
Crosslanes Shrops 110 D2
Crosslee Borders 185 A6
Crosslee Renfs 205 B4
Crossmichael Dumfries 173 B5
Crossmoor Lancs 144 D4
Crossroads Aberds 245 C4
Crossroads E Ayrs 193 B5
Crossway Hereford 79 D4
Crossway Mon 61 B6
Crossway Powys 77 B4
Crossway Green Worcs 79 A6
Crossways Dorset 16 C1
Crosswell Pembs 72 C4
Crosswood Ceredig 75 A5
Crosthwaite Cumb 154 B3
Croston Lancs 136 B3
Crostwick Norf 121 D4
Crostwight Norf 121 C5
Crothair W Isles 288 D2
Crouch Kent 36 A4
Crouch Hill Dorset 29 D7
Crouch House Green Kent 36 B2
Croucheston Wilts 31 C4
Croughton Northants 82 D2
Crovie Aberds 268 C3
Crow Edge S Yorks 139 C4
Crow Hill Hereford 62 A2
Crowan Corn 3 B4
Crowborough E Sus 36 C3
Crowcombe Som 27 B6
Crowdecote Derbys 129 C6
Crowden Derbys 138 C3
Crowell Oxon 66 D2
Crowfield Northants 82 C3
Crowfield Suff 88 B2
Crowhurst E Sus 23 A5
Crowhurst Sur 36 B1
Crowhurst Lane End Sur 36 B1
Crowland Lincs 117 D5
Crowlas Corn 2 B3
Crowle N Lincs 141 B5
Crowle Worcs 80 B2
Crowmarsh Gifford Oxon 47 A4
Crown Corner Suff 104 D3

Place	Ref	Place	Ref
Crownhill Plym	6 B3	Cullipool Argyll	213 A5
Crownland Suff	103 E6	Cullivoe Shetland	284 C7
Crownthorpe Norf	104 A1	Culloch Perth	218 C2
Crowntown Corn	3 B4	Culloden Highld	252 B3
Crows-an-wra Corn	2 C1	Culloden Battlefield, Inverness Highld	252 B3
Crowshill Norf	103 A5	Cullompton Devon	13 A5
Crowsnest Shrops	94 A1	Culmaily Highld	265 A4
Crowthorne Brack	47 C6	Culmazie Dumfries	171 B5
Crowton Ches	127 B5	Culmington Shrops	94 C2
Croxall Staffs	113 D5	Culmstock Devon	27 D6
Croxby Lincs	142 D3	Culnacraig Highld	270 D3
Croxdale Durham	167 B5	Culnaknock Highld	259 B5
Croxden Staffs	113 B4	Culpho Suff	88 C3
Croxley Green Herts	67 D5	Culrain Highld	264 A1
Croxton Cambs	84 A4	Culross Fife	208 B2
Croxton N Lincs	142 B2	Culroy S Ayrs	192 D3
Croxton Norf	103 C4	Culsh Aberds	256 B3
Croxton Staffs	112 B1	Culsh Aberds	243 C6
Croxton Kerrial Leics	115 C6	Culshabbin Dumfries	171 B5
Croxtonbank Staffs	112 B1	Culswick Shetland	285 J4
Croy Highld	252 B3	Cultercullen Aberds	257 D4
Croy N Lnrk	207 C5	Cults Aberdeen	245 B5
Croyde Devon	25 B5	Cults Aberds	255 C6
Croydon Cambs	85 C5	Cults Dumfries	171 C6
Croydon London	49 C6	Culverstone Green Kent	50 C3
Crubenmore Lodge Highld	241 C4	Culverthorpe Lincs	116 A3
Cruckmeole Shrops	94 A2	Culworth Northants	82 C2
Cruckton Shrops	110 D3	Culzean Castle, Maybole S Ayrs	192 E2
Cruden Bay Aberds	257 C5	Culzie Lodge Highld	263 C7
Crudgington Telford	111 D5	Cumberhead S Lnrk	207 C5
Crudwell Wilts	63 D5	Cumbernauld N Lnrk	207 C5
Crug Powys	93 D5	Cumbernauld Village N Lnrk	207 C5
Crugmeer Corn	9 D5	Cumberworth Lincs	135 B5
Crugybar Carms	58 B3	Cuminestown Aberds	268 D3
Crulabhig W Isles	288 D2	Cumlewick Shetland	285 L6
Crumlin = Crymlyn Caerph	41 B7	Cummersdale Cumb	175 C6
Crumpsall Gtr Man	138 C1	Cummertrees Dumfries	174 B4
Crundale Kent	38 A2	Cummingston Moray	266 C2
Crundale Pembs	55 C5	Cumnock E Ayrs	193 C5
Cruwys Morchard Devon	26 D3	Cumnor Oxon	65 C5
Crux Easton Hants	46 D2	Cumrew Cumb	176 D3
Crwbin Carms	57 A4	Cumwhinton Cumb	176 D2
Crya Orkney	283 G4	Cumwhitton Cumb	176 D3
Cryers Hill Bucks	66 D3	Cundall N Yorks	158 D3
Crymlyn Gwyn	123 C6	Cunninghamhead N Ayrs	204 D3
Crymlyn = Crumlin Caerph	41 B7	Cunnister Shetland	284 D7
Crymych Pembs	73 C4	Cupar Fife	220 C3
Crynant Neath	40 A2	Cupar Muir Fife	220 C3
Crynfryn Ceredig	75 B4	Cupernham Hants	32 C2
Crystal Palace National Sports Centre London	49 B6	Curbar Derbys	130 B2
Cuaig Highld	249 A4	Curbridge Hants	32 D4
Cuan Argyll	213 A5	Curbridge Oxon	64 C4
Cubbington Warks	81 A6	Curdridge Hants	32 D4
Cubeck N Yorks	156 C3	Curdworth Warks	97 B4
Cubert Corn	4 B2	Curland Som	28 D2
Cubley S Yorks	139 C5	Curlew Green Suff	89 A4
Cubley Common Derbys	113 B5	Currarie S Ayrs	180 B3
Cublington Bucks	66 A3	Curridge W Berks	46 B2
Cublington Hereford	78 D2	Currie Edin	209 D4
Cuckfield W Sus	35 D6	Curry Mallet Som	28 C3
Cucklington Som	30 C1	Curry Rivel Som	28 C3
Cuckney Notts	131 B5	Curtisden Green Kent	37 B5
Cuckoo Hill Notts	141 D5	Curtisknowle Devon	7 B6
Cuddesdon Oxon	65 C7	Cury Corn	3 C4
Cuddington Bucks	66 B2	Cushnie Aberds	268 C2
Cuddington Ches	127 B6	Cushuish Som	28 B1
Cuddington Heath Ches	110 A3	Cusop Hereford	77 C6
Cuddy Hill Lancs	145 D4	Cutcloy Dumfries	171 D6
Cudham London	36 A2	Cutcombe Som	27 B4
Cudliptown Devon	11 D6	Cutgate Gtr Man	138 B1
Cudworth Som	28 D3	Cutiau Gwyn	90 A4
Cudworth S Yorks	140 C1	Cutlers Green Essex	86 D1
Cuffley Herts	68 C3	Cutnall Green Worcs	80 A1
Cuiashader W Isles	288 B6	Cutsdean Glos	80 D3
Cuidhir W Isles	286 F2	Cutthorpe Derbys	130 B3
Cuidhtinis W Isles	287 F5	Cutts Shetland	285 K6
Culag Highld	264 D2	Cutty Sark, Greenwich London	49 B6
Culbokie Highld	252 A2	Cuxham Oxon	66 D1
Culburnie Highld	251 B6	Cuxton Medway	51 C4
Culcabock Highld	252 B2	Cuxwold Lincs	142 C3
Culcairn Highld	264 D2	Cwm Bl Gwent	60 C3
Culcharry Highld	253 A4	Cwm Denb	125 B5
Culcheth Warr	137 D5	Cwm Swansea	40 B1
Culdrain Aberds	255 C6	Cwm-byr Carms	58 B3
Culduie Highld	249 B4	Cwm-Cewydd Gwyn	91 A6
Culford Suff	103 D4	Cwm-cou Ceredig	73 B5
Culgaith Cumb	165 C4	Cwm-Dulais Swansea	57 B6
Culham Oxon	65 D6	Cwm-felin-fach Caerph	41 B6
Culkein Highld	270 A3	Cwm Ffrwd-oer Torf	61 C4
Culkein Drumbeg Highld	270 A4	Cwm-hesgen Gwyn	108 C2
Culkerton Glos	63 D5	Cwm-hwnt Rhondda	59 E6
Cullachie Highld	253 D5	Cwm Irfon Powys	76 C2
Cullen Moray	267 C6	Cwm-Llinau Powys	91 B6
Cullercoats T & W	179 B5	Cwm-mawr Carms	57 A5
Cullicudden Highld	264 D2	Cwm-parc Rhondda	40 B4
Cullingworth W Yorks	147 D4		

Place	Ref	Place	Ref
Cwm Penmachno Conwy	108 A2	Dalchalloch Perth	229 B6
Cwm-y-glo Carms	57 A5	Dalchalm Highld	274 D3
Cwm-y-glo Gwyn	123 D5	Dalchenna Argyll	214 B3
Cwmafan Neath	40 B2	Dalchirach Moray	254 C2
Cwmaman Rhondda	41 B5	Dalchork Highld	272 C3
Cwmann Carms	75 D4	Dalchreichart Highld	239 A6
Cwmavon Torf	61 C4	Dalchruin Perth	218 C2
Cwmbach Carms	73 D5	Dalderby Lincs	134 C2
Cwmbach Carms	57 B4	Dale Pembs	54 D4
Cwmbach Powys	76 B4	Dale Abbey Derbys	114 B2
Cwmbach Powys	77 D5	Dale Head Cumb	164 D2
Cwmbâch Rhondda	41 A5	Dale of Walls Shetland	285 H3
Cwmbelan Powys	92 C3	Dalelia Highld	235 D6
Cwmbran = Cwmbrân Torf	61 D4	Daless Highld	253 C4
Cwmbrân = Cwmbran Torf	61 D4	Dalfaber Highld	242 A2
Cwmbrwyno Ceredig	91 D5	Dalgarven N Ayrs	204 D2
Cwmcarn Caerph	41 B7	Dalgety Bay Fife	209 B4
Cwmcarvan Mon	61 C6	Dalginross Perth	218 B2
Cwmcych Pembs	73 C5	Dalguise Perth	230 D3
Cwmdare Rhondda	41 A4	Dalhalvaig Highld	279 C4
Cwmderwen Powys	92 A3	Dalham Suff	86 A3
Cwmdu Carms	58 B3	Dalinlongart Argyll	215 D4
Cwmdu Powys	60 A3	Dalkeith Midloth	209 D6
Cwmdu Swansea	57 C6	Dallam Warr	137 D4
Cwmduad Carms	73 C6	Dallas Moray	266 D2
Cwmdwr Carms	59 B4	Dalleagles E Ayrs	182 A3
Cwmfelin Bridgend	40 C3	Dallinghoo Suff	88 B3
Cwmfelin M Tydf	41 A5	Dallington E Sus	23 A4
Cwmfelin Boeth Carms	56 A1	Dallington Northants	83 A4
Cwmfelin Mynach Carms	73 D5	Dallow N Yorks	157 D5
Cwmffrwd Carms	57 A4	Dalmadilly Aberds	245 A4
Cwmgiedd Powys	59 D4	Dalmally Argyll	227 D6
Cwmgors Neath	59 D4	Dalmarnock Glasgow	205 B6
Cwmgwili Carms	57 A5	Dalmary Stirl	206 A3
Cwmgwrach Neath	40 A3	Dalmellington E Ayrs	182 B2
Cwmhiraeth Carms	73 C6	Dalmeny Edin	208 C4
Cwmifor Carms	58 C3	Dalmigavie Highld	241 A5
Cwmisfael Carms	57 A4	Dalmigavie Lodge Highld	252 D3
Cwmllynfell Neath	59 D4	Dalmore Highld	264 D2
Cwmorgan Carms	73 C5	Dalmuir W Dunb	205 A4
Cwmpengraig Carms	73 C6	Dalnabreck Highld	235 D5
Cwmrhos Powys	60 A3	Dalnacardoch Lodge Perth	229 A6
Cwmsychpant Ceredig	74 D3	Dalnacroich Highld	251 A5
Cwmtillery Bl Gwent	60 C4	Dalnaglar Castle Perth	231 B5
Cwmwysg Powys	59 C5	Dalnahaitnach Highld	253 D4
Cwmyoy Mon	61 A4	Dalnaspidal Lodge Perth	229 A5
Cwmystwyth Ceredig	92 D1	Dalnavaid Perth	230 B4
Cwrt Gwyn	91 B4	Dalnavie Highld	264 C2
Cwrt-newydd Ceredig	74 D3	Dalnawillan Lodge Highld	279 D6
Cwrt-y-cadno Carms	58 A3	Dalness Highld	237 D5
Cwrt-y-gollen Powys	60 B4	Dalnessie Highld	273 C4
Cydweli = Kidwelly Carms	57 B4	Dalqueich Perth	219 D5
Cyffordd Llandudno = Llandudno Junction Conwy	124 B2	Dalreavoch Highld	273 D5
		Dalry N Ayrs	204 D2
Cyffylliog Denb	125 D5	Dalrymple E Ayrs	192 D3
Cyfronydd Powys	93 A5	Dalserf S Lnrk	194 A3
Cymer Neath	40 B3	Dalston Cumb	175 C6
Cyncoed Cardiff	41 C6	Dalswinton Dumfries	184 D2
Cynghordy Carms	59 A5	Dalton Dumfries	174 A4
Cynheidre Carms	57 B4	Dalton Lancs	136 C3
Cynwyd Denb	109 A5	Dalton Northumb	177 D7
Cynwyl Elfed Carms	73 D6	Dalton Northumb	178 B3
Cywarch Gwyn	91 A6	Dalton N Yorks	158 D3
		Dalton N Yorks	157 A5
D		Dalton S Yorks	140 D2
		Dalton-in-Furness Cumb	153 C3
Dacre Cumb	164 C2	Dalton-le-Dale Durham	168 A2
Dacre N Yorks	147 A5	Dalton-on-Tees N Yorks	157 A6
Dacre Banks N Yorks	147 A5	Dalton Piercy Hrtlpl	168 B2
Daddry Shield Durham	166 B1	Dalveich Stirl	217 B6
Dadford Bucks	82 D3	Dalvina Lodge Highld	278 D2
Dadlington Leics	97 B7	Dalwhinnie Highld	241 D4
Dafarn Faig Gwyn	107 B4	Dalwood Devon	14 A2
Dafen Carms	57 B5	Dalwyne S Ayrs	181 B5
Daffy Green Norf	103 A5	Dam Green Norf	103 C6
Dagenham London	50 A1	Dam Side Lancs	144 C4
Daglingworth Glos	63 C5	Damerham Hants	31 D5
Dagnall Bucks	67 B4	Damgate Norf	105 A5
Dail Beag W Isles	288 C3	Damnaglaur Highld	170 D3
Dail bho Dheas W Isles	288 A5	Damside Borders	195 B6
Dail bho Thuath W Isles	288 A5	Danbury Essex	70 C1
Dail Mor W Isles	288 C3	Danby N Yorks	159 A6
Daill Argyll	200 B3	Danby Wiske N Yorks	158 B2
Dailly S Ayrs	181 A4	Dandaleith Moray	254 B3
Dairsie or Osnaburgh Fife	220 C4	Danderhall Midloth	209 D6
Daisy Hill Gtr Man	137 C5	Dane End Herts	68 A3
Dalabrog W Isles	286 D3	Danebridge Ches	129 C4
Dalavich Argyll	214 A2	Danehill E Sus	36 D2
Dalbeattie Dumfries	173 B6	Danemoor Green Norf	103 A6
Dalblair E Ayrs	182 A4	Danesford Shrops	95 B5
Dalbog Angus	232 A3	Daneshill Hants	47 D4
Dalbury Derbys	113 B6	Dangerous Corner Lancs	136 B4
Dalby I o M	152 D2	Danskine E Loth	210 D2
Dalby N Yorks	159 D5	Darcy Lever Gtr Man	137 C6
Darfield S Yorks	140 C2	Darenth Kent	50 B2
		Daresbury Halton	127 A5

Place	Ref	Place	Ref
Darfoulds Notts	131 B5	Deebank Aberds	244 C3
Dargate Kent	52 C2		
Darite Corn	6 A1		
Darlaston W Mid	96 B2		
Darley N Yorks	147 B6		
Darley Bridge Derbys	130 C2		
Darley Head N Yorks	147 B5		
Darlingscott Warks	81 C5		
Darlington Darl	167 D5		
Darliston Shrops	111 B4		
Darlton Notts	132 B2		
Darnall S Yorks	130 A3		
Darnick Borders	197 C4		
Darowen Powys	91 B6		
Darra Aberds	256 B2		
Darracott Devon	25 B5		
Darras Hall Northumb	178 B3		
Darrington N Yorks	140 A2		
Darsham Suff	89 A5		
Dartford Kent	50 B2		
Dartford Crossing Kent	50 B2		
Dartington Devon	8 A1		
Dartington Cider Press Centre Devon	8 A1		
Dartington Crystal Devon	25 D5		
Dartmeet Devon	12 D1		
Dartmouth Devon	8 B2		
Darton S Yorks	139 C6		
Darvel E Ayrs	193 B5		
Darwell Hole E Sus	23 A4		
Darwen Blkburn	137 A5		
Datchet Windsor	48 B2		
Datchworth Herts	68 B2		
Datchworth Green Herts	68 B2		
Daubhill Gtr Man	137 C6		
Daugh of Kinermony Moray	254 B3		
Dauntsey Wilts	44 A3		
Dava Moray	253 C6		
Davenham Ches	127 B6		
Davenport Green Ches	128 B3		
Daventry Northants	82 A2		
David's Well Powys	93 D4		
Davidson's Mains Edin	209 C5		
Davidstow Corn	10 C2		
Davington Dumfries	185 B5		
Daviot Aberds	256 D2		
Daviot Highld	252 C3		
Davoch of Grange Moray	267 D5		
Davyhulme Gtr Man	137 D6		
Dawley Telford	95 A4		
Dawlish Devon	13 D4		
Dawlish Warren Devon	13 D4		
Dawn Conwy	124 B3		
Daws Heath Essex	51 A5		
Daw's House Corn	10 C4		
Dawsmere Lincs	118 B1		
Dayhills Staffs	112 B3		
Daylesford Glos	64 A3		
Ddôl-Cownwy Powys	109 D5		
Ddrydwy Anglesey	122 C3		
Deadwater Northumb	187 D5		
Deaf Hill Durham	167 B6		
Deal Kent	53 D5		
Deal Hall Essex	71 D4		
Dean Cumb	162 B3		
Dean Devon	7 A6		
Dean Devon	25 A6		
Dean Dorset	30 D3		
Dean Hants	33 D4		
Dean Som	29 A6		
Dean Prior Devon	7 A6		
Dean Row Ches	128 A3		
Deanburnhaugh Borders	186 B2		
Deane Gtr Man	137 C5		
Deane Hants	46 D3		
Deanich Lodge Highld	263 B5		
Deanland Dorset	30 D3		
Deans W Loth	208 D3		
Deanscales Cumb	162 B3		
Deanshanger Northants	83 D4		
Deanston Stirl	218 D2		
Dearham Cumb	162 A3		
Debach Suff	88 B3		
Debden Essex	86 D1		
Debden Essex	68 D4		
Debden Cross Essex	86 D1		
Debenham Suff	88 A2		
Dechmont W Loth	208 C3		
Deddington Oxon	82 D1		
Dedham Essex	87 D6		
Dedham Heath Essex	87 D6		

Deene Northants 99 B6
Deenethorpe Northants 99 B6
Deep Sea World, North
 Queensferry Fife 208 B4
Deepcar S Yorks 139 D5
Deepcut Sur 34 A2
Deepdale Cumb 155 C6
Deeping Gate Lincs 100 A3
Deeping St James Lincs 100 A3
Deeping St Nicholas
 Lincs 117 D5
Deerhill Moray 267 D5
Deerhurst Glos 63 A4
Deerness Orkney 283 G6
Defford Worcs 80 C2
Defynnog Powys 59 C6
Deganwy Conwy 124 B2
Deighton N Yorks 158 A2
Deighton W Yorks 139 B4
Deighton York 149 C5
Deiniolen Gwyn 123 D5
Delabole Corn 9 C6
Delamere Ches 127 C5
Delfrigs Aberds 257 D4
Dell Lodge Highld 242 A3
Delliefure Highld 254 C1
Delnabo Moray 243 A4
Delnadamph Aberds 243 B5
Delph Gtr Man 138 C2
Delves Durham 166 A4
Delvine Perth 231 D5
Dembleby Lincs 116 B3
Denaby Main S Yorks 140 D2
Denbigh = Dinbych Denb 125 C5
Denbury Devon 8 A2
Denby Derbys 114 A1
Denby Dale W Yorks 139 C5
Denchworth Oxon 65 D4
Dendron Cumb 153 C3
Denel End Beds 84 D2
Denend Aberds 255 C7
Denford Northants 100 D1
Dengie Essex 70 C3
Denham Bucks 48 A3
Denham Suff 86 A3
Denham Suff 104 D2
Denham Green Bucks 48 A3
Denham Street Suff 104 D2
Denhead Aberds 269 D4
Denhead Fife 221 C4
Denhead of Arbilot
 Angus 232 D3
Denhead of Gray Dundee 220 A3
Denholm Borders 187 B4
Denholme W Yorks 147 D4
Denholme Clough
 W Yorks 147 D4
Denio Gwyn 106 C3
Denmead Hants 33 D5
Denmore Aberdeen 245 A6
Denmoss Aberds 256 B1
Dennington Suff 88 A3
Denny Falk 207 B6
Denny Lodge Hants 18 A2
Dennyloanhead Falk 207 B6
Denshaw Gtr Man 138 B2
Denside Aberds 245 C5
Densole Kent 39 A4
Denston Suff 86 B3
Denstone Staffs 113 A5
Dent Cumb 155 C6
Denton Cambs 100 C3
Denton Darl 167 D5
Denton E Sus 22 B2
Denton Gtr Man 138 D2
Denton Kent 39 A4
Denton Lincs 115 B6
Denton Norf 104 C3
Denton Northants 83 B5
Denton N Yorks 147 C5
Denton Oxon 65 C6
Denton's Green Mers 136 D3
Denver Norf 102 A2
Denwick Northumb 189 B5
Deopham Norf 103 A6
Deopham Green Norf 103 B6
Depden Suff 86 B3
Depden Green Suff 86 B3
Deptford London 49 B6
Deptford Wilts 31 B4
Derby Derby 114 B1
Derbyhaven I o M 152 E2
Dereham Norf 120 D1
Deri Caerph 41 A6
Derril Devon 10 A4

Derringstone Kent 39 A4
Derrington Staffs 112 C2
Derriton Devon 10 A1
Derry Hill Wilts 44 B3
Derryguaig Argyll 224 C3
Derrythorpe N Lincs 141 C6
Dersingham Norf 118 B3
Dervaig Argyll 224 A3
Derwen Denb 125 D5
Derwenlas Powys 91 C5
Desborough Northants 99 C5
Desford Leics 98 A1
Detchant Northumb 199 C4
Detling Kent 37 A5
Deuddwr Powys 110 D1
Devauden Mon 61 D6
Devil's Bridge Ceredig 75 A6
Devizes Wilts 44 C4
Devol Invclyd 204 A3
Devon & Exeter
 Racecourse Devon 13 C4
Devonport Plym 6 B3
Devonside Clack 208 A2
Devoran Corn 4 D2
Dewar Borders 196 B2
Dewlish Dorset 16 B1
Dewsbury W Yorks 139 A5
Dewsbury Moor W Yorks 139 A5
Dewshall Court Hereford 78 D2
Dhoon I o M 152 C4
Dhoor I o M 152 B4
Dhowin I o M 152 A4
Dial Post W Sus 21 A4
Dibden Hants 18 A3
Dibden Purlieu Hants 18 A3
Dickleburgh Norf 104 C2
Didbrook Glos 80 D3
Didcot Oxon 46 A3
Diddington Cambs 84 A3
Diddlebury Shrops 94 C3
Didley Hereford 78 D2
Didling W Sus 20 A1
Didmarton Glos 44 A2
Didsbury Gtr Man 138 D1
Didworthy Devon 7 A5
Digby Lincs 133 D5
Digg Highld 259 B4
Diggerland, Cullompton
 Devon 13 A5
Diggerland, Langley Park
 Durham 167 A5
Diggle Gtr Man 138 C3
Digmoor Lancs 136 C3
Digswell Park Herts 68 B2
Dihewyd Ceredig 74 C3
Dilham Norf 121 C5
Dilhorne Staffs 112 A3
Dillarburn S Lnrk 194 B3
Dillington Cambs 84 A3
Dilston Northumb 178 C1
Dilton Marsh Wilts 30 A2
Dilwyn Hereford 78 B2
Dinas Carms 73 C5
Dinas Gwyn 106 C2
Dinas Cross Pembs 72 C3
Dinas Dinlle Gwyn 107 A4
Dinas-Mawddwy Gwyn 91 A6
Dinas Powys V Glam 41 D6
Dinbych = Denbigh Denb 125 C5
Dinbych-y-Pysgod =
 Tenby Pembs 56 B1
Dinder Som 29 A5
Dinedor Hereford 78 D3
Dingestow Mon 61 B6
Dingle Mers 126 A3
Dingleden Kent 37 C6
Dingley Northants 99 C4
Dingwall Highld 252 A1
Dinlabyre Borders 186 D4
Dinmael Conwy 109 A5
Dinnet Aberds 244 C1
Dinnington Som 28 D4
Dinnington S Yorks 131 A5
Dinnington T & W 179 B4
Dinorwic Gwyn 123 D5
Dinton Bucks 66 B2
Dinton Wilts 31 B4
Dinwoodie Mains
 Dumfries 185 C4
Dinworthy Devon 24 D4
Dippen N Ayrs 191 C6
Dippenhall Sur 33 A7
Dipple Moray 266 D4
Dipple S Ayrs 181 A4
Diptford Devon 7 B6
Dipton Durham 178 D3
Dirdhu Highld 254 D1
Dirleton E Loth 210 B2

Dirt Pot Northumb 165 A6
Discoed Powys 77 A6
Discovery Point Dundee 220 B1
Diseworth Leics 114 C2
Dishes Orkney 282 E7
Dishforth N Yorks 158 D2
Disley Ches 129 A4
Diss Norf 104 D2
Disserth Powys 76 B4
Distington Cumb 162 B3
Ditchampton Wilts 31 B4
Ditcheat Som 29 B6
Ditchingham Norf 104 B4
Ditchling E Sus 21 A6
Ditherington Shrops 111 D4
Dittisham Devon 8 B2
Ditton Halton 127 A4
Ditton Kent 37 A5
Ditton Green Cambs 86 B2
Ditton Priors Shrops 95 C4
Divach Highld 251 D6
Divlyn Carms 59 B4
Dixton Glos 80 D2
Dixton Mon 61 B7
Dobcross Gtr Man 138 C2
Dobwalls Corn 5 A7
Doc Penfro = Pembroke
 Dock Pembs 55 D5
Doccombe Devon 12 C2
Dochfour Ho. Highld 252 C2
Dochgarroch Highld 252 B2
Docking Norf 119 B4
Docklow Hereford 78 B3
Dockray Cumb 164 C1
Dockroyd W Yorks 147 D4
Dodburn Borders 186 C3
Doddinghurst Essex 69 D5
Doddington Cambs 101 B5
Doddington Kent 51 D6
Doddington Lincs 133 B4
Doddington Northumb 198 C3
Doddington Shrops 95 D4
Doddiscombsleigh Devon 12 C3
Dodford Northants 82 A3
Dodford Worcs 96 D2
Dodington S Glos 43 A6
Dodleston Ches 126 C3
Dods Leigh Staffs 112 B4
Dodworth S Yorks 139 C6
Doe Green Warr 127 A5
Doe Lea Derbys 131 C4
Dog Village Devon 13 B4
Dogdyke Lincs 134 D2
Dogmersfield Hants 47 D5
Dogridge Wilts 45 A4
Dogsthorpe P'boro 100 A3
Dolanog Powys 109 D5
Dolau Powys 77 A5
Dolau Rhondda 41 C4
Dolbenmaen Gwyn 107 B5
Dolfach Powys 91 B7
Dolfor Powys 93 C5
Dolgarrog Conwy 124 C2
Dolgellau Gwyn 91 A5
Dolgran Carms 58 B1
Dolhendre Gwyn 108 B3
Doll Highld 274 D2
Dollar Clack 208 A2
Dolley Green Powys 77 A6
Dollwen Ceredig 91 D4
Dolphin Flint 126 B1
Dolphinholme Lancs 145 B5
Dolphinton S Lnrk 195 B6
Dolton Devon 25 D6
Dolwen Conwy 124 B3
Dolwen Powys 92 A3
Dolwyd Conwy 124 B3
Dolwyddelan Conwy 124 D2
Dolyhir Powys 77 B6
Doncaster S Yorks 140 C3
Doncaster Racecourse
 S Yorks 140 C4
Dones Green Ches 127 B6
Donhead St Andrew Wilts 30 C3
Donhead St Mary Wilts 30 C3
Donibristle Fife 209 B4
Donington Lincs 117 B5
Donington on Bain Lincs 134 A2
Donington Park Motor
 Racing Circuit Leics 114 C2
Donington South Ing
 Lincs 117 B5
Donisthorpe Leics 113 D7
Donkey Town Sur 48 C2
Donnington Glos 64 A2

Donnington Hereford 79 D5
Donnington Shrops 94 A3
Donnington Telford 111 D6
Donnington W Berks 46 C2
Donnington W Sus 20 B1
Donnington Wood
 Telford 111 D6
Donyatt Som 28 D3
Doonfoot S Ayrs 192 D3
Dorback Lodge Highld 242 A3
Dorchester Dorset 15 B6
Dorchester Oxon 65 D6
Dorchester Abbey,
 Wallingford Oxon 65 D6
Dordon Warks 97 A5
Dore S Yorks 130 A3
Dores Highld 252 C1
Dorking Sur 35 B4
Dormansland Sur 36 B2
Dormanstown Redcar 168 C3
Dormington Hereford 78 C3
Dormston Worcs 80 B2
Dorney Bucks 48 B2
Dornie Highld 249 D5
Dornoch Highld 264 B3
Dornock Dumfries 175 B5
Dorrery Highld 279 C6
Dorridge W Mid 97 D4
Dorrington Lincs 133 D5
Dorrington Shrops 94 A2
Dorsington Warks 80 C4
Dorstone Hereford 77 C7
Dorton Bucks 66 B1
Dorusduain Highld 250 D1
Dosthill Staffs 97 B5
Dottery Dorset 15 B4
Doublebois Corn 5 A6
Dougarie N Ayrs 191 B4
Doughton Glos 63 D4
Douglas I o M 152 D3
Douglas S Lnrk 194 C3
Douglas & Angus Dundee 220 A4
Douglas Water S Lnrk 194 C3
Douglas West S Lnrk 194 C3
Douglastown Angus 232 D2
Doulting Som 29 A6
Dounby Orkney 282 E3
Doune Highld 272 D2
Doune Stirl 218 D2
Doune Park Aberds 268 C2
Douneside Aberds 244 B1
Dounie Highld 264 A1
Dounreay Highld 279 B5
Dousland Devon 7 A4
Dovaston Shrops 110 C2
Dove Cottage and
 Wordsworth Museum
 Cumb 154 A2
Dove Holes Derbys 129 B5
Dovenby Cumb 162 A3
Dover Kent 39 A5
Dover Castle Kent 39 A5
Dovercourt Essex 88 D3
Doverdale Worcs 79 A6
Doveridge Derbys 113 B5
Doversgreen Sur 35 B5
Dowally Perth 230 D4
Dowbridge Lancs 144 D4
Dowdeswell Glos 63 B5
Dowlais M Tydf 60 C2
Dowland Devon 25 D6
Dowlish Wake Som 28 D3
Down Ampney Glos 64 D2
Down Hatherley Glos 63 A4
Down St Mary Devon 12 A2
Down Thomas Devon 7 B4
Downcraig Ferry N Ayrs 204 C1
Downderry Corn 6 B2
Downe London 50 C1
Downend I o W 18 C4
Downend S Glos 43 B5
Downend W Berks 46 B2
Downfield Dundee 220 A3
Downgate Corn 11 D4
Downham Essex 70 D1
Downham Lancs 146 C1
Downham Northumb 198 C2
Downham Market Norf 102 A2
Downhead Som 29 A6
Downhill Perth 219 A5
Downhill T & W 179 D5
Downholland Cross Lancs 136 C2
Downholme N Yorks 157 B5
Downies Aberds 245 C6
Downley Bucks 66 D3
Downside Som 29 A6
Downside Sur 35 A4

Downton Hants 17 B6
Downton Wilts 31 C5
Downton on the Rock
 Hereford 94 D2
Dowsby Lincs 116 C4
Dowsdale Lincs 117 D5
Dowthwaitehead Cumb 163 B6
Doxey Staffs 112 C3
Doxford Northumb 189 A4
Doxford Park T & W 179 D5
Doynton S Glos 43 B6
Draffan S Lnrk 194 B2
Dragonby N Lincs 141 B7
Drakeland Corner Devon 7 B4
Drakemyre N Ayrs 204 C2
Drake's Broughton Worcs 80 C2
Drakes Cross Worcs 96 D3
Drakewalls Corn 11 D5
Draughton Northants 99 D4
Draughton N Yorks 147 B6
Drax N Yorks 141 A4
Draycote Warks 98 D1
Draycott Derbys 114 B2
Draycott Glos 81 D4
Draycott Som 42 D3

Draycott in the Clay
 Staffs 113 C5
Draycott in the Moors
 Staffs 112 A3
Drayford Devon 26 D3
Drayton Leics 99 B5
Drayton Lincs 117 B5
Drayton Norf 120 D3
Drayton Oxon 82 C3
Drayton Oxon 65 D5
Drayton Ptsmth 19 A5
Drayton Som 28 C4
Drayton Worcs 96 D2
Drayton Bassett Staffs 97 A4
Drayton Beauchamp Bucks 67 B4
Drayton Manor Park,
 Tamworth Staffs 97 A4
Drayton Parslow Bucks 66 A3
Drayton St Leonard Oxon 65 D6
Dre-fach Ceredig 75 D5
Dre-fach Carms 57 A5
Dreamland Theme Park,
 Margate Kent 53 B5
Drebley N Yorks 147 B4
Dreemskerry I o M 152 B4
Dreenhill Pembs 55 C5
Drefach Carms 73 C6
Drefach Carms 57 A5
Drefelin Carms 73 C6
Dreghorn N Ayrs 192 B3
Drellingore Kent 39 A4
Drem E Loth 210 C2
Dresden Stoke 112 A3
Dreumasdal W Isles 286 C3
Drewsteignton Devon 12 B2
Driby Lincs 134 B3
Driffield E Yorks 150 B3
Driffield Glos 63 D6
Drigg Cumb 153 A1
Drighlington W Yorks 139 A5
Drimnin Highld 225 A4
Drimpton Dorset 14 D4
Drimsynie Argyll 215 B5
Drinisiadar W Isles 288 H2
Drinkstone Suff 87 A5
Drinkstone Green Suff 87 A5
Drishaig Argyll 215 A5
Drissaig Argyll 214 A2
Drochil Borders 195 B6
Drointon Staffs 112 C4
Droitwich Spa Worcs 80 A1
Droman Highld 276 C2
Dron Perth 219 C6
Dronfield Derbys 130 B3
Dronfield Woodhouse
 Derbys 130 B3
Drongan E Ayrs 182 A2
Dronley Angus 220 A3
Droxford Hants 33 D5
Droylsden Gtr Man 138 D2
Druid Denb 109 A5
Druidston Pembs 55 C4
Druimarbin Highld 237 B4
Druimavuic Argyll 227 B5
Druimdrishaig Argyll 202 A2
Druimindarroch Highld 235 B5
Druimyeon More Argyll 202 C1
Drum Argyll 202 A3
Drum Perth 219 D5
Drumbeg Highld 270 A4
Drumblade Aberds 255 C6
Drumblair Aberds 256 B1
Drumbuie Dumfries 18

Drumbuie Highld 249 C4
Drumburgh Cumb 175 C5
Drumburn Dumfries 174 B2
Drumchapel Glasgow 205 A5
Drumchardine Highld 252 B1
Drumchork Highld 261 B5
Drumclog S Lnrk 193 B6
Drumderfit Highld 252 A2
Drumeldrie Fife 220 D4
Drumelzier Borders 195 C6
Drumfearn Highld 247 C5
Drumgask Highld 241 C4
Drumgley Angus 232 C2
Drumguish Highld 241 C5
Drumin Moray 254 C2
Drumlasie Aberds 244 B3
Drumlemble Argyll 190 D2
Drumligair Aberds 245 A6
Drumlithie Aberds 245 D4
Drummoddie Dumfries 171 C5
Drummond Highld 264 D2
Drummore Dumfries 170 D3
Drummuir Moray 255 B4
Drummuir Castle Moray 255 B4
Drumnadrochit Highld 251 D7
Drumnagorrach Moray 267 D6
Drumoak Aberds 245 C4
Drumpark Dumfries 183 D6
Drumphail Dumfries 171 A4
Drumrash Dumfries 173 A4
Drumrunie Highld 271 D4
Drums Aberds 257 D4
Drumsallie Highld 236 B3
Drumstinchall Dumfries 173 C6
Drumsturdy Angus 221 A4
Drumtochty Castle Aberds 244 E3
Drumtroddan Dumfries 171 C5
Drumuie Highld 259 D4
Drumuillie Highld 253 D5
Drumvaich Stirl 217 D6
Drumwhindle Aberds 257 C4
Drury Flint 126 C2
Drury Square Norf 119 D6
Drusillas Park, Polegate E Sus 22 B3
Dry Doddington Lincs 115 A6
Dry Drayton Cambs 85 A5
Drybeck Cumb 165 D4
Drybridge Moray 267 C5
Drybridge N Ayrs 192 B3
Drybrook Glos 62 B2
Dryburgh Borders 197 C4
Dryhope Borders 196 D1
Drylaw Edin 209 C5
Drym Corn 3 B4
Drymen Stirl 206 B2
Drymuir Aberds 257 B4
Drynoch Highld 246 A3
Dryslwyn Carms 58 C2
Dryton Shrops 94 A3
Dubford Aberds 268 C3
Dubton Angus 232 C3
Duchally Highld 271 C6
Duchlage Argyll 206 B1
Duck Corner Suff 89 C4
Duckington Ches 127 D4
Ducklington Oxon 65 C4
Duckmanton Derbys 131 B4
Duck's Cross Beds 84 B3
Duddenhoe End Essex 85 D6
Duddingston Edin 209 C5
Duddington Northants 100 A1
Duddleswell E Sus 36 D2
Duddo Northumb 198 B3
Duddon Ches 127 C5
Duddon Bridge Cumb 153 B3
Dudleston Shrops 110 B2
Dudleston Heath Shrops 110 B2
Dudley T & W 179 B4
Dudley W Mid 96 B2
Dudley Port W Mid 96 B2
Dudley Zoological Gardens W Mid 96 B2
Duffield Derbys 114 A1
Duffryn Newport 42 A1
Duffryn Neath 40 B3
Dufftown Moray 254 C4
Duffus Moray 266 C2
Dufton Cumb 165 C4
Duggleby N Yorks 150 A1
Duirinish Highld 249 C4
Duisdalemore Highld 247 C6
Duisky Highld 237 B4
Dukestown Bl Gwent 60 B3
Dukinfield Gtr Man 138 D2
Dulas Anglesey 123 B4

Dulcote Som 29 A5
Dulford Devon 13 A5
Dull Perth 230 D2
Dullatur N Lnrk 207 C5
Dullingham Cambs 86 B2
Dulnain Bridge Highld 253 D5
Duloe Beds 84 A3
Duloe Corn 6 B1
Dulsie Highld 253 B5
Dulverton Som 27 C4
Dulwich London 49 B6
Dumbarton W Dunb 205 A4
Dumbleton Glos 80 D3
Dumcrieff Dumfries 185 B4
Dumfries Dumfries 174 A2
Dumgoyne Stirl 206 B3
Dummer Hants 33 A4
Dumpford W Sus 34 D1
Dumpton Kent 53 C5
Dun Angus 233 C4
Dun Charlabhaigh W Isles 288 C2
Dunain Ho. Highld 252 B2
Dunalastair Perth 229 C6
Dunan Highld 247 B4
Dunans Argyll 214 C3
Dunball Som 28 A3
Dunbar E Loth 210 C3
Dunbeath Highld 275 B5
Dunbeg Argyll 226 C3
Dunblane Stirl 218 D2
Dunbog Fife 220 C2
Duncanston Aberds 255 D6
Duncanston Highld 252 A1
Dunchurch Warks 98 D1
Duncote Northants 82 B3
Duncow Dumfries 184 D2
Duncraggan Stirl 217 D5
Duncrievie Perth 219 D6
Duncton W Sus 20 A2
Dundas Ho. Orkney 283 K5
Dundee Dundee 220 A4
Dundee Airport Dundee 220 B3
Dundeugh Dumfries 182 D3
Dundon Som 29 B4
Dundonald S Ayrs 192 B3
Dundonnell Highld 262 B2
Dundonnell Hotel Highld 262 B2
Dundonnell House Highld 262 B3
Dundraw Cumb 175 D5
Dundreggan Highld 239 A7
Dundreggan Lodge Highld 240 A1
Dundrennan Dumfries 173 D5
Dundry N Som 43 C4
Dunecht Aberds 245 B4
Dunfermline Fife 208 B3
Dunfield Glos 64 D2
Dunford Bridge S Yorks 139 C4
Dungworth S Yorks 130 A2
Dunham Notts 132 B3
Dunham Massey Gtr Man 128 A2
Dunham-on-the-Hill Ches 127 B4
Dunham Town Gtr Man 128 A2
Dunhampton Worcs 79 A6
Dunholme Lincs 133 B5
Dunino Fife 221 C5
Dunipace Falk 207 B6
Dunira Perth 218 B2
Dunkeld Perth 230 D4
Dunkerton Bath 43 D6
Dunkeswell Devon 13 A6
Dunkeswick N Yorks 148 C2
Dunkirk Kent 52 D2
Dunkirk Norf 120 C4
Dunk's Green Kent 36 A4
Dunlappie Angus 232 B3
Dunley Hants 46 D2
Dunley Worcs 79 A5
Dunlichity Lodge Highld 252 C2
Dunlop E Ayrs 205 D4
Dunmaglass Lodge Highld 252 D1
Dunmore Argyll 202 B2
Dunmore Falk 208 B1
Dunnet Highld 280 A4
Dunnichen Angus 232 D3
Dunninald Angus 233 C5
Dunning Perth 219 C5
Dunnington E Yorks 151 B4
Dunnington Warks 80 B3
Dunnington York 149 B5
Dunnockshaw Lancs 137 A7
Dunollie Argyll 226 C3
Dunoon Argyll 203 A6
Dunragit Dumfries 170 B3

Dunrobin Castle Museum & Gardens Highld 274 D2
Dunrostan Argyll 213 D5
Duns Borders 198 A1
Duns Tew Oxon 65 A5
Dunsby Lincs 116 C4
Dunscore Dumfries 183 D6
Dunscroft S Yorks 141 C4
Dunsdale Redcar 168 D4
Dunsden Green Oxon 47 B5
Dunsfold Sur 34 C3
Dunsford Devon 12 C3
Dunshalt Fife 220 C2
Dunshillock Aberds 257 B4
Dunskey Ho. Dumfries 170 B2
Dunsley N Yorks 169 D6
Dunsmore Bucks 66 C3
Dunsop Bridge Lancs 145 B6
Dunstable Beds 67 A5
Dunstall Staffs 113 C5
Dunstall Common Worcs 80 C1
Dunstall Green Suff 86 A3
Dunstan Northumb 189 B5
Dunstan Steads Northumb 189 A5
Dunster Som 27 A4
Dunster Castle, Minehead Som 27 A4
Dunston Lincs 133 C5
Dunston Norf 104 A3
Dunston Staffs 112 D3
Dunston T & W 179 C4
Dunsville S Yorks 140 C4
Dunswell E Yorks 150 D3
Dunsyre S Lnrk 195 B5
Dunterton Devon 11 D4
Duntisbourne Abbots Glos 63 C5
Duntisbourne Leer Glos 63 C5
Duntisbourne Rouse Glos 63 C5
Duntish Dorset 15 A6
Duntocher W Dunb 205 A4
Dunton Beds 84 C4
Dunton Bucks 66 A3
Dunton Norf 119 B5
Dunton Bassett Leics 98 B2
Dunton Green Kent 36 A3
Dunton Wayletts Essex 69 D6
Duntulm Highld 259 A4
Dunure S Ayrs 192 D2
Dunvant Swansea 57 C5
Dunvegan Highld 258 D2
Dunvegan Castle Highld 258 C2
Dunwich Suff 105 D5
Dunwood Staffs 129 D4
Dupplin Castle Perth 219 C5
Durdar Cumb 175 C7
Durgates E Sus 36 C4
Durham Durham 167 A5
Durham Cathedral Durham 167 A5
Durham Tees Valley Airport Stockton 167 D6
Durisdeer Dumfries 183 B6
Durisdeermill Dumfries 183 B6
Durkar W Yorks 139 B6
Durleigh Som 28 B2
Durley Hants 32 D4
Durley Wilts 45 C6
Durnamuck Highld 262 A2
Durness Highld 277 B5
Durno Aberds 256 D2
Duror Highld 236 D3
Durran Argyll 214 B2
Durran Highld 280 B3
Durrington Wilts 31 A5
Durrington W Sus 21 B4
Dursley Glos 62 D3
Durston Som 28 C2
Durweston Dorset 16 A2
Dury Shetland 285 G6
Duston Northants 83 A4
Duthil Highld 253 D5
Dutlas Powys 93 D6
Duton Hill Essex 69 A6
Dutson Corn 10 C4
Dutton Ches 127 B5
Duxford Cambs 85 C6
Duxford Oxon 65 D4
Duxford Airfield (Imperial War Museum), Sawston Cambs 85 C6
Dwygyfylchi Conwy 124 B2
Dwyran Anglesey 123 D4
Dyce Aberds 245 A5
Dye House Northumb 178 D1
Dyffryn Bridgend 40 B3
Dyffryn Carms 73 D6

Dyffryn Pembs 72 C2
Dyffryn Ardudwy Gwyn 107 D5
Dyffryn Castell Ceredig 91 D5
Dyffryn Ceidrych Carms 59 C4
Dyffryn Cellwen Neath 59 E5
Dyke Lincs 116 C4
Dyke Moray 253 A5
Dykehead Angus 232 B1
Dykehead N Lnrk 207 E6
Dykehead Stirl 206 A2
Dykelands Aberds 233 B5
Dykends Angus 231 C6
Dykeside Aberds 256 B2
Dykesmains N Ayrs 204 D2
Dylife Powys 91 C6
Dymchurch Kent 38 C2
Dymock Glos 79 D5
Dyrham S Glos 43 B6
Dyrham Park S Glos 43 B6
Dysart Fife 209 A6
Dyserth Denb 125 B5

E

Eachwick Northumb 178 B3
Eadar Dha Fhadhail W Isles 287 A5
Eagland Hill Lancs 144 C4
Eagle Lincs 132 C3
Eagle Barnsdale Lincs 132 C3
Eagle Moor Lincs 132 C3
Eaglescliffe Stockton 168 D2
Eaglesfield Cumb 162 B3
Eaglesfield Dumfries 175 A5
Eaglesham E Renf 205 C5
Eaglethorpe Northants 100 B2
Eairy I o M 152 D2
Eakley Lanes M Keynes 83 B5
Eakring Notts 132 C1
Ealand Lincs 141 B5
Ealing London 49 A4
Eals Northumb 177 D4
Eamont Bridge Cumb 164 C3
Earby Lancs 146 C3
Earcroft Blkburn 137 A5
Eardington Shrops 95 B5
Eardisland Hereford 78 B2
Eardisley Hereford 77 C7
Eardiston Shrops 110 C2
Eardiston Worcs 79 A4
Earith Cambs 101 D5
Earl Shilton Leics 98 B1
Earl Soham Suff 88 A3
Earl Sterndale Derbys 129 C5
Earl Stonham Suff 88 B2
Earle Northumb 188 A2
Earley Wokingham 47 B5
Earlham Norf 104 A3
Earlish Highld 258 B3
Earls Barton Northants 83 A5
Earls Colne Essex 70 A2
Earl's Croome Worcs 79 C6
Earl's Green Suff 87 A6
Earlsdon W Mid 97 D6
Earlsferry Fife 221 E4
Earlsfield Lincs 116 B2
Earlsford Aberds 256 C3
Earlsheaton W Yorks 139 A5
Earlsmill Moray 253 A5
Earlston Borders 197 C4
Earlston E Ayrs 193 B4
Earlswood Mon 61 D6
Earlswood Sur 35 B5
Earlswood Warks 96 D4
Earnley W Sus 19 B7
Earsairidh W Isles 286 G3
Earsdon T & W 179 B5
Earsham Norf 104 C4
Earswick York 149 B5
Eartham W Sus 20 B2
Easby N Yorks 159 A4
Easby N Yorks 157 A5
Easdale Argyll 213 A5
Easebourne W Sus 34 D1
Easenhall Warks 98 D1
Eashing Sur 34 B2
Easington Bucks 66 B1
Easington Durham 168 A2
Easington E Yorks 143 B5
Easington Northumb 199 C5
Easington Oxon 82 D1
Easington Oxon 66 D1
Easington Redcar 169 D5
Easington Colliery Durham 168 A2
Easington Lane T & W 167 A6
Easingwold N Yorks 148 A4

Easole Street Kent 53 D4
Eassie Angus 232 D1
East Aberthaw V Glam 41 E5
East Adderbury Oxon 82 D1
East Allington Devon 7 C6
East Anstey Devon 26 C3
East Appleton N Yorks 157 B6
East Ardsley W Yorks 139 A6
East Ashling W Sus 19 A7
East Auchronie Aberds 245 B5
East Ayton N Yorks 160 C3
East Bank Bl Gwent 60 C4
East Barkwith Lincs 133 A6
East Barming Kent 37 A5
East Barnby N Yorks 169 D6
East Barnet London 68 D2
East Barns E Loth 211 C4
East Barsham Norf 119 B6
East Beckham Norf 120 B3
East Bedfont London 48 B3
East Bergholt Suff 87 D6
East Bilney Norf 119 D6
East Blatchington E Sus 22 B2
East Boldre Hants 18 A2
East Brent Som 42 D2
East Bridgford Notts 115 A4
East Buckland Devon 26 B1
East Budleigh Devon 13 C5
East Burrafirth Shetland 285 H5
East Burton Dorset 16 C2
East Butsfield Durham 166 A4
East Butterwick N Lincs 141 C6
East Cairnbeg Aberds 233 A5
East Calder W Loth 208 D3
East Carleton Norf 104 A2
East Carlton Northants 99 C5
East Carlton N Yorks 147 C6
East Chaldon Dorset 16 C1
East Challow Oxon 46 A1
East Chiltington E Sus 21 A6
East Chinnock Som 29 D4
East Chisenbury Wilts 45 D5
East Clandon Sur 34 A3
East Claydon Bucks 66 A2
East Clyne Highld 274 D2
East Coker Som 29 D5
East Combe Som 27 B6
East Common N Yorks 149 D5
East Compton Som 29 A6
East Cottingwith E Yorks 149 C6
East Cowes I o W 18 B4
East Cowick E Yorks 141 A4
East Cowton N Yorks 157 A7
East Cramlington Northumb 179 B4
East Cranmore Som 29 A6
East Creech Dorset 16 C3
East Croachy Highld 252 D2
East Croftmore Highld 242 A2
East Curthwaite Cumb 164 A1
East Dean E Sus 22 C3
East Dean Hants 31 C6
East Dean W Sus 20 A2
East Down Devon 25 A7
East Drayton Notts 132 B2
East Ella Hull 142 A2
East End Dorset 16 B3
East End E Yorks 143 A4
East End Hants 18 B2
East End Hants 33 C5
East End Herts 46 C2
East End Herts 69 A4
East End Kent 37 C6
East End N Som 42 B3
East End Oxon 65 B4
East Farleigh Kent 37 A5
East Farndon Northants 99 C4
East Ferry Lincs 141 D6
East Fortune E Loth 210 C2
East Garston W Berks 46 B1
East Ginge Oxon 46 A2
East Goscote Leics 115 D4
East Grafton Wilts 45 C6
East Grimstead Wilts 31 C5
East Grinstead W Sus 36 C1
East Guldeford E Sus 38 C1
East Haddon Northants 82 A3
East Hagbourne Oxon 46 A3
East Halton N Lincs 142 B3
East Ham London 50 A1
East Hanney Oxon 65 D5
East Hanningfield Essex 70 C1
East Hardwick W Yorks 140 B2
East Harling Norf 103 C5

East Harlsey N Yorks 158 B3
East Harnham Wilts 31 C5
East Harptree Bath 43 D4
East Hartford Northumb 179 B4
East Harting W Sus 33 D6
East Hatley Cambs 85 B?
East Hauxwell N Yorks 157 B5
East Haven Angus 221 A5
East Heckington Lincs 117 A4
East Hedleyhope Durham 167 A4
East Hendred Oxon 46 A2
East Herrington T & W 179 D5
East Heslerton N Yorks 160 D3
East Hoathly E Sus 22 A3
East Horrington Som 29 A5
East Horsley Sur 34 A3
East Horton Northumb 198 C4
East Huntspill Som 28 A3
East Hyde Beds 67 B6
East Ilkerton Devon 28 A2
East Ilsley W Berks 46 A2
East Keal Lincs 134 C3
East Kennett Wilts 45 C5
East Keswick W Yorks 148 C2
East Kilbride S Lnrk 205 C6
East Kirkby Lincs 134 C3
East Knapton N Yorks 160 D2
East Knighton Dorset 16 C2
East Knoyle Wilts 30 B2
East Kyloe Northumb 199 C4
East Lambrook Som 28 D4
East Lamington Highld 264 C3
East Langdon Kent 39 A5
East Langton Leics 99 B4
East Langwell Highld 273 D5
East Lavant W Sus 20 B1
East Lavington W Sus 20 A2
East Layton N Yorks 157 A5
East Leake Notts 114 C3
East Learmouth Northumb 198 C2
East Leigh Devon 12 A1
East Lexham Norf 119 D5
East Lilburn Northumb 188 A3
East Linton E Loth 210 C2
East Liss Hants 33 C6
East Looe Corn 6 B1
East Lound N Lincs 141 D5
East Lulworth Dorset 16 C2
East Lutton N Yorks 150 A2
East Lydford Som 29 B5
East Mains Aberds 244 C3
East Malling Kent 37 A5
East March Angus 220 A4
East Marden W Sus 33 D7
East Markham Notts 132 B2
East Marton N Yorks 146 B3
East Meon Hants 33 C5
East Mere Devon 27 D4
East Mersea Essex 71 B4
East Mey Highld 281 A5
East Molesey Sur 49 C4
East Morden Dorset 16 B3
East Morton W Yorks 147 C4
East Ness N Yorks 159 D5
East Newton E Yorks 151 D5
East Norton Leics 99 A4
East Nynehead Som 27 C6
East Oakley Hants 46 D3
East Ogwell Devon 12 D3
East Orchard Dorset 30 D2
East Ord Northumb 198 A3
East Panson Devon 11 B4
East Peckham Kent 37 B4
East Pennard Som 29 B5
East Perry Cambs 84 A3
East Portlemouth Devon 7 D6
East Prawle Devon 8 D1
East Preston W Sus 20 B3
East Putford Devon 25 D4
East Quantoxhead Som 27 A6
East Rainton T & W 167 A6
East Ravendale NE Lincs 143 D4
East Raynham Norf 119 C5
East Rhidorroch Lodge Highld 262 A4
East Rigton W Yorks 148 C2
East Rounton N Yorks 158 A3
East Row N Yorks 169 D6
East Rudham Norf 119 C5
East Runton Norf 120 A3
East Ruston Norf 121 C5
East Saltoun E Loth 210 D1
East Sleekburn Northumb 179 A4
East Somerton Norf 121 D6

East Stockwith Lincs 141 D5
East Stoke Dorset 16 C2
East Stoke Notts 115 A6
East Stour Dorset 30 C2
East Stourmouth Kent 53 C4
East Stowford Devon 26 C1
East Stratton Hants 32 B4
East Studdal Kent 39 A5
East Suisnish Highld 248 C2
East Taphouse Corn 5 C6
East-the-Water Devon 25 C5
East Thirston Northumb 189 D4
East Tilbury Thurrock 50 B3
East Tisted Hants 33 B6
East Torrington Lincs 133 A6
East Tuddenham Norf 120 D2
East Tytherley Hants 32 C1
East Tytherton Wilts 44 B3
East Village Devon 12 A3
East Wall Shrops 94 B3
East Walton Norf 119 D4
East Wellow Hants 32 C2
East Whitburn W Loth 208 D2
East Williamston Pembs 55 D6
East Winch Norf 118 D3
East Winterslow Wilts 31 B6
East Wittering W Sus 19 B6
East Witton N Yorks 157 C5
East Woodburn Northumb 177 A7
East Woodhay Hants 46 C2
East Worldham Hants 33 B6
East Worlington Devon 26 D2
East Worthing W Sus 21 B4
Eastbourne E Sus 22 C4
Eastbridge Suff 89 A5
Eastburn W Yorks 147 C4
Eastbury Herts 67 D5
Eastbury W Berks 46 B1
Eastby N Yorks 147 B4
Eastchurch Kent 52 B1
Eastcombe Glos 63 C4
Eastcote London 48 A4
Eastcote Northants 82 B3
Eastcote W Mid 97 D4
Eastcott Corn 24 D3
Eastcott Wilts 44 D4
Eastcourt Wilts 63 D5
Eastcourt Wilts 45 C6
Easter Ardross Highld 264 C2
Easter Balmoral Aberds 243 C5
Easter Boleskine Highld 251 D7
Easter Compton S Glos 43 A4
Easter Cringate Stirl 207 B5
Easter Davoch Aberds 244 B1
Easter Earshaig Dumfries 184 B3
Easter Fearn Highld 264 B2
Easter Galcantray Highld 253 B4
Easter Howgate Midloth 209 D5
Easter Howlaws Borders 197 B6
Easter Kinkell Highld 252 A1
Easter Lednathie Angus 232 B1
Easter Milton Highld 253 A5
Easter Moniack Highld 252 B1
Easter Ord Aberds 245 B5
Easter Quarff Shetland 285 K6
Easter Rhynd Perth 219 C6
Easter Row Stirl 207 A5
Easter Silverford Aberds 268 C2
Easter Skeld Shetland 285 J5
Easter Whyntie Aberds 267 C7
Eastergate W Sus 20 B2
Easterhouse Glasgow 207 D4
Eastern Green W Mid 97 C5
Easterton Wilts 44 D4
Eastertown Som 42 D2
Eastertown of Auchleuchries Aberds 257 C5
Eastfield N Lnrk 208 D1
Eastfield N Yorks 160 C4
Eastfield Hall Northumb 189 C5
Eastgate Durham 166 B2
Eastgate Norf 120 C3
Eastham Mers 126 A3
Eastham Ferry Mers 126 A3
Easthampstead Brack 47 C6
Eastheath Wokingham 47 C6
Easthope Shrops 94 B3
Easthorpe Essex 70 A3
Easthorpe Leics 115 B6
Easthorpe Notts 132 D2
Easthouses Midloth 209 D6
Eastington Devon 12 A2
Eastington Glos 62 C3
Eastington Glos 64 B2
Eastleach Martin Glos 64 C3
Eastleach Turville Glos 64 C2

Eastleigh Devon 25 C5
Eastleigh Hants 32 D3
Eastling Kent 51 D6
Eastmoor Derbys 130 B3
Eastmoor Norf 102 A3
Eastney Ptsmth 19 B5
Eastnor Hereford 79 D5
Eastoft N Lincs 141 B6
Eastoke Hants 19 B6
Easton Cambs 100 D3
Easton Cumb 175 C5
Easton Cumb 176 B2
Easton Devon 12 C2
Easton Dorset 15 D6
Easton Hants 32 B4
Easton Lincs 116 C2
Easton Norf 120 D3
Easton Som 29 A5
Easton Suff 88 B3
Easton Wilts 44 B2
Easton Grey Wilts 44 A2
Easton-in-Gordano N Som 43 B4
Easton Maudit Northants 83 B5
Easton on the Hill Northants 100 A2
Easton Royal Wilts 45 C6
Eastpark Dumfries 174 B3
Eastrea Cambs 101 B4
Eastriggs Dumfries 175 B5
Eastrington E Yorks 141 A5
Eastry Kent 53 D5
Eastville Bristol 43 B5
Eastville Lincs 135 D4
Eastwell Leics 115 C5
Eastwick Herts 68 B4
Eastwick Shetland 284 F5
Eastwood Notts 114 A2
Eastwood Sthend 51 A5
Eastwood W Yorks 138 A2
Eathorpe Warks 81 A6
Eaton Ches 127 C5
Eaton Ches 128 C3
Eaton Leics 115 C5
Eaton Norf 104 A3
Eaton Notts 132 B2
Eaton Oxon 65 C5
Eaton Shrops 94 C1
Eaton Shrops 94 C3
Eaton Bishop Hereford 78 D2
Eaton Bray Beds 67 A4
Eaton Constantine Shrops 94 A3
Eaton Green Beds 67 A4
Eaton Hastings Oxon 64 D3
Eaton on Tern Shrops 111 C5
Eaton Socon Cambs 84 B3
Eavestone N Yorks 147 A6
Ebberston N Yorks 160 C2
Ebbesbourne Wake Wilts 30 C3
Ebbw Vale = Glyn Ebwy Bl Gwent 60 C3
Ebchester Durham 178 D3
Ebford Devon 13 C4
Ebley Glos 63 C4
Ebnal Ches 110 A3
Ebrington Glos 81 D4
Ecchinswell Hants 46 D2
Ecclaw Borders 211 D4
Ecclefechan Dumfries 175 A4
Eccles Borders 197 B6
Eccles Gtr Man 137 D6
Eccles Kent 51 C4
Eccles on Sea Norf 121 C6
Eccles Road Norf 103 B6
Ecclesall S Yorks 130 A3
Ecclesfield S Yorks 139 D6
Ecclesgreig Aberds 233 B5
Eccleshall Staffs 112 C2
Eccleshill W Yorks 147 D5
Ecclesmachan W Loth 208 C3
Eccleston Ches 127 C4
Eccleston Lancs 136 B4
Eccleston Mers 136 D3
Eccleston Park Mers 136 D3
Eccup W Yorks 148 C1
Echt Aberds 245 B4
Eckford Borders 187 A6
Eckington Derbys 131 B4
Eckington Worcs 80 C2
Ecton Northants 83 A5
Edale Derbys 129 A6
Edburton W Sus 21 A5
Edderside Cumb 174 D3
Edderton Highld 264 B3
Eddistone Devon 24 C3
Eddleston Borders 196 B1
Eden Camp Museum, Malton N Yorks 159 D6

Eden Park London 49 C6
Edenbridge Kent 36 B2
Edenfield Lancs 137 B6
Edenhall Cumb 164 B3
Edenham Lincs 116 C3
Edensor Derbys 130 C2
Edentaggart Argyll 215 C6
Edenthorpe S Yorks 140 C4
Edentown Cumb 175 C6
Ederline Argyll 214 B1
Edern Gwyn 106 C2
Edgarley Som 29 B5
Edgbaston W Mid 96 C3
Edgcott Bucks 66 A1
Edgcott Som 26 B3
Edge Shrops 94 A1
Edge End Glos 62 B1
Edge Green Ches 127 D4
Edge Hill Mers 136 E2
Edgebolton Shrops 111 C4
Edgefield Norf 120 B2
Edgefield Street Norf 120 B2
Edgeside Lancs 138 A1
Edgeworth Glos 63 C5
Edgmond Telford 111 D6
Edgmond Marsh Telford 111 C6
Edgton Shrops 94 C1
Edgware London 68 D1
Edgworth Blkburn 137 B6
Edinample Stirl 217 B5
Edinbane Highld 258 C3
Edinburgh Edin 209 C5
Edinburgh Airport Edin 209 C4
Edinburgh Castle Edin 209 C5
Edinburgh Crystal Visitor Centre, Penicuik Midloth 209 D5
Edinburgh Zoo Edin 209 C5
Edingale Staffs 113 D6
Edingight Ho. Moray 267 D6
Edingley Notts 131 D6
Edingthorpe Norf 121 B5
Edingthorpe Green Norf 121 B5
Edington Som 28 B3
Edington Wilts 44 D3
Edintore Moray 255 B5
Edith Weston Rutland 99 A6
Edithmead Som 28 A3
Edlesborough Bucks 67 B4
Edlingham Northumb 189 C4
Edlington Lincs 134 B2
Edmondsham Dorset 31 D4
Edmondsley Durham 167 A5
Edmondthorpe Leics 115 D6
Edmonstone Orkney 282 E6
Edmonton London 68 D3
Edmundbyers Durham 178 D2
Ednam Borders 197 C6
Ednaston Derbys 113 A6
Edradynate Perth 230 C2
Edrom Borders 198 A2
Edstaston Shrops 111 B4
Edstone Warks 81 A4
Edvin Loach Hereford 79 B4
Edwalton Notts 114 B3
Edwardstone Suff 87 C5
Edwinsford Carms 58 B3
Edwinstowe Notts 131 C6
Edworth Beds 84 C4
Edwyn Ralph Hereford 79 B4
Edzell Angus 232 B3
Efail Isaf Rhondda 41 C5
Efailnewydd Gwyn 106 C3
Efailwen Carms 72 D4
Efenechtyd Denb 125 D6
Effingham Sur 35 A4
Effirth Shetland 285 H5
Efford Devon 12 A3
Egdon Worcs 80 B2
Egerton Gtr Man 137 B6
Egerton Kent 37 B7
Egerton Forstal Kent 37 B6
Eggborough N Yorks 140 A3
Eggbuckland Plym 7 B4
Eggington Beds 67 A4
Egginton Derbys 113 C6
Egglescliffe Stockton 168 D2
Eggleston Durham 166 C2
Egham Sur 48 B3
Egleton Rutland 99 A5
Eglingham Northumb 189 B4
Egloshayle Corn 9 D6
Egloskerry Corn 10 C3
Eglwys-Brewis V Glam 41 E5
Eglwys Cross Wrex 110 A3
Eglwys Fach Ceredig 91 C4
Eglwysbach Conwy 124 B3

Eglwyswen Pembs 73 C4
Eglwyswrw Pembs 72 C4
Egmanton Notts 132 C2
Egremont Cumb 162 C3
Egremont Mers 136 D2
Egton N Yorks 159 A7
Egton Bridge N Yorks 159 A7
Eight Ash Green Essex 70 A3
Eignaig Highld 226 B2
Eil Highld 241 B1
Eilanreach Highld 238 A2
Eilean Darach Highld 262 B3
Eileanach Lodge Highld 264 D1
Einacleite W Isles 288 E2
Eisgean W Isles 288 F4
Eisingrug Gwyn 107 C5
Elan Village Powys 76 A3
Elberton S Glos 43 A4
Elburton Plym 7 B4
Elcho Perth 219 B6
Elcombe Thamesdown 45 A4
Eldernell Cambs 101 B5
Eldersfield Worcs 79 D5
Elderslie Renfs 205 B4
Eldon Durham 167 C5
Eldrick S Ayrs 181 C4
Eldroth N Yorks 146 A1
Eldwick W Yorks 147 C5
Elfhowe Cumb 154 B3
Elford Northumb 199 C5
Elford Staffs 113 D5
Elgin Moray 266 C3
Elgol Highld 247 C4
Elham Kent 38 A3
Elie Fife 221 D5
Elim Anglesey 122 B3
Eling Hants 32 D2
Elishader Highld 259 B5
Elishaw Northumb 188 D1
Elkesley Notts 132 B1
Elkstone Glos 63 B5
Ellan Highld 253 D5
Elland W Yorks 139 A4
Ellary Argyll 202 A2
Ellastone Staffs 113 A5
Ellemford Borders 211 D4
Ellenbrook I o M 152 D3
Ellenhall Staffs 112 C2
Ellen's Green Sur 34 C3
Ellerbeck N Yorks 158 B3
Ellerburn N Yorks 160 C2
Ellerby N Yorks 169 D5
Ellerdine Heath Telford 111 C5
Ellerhayes Devon 13 A4
Elleric Argyll 227 B5
Ellerker E Yorks 141 A7
Ellerton E Yorks 149 D6
Ellerton Shrops 111 C6
Ellesborough Bucks 66 C3
Ellesmere Shrops 110 B3
Ellesmere Port Ches 127 B4
Ellingham Norf 105 B4
Ellingham Northumb 189 A5
Ellingstring N Yorks 157 C5
Ellington Cambs 100 D3
Ellington Northumb 189 D5
Elliot Angus 221 A6
Ellisfield Hants 33 A5
Ellistown Leics 114 D2
Ellon Aberds 257 C4
Ellonby Cumb 164 B2
Ellough Suff 105 C5
Elloughton E Yorks 141 A7
Ellwood Glos 62 C4
Elm Cambs 101 A6
Elm Hill Dorset 30 C2
Elm Park London 50 A2
Elmbridge Worcs 80 A2
Elmdon Essex 85 D6
Elmdon W Mid 97 C4
Elmdon Heath W Mid 97 C4
Elmers End London 49 C6
Elmesthorpe Leics 98 B1
Elmfield I o W 19 B5
Elmhurst Staffs 113 D5
Elmley Castle Worcs 80 C2
Elmley Lovett Worcs 79 A6
Elmore Glos 62 B3
Elmore Back Glos 62 B3
Elmscott Devon 24 C3
Elmsett Suff 87 C6
Elmstead Market Essex 71 A4
Elmsted Kent 38 A3
Elmstone Kent 53 C4
Elmstone Hardwicke Glos 63 A5
Elmswell E Yorks 150 B2
Elmswell Suff 87 A5

Elmton Derbys 131 B5
Elphin Highld 271 C5
Elphinstone E Loth 209 C6
Elrick Aberds 245 B5
Elrig Dumfries 171 C5
Elsdon Northumb 188 D2
Elsecar S Yorks 140 D1
Elsenham Essex 69 A5
Elsfield Oxon 65 B6
Elsham N Lincs 142 B2
Elsing Norf 120 D2
Elslack N Yorks 146 C3
lson Shrops 110 B2
lsrickle S Lnrk 195 B5
lstead Sur 34 B2
lsted W Sus 33 D7
lsthorpe Lincs 116 C3
lstob Durham 167 C6
lston Notts 115 A5
lston Wilts 31 A4
lstone Devon 26 D1
lstow Beds 84 C2
lstree Herts 68 D1
lstronwick E Yorks 151 D5
swick Lancs 144 D4
sworth Cambs 85 A5
terwater Cumb 154 A2
tham London 50 B1
tisley Cambs 85 B4
ton Cambs 100 B2
ton Ches 127 B4
ton Derbys 130 C2
ton Glos 62 B3
ton Hereford 94 D2
ton Notts 115 B5
ton Stockton 168 D2
ton Green Ches 127 B4
vanfoot S Lnrk 184 A2
vaston Derbys 114 B2
veden Suff 103 D4
vingston E Loth 210 C1
vington Kent 53 D4
vington York 149 C5
wick Hrtlpl 168 B2
wick Northumb 199 C5
worth Ches 128 C2
worthy Som 27 B5
Cambs 102 C1
Cardiff 41 D6
Cathedral and
Museum Cambs 102 C1
berton M Keynes 83 C5
bleton Cumb 163 A4
bleton Northumb 189 A5
bo Highld 265 A4
bo Street Highld 265 A4
borough Som 43 D5
bsay N Yorks 147 B4
ery Down Hants 18 A1
ley W Yorks 139 B5
mbrook Wokingham 47 C5
mer Green Reading 47 B5
mington Oxon 66 C2
neth Norf 101 A6
neth Hungate Norf 101 A7
pingham Rutland 99 A6
shott Hants 33 B6
strey Shrops 111 D4
sworth Hants 19 A6
orne W Berks 46 C2
hmarsh Shrops 94 B3
erby Leics 98 B2
moor Cumb 154 C4
on Staffs 129 D4
on Bank Staffs 129 D4
eld London 68 D3
eld Wash London 68 D3
rd Wilts 45 D5
moor Shetland 285 H4
ne Common S Glos 43 A5
efield W Berks 47 B4
efield Green Sur 48 B2
esea-brook Ches 128 D2
ish Bicknor Glos 62 B1
ish Frankton Shrops 110 C3
ishcombe Bath 43 C6
m Alamein Hants 32 A2
ore Som 28 B2
rdale Bridge Cumb 162 C3
h Dumfries 183 B6
hdhu Perth 231 B4
y Argyll 224 B2
ury Bmouth 17 B4
on Shrops 110 D3
Devon 25 C6
one Oxon 65 A4
kinfoot Dumfries 183 B6
Enterpen N Yorks 158 A3
Enville Staffs 95 C6
Eolaigearraidh W Isles 286 F3
Eorabus Argyll 224 D2
Eòropaidh W Isles 288 A6
Epperstone Notts 115 A4
Epping Essex 69 C4
Epping Green Essex 68 C4
Epping Green Herts 68 C2
Epping Upland Essex 68 C4
Eppleby N Yorks 167 D4
Eppleworth E Yorks 150 D3
Epsom Sur 49 C5
Epsom Racecourse Sur 35 A5
Epwell Oxon 81 C6
Epworth N Lincs 141 C5
Epworth Turbary N Lincs 141 C5
Erbistock Wrex 110 A2
Erbusaig Highld 249 D4
Erchless Castle Highld 251 B6
Erddig Wrex 110 A2
Erdington W Mid 96 B4
Eredine Argyll 214 B2
Eriboll Highld 277 C5
Ericstane Dumfries 184 A3
Eridge Green E Sus 36 C3
Erines Argyll 202 A3
Eriswell Suff 102 D3
Erith London 50 B2
Erlestoke Wilts 44 D3
Ermine Lincs 133 B4
Ermington Devon 7 B5
Erpingham Norf 120 B3
Errogie Highld 252 D1
Errol Perth 220 B2
Erskine Renfs 205 A4
Erskine Bridge Renfs 205 A4
Ervie Dumfries 170 A2
Erwarton Suff 88 D3
Erwood Powys 77 C4
Eryholme N Yorks 157 A7
Eryrys Denb 126 D2
Escomb Durham 167 C4
Escrick N Yorks 149 C5
Esgairdawe Carms 58 A3
Esgairgeiliog Powys 91 B5
Esh Durham 167 A4
Esh Winning Durham 167 A4
Esher Sur 48 C4
Esholt W Yorks 147 C5
Eshott Northumb 189 D5
Eshton N Yorks 146 B3
Esk Valley N Yorks 159 A7
Eskadale Highld 251 C6
Eskbank Midloth 209 D6
Eskdale Green Cumb 163 D4
Eskdalemuir Dumfries 185 C5
Eske E Yorks 150 C3
Eskham Lincs 143 D5
Esprick Lancs 144 D4
Essendine Rutland 116 D3
Essendon Herts 68 C2
Essich Highld 252 C2
Essington Staffs 96 A2
Esslemont Aberds 257 D4
Eston Redcar 168 D3
Eswick Shetland 285 H6
Etal Northumb 198 C3
Etchilhampton Wilts 44 C4
Etchingham E Sus 37 D5
Etchinghill Kent 38 B3
Etchinghill Staffs 112 D4
Ethie Castle Angus 233 D4
Ethie Mains Angus 233 D4
Etling Green Norf 120 D2
Eton Windsor 48 B2
Eton Wick Windsor 48 B2
Etteridge Highld 241 C4
Ettersgill Durham 166 C1
Ettingshall W Mid 96 B2
Ettington Warks 81 C5
Etton E Yorks 150 C2
Etton P'boro 100 A3
Ettrick Borders 185 A5
Ettrickbridge Borders 186 A2
Ettrickhill Borders 185 A5
Etwall Derbys 113 B6
Eureka!, Halifax W Yorks 138 A3
Euston Suff 103 D4
Euximoor Drove Cambs 101 B6
Euxton Lancs 137 B4
Evanstown Bridgend 41 C4
Evanton Highld 264 D2
Evedon Lincs 116 A3
Evelix Highld 264 A3
Evenjobb Powys 77 A6
Evenley Northants 82 D2
Evenlode Glos 64 A3
Evenwood Durham 167 C4
Evenwood Gate Durham 167 C4
Everbay Orkney 282 E7
Evercreech Som 29 B6
Everdon Northants 82 B2
Everingham E Yorks 149 C7
Everleigh Wilts 45 D6
Everley N Yorks 160 C3
Eversholt Beds 84 D1
Evershot Dorset 15 A5
Eversley Hants 47 C5
Eversley Cross Hants 47 C5
Everthorpe E Yorks 150 D2
Everton Beds 84 B4
Everton Hants 18 B1
Everton Mers 136 D2
Everton Notts 141 D4
Evertown Dumfries 175 A6
Evesbatch Hereford 79 C4
Evesham Worcs 80 C3
Evington Leicester 98 A3
Ewden Village S Yorks 139 D5
Ewell Sur 49 C5
Ewell Minnis Kent 39 A4
Ewelme Oxon 66 D1
Ewen Glos 63 D6
Ewenny V Glam 40 D4
Ewerby Lincs 116 A4
Ewerby Thorpe Lincs 116 A4
Ewes Dumfries 185 C6
Ewesley Northumb 188 D3
Ewhurst Sur 34 B3
Ewhurst Green E Sus 37 D5
Ewhurst Green Sur 34 C3
Ewloe Flint 126 C3
Ewloe Green Flint 126 C2
Ewood Blkburn 137 A5
Eworthy Devon 11 B5
Ewshot Hants 33 A7
Ewyas Harold Hereford 61 A5
Exbourne Devon 11 A7
Exbury Hants 18 B3
Exbury Gardens, Fawley Hants 18 A3
Exebridge Som 27 C4
Exelby N Yorks 157 C6
Exeter Devon 13 B4
Exeter Cathedral Devon 13 B4
Exeter International Airport Devon 13 B4
Exford Som 26 B3
Exhall Warks 80 B4
Exley Head W Yorks 147 D4
Exminster Devon 13 C4
Exmouth Devon 13 C5
Exnaboe Shetland 285 M5
Exning Suff 86 A2
Explosion, Gosport Hants 19 A5
Exton Devon 13 C4
Exton Hants 33 C5
Exton Rutland 116 D2
Exton Som 27 B4
Exwick Devon 13 B4
Eyam Derbys 130 B2
Eydon Northants 82 B2
Eye Hereford 78 A2
Eye P'boro 100 A4
Eye Suff 104 D2
Eye Green P'boro 100 A4
Eyemouth Borders 211 D6
Eyeworth Beds 85 C4
Eyhorne Street Kent 37 A6
Eyke Suff 88 B4
Eynesbury Cambs 84 B3
Eynort Highld 246 B2
Eynsford Kent 50 C2
Eynsham Oxon 65 C5
Eype Dorset 14 B4
Eyre Highld 259 C4
Eyre Highld 248 C2
Eythorne Kent 39 A4
Eyton Hereford 78 A2
Eyton Shrops 94 C1
Eyton Wrex 110 A2
Eyton upon the Weald Moors Telford 111 D5

F

Faccombe Hants 46 D1
Faceby N Yorks 158 A3
Facit Lancs 138 B1
Faddiley Ches 127 D5
Fadmoor N Yorks 159 C5
Faerdre Swansea 40 A1
Failand N Som 43 B4
Failford S Ayrs 193 C4
Failsworth Gtr Man 138 C1
Fain Highld 262 C3
Fair Green Norf 118 D3
Fair Hill Cumb 164 B3
Fair Oak Hants 32 D3
Fair Oak Green Hants 47 C4
Fairbourne Gwyn 90 A4
Fairburn N Yorks 140 A2
Fairfield Derbys 129 B5
Fairfield Stockton 168 D2
Fairfield Worcs 80 C3
Fairfield Worcs 96 D2
Fairford Glos 64 C2
Fairhaven Lancs 136 A2
Fairlie N Ayrs 204 C2
Fairlight E Sus 23 A6
Fairlight Cove E Sus 23 A6
Fairmile Devon 13 B5
Fairmilehead Edin 209 D5
Fairoak Staffs 111 B6
Fairseat Kent 50 C3
Fairstead Essex 70 B1
Fairstead Norf 118 D3
Fairwarp E Sus 36 D2
Fairy Cottage I o M 152 C4
Fairy Cross Devon 25 C5
Fakenham Norf 119 C6
Fakenham Magna Suff 103 D5
Fakenham Racecourse Norf 119 C6
Fala Midloth 210 D1
Fala Dam Midloth 210 D1
Falahill Borders 196 A2
Falcon Hereford 79 D4
Faldingworth Lincs 133 A5
Falfield S Glos 62 D2
Falkenham Suff 88 D3
Falkirk Falk 208 C1
Falkland Fife 220 D2
Falkland Palace Fife 220 D2
Falla Borders 187 B6
Fallgate Derbys 130 C3
Fallin Stirl 207 A6
Fallowfield Gtr Man 138 D1
Fallsidehill Borders 197 B5
Falmer E Sus 21 B6
Falmouth Corn 4 D3
Falsgrave N Yorks 160 C4
Falstone Northumb 177 A5
Fanagmore Highld 276 D2
Fangdale Beck N Yorks 159 B4
Fangfoss E Yorks 149 B6
Fankerton Falk 207 B5
Fanmore Argyll 224 B3
Fannich Lodge Highld 262 D4
Fans Borders 197 B5
Far Bank S Yorks 140 B4
Far Bletchley M Keynes 83 D5
Far Cotton Northants 83 B4
Far Forest Worcs 95 D5
Far Laund Derbys 114 A1
Far Sawrey Cumb 154 B2
Farcet Cambs 100 B4
Farden Shrops 94 D3
Fareham Hants 19 A4
Farewell Staffs 113 D4
Farforth Lincs 134 B3
Faringdon Oxon 64 D3
Farington Lancs 136 A4
Farlam Cumb 176 D3
Farlary Highld 273 D5
Farleigh N Som 42 C3
Farleigh Sur 49 C6
Farleigh Hungerford Som 44 D2
Farleigh Wallop Hants 33 A5
Farlesthorpe Lincs 135 B4
Farleton Cumb 154 C4
Farleton Lancs 145 A5
Farley Shrops 94 A1
Farley Staffs 113 A4
Farley Wilts 31 C6
Farley Green Sur 34 B3
Farley Hill Luton 67 A5
Farley Hill Wokingham 47 C5
Farleys End Glos 62 B3
Farlington N Yorks 149 A5
Farlow Shrops 95 C4
Farmborough Bath 43 C5
Farmcote Glos 63 A6
Farmcote Shrops 95 B5
Farmington Glos 64 B2
Farmoor Oxon 65 C5
Farmtown Moray 267 D6
Farnborough London 50 C1
Farnborough Hants 34 A1
Farnborough Warks 82 C1
Farnborough W Berks 46 A2
Farnborough Green Hants 34 A1
Farncombe Sur 34 B2
Farndish Beds 83 A6
Farndon Ches 127 D4
Farndon Notts 132 D2
Farnell Angus 233 C4
Farnham Dorset 30 D3
Farnham Essex 69 A4
Farnham N Yorks 148 A2
Farnham Suff 89 A4
Farnham Sur 34 B1
Farnham Common Bucks 48 A2
Farnham Green Essex 69 A4
Farnham Royal Bucks 48 A2
Farnhill N Yorks 147 C4
Farningham Kent 50 C2
Farnley N Yorks 147 C6
Farnley W Yorks 147 D6
Farnley Tyas W Yorks 139 B4
Farnsfield Notts 131 D6
Farnworth Gtr Man 137 C6
Farnworth Halton 127 A5
Farr Highld 252 C2
Farr Highld 241 B6
Farr Highld 278 B3
Farr House Highld 252 C2
Farringdon Devon 13 B5
Farrington Gurney Bath 43 D5
Farsley W Yorks 147 D6
Farthinghoe Northants 82 D2
Farthingloe Kent 39 A4
Farthingstone Northants 82 B3
Fartown W Yorks 139 B4
Farway Devon 14 B1
Fasag Highld 249 A5
Fascadale Highld 235 C4
Faslane Port Argyll 215 D5
Fasnacloich Argyll 227 B5
Fasnakyle Ho. Highld 251 D5
Fassfern Highld 237 B4
Fatfield T & W 179 D5
Fattahead Aberds 268 D1
Faugh Cumb 176 D3
Fauldhouse W Loth 208 D2
Faulkbourne Essex 70 B1
Faulkland Som 43 D6
Fauls Shrops 111 B4
Faversham Kent 52 C2
Favillar Moray 254 C3
Fawdington N Yorks 158 D3
Fawfieldhead Staffs 129 C5
Fawkham Green Kent 50 C2
Fawler Oxon 65 B4
Fawley Bucks 47 A5
Fawley Hants 18 A3
Fawley W Berks 46 A1
Fawley Chapel Hereford 62 A1
Faxfleet E Yorks 141 A6
Faygate W Sus 35 C5
Fazakerley Mers 136 D2
Fazeley Staffs 97 A5
Fearby N Yorks 157 C5
Fearn Highld 265 C4
Fearn Lodge Highld 264 B2
Fearn Station Highld 265 C4
Fearnan Perth 229 D6
Fearnbeg Highld 249 A4
Fearnhead Warr 137 D5
Fearnmore Highld 261 D4
Featherstone Staffs 96 A2
Featherstone W Yorks 140 A2
Featherwood Northumb 187 C7
Feckenham Worcs 80 A3
Feering Essex 70 A2
Feetham N Yorks 156 B3
Feizor N Yorks 146 A1
Felbridge Sur 35 C6
Felbrigg Norf 120 B4
Felcourt Sur 36 B1
Felden Herts 67 C5
Felin-Crai Powys 59 C5
Felindre Ceredig 75 C4
Felindre Carms 58 C2
Felindre Carms 58 B3
Felindre Carms 59 C4
Felindre Carms 73 C6
Felindre Powys 93 C5
Felindre Swansea 57 B6
Felindre Farchog Pembs 72 C4
Felinfach Ceredig 75 C4
Felinfach Powys 77 D4
Felinfoel Carms 57 B5
Felingwm isaf Carms 58 C2

Felingwm uchaf Carms 58 C2
Felinwynt Ceredig 73 A5
Felixkirk N Yorks 158 C3
Felixstowe Suff 88 D3
Felixstowe Ferry Suff 88 D4
Felkington Northumb 198 B3
Felkirk W Yorks 140 B1
Fell Side Cumb 163 A6
Felling T & W 179 C4
Felmersham Beds 84 B1
Felmingham Norf 120 C4
Felpham W Sus 20 C2
Felsham Suff 87 B5
Felsted Essex 69 A6
Feltham London 48 B4
Felthorpe Norf 120 D3
Felton Hereford 78 C3
Felton Northumb 189 C4
Felton N Som 43 C4
Felton Butler Shrops 110 D2
Feltwell Norf 102 B3
Fen Ditton Cambs 85 A6
Fen Drayton Cambs 85 A5
Fen End W Mid 97 D5
Fen Side Lincs 134 D3
Fenay Bridge W Yorks 139 B4
Fence Lancs 146 D2
Fence Houses T & W 179 D5
Fengate Norf 120 C3
Fengate P'boro 100 B4
Fenham Northumb 199 B4
Fenhouses Lincs 117 A5
Feniscliffe Blkburn 137 A5
Feniscowles Blkburn 137 A5
Feniton Devon 13 B6
Fenlake Beds 84 C2
Fenny Bentley Derbys 130 D6
Fenny Bridges Devon 13 B6
Fenny Compton Warks 81 B7
Fenny Drayton Leics 97 B6
Fenny Stratford M Keynes 83 D5
Fenrother Northumb 189 D4
Fenstanton Cambs 85 A5
Fenton Cambs 101 D5
Fenton Lincs 132 D3
Fenton Lincs 132 D3
Fenton Stoke 112 A2
Fenton Barns E Loth 210 B2
Fenton Town Northumb 198 C3
Fenwick E Ayrs 205 D4
Fenwick Northumb 178 B2
Fenwick Northumb 199 B4
Fenwick S Yorks 140 B3
Feochaig Argyll 190 D3
Feock Corn 4 D3
Feolin Ferry Argyll 201 B4
Ferens Art Gallery, Hull
  Hull 142 A2
Ferindonald Highld 247 D5
Feriniquarrie Highld 258 C1
Ferlochan Argyll 226 B4
Fern Angus 232 B2
Ferndale Rhondda 41 B5
Ferndown Dorset 17 A4
Ferness Highld 253 B5
Ferney Green Cumb 154 B3
Fernham Oxon 64 D3
Fernhill Heath Worcs 79 B6
Fernhurst W Sus 34 D1
Fernie Fife 220 C3
Ferniegair S Lnrk 194 A2
Fernilea Highld 246 A2
Fernilee Derbys 129 B5
Ferrensby N Yorks 148 A2
Ferring W Sus 20 B3
Ferry Hill Cambs 101 C5
Ferry Point Highld 264 B3
Ferrybridge W Yorks 140 A2
Ferryden Angus 233 C5
Ferryhill Aberdeen 245 B6
Ferryhill Durham 167 B5
Ferryhill Station Durham 167 B6
Ferryside Carms 56 A3
Fersfield Norf 103 C6
Fersit Highld 228 C5
Ferwig Ceredig 73 B4
Feshiebridge Highld 241 B6
Festival Park Visitor
  Centre, Ebbw Vale
  Bl Gwent 60 C3
Fetcham Sur 35 A4
Fetlar Airport Shetland 284 D8
Fetterangus Aberds 269 D4
Fettercairn Aberds 233 A4

Fettes Highld 252 A1
Fewcott Oxon 65 A6
Fewston N Yorks 147 B5
Ffair-Rhos Ceredig 75 B6
Ffairfach Carms 58 C3
Ffaldybrenin Carms 58 A3
Ffarmers Carms 58 A3
Ffawyddog Powys 60 B4
Ffestiniog Railway,
  Porthmadog Gwyn 107 B6
Fforest Carms 57 B5
Fforest-fâch Swansea 57 C6
Ffos-y-ffin Ceredig 74 B3
Ffostrasol Ceredig 73 B6
Ffridd-Uchaf Gwyn 107 A5
Ffrith Flint 126 D2
Ffrwd Gwyn 107 A4
Ffynnon ddrain Carms 73 D7
Ffynnon-oer Ceredig 75 C4
Ffynnongroyw Flint 125 A6
Fidden Argyll 224 D2
Fiddes Aberds 245 D5
Fiddington Glos 80 D2
Fiddington Som 28 A2
Fiddleford Dorset 30 D2
Fiddlers Hamlet Essex 69 C4
Field Staffs 112 B4
Field Broughton Cumb 154 C2
Field Dalling Norf 120 B2
Field Head Leics 98 A1
Fifehead Magdalen Dorset 30 C1
Fifehead Neville Dorset 30 D1
Fifield Oxon 64 B3
Fifield Wilts 45 D5
Fifield Windsor 48 B2
Fifield Bavant Wilts 31 C4
Figheldean Wilts 31 A5
Filands Wilts 44 A3
Filby Norf 121 D6
Filey N Yorks 161 C5
Filgrave M Keynes 83 C5
Filkins Oxon 64 C3
Filleigh Devon 26 C1
Filleigh Devon 26 D2
Fillingham Lincs 133 A4
Fillongley Warks 97 C5
Filton S Glos 43 B5
Fimber E Yorks 150 A1
Finavon Angus 232 C2
Fincharn Argyll 214 B2
Fincham Norf 102 A2
Finchampstead Wokingham 47 C5
Finchdean Hants 33 D6
Finchingfield Essex 86 D2
Finchley London 68 D2
Findern Derbys 113 B7
Findhorn Moray 265 D6
Findhorn Bridge Highld 253 D4
Findo Gask Perth 219 B5
Findochty Moray 267 C5
Findon Aberds 245 C6
Findon W Sus 21 B4
Findon Mains Highld 264 D2
Findrack Ho. Aberds 244 B3
Finedon Northants 99 D6
Fingal Street Suff 88 A3
Fingask Aberds 256 D2
Fingerpost Worcs 95 D5
Fingest Bucks 66 D2
Finghall N Yorks 157 C5
Fingland Cumb 175 C5
Fingland Dumfries 183 A5
Finglesham Kent 53 D5
Fingringhoe Essex 71 A4
Finlarig Stirl 217 A5
Finmere Oxon 82 D3
Finnart Perth 229 C4
Finningham Suff 87 A6
Finningley S Yorks 141 D4
Finnygaud Aberds 267 D6
Finsbury London 49 A6
Finstall Worcs 80 A2
Finsthwaite Cumb 154 C2
Finstock Oxon 65 B4
Finstown Orkney 282 F4
Fintry Aberds 268 D2
Fintry Dundee 220 A4
Fintry Stirl 207 B4
Finzean Aberds 244 C3
Fionnphort Argyll 224 D2
Fionnsbhagh W Isles 287 F5
Fir Tree Durham 166 B4
Firbeck S Yorks 131 A5
Firby N Yorks 157 C6
Firby N Yorks 149 A6
Firgrove Gtr Man 138 B2
Firsby Lincs 135 C4

Firsdown Wilts 31 B6
First Coast Highld 261 A6
Fishbourne I o W 19 B4
Fishbourne W Sus 20 B1
Fishbourne Palace W Sus 20 B1
Fishburn Durham 167 B6
Fishcross Clack 208 A1
Fisher Place Cumb 163 C6
Fisherford Aberds 256 C1
Fisher's Pond Hants 32 C3
Fisherstreet W Sus 34 C2
Fisherton Highld 252 A3
Fisherton S Ayrs 192 D2
Fishguard = Abergwaun
  Pembs 72 C2
Fishlake S Yorks 141 B4
Fishleigh Barton Devon 25 C6
Fishponds Bristol 43 B5
Fishpool Glos 62 A2
Fishtoft Lincs 117 A6
Fishtoft Drove Lincs 117 A6
Fishtown of Usan Angus 233 C5
Fishwick Borders 198 A3
Fiskavaig Highld 246 A2
Fiskerton Lincs 133 B5
Fiskerton Notts 132 D2
Fitling E Yorks 151 D5
Fittleton Wilts 31 A5
Fittleworth W Sus 20 A3
Fitton End Cambs 118 D1
Fitz Shrops 110 D3
Fitzhead Som 27 C6
Fitzwilliam W Yorks 140 B2
Fitzwilliam Museum,
  Cambridge Cambs 85 B6
Fiunary Highld 225 B5
Five Acres Glos 62 B1
Five Ashes E Sus 36 D3
Five Oak Green Kent 36 B4
Five Oaks Jersey 6
Five Oaks W Sus 34 D3
Five Roads Carms 57 B4
Fivecrosses Ches 127 B5
Fivehead Som 28 C3
Flack's Green Essex 70 B1
Flackwell Heath Bucks 48 A1
Fladbury Worcs 80 C2
Fladdabister Shetland 285 K6
Flagg Derbys 129 C6
Flambards Experience,
  Helston Corn 3 C4
Flamborough E Yorks 161 D6
Flamingo Land,
  Pickering N Yorks 159 D6
Flamstead Herts 67 B5
Flamstead End Herts 68 C3
Flansham W Sus 20 B2
Flanshaw W Yorks 139 A6
Flasby N Yorks 146 B3
Flash Staffs 129 C5
Flashader Highld 258 C3
Flask Inn N Yorks 160 A3
Flaunden Herts 67 C5
Flawborough Notts 115 A5
Flawith N Yorks 148 A3
Flax Bourton N Som 43 C4
Flaxby N Yorks 148 B2
Flaxholme Derbys 114 A1
Flaxley Glos 62 B2
Flaxpool Som 27 B6
Flaxton N Yorks 149 A5
Fleckney Leics 98 B3
Flecknoe Warks 82 A2
Fledborough Notts 132 B3
Fleet Hants 47 D6
Fleet Hants 19 A6
Fleet Lincs 117 C6
Fleet Air Arm Museum,
  Yeovil Som 29 C5
Fleet Hargate Lincs 117 C6
Fleetham Northumb 189 A4
Fleetlands Hants 19 A4
Fleetville Herts 67 C6
Fleetwood Lancs 144 C3
Flemingston V Glam 41 D5
Flemington S Lnrk 205 C6
Flempton Suff 87 A4
Fleoideabhagh W Isles 287 F5
Fletchertown Cumb 175 D5
Fletching E Sus 36 D2
Flexbury Corn 10 A3
Flexford Sur 34 B2
Flimby Cumb 162 A3
Flimwell E Sus 37 C5
Flint = Y Fflint Flint 126 B2
Flint Mountain Flint 126 B2
Flintham Notts 115 A5

Flinton E Yorks 151 D5
Flintsham Hereford 77 B7
Flitcham Norf 119 C4
Flitton Beds 84 D2
Flitwick Beds 84 D2
Flixborough N Lincs 141 B6
Flixborough Stather
  N Lincs 141 B6
Flixton Gtr Man 137 D6
Flixton N Yorks 160 D4
Flixton Suff 104 C4
Flockton W Yorks 139 B5
Flodaigh W Isles 286 A4
Flodden Northumb 198 C3
Flodigarry Highld 259 A4
Flood's Ferry Cambs 101 B5
Flookburgh Cumb 154 D2
Florden Norf 104 B2
Flore Northants 82 A3
Flotterton Northumb 188 C2
Flowton Suff 88 C1
Flush House W Yorks 139 C4
Flushing Aberds 257 B5
Flushing Corn 4 D3
Flyford Flavell Worcs 80 B2
Foals Green Suff 104 D3
Fobbing Thurrock 51 A4
Fochabers Moray 266 D4
Fochriw Caerph 60 C3
Fockerby N Lincs 141 B6
Fodderletter Moray 254 D2
Fodderty Highld 251 A7
Foel Powys 109 D4
Foel-gastell Carms 57 A5
Foffarty Angus 232 D2
Foggathorpe E Yorks 149 D6
Fogo Borders 197 B6
Fogorig Borders 198 B1
Foindle Highld 276 D2
Folda Angus 231 B5
Fole Staffs 112 B4
Foleshill W Mid 97 C6
Folke Dorset 29 D6
Folkestone Kent 39 B4
Folkestone Racecourse
  Kent 38 B3
Folkingham Lincs 116 B3
Folkington E Sus 22 B3
Folksworth Cambs 100 C3
Folkton N Yorks 161 D4
Folla Rule Aberds 256 C2
Follifoot N Yorks 148 B2
Folly Gate Devon 11 B6
Fonthill Bishop Wilts 30 B3
Fonthill Gifford Wilts 30 B3
Fontmell Magna Dorset 30 D2
Fontwell W Sus 20 B2
Fontwell Park
  Racecourse W Sus 20 B2
Foolow Derbys 130 B1
Foots Cray London 50 B1
Forbestown Aberds 243 A6
Force Mills Cumb 154 B2
Forcett N Yorks 167 D4
Ford Argyll 214 B1
Ford Bucks 66 C2
Ford Devon 25 C5
Ford Glos 64 A1
Ford Northumb 198 C3
Ford Shrops 110 D3
Ford Staffs 129 D5
Ford Wilts 44 B2
Ford W Sus 20 B2
Ford End Essex 69 B6
Ford Street Som 27 D6
Fordcombe Kent 36 B3
Fordell Fife 209 B4
Forden Powys 93 A6
Forder Green Devon 8 A1
Fordham Cambs 102 D2
Fordham Essex 70 A3
Fordham Norf 102 B2
Fordhouses W Mid 96 A2
Fordingbridge Hants 31 D5
Fordon E Yorks 160 D4
Fordoun Aberds 233 A5
Ford's Green Suff 87 A6
Fordstreet Essex 70 A3
Fordwells Oxon 64 B4
Fordwich Kent 52 D3
Fordyce Aberds 267 C6
Forebridge Staffs 112 C3
Forest Durham 165 B6
Forest Becks Lancs 146 B1
Forest Gate London 49 A7
Forest Green Sur 35 B4
Forest Hall Cumb 154 A4

Forest Head Cumb 176 D4
Forest Hill Oxon 65 C6
Forest Lane Head N Yorks 148 B2
Forest Lodge Argyll 228 D1
Forest Lodge Highld 242 A3
Forest Lodge Perth 230 A3
Forest Mill Clack 208 A2
Forest Row E Sus 36 C2
Forest Town Notts 131 C5
Forestburn Gate
  Northumb 188 D3
Foresterseat Moray 266 D2
Forestside W Sus 33 D6
Forfar Angus 232 C2
Forgandenny Perth 219 C5
Forge Powys 91 C5
Forge Side Torf 60 C4
Forgewood N Lnrk 194 A3
Forgie Moray 267 D4
Forglen Ho. Aberds 268 D1
Formby Mers 136 C1
Forncett End Norf 104 B1
Forncett St Mary Norf 104 B1
Forncett St Peter Norf 104 B1
Forneth Perth 231 D5
Fornham All Saints Suff 87 A4
Fornham St Martin Suff 87 A4
Forres Moray 253 A6
Forrest Lodge Dumfries 182 D3
Forrestfield N Lnrk 207 D6
Forsbrook Staffs 112 A3
Forse Highld 275 A6
Forse Ho. Highld 275 A6
Forsinain Highld 279 D5
Forsinard Highld 279 D4
Forsinard Station Highld 279 D4
Forston Dorset 15 B6
Fort Augustus Highld 240 B6
Fort George Guern 6
Fort George Highld 252 A3
Fort Victoria Country
  Park & Marine
  Aquarium I o W 18 B2
Fort William Highld 237 B5
Forteviot Perth 219 C5
Forth S Lnrk 194 A4
Forth Road Bridge Fife 208 C4
Forthampton Glos 79 D6
Fortingall Perth 229 D6
Forton Hants 32 A2
Forton Lancs 145 B4
Forton Shrops 110 D3
Forton Som 14 A3
Forton Staffs 111 C6
Forton Heath Shrops 110 D3
Fortrie Aberds 256 B1
Fortrose Highld 252 A3
Fortuneswell Dorset 15 D6
Forty Green Bucks 67 D4
Forty Hill London 68 D3
Forward Green Suff 88 B1
Fosbury Wilts 45 D7
Fosdyke Lincs 117 B6
Foss Perth 230 C2
Foss Cross Glos 63 C6
Fossebridge Glos 64 C1
Foster Street Essex 69 C5
Fosterhouses S Yorks 141 B4
Foston Derbys 113 B6
Foston Lincs 115 A6
Foston N Yorks 149 A5
Foston on the Wolds
  E Yorks 151 B4
Fotherby Lincs 143 D5
Fotheringhay Northants 100 B2
Foubister Orkney 283 G6
Foul Mile E Sus 22 A4
Foulby W Yorks 140 B1
Foulden Borders 198 A3
Foulden Norf 102 B3
Foulis Castle Highld 264 D1
Foulridge Lancs 146 C2
Foulsham Norf 120 C2
Fountainhall Borders 196 B3
Fountains Abbey, Ripon
  N Yorks 147 A6
Four Ashes Staffs 95 C6
Four Ashes Suff 104 D1
Four Crosses Powys 109 D7
Four Crosses Powys 93 A5
Four Crosses Wrex 126 D2
Four Elms Kent 36 B2
Four Forks Som 28 B2
Four Gotes Cambs 118 D1
Four Lane Ends Ches 127 C5
Four Lanes Corn 3 B4
Four Marks Hants 33 B5

Four Mile Bridge Anglesey 122 C2
Four Oaks E Sus 37 D6
Four Oaks W Mid 97 C5
Four Oaks W Mid 96 B4
Four Roads Carms 57 B4
Four Roads I o M 152 E2
Four Throws Kent 37 D5
Fourlane Ends Derbys 130 D3
Fourlanes End Ches 128 D3
Fourpenny Highld 265 J4
Fourstones Northumb 177 C6
Fovant Wilts 31 C4
Foveran Aberds 257 D4
Fowey Corn 5 B6
Fowley Common Warr 137 D5
Fowlis Angus 220 A3
Fowlis Wester Perth 218 B4
Fowlmere Cambs 85 C6
Fownhope Hereford 78 D3
Fox Corner Sur 34 A2
Fox Lane Hants 34 A1
Fox Street Essex 71 A4
Foxbar Renfs 205 B4
Foxcombe Hill Oxon 65 C5
Foxdale I o M 152 D2
Foxearth Essex 87 C4
Foxfield Cumb 153 B3
Foxham Wilts 44 B3
Foxhole Corn 5 B4
Foxhole Swansea 57 C6
Foxholes N Yorks 160 D4
Foxhunt Green E Sus 22 A3
Foxley Norf 120 C2
Foxley Wilts 44 A2
Foxt Staffs 112 A4
Foxton Cambs 85 C6
Foxton Durham 167 C6
Foxton Leics 99 B4
Foxton Canal Locks Leics 98 C3
Foxup N Yorks 156 D2
Foxwist Green Ches 127 C6
Foxwood Shrops 95 D4
Foy Hereford 62 A1
Foyers Highld 251 D6
Fraddam Corn 2 B3
Fraddon Corn 4 B4
Fradley Staffs 113 D5
Fradswell Staffs 112 B3
Fraisthorpe E Yorks 151 A4
Framfield E Sus 36 D2
Framingham Earl Norf 104 A3
Framingham Pigot Norf 104 A3
Framlingham Suff 88 A3
Framlingham Castle Suff 88 A3
Frampton Dorset 15 B6
Frampton Lincs 117 B6
Frampton Cotterell S Glos 43 A5
Frampton Mansell Glos 63 C5
Frampton on Severn Glos 62 C3
Frampton West End Lincs 117 A5
Framsden Suff 88 B2
Framwellgate Moor Durham 167 A5
Franche Worcs 95 D6
Frankby Mers 126 A2
Frankley Worcs 96 C2
Frank's Bridge Powys 77 B5
Frankton Warks 98 D1
Frant E Sus 36 C3
Fraserburgh Aberds 269 C4
Frating Green Essex 71 A4
Fratton Ptsmth 19 B5
Freathy Corn 6 B3
Freckenham Suff 102 D2
Freckleton Lancs 136 A3
Freeby Leics 115 C6
Freehay Staffs 112 A4
Freeland Oxon 65 B5
Freeport Hornsea Outlet village E Yorks 151 C5
Freester Shetland 285 H6
Freethorpe Norf 105 A5
Freiston Lincs 117 A6
Frenchay S Glos 43 B5
Frenchbeer Devon 12 C1
Frensham Sur 34 B1
Fresgoe Highld 279 B5
Freshfield Mers 136 C1
Freshford Bath 44 C1
Freshwater I o W 18 C2
Freshwater Bay I o W 18 C2
Freshwater East Pembs 55 E6
Fressingfield Suff 104 D3

Freston Suff 88 D2
Freswick Highld 281 B5
Fretherne Glos 62 C3
Frettenham Norf 120 D4
Freuchie Fife 220 D2
Freuchies Angus 231 B6
Freystrop Pembs 55 C5
Friar's Gate E Sus 36 C2
Friarton Perth 219 B6
Friday Bridge Cambs 101 A6
Friday Street E Sus 22 B4
Fridaythorpe E Yorks 150 B1
Friern Barnet London 68 D2
Friesland Argyll 223 B4
Friesthorpe Lincs 133 A5
Frieston Lincs 116 A2
Frieth Bucks 66 D2
Frilford Oxon 65 D5
Frilsham W Berks 46 B3
Frimley Sur 34 A1
Frimley Green Sur 34 A1
Frindsbury Medway 51 B4
Fring Norf 119 B4
Fringford Oxon 65 A7
Frinsted Kent 37 A6
Frinton-on-Sea Essex 71 A6
Friockheim Angus 232 D3
Friog Gwyn 90 A4
Frisby on the Wreake Leics 115 D4
Friskney Lincs 135 D4
Friskney Eaudike Lincs 135 D4
Friskney Tofts Lincs 135 D4
Friston E Sus 22 C3
Friston Suff 89 A5
Fritchley Derbys 130 D3
Frith Bank Lincs 117 A6
Frith Common Worcs 79 A4
Fritham Hants 31 D6
Frithelstock Devon 25 D5
Frithelstock Stone Devon 25 D5
Frithville Lincs 134 D3
Frittenden Kent 37 B6
Frittiscombe Devon 8 C2
Fritton Norf 104 B3
Fritton Norf 105 A5
Fritwell Oxon 65 A6
Frizinghall W Yorks 147 D5
Frizington Cumb 162 C3
Frocester Glos 62 C3
Frodesley Shrops 94 A3
Frodingham N Lincs 141 B6
Frodsham Ches 127 B5
Frogden Borders 187 A6
Froggatt Derbys 130 B2
Froghall Staffs 112 A4
Frogmore Devon 7 C6
Frogmore Hants 34 A1
Frognall Lincs 117 D4
Frogshail Norf 121 B4
Frolesworth Leics 98 B2
Frome Som 30 A1
Frome St Quintin Dorset 15 A5
Fromes Hill Hereford 79 C4
Fron Denb 125 C5
Fron Gwyn 107 A5
Fron Gwyn 106 C3
Fron Powys 77 A4
Fron Powys 93 A6
Fron Powys 93 B5
Froncysyllte Wrex 110 A1
Frongoch Gwyn 108 B4
Frostenden Suff 105 C5
Frosterley Durham 166 B3
Frotoft Orkney 282 E5
Froxfield Wilts 45 C6
Froxfield Green Hants 33 C6
Froyle Hants 33 A6
Fryerning Essex 69 C6
Fryton N Yorks 159 D5
Fulbeck Lincs 133 D4
Fulbourn Cambs 85 B7
Fulbrook Oxon 64 B3
Fulford Som 28 C2
Fulford Staffs 112 B3
Fulford York 149 C5
Fulham London 49 B5
Fulking W Sus 21 A5
Full Sutton E Yorks 149 B6
Fullarton Glasgow 205 B6
Fullarton N Ayrs 192 B3
Fuller Street Essex 70 B1
Fuller's Moor Ches 127 D4
Fullerton Hants 32 B2
Fulletby Lincs 134 B2
Fullwood E Ayrs 205 C4
Fulmer Bucks 48 A2

Fulmodeston Norf 120 B1
Fulnetby Lincs 133 B5
Fulstow Lincs 143 D5
Fulwell T & W 179 D5
Fulwood Lancs 145 D5
Fulwood S Yorks 130 A3
Fundenhall Norf 104 B2
Fundenhall Street Norf 104 B2
Funtington W Sus 19 A6
Funtley Hants 19 A4
Funzie Shetland 284 D8
Furley Devon 14 A2
Furnace Argyll 214 B3
Furnace Carms 57 B5
Furnace End Warks 97 B5
Furneaux Pelham Herts 68 A4
Furness Vale Derbys 129 A5
Furze Platt Windsor 48 A1
Furzehill Devon 26 A2
Fyfett Som 28 D2
Fyfield Essex 69 C5
Fyfield Glos 64 C3
Fyfield Hants 32 A1
Fyfield Oxon 65 D5
Fyfield Wilts 45 C5
Fylingthorpe N Yorks 160 A3
Fyvie Aberds 256 C2

G

Gabhsann bho Dheas W Isles 288 B5
Gabhsann bho Thuath W Isles 288 B5
Gablon Highld 264 A3
Gabroc Hill E Ayrs 205 C4
Gaddesby Leics 115 D4
Gadebridge Herts 67 C5
Gaer Powys 60 A3
Gaerllwyd Mon 61 D6
Gaerwen Anglesey 123 C4
Gagingwell Oxon 65 A5
Gaick Lodge Highld 241 D5
Gailey Staffs 112 D3
Gainford Durham 167 D4
Gainsborough Lincs 141 D6
Gainsborough Suff 88 C2
Gainsford End Essex 86 D3
Gairloch Highld 261 C5
Gairlochy Highld 239 D5
Gairney Bank Perth 208 A4
Gairnshiel Lodge Aberds 243 B5
Gaisgill Cumb 155 A5
Gaitsgill Cumb 164 A1
Galashiels Borders 196 C3
Galgate Lancs 145 B4
Galhampton Som 29 C6
Gallaberry Dumfries 184 D2
Gallachoille Argyll 213 D5
Gallanach Argyll 226 D3
Gallanach Argyll 223 A5
Gallantry Bank Ches 127 D5
Gallatown Fife 209 A5
Galley Common Warks 97 B6
Galley Hill Cambs 85 A5
Galleyend Essex 69 C7
Galleywood Essex 69 C7
Gallin Perth 229 D4
Gallowfauld Angus 232 D2
Gallows Green Staffs 113 A4
Galltair Highld 249 D5
Galmisdale Highld 234 B3
Galmpton Devon 7 C5
Galmpton Torbay 8 B2
Galphay N Yorks 157 D6
Galston E Ayrs 193 B5
Galtrigill Highld 258 C1
Gamblesby Cumb 165 B4
Gamesley Derbys 138 D3
Gamlingay Cambs 85 B4
Gammersgill N Yorks 157 C4
Gamston Notts 132 B2
Ganarew Hereford 62 B1
Ganavan Argyll 226 C3
Gang Corn 6 A2
Ganllwyd Gwyn 108 C2
Gannochy Angus 232 A3
Gannochy Perth 219 B6
Gansclet Highld 281 D5
Ganstead E Yorks 151 D4
Ganthorpe N Yorks 159 D5
Ganton N Yorks 160 D3
Garbat Highld 263 D6
Garbhallt Argyll 214 C3
Garboldisham Norf 103 C6
Garden City Flint 126 C3

Garden Village Wrex 126 D3
Garden Village W Yorks 148 D3
Gardenstown Aberds 268 C2
Garderhouse Shetland 285 J5
Gardham E Yorks 150 C2
Gardin Shetland 284 G6
Gare Hill Som 30 A1
Garelochhead Argyll 215 C5
Garford Oxon 65 D5
Garforth W Yorks 148 D3
Gargrave N Yorks 146 B3
Gargunnock Stirl 207 A5
Garlic Street Norf 104 C3
Garlieston Dumfries 171 C6
Garlinge Green Kent 52 D3
Garlogie Aberds 245 B4
Garmond Aberds 268 D3
Garmony Argyll 225 B5
Garmouth Moray 266 C4
Garn-yr-erw Torf 60 B4
Garnant Carms 58 D3
Garndiffaith Torf 61 C4
Garndolbenmaen Gwyn 107 B4
Garnedd Conwy 124 D2
Garnett Bridge Cumb 154 B4
Garnfadryn Gwyn 106 C2
Garnkirk N Lnrk 207 D4
Garnlydan Bl Gwent 60 B3
Garnswllt Swansea 57 B6
Garrabost W Isles 288 D6
Garraron Argyll 213 B6
Garras Corn 3 C5
Garreg Gwyn 107 B6
Garrick Perth 218 C3
Garrigill Cumb 165 A5
Garriston N Yorks 157 B5
Garroch Dumfries 182 D3
Garrogie Lodge Highld 240 A3
Garros Highld 259 B4
Garrow Perth 230 D2
Garryhorn Dumfries 182 C3
Garsdale Cumb 155 C6
Garsdale Head Cumb 155 B6
Garsdon Wilts 44 A3
Garshall Green Staffs 112 B3
Garsington Oxon 65 C6
Garstang Lancs 145 C4
Garston Mers 127 A4
Garswood Mers 137 D4
Gartcosh N Lnrk 207 D4
Garth Bridgend 40 B3
Garth Gwyn 123 C5
Garth Powys 76 C3
Garth Shetland 285 H4
Garth Wrex 110 A1
Garth Row Cumb 154 B4
Garthamlock Glasgow 205 B6
Garthbrengy Powys 76 D4
Garthdee Aberdeen 245 B6
Gartheli Ceredig 75 C4
Garthmyl Powys 93 B5
Garthorpe Leics 115 C6
Garthorpe N Lincs 141 B6
Gartly Aberds 255 C6
Gartmore Stirl 206 A3
Gartnagrenach Argyll 202 C2
Gartness N Lnrk 207 D5
Gartness Stirl 206 B3
Gartocharn W Dunb 206 B2
Garton E Yorks 151 D5
Garton-on-the-Wolds E Yorks 150 B2
Gartsherrie N Lnrk 207 D5
Gartymore Highld 274 C4
Garvald E Loth 210 C2
Garvamore Highld 240 C3
Garvard Argyll 212 C1
Garvault Hotel Highld 273 A5
Garve Highld 263 D5
Garvestone Norf 103 A6
Garvock Aberds 233 A5
Garvock Inverclyd 204 A2
Garway Hereford 61 A6
Garway Hill Hereford 61 A6
Gaskan Highld 236 B1
Gastard Wilts 44 C2
Gasthorpe Norf 103 C5
Gatcombe I o W 18 C3
Gate Burton Lincs 132 A3
Gate Helmsley N Yorks 149 B5
Gateacre Mers 127 A4
Gatebeck Cumb 154 C4
Gateford Notts 131 A5
Gateforth N Yorks 140 A3
Gatehead E Ayrs 192 B3
Gatehouse Northumb 177 A5
Gatehouse of Fleet Dumfries 172 C4

Gatelawbridge Dumfries 183 C7
Gateley Norf 119 C6
Gatenby N Yorks 158 C2
Gateshead T & W 179 C4
Gateshead International Stadium T & W 179 C4
Gatesheath Ches 127 C4
Gateside Aberds 244 A3
Gateside Angus 232 D2
Gateside E Renf 205 C4
Gateside Fife 219 D6
Gateside N Ayrs 204 C3
Gathurst Gtr Man 136 C4
Gatley Gtr Man 128 A3
Gattonside Borders 197 C4
Gatwick Airport W Sus 35 B5
Gaufron Powys 76 A3
Gaulby Leics 98 A3
Gauldry Fife 220 B3
Gaunt's Common Dorset 17 A4
Gautby Lincs 134 B1
Gavinton Borders 197 A6
Gawber S Yorks 139 C6
Gawcott Bucks 82 D3
Gawsworth Ches 128 C3
Gawthorpe W Yorks 139 A5
Gawthrop Cumb 155 C5
Gawthwaite Cumb 153 B3
Gay Street W Sus 34 D3
Gaydon Warks 81 B6
Gayfield Orkney 282 B5
Gayhurst M Keynes 83 C5
Gayle N Yorks 156 C2
Gayles N Yorks 157 A5
Gayton Mers 126 A2
Gayton Norf 119 D4
Gayton Northants 83 B4
Gayton Staffs 112 C3
Gayton le Marsh Lincs 135 A4
Gayton le Wold Lincs 134 A2
Gayton Thorpe Norf 119 D4
Gaywood Norf 118 C3
Gazeley Suff 86 A3
Geanies House Highld 265 C4
Gearraidh Bhailteas W Isles 286 D3
Gearraidh Bhaird W Isles 288 E4
Gearraidh na h-Aibhne W Isles 288 D3
Gearraidh na Monadh W Isles 286 E3
Geary Highld 258 B2
Geddes House Highld 253 A4
Gedding Suff 87 B5
Geddington Northants 99 C5
Gedintailor Highld 247 A4
Gedling Notts 115 A4
Gedney Lincs 117 C7
Gedney Broadgate Lincs 117 C7
Gedney Drove End Lincs 118 C1
Gedney Dyke Lincs 117 C7
Gedney Hill Lincs 117 D6
Gee Cross Gtr Man 138 D2
Geilston Argyll 206 C1
Geirinis W Isles 286 B3
Geise Highld 280 B3
Geisiadar W Isles 288 D2
Geldeston Norf 105 B4
Gell Conwy 124 C3
Gelli Pembs 55 C6
Gelli Rhondda 41 B4
Gellideg M Tydf 60 C2
Gellifor Denb 125 C6
Gelligaer Caerph 41 B6
Gellilydan Gwyn 107 C6
Gellinudd Neath 40 A2
Gellyburn Perth 219 A5
Gellywen Carms 73 D5
Gelston Dumfries 173 C5
Gelston Lincs 116 A2
Gembling E Yorks 151 B4
Gentleshaw Staffs 113 D4
Geocrab W Isles 288 H2
George Green Bucks 48 A3
George Nympton Devon 26 C2
George Town Bl Gwent 60 C3
Georgefield Dumfries 185 C5
Georgeham Devon 25 B5
Gerlan Gwyn 123 D6
Germansweek Devon 11 B5
Germoe Corn 2 C3
Gerrans Corn 4 D3
Gerrards Cross Bucks 48 A3
Gestingthorpe Essex 87 D4

Geuffordd Powys 109 D7
Gib Hill Ches 127 B6
Gibbet Hill Warks 98 C2
Gibbshill Dumfries 173 A5
Gidea Park London 50 A2
Gidleigh Devon 12 C1
Giffnock E Renf 205 C5
Gifford E Loth 210 D2
Giffordland N Ayrs 204 D2
Giffordtown Fife 220 C2
Giggleswick N Yorks 146 A2
Gilberdyke E Yorks 141 A6
Gilchriston E Loth 210 D1
Gilcrux Cumb 163 A4
Gildersome W Yorks 139 A5
Gildingwells S Yorks 131 A5
Gileston V Glam 41 E5
Gilfach Caerph 41 B6
Gilfach Goch Rhondda 41 C4
Gilfachrheda Ceredig 73 A7
Gillamoor N Yorks 159 C5
Gillar's Green Mers 136 D3
Gillen Highld 258 C2
Gilling East N Yorks 159 D5
Gilling West N Yorks 157 A5
Gillingham Dorset 30 C2
Gillingham Medway 51 C4
Gillingham Norf 105 B5
Gillock Highld 280 C4
Gillow Heath Staffs 128 D3
Gills Highld 281 A5
Gill's Green Kent 37 C5
Gilmanscleuch Borders 196 D2
Gilmerton Edin 209 D5
Gilmerton Perth 218 B3
Gilmonby Durham 166 D2
Gilmorton Leics 98 C2
Gilmourton S Lnrk 205 D6
Gilsland Cumb 176 C4
Gilsland Spa Cumb 176 C4
Gilston Borders 196 A3
Gilston Herts 68 B4
Gilwern Mon 60 B4
Gimingham Norf 121 B4
Giosla W Isles 288 E2
Gipping Suff 87 A6
Gipsey Bridge Lincs 117 A5
Girdle Toll N Ayrs 204 D3
Girlsta Shetland 285 H6
Girsby N Yorks 158 A2
Girtford Beds 84 B3
Girthon Dumfries 172 C4
Girton Cambs 85 A6
Girton Notts 132 C3
Girvan S Ayrs 180 B3
Gisburn Lancs 146 C2
Gisleham Suff 105 C6
Gislingham Suff 104 D1
Gissing Norf 104 C2
Gittisham Devon 13 B6
Gladestry Powys 77 B6
Gladsmuir E Loth 210 C1
Glais Swansea 40 A2
Glaisdale N Yorks 159 A6
Glame Highld 248 B2
Glamis Angus 232 D1
Glamis Castle Angus 232 D1
Glan Adda Gwyn 123 C5
Glan-Conwy Conwy 124 D3
Glan Conwy Conwy 124 B3
Glan-Duar Carms 58 A2
Glan-Dwyfach Gwyn 107 B4
Glan Gors Anglesey 123 C4
Glan-rhyd Gwyn 107 A4
Glan-traeth Anglesey 122 C2
Glan-y-don Flint 125 B6
Glan-y-nant Powys 92 C3
Glan-y-wern Gwyn 107 C6
Glan-yr-afon Anglesey 123 B6
Glan-yr-afon Gwyn 108 A4
Glan-yr-afon Gwyn 109 A5
Glanaman Carms 57 A6
Glandford Norf 120 A2
Glandwr Pembs 73 D4
Glandy Cross Carms 72 D4
Glandyfi Ceredig 91 C4
Glangrwyney Powys 60 B4
Glanmule Powys 93 B5
Glanrafon Ceredig 90 D4
Glanrhyd Gwyn 106 C2
Glanrhyd Pembs 72 B4
Glanton Northumb 188 B3
Glanton Pike Northumb 188 B3
Glanvilles Wootton Dorset 15 A6

Glapthorn Northants 100 B2
Glapwell Derbys 131 C4
Glas-allt Shiel Aberds 243 D5
Glasbury Powys 77 D5
Glaschoil Highld 253 C6
Glascoed Denb 125 B4
Glascoed Mon 61 C5
Glascoed Powys 109 D6
Glascorrie Aberds 243 C6
Glascote Staffs 97 A5
Glascwm Powys 77 B5
Glasdrum Argyll 227 B5
Glasfryn Conwy 125 D4
Glasgow Glasgow 205 B5
Glasgow Airport Renfs 205 B4
Glasgow Art Gallery & Museum Glasgow 205 B5
Glasgow Botanic Gardens Glasgow 205 B5
Glasgow Cathedral Glasgow 205 B6
Glasgow Prestwick International Airport S Ayrs 192 C3
Glashvin Highld 259 B4
Glasinfryn Gwyn 123 D5
Glasnacardoch Highld 235 A5
Glasnakille Highld 247 C4
Glasphein Highld 258 D1
Glaspwll Powys 91 C5
Glassburn Highld 251 C5
Glasserton Dumfries 171 D6
Glassford S Lnrk 194 B2
Glasshouse Hill Glos 62 A3
Glasshouses N Yorks 147 A5
Glasslie Fife 220 D2
Glasson Cumb 175 B5
Glasson Lancs 144 B4
Glassonby Cumb 164 B3
Glasterlaw Angus 232 C3
Glaston Rutland 99 A5
Glastonbury Som 29 B5
Glastonbury Abbey Som 29 B4
Glatton Cambs 100 C3
Glazebrook Warr 137 D5
Glazebury Warr 137 D5
Glazeley Shrops 95 C5
Gleadless S Yorks 130 A3
Gleadsmoss Ches 128 C3
Gleann Tholàstaidh W Isles 288 C6
Gleaston Cumb 153 C3
Gleiniant Powys 92 B3
Glemsford Suff 87 C4
Glen Dumfries 172 C3
Glen Dumfries 173 A6
Glen Auldyn I o M 152 B4
Glen Bernisdale Highld 259 D4
Glen Ho. Borders 176 A2
Glen Mona I o M 152 C4
Glen Nevis House Highld 237 B5
Glen Parva Leics 98 B2
Glen Sluain Argyll 214 C3
Glen Tanar House Aberds 244 C1
Glen Trool Lodge Dumfries 181 C6
Glen Village Falk 208 C1
Glen Vine I o M 152 D3
Glenamachrie Argyll 226 D4
Glenbarr Argyll 190 B2
Glenbeg Highld 235 D4
Glenbeg Highld 253 D6
Glenbervie Aberds 245 D4
Glenboig N Lnrk 207 D5
Glenborrodale Highld 235 D5
Glenbranter Argyll 215 C4
Glenbreck Borders 195 D5
Glenbrein Lodge Highld 240 A2
Glenbrittle House Highld 246 B3
Glenbuchat Lodge Aberds 243 A6
Glenbuck E Ayrs 194 D2
Glenburn Renfs 205 B4
Glencalvie Lodge Highld 263 B6
Glencanisp Lodge Highld 270 B4
Glencaple Dumfries 174 B2
Glencarron Lodge Highld 250 A2
Glencarse Perth 219 B6
Glencassley Castle Highld 272 D2
Glenceitlein Highld 227 B6
Glencoe Highld 237 D4
Glencraig Fife 209 A4
Glencripesdale Highld 225 A5
Glencrosh Dumfries 183 D5
Glendavan Ho. Aberds 244 B1
Glendevon Perth 219 D4
Glendoe Lodge Highld 240 B2
Glendoebeg Highld 240 B2

Glendoick Perth 220 B2
Glendoll Lodge Angus 231 A6
Glendoune S Ayrs 180 B3
Glenduckie Fife 220 C2
Glendye Lodge Aberds 244 D3
Gleneagles Hotel Perth 218 C4
Gleneagles House Perth 218 D4
Glenegedale Argyll 200 C3
Glenelg Highld 238 A2
Glenernie Moray 253 B6
Glenfarg Perth 219 C6
Glenfarquhar Lodge Aberds 245 D4
Glenferness House Highld 253 B5
Glenfeshie Lodge Highld 241 C6
Glenfiddich Distillery, Dufftown Moray 254 B4
Glenfield Leics 98 A2
Glenfinnan Highld 238 D3
Glenfoot Perth 219 C6
Glenfyne Lodge Argyll 215 A5
Glengap Dumfries 173 C4
Glengarnock N Ayrs 204 C3
Glengorm Castle Argyll 224 A3
Glengrasco Highld 259 D4
Glenhead Farm Angus 231 B6
Glenhoul Dumfries 182 D4
Glenhurich Highld 236 C2
Glenkerry Borders 185 A5
Glenkiln Dumfries 173 A6
Glenkindie Aberds 244 A1
Glenlatterach Moray 266 D2
Glenlee Dumfries 182 D4
Glenlichorn Perth 218 C2
Glenlivet Moray 254 D2
Glenlochsie Perth 231 A4
Glenloig N Ayrs 191 B5
Glenluce Dumfries 171 B4
Glenmallan Argyll 215 C5
Glenmarksie Highld 251 A5
Glenmassan Argyll 215 D4
Glenmavis N Lnrk 207 D5
Glenmaye I o M 152 D2
Glenmidge Dumfries 183 D6
Glenmore Argyll 213 A6
Glenmore Highld 259 D4
Glenmore Lodge Highld 242 B2
Glenmoy Angus 232 B2
Glenogil Angus 232 B2
Glenprosen Lodge Angus 231 B6
Glenprosen Village Angus 232 B1
Glenquiech Angus 232 B2
Glenreasdell Mains Argyll 202 C3
Glenree N Ayrs 191 C5
Glenridding Cumb 164 D1
Glenrossal Highld 272 D2
Glenrothes Fife 220 D2
Glensanda Highld 226 B3
Glensaugh Aberds 233 A4
Glenshero Lodge Highld 240 C3
Glenstockadale Dumfries 170 A2
Glenstriven Argyll 203 A5
Glentaggart S Lnrk 194 D3
Glentham Lincs 142 D2
Glentirranmuir Stirl 207 A4
Glenton Aberds 256 D1
Glentress Borders 196 C1
Glentromie Lodge Highld 241 C5
Glentrool Village Dumfries 181 D5
Glentruan I o M 152 A4
Glentrum House Highld 241 C4
Glenturret Distillery, Crieff Perth 218 B3
Glentworth Lincs 133 A4
Glenuig Highld 235 C5
Glenurquhart Highld 264 D3
Glespin S Lnrk 194 D3
Gletness Shetland 285 H6
Glewstone Hereford 62 A1
Glinton P'boro 100 A3
Glooston Leics 99 B4
Glororum Northumb 199 C5
Glossop Derbys 138 D3
Gloster Hill Northumb 189 C5
Gloucester Glos 63 B4
Gloucester Cathedral Glos 63 B4
Gloucestershire Airport Glos 63 A4
Gloup Shetland 284 C7
Glusburn N Yorks 147 C4
Glutt Lodge Highld 274 A3
Glutton Bridge Derbys 129 C5
Glympton Oxon 65 A5
Glyn-Ceiriog Wrex 109 B7
Glyn-cywarch Gwyn 107 C6
Glyn Ebwy = Ebbw Vale Bl Gwent 60 C3

Glyn-Neath = Glynedd Neath 59 E5
Glynarthen Ceredig 73 B6
Glynbrochan Powys 92 C3
Glyncoch Rhondda 41 B5
Glyncorrwg Neath 40 B3
Glynde E Sus 22 B2
Glyndebourne E Sus 22 A2
Glyndyfrdwy Denb 109 A6
Glynedd = Glyn-Neath Neath 59 E5
Glynogwr Bridgend 41 C4
Glyntaff Rhondda 41 C5
Glyntawe Powys 59 D5
Gnosall Staffs 112 C2
Gnosall Heath Staffs 112 C2
Goadby Leics 99 B4
Goadby Marwood Leics 115 C5
Goat Lees Kent 38 A2
Goatacre Wilts 44 B4
Goathill Dorset 29 D6
Goathland N Yorks 160 A2
Goathurst Som 28 B2
Gobernuisgach Lodge Highld 277 D5
Gobhaig W Isles 287 D5
Gobowen Shrops 110 B2
Godalming Sur 34 B2
Godley Gtr Man 138 D2
Godmanchester Cambs 100 D4
Godmanstone Dorset 15 B6
Godmersham Kent 52 D2
Godney Som 29 A4
Godolphin Cross Corn 3 B4
Godre'r-graig Neath 59 E4
Godshill Hants 31 D5
Godshill I o W 18 C4
Godstone Sur 35 A6
Godstone Farm Sur 35 A6
Godwinscroft Hants 17 B5
Goetre Mon 61 C5
Goferydd Anglesey 122 B2
Goff's Oak Herts 68 C3
Gogar Edin 209 C4
Goginan Ceredig 91 D4
Golan Gwyn 107 B5
Golant Corn 5 B6
Golberdon Corn 10 D4
Golborne Gtr Man 137 D5
Golcar W Yorks 139 B4
Gold Hill Norf 102 B1
Goldcliff Newport 42 A2
Golden Cross E Sus 22 A3
Golden Green Kent 36 B4
Golden Grove Carms 57 A5
Golden Hill Hants 17 B6
Golden Pot Hants 33 A6
Golden Valley Glos 63 A5
Goldenhill Stoke 128 D3
Golders Green London 49 A5
Goldhanger Essex 70 C3
Golding Shrops 94 A3
Goldington Beds 84 B2
Goldsborough N Yorks 148 B2
Goldsborough N Yorks 169 D6
Goldsithney Corn 2 B3
Goldsworthy Devon 25 C4
Goldthorpe S Yorks 140 C2
Gollanfield Highld 253 A4
Golspie Highld 274 D2
Golval Highld 279 B4
Gomeldon Wilts 31 B5
Gomersal W Yorks 139 A5
Gomshall Sur 34 B3
Gonalston Notts 115 A4
Gonfirth Shetland 285 G5
Good Easter Essex 69 B6
Gooderstone Norf 102 A3
Goodleigh Devon 25 B7
Goodmanham E Yorks 150 C1
Goodnestone Kent 52 C2
Goodnestone Kent 53 D4
Goodrich Hereford 62 B1
Goodrington Torbay 8 B2
Goodshaw Lancs 137 A7
Goodwick = Wdig Pembs 72 C2
Goodwood Racecourse W Sus 20 A1
Goodworth Clatford Hants 32 A2
Goole E Yorks 141 A5
Goonbell Corn 4 C2
Goonhavern Corn 4 B2
Goose Eye W Yorks 147 C4
Goose Green Gtr Man 137 C4
Goose Green Norf 104 C2
Goose Green W Sus 21 A4
Gooseham Corn 24 D3

Goosey Oxon 65 D4
Goosnargh Lancs 145 D5
Goostrey Ches 128 B2
Gorcott Hill Warks 80 A3
Gord Shetland 285 L6
Gordon Borders 197 B5
Gordonbush Highld 274 D2
Gordonsburgh Moray 267 C5
Gordonstoun Moray 266 C2
Gordonstown Aberds 267 D6
Gordonstown Aberds 256 C2
Gore Kent 53 D5
Gore Cross Wilts 44 D4
Gore Pit Essex 70 B2
Gorebridge Midloth 209 D6
Gorefield Cambs 117 D7
Gorey Jersey 6
Gorgie Edin 209 C5
Goring Oxon 47 A4
Goring-by-Sea W Sus 21 B6
Goring Heath Oxon 47 B
Gorleston-on-Sea Norf 105 A6
Gornalwood W Mid 96 B
Gorrachie Aberds 268 D?
Gorran Churchtown Corn 5 C
Gorran Haven Corn 5 C
Gorrenberry Borders 186 D6
Gors Ceredig 75 A
Gorse Hill Thamesdown 45 A
Gorsedd Flint 125 B
Gorseinon Swansea 57 C
Gorseness Orkney 282 F
Gorsgoch Ceredig 74 C
Gorslas Carms 57 A
Gorsley Glos 62 A
Gorstan Highld 263 D
Gorstanvorran Highld 236 B
Gorsteyhill Staffs 128 D
Gorsty Hill Staffs 113 C
Gortantaoid Argyll 200 A
Gorton Gtr Man 138 D
Gosbeck Suff 88
Gosberton Lincs 117
Gosberton Clough Lincs 117 A
Gosfield Essex 70 A
Gosford Hereford 78
Gosforth Cumb 162
Gosforth T & W 179 B
Gosmore Herts 68
Gosport Hants 19
Gossabrough Shetland 284 D
Gossington Glos 62 C
Goswick Northumb 199 B
Gotham Notts 114 B
Gotherington Glos 63 A
Gott Shetland 285 H
Goudhurst Kent 37 C
Goulceby Lincs 134 B
Gourdas Aberds 256 B
Gourdon Aberds 233 A
Gourock Inclyd 204 A
Govan Glasgow 205 B
Govanhill Glasgow 205 B
Goveton Devon 7
Govilon Mon 61
Gowanhill Aberds 269 C
Gowdall E Yorks 140 A
Gowerton Swansea 57 C
Gowkhall Fife 208
Gowthorpe E Yorks 149
Goxhill E Yorks 151
Goxhill N Lincs 142
Goxhill Haven N Lincs 142
Goybre Neath 40
Grabhair W Isles 288
Graby Lincs 116
Grade Corn
Graffham W Sus 20
Grafham Cambs 84
Grafham Sur 34
Grafton Hereford 78
Grafton N Yorks 148
Grafton Oxon 64
Grafton Shrops 110
Grafton Worcs 78
Grafton Flyford Worcs 80
Grafton Regis Northants 83
Grafton Underwood Northants 99
Grafty Green Kent 37
Graianrhyd Denb 126
Graig Conwy 124
Graig Denb 125
Graig-fechan Denb 125
Grain Medway 51
Grainsby Lincs 143
Grainthorpe Lincs 143

rampound Corn 4 C4
rampound Road Corn 4 B4
ramsdal W Isles 286 A4
ranborough Bucks 66 A2
ranby Notts 115 B5
randborough Warks 82 A1
randtull Perth 230 C3
range Cumb 163 C5
range E Ayrs 193 B4
range Medway 51 C4
range Mers 126 A2
range Perth 220 B2
range Crossroads Moray 267 D5
range Hall Moray 265 D6
range Hill Essex 68 D4
range Moor W Yorks 139 B5
range of Lindores Fife 220 C2
range-over-Sands Cumb 154 D3
range Villa Durham 179 D4
rangemill Derbys 130 D2
rangemouth Falk 208 B2
rangepans Falk 208 B3
rangetown Cardiff 41 D6
rangetown Redcar 168 C3
ranish Highld 242 A2
ransmoor E Yorks 151 B4
ranston Pembs 55 A4
rantchester Cambs 85 B6
rantham Lincs 116 B2
rantley N Yorks 147 A6
rantlodge Aberds 245 A4
ranton Dumfries 184 B3
ranton Edin 209 C5
rantown-on-Spey Highld 253 D6
rantshouse Borders 211 D5
rappenhall Warr 127 A6
rasby Lincs 142 C2
rasmere Cumb 154 A2
rasscroft Gtr Man 138 C2
rassendale Mers 126 A3
rassholme Durham 166 C2
rassington N Yorks 147 A4
rassmoor Derbys 131 C4
rassthorpe Notts 132 C2
rately Hants 32 A1
ratwich Staffs 112 B4
raveley Cambs 84 A4
raveley Herts 68 A2
ravelly Hill W Mid 96 B4
ravels Shrops 94 A1
raven Shetland 284 F6
raveney Kent 52 C2
ravesend Kent 50 B3
rayingham Lincs 142 D1
rayrigg Cumb 155 B4
rays Thurrock 50 B3
rayshott Hants 34 C1
rayswood Sur 34 C2
raythorp Hrtlpl 168 C3
razeley Wokingham 47 C4
rasbrough S Yorks 140 D2
rasby Mers 126 A2
rat Abington Cambs 86 C1
rat Addington Northants 99 D6
rat Alne Warks 80 B4
rat Altcar Lancs 136 C2
rat Amwell Herts 68 B3
rat Asby Cumb 165 D4
rat Ashfield Suff 87 A5
rat Ayton N Yorks 168 D3
rat Baddow Essex 70 C1
rat Bardfield Essex 86 D2
rat Barford Beds 84 B3
rat Barr W Mid 96 B3
rat Barrington Glos 64 B3
rat Barrow Ches 127 C4
rat Barton Suff 87 A4
rat Barugh N Yorks 159 D6
rat Bavington Northumb 178 A1
rat Bealings Suff 88 C3
rat Bedwyn Wilts 45 C6
rat Bentley Essex 71 A5
rat Billing Northants 83 A4
rat Bircham Norf 119 B4
rat Blakenham Suff 88 B2
rat Blencow Cumb 164 B2
rat Bolas Telford 111 C5
rat Bookham Sur 35 A4
rat Bourton Oxon 82 C1
rat Bowden Leics 99 C4
rat Bradley Suff 86 B2
rat Braxted Essex 70 B2
rat Bricett Suff 87 B6

Great Brickhill Bucks 83 D6
Great Bridge W Mid 96 B2
Great Bridgeford Staffs 112 C2
Great Brington Northants 82 A3
Great Bromley Essex 71 A4
Great Broughton Cumb 162 A3
Great Broughton N Yorks 158 A4
Great Budworth Ches 127 B6
Great Burdon Darl 167 D6
Great Burgh Sur 35 A5
Great Burstead Essex 69 D6
Great Busby N Yorks 158 A4
Great Canfield Essex 69 B5
Great Carlton Lincs 135 A4
Great Casterton Rutland 100 A2
Great Chart Kent 38 A1
Great Chatwell Staffs 112 D1
Great Chesterford Essex 85 C7
Great Cheverell Wilts 44 D3
Great Chishill Cambs 85 D6
Great Clacton Essex 71 B5
Great Cliff W Yorks 139 B6
Great Clifton Cumb 162 B3
Great Coates NE Lincs 143 C4
Great Comberton Worcs 80 C2
Great Corby Cumb 176 D2
Great Cornard Suff 87 C4
Great Cowden E Yorks 151 C5
Great Coxwell Oxon 64 D3
Great Crakehall N Yorks 157 B6
Great Cransley Northants 99 D5
Great Cressingham Norf 103 A4
Great Crosby Mers 136 D2
Great Cubley Derbys 113 B5
Great Dalby Leics 115 D5
Great Denham Beds 84 C2
Great Doddington Northants 83 A5
Great Dunham Norf 119 D5
Great Dunmow Essex 69 A6
Great Durnford Wilts 31 B5
Great Easton Essex 69 A6
Great Easton Leics 99 B5
Great Eccleston Lancs 144 C4
Great Edstone N Yorks 159 C6
Great Ellingham Norf 103 B6
Great Elm Som 30 A1
Great Eversden Cambs 85 B5
Great Fencote N Yorks 157 B6
Great Finborough Suff 87 B6
Great Fransham Norf 119 D5
Great Gaddesden Herts 67 B5
Great Gidding Cambs 100 C3
Great Givendale E Yorks 149 B7
Great Glemham Suff 88 A4
Great Glen Leics 98 B3
Great Gonerby Lincs 116 B1
Great Gransden Cambs 85 B4
Great Green Norf 104 C3
Great Green Suff 87 B5
Great Habton N Yorks 159 D6
Great Hale Lincs 116 A4
Great Hallingbury Essex 69 B5
Great Hampden Bucks 66 C3
Great Harrowden Northants 99 D5
Great Harwood Lancs 146 D1
Great Haseley Oxon 66 C1
Great Hatfield E Yorks 151 C4
Great Haywood Staffs 112 C3
Great Heath W Mid 97 C6
Great Heck N Yorks 140 A3
Great Henny Essex 87 D4
Great Hinton Wilts 44 D3
Great Hockham Norf 103 B5
Great Holland Essex 71 B6
Great Horkesley Essex 87 D5
Great Hormead Herts 68 A3
Great Horton W Yorks 147 D5
Great Horwood Bucks 83 D4
Great Houghton Northants 83 B4
Great Houghton S Yorks 140 C2
Great Hucklow Derbys 130 B1
Great Kelk E Yorks 151 B4
Great Kimble Bucks 66 C3
Great Kingshill Bucks 66 D3
Great Langton N Yorks 157 B6
Great Leighs Essex 70 B1
Great Lever Gtr Man 137 C6
Great Limber Lincs 142 C3
Great Linford M Keynes 83 C5
Great Livermere Suff 103 D4
Great Longstone Derbys 130 B2
Great Lumley Durham 167 A5
Great Lyth Shrops 94 A2
Great Malvern Worcs 79 C5
Great Maplestead Essex 87 D4

Great Marton Blkpool 144 D3
Great Massingham Norf 119 C4
Great Melton Norf 104 A2
Great Milton Oxon 66 C1
Great Missenden Bucks 66 C3
Great Mitton Lancs 145 D7
Great Mongeham Kent 53 D5
Great Moulton Norf 104 B2
Great Munden Herts 68 A3
Great Musgrave Cumb 165 D5
Great Ness Shrops 110 D2
Great Notley Essex 70 A1
Great Oakley Essex 71 A5
Great Oakley Northants 99 C5
Great Offley Herts 67 A6
Great Ormside Cumb 165 D5
Great Orton Cumb 175 C6
Great Ouseburn N Yorks 148 A3
Great Oxendon Northants 99 C4
Great Oxney Green Essex 69 C6
Great Palgrave Norf 119 D5
Great Parndon Essex 68 C4
Great Paxton Cambs 84 A4
Great Plumpton Lancs 144 D3
Great Plumstead Norf 121 D5
Great Ponton Lincs 116 B2
Great Preston W Yorks 140 A2
Great Raveley Cambs 101 C4
Great Rissington Glos 64 B2
Great Rollright Oxon 81 D6
Great Ryburgh Norf 119 C6
Great Ryle Northumb 188 B3
Great Ryton Shrops 94 A2
Great Saling Essex 69 A7
Great Salkeld Cumb 164 B3
Great Sampford Essex 86 D2
Great Sankey Warr 127 A5
Great Saxham Suff 86 A3
Great Shefford W Berks 46 B1
Great Shelford Cambs 85 B6
Great Smeaton N Yorks 158 A2
Great Snoring Norf 119 B6
Great Somerford Wilts 44 A3
Great Stainton Darl 167 C6
Great Stambridge Essex 70 D2
Great Staughton Cambs 84 A3
Great Steeping Lincs 135 C4
Great Stonar Kent 53 D5
Great Strickland Cumb 164 C3
Great Stukeley Cambs 100 D4
Great Sturton Lincs 134 B2
Great Sutton Ches 126 B3
Great Sutton Shrops 94 C3
Great Swinburne Northumb 178 B1
Great Tew Oxon 65 A4
Great Tey Essex 70 A2
Great Thurkleby N Yorks 158 D3
Great Thurlow Suff 86 B2
Great Torrington Devon 25 D5
Great Tosson Northumb 188 C3
Great Totham Essex 70 B2
Great Totham Essex 70 B2
Great Tows Lincs 143 D4
Great Urswick Cumb 153 C3
Great Wakering Essex 51 A6
Great Waldingfield Suff 87 C5
Great Walsingham Norf 119 B6
Great Waltham Essex 69 B6
Great Warley Essex 69 D6
Great Washbourne Glos 80 D2
Great Weldon Northants 99 C6
Great Welnetham Suff 87 B4
Great Wenham Suff 87 D6
Great Whittington Northumb 178 B2
Great Wigborough Essex 70 B3
Great Wilbraham Cambs 86 B1
Great Wishford Wilts 31 B4
Great Witcombe Glos 63 B5
Great Witley Worcs 79 A5
Great Wolford Warks 81 D5
Great Wratting Suff 86 C2
Great Wymondley Herts 68 A2
Great Wyrley Staffs 96 A2
Great Wytheford Shrops 111 D4
Great Yarmouth Norf 105 A6
Great Yarmouth Sea Life Centre Norf 105 A6
Great Yeldham Essex 86 D3
Greater Doward Hereford 62 B1
Greatford Lincs 116 D3
Greatgate Staffs 113 A4
Greatham Hants 33 B6
Greatham Hrtlpl 168 C2

Greatham W Sus 20 A3
Greatstone on Sea Kent 38 C2
Greatworth Northants 82 C2
Greave Lancs 138 A1
Greeba I o M 152 C3
Green End Beds 84 B3
Green Hammerton N Yorks 148 B3
Green Lane Powys 93 B5
Green Ore Som 43 D4
Green St Green London 50 C1
Green Street Herts 68 D1
Greenbank Shetland 284 C7
Greenburn W Loth 208 D2
Greendikes Northumb 188 A3
Greenfield Beds 84 D2
Greenfield Flint 126 B1
Greenfield Gtr Man 138 C2
Greenfield Highld 239 B6
Greenfield Oxon 66 D2
Greenford London 48 A4
Greengairs N Lnrk 207 C5
Greenham W Berks 46 C2
Greenhaugh Northumb 177 A5
Greenhead Northumb 177 A5
Greenhill Falk 207 C6
Greenhill London 49 A4
Greenhill Kent 52 C3
Greenhill Leics 114 D2
Greenhills N Ayrs 204 C3
Greenhithe Kent 50 B2
Greenholm E Ayrs 193 B5
Greenholme Cumb 155 A4
Greenhouse Borders 187 A4
Greenhow Hill N Yorks 147 A5
Greenigoe Orkney 283 G5
Greenland Highld 280 B4
Greenlands Bucks 47 A5
Greenlaw Aberds 268 D1
Greenlaw Borders 197 B6
Greenlea Dumfries 174 A3
Greenloaning Perth 218 D3
Greenmeadow Community Farm, Pontnewydd Torf 61 D4
Greenmount Gtr Man 137 B6
Greenmow Shetland 285 L6
Greenock Inverclyd 204 A2
Greenock West Inverclyd 204 A2
Greenodd Cumb 154 C2
Greenrow Cumb 174 C4
Greens Norton Northants 82 C3
Greenside T & W 178 C3
Greensidehill Northumb 188 B2
Greenstead Green Essex 70 A2
Greensted Essex 69 C5
Greensted Church, Chipping Ongar Essex 69 C5
Greenwich London 49 B6
Greet Glos 80 D3
Greete Shrops 94 D3
Greetham Lincs 134 B3
Greetham Rutland 116 D2
Greetland W Yorks 138 A3
Gregg Hall Cumb 154 B3
Gregson Lane Lancs 137 A4
Greinetobht W Isles 287 G3
Greinton Som 28 B4
Gremista Shetland 285 J6
Grenaby I o M 152 D2
Grendon Northants 83 A5
Grendon Warks 97 A5
Grendon Common Warks 97 B5
Grendon Green Hereford 78 B3
Grendon Underwood Bucks 66 A1
Grenofen Devon 11 D5
Grenoside S Yorks 139 D6
Greosabhagh W Isles 288 H2
Gresford Wrex 126 D3
Gresham Norf 120 B3
Greshornish Highld 258 C3
Gressenhall Norf 119 D6
Gressingham Lancs 145 A5
Gresty Green Ches 128 D2
Greta Bridge Durham 166 D3
Gretna Dumfries 175 B6
Gretna Green Dumfries 175 B6
Gretton Glos 80 D3
Gretton Northants 99 B5
Gretton Shrops 94 B3
Grewelthorpe N Yorks 157 D6
Grey Green N Lincs 141 C5
Greygarth N Yorks 157 D5
Greynor Carms 57 B5
Greysouthen Cumb 162 B3

Greystoke Cumb 164 B2
Greystone Angus 232 D3
Greystone Dumfries 174 A2
Greywell Hants 47 D5
Griais W Isles 288 C5
Grianan W Isles 288 D5
Gribthorpe E Yorks 149 D6
Gridley Corner Devon 11 B4
Griff Warks 97 C6
Griffithstown Torf 61 D4
Grimbister Orkney 282 F4
Grimblethorpe Lincs 134 A2
Grimeford Village Lancs 137 B5
Grimethorpe S Yorks 140 C2
Griminis W Isles 286 A3
Grimister Shetland 284 D6
Grimley Worcs 79 A6
Grimness Orkney 283 H5
Grimoldby Lincs 134 A3
Grimpo Shrops 110 C2
Grimsargh Lancs 145 D5
Grimsbury Oxon 82 C1
Grimsby NE Lincs 143 B4
Grimscote Northants 82 B3
Grimscott Corn 10 A3
Grimsthorpe Lincs 116 C3
Grimston E Yorks 151 D5
Grimston Leics 115 C4
Grimston Norf 119 C4
Grimston York 149 B5
Grimstone Dorset 15 B6
Grinacombe Moor Devon 11 B5
Grindale E Yorks 161 D5
Grindigar Orkney 283 G6
Grindiscol Shetland 285 K6
Grindle Shrops 95 A5
Grindleford Derbys 130 B2
Grindleton Lancs 146 C1
Grindley Staffs 112 C4
Grindley Brook Shrops 111 A4
Grindlow Derbys 130 B1
Grindon Northumb 198 B3
Grindon Staffs 129 D5
Grindonmoor Gate Staffs 129 D5
Gringley on the Hill Notts 141 D5
Grinsdale Cumb 175 C6
Grinshill Shrops 111 C4
Grinton N Yorks 156 B4
Griomsidar W Isles 288 E4
Grishipoll Argyll 223 B4
Grisling Common E Sus 36 D2
Gristhorpe N Yorks 161 C4
Griston Norf 103 B5
Gritley Orkney 283 G6
Grittenham Wilts 44 A4
Grittleton Wilts 44 A2
Grizebeck Cumb 153 B3
Grizedale Cumb 154 B2
Grobister Orkney 282 E7
Groby Leics 98 A2
Groes Conwy 125 C5
Groes Neath 40 C2
Groes-faen Rhondda 41 C5
Groes-lwyd Powys 109 D7
Groesffordd Marli Denb 125 B5
Groeslon Gwyn 123 D5
Groeslon Gwyn 107 A4
Grogport Argyll 202 D3
Gromford Suff 89 B4
Gronant Flint 125 A5
Groombridge E Sus 36 C3
Grosmont Mon 61 A6
Grosmont N Yorks 160 A2
Grosvenor Museum, Chester Ches 127 C4
Groton Suff 87 C5
Groudle Glen Railway I o M 152 D4
Grougfoot Falk 208 C3
Grouville Jersey 6
Grove Dorset 15 D7
Grove Kent 53 C4
Grove Notts 132 B2
Grove Oxon 65 D5
Grove Park London 49 B7
Grove Vale W Mid 96 B3
Grovesend Swansea 57 B5
Grudie Highld 263 D5
Gruids Highld 272 D3
Gruinard House Highld 261 A6
Grula Highld 246 B2
Gruline Argyll 225 B4
Grunasound Shetland 285 K5
Grundisburgh Suff 88 B3

H

Grunsaglll Lancs 146 B1
Gruting Shetland 285 J4
Grutness Shetland 285 N6
Gualachulain Highld 227 B6
Gualin Ho. Highld 276 C4
Guardbridge Fife 221 C4
Guarlford Worcs 79 C6
Guay Perth 230 D4
Guernsey Airport Guern 6
Guestling Green E Sus 23 A6
Guestling Thorn E Sus 23 A6
Guestwick Norf 120 C2
Guestwick Green Norf 120 C2
Guide Blkburn 137 A6
Guide Post Northumb 179 A4
Guilden Morden Cambs 85 C4
Guilden Sutton Ches 127 C4
Guildford Sur 34 B2
Guildtown Perth 219 A6
Guilsborough Northants 98 D3
Guilsfield Powys 109 D7
Guilton Kent 53 D4
Guineaford Devon 25 B6
Guisborough Redcar 168 D4
Guiseley W Yorks 147 C5
Guist Norf 120 C1
Guith Orkney 282 D6
Guiting Power Glos 64 A1
Gulberwick Shetland 285 K6
Gullane E Loth 210 B1
Gulval Corn 2 B2
Gulworthy Devon 11 D5
Gumfreston Pembs 55 D7
Gumley Leics 98 B3
Gummow's Shop Corn 4 B3
Gun Hill E Sus 22 A3
Gunby E Yorks 149 D6
Gunby Lincs 116 C2
Gundleton Hants 33 B5
Gunn Devon 26 B1
Gunnerside N Yorks 156 B3
Gunnerton Northumb 177 B7
Gunness N Lincs 141 B6
Gunnislake Corn 11 D5
Gunnista Shetland 285 J7
Gunthorpe Norf 120 B2
Gunthorpe Notts 115 A4
Gunthorpe P'boro 100 A3
Gunville I o W 18 C3
Gunwalloe Corn 3 C4
Gurnard I o W 18 B3
Gurnett Ches 129 B4
Gurney Slade Som 29 A6
Gurnos Powys 59 E4
Gussage All Saints Dorset 31 D4
Gussage St Michael Dorset 30 D3
Guston Kent 39 A5
Gutcher Shetland 284 D7
Guthrie Angus 232 C3
Guyhirn Cambs 101 A5
Guyhirn Gull Cambs 101 A5
Guy's Head Lincs 118 C1
Guy's Marsh Dorset 30 C2
Guyzance Northumb 189 C5
Gwaenysgor Flint 125 A5
Gwalchmai Anglesey 122 C3
Gwaun-Cae-Gurwen Neath 59 D4
Gwaun-Leision Neath 59 D4
Gwbert Ceredig 73 B4
Gweek Corn 3 C5
Gwehelog Mon 61 C5
Gwenddwr Powys 77 C4
Gwennap Corn 4 D2
Gwenter Corn 3 D5
Gwernaffield Flint 126 C2
Gwernesney Mon 61 C6
Gwernogle Carms 58 B2
Gwernymynydd Flint 126 C2
Gwersyllt Wrex 126 D3
Gwespyr Flint 125 A6
Gwithian Corn 2 A3
Gwredog Anglesey 123 B4
Gwyddelwern Denb 109 A5
Gwyddgrug Carms 58 B1
Gwydyr Uchaf Conwy 124 C2
Gwynfryn Wrex 126 D2
Gwystre Powys 77 A4
Gwytherin Conwy 124 C3
Gyfelia Wrex 110 A2
Gyffin Conwy 124 B2
Gyre Orkney 283 G4
Gyrn-goch Gwyn 107 B4

Habberley Shrops 94 A1
Habergham Lancs 146 D2
Habrough NE Lincs 142 B3
Haceby Lincs 116 B3
Hacheston Suff 88 B4
Hackbridge London 49 C5
Hackenthorpe S Yorks 131 A4
Hackford Norf 103 A6
Hackforth N Yorks 157 B6
Hackland Orkney 282 E4
Hackleton Northants 83 B5
Hackness N Yorks 160 B3
Hackness Orkney 283 H4
Hackney London 49 A6
Hackthorn Lincs 133 A4
Hackthorpe Cumb 164 C3
Haconby Lincs 116 C4
Hacton London 50 A2
Hadden Borders 198 C1
Haddenham Bucks 66 C2
Haddenham Cambs 101 D6
Haddington E Loth 210 C2
Haddington Lincs 133 C4
Haddiscoe Norf 105 B5
Haddon Cambs 100 B3
Haddon Ches 129 C4
Haddon Hall Derbys 130 C2
Hade Edge W Yorks 139 C4
Hademore Staffs 97 A4
Hadfield Derbys 138 D3
Hadham Cross Herts 68 B4
Hadham Ford Herts 68 A4
Hadleigh Essex 51 A5
Hadleigh Suff 87 C6
Hadley Telford 111 D5
Hadley End Staffs 113 C5
Hadlow Kent 36 B4
Hadlow Down E Sus 36 D3
Hadnall Shrops 111 D4
Hadstock Essex 86 C1
Hady Derbys 130 B3
Hadzor Worcs 80 A2
Haffenden Quarter Kent 37 B6
Hafod-Dinbych Conwy 124 D3
Hafod-Iom Conwy 124 B3
Haggate Lancs 146 D2
Haggbeck Cumb 176 B2
Haggerston Northumb 198 B4
Haggrister Shetland 284 F5
Hagley Hereford 78 C3
Hagley Worcs 96 C2
Hagworthingham Lincs 134 C3
Haigh Gtr Man 137 C5
Haigh S Yorks 139 B5
Haigh Moor W Yorks 139 A5
Haighton Green Lancs 145 D5
Hail Weston Cambs 84 A3
Haile Cumb 162 D3
Hailes Glos 80 D3
Hailey Herts 68 B3
Hailey Oxon 65 B4
Hailsham E Sus 22 B3
Haimer Highld 280 B3
Hainault London 69 D4
Hainford Norf 120 D4
Hainton Lincs 134 A1
Hairmyres S Lnrk 205 C6
Haisthorpe E Yorks 151 A4
Hakin Pembs 55 D4
Halam Notts 132 D1
Halbeath Fife 208 B4
Halberton Devon 27 D5
Halcro Highld 280 B4
Hale Gtr Man 128 A2
Hale Halton 127 A4
Hale Hants 31 D5
Hale Bank Halton 127 A4
Hale Street Kent 37 B4
Halebarns Gtr Man 128 A2
Hales Norf 105 B4
Hales Staffs 111 B6
Hales Place Kent 52 D3
Halesfield Telford 95 A5
Halesgate Lincs 117 C6
Halesowen W Mid 96 C2
Halesworth Suff 105 D4
Halewood Mers 127 A4
Halford Shrops 94 C2
Halford Warks 81 C5
Halfpenny Furze Carms 56 A2
Halfpenny Green Staffs 95 B6
Halfway Carms 58 B3
Halfway Carms 59 B5
Halfway W Berks 46 C2
Halfway Bridge W Sus 34 D2

Halfway House Shrops 110 D2
Halfway Houses Kent 51 B6
Halifax W Yorks 138 A3
Halket E Ayrs 205 C4
Halkirk Highld 280 C3
Halkyn Flint 126 B2
Hall Dunnerdale Cumb 153 A3
Hall Green W Mid 96 C4
Hall Green W Yorks 139 B6
Hall Grove Herts 68 B2
Hall of Tankerness Orkney 283 G6
Hall of the Forest Shrops 93 C6
Halland E Sus 22 A2
Hallaton Leics 99 B4
Hallatrow Bath 43 D5
Hallbankgate Cumb 176 D3
Hallen S Glos 43 A4
Halliburton Borders 197 B5
Hallin Highld 258 C2
Halling Medway 51 C4
Hallington Lincs 134 A3
Hallington Northumb 178 B1
Halliwell Gtr Man 137 B6
Halloughton Notts 132 D1
Hallow Worcs 79 B6
Hallrule Borders 187 B4
Halls E Loth 210 C3
Hall's Green Herts 68 A2
Hallsands Devon 8 D2
Hallthwaites Cumb 153 B2
Hallworthy Corn 10 C2
Hallyburton House Perth 220 A2
Hallyne Borders 195 B6
Halmer End Staffs 112 A1
Halmore Glos 62 C2
Halmyre Mains Borders 195 B6
Halnaker W Sus 20 B2
Halsall Lancs 136 B2
Halse Northants 82 C2
Halse Som 27 C6
Halsetown Corn 2 B3
Halsham E Yorks 143 A4
Halsinger Devon 25 B6
Halstead Essex 87 D4
Halstead Kent 50 C1
Halstead Leics 99 A4
Halstock Dorset 15 A5
Haltham Lincs 134 C2
Haltoft End Lincs 117 A6
Halton Bucks 66 B3
Halton Halton 127 A5
Halton Lancs 145 A5
Halton Northumb 178 C1
Halton Wrex 110 B2
Halton W Yorks 148 D2
Halton East N Yorks 147 B4
Halton Gill N Yorks 156 D2
Halton Holegate Lincs 135 C4
Halton Lea Gate Northumb 176 D4
Halton West N Yorks 146 B2
Haltwhistle Northumb 177 C5
Halvergate Norf 105 A5
Halwell Devon 8 B1
Halwill Devon 11 B5
Halwill Junction Devon 11 A5
Ham Devon 14 A2
Ham Glos 62 D2
Ham London 49 B4
Ham Highld 280 A4
Ham Kent 53 D5
Ham Shetland 285 K1
Ham Wilts 46 C1
Ham Common Dorset 30 C2
Ham Green Hereford 79 C5
Ham Green Kent 37 D6
Ham Green Kent 51 C5
Ham Green N Som 43 B4
Ham Green Worcs 80 A3
Ham Street Som 29 B5
Hamble-le-Rice Hants 18 A3
Hambleden Bucks 47 A5
Hambledon Hants 33 D5
Hambledon Sur 34 C2
Hambleton Lancs 144 C3
Hambleton N Yorks 149 D4
Hambridge Som 28 C3
Hambrook S Glos 43 B5
Hambrook W Sus 19 A6
Hameringham Lincs 134 C3
Hamerton Cambs 100 D3
Hametoun Shetland 285 K1
Hamilton S Lnrk 194 A2
Hamilton Park Racecourse S Lnrk 194 A2
Hammer W Sus 34 C1

Hammerpot W Sus 20 B3
Hammersmith London 49 B5
Hammerwich Staffs 96 A3
Hammerwood E Sus 36 C2
Hammond Street Herts 68 C3
Hammoon Dorset 30 D2
Hamnavoe Shetland 284 E4
Hamnavoe Shetland 284 E4
Hamnavoe Shetland 285 K5
Hamnavoe Shetland 284 E6
Hamnavoe Shetland 284 F6
Hampden National Stadium Glasgow 205 B5
Hampden Park E Sus 22 B4
Hamperden End Essex 86 D1
Hampnett Glos 64 B1
Hampole S Yorks 140 B3
Hampreston Dorset 17 B4
Hampstead London 49 A5
Hampstead Norreys W Berks 46 B3
Hampsthwaite N Yorks 147 B6
Hampton London 48 C4
Hampton Shrops 95 C5
Hampton Worcs 80 C3
Hampton Bishop Hereford 78 D3
Hampton Court Palace, Teddington London 52 C3
Hampton Heath Ches 110 A3
Hampton in Arden W Mid 97 C5
Hampton Loade Shrops 95 C5
Hampton Lovett Worcs 80 A1
Hampton Lucy Warks 81 B5
Hampton on the Hill Warks 81 A5
Hampton Poyle Oxon 65 B6
Hamrow Norf 119 C6
Hamsey E Sus 22 A2
Hamsey Green Sur 35 A6
Hamstall Ridware Staffs 113 D5
Hamstead I o W 18 B3
Hamstead W Mid 96 B3
Hamstead Marshall W Berks 46 C2
Hamsterley Durham 166 B4
Hamsterley Durham 178 D3
Hamstreet Kent 38 B2
Hamworthy Poole 16 B3
Hanbury Staffs 113 C5
Hanbury Worcs 80 A2
Hanbury Woodend Staffs 113 C5
Hanby Lincs 116 B3
Hanchurch Staffs 112 A2
Handbridge Ches 127 C4
Handcross W Sus 35 D5
Handforth Ches 128 A3
Handley Ches 127 D4
Handsacre Staffs 113 D4
Handsworth S Yorks 131 A4
Handsworth W Mid 96 B3
Handy Cross Devon 25 C5
Hanford Stoke 112 A2
Hanging Langford Wilts 31 B4
Hangleton W Sus 20 B3
Hanham S Glos 43 B5
Hankelow Ches 111 A5
Hankerton Wilts 63 D5
Hankham E Sus 22 B4
Hanley Stoke 112 A2
Hanley Castle Worcs 79 C6
Hanley Child Worcs 79 A4
Hanley Swan Worcs 79 C6
Hanley William Worcs 79 A4
Hanlith N Yorks 146 A3
Hanmer Wrex 110 B3
Hannah Lincs 135 B5
Hannington Hants 46 D3
Hannington Northants 99 D5
Hannington Thamesdown 64 D2
Hannington Wick Thamesdown 64 D2
Hansel Village S Ayrs 192 B3
Hanslope M Keynes 83 C5
Hanthorpe Lincs 116 C3
Hanwell London 49 A4
Hanwell Oxon 82 C1
Hanwood Shrops 94 A2
Hanworth London 48 B4
Hanworth Norf 120 B3
Happendon S Lnrk 194 C3
Happisburgh Norf 121 B5
Happisburgh Common Norf 121 C5
Hapsford Ches 127 B4
Hapton Lancs 146 D1
Hapton Norf 104 B2
Harberton Devon 8 B1
Harbertonford Devon 8 B1

Harbledown Kent 52 D
Harborne W Mid 96 C
Harborough Magna Warks 98 D
Harbottle Northumb 188 C
Harbour Park, Littlehampton W Sus 20 C
Harbury Warks 81 B
Harby Leics 115 B
Harby Notts 132 B
Harcombe Devon 13 B
Harden W Mid 96 A
Harden W Yorks 147 D
Hardenhuish Wilts 44 B
Hardgate Aberds 245 B
Hardham W Sus 20 A
Hardingham Norf 103 A
Hardingstone Northants 83 B
Hardington Som 43 D
Hardington Mandeville Som 29 D
Hardington Marsh Som 15 A
Hardley Hants 18 A
Hardley Street Norf 105 A
Hardmead M Keynes 83 C
Hardrow N Yorks 156 B
Hardstoft Derbys 131 C
Hardway Hants 19 A
Hardway Som 29 B
Hardwick Bucks 66 B
Hardwick Cambs 85 B
Hardwick Norf 118 D
Hardwick Norf 104
Hardwick Notts 131
Hardwick Northants 83 A
Hardwick Oxon 65
Hardwick Oxon 65
Hardwick W Mid 96
Hardwick Hall Derbys 131
Hardwicke Glos 62
Hardwicke Glos 63
Hardwicke Hereford 77
Hardy's Green Essex 70
Hare Green Essex 71
Hare Hatch Wokingham 47
Hare Street Herts 68
Hareby Lincs 134
Hareden Lancs 145
Harefield London 67
Harehills W Yorks 148
Harehope Northumb 188
Harescombe Glos 63
Haresfield Glos 63
Hareshaw N Lnrk 207
Hareshaw Head Northumb 177
Harewood W Yorks 148
Harewood End Hereford 62
Harewood House, Wetherby W Yorks 148
Harford Carms 58
Harford Devon 7
Hargate Norf 104
Hargatewall Derbys 129
Hargrave Ches 127
Hargrave Northants 100
Hargrave Suff 86
Harker Cumb 175
Harkland Shetland 284
Harkstead Suff 88
Harlaston Staffs 113
Harlaw Ho. Aberds 256
Harlaxton Lincs 116
Harle Syke Lancs 146
Harlech Gwyn 107
Harlech Castle Gwyn 107
Harlequin Notts 115
Harlescott Shrops 111
Harlesden London 49
Harleston Devon 8
Harleston Norf 104
Harleston Suff 87
Harlestone Northants 83
Harley Shrops 94
Harley S Yorks 139
Harleyholm S Lnrk 195
Harlington Beds 84
Harlington London 48
Harlington S Yorks 140
Harlosh Highld 258
Harlow Essex 69
Harlow Carr RHS Garden, Harrogate N Yorks 147
Harlow Hill Northumb 178
Harlow Hill N Yorks 148
Harlthorpe E Yorks 149
Harlton Cambs 85
Harman's Cross Dorset 16

Harmby N Yorks 157 C5
Harmer Green Herts 68 B2
Harmer Hill Shrops 110 C3
Harmondsworth London 48 B3
Harmston Lincs 133 C4
Harnham Northumb 178 B2
Harnhill Glos 63 C6
Harold Hill London 69 D5
Harold Wood London 69 D5
Haroldston West Pembs 55 C4
Haroldswick Shetland 284 B8
Harome N Yorks 159 C5
Harpenden Herts 67 B6
Harpford Devon 13 B5
Harpham E Yorks 150 A3
Harpley Norf 119 C4
Harpley Worcs 79 A4
Harpole Northants 82 A3
Harpsdale Highld 280 C3
Harpsden Oxon 47 A5
Harpswell Lincs 133 A4
Harpur Hill Derbys 129 B5
Harpurhey Gtr Man 138 C1
Harraby Cumb 175 C7
Harrapool Highld 247 B5
Harrier Shetland 285 J1
Harrietfield Perth 219 B4
Harrietsham Kent 37 A6
Harrington Cumb 162 B2
Harrington Lincs 134 B3
Harrington Northants 99 C4
Harringworth Northants 99 B6
Harris Highld 234 A2
Harris Museum, Preston Lancs 136 A4
Harrogate N Yorks 148 B2
Harrold Beds 83 B6
Harrow London 49 A4
Harrow on the Hill London 49 A4
Harrow Street Suff 87 D5
Harrow Weald London 67 D6
Harrowbarrow Corn 6 A2
Harrowden Beds 84 C2
Harrowgate Hill Darl 167 D5
Harston Cambs 85 B6
Harston Leics 115 B6
Harswell E Yorks 150 C1
Hart Hrtlpl 168 B2
Hart Common Gtr Man 137 C5
Hart Hill Luton 67 A6
Hart Station Hrtlpl 168 B2
Hartburn Northumb 178 A2
Hartburn Stockton 168 D2
Hartest Suff 87 B4
Hartfield E Sus 36 C2
Hartford Cambs 101 D4
Hartford Ches 127 B6
Hartford End Essex 69 B6
Hartfordbridge Hants 47 D5
Hartforth N Yorks 157 A5
Harthill Ches 127 D5
Harthill N Lnrk 208 D2
Harthill S Yorks 131 A4
Hartington Derbys 129 C6
Hartland Devon 24 C3
Hartlebury Worcs 95 D6
Hartlepool Hrtlpl 168 B3
Hartlepool's Maritime Experience Hrtlpl 168 B3
Hartley Cumb 155 A6
Hartley Kent 50 C3
Hartley Kent 37 C5
Hartley Northumb 179 B5
Hartley Westpall Hants 47 D4
Hartley Wintney Hants 47 D5
Hartlip Kent 51 C5
Hartoft End N Yorks 159 B6
Harton N Yorks 149 A6
Harton Shrops 94 C2
Harton T & W 179 C5
Hartpury Glos 62 A3
Hartshead W Yorks 139 A4
Hartshill Warks 97 B6
Hartshorne Derbys 113 C7
Hartsop Cumb 164 D2
Hartwell Northants 83 B4
Hartwood N Lnrk 194 A3
Harvieston Stirl 206 B3
Harvington Worcs 80 C3
Harvington Cross Worcs 80 C3
Harwell Oxon 46 A2
Harwich Essex 88 D3
Harwood Durham 165 B6
Harwood Gtr Man 137 B6
Harwood Dale N Yorks 160 B3
Harworth Notts 140 D4
Hasbury W Mid 96 C2

Hascombe Sur 34 B2
Haselbech Northants 99 D4
Haselbury Plucknett Som 29 D4
Haseley Warks 81 A5
Haselor Warks 80 B4
Hasfield Glos 63 A4
Hasguard Pembs 55 D4
Haskayne Lancs 136 C2
Hasketon Suff 88 B3
Hasland Derbys 130 C3
Haslemere Sur 34 C2
Haslingden Lancs 137 A6
Haslingfield Cambs 85 B6
Haslington Ches 128 D2
Hassall Ches 128 D2
Hassall Green Ches 128 D2
Hassell Street Kent 38 A2
Hassendean Borders 186 A4
Hassingham Norf 105 A4
Hassocks W Sus 21 A5
Hassop Derbys 130 B2
Hastigrow Highld 281 B4
Hastingleigh Kent 38 A2
Hastings E Sus 23 B6
Hastings Castle E Sus 23 A6
Hastings Sea Life Centre E Sus 23 B6
Hastingwood Essex 69 C4
Hastoe Herts 67 C4
Haswell Durham 167 A6
Haswell Plough Durham 167 A6
Hatch Beds 84 C3
Hatch Hants 47 D4
Hatch Wilts 30 C3
Hatch Beauchamp Som 28 C3
Hatch End London 67 D6
Hatch Green Som 28 D3
Hatchet Gate Hants 18 A2
Hatching Green Herts 67 B6
Hatchmere Ches 127 B5
Hatcliffe NE Lincs 143 C4
Hatfield Hereford 78 B3
Hatfield Herts 68 C2
Hatfield S Yorks 141 C4
Hatfield Worcs 80 B1
Hatfield Broad Oak Essex 69 B5
Hatfield Garden Village Herts 68 C2
Hatfield Heath Essex 69 B5
Hatfield House Herts 68 C2
Hatfield Peverel Essex 70 B1
Hatfield Woodhouse S Yorks 141 C4
Hatford Oxon 64 D4
Hatherden Hants 46 D1
Hatherleigh Devon 11 A6
Hathern Leics 114 C2
Hatherop Glos 64 C2
Hathersage Derbys 130 A2
Hathershaw Gtr Man 138 C2
Hatherton Ches 111 A5
Hatherton Staffs 112 D3
Hatley St George Cambs 85 B4
Hatt Corn 6 A2
Hattingley Hants 33 B5
Hatton Aberds 257 C5
Hatton Derbys 113 C6
Hatton Lincs 134 B1
Hatton Shrops 94 B2
Hatton Warks 81 A5
Hatton Warr 127 A5
Hatton Castle Aberds 256 B2
Hatton Country World Warks 81 A5
Hatton Heath Ches 127 C4
Hatton of Fintray Aberds 245 A5
Hattoncrook Aberds 256 D3
Haugh E Ayrs 193 C4
Haugh Gtr Man 138 B2
Haugh Lincs 135 B4
Haugh Head Northumb 188 A3
Haugh of Glass Moray 255 C5
Haugh of Urr Dumfries 173 B6
Haugham Lincs 134 A3
Haughley Suff 87 A6
Haughley Green Suff 87 A6
Haughs of Clinterty Aberdeen 245 A5
Haughton Notts 132 B1
Haughton Shrops 95 B4
Haughton Shrops 110 C2
Haughton Shrops 111 D4
Haughton Shrops 95 A5
Haughton Staffs 112 C2
Haughton Castle Northumb 177 B7

Haughton Green Gtr Man 138 D2
Haughton Le Skerne Darl 167 D6
Haughton Moss Ches 127 D5
Haultwick Herts 68 A3
Haunn Argyll 224 B2
Haunn W Isles 286 E3
Haunton Staffs 113 D6
Hauxley Northumb 189 C5
Hauxton Cambs 85 B6
Havant Hants 19 A6
Haven Hereford 78 B2
Haven Bank Lincs 134 D2
Haven Side E Yorks 142 A3
Havenstreet I o W 19 B4
Havercroft W Yorks 140 B1
Haverfordwest = Hwlffordd Pembs 55 C5
Haverhill Suff 86 C2
Haverigg Cumb 153 C2
Havering-atte-Bower London 69 D5
Haveringland Norf 120 C3
Haversham M Keynes 83 C5
Haverthwaite Cumb 154 C2
Haverton Hill Stockton 168 C2
Hawarden = Penarlâg Flint 126 C3
Hawcoat Cumb 153 C3
Hawen Ceredig 73 B6
Hawes N Yorks 156 C2
Hawes Side Blkpool 144 D3
Hawes'Green Norf 104 B3
Hawford Worcs 79 A6
Hawick Borders 186 B4
Hawk Green Gtr Man 129 A4
Hawkchurch Devon 14 A3
Hawkedon Suff 86 B3
Hawkenbury Kent 37 B6
Hawkenbury Kent 36 C3
Hawkeridge Wilts 44 D2
Hawkerland Devon 13 C5
Hawkes End W Mid 97 C6
Hawkesbury S Glos 43 A6
Hawkesbury Warks 97 C6
Hawkesbury Upton S Glos 44 A1
Hawkhill Northumb 189 B5
Hawkhurst Kent 37 C5
Hawkinge Kent 39 B4
Hawkley Hants 33 C6
Hawkridge Som 26 B3
Hawkshead Cumb 154 B2
Hawkshead Hill Cumb 154 B2
Hawksland S Lnrk 194 C3
Hawkswick N Yorks 156 D3
Hawksworth Notts 115 A5
Hawksworth W Yorks 147 C5
Hawksworth W Yorks 147 D6
Hawkwell Essex 70 D2
Hawley Hants 34 A1
Hawley Kent 50 B2
Hawling Glos 63 A6
Hawnby N Yorks 158 C4
Haworth W Yorks 147 D4
Hawstead Suff 87 B4
Hawthorn Durham 168 A2
Hawthorn Rhondda 41 C6
Hawthorn Wilts 44 C2
Hawthorn Hill Brack 48 B1
Hawthorn Hill Lincs 134 D2
Hawthorpe Lincs 116 C3
Hawton Notts 132 D2
Haxby York 149 B5
Haxey N Lincs 141 C5
Hay Green Norf 118 D2
Hay-on-Wye = Y Gelli Gandryll Powys 77 C6
Hay Street Herts 68 A3
Haydock Mers 137 D4
Haydock Park Racecourse Mers 137 D4
Haydon Dorset 29 D6
Haydon Bridge Northumb 177 C6
Haydon Wick Thamesdown 45 A5
Haye Corn 6 A2
Hayes London 49 C7
Hayes London 48 A4
Hayfield Derbys 129 A5
Hayfield Fife 209 A5
Hayhill E Ayrs 182 A2
Hayhillock Angus 232 D3
Hayle Corn 2 B3
Haynes Beds 84 C2
Haynes Church End Beds 84 C2
Hayscastle Pembs 55 B4
Hayscastle Cross Pembs 55 B5
Hayshead Angus 233 D4
Hayton Aberdeen 245 B6

Hayton Cumb 174 D4
Hayton Cumb 176 D3
Hayton E Yorks 149 C7
Hayton Notts 132 A2
Hayton's Bent Shrops 94 C3
Haytor Vale Devon 12 D2
Haywards Heath W Sus 35 D6
Haywood S Yorks 140 B3
Haywood Oaks Notts 131 D6
Hazel Grove Gtr Man 129 A4
Hazel Street Kent 37 C4
Hazelbank S Lnrk 194 B3
Hazelbury Bryan Dorset 16 A1
Hazeley Hants 47 D5
Hazelhurst Gtr Man 138 C2
Hazelslade Staffs 112 D4
Hazelton Glos 64 B1
Hazelton Walls Fife 220 B3
Hazelwood Derbys 114 A1
Hazlemere Bucks 66 D3
Hazlerigg T & W 179 B4
Hazlewood N Yorks 147 B4
Hazon Northumb 189 C4
Heacham Norf 118 B3
Head of Muir Falk 207 B6
Headbourne Worthy Hants 32 B3
Headbrook Hereford 77 B7
Headcorn Kent 37 B6
Headingley W Yorks 148 D1
Headington Oxon 65 C6
Headlam Durham 167 D4
Headless Cross Worcs 80 A3
Headley Hants 46 C3
Headley Hants 33 B7
Headley Sur 35 A5
Headon Notts 132 B2
Heads S Lnrk 194 B2
Heads Nook Cumb 176 D2
Heage Derbys 130 D3
Healaugh N Yorks 148 C3
Healaugh N Yorks 156 B4
Heald Green Gtr Man 128 A3
Heale Devon 26 A1
Heale Som 29 A6
Healey Gtr Man 138 B1
Healey Northumb 178 D2
Healey N Yorks 157 C5
Healing NE Lincs 143 B4
Heamoor Corn 2 B2
Heanish Argyll 222 C3
Heanor Derbys 114 A2
Heanton Punchardon Devon 25 B6
Heapham Lincs 132 A3
Heart of the National Forest Leics 113 D7
Hearthstane Borders 195 D6
Heasley Mill Devon 26 B2
Heast Highld 247 C5
Heath Cardiff 41 D6
Heath Derbys 131 C4
Heath and Reach Beds 67 A4
Heath End Hants 46 C3
Heath End Sur 34 B1
Heath End Warks 81 A5
Heath Hayes Staffs 112 D4
Heath Hill Shrops 111 D6
Heath House Som 28 A4
Heath Town W Mid 96 B2
Heathcote Derbys 129 C6
Heather Leics 114 D1
Heatherfield Highld 259 D4
Heathfield Devon 12 D3
Heathfield E Sus 36 D3
Heathfield Som 27 C6
Heathhall Dumfries 174 A2
Heathrow Airport London 48 B3
Heathstock Devon 14 A2
Heathton Shrops 95 B6
Heatley Warr 128 A2
Heaton Lancs 144 A4
Heaton Staffs 129 C4
Heaton T & W 179 C4
Heaton W Yorks 147 D5
Heaton Moor Gtr Man 138 D1
Heaverham Kent 36 A3
Heaviley Gtr Man 129 A4
Heavitree Devon 13 B4
Hebburn T & W 179 C5
Hebden N Yorks 147 A4
Hebden Bridge W Yorks 138 A2
Hebron Anglesey 123 B4
Hebron Carms 73 D4
Hebron Northumb 178 A3
Heck Dumfries 184 D3
Heckfield Hants 47 C5
Heckfield Green Suff 104 D2

Heckfordbridge Essex 70 A3
Heckington Lincs 116 A4
Heckmondwike W Yorks 139 A5
Heddington Wilts 44 C3
Heddle Orkney 282 F4
Heddon-on-the-Wall Northumb 178 C3
Hedenham Norf 104 B4
Hedge End Hants 32 D3
Hedgerley Bucks 48 A2
Hedging Som 28 C3
Hedley on the Hill Northumb 178 D2
Hednesford Staffs 112 D3
Hedon E Yorks 142 A3
Hedsor Bucks 48 A2
Hedworth T & W 179 C5
Heeley City Farm, Sheffield S Yorks 130 A3
Hegdon Hill Hereford 78 B3
Heggerscales Cumb 165 D6
Heglibister Shetland 285 H5
Heighington Darl 167 C5
Heighington Lincs 133 C5
Heights of Brae Highld 263 D7
Heights of Kinlochewe Highld 262 D2
Heilam Highld 277 B5
Heiton Borders 197 C6
Hele Devon 25 A6
Hele Devon 13 A4
Helensburgh Argyll 215 D5
Helford Corn 3 C5
Helford Passage Corn 3 C5
Helhoughton Norf 119 C5
Helions Bumpstead Essex 86 C2
Hellaby S Yorks 140 D3
Helland Corn 10 D1
Hellesdon Norf 120 D4
Hellidon Northants 82 B2
Hellifield N Yorks 146 B2
Hellingly E Sus 22 A3
Hellington Norf 104 A4
Hellister Shetland 285 J5
Helm Northumb 189 D4
Helmdon Northants 82 C2
Helmingham Suff 88 B2
Helmington Row Durham 167 B4
Helmsdale Highld 274 C4
Helmshore Lancs 137 A6
Helmsley N Yorks 159 C5
Helperby N Yorks 148 A3
Helperthorpe N Yorks 160 D3
Helpringham Lincs 116 A4
Helpston P'boro 100 A3
Helsby Ches 127 B4
Helsey Lincs 135 B5
Helston Corn 3 C4
Helstone Corn 10 C1
Helton Cumb 164 C3
Helwith Bridge N Yorks 146 A2
Hemblington Norf 121 D5
Hemel Hempstead Herts 67 C5
Hemingbrough N Yorks 149 D5
Hemingby Lincs 134 B2
Hemingford Abbots Cambs 101 D4
Hemingford Grey Cambs 101 D4
Hemingstone Suff 88 B2
Hemington Leics 114 C2
Hemington Northants 100 C2
Hemington Som 43 D6
Hemley Suff 88 C3
Hemlington M'bro 168 D3
Hemp Green Suff 89 A4
Hempholme E Yorks 150 B3
Hempnall Norf 104 B3
Hempnall Green Norf 104 B3
Hempriggs House Highld 281 D5
Hempstead Essex 86 D2
Hempstead Medway 51 C4
Hempstead Norf 120 B3
Hempstead Norf 121 C6
Hempsted Glos 63 B4
Hempton Norf 119 C6
Hempton Oxon 82 D1
Hemsby Norf 121 D6
Hemswell Lincs 142 D1
Hemswell Cliff Lincs 133 A4
Hemsworth W Yorks 140 B2
Hemyock Devon 27 D6
Hen-feddau fawr Pembs 73 C5
Henbury Bristol 43 B4
Henbury Ches 128 B3

Hendon London 49 A5
Hendon T & W 179 D6
Hendre Flint 126 C1
Hendre-ddu Conwy 124 C3
Hendreforgan Rhondda 41 C4
Hendy Carms 57 B5
Heneglwys Anglesey 123 C4
Henfield W Sus 21 A5
Henford Devon 11 B4
Henghurst Kent 38 B1
Hengoed Caerph 41 B6
Hengoed Powys 77 B6
Hengoed Shrops 110 B1
Hengrave Suff 87 A4
Henham Essex 69 A5
Heniarth Powys 93 A5
Henlade Som 28 C2
Henley Shrops 94 D3
Henley Som 28 B4
Henley Suff 88 B2
Henley W Sus 34 D1
Henley-in-Arden Warks 81 A4
Henley-on-Thames Oxon 47 A5
Henley's Down E Sus 23 A5
Henllan Ceredig 73 B6
Henllan Denb 125 C5
Henllan Amgoed Carms 73 D4
Henllys Torf 61 D4
Henlow Beds 84 D3
Hennock Devon 12 C3
Henny Street Essex 87 D4
Henryd Conwy 124 B2
Henry's Moat Pembs 55 B6
Hensall N Yorks 140 A3
Henshaw Northumb 177 C5
Hensingham Cumb 162 C2
Henstead Suff 105 C5
Henstridge Som 30 D1
Henstridge Ash Som 29 C7
Henstridge Marsh Som 30 C1
Henton Oxon 66 C2
Henton Som 29 A4
Henwood Corn 10 D3
Heogan Shetland 285 J6
Heol-las Swansea 40 B1
Heol Senni Powys 59 C6
Heol-y-Cyw Bridgend 40 C4
Hepburn Northumb 188 A3
Hepple Northumb 188 C2
Hepscott Northumb 179 A4
Heptonstall W Yorks 138 A2
Hepworth Suff 103 D5
Hepworth W Yorks 139 C4
Herbrandston Pembs 55 D4
Hereford Hereford 78 C3
Hereford Cathedral
  Hereford 78 D3
Hereford Racecourse
  Hereford 78 C3
Heriot Borders 196 A2
Heritage Motor Centre,
  Gaydon Warks 81 B6
Hermiston Edin 209 C4
Hermitage Borders 186 D4
Hermitage Dorset 15 A6
Hermitage W Berks 46 B3
Hermitage W Sus 19 A6
Hermon Anglesey 122 D3
Hermon Carms 73 C6
Hermon Carms 58 C3
Hermon Pembs 73 C5
Herne Kent 52 C3
Herne Bay Kent 52 C3
Herner Devon 25 C6
Hernhill Kent 52 C2
Herodsfoot Corn 5 A7
Herongate Essex 69 D6
Heronsford S Ayrs 180 C3
Herriard Hants 33 A5
Herringfleet Suff 105 B5
Herringswell Suff 102 D3
Hersden Kent 53 C4
Hersham Corn 10 A3
Hersham Sur 48 C4
Herstmonceux E Sus 22 A4
Herston Orkney 283 H5
Hertford Herts 68 B3
Hertford Heath Herts 68 B3
Hertingfordbury Herts 68 B3
Hesket Newmarket Cumb 163 A6
Hesketh Bank Lancs 136 A3
Hesketh Lane Lancs 145 C6
Heskin Green Lancs 136 B4
Hesleden Durham 168 B2

Hesleyside Northumb 177 A6
Heslington York 149 B5
Hessay York 148 B4
Hessenford Corn 6 B2
Hessett Suff 87 A5
Hessle E Yorks 142 A2
Hest Bank Lancs 145 A4
Heston London 48 B4
Hestwall Orkney 282 F3
Heswall Mersey 126 A2
Hethe Oxon 65 A6
Hethersett Norf 104 A2
Hethersgill Cumb 176 C2
Hethpool Northumb 188 A1
Hett Durham 167 B5
Hetton N Yorks 146 B3
Hetton-le-Hole T & W 167 A6
Hetton Steads Northumb 198 C4
Heugh Northumb 178 B2
Heugh-head Aberds 243 A6
Heveningham Suff 104 D4
Hever Kent 36 B2
Hever Castle and
  Gardens Kent 36 B2
Heversham Cumb 154 C3
Hevingham Norf 120 C3
Hewas Water Corn 5 C4
Hewelsfield Glos 62 C1
Hewish N Som 42 C3
Hewish Som 14 A4
Heworth York 149 B5
Hexham Northumb 178 C1
Hexham Abbey Northumb 178 C1
Hexham Racecourse
  Northumb 177 C7
Hextable Kent 50 B2
Hexton Herts 84 D3
Hexworthy Devon 12 D1
Hey Lancs 146 C2
Heybridge Essex 69 D6
Heybridge Essex 70 C2
Heybridge Basin Essex 70 C2
Heybrook Bay Devon 7 C4
Heydon Cambs 85 C6
Heydon Norf 120 C3
Heydour Lincs 116 B3
Heylipol Argyll 222 C2
Heylor Shetland 284 E4
Heysham Lancs 144 A4
Heyshott W Sus 20 A1
Heyside Gtr Man 138 C2
Heytesbury Wilts 30 A3
Heythrop Oxon 64 A4
Heywood Gtr Man 138 B1
Heywood Wilts 44 D2
Hibaldstow N Lincs 142 C1
Hickleton S Yorks 140 C2
Hickling Norf 121 C6
Hickling Notts 115 C4
Hickling Green Norf 121 C6
Hickling Heath Norf 121 C6
Hickstead W Sus 35 D5
Hidcote Boyce Glos 81 C4
Hidcote Manor Garden,
  Moreton-in-Marsh Glos 81 C4
High Ackworth W Yorks 140 B2
High Angerton Northumb 178 A2
High Bankhill Cumb 164 A3
High Barnes T & W 179 D5
High Beach Essex 68 D4
High Bentham N Yorks 145 A6
High Bickington Devon 25 C7
High Birkwith N Yorks 155 D6
High Blantyre S Lnrk 194 A1
High Bonnybridge Falk 207 C6
High Bradfield S Yorks 139 D5
High Bray Devon 26 B1
High Brooms Kent 36 B3
High Bullen Devon 25 C6
High Buston Northumb 189 C5
High Callerton Northumb 178 B3
High Catton E Yorks 149 B6
High Cogges Oxon 65 C4
High Coniscliffe Darl 167 D5
High Cross Hants 33 C6
High Cross Herts 68 B3
High Easter Essex 69 B6
High Eggborough N Yorks 140 A3
High Ellington N Yorks 157 C5
High Ercall Telford 111 D4
High Etherley Durham 167 C4
High Garrett Essex 70 A1
High Grange Durham 167 B4
High Green Norf 104 A2
High Green S Yorks 139 D6
High Green Worcs 80 C1
High Halden Kent 37 C6

High Halstow Medway 51 B4
High Ham Som 28 B4
High Harrington Cumb 162 B3
High Hatton Shrops 111 C5
High Hawsker N Yorks 160 A3
High Hesket Cumb 164 A2
High Hesleden Durham 168 B2
High Hoyland S Yorks 139 B5
High Hunsley E Yorks 150 D2
High Hurstwood E Sus 36 D2
High Hutton N Yorks 149 A6
High Ireby Cumb 163 A5
High Kelling Norf 120 A3
High Kilburn N Yorks 158 D4
High Lands Durham 166 C4
High Lane Gtr Man 129 A4
High Lane Hereford 79 A4
High Laver Essex 69 C5
High Legh Ches 128 A2
High Leven Stockton 168 D2
High Littleton Bath 43 D5
High Lorton Cumb 163 B4
High Marishes N Yorks 159 D7
High Marnham Notts 132 B3
High Melton S Yorks 140 C3
High Mickley Northumb 178 C2
High Mindork Dumfries 171 B5
High Moorland Visitor
  Centre, Princetown
  Devon 11 D6
High Newton Cumb 154 C3
High Newton-by-the-Sea
  Northumb 189 A5
High Nibthwaite Cumb 154 C1
High Offley Staffs 112 C1
High Ongar Essex 69 C5
High Onn Staffs 112 D2
High Roding Essex 69 B6
High Row Cumb 163 A6
High Salvington W Sus 21 B4
High Sellafield Cumb 162 D3
High Shaw N Yorks 156 B2
High Spen T & W 178 D3
High Stoop Durham 166 A4
High Street Corn 5 B4
High Street Kent 37 C5
High Street Suff 89 B5
High Street Suff 105 D5
High Street Suff 87 C4
High Street Green Suff 87 B6
High Throston Hrtlpl 168 B2
High Toynton Lincs 134 C2
High Trewhitt Northumb 188 C3
High Valleyfield Fife 208 B3
High Westwood Durham 178 D3
High Wray Cumb 154 B2
High Wych Herts 69 B4
High Wycombe Bucks 66 D3
Higham Derbys 130 D3
Higham Kent 51 B4
Higham Lancs 146 D2
Higham Suff 87 D6
Higham Suff 86 A3
Higham Dykes Northumb 178 B3
Higham Ferrers Northants 83 A6
Higham Gobion Beds 84 D3
Higham on the Hill Leics 97 B6
Higham Wood Kent 36 B3
Highampton Devon 11 A5
Highbridge Hrtlpl 239 D5
Highbridge Som 28 A3
Highbrook W Sus 35 C6
Highburton W Yorks 139 B4
Highbury Som 29 A6
Highclere Hants 46 C2
Highcliffe Dorset 17 B6
Higher Ansty Dorset 16 A1
Higher Ashton Devon 12 C3
Higher Ballam Lancs 144 D3
Higher Bartle Lancs 145 D5
Higher Boscaswell Corn 2 B1
Higher Burwardsley Ches 127 D5
Higher Clovelly Devon 24 C4
Higher End Gtr Man 136 C4
Higher Kinnerton Flint 126 C3
Higher Penwortham
  Lancs 136 A4
Higher Town Scilly 2 E4
Higher Walreddon Devon 11 D5
Higher Walton Lancs 137 A4
Higher Walton Warr 127 A5
Higher Wheelton Lancs 137 A5
Higher Whitley Ches 127 A6
Higher Wincham Ches 128 B1
Higher Wych Ches 110 A3
Highfield E Yorks 149 D6
Highfield Gtr Man 137 C6

Highfield N Ayrs 204 C3
Highfield Oxon 65 A6
Highfield S Yorks 130 A3
Highfield T & W 178 D3
Highfields Cambs 85 B5
Highfields Northumb 198 A3
Highgate London 49 A5
Highland Folk Museum,
  Aultlairie Highld 241 C5
Highland Folk Museum,
  Kingussie Highld 241 B5
Highlane Ches 128 C3
Highlane Derbys 131 A4
Highlaws Cumb 174 D4
Highleadon Glos 62 A3
Highleigh W Sus 20 C1
Highley Shrops 95 C5
Highmoor Cross Oxon 47 A5
Highmoor Hill Mon 42 A3
Highnam Glos 62 B3
Highnam Green Glos 62 A3
Highsted Kent 51 C6
Highstreet Green Essex 86 D3
Hightae Dumfries 174 A3
Hightown Ches 128 C3
Hightown Mers 136 C2
Hightown Green Suff 87 B5
Highway Wilts 44 B4
Highweek Devon 12 D3
Highworth Thamesdown 64 D3
Hilborough Norf 103 A4
Hilcote Derbys 131 D4
Hilcott Wilts 45 D5
Hilden Park Kent 36 B3
Hildenborough Kent 36 B3
Hildersham Cambs 86 C1
Hilderstone Staffs 112 B3
Hilderthorpe E Yorks 151 A4
Hilfield Dorset 15 A6
Hilgay Norf 102 B2
Hill Pembs 55 D7
Hill S Glos 62 D2
Hill W Mid 96 B4
Hill Brow W Sus 33 C6
Hill Dale Lancs 136 B3
Hill Dyke Lincs 117 A6
Hill End Durham 166 B3
Hill End Fife 208 A3
Hill End N Yorks 147 B4
Hill Head Hants 18 A4
Hill Head Northumb 178 C1
Hill Mountain Pembs 55 D5
Hill of Beath Fife 209 A4
Hill of Fearn Highld 265 C4
Hill of Mountblairy
  Aberds 268 D1
Hill Ridware Staffs 113 D4
Hill Top Hants 18 A3
Hill Top N Yorks 166 C2
Hill Top W Mid 96 B2
Hill Top W Yorks 139 B6
Hill Top, Sawrey Cumb 154 B2
Hill View Dorset 16 B3
Hillam N Yorks 140 A3
Hillbeck Cumb 165 D5
Hillborough Kent 53 C4
Hillbrae Aberds 256 D2
Hillbrae Aberds 255 B7
Hillbutts Dorset 16 A3
Hillclifflane Derbys 113 A6
Hillcommon Som 27 C6
Hillend Fife 208 B4
Hillerton Devon 12 B2
Hillesden Bucks 66 A1
Hillesley Glos 43 A6
Hillfarance Som 27 C6
Hillhead Aberds 255 C6
Hillhead Devon 8 B3
Hillhead S Ayrs 182 A2
Hillhead of Auchentumb
  Aberds 269 D4
Hillhead of Cocklaw
  Aberds 257 B5
Hillhouse Borders 197 A4
Hilliclachy Highld 280 B3
Hillier Gardens and
  Arboretum Hants 32 C2
Hillingdon London 48 A3
Hillington Glasgow 205 B5
Hillington Norf 119 C4
Hillmorton Warks 98 D2
Hillockhead Aberds 244 A1
Hillockhead Aberds 243 B6
Hillside Aberds 245 C6
Hillside Angus 233 B5
Hillside Orkney 283 H5

Hillside Shetland 285 G6
Hillswick Shetland 284 F4
Hillway I o W 19 C5
Hillwell Shetland 285 M5
Hilmarton Wilts 44 B4
Hilperton Wilts 44 D2
Hilsea Ptsmth 19 A5
Hilston E Yorks 151 D5
Hilton Aberds 257 C4
Hilton Cambs 85 A4
Hilton Cumb 165 C5
Hilton Derbys 113 B6
Hilton Dorset 16 A1
Hilton Durham 167 C4
Hilton Highld 264 B3
Hilton Shrops 95 B5
Hilton Stockton 168 D3
Hilton of Cadboll Highld 265 C4
Himbleton Worcs 80 B5
Himley Staffs 96 B6
Hincaster Cumb 154 C4
Hinckley Leics 98 B1
Hinderclay Suff 103 D6
Hinderton Ches 126 B3
Hinderwell N Yorks 169 D5
Hindford Shrops 110 B2
Hindhead Sur 34 C6
Hindley Gtr Man 137 C5
Hindley Green Gtr Man 137 C5
Hindlip Worcs 80 B1
Hindolveston Norf 120 C2
Hindon Wilts 30 B3
Hindringham Norf 120 B1
Hingham Norf 103 A6
Hinstock Shrops 111 C5
Hintlesham Suff 88 C1
Hinton Hants 17 B6
Hinton Hereford 78 D1
Hinton Northants 82 B2
Hinton Shrops 94 A2
Hinton S Glos 43 B6
Hinton Ampner Hants 33 C4
Hinton Blewett Bath 43 D4
Hinton Charterhouse Bath 43 D6
Hinton-in-the-Hedges
  Northants 82 D2
Hinton Martell Dorset 17 A4
Hinton on the Green
  Worcs 80 C3
Hinton Parva Thamesdown 45 A6
Hinton St George Som 28 D4
Hinton St Mary Dorset 30 D1
Hinton Waldrist Oxon 65 D4
Hints Shrops 95 D5
Hints Staffs 97 A4
Hinwick Beds 83 A6
Hinxhill Kent 38 A2
Hinxton Cambs 85 C6
Hinxworth Herts 84 D4
Hipperholme W Yorks 139 A4
Hipswell N Yorks 157 B5
Hirael Gwyn 123 C5
Hiraeth Carms 73 D4
Hirn Aberds 245 B5
Hirnant Powys 109 C5
Hirst N Lnrk 207 D6
Hirst Northumb 179 A4
Hirst Courtney N Yorks 140 A4
Hirwaen Denb 125 C5
Hirwaun Rhondda 59 E6
Hiscott Devon 25 C6
Histon Cambs 85 A6
Hitcham Suff 87 B5
Hitchin Herts 68 A1
Hither Green London 49 B6
Hittisleigh Devon 12 B1
Hive E Yorks 149 D7
Hixon Staffs 112 C4
HMS Victory Ptsmth 19 A5
HMY Britannia Edin 209 C5
Hoaden Kent 53 D4
Hoaldalbert Mon 61 A5
Hoar Cross Staffs 113 C5
Hoarwithy Hereford 62 A1
Hoath Kent 53 C4
Hobarris Shrops 93 D7
Hobbister Orkney 283 G4
Hobkirk Borders 187 B4
Hobson Durham 178 D3
Hoby Leics 115 D4
Hockering Norf 120 D2
Hockerton Notts 132 D2
Hockley Essex 70 D2
Hockley Heath W Mid 97 D4
Hockliffe Beds 67 A4
Hockwold cum Wilton
  Norf 102 C3

Hockworthy Devon 27 D5
Hoddesdon Herts 68 C3
Hoddlesden Blkburn 137 A6
Hoddom Mains Dumfries 175 A4
Hoddomcross Dumfries 175 A4
Hodgeston Pembs 55 E6
Hodley Powys 93 B5
Hodnet Shrops 111 C5
Hodthorpe Derbys 131 B5
Hoe Hants 33 D4
Hoe Norf 120 D1
Hoe Gate Hants 33 D5
Hoff Cumb 165 D4
Hog Patch Sur 34 B1
Hoggard's Green Suff 87 B4
Hoggeston Bucks 66 A3
Hogha Gearraidh W Isles 287 G2
oghton Lancs 137 A5
ognaston Derbys 130 D2
ogsthorpe Lincs 135 B5
olbeach Lincs 117 C6
olbeach Bank Lincs 117 C6
olbeach Clough Lincs 117 C6
olbeach Drove Lincs 117 D6
olbeach Hurn Lincs 117 C6
olbeach St Johns Lincs 117 D6
olbeach St Marks Lincs 117 B6
olbeach St Matthew Lincs 117 B7
olbeck Notts 131 B5
olbeck W Yorks 148 D1
olbeck Woodhouse Notts 131 B5
olberrow Green Worcs 80 B3
olbeton Devon 7 B5
olborn London 49 A6
olbrook Derbys 114 A1
olbrook Suff 88 D2
olbrook S Yorks 131 A4
olburn Northumb 198 C4
olbury Hants 18 A3
olcombe Devon 13 D4
olcombe Som 29 A6
olcombe Rogus Devon 27 D5
olcot Northants 83 A4
olden Lancs 146 C1
oldenby Northants 82 A3
oldenhurst Bmouth 17 B5
oldgate Shrops 94 C3
oldingham Lincs 116 A3
olditch Dorset 14 A3
ole-in-the-Wall Hereford 62 A2
olefield Borders 198 C2
olehouses Ches 128 B2
lemoor Devon 11 A5
lestane Dumfries 183 C6
lford Som 27 A6
lgate York 149 B4
lker Cumb 154 D2
lkham Norf 119 A5
llacombe Devon 11 A4
lland Orkney 282 B5
lland Orkney 282 E7
lland Fen Lincs 117 A5
land-on-Sea Essex 71 B6
landstoun Orkney 282 B8
lee Dumfries 175 B5
lesley Suff 89 C4
licombe Torbay 8 A2
lingbourne Kent 37 A6
lington Derbys 113 B6
lington E Sus 23 A5
lington Staffs 113 B4
lington Grove Derbys 113 B6
lingworth Gtr Man 138 D3
lins Gtr Man 137 C7
lins Green Warr 137 D5
lins Lane Lancs 145 B4
linsclough Staffs 129 C5
inwood Gtr Man 138 C2
inwood Shrops 111 B4
ocombe Devon 26 D1
ow Meadows S Yorks 130 A2
oway Derbys 130 D3
owell Northants 98 D3
y End Norf 101 A6
y Green Worcs 79 C6
ybush Caerph 41 A6
ybush E Ayrs 182 A1
ybush Worcs 79 D5
ym E Yorks 143 A5
ywood Worcs 96 D3
nbridge W Yorks 139 C4
nbury St Mary Sur 35 B4
nbush Corn 5 B5
ncroft Staffs 112 C3
ne Cambs 100 C3
Holme Cumb 154 D4
Holme Notts 132 D3
Holme N Yorks 158 C2
Holme W Yorks 139 C4
Holme Chapel Lancs 138 A1
Holme Green N Yorks 149 C4
Holme Hale Norf 103 A4
Holme Lacy Hereford 78 D3
Holme Marsh Hereford 78 B1
Holme next the Sea Norf 119 A4
Holme-on-Spalding-Moor E Yorks 149 D7
Holme on the Wolds E Yorks 150 C2
Holme Pierrepont Notts 115 B4
Holme St Cuthbert Cumb 174 D4
Holme Wood W Yorks 147 D5
Holmer Hereford 78 C3
Holmer Green Bucks 67 D4
Holmes Chapel Ches 128 C2
Holmesfield Derbys 130 B3
Holmeswood Lancs 136 B3
Holmewood Derbys 131 C4
Holmfirth W Yorks 139 C4
Holmhead Dumfries 183 D5
Holmhead E Ayrs 193 C5
Holmisdale Highld 258 D1
Holmpton E Yorks 143 A5
Holmrook Cumb 153 A1
Holmsgarth Shetland 285 J6
Holmwrangle Cumb 164 A3
Holne Devon 7 A6
Holnest Dorset 15 A6
Holsworthy Devon 10 A4
Holsworthy Beacon Devon 11 A4
Holt Dorset 17 A4
Holt Norf 120 B2
Holt Wilts 44 C2
Holt Worcs 79 A6
Holt Wrex 127 D4
Holt End Hants 33 B5
Holt End Worcs 80 A3
Holt Fleet Worcs 79 A6
Holt Heath Worcs 79 A6
Holt Park W Yorks 147 C6
Holtby York 149 B5
Holton Oxon 65 C7
Holton Som 29 C6
Holton Suff 105 D4
Holton cum Beckering Lincs 133 A6
Holton Heath Dorset 16 B3
Holton le Clay Lincs 143 C4
Holton le Moor Lincs 142 D2
Holton St Mary Suff 87 D6
Holwell Dorset 29 D7
Holwell Herts 84 D3
Holwell Leics 115 C5
Holwell Oxon 64 C3
Holwick Durham 166 C2
Holworth Dorset 16 C1
Holy Cross Worcs 96 D2
Holy Island Northumb 199 B5
Holybourne Hants 33 A6
Holyhead = Caergybi Anglesey 122 B2
Holymoorside Derbys 130 C3
Holyport Windsor 48 B1
Holystone Northumb 188 C2
Holytown N Lnrk 207 D5
Holywell Cambs 101 D5
Holywell Corn 4 B2
Holywell Dorset 15 A5
Holywell E Sus 22 C3
Holywell Northumb 179 B5
Holywell = Treffynnon Flint 126 B1
Holywell Bay Fun Park, Newquay Corn 4 B2
Holywell Green W Yorks 138 B3
Holywell Lake Som 27 C6
Holywell Row Suff 102 D3
Holywood Dumfries 184 D2
Hom Green Hereford 62 A1
Homer Shrops 95 A4
Homersfield Suff 104 C3
Homington Wilts 31 C5
Honey Hill Kent 52 C3
Honey Street Wilts 45 C5
Honey Tye Suff 87 D5
Honeyborough Pembs 55 D5
Honeybourne Worcs 80 C4
Honeychurch Devon 12 A1
Honiley Warks 97 D5
Honing Norf 121 C5
Honingham Norf 120 D3
Honington Lincs 116 A2
Honington Suff 103 D5
Honington Warks 81 C5
Honiton Devon 13 A6
Honley W Yorks 139 B4
Hoo Green Ches 128 A2
Hoo St Werburgh Medway 51 B4
Hood Green S Yorks 139 C6
Hooe E Sus 23 B4
Hooe Plym 7 B4
Hooe Common E Sus 23 A4
Hook E Yorks 141 A5
Hook London 49 C4
Hook Hants 47 D5
Hook Pembs 55 C5
Hook Wilts 45 A4
Hook Green Kent 37 C4
Hook Green Kent 50 C3
Hook Norton Oxon 81 D6
Hooke Dorset 15 B5
Hookgate Staffs 111 B6
Hookway Devon 12 B3
Hookwood Sur 35 B5
Hoole Ches 127 C4
Hooley Sur 35 A5
Hooton Ches 126 B3
Hooton Levitt S Yorks 140 D3
Hooton Pagnell S Yorks 140 C2
Hooton Roberts S Yorks 140 D2
Hop Pole Lincs 117 D4
Hope Derbys 129 A6
Hope Devon 7 D5
Hope Highld 277 C5
Hope Powys 93 A6
Hope Shrops 94 A1
Hope Staffs 129 D6
Hope = Yr Hôb Flint 126 D3
Hope Bagot Shrops 94 D3
Hope Bowdler Shrops 94 B2
Hope End Green Essex 69 A5
Hope Green Ches 129 A4
Hope Mansell Hereford 62 B2
Hope under Dinmore Hereford 78 B3
Hopeman Moray 266 C2
Hope's Green Essex 51 A4
Hopesay Shrops 94 C1
Hopley's Green Hereford 78 B1
Hopperton N Yorks 148 B3
Hopstone Shrops 95 B5
Hopton Shrops 110 C2
Hopton Shrops 111 C4
Hopton Staffs 112 C3
Hopton Suff 103 D5
Hopton Cangeford Shrops 94 C3
Hopton Castle Shrops 94 D1
Hopton on Sea Norf 105 A6
Hopton Wafers Shrops 95 D4
Hoptonheath Shrops 94 D1
Hopwas Staffs 97 A4
Hopwood Gtr Man 138 C1
Hopwood Worcs 96 D3
Horam E Sus 22 A3
Horbling Lincs 116 B4
Horbury W Yorks 139 B5
Horcott Glos 64 C2
Horden Durham 168 A2
Horderley Shrops 94 C2
Hordle Hants 17 B6
Hordley Shrops 110 B2
Horeb Ceredig 73 B6
Horeb Carms 57 B4
Horeb Carms 58 C2
Horfield Bristol 43 B5
Horham Suff 104 D3
Horkesley Heath Essex 70 A3
Horkstow N Lincs 142 B1
Horley Oxon 81 C7
Horley Sur 35 B5
Hornblotton Green Som 29 B5
Hornby Lancs 145 A5
Hornby N Yorks 157 B6
Hornby N Yorks 158 A2
Horncastle Lincs 134 C2
Hornchurch London 50 A2
Horncliffe Northumb 198 B3
Horndean Borders 198 B2
Horndean Hants 33 D6
Horndon Devon 11 D6
Horndon on the Hill Thurrock 50 A3
Horne Sur 35 B6
Horniehaugh Angus 232 B2
Horning Norf 121 D5
Horninghold Leics 99 B5
Horninglow Staffs 113 C6
Horningsea Cambs 85 A6
Horningsham Wilts 30 A2
Horningtoft Norf 119 C6
Horns Corner Kent 37 D5
Horns Cross Devon 25 C4
Horns Cross E Sus 37 D6
Hornsby Cumb 176 D3
Hornsea E Yorks 151 C5
Hornsea Bridge E Yorks 151 C5
Hornsey London 49 A6
Hornton Oxon 81 C6
Horrabridge Devon 7 A4
Horringer Suff 87 A4
Horringford I o W 18 C4
Horse Bridge Staffs 129 D4
Horsebridge Devon 11 D5
Horsebridge Hants 32 B2
Horsebrook Staffs 112 D2
Horsehay Telford 95 A4
Horseheath Cambs 86 C2
Horsehouse N Yorks 156 C4
Horsell Sur 34 A2
Horseman's Green Wrex 110 A3
Horseway Cambs 101 C6
Horsey Norf 121 C6
Horsford Norf 120 D3
Horsforth W Yorks 147 D6
Horsham Worcs 79 B5
Horsham W Sus 35 C4
Horsham St Faith Norf 120 D4
Horsington Lincs 134 C1
Horsington Som 29 C7
Horsley Derbys 114 A1
Horsley Glos 63 D4
Horsley Northumb 178 C2
Horsley Northumb 188 D1
Horsley Cross Essex 71 A5
Horsley Woodhouse Derbys 114 A1
Horsleycross Street Essex 71 A5
Horsleyhill Borders 186 B4
Horsleyhope Durham 166 A3
Horsmonden Kent 37 B4
Horspath Oxon 65 C6
Horstead Norf 121 D4
Horsted Keynes W Sus 36 D1
Horton Bucks 67 B4
Horton Dorset 17 A4
Horton Lancs 146 B2
Horton Northants 83 B5
Horton Shrops 110 C3
Horton S Glos 43 A6
Horton Som 28 D3
Horton Staffs 129 D4
Horton Swansea 57 D4
Horton Wilts 45 C4
Horton Windsor 48 B3
Horton-cum-Studley Oxon 65 B6
Horton Green Ches 110 A3
Horton Heath Hants 32 D3
Horton in Ribblesdale N Yorks 155 D7
Horton Kirby Kent 50 C2
Hortonlane Shrops 110 D3
Horwich Gtr Man 137 B5
Horwich End Derbys 129 A5
Horwood Devon 25 C6
Hose Leics 115 C5
Hoselaw Borders 198 C2
Hoses Cumb 153 A3
Hosh Perth 218 B3
Hosta W Isles 287 G2
Hoswick Shetland 285 L6
Hotham E Yorks 150 D1
Hothfield Kent 38 A1
Hoton Leics 114 C3
Houbie Shetland 284 D8
Houdston S Ayrs 181 B3
Hough Ches 128 D2
Hough Ches 128 B3
Hough Green Halton 127 A4
Hough-on-the-Hill Lincs 116 A2
Hougham Lincs 116 A1
Houghton Cambs 101 D4
Houghton Cumb 175 C7
Houghton Hants 32 B2
Houghton Pembs 55 D5
Houghton W Sus 20 A3
Houghton Conquest Beds 84 C2
Houghton Green E Sus 37 D7
Houghton Green Warr 137 D5
Houghton-le-Side Darl 167 C5
Houghton-Le-Spring T & W 167 A6
Houghton on the Hill Leics 98 A3
Houghton Regis Beds 67 A5
Houghton St Giles Norf 119 B6
Houlland Shetland 285 H5
Houlland Shetland 284 F7
Houlsyke N Yorks 159 A6
Hound Hants 18 A3
Hound Green Hants 47 D5
Houndslow Borders 197 B5
Houndwood Borders 211 D5
Hounslow London 48 B4
Hounslow Green Essex 69 B6
Housay Shetland 284 F8
House of Daviot Highld 252 B3
House of Glenmuick Aberds 243 C6
Housesteads Roman Fort Northumb 177 C5
Housetter Shetland 284 E5
Houss Shetland 285 K5
Houston Renfs 205 B4
Houstry Highld 275 A5
Houton Orkney 283 G4
Hove Brighton 21 B5
Hoveringham Notts 115 A4
Hoveton Norf 121 D5
Hovingham N Yorks 159 D5
How Cumb 176 D3
How Caple Hereford 79 D4
How End Beds 84 C2
How Green Kent 36 B2
Howbrook S Yorks 139 D6
Howden Borders 187 A5
Howden E Yorks 141 A5
Howden-le-Wear Durham 167 B4
Howe Highld 281 B5
Howe Norf 104 A3
Howe N Yorks 158 C2
Howe Bridge Gtr Man 137 C5
Howe Green Essex 70 C1
Howe of Teuchar Aberds 256 B2
Howe Street Essex 69 B6
Howe Street Essex 86 D2
Howell Lincs 116 A4
Howey Powys 77 B4
Howgate Midloth 196 A1
Howick Northumb 189 B5
Howle Durham 166 C3
Howle Telford 111 C5
Howlett End Essex 86 D1
Howley Som 14 A2
Hownam Borders 187 B6
Hownam Mains Borders 187 A6
Howpasley Borders 185 B6
Howsham N Lincs 142 C2
Howsham N Yorks 149 A6
Howslack Dumfries 184 B3
Howtel Northumb 198 C2
Howton Hereford 61 A6
Howtown Cumb 164 D2
Howwood Renfs 204 B3
Hoxne Suff 104 D2
Hoy Orkney 283 G3
Hoylake Mers 126 A2
Hoyland S Yorks 139 C6
Hoylandswaine S Yorks 139 C5
Hubberholme N Yorks 156 D3
Hubbert's Bridge Lincs 117 A5
Huby N Yorks 147 C6
Huby N Yorks 149 A4
Hucclecote Glos 63 B4
Hucking Kent 37 A6
Hucknall Notts 114 A3
Huddersfield W Yorks 139 B4
Huddington Worcs 80 B2
Hudswell N Yorks 157 A5
Huggate E Yorks 150 B1
Hugglescote Leics 114 D2
Hugh Town Scilly 2 E4
Hughenden Valley Bucks 66 D3
Hughley Shrops 94 B3
Huish Devon 25 D6
Huish Wilts 45 C5
Huish Champflower Som 27 C5
Huish Episcopi Som 28 C4
Huisinis W Isles 287 C4
Hulcott Bucks 66 B3
Hulland Derbys 113 A6
Hulland Ward Derbys 113 A6
Hullavington Wilts 44 A2
Hullbridge Essex 70 D2
Hulme Gtr Man 138 D1
Hulme End Staffs 129 D6
Hulme Walfield Ches 128 C3
Hulver Street Suff 105 C5
Hulverstone I o W 18 C2
Humber Hereford 78 B3
Humber Bridge E Yorks 142 A2
Humberside International Airport N Lincs 142 B2

Humberston NE Lincs 143 C5
Humbie E Loth 210 D1
Humbleton E Yorks 151 D5
Humbleton Northumb 188 A2
Humby Lincs 116 B3
Hume Borders 197 B6
Humshaugh Northumb 177 B7
Huna Highld 281 A5
Huncoat Lancs 146 D1
Huncote Leics 98 B2
Hundalee Borders 187 B5
Hunderthwaite Durham 166 C2
Hundle Houses Lincs 134 D2
Hundleby Lincs 134 C3
Hundleton Pembs 55 D5
Hundon Suff 86 C3
Hundred Acres Hants 33 D4
Hundred End Lancs 136 A3
Hundred House Powys 77 B5
Hungarton Leics 98 A3
Hungerford Hants 31 D5
Hungerford W Berks 46 C1
Hungerford Newtown
  W Berks 46 B1
Hungerton Lincs 116 C1
Hungladder Highld 258 A3
Hunmanby N Yorks 161 D4
Hunmanby Moor N Yorks 161 D5
Hunningham Warks 81 A6
Hunny Hill I o W 18 C3
Hunsdon Herts 68 B4
Hunsingore N Yorks 148 B3
Hunslet W Yorks 148 D2
Hunsonby Cumb 164 B3
Hunspow Highld 280 A4
Hunstanton Norf 118 A3
Hunstanworth Durham 166 A2
Hunsterson Ches 111 A5
Hunston Suff 87 A5
Hunston W Sus 20 B1
Hunstrete Bath 43 C5
Hunt End Worcs 80 A3
Hunter's Quay Argyll 203 A6
Hunthill Lodge Angus 232 A2
Hunting-tower Perth 219 B5
Huntingdon Cambs 100 D4
Huntingdon Racecourse
  Cambs 100 D4
Huntingfield Suff 104 D4
Huntingford Dorset 30 B2
Huntington E Loth 210 C1
Huntington Hereford 77 B6
Huntington Staffs 112 D3
Huntington York 149 B5
Huntley Glos 62 B3
Huntly Aberds 255 C6
Huntlywood Borders 197 B5
Hunton Kent 37 B5
Hunton N Yorks 157 B5
Hunt's Corner Norf 103 C6
Hunt's Cross Mers 127 A4
Huntsham Devon 27 C5
Huntspill Som 28 A3
Huntworth Som 28 B3
Hunwick Durham 167 B4
Hunworth Norf 120 B2
Hurdsfield Ches 129 B4
Hurley Warks 97 B5
Hurley Windsor 47 A6
Hurlford E Ayrs 193 B4
Hurliness Orkney 283 K3
Hurn Dorset 17 B5
Hurn's End Lincs 118 A1
Hursley Hants 32 C3
Hurst N Yorks 156 A4
Hurst Som 29 D4
Hurst Wokingham 47 B5
Hurst Green E Sus 37 D5
Hurst Green Lancs 145 D6
Hurst Wickham W Sus 21 A5
Hurstbourne Priors Hants 32 A3
Hurstbourne Tarrant
  Hants 46 D1
Hurstpierpoint W Sus 21 A5
Hurstway Common
  Hereford 77 C6
Hurstwood Lancs 146 D2
Hurtmore Sur 34 B2
Hurworth Place Darl 157 A6
Hury Durham 166 D2
Husabost Highld 258 C2
Husbands Bosworth Leics 98 C3
Husborne Crawley Beds 83 D6
Husthwaite N Yorks 158 D4

Hutchwns Bridgend 40 D3
Huthwaite Notts 131 D4
Huttoft Lincs 135 B5
Hutton Borders 198 A3
Hutton Cumb 164 C2
Hutton E Yorks 150 B3
Hutton Essex 69 D6
Hutton Lancs 136 A3
Hutton N Som 42 D2
Hutton Buscel N Yorks 160 C3
Hutton Conyers N Yorks 158 D2
Hutton Cranswick E Yorks 150 B3
Hutton End Cumb 164 B2
Hutton Gate Redcar 168 D3
Hutton Henry Durham 168 B2
Hutton-le-Hole N Yorks 159 B6
Hutton Magna Durham 166 D4
Hutton Roof Cumb 163 A6
Hutton Roof Cumb 155 D4
Hutton Rudby N Yorks 158 A3
Hutton Sessay N Yorks 158 D3
Hutton Village Redcar 168 D3
Hutton Wandesley
  N Yorks 148 B4
Huxley Ches 127 C5
Huxter Shetland 285 H5
Huxter Shetland 285 G7
Huxton Borders 211 D5
Huyton Mers 136 D3
Hwlffordd =
  Haverfordwest Pembs 55 C5
Hycemoor Cumb 153 B1
Hyde Glos 63 C4
Hyde Gtr Man 138 D2
Hyde Hants 31 D5
Hyde Heath Bucks 67 C4
Hyde Park S Yorks 140 C3
Hydestile Sur 34 B2
Hylton Castle T & W 179 D5
Hyndford Bridge S Lnrk 194 B4
Hynish Argyll 222 D2
Hyssington Powys 93 B7
Hythe Hants 18 A3
Hythe Kent 38 B3
Hythe End Windsor 48 B3
Hythie Aberds 269 D5

I

Ibberton Dorset 16 A1
Ible Derbys 130 D2
Ibsley Hants 17 A5
Ibstock Leics 114 D2
Ibstone Bucks 66 D2
Ibthorpe Hants 46 D1
Ibworth Hants 46 D3
Ichrachan Argyll 227 C5
Ickburgh Norf 103 B4
Ickenham London 48 A3
Ickford Bucks 66 C1
Ickham Kent 53 D4
Ickleford Herts 84 D3
Icklesham E Sus 23 A6
Ickleton Cambs 85 C6
Icklingham Suff 102 D3
Ickwell Green Beds 84 C3
Ickworth House Suff 87 A4
Icomb Glos 64 A3
Idbury Oxon 64 B3
Iddesleigh Devon 11 A6
Ide Devon 12 B3
Ide Hill Kent 36 A2
Ideford Devon 12 D3
Iden E Sus 37 D7
Iden Green Kent 37 C6
Iden Green Kent 37 C5
Idle W Yorks 147 D5
Idlicote Warks 81 C5
Idmiston Wilts 31 B5
Idole Carms 57 A4
Idridgehay Derbys 113 A6
Idrigill Highld 258 B3
Idstone Oxon 45 A6
Idvies Angus 232 D3
Iffley Oxon 65 C6
Ifield W Sus 35 C5
Ifold W Sus 34 C3
Iford E Sus 22 B2
Ifton Heath Shrops 110 B2
Ightfield Shrops 111 B4
Ightham Kent 36 A3
Ightham Mote,
  Sevenoaks Kent 49 B6
Iken Suff 89 B5
Ilam Staffs 129 D6
Ilchester Som 29 C5
Ilderton Northumb 188 A3

Ilford London 50 A1
Ilfracombe Devon 25 A6
Ilkeston Derbys 114 A2
Ilketshall St Andrew Suff 105 C4
Ilketshall St Lawrence
  Suff 105 C4
Ilketshall St Margaret
  Suff 104 C4
Ilkley W Yorks 147 C5
Illey W Mid 96 C2
Illingworth W Yorks 138 A3
Illogan Corn 3 A4
Illston on the Hill Leics 99 B4
Ilmer Bucks 66 C2
Ilmington Warks 81 C5
Ilminster Som 28 D3
Ilsington Devon 12 D2
Ilston Swansea 57 C5
Ilton N Yorks 157 D5
Ilton Som 28 D3
Imachar N Ayrs 202 D3
Imeraval Argyll 200 D3
Immingham NE Lincs 142 B3
Imperial War Museum
  London 36 A3
Imperial War Museum
  North Gtr Man 137 D7
Impington Cambs 85 A6
Ince Ches 127 B4
Ince Blundell Mers 136 C2
Ince in Makerfield
  Gtr Man 137 C4
Inch of Arnhall Aberds 233 A4
Inchbare Angus 233 B4
Inchberry Moray 266 D4
Inchbraoch Angus 233 C5
Incheril Highld 262 D2
Inchgrundle Angus 232 A2
Inchina Highld 261 A6
Inchinnan Renfs 205 B4
Inchkinloch Highld 277 D6
Inchlaggan Highld 239 B5
Inchlumpie Highld 264 C1
Inchmore Highld 251 B5
Inchnacardoch Hotel
  Highld 240 A1
Inchnadamph Highld 271 B5
Inchree Highld 237 C4
Inchture Perth 220 B2
Inchyra Perth 219 B6
Indian Queens Corn 4 B4
Inerval Argyll 200 D3
Ingatestone Essex 69 D6
Ingbirchworth S Yorks 139 C5
Ingestre Staffs 112 C3
Ingham Lincs 133 A4
Ingham Norf 121 C5
Ingham Suff 103 D4
Ingham Corner Norf 121 C5
Ingleborough Norf 118 D1
Ingleby Derbys 114 C1
Ingleby Lincs 132 B3
Ingleby Arncliffe N Yorks 158 A3
Ingleby Barwick Stockton 168 D2
Ingleby Greenhow
  N Yorks 159 A4
Inglemire Hull 150 D3
Inglesbatch Bath 43 C6
Inglesham Thamesdown 64 D3
Ingleton Durham 167 C4
Ingleton N Yorks 155 D5
Inglewhite Lancs 145 C5
Ingliston Edin 208 C4
Ingoe Northumb 178 B2
Ingol Lancs 145 D5
Ingoldisthorpe Norf 118 B3
Ingoldmells Lincs 135 C5
Ingoldsby Lincs 116 B3
Ingon Warks 81 B5
Ingram Northumb 188 B3
Ingrave Essex 69 D6
Ingrow W Yorks 147 D4
Ings Cumb 154 B3
Ingst S Glos 43 A4
Ingworth Norf 120 C3
Inham's End Cambs 101 B4
Inkberrow Worcs 80 B3
Inkpen W Berks 46 C1
Inkstack Highld 281 A4
Inn Cumb 154 A3
Innellan Argyll 203 A6
Innerleithen Borders 196 C2
Innerleven Fife 220 D3
Innermessan Dumfries 170 A2
Innerwick E Loth 211 C4
Innerwick Perth 229 D4
Innis Chonain Argyll 227 D6

Insh Aberds 256 D1
Insh Highld 241 B6
Inshore Highld 276 B4
Inskip Lancs 145 D4
Instoneville S Yorks 140 B3
Instow Devon 25 B5
Intake S Yorks 140 C3
Inver Aberds 243 C5
Inver Highld 265 B4
Inver Perth 230 D4
Inver Mallie Highld 239 D5
Inverailort Highld 235 B6
Inveraldie Angus 220 A4
Inveralligin Highld 249 A5
Inverallochy Aberds 269 C5
Inveran Highld 264 A1
Inveraray Argyll 214 B3
Inveraray Jail Argyll 214 B3
Inverarish Highld 248 C2
Inverarity Angus 232 D2
Inverarnan Stirl 215 A6
Inverasdale Highld 261 B5
Inverbeg Argyll 206 A1
Inverbervie Aberds 233 A6
Inverboyndie Aberds 268 C1
Inverbroom Highld 262 B3
Invercassley Highld 272 D2
Invercauld House Aberds 243 C4
Inverchaolain Argyll 203 A5
Invercharnan Highld 227 B6
Inverchoran Highld 251 A4
Invercreran Argyll 227 B5
Inverdruie Highld 242 A2
Inverebrie Aberds 257 C4
Invereck Argyll 215 D4
Inverenan Ho. Aberds 243 A6
Invereshie House Highld 241 B6
Inveresk E Loth 209 C6
Inverewe Gardens,
  Gairloch Highld 261 B5
Inverey Aberds 242 D3
Inverfarigaig Highld 251 D7
Invergarry Highld 239 B7
Invergelder Aberds 243 C5
Invergeldie Perth 218 B2
Invergordon Highld 264 D3
Invergowrie Perth 220 A3
Inverguseran Highld 247 D6
Inverhadden Perth 229 C5
Inverharroch Moray 255 C4
Inverherive Stirl 216 B3
Inverie Highld 247 E6
Inverinan Argyll 214 A2
Inverinate Highld 249 D6
Inverkeilor Angus 233 D4
Inverkeithing Fife 208 B4
Inverkeithny Aberds 256 B1
Inverkip Invclyd 204 A2
Inverkirkaig Highld 270 C3
Inverlael Highld 262 B3
Inverlochlarig Stirl 216 C4
Inverlochy Argyll 227 D6
Inverlochy Highld 237 B5
Inverlussa Argyll 213 D4
Invermark Lodge Angus 244 D1
Invermoidart Highld 235 C5
Invermoriston Highld 240 A2
Invernaver Highld 278 B3
Inverneill Argyll 213 D6
Inverness Highld 252 B2
Inverness Airport Highld 252 A3
Invernettie Aberds 257 B6
Invernoaden Argyll 215 C4
Inveroran Hotel Argyll 228 D1
Inverpolly Lodge Highld 270 C3
Inverquharity Angus 232 C2
Inverquhomery Aberds 257 B5
Inverroy Highld 239 D6
Inversanda Highld 236 D3
Invershiel Highld 238 A3
Invershin Highld 264 A1
Inversnaid Hotel Stirl 215 B6
Inveruglas Argyll 215 B6
Inveruglass Highld 241 B6
Inverurie Aberds 256 D2
Invervar Perth 229 D5
Inverythan Aberds 256 B2
Inwardleigh Devon 11 B6
Inworth Essex 70 B2
Iochdar W Isles 286 B3
Iona Abbey and
  Cathedral Argyll 224 D1
Iping W Sus 34 D1
Ipplepen Devon 8 A2
Ipsden Oxon 47 A4
Ipsley Worcs 80 A3

Ipstones Staffs 129 D5
Ipswich Suff 88 C2
Irby Mers 126 A2
Irby in the Marsh Lincs 135 C4
Irby upon Humber
  NE Lincs 142 C3
Irchester Northants 83 A6
Ireby Cumb 163 A5
Ireby Lancs 155 D5
Ireland Orkney 283 G4
Ireland Shetland 285 L5
Ireland's Cross Shrops 111 A6
Ireleth Cumb 153 C3
Ireshopeburn Durham 165 B6
Irlam Gtr Man 137 D6
Irnham Lincs 116 C3
Iron Acton S Glos 43 A4
Iron Cross Warks 80 B3
Ironbridge Telford 95 A4
Ironbridge Gorge
  Museum, Telford Shrops 95 A4
Irongray Dumfries 173 A4
Ironmacannie Dumfries 173 A4
Ironside Aberds 268 D3
Ironville Derbys 131 D4
Irstead Norf 121 C5
Irthington Cumb 176 C2
Irthlingborough Northants 99 D6
Irton N Yorks 160 C4
Irvine N Ayrs 192 B3
Isauld Highld 279 B5
Isbister Orkney 282 E4
Isbister Orkney 282 F3
Isbister Shetland 284 D5
Isbister Shetland 285 G6
Isfield E Sus 22 A2
Isham Northants 99 D5
Islay Airport Argyll 200 C3
Isle Abbotts Som 28 C3
Isle Brewers Som 28 C3
Isle of Man Airport I o M 152 E2
Isle of Man Steam
  Railway I o M 152 D3
Isle of Whithorn Dumfries 171 D6
Isleham Cambs 102 D1
Isleornsay Highld 247 C6
Islesburgh Shetland 284 G5
Islesteps Dumfries 174 A2
Isleworth London 49 B4
Isley Walton Leics 114 C2
Islibhig W Isles 287 B4
Islington London 49 A6
Islip Northants 100 D1
Islip Oxon 65 B6
Istead Rise Kent 50 C3
Isycoed Wrex 127 D4
Itchen Soton 32 D3
Itchen Abbas Hants 32 B4
Itchen Stoke Hants 33 B4
Itchingfield W Sus 35 D4
Itchington S Glos 43 A5
Itteringham Norf 120 B3
Itton Devon 12 B1
Itton Common Mon 61 D6
Ivegill Cumb 164 A2
Iver Bucks 48 A3
Iver Heath Bucks 48 A3
Iveston Durham 178 D3
Ivinghoe Bucks 67 B4
Ivinghoe Aston Bucks 67 B4
Ivington Hereford 78 B2
Ivington Green Hereford 78 B2
Ivy Chimneys Essex 68 C4
Ivy Cross Dorset 30 C2
Ivy Hatch Kent 36 A3
Ivybridge Devon 7 B5
Ivychurch Kent 38 C2
Iwade Kent 51 C5
Iwerne Courtney or
  Shroton Dorset 30 D2
Iwerne Minster Dorset 30 D2
Ixworth Suff 103 D5
Ixworth Thorpe Suff 103 D5

J

Jack Hill N Yorks 147 B6
Jack in the Green Devon 13 B5
Jacksdale Notts 131 D4
Jackstown Aberds 256 C2
Jacobstow Corn 10 B2
Jacobstowe Devon 11 A6
Jameston Pembs 55 E6
Jamestown Dumfries 185 D6
Jamestown Highld 251 A6
Jamestown W Dunb 206 B1
Jarlshof Prehistoric Site
  Shetland 285 N5

Jarrow T & W 179 C5
Jarvis Brook E Sus 36 D3
Jasper's Green Essex 69 A7
Java Argyll 225 C6
Jawcraig Falk 207 C6
Jaywick Essex 71 B5
Jealott's Hill Brack 47 B6
Jedburgh Borders 187 A5
Jeffreyston Pembs 55 D6
Jellyhill E Dunb 205 A6
Jenkinsville Highld 104 D3
Jersey Airport Jersey 6
Jersey Farm Herts 67 C6
Jersey Zoo & Wildlife
Park Jersey 6
Jesmond T & W 179 C4
Jevington E Sus 22 B3
Jockey End Herts 67 B5
Jodrell Bank Visitor
Centre, Holmes Chapel
Ches 128 B2
John o'Groats Highld 281 A5
Johnby Cumb 164 B2
John's Cross E Sus 37 D5
Johnshaven Aberds 233 B5
Johnston Pembs 55 C5
Johnstone Renfs 205 B4
Johnstonebridge
Dumfries 184 C3
Johnstown Carms 57 A4
Johnstown Wrex 110 A2
Joppa Edin 209 C6
Joppa S Ayrs 182 A2
Jordans Bucks 67 D4
Jordanthorpe S Yorks 130 A3
Jorvik Centre York 149 B5
Judges Lodging,
Presteigne Powys 77 A7
Jump S Yorks 140 C1
Jumpers Green Dorset 17 B5
Juniper Green Edin 209 D4
Jurby East I o M 152 B3
Jurby South Motor
Racing Circuit I o M 152 B3
Jurby West I o M 152 B3

K

...ber Cumb 165 D5
...imend S Lnrk 195 B4
...imes Edin 209 D5
...lemouth Borders 187 A6
...mes Argyll 203 A4
...mes Argyll 213 A6
...mes E Ayrs 194 D1
...a Corn 4 C3
...adby N Lincs 141 B6
...al Cotes Lincs 134 C3
...arsley Gtr Man 137 C6
...arstwick Cumb 155 C5
...arton N Yorks 156 B3
...arvaig Highld 276 A3
...asden N Yorks 145 A7
...ckwick Halton 127 A5
...ddington Lincs 134 A3
...dington Suff 86 C3
...dleston Derbys 113 A7
...dleston Hall Derbys 113 A7
...elby Lincs 142 B3
...ele Staffs 112 A2
...eley Green Beds 84 C2
...eston Pembs 55 C5
...evil Wilts 44 D3
...gworth Leics 114 C2
...helland Corn 3 A4
...g Aberds 244 A3
...ghley W Yorks 147 C4
...ghley and Worth
Valley Railway W Yorks 147 D4
...Highld 236 D3
...arsbrae Clack 208 A1
...hill Aberds 268 D2
...lmore Argyll 213 D4
...lor Perth 231 D6
...lour Perth 219 B4
...ls Argyll 201 B4
...s Argyll 201 B5
...nton Mandeville Som 29 B5
...Mill Dumfries 183 C6
...by Lincs 116 C3
...s Highld 281 B5
...h Aberds 267 D5
...n Inch Aberds 257 B6
...nock Angus 233 B4
...brook Lancs 146 C3
...y Lincs 116 A3
...Cumb 164 D3

Keld N Yorks 156 A2
Keldholme N Yorks 159 C6
Kelfield N Lincs 141 C6
Kelfield N Yorks 149 D4
Kelham Notts 132 D2
Kellan Argyll 225 B4
Kellas Angus 221 A4
Kellas Moray 266 D2
Kellaton Devon 8 D2
Kelleth Cumb 155 A5
Kelleythorpe E Yorks 150 B2
Kelling Norf 120 A2
Kellingley N Yorks 140 A3
Kellington N Yorks 140 A3
Kelloe Durham 167 B6
Kelloholm Dumfries 183 A5
Kelly Devon 11 C4
Kelly Bray Corn 11 D4
Kelmarsh Northants 99 D4
Kelmscot Oxon 64 D3
Kelsale Suff 89 A4
Kelsall Ches 127 C5
Kelsall Hill Ches 127 C5
Kelshall Herts 85 D5
Kelsick Cumb 175 C4
Kelso Borders 197 C6
Kelso Racecourse
Borders 197 C6
Kelstedge Derbys 130 C3
Kelstern Lincs 143 D4
Kelston Bath 43 C6
Keltneyburn Perth 229 D6
Kelton Dumfries 174 A2
Kelty Fife 208 A4
Kelvedon Essex 70 B2
Kelvedon Hatch Essex 69 D5
Kelvin S Lnrk 205 C6
Kelvinside Glasgow 205 B5
Kelynack Corn 2 B1
Kemback Fife 220 C4
Kemberton Shrops 95 A5
Kemble Glos 63 D5
Kemerton Worcs 80 D2
Kemeys Commander Mon 61 C5
Kemnay Aberds 245 A4
Kemp Town Brighton 21 B6
Kempley Glos 62 A2
Kemps Green Warks 96 D4
Kempsey Worcs 79 C6
Kempsford Glos 64 D2
Kempshott Hants 47 D4
Kempston Beds 84 C2
Kempston Hardwick Beds 84 C2
Kempton Shrops 94 C1
Kempton Park
Racecourse Sur 48 B4
Kemsing Kent 36 A3
Kemsley Kent 51 C6
Kenardington Kent 38 B1
Kenchester Hereford 78 C2
Kencot Oxon 64 C3
Kendal Cumb 154 B4
Kendoon Dumfries 182 D4
Kendray S Yorks 139 C6
Kenfig Bridgend 40 C3
Kenfig Hill Bridgend 40 C3
Kenilworth Warks 97 D5
Kenilworth Castle Warks 97 D5
Kenknock Stirl 217 A4
Kenley London 35 A6
Kenley Shrops 94 A3
Kenmore Highld 249 A4
Kenmore Perth 230 D1
Kenn Devon 13 C4
Kenn N Som 42 C3
Kennacley W Isles 288 H2
Kennacraig Argyll 202 B3
Kennerleigh Devon 12 A3
Kennet Clack 208 A2
Kennethmont Aberds 255 D6
Kennett Cambs 86 A2
Kennford Devon 13 C4
Kenninghall Norf 103 C6
Kenninghall Heath Norf 103 C6
Kennington Kent 38 A2
Kennington Oxon 65 C6
Kennoway Fife 220 D3
Kenny Hill Suff 102 D2
Kennythorpe N Yorks 149 A6
Kenovay Argyll 222 C2
Kensaleyre Highld 259 C4
Kensington London 49 B5
Kensworth Beds 67 B5
Kensworth Common Beds 67 B5
Kent International
Airport Kent 53 C5
Kent Street E Sus 23 A5

Kent Street Kent 37 A4
Kent Street W Sus 35 D5
Kentallen Highld 237 D4
Kentchurch Hereford 61 A6
Kentford Suff 86 A3
Kentisbeare Devon 13 A5
Kentisbury Devon 25 A7
Kentisbury Ford Devon 25 A7
Kentmere Cumb 154 A3
Kenton Devon 13 C4
Kenton Suff 88 A2
Kenton T & W 179 C4
Kenton Bankfoot T & W 179 C4
Kentra Highld 235 D5
Kents Bank Cumb 154 D2
Kent's Green Glos 62 A3
Kent's Oak Hants 32 C2
Kenwick Shrops 110 B3
Kenwyn Corn 4 C3
Keoldale Highld 277 B4
Keppanach Highld 237 C4
Keppoch Highld 249 D6
Keprigan Argyll 190 D2
Kepwick N Yorks 158 B3
Kerchesters Borders 197 C6
Keresley W Mid 97 C6
Kernborough Devon 8 C1
Kerne Bridge Hereford 62 B1
Kerris Corn 2 C2
Kerry Powys 93 C5
Kerrycroy Argyll 203 B6
Kerry's Gate Hereford 78 D1
Kerrysdale Highld 261 C5
Kersall Notts 132 C2
Kersey Suff 87 C6
Kershopefoot Cumb 176 A2
Kersoe Worcs 80 D2
Kerswell Devon 13 A5
Kerswell Green Worcs 79 C6
Kesgrave Suff 88 C3
Kessingland Suff 105 C6
Kessingland Beach Suff 105 C6
Kessington E Dunb 205 A5
Kestle Corn 5 C4
Kestle Mill Corn 4 B3
Keston London 49 C7
Keswick Cumb 163 B5
Keswick Norf 104 A3
Keswick Norf 121 B5
Ketley Telford 111 D5
Ketley Bank Telford 111 D5
Ketsby Lincs 134 B3
Kettering Northants 99 D5
Ketteringham Norf 104 A2
Kettins Perth 220 A2
Kettlebaston Suff 87 B5
Kettlebridge Fife 220 D3
Kettleburgh Suff 88 A3
Kettlehill Fife 220 D3
Kettleholm Dumfries 174 A4
Kettleness N Yorks 169 D6
Kettleshume Ches 129 B4
Kettlesing Bottom
N Yorks 147 B6
Kettlesing Head N Yorks 147 B6
Kettlestone Norf 119 B6
Kettlethorpe Lincs 132 B3
Kettletoft Orkney 282 D7
Kettlewell N Yorks 156 D3
Ketton Rutland 100 A1
Kew London 49 B4
Kew Br. London 49 B4
Kew Gardens London 48 B4
Kewstoke N Som 42 C2
Kexbrough S Yorks 139 C6
Kexby Lincs 132 A3
Kexby York 149 B6
Key Green Ches 128 C3
Keyham Leics 98 A3
Keyhaven Hants 18 B2
Keyingham E Yorks 143 A4
Keymer W Sus 21 A6
Keynsham Bath 43 C5
Keysoe Beds 84 A2
Keysoe Row Beds 84 A2
Keyston Cambs 100 D2
Keyworth Notts 115 B4
Kibblesworth T & W 179 D4
Kibworth Beauchamp
Leics 98 B3
Kibworth Harcourt Leics 98 B3
Kidbrooke London 49 B7
Kiddemore Green Staffs 95 A6
Kidderminster Worcs 95 D6
Kiddington Oxon 65 A5
Kidlington Oxon 65 B5
Kidmore End Oxon 47 B4

Kidsgrove Staffs 128 D3
Kidstones N Yorks 156 C3
Kidwelly = Cydweli Carms 57 B4
Kiel Crofts Argyll 226 C4
Kielder Northumb 187 D5
Kielder Castle Visitor
Centre Northumb 187 D5
Kierfiold Ho. Orkney 282 F3
Kilbagie Clack 208 B2
Kilbarchan Renfs 205 B4
Kilbeg Highld 247 D5
Kilberry Argyll 202 B2
Kilbirnie N Ayrs 204 C3
Kilbride Argyll 226 D3
Kilbride Argyll 226 D4
Kilbride Highld 247 B4
Kilburn Angus 232 B1
Kilburn Derbys 114 A1
Kilburn London 49 A5
Kilburn N Yorks 158 D4
Kilby Leics 98 B3
Kilchamaig Argyll 202 B3
Kilchattan Argyll 212 C1
Kilchattan Bay Argyll 203 C6
Kilchenzie Argyll 190 C2
Kilcheran Argyll 226 C3
Kilchiaran Argyll 200 B2
Kilchoan Argyll 213 A5
Kilchoan Highld 234 D3
Kilchoman Argyll 200 B2
Kilchrenan Argyll 227 D5
Kilconquhar Fife 221 D4
Kilcot Glos 62 A2
Kilcoy Highld 252 A1
Kilcreggan Argyll 215 D5
Kildale N Yorks 159 A5
Kildalloig Argyll 190 D3
Kildary Highld 264 C3
Kildermorie Lodge Highld 263 C7
Kildonan N Ayrs 191 C6
Kildonan Lodge Highld 274 B3
Kildonnan Highld 234 B3
Kildrummy Aberds 244 A1
Kildwick N Yorks 147 C4
Kilfinan Argyll 203 A4
Kilfinnan Highld 239 C6
Kilgetty Pembs 56 B1
Kilgwrrwg Common Mon 61 D6
Kilham E Yorks 150 A3
Kilham Northumb 198 C2
Kilkenneth Argyll 222 C2
Kilkerran Argyll 190 D3
Kilkhampton Corn 24 D3
Killamarsh Derbys 131 A4
Killay Swansea 57 C6
Killbeg Argyll 225 B5
Killean Argyll 202 D1
Killearn Stirl 206 B3
Killen Highld 252 A2
Killerby Darl 167 D4
Killerton House, Exeter
Devon 13 A4
Killichonan Perth 229 C4
Killiechonate Highld 239 D6
Killiechronan Argyll 225 B4
Killiecrankie Perth 230 B3
Killiemor Argyll 224 C3
Killiemore House Argyll 224 D3
Killilan Highld 249 C6
Killimster Highld 281 C5
Killin Stirl 217 A5
Killin Lodge Highld 240 B3
Killinallan Argyll 200 A3
Killinghall N Yorks 148 B1
Killington Cumb 155 C5
Killingworth T & W 179 B4
Killmahumaig Argyll 213 C5
Killochyett Borders 196 B3
Killocraw Argyll 190 B2
Killundine Highld 225 B4
Kilmacolm Invclyd 204 B3
Kilmaha Argyll 214 B2
Kilmahog Stirl 217 D6
Kilmalieu Highld 236 D2
Kilmaluag Highld 259 A4
Kilmany Fife 220 B3
Kilmarie Highld 247 C4
Kilmarnock E Ayrs 193 B4
Kilmaron Castle Fife 220 C3
Kilmartin Argyll 213 C6
Kilmaurs E Ayrs 205 D4
Kilmelford Argyll 213 A6
Kilmeny Argyll 200 B3
Kilmersdon Som 43 D5
Kilmeston Hants 33 C4
Kilmichael Argyll 190 C2
Kilmichael Glassary
Argyll 214 C1

Kilmichael of Inverlussa
Argyll 213 D5
Kilmington Devon 14 B2
Kilmington Wilts 30 B1
Kilmonivaig Highld 239 D5
Kilmorack Highld 251 B6
Kilmore Argyll 226 D3
Kilmore Highld 247 D5
Kilmory Argyll 202 A2
Kilmory Argyll 235 C4
Kilmory Highld 235 C4
Kilmory Highld 246 D2
Kilmory N Ayrs 191 C5
Kilmuir Highld 258 D2
Kilmuir Highld 252 B2
Kilmuir Highld 264 C3
Kilmuir Highld 258 A3
Kilmun Argyll 215 D4
Kilmun Argyll 214 A2
Kiln Pit Hill Northumb 178 D2
Kilncadzow S Lnrk 194 B3
Kilndown Kent 37 C5
Kilnhurst S Yorks 140 D2
Kilninian Argyll 224 B2
Kilninver Argyll 226 D3
Kilnsea E Yorks 143 B6
Kilnsey N Yorks 146 A3
Kilnwick E Yorks 150 C2
Kilnwick Percy E Yorks 149 B1
Kiloran Argyll 212 C1
Kilpatrick N Ayrs 191 C5
Kilpeck Hereford 78 D2
Kilphedir Highld 274 C2
Kilpin E Yorks 141 A5
Kilpin Pike E Yorks 141 A5
Kilrenny Fife 221 D5
Kilsby Northants 98 D2
Kilspindie Perth 220 B2
Kilsyth N Lnrk 207 C5
Kiltarlity Highld 251 B7
Kilton Notts 131 B5
Kilton Som 27 A6
Kilton Thorpe Redcar 169 D4
Kilvaxter Highld 258 B3
Kilve Som 27 A6
Kilvington Notts 115 A5
Kilwinning N Ayrs 204 D3
Kimber worth S Yorks 140 D2
Kimberley Norf 103 A6
Kimberley Notts 114 A3
Kimble Wick Bucks 66 C3
Kimblesworth Durham 167 A5
Kimbolton Cambs 84 A2
Kimbolton Hereford 78 A3
Kimcote Leics 98 C2
Kimmeridge Dorset 16 D3
Kimmerston Northumb 198 C3
Kimpton Hants 32 A1
Kimpton Herts 68 B1
Kinbrace Highld 274 A2
Kinbuck Stirl 218 D2
Kincaple Fife 221 C4
Kincardine Fife 208 B2
Kincardine Highld 264 B2
Kincardine Bridge Fife 208 B2
Kincardine O'Neil Aberds 244 C2
Kinclaven Perth 219 A6
Kincorth Aberdeen 245 B6
Kincorth Ho. Moray 265 D6
Kincraig Highld 241 B6
Kincraigie Perth 230 D3
Kindallachan Perth 230 D3
Kinderland, Scarborough
N Yorks 160 B4
Kineton Glos 64 A1
Kineton Warks 81 B6
Kinfauns Perth 219 B6
King Edward Aberds 268 D2
King Sterndale Derbys 129 B5
Kingairloch Highld 236 D2
Kingarth Argyll 203 C5
Kingcoed Mon 61 C6
Kingerby Lincs 142 D2
Kingham Oxon 64 A3
Kingholm Quay Dumfries 174 A2
Kinghorn Fife 209 B5
Kingie Highld 239 B5
Kinglassie Fife 209 A5
Kingoodie Perth 220 B3
King's Acre Hereford 78 C2
King's Bromley Staffs 113 D5
King's Caple Hereford 62 A1
King's Cliffe Northants 100 B2
Kings College Chapel,
Cambridge Cambs 85 B6

King's Coughton Warks 80 B3
King's Heath W Mid 96 C3
Kings Hedges Cambs 85 A6
Kings Langley Herts 67 C5
King's Lynn Norf 118 C3
King's Meaburn Cumb 165 C4
Kings Muir Borders 196 C1
King's Newnham Warks 98 D1
King's Newton Derbys 114 C1
King's Norton Leics 98 A3
King's Norton W Mid 96 D3
King's Nympton Devon 26 D1
King's Pyon Hereford 78 B2
King's Ripton Cambs 101 D4
King's Somborne Hants 32 B2
King's Stag Dorset 30 D1
King's Stanley Glos 63 C4
King's Sutton Northants 82 D1
King's Thorn Hereford 78 D3
King's Walden Herts 67 A6
Kings Worthy Hants 32 B3
Kingsand Corn 6 B3
Kingsbarns Fife 221 C5
Kingsbridge Devon 7 C6
Kingsbridge Som 28 B2
Kingsburgh Highld 258 C3
Kingsbury London 49 A5
Kingsbury Warks 97 B5
Kingsbury Episcopi Som 28 C4
Kingsclere Hants 46 D3
Kingscote Glos 63 D4
Kingscott Devon 25 D6
Kingscross N Ayrs 191 C6
Kingsdon Som 29 C5
Kingsdown Kent 39 A5
Kingseat Fife 208 A4
Kingsey Bucks 66 C2
Kingsfold W Sus 35 C4
Kingsford E Ayrs 205 D4
Kingsford Worcs 95 C6
Kingsforth N Lincs 142 B2
Kingsgate Kent 53 B5
Kingsheanton Devon 25 B6
Kingshouse Hotel Highld 237 D6
Kingside Hill Cumb 175 C4
Kingskerswell Devon 8 A2
Kingskettle Fife 220 D3
Kingsland Anglesey 122 B2
Kingsland Hereford 78 A2
Kingsley Ches 127 B5
Kingsley Hants 33 B6
Kingsley Staffs 112 A4
Kingsley Green W Sus 34 C1
Kingsley Holt Staffs 112 A4
Kingsley Park Northants 83 A4
Kingsmuir Angus 232 D2
Kingsmuir Fife 221 D5
Kingsnorth Kent 38 B2
Kingstanding W Mid 96 B3
Kingsteignton Devon 12 D3
Kingsthorpe Northants 83 A4
Kingston Cambs 85 B5
Kingston Devon 7 C5
Kingston Dorset 16 A1
Kingston Dorset 16 D3
Kingston E Loth 210 B2
Kingston Hants 17 A5
Kingston I o W 18 C3
Kingston Kent 52 D3
Kingston Moray 266 C4
Kingston Bagpuize Oxon 65 D5
Kingston Blount Oxon 66 D2
Kingston by Sea W Sus 21 B5
Kingston Deverill Wilts 30 B2
Kingston Gorse W Sus 20 B3
Kingston Lacy,
   Wimborne Minster
   Dorset 16 A3
Kingston Lisle Oxon 45 A7
Kingston Maurward Dorset 15 B7
Kingston near Lewes E Sus 22 B1
Kingston on Soar Notts 114 C3
Kingston Russell Dorset 15 B5
Kingston St Mary Som 28 C2
Kingston Seymour N Som 42 C3
Kingston Upon Hull Hull 142 A2
Kingston upon Thames
   London 49 C4
Kingston Vale London 49 B5
Kingstone Hereford 78 D2
Kingstone Som 28 D3
Kingstone Staffs 113 C4
Kingstown Cumb 175 C6

Kingswear Devon 8 B2
Kingswells Aberdeen 245 B5
Kingswinford W Mid 96 C1
Kingswood Bucks 66 B1
Kingswood Glos 62 D3
Kingswood Hereford 77 B6
Kingswood Kent 37 A6
Kingswood Powys 93 A6
Kingswood S Glos 43 B5
Kingswood Som 27 B6
Kingswood Sur 35 A5
Kingswood Warks 97 D4
Kingthorpe Lincs 133 B6
Kington Hereford 77 B6
Kington Worcs 80 B2
Kington Langley Wilts 44 B3
Kington Magna Dorset 30 C1
Kington St Michael Wilts 44 B3
Kingussie Highld 241 B5
Kingweston Som 29 B5
Kininvie Ho. Moray 254 B4
Kinkell Bridge Perth 218 C4
Kinknockie Aberds 257 B5
Kinlet Shrops 95 C5
Kinloch Fife 220 C2
Kinloch Highld 234 A2
Kinloch Highld 271 A6
Kinloch Highld 247 C5
Kinloch Highld 231 D5
Kinloch Perth 231 D6
Kinloch Hourn Highld 238 B3
Kinloch Laggan Highld 240 D3
Kinloch Lodge Highld 277 C6
Kinloch Rannoch Perth 229 C5
Kinlochan Highld 236 C2
Kinlochard Stirl 217 D4
Kinlochbeoraid Highld 238 D2
Kinlochbervie Highld 276 C3
Kinlocheil Highld 236 B3
Kinlochewe Highld 262 D2
Kinlochleven Highld 237 C5
Kinlochmoidart Highld 235 C6
Kinlochmorar Highld 238 C2
Kinlochmore Highld 237 C5
Kinlochspelve Argyll 225 D5
Kinloid Highld 235 B5
Kinloss Moray 265 D6
Kinmel Bay Conwy 125 A4
Kinmuck Aberds 256 E3
Kinmundy Aberds 245 A5
Kinnadie Aberds 257 B4
Kinnaird Perth 220 B2
Kinnaird Castle Angus 233 C4
Kinneff Aberds 233 A6
Kinnelhead Dumfries 184 B3
Kinnell Angus 233 C4
Kinnerley Shrops 110 C2
Kinnersley Hereford 78 C1
Kinnersley Worcs 79 C6
Kinnerton Powys 77 A6
Kinnesswood Perth 219 D6
Kinninvie Durham 166 C3
Kinnordy Angus 232 C1
Kinoulton Notts 115 B4
Kinross Perth 219 D6
Kinrossie Perth 219 A6
Kinsbourne Green Herts 67 B6
Kinsey Heath Ches 111 A5
Kinsham Hereford 78 A1
Kinsham Worcs 80 D2
Kinsley W Yorks 140 B2
Kinson Bmouth 17 B4
Kintbury W Berks 46 C1
Kintessack Moray 265 D5
Kintillo Perth 219 C6
Kintocher Aberds 244 B2
Kinton Hereford 94 D2
Kinton Shrops 110 D2
Kintore Aberds 245 A4
Kintour Argyll 201 C4
Kintra Argyll 224 D2
Kintra Argyll 200 D3
Kintraw Argyll 213 B6
Kinuachdrachd Argyll 213 C5
Kinveachy Highld 242 A2
Kinver Staffs 95 C6
Kippax W Yorks 148 D3
Kippen Stirl 207 A4
Kippford or Scaur
   Dumfries 173 C6
Kirbister Orkney 283 G4
Kirbister Orkney 282 E7
Kirbuster Orkney 282 E3
Kirby Bedon Norf 104 A3
Kirby Bellars Leics 115 D5
Kirby Cane Norf 105 B4
Kirby Cross Essex 71 A6
Kirby Grindalythe N Yorks 150 A2

Kirby Hill N Yorks 148 A2
Kirby Hill N Yorks 157 A5
Kirby Knowle N Yorks 158 C3
Kirby-le-Soken Essex 71 A6
Kirby Misperton N Yorks 159 D6
Kirby Muxloe Leics 98 A2
Kirby Overblow N Yorks 148 C2
Kirby Row Norf 105 B4
Kirby Sigston N Yorks 158 B3
Kirby Underdale
   E Yorks 150 B1
Kirby Wiske N Yorks 158 C2
Kirdford W Sus 34 D3
Kirk Highld 281 C4
Kirk Bramwith S Yorks 140 B4
Kirk Deighton N Yorks 148 B2
Kirk Ella E Yorks 142 A2
Kirk Hallam Derbys 114 A2
Kirk Hammerton N Yorks 148 B3
Kirk Ireton Derbys 130 D2
Kirk Langley Derbys 113 B6
Kirk Merrington Durham 167 B5
Kirk Michael I o M 152 B3
Kirk of Shotts N Lnrk 207 D6
Kirk Sandall S Yorks 140 C4
Kirk Smeaton N Yorks 140 B3
Kirk Yetholm Borders 188 A1
Kirkabister Shetland 285 K6
Kirkandrews Dumfries 172 D4
Kirkandrews upon Eden
   Cumb 175 C6
Kirkbampton Cumb 175 C6
Kirkbean Dumfries 174 C2
Kirkbride Cumb 175 C5
Kirkbuddo Angus 232 D3
Kirkburn Borders 196 C1
Kirkburn E Yorks 150 B2
Kirkburton W Yorks 139 B4
Kirkby Lincs 142 D2
Kirkby Mers 136 D3
Kirkby N Yorks 158 A4
Kirkby Fleetham N Yorks 157 B6
Kirkby Green Lincs 133 D5
Kirkby In Ashfield Notts 131 D5
Kirkby-in-Furness Cumb 153 B3
Kirkby la Thorpe Lincs 116 A4
Kirkby Lonsdale Cumb 155 D5
Kirkby Malham N Yorks 146 A2
Kirkby Mallory Leics 98 A1
Kirkby Malzeard N Yorks 157 D6
Kirkby Mills N Yorks 159 C6
Kirkby on Bain Lincs 134 C2
Kirkby Stephen Cumb 155 A6
Kirkby Thore Cumb 165 C4
Kirkby Underwood Lincs 116 C3
Kirkby Wharfe N Yorks 148 C4
Kirkbymoorside N Yorks 159 C5
Kirkcaldy Fife 209 A5
Kirkcambeck Cumb 176 C3
Kirkcarswell Dumfries 173 D5
Kirkcolm Dumfries 170 A2
Kirkconnel Dumfries 183 A5
Kirkconnell Dumfries 174 B2
Kirkcowan Dumfries 171 A5
Kirkcudbright Dumfries 173 C4
Kirkdale Mers 136 D2
Kirkfieldbank S Lnrk 194 B3
Kirkgunzeon Dumfries 173 B6
Kirkham Lancs 144 D4
Kirkham N Yorks 149 A6
Kirkhamgate W Yorks 139 A5
Kirkharle Northumb 178 A2
Kirkheaton Northumb 178 B2
Kirkheaton W Yorks 139 B4
Kirkhill Angus 233 B4
Kirkhill Highld 252 B1
Kirkhill Midloth 209 D5
Kirkhill Moray 254 C3
Kirkhope Borders 186 A2
Kirkhouse Borders 196 C2
Kirkiboll Highld 277 C6
Kirkibost Highld 247 C4
Kirkinch Angus 231 D7
Kirkinner Dumfries 171 B6
Kirkintilloch E Dunb 205 A6
Kirkland Cumb 162 C3
Kirkland Cumb 165 B4
Kirkland Dumfries 183 C6
Kirkland Dumfries 183 A5
Kirkleatham Redcar 168 C3
Kirklevington Stockton 158 A3
Kirkley Suff 105 B6
Kirklington Notts 132 C1
Kirklington N Yorks 157 C7
Kirklinton Cumb 176 C2
Kirkliston Edin 208 C4
Kirkmaiden Dumfries 170 D3
Kirkmichael Perth 231 C4

Kirkmichael S Ayrs 192 E3
Kirkmuirhill S Lnrk 194 B2
Kirknewton Northumb 198 C3
Kirknewton W Loth 208 D4
Kirkney Aberds 255 C6
Kirkoswald Cumb 164 A3
Kirkoswald S Ayrs 192 E2
Kirkpatrick Durham
   Dumfries 173 A5
Kirkpatrick-Fleming
   Dumfries 175 A5
Kirksanton Cumb 153 B2
Kirkstall W Yorks 147 D6
Kirkstead Lincs 134 C1
Kirkstile Aberds 255 C6
Kirkstyle Highld 281 A5
Kirkton Aberds 256 D1
Kirkton Aberds 268 E1
Kirkton Angus 232 D2
Kirkton Angus 220 A4
Kirkton Borders 186 B4
Kirkton Dumfries 184 D2
Kirkton Fife 220 B3
Kirkton Highld 249 D5
Kirkton Highld 249 B6
Kirkton Highld 265 A4
Kirkton Highld 252 A3
Kirkton Perth 219 C4
Kirkton S Lnrk 194 D4
Kirkton Stirl 217 D5
Kirkton Manor Borders 195 C7
Kirkton of Airlie Angus 231 C7
Kirkton of Auchterhouse
   Angus 220 A3
Kirkton of Auchterless
   Aberds 256 B2
Kirkton of Barevan Highld 253 B4
Kirkton of Bourtie Aberds 256 D3
Kirkton of Collace Perth 219 A6
Kirkton of Craig Angus 233 C5
Kirkton of Culsalmond
   Aberds 256 C1
Kirkton of Durris Aberds 245 C4
Kirkton of Glenbuchat
   Aberds 243 A6
Kirkton of Glenisla Angus 231 B6
Kirkton of Kingoldrum
   Angus 232 C1
Kirkton of Largo Fife 220 D4
Kirkton of Lethendy
   Perth 231 D5
Kirkton of Logie Buchan
   Aberds 257 D4
Kirkton of Maryculter
   Aberds 245 C5
Kirkton of Menmuir
   Angus 232 B3
Kirkton of Monikie Angus 221 A5
Kirkton of Oyne Aberds 256 D1
Kirkton of Rayne Aberds 256 D1
Kirkton of Skene Aberds 245 B5
Kirkton of Tough Aberds 244 A3
Kirktonhill Borders 196 A3
Kirktown Aberds 269 D5
Kirktown of Alvah Aberds 268 C1
Kirktown of Deskford
   Moray 267 C6
Kirktown of Fetteresso
   Aberds 245 D5
Kirktown of Mortlach
   Moray 254 C4
Kirktown of Slains
   Aberds 257 D5
Kirkurd Borders 195 B6
Kirkwall Orkney 282 F5
Kirkwall Airport Orkney 283 G5
Kirkwhelpington
   Northumb 178 A1
Kirmington N Lincs 142 B3
Kirmond le Mire Lincs 142 D3
Kirn Argyll 203 A6
Kirriemuir Angus 232 C1
Kirstead Green Norf 104 B3
Kirtlebridge Dumfries 175 A5
Kirtleton Dumfries 185 D5
Kirtling Cambs 86 B2
Kirtling Green Cambs 86 B2
Kirtlington Oxon 65 B5
Kirtomy Highld 278 B3
Kirton Lincs 117 B6
Kirton Notts 132 C1
Kirton Suff 88 D3
Kirton End Lincs 117 A5
Kirton Holme Lincs 117 A5
Kirton in Lindsey N Lincs 142 D1
Kislingbury Northants 82 B3
Kites Hardwick Warks 82 A1

Kittisford Som 27 C5
Kittle Swansea 57 D5
Kitt's Green W Mid 97 C4
Kitt's Moss Gtr Man 128 A3
Kitwood Hants 33 B5
Kivernoll Hereford 78 D2
Kiveton Park S Yorks 131 A4
Knaith Lincs 132 A3
Knaith Park Lincs 132 A3
Knap Corner Dorset 30 C2
Knaphill Sur 34 A2
Knapp Perth 220 A2
Knapp Som 28 C3
Knapthorpe Notts 132 D2
Knapton Norf 121 B5
Knapton York 149 B4
Knapton Green Hereford 78 B2
Knapwell Cambs 85 A5
Knaresborough N Yorks 148 B2
Knarsdale Northumb 177 D4
Knauchland Moray 267 D7
Knaven Aberds 256 B3
Knayton N Yorks 158 C3
Knebworth Herts 68 A2
Knebworth House,
   Stevenage Herts 68 A2
Knedlington E Yorks 141 A5
Kneesall Notts 132 C2
Kneesworth Cambs 85 C5
Kneeton Notts 115 A5
Knelston Swansea 57 D4
Knenhall Staffs 112 B3
Knettishall Suff 103 C5
Knightacott Devon 26 B1
Knightcote Warks 81 B6
Knightley Dale Staffs 112 C2
Knighton Devon 7 C4
Knighton Leicester 98 A2
Knighton Staffs 111 A6
Knighton Staffs 111 C6
Knighton =
   Tref-y-Clawdd Powys 93 D6
Knightshayes Court Devon 27 D4
Knightswood Glasgow 205 B5
Knightwick Worcs 79 B5
Knill Hereford 77 A6
Knipton Leics 115 B6
Knitsley Durham 166 A4
Kniveton Derbys 130 D2
Knock Argyll 225 C4
Knock Cumb 165 C4
Knock Moray 267 D7
Knockally Highld 275 B5
Knockan Highld 271 C5
Knockandhu Moray 254 D3
Knockando Moray 254 B2
Knockando Ho. Moray 254 B3
Knockbain Highld 252 A2
Knockbreck Highld 258 B2
Knockbrex Dumfries 172 D3
Knockdee Highld 280 B3
Knockdolian S Ayrs 180 C3
Knockenkelly N Ayrs 191 C6
Knockentiber E Ayrs 192 B3
Knockespock Ho. Aberds 255 D6
Knockfarrel Highld 251 A6
Knockglass Dumfries 170 B2
Knockhill Motor Racing
   Circuit Fife 208 A3
Knockholt Kent 36 A2
Knockholt Pound Kent 36 A2
Knockie Lodge Highld 240 B3
Knockin Shrops 110 C2
Knockinlaw E Ayrs 193 B4
Knocklearn Dumfries 173 A5
Knocknaha Argyll 190 D2
Knocknain Dumfries 170 A1
Knockrome Argyll 201 A5
Knocksharry I o M 152 C2
Knodishall Suff 89 A5
Knole House & Gardens
   Kent 36 A3
Knolls Green Ches 128 B3
Knolton Wrex 110 B2
Knolton Bryn Wrex 110 B2
Knook Wilts 30 A3
Knossington Leics 99 A5
Knott End-on-Sea Lancs 144 C3
Knotting Beds 84 A2
Knotting Green Beds 84 A2
Knottingley W Yorks 140 A3
Knotts Cumb 164 C2
Knotts Lancs 146 B1
Knotty Ash Mers 136 D3
Knotty Green Bucks 67 D4
Knowbury Shrops 94 D3

Knowe Dumfries 181 D5
Knowehead Dumfries 182 C4
Knowes of Elrick Aberds 267 D7
Knowesgate Northumb 178 A1
Knoweton N Lnrk 194 A2
Knowhead Aberds 269 D4
Knowl Hill Windsor 47 B6
Knowle Bristol 43 B5
Knowle Devon 12 A2
Knowle Devon 13 C5
Knowle Devon 08 B1
Knowle Shrops 94 D3
Knowle W Mid 97 D4
Knowle Green Lancs 145 D6
Knowle Park W Yorks 147 C4
Knowlton Dorset 31 D4
Knowlton Kent 53 D4
Knowsley Mers 136 D3
Knowsley Safari Park Mers 136 D3
Knowstone Devon 26 C3
Knox Bridge Kent 37 B5
Knucklas Powys 93 D6
Knuston Northants 83 A6
Knutsford Ches 128 B2
Knutton Staffs 112 A2
Knypersley Staffs 128 D3
Kuggar Corn 3 D5
Kyle of Lochalsh Highld 249 D4
Kyleakin Highld 247 B6
Kylerhea Highld 247 B6
Kylesknoydart Highld 238 C2
Kylesku Highld 271 A5
Kylesmorar Highld 238 C2
Kylestrome Highld 271 A5
Kyllachy House Highld 252 D3
Kynaston Shrops 110 C2
Kynnersley Telford 111 D5
Kyre Magna Worcs 79 A4

L

a Fontenelle Guern 6
a Planque Guern 6
abost W Isles 288 C3
acasaidh W Isles 288 E4
acasdal W Isles 288 D5
aceby NE Lincs 143 C4
acey Green Bucks 66 D3
ach Dennis Ches 128 B2
ackford Suff 102 D3
acock Wilts 44 C3
adbroke Warks 81 B7
ddingford Kent 37 B4
de Bank Lincs 134 D3
adock Corn 4 B3
dy Orkney 282 C7
dybank Fife 220 C3
dykirk Borders 198 B2
dysford Aberds 269 C4
ga Highld 235 D5
galochan Argyll 214 A1
gavulin Argyll 201 B4
gg Argyll 201 A5
gg N Ayrs 191 C5
ggan Argyll 200 C2
ggan Highld 239 C6
ggan Highld 241 C4
ggan Highld 235 C6
ggan S Ayrs 181 C4
gganulva Argyll 224 B3
de Highld 261 A5
gh Fenwick E Ayrs 205 D4
gh Glengall S Ayrs 192 D3
ghmuir E Ayrs 205 D4
ndon Essex 50 A3
 Highld 250 B2
rg Highld 272 D3
rg Highld 272 D3
rg Muir Highld 272 D3
gmore Highld 252 C1
sterdyke W Yorks 147 D5
ches Cumb 164 B2
e I o W 19 C4
e Wilts 31 B5
enham Norf 104 A3
enheath Suff 102 C3
esend Norf 101 B7
eside Cumb 154 C2
aside and
averthwaite Railway
mb 153 B2
ham Sur 48 C3
ston Bridgend 40 D3
arsh Essex 87 D4
as Norf 120 C4
bden Borders 197 B6

Lamberhurst Kent 37 C4
Lamberhurst Quarter Kent 37 C4
Lamberton Borders 198 A3
Lambeth London 49 B6
Lambhill Glasgow 205 B5
Lambley Notts 115 A4
Lambley Northumb 177 D4
Lamborough Hill Oxon 65 C5
Lambourn W Berks 46 B1
Lambourne End Essex 69 D4
Lambs Green W Sus 35 C5
Lambston Pembs 55 C5
Lambton T & W 179 D4
Lamerton Devon 11 D5
Lamesley T & W 179 D4
Laminess Orkney 282 D7
Lamington Highld 264 C3
Lamington S Lnrk 195 C4
Lamlash N Ayrs 191 B6
Lamloch Dumfries 182 C3
Lamonby Cumb 164 B2
Lamorna Corn 2 C2
Lamorran Corn 4 C3
Lampardbrook Suff 88 A3
Lampeter = Llanbedr
 Pont Steffan Ceredig 75 D4
Lampeter Velfrey Pembs 56 A1
Lamphey Pembs 55 D6
Lamplugh Cumb 162 B3
Lamport Northants 99 D4
Lamyatt Som 29 B6
Lana Devon 10 B4
Lanark S Lnrk 194 B3
Lancaster Lancs 145 A4
Lancaster Leisure Park Lancs 145 A4
Lanchester Durham 167 A4
Lancing W Sus 21 B4
Landbeach Cambs 85 A6
Landcross Devon 25 C5
Landerberry Aberds 245 B4
Landford Wilts 31 D6
Landford Manor Wilts 31 C6
Landimore Swansea 57 C4
Landkey Devon 25 B6
Landore Swansea 57 C6
Landrake Corn 6 A2
Land's End Corn 2 C1
Land's End Airport Corn 2 C1
Landscove Devon 8 A1
Landshipping Pembs 55 C6
Landshipping Quay Pembs 55 C6
Landulph Corn 6 A3
Landwade Suff 86 A2
Lane Corn 4 A3
Lane End Bucks 66 D3
Lane End Cumb 153 A2
Lane End Dorset 16 B2
Lane End Hants 33 C4
Lane End I o W 19 C5
Lane End Lancs 146 C2
Lane Ends Lancs 146 D1
Lane Ends Lancs 146 B1
Lane Ends N Yorks 146 C3
Lane Head Derbys 129 B6
Lane Head Durham 166 D4
Lane Head Gtr Man 137 D5
Lane Head W Yorks 139 C4
Lane Side Lancs 137 A6
Laneast Corn 10 C3
Laneham Notts 132 B3
Lanehead Durham 165 A6
Lanehead Northumb 177 A5
Lanercost Cumb 176 C3
Laneshaw Bridge Lancs 146 C3
Lanfach Caerph 41 B7
Langar Notts 115 B5
Langbank Renfs 204 A3
Langbar N Yorks 147 B4
Langburnshiels Borders 186 C4
Langcliffe N Yorks 146 A2
Langdale Highld 278 D2
Langdale End N Yorks 160 B3
Langdon Corn 10 C4
Langdon Beck Durham 165 B6
Langdon Hills Essex 50 A3
Langdyke Fife 220 D3
Langenhoe Essex 71 B4
Langford Beds 84 C3
Langford Devon 13 A5
Langford Essex 70 C2
Langford Notts 132 D3
Langford Oxon 64 C3
Langford Budville Som 27 C6
Langham Essex 87 D6
Langham Norf 120 A2
Langham Rutland 115 D6

Langham Suff 103 E5
Langhaugh Borders 195 C7
Langho Lancs 145 D7
Langholm Dumfries 185 D6
Langleeford Northumb 188 A2
Langley Ches 129 B4
Langley Hants 18 A3
Langley Herts 68 A2
Langley Kent 37 A6
Langley Northumb 177 C6
Langley Slough 48 B3
Langley Warks 81 A4
Langley W Sus 33 C7
Langley Burrell Wilts 44 B3
Langley Common Derbys 113 B6
Langley Heath Kent 37 A6
Langley Lower Green Essex 85 D6
Langley Marsh Som 27 C5
Langley Park Durham 167 A5
Langley Street Norf 105 A4
Langley Upper Green Essex 85 D6
Langney E Sus 22 B4
Langold Notts 131 A5
Langore Corn 10 C4
Langport Som 28 C4
Langrick Lincs 117 A5
Langridge Bath 43 C6
Langridge Ford Devon 25 C6
Langrigg Cumb 175 D4
Langrish Hants 33 C6
Langsett S Yorks 139 C5
Langshaw Borders 197 C4
Langside Perth 218 C2
Langskaill Orkney 282 C5
Langstone Hants 19 A6
Langstone Newport 61 D5
Langthorne N Yorks 157 B6
Langthorpe N Yorks 148 A2
Langthwaite N Yorks 156 A4
Langtoft E Yorks 150 A3
Langtoft Lincs 116 D4
Langton Durham 167 D4
Langton Lincs 134 C2
Langton Lincs 134 B3
Langton N Yorks 149 A6
Langton by Wragby Lincs 133 B6
Langton Green Kent 36 C3
Langton Green Suff 104 D2
Langton Herring Dorset 15 C6
Langton Matravers Dorset 17 D4
Langtree Devon 25 D5
Langwathby Cumb 164 B3
Langwell Ho. Highld 275 B5
Langwell Lodge Highld 271 D4
Langwith Derbys 131 C5
Langwith Junction Derbys 131 C5
Langworth Lincs 133 B5
Lanhydrock House,
 Bodmin Corn 5 A5
Lanivet Corn 5 A5
Lanlivery Corn 5 B5
Lanner Corn 4 D2
Lanreath Corn 5 B6
Lansallos Corn 5 B6
Lansdown Glos 63 A5
Lanteglos Highway Corn 5 B6
Lanton Borders 187 A5
Lanton Northumb 198 C3
Lapford Devon 12 A2
Laphroaig Argyll 200 D3
Lapley Staffs 112 D2
Lapworth Warks 97 D4
Larachbeg Highld 225 B5
Larbert Falk 207 B6
Larden Green Ches 127 D5
Largie Aberds 255 C7
Largiemore Argyll 214 D2
Largoward Fife 221 D4
Largs N Ayrs 204 C2
Largybeg N Ayrs 191 C6
Largymore N Ayrs 191 C6
Larkfield Inclyd 204 A2
Larkhall S Lnrk 194 A2
Larkhill Wilts 31 A5
Larling Norf 103 C5
Larriston Borders 186 D4
Lartington Durham 166 D3
Lary Aberds 243 B6
Lasham Suff 33 A5
Lashenden Kent 37 B6
Lassington Glos 62 A3
Lassodie Fife 208 A4
Lastingham N Yorks 159 B6
Latcham Som 29 A4

Latchford Herts 68 A3
Latchford Warr 127 A6
Latchingdon Essex 70 C2
Latchley Corn 11 D5
Lately Common Warr 137 D5
Lathbury M Keynes 83 C5
Latheron Highld 275 A5
Latheronwheel Highld 275 A5
Latheronwheel Ho.
 Highld 275 A5
Lathones Fife 221 D4
Latimer Bucks 67 D5
Latteridge S Glos 43 A5
Lattiford Som 29 C6
Latton Wilts 64 D1
Latton Bush Essex 69 C4
Lauchintilly Aberds 245 A4
Lauder Borders 197 B4
Laugharne Carms 56 A3
Laughterton Lincs 132 B3
Laughton E Sus 22 A3
Laughton Leics 98 C3
Laughton Lincs 116 B3
Laughton Lincs 141 D6
Laughton Common
 S Yorks 131 A5
Laughton en le Morthen
 S Yorks 131 A5
Launcells Corn 10 A3
Launceston Corn 10 C4
Launton Oxon 65 A7
Laurencekirk Aberds 233 A5
Laurieston Dumfries 173 B4
Laurieston Falk 208 C2
Lavendon M Keynes 83 B6
Lavenham Suff 87 C5
Laverhay Dumfries 185 C4
Laversdale Cumb 176 C2
Laverstock Wilts 31 B5
Laverstoke Hants 32 A3
Laverton Glos 80 D3
Laverton N Yorks 157 D6
Laverton Som 44 D1
Lavister Wrex 126 D3
Law S Lnrk 194 A3
Lawers Perth 217 A6
Lawers Perth 218 B2
Lawford Essex 88 D1
Lawhitton Corn 11 C4
Lawkland N Yorks 146 A1
Lawley Telford 95 A4
Lawnhead Staffs 112 C2
Lawrenny Pembs 55 D6
Lawshall Suff 87 B4
Lawton Hereford 78 B2
Laxey I o M 152 C4
Laxey Wheel and Mines
 I o M 152 C4
Laxfield Suff 104 D3
Laxfirth Shetland 285 J6
Laxfirth Shetland 285 H6
Laxford Bridge Highld 276 D3
Laxo Shetland 285 G6
Laxobigging Shetland 284 F6
Laxton E Yorks 141 A5
Laxton Notts 132 C2
Laxton Northants 99 B6
Laycock W Yorks 147 C4
Layer Breton Essex 70 B3
Layer de la Haye Essex 70 B3
Layer Marney Essex 70 B3
Layham Suff 87 C6
Laylands Green W Berks 46 C1
Laytham E Yorks 149 D6
Layton Blkpool 144 D3
Lazenby Redcar 168 C3
Lazonby Cumb 164 B3
Le Planel Guern 6
Le Villocq Guern 6
Lea Derbys 130 D3
Lea Hereford 62 A2
Lea Lincs 132 A3
Lea Shrops 94 C1
Lea Shrops 94 A2
Lea Wilts 44 A3
Lea Marston Warks 97 B5
Lea Town Lancs 145 D4
Leabrooks Derbys 131 D4
Leac a Li W Isles 288 H2
Leachkin Highld 252 B2
Leadburn Midloth 196 A1
Leaden Roding Essex 69 B5
Leadenham Lincs 133 D4
Leadgate Cumb 165 A5
Leadgate Durham 178 D3
Leadgate Northumb 178 D3
Leadhills S Lnrk 183 A6

Leafield Oxon 64 B4
Leagrave Luton 67 A5
Leake N Yorks 158 B3
Leake Commonside Lincs 134 D3
Lealholm N Yorks 159 A6
Lealt Argyll 213 C4
Lealt Highld 259 B5
Leamington Hastings
 Warks 82 A1
Leamonsley Staffs 96 A4
Leamside Durham 167 A6
Leanaig Highld 252 A1
Leargybreck Argyll 201 A5
Leasgill Cumb 154 C3
Leasingham Lincs 116 A3
Leasingthorne Durham 167 C5
Leasowe Mers 136 D1
Leatherhead Sur 35 A4
Leatherhead Common Sur 35 A4
Leathley N Yorks 147 C6
Leaton Shrops 110 D3
Leaveland Kent 52 D2
Leavening N Yorks 149 A6
Leaves Green London 49 C7
Leazes Durham 178 D3
Lebberston N Yorks 161 C4
Lechlade-on-Thames Glos 64 D3
Leck Lancs 155 D5
Leckford Hants 32 B2
Leckfurin Highld 278 C3
Leckgruinart Argyll 200 B2
Leckhampstead Bucks 83 D4
Leckhampstead W Berks 46 B2
Leckhampstead Thicket
 W Berks 46 B2
Leckhampton Glos 63 B5
Leckie Highld 262 D2
Leckmelm Highld 262 A3
Leckwith V Glam 41 D6
Leconfield E Yorks 150 C3
Ledaig Argyll 226 C4
Ledburn Bucks 67 A4
Ledbury Hereford 79 D5
Ledcharrie Stirl 217 B5
Ledgemoor Hereford 78 B2
Ledicot Hereford 78 A2
Ledmore Highld 271 C5
Lednagullin Highld 278 B3
Ledsham Ches 126 B3
Ledsham W Yorks 140 A2
Ledston W Yorks 140 A2
Ledston Luck W Yorks 148 D3
Ledwell Oxon 65 A5
Lee Argyll 224 D3
Lee Devon 25 A5
Lee Hants 32 D2
Lee Lancs 145 B5
Lee Shrops 110 B3
Lee Brockhurst Shrops 111 C4
Lee Clump Bucks 67 C4
Lee Mill Devon 7 B5
Lee Moor Devon 7 A4
Lee-on-the-Solent Hants 19 A4
Leeans Shetland 285 J5
Leebotten Shetland 285 L6
Leebotwood Shrops 94 B2
Leece Lancs 153 D3
Leechpool Pembs 55 C5
Leeds Kent 37 A6
Leeds W Yorks 148 D1
Leeds Bradford
 International Airport
 W Yorks 147 C6
Leeds Castle Kent 37 A6
Leeds City Art Gallery
 W Yorks 148 D1
Leedstown Corn 3 B4
Leek Staffs 129 D4
Leek Wootton Warks 81 A5
Leekbrook Staffs 129 D4
Leeming N Yorks 157 C6
Leeming Bar N Yorks 157 B6
Lees Derbys 113 B6
Lees Gtr Man 138 C2
Lees W Yorks 147 D4
Leeswood Flint 126 C2
Legbourne Lincs 134 A3
Legerwood Borders 197 B4
Legoland Windsor 48 B2
Legsby Lincs 133 A6
Leicester Leics 98 A2
Leicester Forest East Leics 98 A2
Leicester Racecourse
 Leics 98 A3

Leigh Dorset 15 A6
Leigh Glos 63 A4
Leigh Gtr Man 137 C5
Leigh Kent 36 B3
Leigh Shrops 94 A1
Leigh Sur 35 B5
Leigh Wilts 63 D6
Leigh Worcs 79 B5
Leigh Beck Essex 51 A5
Leigh Common Som 30 C1
Leigh Delamere Wilts 44 B2
Leigh Green Kent 37 C7
Leigh on Sea Sthend 51 A5
Leigh Park Hants 19 A6
Leigh Sinton Worcs 79 B5
Leigh upon Mendip Som 29 A6
Leigh Woods N Som 43 B4
Leighswood W Mid 96 A3
Leighterton Glos 63 D4
Leighton N Yorks 157 D5
Leighton Powys 93 A6
Leighton Shrops 95 A4
Leighton Som 29 A7
Leighton Bromswold Cambs 100 D3
Leighton Buzzard Beds 67 A4
Leinthall Earls Hereford 78 A2
Leinthall Starkes Hereford 78 A2
Leintwardine Hereford 94 D2
Leire Leics 98 B2
Leirinmore Highld 277 B5
Leiston Suff 89 A5
Leitfie Perth 231 D6
Leith Edin 209 C5
Leitholm Borders 198 B1
Lelant Corn 2 B3
Lelley E Yorks 151 D5
Lem Hill Worcs 95 D5
Lemmington Hall Northumb 189 B4
Lempitlaw Borders 198 C1
Lenchwick Worcs 80 C3
Lendalfoot S Ayrs 180 C3
Lendrick Lodge Stirl 217 D5
Lenham Kent 37 A6
Lenham Heath Kent 37 B7
Lennel Borders 198 B2
Lennoxtown E Dunb 205 A6
Lenton Lincs 116 B3
Lenton Nottingham 114 B3
Lentran Highld 252 B1
Lenwade Norf 120 D2
Leny Ho. Stirl 217 D6
Lenzie E Dunb 205 A6
Leoch Angus 220 A3
Leochel-Cushnie Aberds 244 A2
Leominster Hereford 78 B2
Leonard Stanley Glos 63 C4
Leonardslee Gardens W Sus 35 D3
Leorin Argyll 200 D3
Lepe Hants 18 B3
Lephin Highld 258 D1
Lephinchapel Argyll 214 C2
Lephinmore Argyll 214 C2
Leppington N Yorks 149 A6
Lepton W Yorks 139 B5
Lerryn Corn 5 B6
Lerwick Shetland 285 J6
Lerwick (Tingwall) Airport Shetland 285 J6
Lesbury Northumb 189 B5
Leslie Aberds 255 D6
Leslie Fife 220 D2
Lesmahagow S Lnrk 194 C3
Lesnewth Corn 10 B2
Lessendrum Aberds 255 B6
Lessingham Norf 121 C5
Lessonhall Cumb 175 C5
Leswalt Dumfries 170 A2
Letchmore Heath Herts 67 D6
Letchworth Herts 84 D4
Letcombe Bassett Oxon 46 A1
Letcombe Regis Oxon 46 A1
Letham Angus 232 D3
Letham Falk 208 B1
Letham Fife 220 C3
Letham Perth 219 B5
Letham Grange Angus 233 D4
Lethenty Aberds 256 B3
Letheringham Suff 88 B3
Letheringsett Norf 120 B2
Lettaford Devon 12 C2
Lettan Orkney 282 C8

Letterewe Highld 261 C6
Letterfearn Highld 249 D5
Letterfinlay Highld 239 C6
Lettermorar Highld 235 B6
Lettermore Argyll 224 B3
Letters Highld 262 B3
Letterston Pembs 55 B5
Lettoch Highld 242 A3
Lettoch Highld 254 C1
Letton Hereford 78 C1
Letton Hereford 94 D1
Letton Green Norf 103 A5
Letty Green Herts 68 B2
Letwell S Yorks 131 A5
Leuchars Fife 221 B4
Leuchars Ho. Moray 266 C3
Leumrabhagh W Isles 288 F4
Levan Invclyd 204 A2
Levaneap Shetland 285 G6
Levedale Staffs 112 D2
Leven E Yorks 151 C4
Leven Fife 220 D3
Levencorroch N Ayrs 191 C6
Levens Cumb 154 C3
Levens Green Herts 68 A3
Levenshulme Gtr Man 138 D1
Levenwick Shetland 285 L6
Leverburgh = An t-Ob W Isles 287 F5
Leverington Cambs 118 D1
Leverton Lincs 117 A7
Leverton Highgate Lincs 117 A7
Leverton Lucasgate Lincs 117 A7
Leverton Outgate Lincs 117 A7
Levington Suff 88 D3
Levisham N Yorks 160 B2
Levishie Highld 240 A2
Lew Oxon 64 C4
Lewannick Corn 10 C3
Lewdown Devon 11 C5
Lewes E Sus 22 A2
Leweston Pembs 55 B5
Lewisham London 49 B6
Lewiston Highld 251 D7
Lewistown Bridgend 40 C4
Lewknor Oxon 66 D2
Leworthy Devon 10 A4
Leworthy Devon 26 B1
Lewtrenchard Devon 11 C5
Lexden Essex 70 A3
Ley Aberds 244 A2
Ley Corn 5 A6
Leybourne Kent 37 A4
Leyburn N Yorks 157 B5
Leyfields Staffs 97 A5
Leyhill Bucks 67 C4
Leyland Lancs 136 A4
Leylodge Aberds 245 A4
Leymoor W Yorks 139 B4
Leys Aberds 269 D5
Leys Perth 220 A2
Leys Castle Highld 252 B2
Leys of Cossans Angus 232 D1
Leysdown-on-Sea Kent 52 B2
Leysmill Angus 233 D4
Leysters Pole Hereford 78 A3
Leyton London 49 A6
Leytonstone London 49 A6
Lezant Corn 10 D4
Leziate Norf 118 D3
Lhanbryde Moray 266 C3
Liatrie Highld 250 C4
Libanus Powys 60 A1
Libberton S Lnrk 195 B4
Liberton Edin 209 D5
Liceasto W Isles 288 H2
Lichfield Staffs 96 A4
Lichfield Cathedral Staffs 113 D5
Lickey Worcs 96 D2
Lickey End Worcs 96 D2
Lickfold W Sus 34 D2
Liddel Orkney 283 K5
Liddesdale Highld 236 D1
Liddington Thamesdown 45 A6
Lidgate Suff 86 B3
Lidget S Yorks 141 C4
Lidget Green W Yorks 147 D5
Lidgett Notts 131 C6
Lidlington Beds 84 D1
Lidstone Oxon 65 A4
Lieurary Highld 279 B6
Liff Angus 220 A3
Lifton Devon 11 C4
Liftondown Devon 11 C4
Lighthorne Warks 81 B6
Lightwater Sur 48 C2
Lightwater Valley N Yorks 157 D6

Lightwood Stoke 112 A3
Lightwood Green Ches 111 A5
Lightwood Green Wrex 110 A2
Lilbourne Northants 98 D2
Lilburn Tower Northumb 188 A3
Lilleshall Telford 111 D6
Lilley Herts 67 A6
Lilley W Berks 46 B2
Lilliesleaf Borders 186 A4
Lillingstone Dayrell Bucks 83 D4
Lillingstone Lovell Bucks 83 C4
Lillington Dorset 29 D6
Lillington Warks 81 A6
Lilliput Poole 17 B4
Lilstock Som 27 A6
Lilyhurst Shrops 111 D6
Limbury Luton 67 A5
Limebrook Hereford 78 A1
Limefield Gtr Man 137 B7
Limekilnburn S Lnrk 194 A2
Limekilns Fife 208 B3
Limerigg Falk 207 C6
Limerstone I o W 18 C3
Limington Som 29 C5
Limpenhoe Norf 105 A4
Limpley Stoke Wilts 44 C1
Limpsfield Sur 36 A2
Limpsfield Chart Sur 36 A2
Linby Notts 131 D5
Linchmere W Sus 34 C1
Lincluden Dumfries 174 A2
Lincoln Lincs 133 B4
Lincoln Castle Lincs 133 B4
Lincoln Cathedral Lincs 133 B4
Lincomb Worcs 79 A6
Lincombe Devon 7 B6
Lindal in Furness Cumb 153 C3
Lindale Cumb 154 C3
Lindean Borders 196 C3
Lindfield W Sus 35 D6
Lindford Hants 33 B7
Lindifferon Fife 220 C3
Lindisfarne Priory, Holy Island Northumb 199 B5
Lindley W Yorks 139 B4
Lindley Green N Yorks 147 C6
Lindores Fife 220 C2
Lindridge Worcs 79 A4
Lindsell Essex 69 A6
Lindsey Suff 87 C5
Linford Hants 17 A5
Linford Thurrock 50 B3
Lingague I o M 152 D2
Lingards Wood W Yorks 138 B3
Lingbob W Yorks 147 D4
Lingdale Redcar 169 D4
Lingen Hereford 78 A1
Lingfield Sur 36 B1
Lingfield Park Racecourse Sur 36 B1
Lingreabhagh W Isles 287 F5
Lingwood Norf 105 A4
Linicro Highld 258 B3
Linkenholt Hants 46 D1
Linkhill Kent 37 D6
Linkinhorne Corn 10 D4
Linklater Orkney 283 K5
Linksness Orkney 283 G3
Linktown Fife 209 A5
Linley Shrops 94 B1
Linley Green Hereford 79 B4
Linlithgow W Loth 208 C3
Linlithgow Bridge W Loth 208 C2
Linshiels Northumb 188 C1
Linsiadar W Isles 288 D3
Linsidemore Highld 264 A1
Linslade Beds 67 A4
Linstead Parva Suff 104 D4
Linstock Cumb 176 D2
Linthwaite W Yorks 139 B4
Lintlaw Borders 198 A2
Lintmill Moray 267 C6
Linton Borders 187 A6
Linton Cambs 86 C1
Linton Derbys 113 D6
Linton Hereford 62 A2
Linton Kent 37 B5
Linton Northumb 189 D5
Linton N Yorks 146 A3
Linton W Yorks 148 C3
Linton-on-Ouse N Yorks 148 A3
Linwood Hants 17 A5
Linwood Lincs 133 A6
Linwood Renfs 205 B4
Lional W Isles 288 A6
Liphook Hants 34 C1

Liscard Mers 136 D2
Liscombe Som 26 B3
Liskeard Corn 6 A1
L'islet Guern 6
Liss Hants 33 C6
Liss Forest Hants 33 C6
Lissett E Yorks 151 B4
Lissington Lincs 133 A6
Lisvane Cardiff 41 C6
Liswerry Newport 42 A2
Litcham Norf 119 D5
Litchborough Northants 82 B3
Litchfield Hants 46 D2
Litherland Mers 136 D2
Litlington Cambs 85 C5
Litlington E Sus 22 B3
Little Abington Cambs 86 C1
Little Addington Northants 99 D6
Little Alne Warks 80 A4
Little Altcar Mers 136 C2
Little Asby Cumb 155 A5
Little Assynt Highld 271 B4
Little Aston Staffs 96 A3
Little Atherfield I o W 18 C3
Little Ayre Orkney 283 H4
Little Ayton N Yorks 168 D3
Little Baddow Essex 70 C1
Little Badminton S Glos 44 A2
Little Ballinluig Perth 230 C3
Little Bampton Cumb 175 C5
Little Bardfield Essex 86 D2
Little Barford Beds 84 B3
Little Barningham Norf 120 B3
Little Barrington Glos 64 B3
Little Barrow Ches 127 B4
Little Barugh N Yorks 159 D6
Little Bavington Northumb 178 B1
Little Bealings Suff 88 C3
Little Bedwyn Wilts 45 C6
Little Bentley Essex 71 A5
Little Berkhamsted Herts 68 C2
Little Billing Northants 83 A5
Little Birch Hereford 78 D3
Little Blakenham Suff 88 C2
Little Blencow Cumb 164 B2
Little Bollington Ches 128 A2
Little Bookham Sur 35 A4
Little Bowden Leics 99 C4
Little Bradley Suff 86 B2
Little Brampton Shrops 94 C1
Little Brechin Angus 232 B3
Little Brickhill M Keynes 83 D6
Little Brington Northants 82 A3
Little Bromley Essex 71 A4
Little Broughton Cumb 162 A3
Little Budworth Ches 127 C5
Little Burstead Essex 69 D6
Little Bytham Lincs 116 D3
Little Carlton Lincs 134 A3
Little Carlton Notts 132 D2
Little Casterton Rutland 100 A2
Little Cawthorpe Lincs 134 A3
Little Chalfont Bucks 67 D4
Little Chart Kent 38 A1
Little Chesterford Essex 85 C7
Little Cheverell Wilts 44 D3
Little Chishill Cambs 85 D6
Little Clacton Essex 71 B5
Little Clifton Cumb 162 B3
Little Colp Aberds 256 B2
Little Comberton Worcs 80 C2
Little Common E Sus 23 B5
Little Compton Warks 81 D5
Little Cornard Suff 87 D4
Little Cowarne Hereford 79 B4
Little Coxwell Oxon 64 D3
Little Crakehall N Yorks 157 B6
Little Cressingham Norf 103 A4
Little Crosby Mers 136 C2
Little Dalby Leics 115 D5
Little Dawley Telford 95 A4
Little Dens Aberds 257 B5
Little Dewchurch Hereford 78 D3
Little Downham Cambs 101 C7
Little Driffield E Yorks 150 B3
Little Dunham Norf 119 D5
Little Dunkeld Perth 230 D4
Little Dunmow Essex 69 A6
Little Easton Essex 69 A6
Little Eaton Derbys 114 A1
Little Eccleston Lancs 144 C4
Little Ellingham Norf 103 B6
Little End Essex 69 C5
Little Eversden Cambs 85 B5
Little Faringdon Oxon 64 C3
Little Fencote N Yorks 157 B6

Little Fenton N Yorks 148 D4
Little Finborough Suff 87 B6
Little Fransham Norf 119 D6
Little Gaddesden Herts 67 B4
Little Gidding Cambs 100 C3
Little Glemham Suff 88 B4
Little Glenshee Perth 219 A4
Little Gransden Cambs 85 B4
Little Green Som 29 A7
Little Grimsby Lincs 143 D5
Little Gruinard Highld 261 B6
Little Habton N Yorks 159 D6
Little Hadham Herts 68 A4
Little Hale Lincs 116 A4
Little Hallingbury Essex 69 B4
Little Hampden Bucks 66 C3
Little Harrowden Northants 99 D5
Little Haseley Oxon 66 C1
Little Hatfield E Yorks 151 C4
Little Hautbois Norf 121 C4
Little Haven Pembs 55 C4
Little Hay Staffs 96 A4
Little Hayfield Derbys 129 A5
Little Haywood Staffs 112 C4
Little Heath W Mid 97 C6
Little Hereford Hereford 78 A3
Little Horkesley Essex 87 D5
Little Horsted E Sus 22 A2
Little Horton W Yorks 147 D5
Little Horwood Bucks 83 D6
Little Houghton Northants 83 B5
Little Houghton S Yorks 140 C2
Little Hucklow Derbys 129 B6
Little Hulton Gtr Man 137 C6
Little Humber E Yorks 142 A3
Little Hungerford W Berks 46 B3
Little Irchester Northants 83 A6
Little Kimble Bucks 66 C3
Little Kineton Warks 81 B6
Little Kingshill Bucks 66 D3
Little Langdale Cumb 154 A2
Little Langford Wilts 31 B4
Little Laver Essex 69 C5
Little Leigh Ches 127 B5
Little Leighs Essex 69 B7
Little Lever Gtr Man 137 C6
Little London Bucks 66 B1
Little London E Sus 22 A3
Little London Hants 32 A4
Little London Hants 47 D4
Little London Lincs 117 C6
Little London Norf 120 A4
Little London Powys 92 C4
Little Longstone Derbys 130 B1
Little Lynturk Aberds 244 A3
Little Malvern Worcs 79 C5
Little Maplestead Essex 87 D4
Little Marcle Hereford 79 D4
Little Marlow Bucks 47 A6
Little Marsden Lancs 146 D2
Little Massingham Norf 119 C4
Little Melton Norf 104 A2
Little Mill Mon 61 C5
Little Milton Oxon 65 C7
Little Missenden Bucks 67 D4
Little Musgrave Cumb 165 D5
Little Ness Shrops 110 D3
Little Neston Ches 126 B2
Little Newcastle Pembs 55 B5
Little Newsham Durham 166 D4
Little Oakley Essex 71 A6
Little Oakley Northants 99 C5
Little Orton Cumb 175 C6
Little Ouseburn N Yorks 148 A3
Little Paxton Cambs 84 A3
Little Petherick Corn 9 D5
Little Pitlurg Moray 255 B5
Little Plumpton Lancs 144 D3
Little Plumstead Norf 121 D5
Little Ponton Lincs 116 B2
Little Raveley Cambs 101 D4
Little Reedness E Yorks 141 A6
Little Ribston N Yorks 148 B2
Little Rissington Glos 64 B2
Little Ryburgh Norf 119 C6
Little Ryle Northumb 188 B3
Little Salkeld Cumb 164 B3
Little Sampford Essex 86 D2
Little Sandhurst Brack 47 C6
Little Saxham Suff 86 A3
Little Scatwell Highld 251 A5
Little Sessay N Yorks 158 D3
Little Shelford Cambs 85 B6
Little Singleton Lancs 144 D3
Little Skillymarno Aberds 269 D4
Little Smeaton N Yorks 140 B3

Little Snoring Norf 119 B6
Little Sodbury S Glos 43 A6
Little Somborne Hants 32 B2
Little Somerford Wilts 44 A3
Little Stainforth N Yorks 146 A2
Little Stainton Darl 167 C6
Little Stanney Ches 127 B4
Little Staughton Beds 84 A3
Little Steeping Lincs 135 C4
Little Stoke Staffs 112 B3
Little Stonham Suff 88 A2
Little Stretton Leics 98 A3
Little Stretton Shrops 94 B2
Little Strickland Cumb 164 D3
Little Stukeley Cambs 100 D4
Little Sutton Ches 126 B3
Little Tew Oxon 65 A4
Little Thetford Cambs 102 D1
Little Thirkleby N Yorks 158 D3
Little Thurlow Suff 86 B2
Little Thurrock Thurrock 50 B3
Little Torboll Highld 264 A3
Little Torrington Devon 25 D5
Little Totham Essex 70 B2
Little Toux Aberds 267 D6
Little Town Cumb 163 C5
Little Town Lancs 145 D6
Little Urswick Cumb 153 C3
Little Wakering Essex 51 A6
Little Walden Essex 86 C1
Little Waldingfield Suff 87 C5
Little Walsingham Norf 119 B6
Little Waltham Essex 69 B7
Little Warley Essex 69 D6
Little Weighton E Yorks 150 D2
Little Weldon Northants 99 C6
Little Welnetham Suff 87 A4
Little Wenlock Telford 95 A4
Little Whittingham Green Suff 104 D3
Little Wilbraham Cambs 86 B1
Little Wishford Wilts 31 B4
Little Witley Worcs 79 A5
Little Wittenham Oxon 65 D6
Little Wolford Warks 81 D5
Little Wratting Suff 86 C2
Little Wymington Beds 83 A6
Little Wymondley Herts 68 A2
Little Wyrley Staffs 96 A3
Little Yeldham Essex 86 D3
Littlebeck N Yorks 160 A2
Littleborough Gtr Man 138 B2
Littleborough Notts 132 A3
Littlebourne Kent 53 D4
Littlebredy Dorset 15 C5
Littlebury Essex 85 D7
Littlebury Green Essex 85 D6
Littledean Glos 62 B2
Littleferry Highld 265 A4
Littleham Devon 13 C5
Littleham Devon 25 C5
Littlehampton W Sus 20 B3
Littlehempston Devon 8 A2
Littlehoughton Northumb 189 B5
Littlemill Aberds 243 C6
Littlemill E Ayrs 182 A2
Littlemill Highld 253 A5
Littlemill Northumb 189 B5
Littlemoor Dorset 15 C6
Littlemore Oxon 65 C6
Littleover Derby 114 B1
Littleport Cambs 102 C1
Littlestone on Sea Kent 38 C2
Littlethorpe Leics 98 B2
Littlethorpe N Yorks 148 A2
Littleton Ches 127 C4
Littleton Hants 32 B3
Littleton Perth 220 A2
Littleton Som 29 B4
Littleton Sur 48 C3
Littleton Sur 34 B2
Littleton Drew Wilts 44 A2
Littleton-on-Severn S Glos 43 A4
Littleton Pannell Wilts 44 D4
Littletown Durham 167 A6
Littlewick Green Windsor 47 B6
Littleworth Beds 84 C2
Littleworth Glos 63 C4
Littleworth Oxon 64 D4
Littleworth Staffs 112 D4
Littleworth Worcs 80 B1
Litton Derbys 129 B6
Litton N Yorks 156 D3
Litton Som 43 D4
Litton Cheney Dorset 15 B5
Liurbost W Isles 288 E4
Liverpool Mers 136 D2

Liverpool Airport Mers 127 A4
Liverpool Cathedral (C of E) Mers 126 A3
Liverpool Cathedral (RC) Mers 136 D2
Liverpool John Lennon Airport Mers 127 A4
Liversedge W Yorks 139 A5
Liverton Devon 12 D3
Liverton Redcar 169 D5
Livingston W Loth 208 D3
Livingston Village W Loth 208 D3
Lixwm Flint 125 B6
Lizard Corn 3 D5
Llaingoch Anglesey 122 B2
Laithddu Powys 93 C4
Llan Powys 91 B6
Llan Ffestiniog Gwyn 108 A2
Llan-y-pwll Wrex 126 D3
Llanaber Gwyn 90 A4
Llanaelhaearn Gwyn 106 B3
Llanafan Ceredig 75 A5
Llanafan-fawr Powys 76 B3
Llanallgo Anglesey 123 B4
Llanandras = Presteigne Powys 77 A7
Llanarmon Gwyn 107 C4
Llanarmon Dyffryn Ceiriog Wrex 109 B6
Llanarmon-yn-Ial Denb 126 D1
Llanarth Ceredig 73 A7
Llanarth Mon 61 B5
Llanarthne Carms 58 C2
Llanasa Flint 125 A6
Llanbabo Anglesey 122 B3
Llanbadarn Fawr Ceredig 90 D4
Llanbadarn Fynydd Powys 93 D5
Llanbadarn-y-Garreg Powys 77 C5
Llanbadoc Mon 61 C5
Llanbadrig Anglesey 122 A3
Llanbeder Newport 61 D5
Llanbedr Gwyn 107 D5
Llanbedr Powys 77 C5
Llanbedr Powys 60 A4
Llanbedr-Dyffryn-Clwyd Denb 125 D6
Llanbedr Pont Steffan = Lampeter Ceredig 75 D4
Llanbedr-y-cennin Conwy 124 C2
Llanbedrgoch Anglesey 123 B5
Llanbedrog Gwyn 106 C3
Llanberis Gwyn 123 D5
Llanbethêry V Glam 41 E5
Llanbister Powys 93 D5
Llanblethian V Glam 41 D5
Llanboidy Carms 73 D5
Llanbradach Caerph 41 B6
Llanbrynmair Powys 91 B6
Llancarfan V Glam 41 D5
Llancayo Mon 61 C5
Llancloudy Hereford 61 A6
Llancynfelyn Ceredig 90 C4
Llandaff Cardiff 41 D6
Llandanwg Gwyn 107 D5
Llandarcy Neath 40 B2
Llandawke Carms 56 A2
Llanddaniel Fab Anglesey 123 C4
Llanddarog Carms 57 A5
Llanddeiniol Ceredig 75 A4
Llanddeiniolen Gwyn 123 D5
Llandderfel Gwyn 109 B4
Llanddeusant Anglesey 122 B3
Llanddeusant Carms 59 C4
Llanddew Powys 77 D4
Llanddewi Swansea 57 D4
Llanddewi-Brefi Ceredig 75 C5
Llanddewi Rhydderch Mon 61 B5
Llanddewi Velfrey Pembs 56 A1
Llanddewi'r Cwm Powys 76 C4
Llanddoged Conwy 124 C3
Llanddona Anglesey 123 C5
Llanddowror Carms 56 A2
Llanddulas Conwy 125 B4
Llanddwywe Gwyn 107 D5
Llanddyfnan Anglesey 123 C5
Llandefaelog Fach Powys 76 D4
Llandefaelog-tre'r-graig Powys 77 E5
Llandefalle Powys 77 D4
Llandegai Gwyn 123 C5
Llandegfan Anglesey 123 C5
Llandegla Denb 126 D1
Llandegley Powys 77 A5
Llandegveth Mon 61 D5
Llandegwning Gwyn 106 C2

Llandeilo Carms 58 C3
Llandeilo Graban Powys 77 C4
Llandeilo'r Fan Powys 59 B5
Llandeloy Pembs 55 B4
Llandenny Mon 61 C6
Llandevenny Mon 42 A3
Llandewednock Corn 3 D5
Llandewi Ystradenny Powys 77 A5
Llandinabo Hereford 61 A7
Llandinam Powys 92 C4
Llandissilio Pembs 55 B7
Llandogo Mon 62 C1
Llandough V Glam 41 D4
Llandough V Glam 41 D6
Llandovery = Llanymddyfri Carms 59 B4
Llandow V Glam 40 D4
Llandre Ceredig 90 D4
Llandre Carms 58 A3
Llandrillo Denb 109 B5
Llandrillo-yn-Rhos Conwy 124 A3
Llandrindod = Llandrindod Wells Powys 77 A4
Llandrindod Wells = Llandrindod Powys 77 A4
Llandrinio Powys 110 D1
Llandudno Conwy 124 A2
Llandudno Junction = Cyffordd Llandudno Conwy 124 B2
Llandwrog Gwyn 107 A4
Llandybie Carms 57 A6
Llandyfaelog Carms 57 A4
Llandyfan Carms 57 A6
Llandyfriog Ceredig 73 B6
Llandyfrydog Anglesey 123 B4
Llandygwydd Ceredig 73 B5
Llandynan Denb 109 A6
Llandyrnog Denb 125 C6
Llandysilio Powys 110 D1
Llandyssil Powys 93 B5
Llandysul Ceredig 73 B7
Llanedeyrn Cardiff 41 C7
Llanedy Carms 57 B5
Llaneglwys Powys 77 D4
Llanegryn Gwyn 90 B3
Llanegwad Carms 58 C2
Llaneilian Anglesey 123 A4
Llanelian-yn-Rhos Conwy 124 B3
Llanelidan Denb 125 D6
Llanelieu Powys 77 D5
Llanellen Mon 61 B5
Llanelli Carms 57 C5
Llanelli Mon 60 D4
Llanelltyd Gwyn 91 A5
Llanelly Hill Mon 60 B4
Llanelwedd Powys 76 B4
Llanelwy = St Asaph Denb 125 B5
Llanenddwyn Gwyn 107 D5
Llanengan Gwyn 106 D2
Llanerchymedd Anglesey 123 B4
Llanerfyl Powys 92 A4
Llanfachraeth Anglesey 122 B3
Llanfachreth Gwyn 108 C2
Llanfaelog Anglesey 122 C3
Llanfaelrhys Gwyn 106 D2
Llanfaenor Mon 61 B6
Llanfaes Powys 76 D4
Llanfaes Anglesey 123 C6
Llanfaethlu Anglesey 122 B3
Llanfaglan Gwyn 123 D4
Llanfair Gwyn 107 D5
Llanfair-ar-y-bryn Carms 59 B5
Llanfair Caereinion Powys 93 A5
Llanfair Clydogau Ceredig 75 C5
Llanfair-Dyffryn-Clwyd Denb 125 D6
Llanfair-Nant-Gwyn Pembs 73 C4
Llanfair Talhaiarn Conwy 125 B4
Llanfair Waterdine Shrops 93 D6
Llanfair-ym-Muallt = Builth Wells Powys 76 B4
Llanfairfechan Conwy 124 B1
Llanfairpwll-gwyngyll Anglesey 123 C5
Llanfairyneubwll Anglesey 122 C3
Llanfairynghornwy Anglesey 122 A3
Llanfallteg Carms 56 A1
Llanfaredd Powys 77 B5
Llanfarian Ceredig 75 A4
Llanfechain Powys 109 C6

Llanfechan Powys 76 B3
Llanfechell Anglesey 122 A3
Llanfendigaid Gwyn 90 B3
Llanferres Denb 126 C1
Llanfflewyn Anglesey 122 B3
Llanfihangel-ar-arth Carms 58 B1
Llanfihangel-Crucorney Mon 61 A5
Llanfihangel Glyn Myfyr Conwy 109 A4
Llanfihangel Nant Bran Powys 59 B6
Llanfihangel-nant-Melan Powys 77 B5
Llanfihangel Rhydithon Powys 77 A5
Llanfihangel Rogiet Mon 42 A3
Llanfihangel Tal-y-llyn Powys 60 A3
Llanfihangel-uwch-Gwili Carms 58 C1
Llanfihangel-y-Creuddyn Ceredig 75 A5
Llanfihangel-y-pennant Gwyn 107 B5
Llanfihangel-y-pennant Gwyn 91 B4
Llanfihangel-y-traethau Gwyn 107 C5
Llanfihangel-yn-Ngwynfa Powys 109 D5
Llanfihangel yn Nhowyn Anglesey 122 C3
Llanfilo Powys 77 D5
Llanfoist Mon 61 B4
Llanfor Gwyn 108 B4
Llanfrechfa Torf 61 D5
Llanfrothen Gwyn 107 B6
Llanfrynach Powys 60 A2
Llanfwrog Anglesey 122 B3
Llanfwrog Denb 125 D6
Llanfyllin Powys 109 D6
Llanfynydd Carms 58 C2
Llanfynydd Flint 126 D2
Llanfyrnach Pembs 73 C5
Llangadfan Powys 109 D5
Llangadog Carms 59 C4
Llangadwaladr Anglesey 122 D3
Llangadwaladr Powys 109 B6
Llangaffo Anglesey 123 D4
Llangain Carms 56 A3
Llangammarch Wells Powys 76 C3
Llangan V Glam 41 D4
Llangarron Hereford 62 A1
Llangasty Talyllyn Powys 60 A3
Llangathen Carms 58 C2
Llangattock Powys 60 B4
Llangattock Lingoed Mon 61 A5
Llangattock nigh Usk Mon 61 C5
Llangattock-Vibon-Avel Mon 61 B6
Llangedwyn Powys 109 C6
Llangefni Anglesey 123 C4
Llangeinor Bridgend 40 C4
Llangeitho Ceredig 75 C5
Llangeler Carms 73 C6
Llangelynin Gwyn 90 B3
Llangendeirne Carms 57 A4
Llangennech Carms 57 B5
Llangennith Swansea 57 C4
Llangenny Powys 60 B4
Llangernyw Conwy 124 C3
Llangian Gwyn 106 D2
Llanglydwen Carms 73 D4
Llangoed Anglesey 123 C6
Llangoedmor Ceredig 73 B4
Llangollen Denb 109 A7
Llangolman Pembs 55 B7
Llangors Powys 60 A3
Llangovan Mon 61 C6
Llangower Gwyn 108 B4
Llangrannog Ceredig 73 A6
Llangristiolus Anglesey 123 C4
Llangrove Hereford 62 B1
Llangua Mon 61 A5
Llangunllo Powys 93 D6
Llangunnor Carms 57 A4
Llangurig Powys 92 D3
Llangwm Conwy 109 A4
Llangwm Mon 61 C6
Llangwm Pembs 55 D5
Llangwnnadl Gwyn 106 C2
Llangwyfan Denb 125 C5
Llangwyfan-isaf Anglesey 122 D3
Llangwyllog Anglesey 123 C4

Llangwyryfon Ceredig 75 A4
Llangybi Ceredig 75 C5
Llangybi Gwyn 107 B4
Llangybi Mon 61 D5
Llangyfelach Swansea 57 C6
Llangynhafal Denb 125 C6
Llangynidr Powys 60 B3
Llangynin Carms 56 A2
Llangynog Carms 56 A3
Llangynog Powys 109 C5
Llangynwyd Bridgend 40 C3
Llanhamlach Powys 60 A2
Llanharan Rhondda 41 C5
Llanharry Rhondda 41 C5
Llanhennock Mon 61 D5
Llanhiledd = Llanhilleth Bl Gwent 41 A7
Llanhilleth = Llanhiledd Bl Gwent 41 A7
Llanidloes Powys 92 C3
Llaniestyn Gwyn 106 C2
Llanifyny Powys 91 D6
Llanigon Powys 77 D6
Llanilar Ceredig 75 A5
Llanilid Rhondda 41 C4
Llanilltud Fawr = Llantwit Major V Glam 41 E4
Llanishen Cardiff 41 C6
Llanishen Mon 61 C6
Llanllawddog Carms 58 C1
Llanllechid Gwyn 123 D6
Llanllowell Mon 61 D5
Llanllugan Powys 93 A4
Llanllwch Carms 56 A3
Llanllwchaiarn Powys 93 B5
Llanllwni Carms 58 B1
Llanllyfni Gwyn 107 A4
Llanmadoc Swansea 57 C4
Llanmaes V Glam 41 E4
Llanmartin Newport 42 A2
Llanmihangel V Glam 41 D4
Llanmorlais Swansea 57 C5
Llannefydd Conwy 125 B4
Llannon Carms 57 B5
Llannor Gwyn 106 C3
Llanon Ceredig 75 B4
Llanover Mon 61 C5
Llanpumsaint Carms 73 D7
Llanreithan Pembs 55 B4
Llanrhaeadr Denb 125 C5
Llanrhaeadr-ym-Mochnant Powys 109 C6
Llanrhian Pembs 54 A4
Llanrhidian Swansea 57 C4
Llanrhos Conwy 124 A2
Llanrhyddlad Anglesey 122 B3
Llanrhystud Ceredig 75 B4
Llanrosser Hereford 77 D6
Llanrothal Hereford 61 B6
Llanrug Gwyn 123 D5
Llanrumney Cardiff 41 C7
Llanrwst Conwy 124 C3
Llansadurnen Carms 56 A2
Llansadwrn Anglesey 123 C5
Llansadwrn Carms 58 B3
Llansaint Carms 56 B3
Llansamlet Swansea 40 B1
Llansannan Conwy 125 C4
Llansannor V Glam 41 D4
Llansantffraed Ceredig 75 B4
Llansantffraed Powys 60 A3
Llansantffraed Cwmdeuddwr Powys 76 A3
Llansantffraed-in-Elvel Powys 77 B4
Llansantffraid-ym-Mechain Powys 109 C7
Llansawel Carms 58 B3
Llansilin Powys 109 C7
Llansoy Mon 61 C6
Llanspyddid Powys 60 A2
Llanstadwell Pembs 55 D5
Llansteffan Carms 56 A3
Llanstephan Powys 77 C5
Llantarnam Torf 61 D5
Llanteg Pembs 56 A1
Llanthony Mon 61 A4
Llantilio Crossenny Mon 61 B5
Llantilio Pertholey Mon 61 B5
Llantood Pembs 73 B4
Llantrisant Anglesey 122 B3
Llantrisant Mon 61 D5
Llantrisant Rhondda 41 C5
Llantrithyd V Glam 41 D5

Llantwit Fardre Rhondda 41 C5
Llantwit Major =
Llanilltud Fawr V Glam 41 E4
Llanuwchllyn Gwyn 108 B3
Llanvaches Newport 61 D6
Llanvair Discoed Mon 61 D6
Llanvapley Mon 61 B5
Llanvetherine Mon 61 B5
Llanveynoe Hereford 77 D7
Llanvihangel Gobion Mon 61 C5
Llanvihangel-Ystern-
Llewern Mon 61 B6
Llanwarne Hereford 61 A7
Llanwddyn Powys 109 D5
Llanwenog Ceredig 74 D3
Llanwern Newport 42 A2
Llanwinio Carms 73 D5
Llanwnda Gwyn 107 A4
Llanwnda Pembs 72 C2
Llanwnnen Ceredig 75 D4
Llanwnog Powys 92 B4
Llanwrda Carms 59 B4
Llanwrin Powys 91 B5
Llanwrthwl Powys 76 A3
Llanwrtyd = Llanwrtyd
Wells Powys 76 C2
Llanwrtyd Powys 76 C2
Llanwrtyd Wells =
Llanwrtyd Powys 76 C2
Llanwyddelan Powys 93 A4
Llanyblodwel Shrops 110 C1
Llanybri Carms 56 A3
Llanybydder Carms 58 A2
Llanycefn Pembs 55 B6
Llanychaer Pembs 72 C2
Llanycil Gwyn 108 B4
Llanycrwys Carms 75 D5
Llanymawddwy Gwyn 91 A7
Llanymddyfri =
Llandovery Carms 59 B4
Llanymynech Powys 110 C1
Llanynghenedl Anglesey 122 B3
Llanynys Denb 125 C6
Llanyre Powys 76 A4
Llanystumdwy Gwyn 107 C4
Llanywern Powys 60 A3
Llawhaden Pembs 55 C6
Llawnt Shrops 110 B1
Llawr Dref Gwyn 106 D2
Llawryglyn Powys 92 B3
Llay Wrex 126 D3
Llechcynfarwy Anglesey 122 B3
Llecheiddior Gwyn 107 B4
Llechfaen Powys 60 A2
Llechryd Caerph 60 C3
Llechryd Ceredig 73 B5
Llechrydau Powys 110 B1
Llechwedd Slate
Caverns, Blaenau
Ffestiniog Gwyn 108 A2
Lledrod Ceredig 75 A5
Llenmerewig Powys 93 B5
Llethrid Swansea 57 C5
Llidiad Nenog Carms 58 B2
Llidiardau Gwyn 108 B3
Llidiart-y-parc Denb 109 A6
Llithfaen Gwyn 106 B3
Llong Flint 126 C2
Llowes Powys 77 C5
Llundain-fach Ceredig 75 C4
Llwydcoed Rhondda 41 A4
Llwyn Shrops 93 C6
Llwyn-du Mon 61 B4
Llwyn-hendy Carms 57 C5
Llwyn-têg Carms 57 B5
Llwyn-y-brain Carms 76 A1
Llwyn-y-groes Ceredig 75 C4
Llwyncelyn Ceredig 74 C3
Llwyndafydd Ceredig 73 A6
Llwynderw Powys 93 A6
Llwyndyrys Gwyn 106 B3
Llwyngwril Gwyn 90 B3
Llwynmawr Wrex 110 B1
Llwynypia Rhondda 41 B4
Llynclys Shrops 110 C1
Llynfaes Anglesey 123 C4
Llys-y-frân Pembs 55 B6
Llysfaen Conwy 124 B3
Llyswen Powys 77 D5
Llysworney V Glam 41 D4
Llywel Powys 59 B5
Loan Falk 208 C2
Loanend Northumb 198 A3
Loanhead Midloth 209 D5

Loans S Ayrs 192 B3
Loans of Tullich Highld 265 C4
Lobb Devon 25 B5
Loch a Charnain W Isles 286 B4
Loch a'Ghainmhich
W Isles 288 E3
Loch Baghasdail =
Lochboisdale W Isles 286 E3
Loch Choire Lodge Highld 273 A4
Loch Euphoirt W Isles 287 H3
Loch Head Dumfries 171 C5
Loch Loyal Lodge Highld 277 D7
Loch nam Madadh =
Lochmaddy W Isles 287 H4
Loch Ness Monster
Exhibition,
Drumnadrochit Highld 252 C1
Loch Sgioport W Isles 286 C4
Lochailort Highld 235 B6
Lochaline Highld 225 B5
Lochanhully Highld 253 D5
Lochans Dumfries 170 B2
Locharbriggs Dumfries 184 D2
Lochassynt Lodge Highld 271 B4
Lochavich Ho. Argyll 214 A2
Lochawe Argyll 227 D6
Lochboisdale = Loch
Baghasdail W Isles 286 E3
Lochbuie Argyll 225 D5
Lochcarron Highld 249 C5
Lochdhu Highld 279 D6
Lochdochart House Stirl 216 B4
Lochdon Argyll 225 C6
Lochdrum Highld 263 C4
Lochead Argyll 202 A2
Lochearnhead Stirl 217 B5
Lochee Dundee 220 A3
Lochend Highld 252 C1
Lochend Highld 281 B4
Locherben Dumfries 184 C2
Lochfoot Dumfries 173 A6
Lochgair Argyll 214 C2
Lochgarthside Highld 240 A3
Lochgelly Fife 209 A4
Lochgilphead Argyll 214 D1
Lochgoilhead Argyll 215 B5
Lochhill Moray 266 C3
Lochindorb Lodge Highld 253 C5
Lochinver Highld 270 B3
Lochlane Perth 218 B3
Lochluichart Highld 263 D5
Lochmaben Dumfries 184 D3
Lochmaddy = Loch nam
Madadh W Isles 287 H4
Lochmore Cottage Highld 280 D2
Lochmore Lodge Highld 271 A5
Lochore Fife 209 A4
Lochportain W Isles 287 G4
Lochranza N Ayrs 203 C4
Lochs Crofts Moray 266 C4
Lochside Aberds 233 B5
Lochside Highld 277 C5
Lochside Highld 274 A2
Lochside Highld 253 A4
Lochslin Highld 265 B4
Lochstack Lodge Highld 276 D3
Lochton Aberds 245 C4
Lochty Angus 232 B3
Lochty Fife 221 D5
Lochty Perth 219 B5
Lochuisge Highld 236 D1
Lochurr Dumfries 183 D5
Lochwinnoch Renfs 204 C3
Lochwood Dumfries 184 C3
Lochyside Highld 237 B5
Lockengate Corn 5 A5
Lockerbie Dumfries 185 D4
Lockeridge Wilts 45 C5
Lockerley Hants 32 C1
Locking N Som 42 D2
Lockinge Oxon 46 A2
Lockington E Yorks 150 C2
Lockington Leics 114 C2
Lockleywood Shrops 111 C5
Locks Heath Hants 18 A4
Lockton N Yorks 160 B2
Lockwood W Yorks 139 B4
Locomotive Museum,
Shildon Durham 167 C5
Loddington Leics 99 A4
Loddington Northants 99 D5
Loddiswell Devon 7 C6
Loddon Norf 105 B4
Lode Cambs 86 A1
Loders Dorset 15 B4
Lodsworth W Sus 34 D2
Lofthouse N Yorks 157 D5

Lofthouse W Yorks 139 A6
Loftus Redcar 169 D5
Logan F Ayrs 193 C5
Logan Mains Dumfries 170 C2
Loganlea W Loth 208 D2
Loggerheads Staffs 111 B6
Logie Angus 233 B4
Logie Fife 220 B4
Logie Moray 253 A6
Logie Coldstone Aberds 244 B1
Logie Hill Highld 264 C3
Logie Newton Aberds 256 C1
Logie Pert Angus 233 B4
Logiealmond Lodge
Perth 219 A4
Logierait Perth 230 C3
Login Carms 73 D4
Lolworth Cambs 85 A5
Lonbain Highld 248 A3
Londesborough E Yorks 150 C1
London, City of = City of
London London 49 A6
London City Airport
London 50 A1
London Colney Herts 68 C1
London Gatwick Airport
W Sus 35 B5
London Heathrow Airport
London 48 B3
London Luton Airport
Luton 67 A6
London Stansted Airport
Essex 69 A5
London Zoo London 49 A5
Londonderry N Yorks 157 C7
Londonthorpe Lincs 116 B2
Londubh Highld 261 B5
Lonemore Highld 264 B3
Long Ashton N Som 43 B4
Long Bennington Lincs 115 A6
Long Bredy Dorset 15 B5
Long Buckby Northants 82 A3
Long Clawson Leics 115 C5
Long Common Hants 32 D4
Long Compton Staffs 112 C2
Long Compton Warks 81 D5
Long Crendon Bucks 66 C1
Long Crichel Dorset 30 D3
Long Ditton Sur 49 C4
Long Drax N Yorks 141 A4
Long Duckmanton Derbys 131 B4
Long Eaton Derbys 114 B2
Long Green Worcs 79 D6
Long Hanborough Oxon 65 B5
Long Itchington Warks 81 A7
Long Lawford Warks 98 D1
Long Load Som 29 C4
Long Marston Herts 66 B3
Long Marston N Yorks 148 B4
Long Marston Warks 81 C4
Long Marton Cumb 165 C4
Long Melford Suff 87 C4
Long Newnton Glos 63 D5
Long Newton E Loth 210 D2
Long Preston N Yorks 146 B2
Long Riston E Yorks 151 C4
Long Sight Gtr Man 138 C2
Long Stratton Norf 104 B2
Long Street M Keynes 83 C4
Long Sutton Hants 33 A6
Long Sutton Lincs 118 C1
Long Sutton Som 29 C4
Long Thurlow Suff 87 A6
Long Whatton Leics 114 C2
Long Wittenham Oxon 65 D6
Longbar N Ayrs 204 C3
Longbenton T & W 179 C4
Longborough Glos 64 A2
Longbridge Warks 81 A5
Longbridge W Mid 96 D3
Longbridge Deverill Wilts 30 A2
Longburton Dorset 29 D6
Longcliffe Derbys 130 D2
Longcot Oxon 64 D3
Longcroft Falk 207 C5
Longden Shrops 94 A2
Longdon Staffs 113 D4
Longdon Worcs 79 D6
Longdon Green Staffs 113 D4
Longdon on Tern Telford 111 D5
Longdown Devon 12 B3
Longdowns Corn 3 C6
Longfield Kent 50 C3
Longfield Shetland 285 M5
Longford Derbys 113 B6
Longford Glos 63 A4
Longford London 48 B3

Longford Shrops 111 B5
Longford Telford 111 D6
Longford W Mid 97 C6
Longfordlane Derbys 113 B6
Longforgan Perth 220 B3
Longformacus Borders 197 A5
Longframlington
Northumb 189 C4
Longham Dorset 17 B4
Longham Norf 119 D6
Longhaven Aberds 257 C6
Longhill Aberds 269 D4
Longhirst Northumb 179 A4
Longhope Glos 62 B2
Longhope Orkney 283 H4
Longhorsley Northumb 189 D4
Longhoughton Northumb 189 B5
Longlane Derbys 113 B6
Longlane W Berks 46 B2
Longleat, Warminster
Wilts 30 A2
Longlevens Glos 63 A4
Longley W Yorks 129 C4
Longley Green Worcs 79 B5
Longmanhill Aberds 268 C2
Longmoor Camp Hants 33 B6
Longmorn Moray 266 D3
Longnewton Borders 187 A4
Longnewton Stockton 167 D6
Longney Glos 62 B3
Longniddry E Loth 210 C1
Longnor Shrops 94 A2
Longnor Staffs 129 C5
Longparish Hants 32 A3
Longport Stoke 112 A2
Longridge Lancs 145 D6
Longridge Staffs 112 D3
Longridge W Loth 208 D2
Longriggend N Lnrk 207 C6
Longsdon Staffs 129 D4
Longshaw Gtr Man 136 C4
Longside Aberds 257 B5
Longstanton Cambs 85 A5
Longstock Hants 32 B2
Longstone Pembs 56 B1
Longstowe Cambs 85 B5
Longthorpe P'boro 100 B3
Longthwaite Cumb 164 C2
Longton Lancs 136 A3
Longton Stoke 112 A3
Longtown Cumb 175 B6
Longtown Hereford 61 A5
Longview Mers 136 D3
Longville in the Dale
Shrops 94 B3
Longwick Bucks 66 C2
Longwitton Northumb 178 A2
Longwood Shrops 95 A4
Longworth Oxon 65 D4
Longyester E Loth 210 D2
Lonmay Aberds 269 C5
Lonmore Highld 258 D2
Looe Corn 6 B1
Loose Kent 37 A5
Loosley Row Bucks 66 C3
Lopcombe Corner Wilts 31 B6
Lopen Som 28 D4
Loppington Shrops 110 C3
Lopwell Devon 6 A3
Lorbottle Northumb 188 C3
Lorbottle Hall Northumb 188 C3
Lord's Cricket Ground
London 49 A5
Lornty Perth 231 D5
Loscoe Derbys 114 A2
Losgaintir W Isles 287 E5
Lossiemouth Moray 266 B3
Lossit Argyll 200 C1
Lostford Shrops 111 B5
Lostock Gralam Ches 128 B1
Lostock Green Ches 128 B1
Lostock Hall Lancs 136 A4
Lostock Junction Gtr Man 137 C5
Lostwithiel Corn 5 B6
Loth Orkney 282 D7
Lothbeg Highld 274 C3
Lothersdale N Yorks 146 C3
Lothmore Highld 274 C3
Loudwater Bucks 67 D4
Loughborough Leics 114 D3
Loughor Swansea 57 C5
Loughton Essex 68 D4
Loughton M Keynes 83 D5
Loughton Shrops 95 C4
Louis Tussaud's
Waxworks Blkpool 144 D3
Lound Lincs 116 D3

Lound Notts 132 A1
Lound Suff 105 B6
Louth Lincs 134 A3
Love Clough Lancs 137 A7
Lovedean Hants 33 D5
Lover Wilts 31 C6
Loversall S Yorks 140 D3
Loves Green Essex 69 C6
Lovesome Hill N Yorks 158 B2
Loveston Pembs 55 D6
Lovington Som 29 B5
Low Ackworth W Yorks 140 B2
Low Barlings Lincs 133 B5
Low Bentham N Yorks 145 A6
Low Bradfield S Yorks 139 D5
Low Bradley N Yorks 147 C4
Low Braithwaite Cumb 164 A3
Low Brunton Northumb 177 B2
Low Burnham N Lincs 141 C5
Low Burton N Yorks 157 C6
Low Buston Northumb 189 C5
Low Catton E Yorks 149 B6
Low Clanyard Dumfries 170 D3
Low Coniscliffe Darl 167 D5
Low Crosby Cumb 176 D2
Low Dalby N Yorks 160 C2
Low Dinsdale Darl 167 D6
Low Ellington N Yorks 157 C6
Low Etherley Durham 167 C4
Low Fell T & W 179 D4
Low Fulney Lincs 117 C5
Low Garth N Yorks 159 A6
Low Gate Northumb 177 C7
Low Grantley N Yorks 157 D6
Low Habberley Worcs 95 D6
Low Ham Som 28 C4
Low Hesket Cumb 164 A2
Low Hesleyhurst
Northumb 188 D2
Low Hutton N Yorks 149 A6
Low Laithe N Yorks 147 A5
Low Leighton Derbys 129 A5
Low Lorton Cumb 163 B4
Low Marishes N Yorks 159 D6
Low Marnham Notts 132 C3
Low Mill N Yorks 159 B5
Low Moor Lancs 146 C1
Low Moor W Yorks 139 A4
Low Moorsley T & W 167 A6
Low Newton Cumb 154 C3
Low Newton-by-the-Sea
Northumb 189 A5
Low Row Cumb 163
Low Row Cumb 176
Low Row N Yorks 156
Low Salchrie Dumfries 170
Low Smerby Argyll 190
Low Torry Fife 208
Low Worsall N Yorks 158
Low Wray Cumb 154
Lowbridge House Cumb 154
Lowca Cumb 162
Lowdham Notts 115
Lowe Shrops 111
Lowe Hill Staffs 129
Lower Aisholt Som 28
Lower Arncott Oxon 65
Lower Ashton Devon 12
Lower Assendon Oxon 47
Lower Badcall Highld 276
Lower Bartle Lancs 145
Lower Basildon W Berks 47
Lower Beeding W Sus 35
Lower Benefield
Northants 100
Lower Boddington
Northants 82
Lower Brailes Warks 81
Lower Breakish Highld 247
Lower Broadheath Worcs 79
Lower Bullingham
Hereford 78
Lower Cam Glos 62
Lower Chapel Powys 76
Lower Chute Wilts 45
Lower Cragabus Argyll 20
Lower Crossings 12
Lower Cumberworth
W Yorks 13
Lower Cwm-twrch Powys 13
Lower Darwen Blkburn 13
Lower Dean Beds 8
Lower Diabaig Highld 26
Lower Dicker E Sus 2
Lower Dinchope Shrops 9
Lower Down Shrops 9

Lower Drift Corn 2 C2
Lower Dunsforth N Yorks 148 A3
Lower Egleton Hereford 79 C4
Lower Elkstone Staffs 129 D5
Lower End Beds 67 A4
Lower Everleigh Wilts 45 D5
Lower Farringdon Hants 33 B6
Lower Foxdale I o M 152 D2
Lower Frankton Shrops 110 B2
Lower Froyle Hants 33 A6
Lower Gledfield Highld 264 A1
Lower Green Norf 120 B1
Lower Hacheston Suff 88 B4
Lower Halistra Highld 258 C2
Lower Halstow Kent 51 C5
Lower Hardres Kent 52 D3
Lower Hawthwaite Cumb 153 B3
Lower Heath Ches 128 C3
Lower Hempriggs Moray 266 C2
Lower Hergest Hereford 77 B6
Lower Heyford Oxon 65 A5
Lower Higham Kent 51 B4
Lower Holbrook Suff 88 D2
Lower Hordley Shrops 110 C2
Lower Horsebridge E Sus 22 A3
Lower Killeyan Argyll 200 D2
Lower Kingswood Sur 35 A5
Lower Kinnerton Ches 126 C3
Lower Langford N Som 42 C3
Lower Largo Fife 220 D4
Lower Leigh Staffs 112 B4
Lower Lemington Glos 81 D5
Lower Lenie Highld 251 D7
Lower Lydbrook Glos 62 B1
Lower Lye Hereford 78 A2
Lower Machen Newport 42 A1
Lower Maes-coed Hereford 78 D1
Lower Mayland Essex 70 C3
Lower Midway Derbys 113 C7
Lower Milovaig Highld 258 C1
Lower Moor Worcs 80 C2
Lower Nazeing Essex 68 C3
Lower Netchwood Shrops 95 B4
Lower Ollach Highld 247 A4
Lower Penarth V Glam 41 D6
Lower Penn Staffs 95 B6
Lower Pennington Hants 18 B2
Lower Peover Ches 128 B2
Lower Pexhill Ches 128 B3
Lower Place Gtr Man 138 B2
Lower Quinton Warks 81 C4
Lower Rochford Worcs 79 A4
Lower Seagry Wilts 44 A3
Lower Shelton Beds 84 C1
Lower Shiplake Oxon 47 B5
Lower Shuckburgh Warks 82 A1
Lower Slaughter Glos 64 A2
Lower Stanton St Quintin Wilts 44 A3
Lower Stoke Medway 51 B5
Lower Stondon Beds 84 D3
Lower Stow Bedon Norf 103 B5
Lower Street Norf 121 B4
Lower Street Norf 121 D5
Lower Strensham Worcs 80 C2
Lower Stretton Warr 127 A6
Lower Sundon Beds 67 A5
Lower Swanwick Hants 18 A3
Lower Swell Glos 64 A2
Lower Tean Staffs 112 B4
Lower Thurlton Norf 105 B5
Lower Tote Highld 259 B5
Lower Town Pembs 72 C2
Lower Tysoe Warks 81 C6
Lower Upham Hants 32 D4
Lower Vexford Som 27 B6
Lower Weare Som 42 D3
Lower Welson Hereford 77 B6
Lower Whitley Ches 127 B6
Lower Wield Hants 33 A5
Lower Winchendon Bucks 66 B2
Lower Withington Ches 128 C3
Lower Woodend Bucks 47 A6
Lower Woodford Wilts 31 B5
Lower Wyche Worcs 79 C5
Lowesby Leics 99 A4
Lowestoft Suff 105 B6
Loweswater Cumb 163 B4
Lowford Hants 32 D3
Lowgill Cumb 155 B5
Lowgill Lancs 145 A6
Lowick Northants 100 C1
Lowick Northumb 198 C4
Lowick Bridge Cumb 154 C1
Lowick Green Cumb 154 C1
Lowlands Torf 61 D4

Lowmoor Row Cumb 165 C4
Lownie Moor Angus 232 D2
Lowsonford Warks 81 A4
Lowther Cumb 164 C3
Lowthorpe E Yorks 150 A3
Lowton Gtr Man 137 D5
Lowton Common Gtr Man 137 D5
Loxbeare Devon 27 D4
Loxhill Sur 34 C3
Loxhore Devon 25 B7
Loxley Warks 81 B5
Loxton N Som 42 D2
Loxwood W Sus 34 C3
Lubcroy Highld 271 D6
Lubenham Leics 99 C4
Luccombe Som 27 A4
Luccombe Village I o W 19 D4
Lucker Northumb 199 C5
Luckett Corn 11 D4
Luckington Wilts 44 A2
Lucklawhill Fife 220 B4
Luckwell Bridge Som 27 B4
Lucton Hereford 78 A2
Ludag W Isles 286 E3
Ludborough Lincs 143 D4
Ludchurch Pembs 56 A1
Luddenden W Yorks 138 A3
Luddenden Foot W Yorks 138 A3
Luddesdown Kent 50 C3
Luddington N Lincs 141 B6
Luddington Warks 81 B4
Luddington in the Brook Northants 100 C3
Lude House Perth 230 B2
Ludford Lincs 134 A2
Ludford Shrops 94 D3
Ludgershall Bucks 66 B1
Ludgershall Wilts 45 D6
Ludgvan Corn 2 B3
Ludham Norf 121 D5
Ludlow Shrops 94 D3
Ludlow Racecourse Shrops 94 D2
Ludwell Wilts 30 C3
Ludworth Durham 167 A6
Luffincott Devon 10 B4
Lugar E Ayrs 193 C5
Lugg Green Hereford 78 A2
Luggate Burn E Loth 210 C3
Luggiebank N Lanrk 207 C5
Lugton E Ayrs 205 C4
Lugwardine Hereford 78 C3
Luib Highld 247 B4
Lulham Hereford 78 C2
Lullenden Sur 36 B2
Lullington Derbys 113 D6
Lullington Som 44 D1
Lulsgate Bottom N Som 43 C4
Lulsley Worcs 79 B5
Lulworth Castle Dorset 16 C2
Lumb W Yorks 138 A3
Lumby N Yorks 148 D3
Lumloch E Dunb 205 B6
Lumphanan Aberds 244 B2
Lumphinnans Fife 209 A4
Lumsdaine Borders 211 D5
Lumsden Aberds 255 D5
Lunan Angus 233 C4
Lunanhead Angus 232 C2
Luncarty Perth 219 B5
Lund E Yorks 150 C2
Lund N Yorks 149 D5
Lund Shetland 284 C7
Lunderton Aberds 269 E6
Lundie Angus 220 A2
Lundie Highld 239 A5
Lundin Links Fife 220 D4
Lunga Argyll 213 B5
Lunna Shetland 284 G6
Lunning Shetland 284 G7
Lunnon Swansea 57 D5
Lunsford's Cross E Sus 23 A5
Lunt Mers 136 C2
Luntley Hereford 78 B1
Luppitt Devon 13 A6
Lupset W Yorks 139 B6
Lupton Cumb 155 C4
Lurgashall W Sus 34 D2
Lusby Lincs 134 C3
Luson Devon 7 C5
Luss Argyll 206 A1
Lussagiven Argyll 213 D4
Lusta Highld 258 C2
Lustleigh Devon 12 C2
Luston Hereford 78 A2
Luthermuir Aberds 233 B4
Luthrie Fife 220 C3
Luton Devon 13 D4

Luton Luton 67 A5
Luton Medway 51 C4
Lutterworth Leics 98 C2
Lutton Devon 7 B4
Lutton Lincs 118 C1
Lutton Northants 100 C3
Lutworthy Devon 26 D2
Luxborough Som 27 B4
Luxulyan Corn 5 B5
Lybster Highld 275 A6
Lydbury North Shrops 94 C1
Lydcott Devon 26 B1
Lydd Kent 38 C2
Lydd on Sea Kent 38 C2
Lydden Kent 39 A4
Lydden Motor Racing Circuit Kent 39 A4
Lyddington Rutland 99 B5
Lyde Green Hants 47 D5
Lydeard St Lawrence Som 27 B6
Lydford Devon 11 C6
Lydford-on-Fosse Som 29 B5
Lydgate W Yorks 138 A2
Lydham Shrops 94 B1
Lydiard Green Wilts 45 A4
Lydiard Millicent Wilts 45 A4
Lydiate Mers 136 C2
Lydlinch Dorset 30 D1
Lydney Glos 62 C2
Lydstep Pembs 55 E6
Lye W Mid 96 C2
Lye Cross N Som 42 C3
Lye Green Bucks 67 C4
Lye Green E Sus 36 C3
Lyford Oxon 65 D4
Lymbridge Green Kent 38 A3
Lyme Park, Disley Ches 129 A4
Lyme Regis Dorset 14 B3
Lyminge Kent 38 A3
Lymington Hants 18 B2
Lyminster W Sus 20 B3
Lymm Warr 128 A1
Lymore Hants 18 B1
Lympne Kent 38 B3
Lympsham Som 42 D2
Lympstone Devon 13 C4
Lynchat Highld 241 B5
Lyndale Ho. Highld 258 C3
Lyndhurst Hants 18 A2
Lyndon Rutland 99 A6
Lyne Sur 48 C3
Lyne Down Hereford 79 D4
Lyne of Gorthleck Highld 252 D1
Lyne of Skene Aberds 245 A4
Lyneal Shrops 110 B3
Lyneham Oxon 64 A3
Lyneham Wilts 44 B4
Lynemore Highld 253 D6
Lynemouth Northumb 189 D5
Lyness Orkney 283 H4
Lyng Norf 120 D2
Lyng Som 28 C3
Lynmouth Devon 26 A2
Lynsted Kent 51 C6
Lynton Devon 26 A2
Lynton & Lynmouth Cliff Railway Devon 26 A2
Lyon's Gate Dorset 15 A6
Lyonshall Hereford 78 B1
Lytchett Matravers Dorset 16 B3
Lytchett Minster Dorset 16 B3
Lyth Highld 281 B4
Lytham Lancs 136 A2
Lytham St Anne's Lancs 136 A2
Lythe N Yorks 169 D6
Lythes Orkney 283 K5

M

Mabe Burnthouse Corn 4 D2
Mabie Dumfries 174 A2
Mablethorpe Lincs 135 A5
Macclesfield Ches 129 B4
Macclesfield Forest Ches 129 B4
Macduff Aberds 268 C2
Mace Green Suff 88 C2
Macharioch Argyll 190 E3
Machen Caerph 41 C7
Machrihanish Argyll 190 C2
Machynlleth Powys 91 B5
Machynys Carms 57 C5
Mackerel's Common W Sus 34 D3
Mackworth Derbys 113 B7
Macmerry E Loth 210 C1
Madame Tussaud's London 49 A5
Madderty Perth 219 B4

Maddiston Falk 208 C2
Madehurst W Sus 20 A2
Madeley Staffs 111 A6
Madeley Telford 95 A4
Madeley Heath Staffs 112 A1
Madeley Park Staffs 112 A1
Madingley Cambs 85 A5
Madley Hereford 78 D2
Madresfield Worcs 79 C6
Madron Corn 2 B2
Maen-y-groes Ceredig 73 A6
Maenaddwyn Anglesey 123 B4
Maenclochog Pembs 55 B6
Maendy V Glam 41 D5
Maentwrog Gwyn 107 B6
Maer Staffs 112 B1
Maerdy Conwy 109 A5
Maerdy Rhondda 41 B4
Maes-Treylow Powys 77 A6
Maesbrook Shrops 110 C1
Maesbury Shrops 110 C2
Maesbury Marsh Shrops 110 C2
Maesgwyn-Isaf Powys 109 D6
Maesgwynne Carms 73 D5
Maeshafn Denb 126 C2
Maesllyn Ceredig 73 B6
Maesmynis Powys 76 C4
Maesteg Bridgend 40 B3
Maestir Ceredig 75 D4
Maesy cwmmer Caerph 41 B6
Maesybont Carms 57 A5
Maesycrugiau Carms 58 A1
Maesymeillion Ceredig 73 B7
Magdalen Laver Essex 69 C5
Maggieknockater Moray 254 B4
Magham Down E Sus 22 A4
Maghull Mers 136 C2
Magna Science Adventure Centre, Rotherham S Yorks 140 D2
Magor Mon 42 A3
Magpie Green Suff 104 D1
Maiden Bradley Wilts 30 B2
Maiden Law Durham 167 A4
Maiden Newton Dorset 15 B5
Maiden Wells Pembs 55 E5
Maidencombe Torbay 8 A3
Maidenhall Suff 88 C2
Maidenhead Windsor 48 A1
Maidens S Ayrs 192 E2
Maiden's Green Brack 48 B1
Maidensgrave Suff 88 C3
Maidenwell Corn 10 D2
Maidenwell Lincs 134 B3
Maidford Northants 82 B3
Maids Moreton Bucks 83 D4
Maidstone Kent 37 A5
Maidwell Northants 99 D4
Mail Shetland 285 L6
Main Powys 109 D6
Maindee Newport 42 A2
Mains of Airies Dumfries 170 A1
Mains of Allardice Aberds 233 A6
Mains of Annochie Aberds 257 B4
Mains of Ardestie Angus 221 A5
Mains of Balhall Angus 232 B3
Mains of Ballindarg Angus 232 C2
Mains of Balnakettle Aberds 233 A4
Mains of Birness Aberds 257 C4
Mains of Burgie Moray 266 D1
Mains of Clunas Highld 253 B4
Mains of Crichie Aberds 257 B4
Mains of Dalvey Highld 254 C2
Mains of Dellavaird Aberds 245 D4
Mains of Drum Aberds 245 C5
Mains of Edingight Moray 267 D6
Mains of Fedderate Aberds 268 E3
Mains of Inkhorn Aberds 257 C4
Mains of Mayen Moray 255 B6
Mains of Melgund Angus 232 C3
Mains of Thornton Aberds 233 A4
Mains of Watten Highld 281 C4
Mainsforth Durham 167 B6
Mainsriddle Dumfries 174 C2
Mainstone Shrops 93 C6
Maisemore Glos 63 A4
Malacleit W Isles 287 G2
Malborough Devon 7 D6
Malcoff Derbys 129 A5
Maldon Essex 70 C2

Malham N Yorks 146 A3
Maligar Highld 259 B4
Mallaig Highld 235 A5
Malleny Mills Edin 209 D4
Malling Stirl 217 D5
Mallory Park Motor Racing Circuit Leics 98 A1
Mallwyd Gwyn 91 A6
Malmesbury Wilts 44 A3
Malmsmead Devon 26 A2
Malpas Ches 110 A3
Malpas Corn 4 C3
Malpas Newport 61 D5
Malswick Glos 62 A3
Maltby Stockton 168 D2
Maltby S Yorks 140 D3
Maltby le Marsh Lincs 135 A4
Malting Green Essex 70 A3
Maltman's Hill Kent 37 B7
Malton N Yorks 159 D6
Malvern Link Worcs 79 C5
Malvern Wells Worcs 79 C5
Mamble Worcs 95 D4
Man-moel Caerph 41 A6
Manaccan Corn 3 C5
Manafon Powys 93 A5
Manais W Isles 287 F6
Manar Ho. Aberds 256 D2
Manaton Devon 12 C2
Manby Lincs 134 A3
Mancetter Warks 97 B6
Manchester Gtr Man 138 D1
Manchester Airport Gtr Man 128 A3
Manchester National Velodrome Gtr Man 138 D1
Mancot Flint 126 C3
Mandally Highld 239 B6
Manea Cambs 101 C6
Manfield N Yorks 167 D5
Mangaster Shetland 284 F5
Mangotsfield S Glos 43 B5
Mangurstadh W Isles 287 A5
Mankinholes W Yorks 138 A2
Manley Ches 127 B5
Mannal Argyll 222 C2
Mannerston W Loth 208 C3
Manningford Bohune Wilts 45 D5
Manningford Bruce Wilts 45 D5
Manningham W Yorks 147 D5
Mannings Heath W Sus 35 D5
Mannington Dorset 17 A4
Manningtree Essex 88 D1
Mannofield Aberdeen 245 B6
Manor Estate S Yorks 130 A3
Manor Park London 50 A1
Manorbier Pembs 55 E6
Manordeilo Carms 58 C3
Manorhill Borders 197 C5
Manorowen Pembs 72 C2
Mansel Lacy Hereford 78 C2
Manselfield Swansea 57 D5
Mansell Gamage Hereford 78 C1
Mansergh Cumb 155 C5
Mansfield E Ayrs 182 A4
Mansfield Notts 131 C5
Mansfield Woodhouse Notts 131 C5
Mansriggs Cumb 154 C1
Manston Dorset 30 D2
Manston Kent 53 C5
Manston W Yorks 148 D2
Manswood Dorset 16 A3
Manthorpe Lincs 116 D3
Manthorpe Lincs 116 B2
Manton N Lincs 142 C1
Manton Notts 131 B5
Manton Rutland 99 A5
Manton Wilts 45 C5
Manuden Essex 69 A4
Manx Electric Railway I o M 152 B4
Maperton Som 29 C6
Maple Cross Herts 67 D5
Maplebeck Notts 132 C2
Mapledurham Oxon 47 B4
Mapledurwell Hants 47 D4
Maplehurst W Sus 35 D4
Maplescombe Kent 50 C2
Mapleton Derbys 113 A5
Mapleton E Yorks 151 C5
Mapperley Derbys 114 A2

Mapperley Park
Nottingham 114 A3
Mapperton Dorset 15 B5
Mappleborough Green
Warks 80 A3
Mappowder Dorset 16 A1
Mar Lodge Aberds 242 C3
Maraig W Isles 288 G2
Marazanvose Corn 4 B3
Marazion Corn 2 B3
Marbhig W Isles 288 F5
Marbury Ches 111 A4
March Cambs 101 B6
March S Lnrk 184 A2
Marcham Oxon 65 D5
Marchamley Shrops 111 C4
Marchington Staffs 113 B5
Marchington Woodlands
Staffs 113 C5
Marchroes Gwyn 106 D3
Marchwiel Wrex 110 A2
Marchwood Hants 32 D2
Marcross V Glam 40 E4
Marden Hereford 78 C3
Marden Kent 37 B5
Marden T & W 179 B5
Marden Wilts 45 D4
Marden Beech Kent 37 B5
Marden Thorn Kent 37 B5
Mardy Mon 61 B5
Marefield Leics 99 A4
Mareham le Fen Lincs 134 C2
Mareham on the Hill
Lincs 134 C2
Marehay Derbys 114 A1
Marehill W Sus 20 A3
Maresfield E Sus 36 D2
Marfleet Hull 142 A3
Marford Wrex
Margam Neath 40 C2
Margaret Marsh Dorset 30 B2
Margaret Roding Essex 69 B5
Margaretting Essex 69 C6
Margate Kent 53 B5
Margnaheglish N Ayrs 191 B6
Margrove Park Redcar 169 D4
Marham Norf 119 D4
Marhamchurch Corn 10 A3
Marholm P'boro 100 A3
Mariandyrrys Anglesey 123 B6
Marianglas Anglesey 123 B5
Mariansleigh Devon 26 C2
Marionburgh Aberds 245 B4
Marishader Highld 259 B4
Maritime and Industrial
Museum Swansea 57 C6
Marjoriebanks Dumfries 184 D3
Mark Dumfries 170 B3
Mark S Ayrs 180 E2
Mark Som 28 A3
Mark Causeway Som 28 A3
Mark Cross E Sus 22 A2
Mark Cross E Sus 36 C3
Markbeech Kent 36 B2
Markby Lincs 135 B4
Market Bosworth Leics 97 A7
Market Deeping Lincs 116 E4
Market Drayton Shrops 111 B5
Market Harborough Leics 99 C4
Market Lavington Wilts 44 D4
Market Overton Rutland 116 D1
Market Rasen Lincs 133 A6
Market Rasen
Racecourse Lincs 133 A6
Market Stainton Lincs 134 B2
Market Warsop Notts 131 C5
Market Weighton E Yorks 150 C1
Market Weston Suff 103 D5
Markethill Perth 220 A2
Markfield Leics 114 D2
Markham Caerph 41 A6
Markham Moor Notts 132 B2
Markinch Fife 220 D2
Markington N Yorks 148 A1
Marks Tey Essex 70 A3
Marksbury Bath 43 C5
Markyate Herts 67 B5
Marland Gtr Man 138 B1
Marlborough Wilts 45 C5
Marlbrook Hereford 78 B3
Marlbrook Worcs 96 D2
Marlcliff Warks 80 B3
Marldon Devon 8 A2
Marlesford Suff 88 B4

Marley Green Ches 111 A4
Marley Hill T & W 179 D4
Marley Mount Hants 17 B6
Marlingford Norf 104 A2
Marloes Pembs 54 D3
Marlow Bucks 47 A6
Marlow Hereford 94 D2
Marlow Bottom Bucks 47 A6
Marlpit Hill Kent 36 B2
Marlpool Derbys 114 A2
Marnhull Dorset 30 D1
Marnoch Aberds 267 D6
Marnock N Lnrk 207 D5
Marple Gtr Man 129 A4
Marple Bridge Gtr Man 129 A4
Marr S Yorks 140 C3
Marrel Highld 274 C4
Marrick N Yorks 157 B4
Marrister Shetland 285 G7
Marros Carms 56 B2
Marsden T & W 179 C5
Marsden W Yorks 138 B3
Marsett N Yorks 156 C3
Marsh Devon 28 D2
Marsh W Yorks 147 D4
Marsh Baldon Oxon 65 D6
Marsh Gibbon Bucks 66 A1
Marsh Green Devon 13 B5
Marsh Green Kent 36 B2
Marsh Green Staffs 128 D3
Marsh Lane Derbys 131 B4
Marsh Street Som 27 A4
Marshall's Heath Herts 67 B6
Marshalsea Dorset 14 A3
Marshalswick Herts 67 C6
Marsham Norf 120 C3
Marshaw Lancs 145 B5
Marshborough Kent 53 D5
Marshbrook Shrops 94 C2
Marshchapel Lincs 143 D5
Marshfield Newport 42 A1
Marshfield S Glos 44 B1
Marshgate Corn 10 B2
Marshland St James Norf 101 A7
Marshside Mers 136 B2
Marshwood Dorset 14 B3
Marske N Yorks 157 A5
Marske-by-the-Sea
Redcar 168 C4
Marston Ches 127 B6
Marston Hereford 78 B1
Marston Lincs 116 A1
Marston Oxon 65 C6
Marston Staffs 112 D2
Marston Staffs 112 C3
Marston Warks 97 B5
Marston Wilts 44 D3
Marston Doles Warks 82 B1
Marston Green W Mid 97 C4
Marston Magna Som 29 C5
Marston Meysey Wilts 64 D2
Marston Montgomery
Derbys 113 B5
Marston Moretaine Beds 84 C1
Marston on Dove Derbys 113 C6
Marston St Lawrence
Northants 82 C2
Marston Stannett Hereford 78 B3
Marston Trussell Northants 98 C3
Marstow Hereford 62 B1
Marsworth Bucks 67 B4
Marten Wilts 45 D6
Marthall Ches 128 B3
Martham Norf 121 D6
Martin Hants 31 D4
Martin Kent 39 A5
Martin Lincs 133 D6
Martin Lincs 134 C2
Martin Dales Lincs 133 C6
Martin Drove End Hants 31 C4
Martin Hussingtree Worcs 80 A1
Martin Mill Kent 39 A5
Martinhoe Devon 26 A1
Martinhoe Cross Devon 26 A1
Martinscroft Warr 127 A6
Martinstown Dorset 15 C6
Martlesham Suff 88 C3
Martlesham Heath Suff 88 C3
Martletwy Pembs 55 C6
Martley Worcs 79 B5
Martock Som 29 D4
Marton Ches 128 C3
Marton E Yorks 151 D4
Marton Lincs 132 A3
Marton M'bro 168 D3
Marton N Yorks 148 A3
Marton N Yorks 159 D6

Marton Shrops 93 A6
Marton Shrops 110 C3
Marton Warks 81 A7
Marton-le-Moor N Yorks 158 D2
Martyr Worthy Hants 32 B4
Martyr's Green Sur 34 A3
Marwell Zoo, Bishop's
Waltham Hants 32 C4
Marwick Orkney 282 E3
Marwood Devon 25 B6
Mary Arden's House,
Stratford-upon-Avon
Warks 81 B4
Mary Rose Ptsmth 19 A5
Mary Tavy Devon 11 D6
Marybank Highld 251 A6
Maryburgh Highld 252 A1
Maryhill Glasgow 205 B5
Marykirk Aberds 233 B4
Marylebone Gtr Man 137 C4
Marypark Moray 254 C2
Maryport Cumb 162 A3
Maryport Dumfries 170 D3
Maryton Angus 233 C4
Marywell Aberds 244 C2
Marywell Aberds 245 C6
Marywell Angus 233 D4
Masham N Yorks 157 C6
Mashbury Essex 69 B6
Masongill N Yorks 155 D5
Masonhill S Ayrs 192 C3
Mastin Moor Derbys 131 B4
Mastrick Aberdeen 245 B5
Matching Essex 69 B5
Matching Green Essex 69 B5
Matching Tye Essex 69 B5
Matfen Northumb 178 B2
Matfield Kent 37 B4
Mathern Mon 62 D1
Mathon Hereford 79 C5
Mathry Pembs 55 A4
Matlaske Norf 120 B3
Matlock Derbys 130 C2
Matlock Bath Derbys 130 D2
Matson Glos 63 B4
Matterdale End Cumb 164 C1
Mattersey Notts 132 A1
Mattersey Thorpe Notts 132 A1
Mattingley Hants 47 D5
Mattishall Norf 120 D2
Mattishall Burgh Norf 120 D2
Mauchline E Ayrs 193 C4
Maud Aberds 257 B4
Maugersbury Glos 64 A3
Maughold I o M 152 B4
Mauld Highld 251 C6
Maulden Beds 84 D2
Maulds Meaburn Cumb 165 D4
Maunby N Yorks 158 C2
Maund Bryan Hereford 78 B3
Maundown Som 27 C5
Mautby Norf 121 D6
Mavis Enderby Lincs 134 C3
Maw Green Ches 128 D2
Mawbray Cumb 174 D3
Mawdesley Lancs 136 B3
Mawdlam Bridgend 40 C3
Mawgan Corn 3 C5
Mawla Corn 4 C2
Mawnan Corn 3 C5
Mawnan Smith Corn 3 C5
Mawsley Northants 99 D5
Maxey P'boro 100 A3
Maxstoke Warks 97 C5
Maxton Borders 197 C5
Maxton Kent 39 A5
Maxwellheugh Borders 197 C6
Maxwelltown Dumfries 174 A2
Maxworthy Corn 10 B3
May Bank Staffs 112 A2
Mayals Swansea 57 C6
Maybole S Ayrs 192 E3
Mayfield E Sus 36 D3
Mayfield Midloth 209 D6
Mayfield Staffs 113 A5
Mayfield W Loth 208 D2
Mayford Sur 34 A2
Mayland Essex 70 C3
Maynard's Green E Sus 22 A3
Maypole Mon 61 B6
Maypole Scilly 2 E4
Maypole Green Essex 70 A3
Maypole Green Norf 105 B5
Maypole Green Suff 88 A3
Maywick Shetland 285 L5
Meadle Bucks 66 C3
Meadowtown Shrops 93 A7

Meaford Staffs 112 B2
Meal Bank Cumb 154 B4
Mealabost W Isles 288 D5
Mealabost Bhuirgh
W Isles 288 B5
Mealsgate Cumb 175 D5
Meanwood W Yorks 148 D1
Mearbeck N Yorks 146 A2
Meare Som 29 A4
Meare Green Som 28 C3
Mears Ashby Northants 83 A5
Measham Leics 114 D1
Meath Green Sur 35 B5
Meathop Cumb 154 C3
Meaux E Yorks 150 D3
Meavy Devon 7 A4
Medbourne Leics 99 B4
Medburn Northumb 178 B3
Meddon Devon 24 D3
Meden Vale Notts 131 C5
Medlam Lincs 134 D3
Medmenham Bucks 47 A6
Medomsley Durham 178 D3
Medstead Hants 33 B5
Meer End W Mid 97 D5
Meerbrook Staffs 129 C4
Meers Bridge Lincs 135 A4
Meesden Herts 85 D6
Meeth Devon 11 A6
Meggethead Borders 195 D6
Meidrim Carms 73 D5
Meifod Denb 125 D5
Meifod Powys 109 D6
Meigle N Ayrs 204 B1
Meigle Perth 231 D6
Meikle Earnock S Lnrk 194 A2
Meikle Ferry Highld 264 B3
Meikle Forter Angus 231 B5
Meikle Gluich Highld 264 B2
Meikle Pinkerton E Loth 211 C4
Meikle Strath Aberds 233 A4
Meikle Tarty Aberds 257 D4
Meikle Wartle Aberds 256 C2
Meikleour Perth 219 A6
Meinciau Carms 57 A4
Meir Stoke 112 A3
Meir Heath Staffs 112 A3
Melbourn Cambs 85 C5
Melbourne Derbys 114 C1
Melbourne E Yorks 149 C6
Melbourne S Lnrk 195 B5
Melbury Abbas Dorset 30 C2
Melbury Bubb Dorset 15 A5
Melbury Osmond Dorset 15 A5
Melbury Sampford Dorset 15 A5
Melby Shetland 285 H3
Melchbourne Beds 84 A2
Melcombe Bingham
Dorset 16 A1
Melcombe Regis Dorset 15 C6
Meldon Devon 11 B6
Meldon Northumb 178 A3
Meldreth Cambs 85 C5
Meldrum Ho. Aberds 256 D3
Melfort Argyll 213 A6
Melgarve Highld 240 C2
Meliden Denb 125 A5
Melin-y-coed Conwy 124 C3
Melin-y-ddôl Powys 93 A4
Melin-y-grug Powys 93 A4
Melin-y-Wig Denb 109 A5
Melinbyrhedyn Powys 91 C6
Melincourt Neath 40 A3
Melkinthorpe Cumb 164 C3
Melkridge Northumb 177 C5
Melksham Wilts 44 C3
Melldalloch Argyll 203 A4
Melling Lancs 155 D4
Melling Mers 136 C2
Mellis Suff 104 D2
Mellon Charles Highld 261 A5
Mellon Udrigle Highld 261 A5
Mellor Gtr Man 129 A4
Mellor Lancs 145 D6
Mellor Brook Lancs 145 D6
Mells Som 30 A1
Melmerby Cumb 165 B4
Melmerby N Yorks 158 D2
Melmerby N Yorks 157 C4
Meltham W Yorks 139 B4
Melton Suff 88 B3
Melton Constable Norf 120 B2

Melton Mowbray Leics 1
Melton Ross N Lincs 1
Meltonby E Yorks 1
Melvaig Highld 2
Melverley Shrops 1
Melverley Green Shrops 1
Melvich Highld 2
Membury Devon
Memsie Aberds 2
Memus Angus 2
Menabilly Corn
Menai Bridge =
Porthaethwy Anglesey 1
Mendham Suff 1
Mendlesham Suff 1
Mendlesham Green Suff
Menheniot Corn
Mennock Dumfries 1
Menston W Yorks 1
Menstrie Clack 2
Menthorpe N Yorks 1
Mentmore Bucks
Meoble Highld 2
Meole Brace Shrops 1
Meols Mers 1
Meonstoke Hants
Meopham Kent
Meopham Station Kent
Mepal Cambs 1
Meppershall Beds
Merbach Hereford
Mere Ches
Mere Wilts 1
Mere Brow Lancs 1
Mere Green W Mid 1
Mereclough Lancs 1
Mereside Blkpool 1
Mereworth Kent
Mergie Aberds 2
Meriden W Mid
Merkadale Highld 2
Merkland Dumfries 1
Merkland S Ayrs 1
Merkland Lodge Highld 2
Merley Poole
Merlin's Bridge Pembs
Merrington Shrops 1
Merrion Pembs
Merriott Som
Merrivale Devon
Merrow Sur
Merrymeet Corn
Mersey Ferry Merseyside Maritime
Museum Mers 1
Mersham Kent
Merstham Sur
Merston W Sus
Merstone I o W
Merther Corn
Merthyr Carms
Merthyr Cynog Powys
Merthyr-Dyfan V Glam
Merthyr Mawr Bridgend
Merthyr Tudful =
Merthyr Tydfil M Tydf
Merthyr Tydfil = Merthyr
Tudful M Tydf
Merton Devon
Merton London
Merton Norf 1
Merton Oxon
Mervinslaw Borders 1
Meshaw Devon
Messing Essex
Messingham N Lincs 1
Metfield Suff
Metheringham Lincs 1
Methil Fife
Methlem Gwyn 1
Methley W Yorks 1
Methlick Aberds 2
Methven Perth 2
Methwold Norf 1
Methwold Hythe Norf 1
Metroland, Gateshead
T & W 1
Mettingham Suff 1
Mevagissey Corn
Mewith Head N Yorks 1
Mexborough S Yorks 1
Mey Highld 2
Meysey Hampton Glos 2
Miabhag W Isles 2
Miabhag W Isles 2
Miabhig W Isles 2
Michaelchurch Hereford

Michaelchurch Escley Hereford		77 D7
Michaelchurch on Arrow Powys		77 B6
Michaelston-le-Pit	V Glam	41 D6
Michaelston-y-Fedw Newport		42 A1
Michaelstow	Corn	10 D1
Michaelston-super-Ely Cardiff		41 D6
Michdever	Hants	32 B4
Michelmersh	Hants	32 C2
Mickfield	Suff	88 A2
Mickle Trafford	Ches	127 C4
Micklebring	S Yorks	140 D3
Mickleby	N Yorks	169 D6
Mickleham	Sur	35 A4
Mickleover	Derby	113 B7
Micklethwaite	W Yorks	147 C5
Mickleton	Durham	166 C2
Mickleton	Glos	81 C4
Mickletown	W Yorks	140 A1
Mickley	N Yorks	157 D6
Mickley Square	Northumb	178 C2
Mid Ardlaw	Aberds	269 C4
Mid Auchinlech	Invclyd	204 A3
Mid Beltie	Aberds	244 B3
Mid Calder	W Loth	208 D3
Mid Cloch Forbie	Aberds	268 D2
Mid Clyth	Highld	275 A6
Mid-Hants Railway (Watercress Line), New Alresford	Hants	33 B4
Mid Lavant	W Sus	20 B1
Mid Main	Highld	251 C6
Mid Urchany	Highld	253 B4
Mid Walls	Shetland	285 H4
Mid Yell	Shetland	284 D7
Midbea	Orkney	282 C5
Middle Assendon	Oxon	47 A5
Middle Aston	Oxon	65 A5
Middle Barton	Oxon	65 A5
Middle Cairncake	Aberds	256 B3
Middle Claydon	Bucks	66 A2
Middle Drums	Angus	232 C3
Middle Handley	Derbys	131 B4
Middle Littleton	Worcs	80 C3
Middle Maes-coed Hereford		78 D1
Middle Mill	Pembs	54 B4
Middle Rasen	Lincs	133 A5
Middle Rigg	Perth	219 D5
Middle Tysoe	Warks	81 C6
Middle Wallop	Hants	32 B1
Middle Winterslow	Wilts	31 B6
Middle Woodford	Wilts	31 B5
Middlebie	Dumfries	175 A5
Middleforth Green	Lancs	136 A4
Middleham	N Yorks	157 C5
Middlehope	Shrops	94 C2
Middlemarsh	Dorset	15 A6
Middlemuir	Aberds	257 D4
Middlesbrough	M'bro	168 C2
Middleshaw	Cumb	155 C4
Middleshaw	Dumfries	174 A4
Middlesmoor	N Yorks	157 D4
Middlestone	Durham	167 B5
Middlestone Moor Durham		167 B5
Middlestown	W Yorks	139 B5
Middlethird	Borders	197 B5
Middleton	Aberds	245 A5
Middleton	Argyll	222 C2
Middleton	Cumb	155 C5
Middleton	Derbys	130 D2
Middleton	Derbys	130 C1
Middleton	Essex	87 D4
Middleton	Gtr Man	138 C1
Middleton	Hants	32 A3
Middleton	Hereford	78 A3
Middleton	Lancs	144 B4
Middleton	Midloth	196 A2
Middleton	Norf	118 D3
Middleton	Northants	99 C5
Middleton	Northumb	178 A2
Middleton	Northumb	199 C5
Middleton	N Yorks	159 C6
Middleton	Perth	219 D6
Middleton	Perth	231 D5
Middleton	Shrops	94 D3
Middleton	Shrops	93 B6
Middleton	Shrops	110 C2
Middleton	Suff	89 A5
Middleton	Swansea	57 D4
Middleton	Warks	97 B4
Middleton	W Yorks	139 A5
Middleton	W Yorks	147 C5
Middleton Cheney Northants		82 C1
Middleton Green	Staffs	112 B3
Middleton Hall	Northumb	188 A2
Middleton-in-Teesdale Durham		166 C2
Middleton Moor	Suff	89 A5
Middleton-on-Leven N Yorks		158 A3
Middleton-on-Sea	W Sus	20 B2
Middleton on the Hill Hereford		78 A3
Middleton-on-the-Wolds E Yorks		150 C2
Middleton One Row	Darl	167 D6
Middleton Priors	Shrops	95 B4
Middleton Quernham N Yorks		158 D2
Middleton Railway, Hunslet	W Yorks	139 A6
Middleton St George Darl		167 D6
Middleton Scriven	Shrops	95 C4
Middleton Stoney	Oxon	65 A6
Middleton Tyas	N Yorks	157 A6
Middletown	Cumb	162 D2
Middletown	Powys	110 D2
Middlewich	Ches	128 C1
Middlewood Green	Suff	88 A1
Middlezoy	Som	28 B3
Middridge	Durham	167 C5
Midfield	Highld	277 B6
Midge Hall	Lancs	136 A4
Midgeholme	Cumb	176 D4
Midgham	W Berks	46 C3
Midgley	W Yorks	138 A3
Midgley	W Yorks	139 B5
Midhopestones	S Yorks	139 D5
Midhurst	W Sus	34 D1
Midlem	Borders	186 A4
Midmar	Aberds	244 B3
Midsomer Norton	Bath	43 D5
Midton	Invclyd	204 A2
Midtown	Highld	277 B6
Midtown	Highld	261 B5
Midtown of Buchromb Moray		254 B4
Midville	Lincs	134 D3
Midway	Ches	129 A4
Migdale	Highld	264 A2
Migvie	Aberds	244 B1
Milarrochy	Stirl	206 A2
Milborne Port	Som	29 D6
Milborne St Andrew Dorset		16 B2
Milborne Wick	Som	29 C6
Milbourne	Northumb	178 B3
Milburn	Cumb	165 C4
Milbury Heath	S Glos	62 D2
Milcombe	Oxon	81 D7
Milden	Suff	87 C5
Mildenhall	Suff	102 D3
Mildenhall	Wilts	45 C6
Mile Cross	Norf	120 D4
Mile Elm	Wilts	44 C3
Mile End	Essex	70 A3
Mile End	Glos	62 B1
Mile Oak	Brighton	21 B5
Milebrook	Powys	93 D7
Milebush	Kent	37 B5
Mileham	Norf	119 D6
Milesmark	Fife	208 B3
Milestones, Basingstoke Hants		47 D4
Milfield	Northumb	198 C3
Milford	Derbys	114 A1
Milford	Devon	24 C3
Milford	Powys	93 B4
Milford	Staffs	112 C3
Milford	Sur	34 B2
Milford	Wilts	31 C5
Milford Haven = Aberdaugleddau	Pembs	55 D5
Milford on Sea	Hants	18 B1
Milkwall	Glos	62 C1
Milkwell	Wilts	30 C3
Mill Bank	W Yorks	138 A3
Mill Common	Suff	105 C5
Mill End	Bucks	47 A5
Mill End	Herts	85 D5
Mill Green	Essex	69 C6
Mill Green	Norf	104 C2
Mill Green	Suff	87 C5
Mill Hill	London	68 D2
Mill Lane	Hants	47 D5
Mill of Kingoodie	Aberds	256 D3
Mill of Muiresk	Aberds	256 B1
Mill of Sterin	Aberds	243 C6
Mill of Uras	Aberds	245 D5
Mill Place	N Lincs	142 C1
Mill Side	Cumb	154 C3
Mill Street	Norf	120 D2
Milland	W Sus	34 D1
Millarston	Renfs	205 B4
Millbank	Aberds	257 B6
Millbank	Highld	280 B3
Millbeck	Cumb	163 B5
Millbounds	Orkney	282 D6
Millbreck	Aberds	257 B5
Millbridge	Sur	34 B1
Millbrook	Beds	84 D2
Millbrook	Corn	6 B3
Millbrook	Soton	32 D2
Millburn	S Ayrs	193 C4
Millcombe	Devon	8 C2
Millcorner	E Sus	37 D6
Milldale	Staffs	129 D6
Millden Lodge	Angus	232 A3
Milldens	Angus	232 C3
Millennium Stadium Cardiff		41 D6
Millerhill	Midloth	209 D6
Miller's Dale	Derbys	129 B6
Miller's Green	Derbys	130 D2
Millgreen	Shrops	111 C5
Millhalf	Hereford	77 C6
Millhayes	Devon	14 A2
Millhead	Lancs	154 D3
Millheugh	S Lnrk	194 A2
Millholme	Cumb	155 B4
Millhouse	Argyll	203 A4
Millhouse	Cumb	163 A6
Millhouse Green	S Yorks	139 C5
Millhousebridge	Dumfries	185 D4
Millhouses	S Yorks	130 A3
Millikenpark	Renfs	205 B4
Millin Cross	Pembs	55 C5
Millington	E Yorks	150 B1
Millmeece	Staffs	112 B2
Millom	Cumb	153 B2
Millook	Corn	10 B2
Millpool	Corn	10 D2
Millport	N Ayrs	204 C1
Millquarter	Dumfries	182 D4
Millthorpe	Lincs	116 B4
Millthrop	Cumb	155 B5
Milltimber	Aberdeen	245 B5
Milltown	Corn	5 B6
Milltown	Derbys	130 C3
Milltown	Devon	25 B6
Milltown	Dumfries	175 A6
Milltown of Aberdalgie Perth		219 B5
Milltown of Auchindoun Moray		255 B4
Milltown of Craigston Aberds		268 D2
Milltown of Edinville Moray		254 B3
Milltown of Kildrummy Aberds		244 A1
Milltown of Rothiemay Moray		255 B6
Milltown of Towie	Aberds	244 A1
Milnathort	Perth	219 D6
Milner's Heath	Ches	127 C4
Milngavie	E Dunb	205 A5
Milnrow	Gtr Man	138 B2
Milnshaw	Lancs	137 A6
Milnthorpe	Cumb	154 C3
Milo	Corn	57 A5
Milson	Shrops	95 D4
Milstead	Kent	37 A7
Milston	Wilts	31 A5
Milton	Angus	232 D1
Milton	Cambs	85 A6
Milton	Cumb	176 C3
Milton	Derbys	113 C7
Milton	Dumfries	171 B4
Milton	Dumfries	173 A6
Milton	Dumfries	183 D6
Milton	Highld	251 A5
Milton	Highld	251 C6
Milton	Highld	252 B1
Milton	Highld	281 C5
Milton	Highld	264 C3
Milton	Moray	267 C6
Milton	Notts	132 B2
Milton	N Som	42 C2
Milton	Oxon	82 D1
Milton	Oxon	65 D5
Milton	Pembs	55 D6
Milton	Perth	219 C4
Milton	Ptsmth	19 B5
Milton	Stirl	217 D5
Milton	Stoke	129 D4
Milton	W Dunb	205 A4
Milton Abbas	Dorset	16 A2
Milton Abbot	Devon	11 D5
Milton Bridge	Midloth	209 D5
Milton Bryan	Beds	83 D6
Milton Clevedon	Som	29 B6
Milton Coldwells	Aberds	257 C4
Milton Combe	Devon	6 A3
Milton Damerel	Devon	25 D4
Milton End	Glos	64 C2
Milton Ernest	Beds	84 B2
Milton Green	Ches	127 C4
Milton Hill	Oxon	65 D5
Milton Keynes	M Keynes	83 D5
Milton Keynes Village M Keynes		83 D5
Milton Lilbourne	Wilts	45 C5
Milton Malsor	Northants	83 B4
Milton Morenish	Perth	217 A6
Milton of Auchinhove Aberds		244 B2
Milton of Balgonie	Fife	220 D3
Milton of Buchanan	Stirl	206 A2
Milton of Campfield Aberds		244 B3
Milton of Campsie	E Dunb	205 A6
Milton of Corsindae Aberds		244 B3
Milton of Cushnie	Aberds	244 A2
Milton of Dalcapon	Perth	230 C3
Milton of Edradour	Perth	230 C3
Milton of Gollanfield Highld		252 A3
Milton of Lesmore Aberds		255 D5
Milton of Logie	Aberds	244 B1
Milton of Murtle Aberdeen		245 B5
Milton of Noth	Aberds	255 D6
Milton of Tullich	Aberds	243 C6
Milton on Stour	Dorset	30 C1
Milton Regis	Kent	51 C6
Milton under Wychwood Oxon		64 B3
Miltonduff	Moray	266 C2
Miltonhill	Moray	266 C1
Miltonise	Dumfries	180 D3
Milverton	Som	27 C6
Milverton	Warks	81 A6
Milwich	Staffs	112 B3
Minard	Argyll	214 C2
Minchinhampton	Glos	63 C4
Mindrum	Northumb	198 C2
Minehead	Som	27 A4
Minera	Wrex	126 D2
Minety	Wilts	63 D6
Minffordd	Gwyn	107 C5
Minffordd	Gwyn	91 A5
Minffordd	Gwyn	123 C5
Miningsby	Lincs	134 C3
Minions	Corn	10 D3
Minishant	S Ayrs	192 D3
Minllyn	Gwyn	91 A6
Minnes	Aberds	257 D4
Minngearraidh	W Isles	286 D3
Minnigaff	Dumfries	171 A6
Minnonie	Aberds	268 C2
Minskip	N Yorks	148 A2
Minstead	Hants	32 D1
Minsted	W Sus	34 D1
Minster	Kent	51 B6
Minster	Kent	53 C5
Minster Lovell	Oxon	64 B4
Minsterley	Shrops	94 A1
Minsterworth	Glos	62 B3
Minterne Magna	Dorset	15 A6
Minting	Lincs	134 B1
Mintlaw	Aberds	257 B5
Minto	Borders	187 A4
Minton	Shrops	94 B2
Minwear	Pembs	55 C6
Minworth	W Mid	97 B4
Mirbister	Orkney	282 E4
Mirehouse	Cumb	162 C2
Mireland	Highld	281 B5
Mirfield	W Yorks	139 B5
Miserden	Glos	63 C5
Miskin	Rhondda	41 C5
Misson	Notts	141 D4
Misterton	Leics	98 C2
Misterton	Notts	141 D5
Misterton	Som	15 A4
Mistley	Essex	88 D2
Mitcham	London	49 C5
Mitchel Troy	Mon	61 B6
Mitcheldean	Glos	62 B2
Mitchell	Corn	4 B3
Mitcheltroy Common	Mon	61 C6
Mitford	Northumb	178 A3
Mithian	Corn	4 B2
Mitton	Staffs	112 D2
Mixbury	Oxon	82 D3
Moat	Cumb	175 A7
Moats Tye	Suff	87 B6
Mobberley	Ches	128 B2
Mobberley	Staffs	112 A4
Moccas	Hereford	78 C1
Mochdre	Conwy	124 B3
Mochdre	Powys	93 C4
Mochrum	Dumfries	171 C5
Mockbeggar	Hants	17 A5
Mockerkin	Cumb	162 B3
Modbury	Devon	7 B5
Moddershall	Staffs	112 B3
Model Village, Babbacombe	Devon	8 A3
Moelfre	Anglesey	123 B5
Moelfre	Powys	109 C6
Moffat	Dumfries	184 B3
Moggerhanger	Beds	84 C3
Moira	Leics	113 D7
Mol-chlach	Highld	246 C3
Molash	Kent	52 D2
Mold = Yr Wyddgrug Flint		126 C2
Moldgreen	W Yorks	139 B4
Molehill Green	Essex	69 A5
Molescroft	E Yorks	150 C3
Molesden	Northumb	178 A3
Molesworth	Cambs	100 D2
Moll	Highld	247 A4
Molland	Devon	26 C3
Mollington	Ches	126 B3
Mollington	Oxon	82 C1
Mollinsburn	N Lnrk	207 C5
Monachty	Ceredig	75 B4
Monachylemore	Stirl	217 C4
Monar Lodge	Highld	250 B4
Monaughty	Powys	77 A6
Monboddo House	Aberds	233 A5
Mondynes	Aberds	233 A5
Monevechadan	Argyll	215 B4
Monewden	Suff	88 B3
Moneydie	Perth	219 B5
Moniaive	Dumfries	183 C5
Monifieth	Angus	221 A4
Monikie	Angus	221 A4
Monimail	Fife	220 C2
Monington	Pembs	72 B4
Monk Bretton	S Yorks	139 C6
Monk Fryston	N Yorks	140 A3
Monk Sherborne	Hants	47 D4
Monk Soham	Suff	88 A3
Monk Street	Essex	69 A6
Monken Hadley	London	68 D2
Monkhopton	Shrops	95 B4
Monkland	Hereford	78 B2
Monkleigh	Devon	25 C5
Monknash	V Glam	40 D4
Monkokehampton	Devon	11 A6
Monks Eleigh	Suff	87 C5
Monk's Gate	W Sus	35 D5
Monks Heath	Ches	128 B3
Monks Kirby	Warks	98 C1
Monks Risborough	Bucks	66 C3
Monkseaton	T & W	179 B5
Monkshill	Aberds	256 B2
Monksilver	Som	27 B5
Monkspath	W Mid	96 D4
Monkswood	Mon	61 C5
Monkton	Devon	14 A1
Monkton	Kent	53 C4
Monkton	Pembs	55 D5
Monkton	S Ayrs	192 C3
Monkton Combe	Bath	44 C1
Monkton Deverill	Wilts	30 B2
Monkton Farleigh	Wilts	44 C2
Monkton Heathfield	Som	28 C2
Monkton Up Wimborne Dorset		31 D4
Monkwearmouth	T & W	179 D5
Monkwood	Hants	33 B5
Monmouth = Trefynwy Mon		61 B7
Monmouth Cap	Mon	61 A5
Monnington on Wye Hereford		78 C1
Monreith	Dumfries	171 C5
Monreith Mains	Dumfries	171 C5

Mont Saint Guern 6
Montacute Som 29 D4
Montacute House Som 29 D5
Montcoffer Ho. Aberds 268 C1
Montford Argyll 203 B6
Montford Shrops 110 D3
Montford Bridge Shrops 110 D3
Montgarrie Aberds 244 A2
Montgomery = Trefaldwyn Powys 93 B6
Montrave Fife 220 D3
Montrose Angus 233 C5
Montsale Essex 71 D4
Monxton Hants 32 A2
Monyash Derbys 129 C6
Monymusk Aberds 244 A3
Monzie Perth 218 B3
Monzie Castle Perth 218 B3
Moodiesburn N Lnrk 207 C4
Moonzie Fife 220 C3
Moor Allerton W Yorks 148 D1
Moor Crichel Dorset 16 A3
Moor End E Yorks 149 D7
Moor End York 149 B5
Moor Monkton N Yorks 148 B4
Moor of Granary Moray 253 A6
Moor of Ravenstone Dumfries 171 C5
Moor Row Cumb 162 C3
Moor Street Kent 51 C5
Moorby Lincs 134 C2
Moordown Bmouth 17 B4
Moore Halton 127 A5
Moorend Glos 62 C3
Moorends S Yorks 141 B4
Moorgate S Yorks 140 D2
Moorgreen Notts 114 A2
Moorhall Derbys 130 B3
Moorhampton Hereford 78 C1
Moorhead W Yorks 147 D5
Moorhouse Cumb 175 C6
Moorhouse Notts 132 C2
Moorlinch Som 28 B3
Moorsholm Redcar 169 D4
Moorside Gtr Man 138 C2
Moorthorpe W Yorks 140 B2
Moortown Hants 17 A5
Moortown I o W 18 C3
Moortown Lincs 142 D2
Morangie Highld 264 B3
Morar Highld 235 A5
Morborne Cambs 100 B3
Morchard Bishop Devon 12 A2
Morcombelake Dorset 14 B4
Morcott Rutland 99 A6
Morda Shrops 110 C1
Morden Dorset 16 B3
Morden London 49 C5
Mordiford Hereford 78 D3
Mordon Durham 167 C6
More Shrops 94 B1
Morebath Devon 27 C4
Morebattle Borders 187 A6
Morecambe Lancs 144 A4
Morefield Highld 262 A3
Moreleigh Devon 7 B6
Morenish Perth 217 A5
Moresby Cumb 162 B2
Moresby Parks Cumb 162 C2
Morestead Hants 32 C4
Moreton Dorset 16 C2
Moreton Essex 69 C5
Moreton Mers 136 D1
Moreton Oxon 66 C1
Moreton Staffs 112 D1
Moreton Corbet Shrops 111 C4
Moreton-in-Marsh Glos 81 D5
Moreton Jeffries Hereford 79 C4
Moreton Morrell Warks 81 B6
Moreton on Lugg Hereford 78 C3
Moreton Pinkney Northants 82 C2
Moreton Say Shrops 111 B5
Moreton Valence Glos 62 C3
Moretonhampstead Devon 12 C2
Morfa Carms 57 A5
Morfa Carms 57 C5
Morfa Bach Carms 56 A3
Morfa Bychan Gwyn 107 C5
Morfa Dinlle Gwyn 107 A4
Morfa Glas Neath 59 E5
Morfa Nefyn Gwyn 106 B2
Morfydd Denb 109 A6
Morgan's Vale Wilts 31 C5
Moriah Ceredig 75 A5

Morland Cumb 164 C3
Morley Derbys 114 A1
Morley Durham 166 C4
Morley W Yorks 139 A5
Morley Green Ches 128 A3
Morley St Botolph Norf 104 B1
Morningside Edin 209 C5
Morningside N Lnrk 194 A3
Morningthorpe Norf 104 B3
Morpeth Northumb 179 A4
Morphie Aberds 233 B5
Morrey Staffs 113 D5
Morris Green Essex 86 D3
Morriston Swansea 57 C6
Morston Norf 120 A2
Mortehoe Devon 25 A5
Mortimer W Berks 47 C4
Mortimer West End Hants 47 C4
Mortimer's Cross Hereford 78 A2
Mortlake London 49 B5
Morton Cumb 175 C6
Morton Derbys 131 C4
Morton Lincs 116 C3
Morton Lincs 141 D6
Morton Lincs 132 C3
Morton Norf 120 D3
Morton Notts 132 D2
Morton Shrops 110 C1
Morton S Glos 62 D2
Morton Bagot Warks 80 A4
Morton-on-Swale N Yorks 157 B7
Morvah Corn 2 B2
Morval Corn 6 B1
Morvich Highld 249 D6
Morvich Highld 273 D5
Morville Shrops 95 B4
Morville Heath Shrops 95 B4
Morwenstow Corn 24 D3
Mosborough S Yorks 131 A4
Moscow E Ayrs 205 D4
Mosedale Cumb 163 A6
Moseley W Mid 96 C3
Moseley W Mid 96 B2
Moseley Worcs 79 B6
Mosquito Aircraft Museum, London Colney Herts 68 C1
Moss Argyll 222 C2
Moss Highld 235 D5
Moss S Yorks 140 B3
Moss Wrex 126 D3
Moss Bank Mers 136 D4
Moss Edge Lancs 144 C4
Moss End Brack 47 B6
Moss of Barmuckity Moray 266 C3
Moss Pit Staffs 112 C3
Moss-side Highld 253 A4
Moss Side Lancs 144 D3
Mossat Aberds 244 A1
Mossbank Shetland 284 F6
Mossbay Cumb 162 B2
Mossblown S Ayrs 193 C4
Mossbrow Gtr Man 128 A2
Mossburnford Borders 187 B5
Mossdale Dumfries 173 A4
Mossend N Lnrk 207 D5
Mosser Cumb 163 B4
Mossfield Highld 264 C2
Mossgiel E Ayrs 193 C4
Mosside Angus 232 C2
Mossley Ches 128 C3
Mossley Gtr Man 138 C2
Mossley Hill Mers 126 A3
Mosstodloch Moray 266 D4
Mosston Angus 232 D3
Mossy Lea Lancs 136 B4
Mosterton Dorset 15 A4
Moston Gtr Man 138 C1
Moston Shrops 111 C4
Moston Green Ches 128 C2
Mostyn Flint 125 A6
Mostyn Quay Flint 125 A6
Motcombe Dorset 30 C2
Mothecombe Devon 7 C5
Motherby Cumb 164 C2
Motherwell N Lnrk 194 A2
Mottingham London 49 B7
Mottisfont Hants 32 C2
Mottisfont Abbey Garden Hants 32 C2
Mottistone I o W 18 C3
Mottram in Longdendale Gtr Man 138 D2
Mottram St Andrew Ches 128 B3
Mouilpied Guern 6

Mouldsworth Ches 127 B5
Moulin Perth 230 C3
Moulsecoomb Brighton 21 B6
Moulsford Oxon 46 A3
Moulsoe M Keynes 83 C6
Moulton Ches 127 C6
Moulton Lincs 117 C6
Moulton Northants 83 A4
Moulton N Yorks 157 A6
Moulton Suff 86 A3
Moulton V Glam 41 D5
Moulton Chapel Lincs 117 D5
Moulton Eaugate Lincs 117 D6
Moulton St Mary Norf 105 A4
Moulton Seas End Lincs 117 C6
Mounie Castle Aberds 256 D2
Mount Corn 4 B2
Mount Corn 5 A6
Mount Highld 253 B5
Mount Bures Essex 87 D5
Mount Canisp Highld 264 C3
Mount Hawke Corn 4 C2
Mount Pleasant Ches 128 D3
Mount Pleasant Derbys 114 A1
Mount Pleasant Derbys 113 D6
Mount Pleasant Flint 126 B2
Mount Pleasant Hants 18 B1
Mount Pleasant W Yorks 139 A5
Mount Sorrel Wilts 31 C4
Mount Tabor W Yorks 138 A3
Mountain W Yorks 147 D4
Mountain Ash = Aberpennar Rhondda 41 B5
Mountain Cross Borders 195 B6
Mountain Water Pembs 55 B5
Mountbenger Borders 196 D2
Mountfield E Sus 37 D5
Mountgerald Highld 264 D1
Mountjoy Corn 4 A3
Mountnessing Essex 69 D6
Mounton Mon 61 D7
Mountsorrel Leics 114 D3
Mousehole Corn 2 C2
Mousen Northumb 199 C5
Mouswald Dumfries 174 A3
Mow Cop Ches 128 D3
Mowhaugh Borders 187 A7
Mowsley Leics 98 C3
Moxley W Mid 96 B2
Moy Highld 240 D2
Moy Highld 252 C3
Moy Hall Highld 252 C3
Moy Ho. Moray 265 D6
Moy Lodge Highld 240 D2
Moyles Court Hants 17 A5
Moylgrove Pembs 72 B4
Muasdale Argyll 202 D1
Much Birch Hereford 78 D3
Much Cowarne Hereford 79 C4
Much Dewchurch Hereford 78 D2
Much Hadham Herts 68 B4
Much Hoole Lancs 136 A3
Much Marcle Hereford 79 D4
Much Wenlock Shrops 95 A4
Muchalls Aberds 245 C6
Muchelney Som 28 C4
Muchlarnick Corn 5 B7
Muchrachd Highld 251 C4
Muckernich Highld 252 A1
Mucking Thurrock 50 A3
Muckleford Dorset 15 B6
Mucklestone Staffs 111 B6
Muckleton Shrops 111 C4
Muckletown Aberds 255 D6
Muckley Corner Staffs 96 A3
Muckton Lincs 134 A3
Mudale Highld 272 A3
Muddiford Devon 25 B6
Mudeford Dorset 17 B5
Mudford Som 29 D5
Mudgley Som 28 A4
Mugdock Stirl 205 A5
Mugeary Highld 246 A3
Mugginton Derbys 113 A6
Muggleswick Durham 166 A3
Muie Highld 273 D4
Muir Aberds 242 D3
Muir of Fairburn Highld 251 A6
Muir of Fowlis Aberds 244 A2
Muir of Ord Highld 252 A1
Muir of Pert Angus 220 A4
Muirden Aberds 268 D2
Muirdrum Angus 221 A5
Muirhead Angus 220 A3
Muirhead Fife 220 D2
Muirhead N Lnrk 207 D4
Muirhead S Ayrs 192 B3
Muirhouselaw Borders 187 A5

Muirhouses Falk 208 B3
Muirkirk E Ayrs 194 D1
Muirmill Stirl 207 B5
Muirshearlich Highld 239 D5
Muirskie Aberds 245 C5
Muirtack Aberds 257 C4
Muirton Highld 264 D3
Muirton Perth 219 B6
Muirton Perth 218 C4
Muirton Mains Highld 251 A6
Muirton of Ardblair Perth 231 D5
Muirton of Ballochy Angus 233 B4
Muiryfold Aberds 268 D2
Muker N Yorks 156 B3
Mulbarton Norf 104 A2
Mulben Moray 267 D4
Mulindry Argyll 200 C3
Mullardoch House Highld 250 C4
Mullion Corn 3 D4
Mullion Cove Corn 3 D4
Mumby Lincs 135 B5
Muncaster Owl Trust World HQ Cumb 153 A2
Munderfield Row Hereford 79 B4
Munderfield Stocks Hereford 79 B4
Mundesley Norf 121 B5
Mundford Norf 103 B4
Mundham Norf 104 B4
Mundon Essex 70 C2
Mundurno Aberdeen 245 A6
Munerigie Highld 239 B6
Muness Shetland 284 C8
Mungasdale Highld 261 A6
Mungrisdale Cumb 163 A6
Munlochy Highld 252 A2
Munsley Hereford 79 C4
Munslow Shrops 94 C3
Murchington Devon 12 C1
Murcott Oxon 65 B6
Murkle Highld 280 B3
Murlaggan Highld 238 C4
Murlaggan Highld 239 D7
Murra Orkney 283 G3
Murrayfield Edin 209 C5
Murrayfield Stadium Edin 209 C5
Murrays Motorcycle Museum I o M 152 C3
Murrow Cambs 101 A5
Mursley Bucks 66 A3
Murthill Angus 232 C2
Murthly Perth 219 A5
Murton Cumb 165 C5
Murton Durham 167 A6
Murton Northumb 198 B3
Murton York 149 B5
Musbury Devon 14 B2
Muscoates N Yorks 159 C5
Musdale Argyll 226 D4
Museum of Childhood, Bethnal Green London 49 A6
Museum of the Broads, Sutton Norf 121 C5
Musselburgh E Loth 209 C6
Musselburgh Racecourse E Loth 209 C6
Muston Leics 115 B6
Muston N Yorks 161 D4
Mustow Green Worcs 95 D6
Mutehill Dumfries 173 D4
Mutford Suff 105 C5
Muthill Perth 218 C3
Mutterton Devon 13 A5
Muxton Telford 111 D6
Mybster Highld 280 C3
Myddfai Carms 59 C4
Myddle Shrops 110 C3
Mydroilyn Ceredig 74 C3
Myerscough Lancs 145 D4
Mylor Bridge Corn 4 D3
Mynachlog-ddu Pembs 72 C4
Myndtown Shrops 94 C1
Mynydd Bach Ceredig 75 A6
Mynydd-bach Mon 61 D6
Mynydd Bodafon Anglesey 123 B4
Mynydd-isa Flint 126 C2
Mynyddygarreg Carms 57 B4
Mynytho Gwyn 106 C3
Myrebird Aberds 245 C4
Myrelandhorn Highld 281 C4
Myreside Perth 220 B2
Myrtle Hill Carms 59 B4
Mytchett Sur 34 A1
Mytholm W Yorks 138 A2
Mytholmroyd W Yorks 138 A3
Myton-on-Swale N Yorks 148 A3
Mytton Shrops 110 D3

N

Na Gearrannan W Isles 288 C2
Naast Highld 261 B5
Naburn York 149 C4
Nackington Kent 52 D3
Nacton Suff 88 C3
Nafferton E Yorks 150 B3
Nailbridge Glos 62 B2
Nailsbourne Som 28 C2
Nailsea N Som 42 B3
Nailstone Leics 97 A7
Nailsworth Glos 63 D4
Nairn Highld 253 A4
Nalderswood Sur 35 B5
Nancegollan Corn 3 B4
Nancledra Corn 2 B2
Nanhoron Gwyn 106 C2
Nannau Gwyn 108 C2
Nannerch Flint 125 C6
Nanpantan Leics 114 D3
Nanpean Corn 5 B4
Nanstallon Corn 5 A5
Nant-ddu Powys 60 B3
Nant-glas Powys 76 A4
Nant Peris Gwyn 107 A6
Nant Uchaf Denb 125 D6
Nant-y-Bai Carms 59 A4
Nant-y-cafn Neath 59 E5
Nant-y-derry Mon 61 C5
Nant-y-ffin Carms 58 B3
Nant-y-moel Bridgend 40 B4
Nant-y-pandy Conwy 124 B1
Nanternis Ceredig 73 A6
Nantgaredig Carms 58 C1
Nantgarw Rhondda 41 C6
Nantglyn Denb 125 C5
Nantgwyn Powys 92 D3
Nantlle Gwyn 107 A5
Nantmawr Shrops 110 C1
Nantmel Powys 76 A4
Nantmor Gwyn 107 A6
Nantwich Ches 127 D6
Nantycaws Carms 57 A4
Nantyffyllon Bridgend 40 B3
Nantyglo Bl Gwent 60 C3
Naphill Bucks 66 D3
Nappa N Yorks 146 B2
Napton on the Hill Warks 82 A1
Narberth = Arberth Pembs 55 C7
Narborough Leics 98 B2
Narborough Norf 119 D5
Nasareth Gwyn 107 A4
Naseby Northants 98 D3
Nash Bucks 83 D4
Nash Hereford 77 A7
Nash Newport 42 A2
Nash Shrops 95 D4
Nash Lee Bucks 66 C3
Nassington Northants 100 B2
Nasty Herts 68 A3
Nateby Cumb 155 A6
Nateby Lancs 145 C4
National Agricultural Centre, Stoneleigh Warks 97 D6
National Botanic Garden of Wales Carms 57 A5
National Cycle Collection, Llandrindod Wells Powys 77 A4
National Exhibition Centre, Birmingham W Mid 97 C4
National Fishing Heritage Centre, Grimsby NE Lincs 143 B4
National Gallery London 49 B5
National Hockey Stadium M Keynes 83 C5
National Ice Centre Nottingham 114 B3
National Maritime Museum London 49 B7
National Maritime Museum, Falmouth Corn 4 D3
National Motor Museum, Beaulieu Hants 18 B2
National Museum of Photography, Bradford W Yorks 147 D5
National Museum of Wales Cardiff 41 D6
National Portrait Gallery (See National Gallery) London 49 B5

National Railway Museum York 149 B4
National Seal Sanctuary, Gweek Corn 3 C5
National Space Science Centre Leics 98 A2
National Squash Centre Gtr Man 138 D1
Natland Cumb 154 C4
Natural History Museum London 49 B5
Natureland Seal Sanctuary, Skegness Lincs 135 C5
Naughton Suff 87 C6
Naunton Glos 64 A2
Naunton Worcs 80 D1
Naunton Beauchamp Worcs 80 B2
Navenby Lincs 133 D4
Navestock Heath Essex 69 D5
Navestock Side Essex 69 D5
Navidale Highld 274 C4
Nawton N Yorks 159 C5
Nayland Suff 87 D5
Nazeing Essex 68 C4
Neacroft Hants 17 B5
Neal's Green Warks 97 C6
Neap Shetland 285 H7
Near Sawrey Cumb 154 B2
Neasham Darl 167 D6
Neath = Castell-Nedd Neath 40 B2
Neath Abbey Neath 40 B2
Neatishead Norf 121 C5
Nebo Anglesey 123 A4
Nebo Ceredig 75 B4
Nebo Conwy 124 D3
Nebo Gwyn 107 A4
Necton Norf 103 A4
Nedd Highld 270 A4
Nedderton Northumb 179 A4
Nedging Tye Suff 87 C6
Needham Norf 104 C3
Needham Market Suff 88 B1
Needingworth Cambs 101 D5
Needwood Staffs 113 C5
Neen Savage Shrops 95 D4
Neen Sollars Shrops 95 C4
Neenton Shrops 95 C4
Nefyn Gwyn 106 B3
Neilston E Renf 205 C4
Neinthirion Powys 92 A3
Neithrop Oxon 82 C1
Nelly Andrews Green Powys 93 A6
Nelson Caerph 41 B6
Nelson Lancs 146 D2
Nelson Village Northumb 179 B4
Nemphlar S Lnrk 194 B3
Nempnett Thrubwell Bath 43 C4
Nene Terrace Lincs 101 A4
Nenthall Cumb 165 A5
Nenthead Cumb 165 A5
Nenthorn Borders 197 C5
Nerabus Argyll 200 C2
Nercwys Flint 126 C2
Nerston S Lnrk 205 C6
Nesbit Northumb 198 C3
Ness Ches 126 B3
Ness Gardens, Connah's Quay Ches 126 B3
Nesscliffe Shrops 110 D2
Neston Ches 126 B2
Neston Wilts 44 C2
Nether Alderley Ches 128 B3
Nether Blainslie Borders 197 B4
Nether Booth Derbys 129 A6
Nether Broughton Leics 115 C4
Nether Burrow Lancs 155 D5
Nether Cerne Dorset 15 B6
Nether Compton Dorset 29 D5
Nether Crimond Aberds 256 D3
Nether Dalgliesh Borders 185 B5
Nether Dallachy Moray 267 C4
Nether Exe Devon 13 A4
Nether Glasslaw Aberds 268 D3
Nether Handwick Angus 232 D1
Nether Haugh S Yorks 140 D2
Nether Heage Derbys 130 D3
Nether Heyford Northants 82 B3
Nether Hindhope Borders 187 B6
Nether Howecleuch ...nrk 184 A3
Nether Kellet Lancs 145 A5
Nether Kinmundy Aberds 257 B5
Nether Langwith Notts 131 B5

Nether Leask Aberds 257 C5
Nether Lenshie Aberds 256 B1
Nether Monynut Borders 211 D4
Nether Padley Derbys 130 B2
Nether Park Aberds 269 D5
Nether Poppleton N Yorks 149 B4
Nether Silton N Yorks 158 B3
Nether Stowey Som 28 B1
Nether Urquhart Fife 219 D6
Nether Wallop Hants 32 B2
Nether Wasdale Cumb 163 D4
Nether Whitacre Warks 97 B5
Nether Worton Oxon 82 D1
Netheravon Wilts 31 A5
Netherbrae Aberds 268 D2
Netherbrough Orkney 282 F4
Netherburn S Lnrk 194 B3
Netherbury Dorset 15 B4
Netherby Cumb 175 A6
Netherby N Yorks 148 C2
Nethercote Warks 82 A2
Nethercott Devon 25 B5
Netherend Glos 62 C1
Netherfield E Sus 23 A5
Netherhampton Wilts 31 C5
Netherlaw Dumfries 173 D5
Netherley Aberds 245 C5
Netherley Mers 127 A4
Nethermill Dumfries 184 D3
Nethermuir Aberds 257 B4
Netherplace E Renf 205 C5
Netherseal Derbys 113 D6
Netherthird E Ayrs 182 A3
Netherthong W Yorks 139 C4
Netherthorpe S Yorks 131 A5
Netherton Angus 232 C3
Netherton Devon 12 D3
Netherton Hants 46 D1
Netherton Mers 136 C2
Netherton Northumb 188 C2
Netherton Oxon 65 D5
Netherton Perth 231 C5
Netherton Stirl 205 A5
Netherton W Mid 96 C2
Netherton Worcs 80 C2
Netherton N Yorks 139 B4
Netherton W Yorks 139 B5
Nethertown Cumb 162 D2
Nethertown Highld 281 A5
Netherwitton Northumb 189 D4
Netherwood E Ayrs 193 C6
Nethy Bridge Highld 253 D6
Netley Hants 18 A3
Netley Marsh Hants 32 D2
Nettacott Essex 69 B4
Nettlebed Oxon 47 A5
Nettlebridge Som 29 A6
Nettlecombe Dorset 15 B5
Nettleden Herts 67 B5
Nettleham Lincs 133 B5
Nettlestead Kent 37 A4
Nettlestead Green Kent 37 A4
Nettlestone I o W 19 B5
Nettlesworth Durham 167 A5
Nettleton Lincs 142 C3
Nettleton Wilts 44 B2
Neuadd Carms 58 C3
Nevendon Essex 70 D1
Nevern Pembs 72 B3
Nevis Range Ski Centre, Torlundy Highld 237 B5
New Abbey Dumfries 174 B2
New Aberdour Aberds 268 C3
New Addington London 49 C6
New Alresford Hants 33 B4
New Alyth Perth 231 D6
New Arley Warks 97 C5
New Ash Green Kent 50 C3
New Barn Kent 50 C3
New Barnetby N Lincs 142 B2
New Barton Northants 83 A5
New Bewick Northumb 188 A3
New Bilton Warks 98 D1
New Bolingbroke Lincs 134 D3
New Boultham Lincs 133 B4
New Bradwell M Keynes 83 C5
New Brancepeth Durham 167 A5
New Bridge Wrex 110 A1
New Brighton Flint 126 C2
New Brighton Mers 136 D2
New Brinsley Notts 131 D4
New Broughton Wrex 126 D3
New Buckenham Norf 104 B1
New Byth Aberds 268 D3
New Catton Norf 120 D4
New Cheriton Hants 33 C4

New Costessy Norf 120 D3
New Cowper Cumb 174 D4
New Cross Ceredig 75 A5
New Cross London 49 B6
New Cumnock E Ayrs 182 A4
New Deer Aberds 256 B3
New Delaval Northumb 179 B4
New Duston Northants 83 A4
New Earswick York 149 B5
New Edlington S Yorks 140 D3
New Elgin Moray 266 C3
New Ellerby E Yorks 151 D4
New End Worcs 80 B3
New Farnley W Yorks 147 D6
New Ferry Mers 126 A3
New Fryston W Yorks 140 A2
New Galloway Dumfries 172 A4
New Gilston Fife 220 D4
New Grimsby Scilly 2 E3
New Hainford Norf 120 D4
New Hartley Northumb 179 B5
New Haw Sur 48 C3
New Hedges Pembs 56 B1
New Herrington T & W 179 D5
New Hinksey Oxon 65 C6
New Holkham Norf 119 B5
New Holland N Lincs 142 A2
New Houghton Derbys 131 C4
New Houghton Norf 119 C4
New Houses N Yorks 155 D7
New Humberstone Leicester 98 A3
New Hutton Cumb 155 B4
New Hythe Kent 37 A5
New Inn Carms 58 B1
New Inn Mon 61 C6
New Inn Pembs 55 A6
New Inn Torf 61 D5
New Invention Shrops 93 D6
New Invention W Mid 96 A2
New Kelso Highld 249 B6
New Kingston Notts 114 C3
New Lanark S Lnrk 194 B3
New Lanark Village & Visitor Centre, Lanark S Lnrk 194 B3
New Lane Lancs 136 B3
New Lane End Warr 137 D5
New Leake Lincs 135 D4
New Leeds Aberds 269 D4
New Longton Lancs 136 A4
New Luce Dumfries 170 A3
New Malden London 49 C5
New Marske Redcar 168 C4
New Marton Shrops 110 B2
New Micklefield W Yorks 148 D3
New Mill Aberds 245 D4
New Mill Herts 67 B4
New Mill Wilts 45 C5
New Mill W Yorks 139 C4
New Mills Ches 128 A2
New Mills Corn 4 B3
New Mills Derbys 129 A4
New Mills Powys 93 A4
New Milton Hants 17 B6
New Moat Pembs 55 B6
New Ollerton Notts 131 C6
New Oscott W Mid 96 B3
New Park N Yorks 148 B1
New Pitsligo Aberds 268 D3
New Pleasurewood Hills Leisure Park, Lowestoft Suff 105 B6
New Polzeath Corn 9 D5
New Quay = Ceinewydd Ceredig 73 A6
New Rackheath Norf 121 D4
New Radnor Powys 77 A6
New Rent Cumb 164 B2
New Ridley Northumb 178 D2
New Road Side N Yorks 146 C3
New Romney Kent 38 C2
New Rossington S Yorks 140 D4
New Row Ceredig 75 A6
New Row Lancs 145 D6
New Row N Yorks 168 D4
New Sarum Wilts 31 B5
New Silksworth T & W 179 D5
New Stevenston N Lnrk 194 A2
New Street Staffs 129 D5
New Street Lane Shrops 111 B5
New Swanage Dorset 17 C4
New Totley S Yorks 130 B3
New Town E Loth 210 C1
New Tredegar = Tredegar Newydd Caerph 41 A6

New Trows S Lnrk 194 C3
New Ulva Argyll 213 D5
New Walsoken Cambs 101 A6
New Waltham NE Lincs 143 C4
New Whittington Derbys 130 B3
New Wimpole Cambs 85 C5
New Winton E Loth 210 C1
New Yatt Oxon 65 B4
New York Lincs 134 D2
New York N Yorks 147 A5
Newall W Yorks 147 C5
Newark Orkney 282 C8
Newark P'boro 100 A4
Newark Castle Notts 132 D2
Newark-on-Trent Notts 132 D2
Newarthill N Lnrk 194 A2
Newbarns Cumb 153 C3
Newbattle Midloth 209 D6
Newbiggin Cumb 153 A1
Newbiggin Cumb 164 C2
Newbiggin Cumb 164 A3
Newbiggin Cumb 165 C4
Newbiggin Durham 166 C2
Newbiggin N Yorks 156 B3
Newbiggin N Yorks 156 C3
Newbiggin-by-the-Sea Northumb 179 A5
Newbiggin-on-Lune Cumb 155 A6
Newbigging Angus 220 A4
Newbigging Angus 221 A4
Newbigging S Lnrk 195 B5
Newbold Derbys 130 B3
Newbold Leics 114 D2
Newbold on Avon Warks 98 D1
Newbold on Stour Warks 81 C5
Newbold Pacey Warks 81 B5
Newbold Verdon Leics 98 A1
Newborough Anglesey 123 D4
Newborough P'boro 100 A4
Newborough Staffs 113 C5
Newbottle Northants 82 D2
Newbottle T & W 179 D5
Newbourne Suff 88 C3
Newbridge Caerph 41 B7
Newbridge Ceredig 75 C4
Newbridge Corn 2 B2
Newbridge Corn 6 A2
Newbridge Dumfries 174 A2
Newbridge Edin 208 C4
Newbridge Hants 32 D1
Newbridge I o W 18 C3
Newbridge Pembs 55 A5
Newbridge Green Worcs 79 D6
Newbridge-on-Usk Mon 61 D5
Newbridge on Wye Powys 76 B4
Newbrough Northumb 177 C6
Newbuildings Devon 12 A2
Newburgh Aberds 257 D4
Newburgh Aberds 269 D4
Newburgh Borders 185 A6
Newburgh Fife 220 C2
Newburgh Lancs 136 B3
Newburn T & W 178 C3
Newbury W Berks 46 C2
Newbury Park London 50 A1
Newbury Racecourse W Berks 46 C2
Newby Cumb 164 C3
Newby Lancs 146 C2
Newby N Yorks 155 D6
Newby N Yorks 168 D3
Newby N Yorks 160 B4
Newby Bridge Cumb 154 C2
Newby East Cumb 176 D2
Newby Hall, Ripon N Yorks 148 A3
Newby West Cumb 175 C6
Newby Wiske N Yorks 158 C2
Newcastle Mon 61 B6
Newcastle Shrops 93 C6
Newcastle Discovery T & W 179 C4
Newcastle Emlyn = Castell Newydd Emlyn Carms 73 B6
Newcastle International Airport T & W 178 B3
Newcastle Racecourse T & W 179 B4
Newcastle-under-Lyme Staffs 112 A2
Newcastle Upon Tyne T & W 179 C4
Newcastleton = Copshaw Holm Borders 176 A2

Newchapel Pembs 73 C5
Newchapel Powys 92 C3
Newchapel Staffs 128 D3
Newchapel Sur 35 B6
Newchurch Carms 73 D6
Newchurch I o W 19 C4
Newchurch Kent 38 B2
Newchurch Lancs 146 D2
Newchurch Mon 61 D6
Newchurch Powys 77 B6
Newchurch Staffs 113 C5
Newcott Devon 14 A2
Newcraighall Edin 209 C6
Newdigate Sur 35 B4
Newell Green Brack 48 B1
Newenden Kent 37 D6
Newent Glos 62 A3
Newerne Glos 62 C2
Newfield Durham 167 B5
Newfield Highld 264 C3
Newford Scilly 2 E4
Newfound Hants 46 D3
Newgale Pembs 54 B4
Newgate Norf 120 A2
Newgate Street Herts 68 C3
Newhall Ches 111 A5
Newhall Derbys 113 C6
Newhall House Highld 264 D2
Newhall Point Highld 264 D3
Newham Northumb 189 A4
Newham Hall Northumb 189 A4
Newhaven Derbys 129 D6
Newhaven Edin 209 C5
Newhaven E Sus 22 B2
Newhey Gtr Man 138 B2
Newholm N Yorks 169 D6
Newhouse N Lnrk 207 D5
Newick E Sus 36 D2
Newingreen Kent 38 B3
Newington Kent 51 C5
Newington Kent 38 B3
Newington Kent 53 C5
Newington Notts 141 D4
Newington Oxon 65 D7
Newington Shrops 94 C2
Newland Glos 62 C1
Newland Hull 150 D3
Newland N Yorks 141 A4
Newland Worcs 79 C5
Newlandrig Midloth 209 D6
Newlands Borders 186 D4
Newlands Highld 252 B3
Newlands Moray 266 D4
Newlands Northumb 178 D2
Newland's Corner Sur 34 B3
Newlands of Geise Highld 280 B2
Newlands of Tynet Moray 267 C4
Newlands Park Anglesey 122 B2
Newlandsmuir S Lnrk 205 C6
Newlot Orkney 282 F6
Newlyn Corn 2 C2
Newmachar Aberds 245 A5
Newmains N Lnrk 194 A3
Newmarket Suff 86 A2
Newmarket W Isles 288 D5
Newmarket Racecourse Suff 86 A2
Newmill Borders 186 B3
Newmill Corn 2 B2
Newmill Moray 267 D5
Newmill of Inshewan Angus 232 B2
Newmills Mon 61 C7
Newmills of Boyne Aberds 267 D6
Newmiln Perth 219 A6
Newmilns E Ayrs 193 B5
Newnham Cambs 85 B6
Newnham Glos 62 B2
Newnham Hants 47 D5
Newnham Herts 84 D4
Newnham Kent 51 D6
Newnham Northants 82 B2
Newnham Bridge Worcs 79 A4
Newpark Fife 221 C4
Newport Devon 25 B6
Newport E Yorks 150 D1
Newport Essex 85 D7
Newport Highld 275 B5
Newport I o W 18 C4
Newport Norf 121 D7
Newport Telford 111 D6
Newport = Casnewydd Newport 42 A2

Newport = Tretdraeth
Pembs 72 C3
Newport Museum & Art
Gallery Newport 42 A2
Newport-on-Tay Fife 220 B4
Newport Pagnell M Keynes 83 C5
Newpound Common
W Sus 34 D3
Newquay Corn 4 A3
Newquay Airport Corn 4 A3
Newquay Sea Life Centre
Corn 4 A2
Newsbank Ches 128 C3
Newseat Aberds 256 C2
Newseat Aberds 257 B5
Newsham Northumb 179 B5
Newsham N Yorks 166 D4
Newsham N Yorks 158 C2
Newsholme E Yorks 141 A5
Newsholme Lancs 146 B2
Newsome W Yorks 139 B4
Newstead Borders 197 C4
Newstead Notts 131 D5
Newstead Northumb 189 A4
Newstead Abbey, Kirkby
in Ashfield Notts 131 D5
Newthorpe N Yorks 148 D3
Newton Argyll 214 C3
Newton Borders 187 A5
Newton Bridgend 40 D3
Newton Cambs 85 C6
Newton Cambs 118 D1
Newton Cardiff 42 B1
Newton Ches 127 D5
Newton Ches 127 C4
Newton Ches 127 B5
Newton Cumb 153 C3
Newton Derbys 131 D4
Newton Dorset 30 D1
Newton Dumfries 185 C4
Newton Dumfries 175 A5
Newton Gtr Man 138 D2
Newton Hereford 78 D1
Newton Hereford 78 B3
Newton Highld 264 D3
Newton Highld 271 A5
Newton Highld 281 D5
Newton Highld 252 B3
Newton Lancs 144 D4
Newton Lancs 145 B6
Newton Lancs 155 C4
Newton Lincs 116 B3
Newton Moray 266 C2
Newton Norf 119 D5
Newton Notts 115 A4
Newton Northants 99 C5
Newton Northumb 178 C2
Newton Perth 218 A3
Newton S Lnrk 205 B6
Newton S Lnrk 194 C4
Newton Staffs 112 C4
Newton Suff 87 C5
Newton Swansea 57 D6
Newton S Yorks 140 C3
Newton Warks 98 D2
Newton Wilts 31 C6
Newton W Loth 208 C3
Newton Abbot Devon 12 D3
Newton Abbot
Racecourse Devon 12 D3
Newton Arlosh Cumb 175 C4
Newton Aycliffe Durham 167 C5
Newton Bewley Hrtlpl 168 C2
Newton Blossomville
M Keynes 83 B6
Newton Bromswold
Northants 84 A1
Newton Burgoland Leics 97 A6
Newton by Toft Lincs 133 A5
Newton Ferrers Devon 7 C4
Newton Flotman Norf 104 B3
Newton Hall Northumb 178 C2
Newton Harcourt Leics 98 B3
Newton Heath Gtr Man 138 C1
Newton Ho. Aberds 256 D1
Newton Kyme N Yorks 148 C3
Newton-le-Willows Mers 137 D4
Newton-le-Willows
N Yorks 157 B5
Newton Longville Bucks 83 D5
Newton Mearns E Renf 205 C5
Newton Morrell N Yorks 157 A6
Newton Mulgrave
N Yorks 169 D5

Newton of Ardtoe Highld 235 C5
Newton of Balcanquhal
Perth 219 C6
Newton of Falkland Fife 220 D2
Newton on Ayr S Ayrs 192 C3
Newton on Ouse N Yorks 148 B4
Newton-on-Rawcliffe
N Yorks 159 B7
Newton-on-the-Moor
Northumb 189 C4
Newton on Trent Lincs 132 B3
Newton Park Argyll 203 B6
Newton Poppleford Devon 13 C5
Newton Purcell Oxon 82 D3
Newton Regis Warks 97 A5
Newton Reigny Cumb 164 B2
Newton St Cyres Devon 12 B3
Newton St Faith Norf 120 D4
Newton St Loe Bath 43 C6
Newton St Petrock Devon 25 D5
Newton Solney Derbys 113 C6
Newton Stacey Hants 32 A3
Newton Stewart Dumfries 171 A6
Newton Tony Wilts 31 A6
Newton Tracey Devon 25 C6
Newton under Roseberry
Redcar 168 D3
Newton upon Derwent
E Yorks 149 C6
Newton Valence Hants 33 B6
Newtonairds Dumfries 183 D6
Newtongrange Midloth 209 D6
Newtonhill Aberds 245 C6
Newtonhill Highld 252 B1
Newtonmill Angus 233 B4
Newtonmore Highld 241 C5
Newtown Argyll 214 B3
Newtown Ches 127 B5
Newtown Corn 3 C5
Newtown Cumb 174 D3
Newtown Cumb 176 C3
Newtown Derbys 129 A4
Newtown Devon 26 C2
Newtown Glos 62 C2
Newtown Glos 80 D2
Newtown Hants 31 D6
Newtown Hants 32 C2
Newtown Hants 33 D5
Newtown Hants 46 C2
Newtown Hants 32 D4
Newtown Hants 18 A3
Newtown Hereford 79 C4
Newtown Highld 240 B1
Newtown I o M 152 D3
Newtown I o W 18 B3
Newtown Northumb 188 C3
Newtown Northumb 188 A3
Newtown Northumb 198 C3
Newtown Poole 17 B4
Newtown Shrops 110 B3
Newtown Staffs 129 C4
Newtown Staffs 129 C5
Newtown Wilts 30 C3
Newtown = Y
Drenewydd Powys 93 B5
Newtown Linford Leics 98 A2
Newtown St Boswells
Borders 197 C4
Newtown Unthank Leics 98 A1
Newtyle Angus 231 D6
Neyland Pembs 55 D5
Niarbyl I o M 152 D2
Nibley S Glos 43 A5
Nibley Green Glos 62 D3
Nibon Shetland 284 F5
Nicholashayne Devon 27 D6
Nicholaston Swansea 57 D5
Nidd N Yorks 148 A2
Nigg Aberdeen 245 B6
Nigg Highld 265 C4
Nigg Ferry Highld 264 D3
Nightcott Som 26 C3
Nilig Denb 125 D5
Nine Ashes Essex 69 C5
Nine Mile Burn Midloth 195 A6
Nine Wells Pembs 54 B3
Ninebanks Northumb 177 D5
Ninfield E Sus 23 A5
Ningwood I o W 18 C2
Nisbet Borders 187 A5
Nisthouse Orkney 282 F4
Nisthouse Shetland 285 G7
Niton I o W 18 D4
Nitshill Glasgow 205 B5
No Man's Heath Ches 111 A4
No Man's Heath Warks 97 A5
Noak Hill London 69 D5

Noblethorpe S Yorks 139 C5
Nobottle Northants 82 A3
Nocton Lincs 133 C5
Noke Oxon 65 B6
Nolton Pembs 55 C4
Nolton Haven Pembs 55 C4
Nomansland Devon 26 D3
Nomansland Wilts 31 D6
Noneley Shrops 110 C3
Nonikiln Highld 264 C2
Nonington Kent 53 D4
Noonsbrough Shetland 285 H4
Norbreck Blkpool 144 C3
Norbridge Hereford 79 C5
Norbury Ches 111 A4
Norbury Derbys 113 A5
Norbury Shrops 94 B1
Norbury Staffs 112 C1
Nordelph Norf 102 A1
Norden Gtr Man 138 B1
Norden Heath Dorset 16 C3
Nordley Shrops 95 B4
Norham Northumb 198 B3
Norley Ches 127 B5
Norleywood Hants 18 B2
Norman Cross Cambs 100 B3
Normanby N Lincs 141 B6
Normanby N Yorks 159 C6
Normanby Redcar 168 D3
Normanby-by-Spital
Lincs 133 A5
Normanby by Stow Lincs 132 A3
Normanby le Wold Lincs 142 D3
Normandy Sur 34 A2
Norman's Bay E Sus 23 B4
Norman's Green Devon 13 A5
Normanstone Suff 105 B6
Normanton Derby 114 B1
Normanton Leics 115 A6
Normanton Lincs 116 A2
Normanton Notts 132 D2
Normanton Rutland 99 A6
Normanton W Yorks 140 A1
Normanton le Heath
Leics 114 D1
Normanton on Soar
Notts 114 C3
Normanton-on-the-
Wolds Notts 115 B4
Normanton on Trent
Notts 132 C2
Normoss Lancs 144 D3
Norney Sur 34 B2
Norrington Common Wilts 44 C2
Norris Green Mers 136 D2
Norris Hill Leics 114 D1
North Anston S Yorks 131 A5
North Aston Oxon 65 A5
North Baddesley Hants 32 D2
North Ballachulish Highld 237 C4
North Barrow Som 29 C6
North Barsham Norf 119 B6
North Benfleet Essex 51 A4
North Bersted W Sus 20 B2
North Berwick E Loth 210 B2
North Boarhunt Hants 33 D5
North Bovey Devon 12 C2
North Bradley Wilts 44 D2
North Brentor Devon 11 C5
North Brewham Som 29 B7
North Buckland Devon 25 A5
North Burlingham Norf 121 D5
North Cadbury Som 29 C6
North Cairn Dumfries 180 D1
North Carlton Lincs 133 B4
North Carrine Argyll 190 E2
North Cave E Yorks 150 D1
North Cerney Glos 63 C6
North Charford Wilts 31 D5
North Charlton Northumb 189 A4
North Cheriton Som 29 C6
North Cliff E Yorks 151 C5
North Cliffe E Yorks 150 D1
North Clifton Notts 132 B3
North Cockerington Lincs 143 D5
North Coker Som 29 D5
North Collafirth Shetland 284 E5
North Common E Sus 36 D1
North Connel Argyll 226 C4
North Cornelly Bridgend 40 C3
North Cotes Lincs 143 C5
North Cove Suff 105 C5
North Cowton N Yorks 157 A6
North Crawley M Keynes 83 C6
North Cray London 50 B1
North Creake Norf 119 B5
North Curry Som 28 C3

North Dalton E Yorks 150 B2
North Dawn Orkney 283 G5
North Deighton N Yorks 148 R?
North Duffield N Yorks 149 D5
North Elkington Lincs 143 D4
North Elmham Norf 120 C1
North Elmshall W Yorks 140 B2
North End Bucks 66 A3
North End E Yorks 151 D5
North End Essex 69 B6
North End Hants 46 C2
North End Lincs 117 A5
North End N Som 42 C3
North End Ptsmth 19 A5
North End Som 28 C2
North End W Sus 21 B4
North Erradale Highld 261 B4
North Fambridge Essex 70 D2
North Fearns Highld 248 C2
North Featherstone
W Yorks 140 A2
North Ferriby E Yorks 142 A1
North Frodingham
E Yorks 151 B4
North Gluss Shetland 284 F5
North Gorley Hants 31 D5
North Green Norf 104 C3
North Green Suff 89 A4
North Greetwell Lincs 133 B5
North Grimston N Yorks 150 A1
North Halley Orkney 283 G6
North Halling Medway 51 C4
North Hayling Hants 19 A6
North Hazelrigg Northumb 199 C4
North Heasley Devon 26 B2
North Heath W Sus 34 D3
North Hill Cambs 101 D6
North Hill Corn 10 D3
North Hinksey Oxon 65 C5
North Holmwood Sur 35 B4
North Howden E Yorks 149 D6
North Huish Devon 7 B6
North Hykeham Lincs 133 C4
North Johnston Pembs 55 C5
North Kelsey Lincs 142 C2
North Kelsey Moor Lincs 142 C2
North Killingholme
N Lincs 142 B3
North Kilvington N Yorks 158 C3
North Kilworth Leics 98 C3
North Kirkton Aberds 269 D6
North Kiscadale N Ayrs 191 C6
North Kyme Lincs 133 D6
North Lancing W Sus 21 B4
North Lee Bucks 66 C3
North Leigh Oxon 65 B4
North Leverton with
Habblesthorpe Notts 132 A2
North Littleton Worcs 80 C3
North Lopham Norf 103 C6
North Luffenham Rutland 99 A6
North Marden W Sus 33 D7
North Marston Bucks 66 A2
North Middleton Midloth 196 A2
North Middleton
Northumb 188 A3
North Molton Devon 26 C2
North Moreton Oxon 46 A3
North Mundham W Sus 20 B1
North Muskham Notts 132 D2
North Newbald E Yorks 150 D2
North Newington Oxon 81 D7
North Newnton Wilts 45 D5
North Newton Som 28 B2
North Nibley Glos 62 D3
North Norfolk Railway,
Sheringham Norf 120 A3
North Oakley Hants 46 D3
North Ockendon London 50 A2
North Ormesby M'boro 168 C3
North Ormsby Lincs 143 D4
North Otterington
N Yorks 158 C2
North Owersby Lincs 142 D2
North Perrott Som 15 A4
North Petherton Som 28 B2
North Petherwin Corn 10 C3
North Pickenham Norf 103 A4
North Piddle Worcs 80 B2
North Poorton Dorset 15 B5
North Port Argyll 227 D5
North Queensferry Fife 208 B4
North Radworthy Devon 26 B2
North Rauceby Lincs 116 A3
North Reston Lincs 134 A3
North Rigton N Yorks 148 C1

North Rode Ches 128 C3
North Roe Shetland 284 E5
North Ronaldsay Airport
Orkney 282 B6
North Runcton Norf 118 D3
North Sandwick Shetland 284 D7
North Scale Cumb 153 D2
North Scarle Lincs 132 C3
North Seaton Northumb 179 A4
North Shian Argyll 226 B4
North Shields T & W 179 C5
North Shoebury Sthend 51 A6
North Shore Blkpool 144 D7
North Side Cumb 162 B
North Side P'boro 101 B
North Skelton Redcar 169 D
North Somercotes Lincs 143 D6
North Stainley N Yorks 157 D
North Stainmore Cumb 165 D
North Stifford Thurrock 50 A
North Stoke Bath 43 C
North Stoke Oxon 47 A
North Stoke W Sus 20 A
North Street Hants 33 B
North Street Kent 52 D
North Street Medway 51 B
North Street W Berks 47 B
North Sunderland
Northumb 199 C
North Tamerton Corn 10 B
North Tawton Devon 12 A
North Thoresby Lincs 143 D
North Tidworth Wilts 31 A
North Togston Northumb 189 C
North Tuddenham Norf 120 D
North Walbottle T & W 178 C
North Walsham Norf 121 B
North Waltham Hants 33 A
North Warnborough Hants 47 D
North Water Bridge
Angus 233 B
North Watten Highld 280 C
North Weald Bassett Essex 69 C
North Wheatley Notts 132 A
North Whilborough Devon 8 A
North Wick Bath 43 C
North Willingham Lincs 133 A
North Wingfield Derbys 131 C
North Witham Lincs 116 C
North Woolwich London 50 B
North Wootton Dorset 29 D
North Wootton Norf 118 C
North Wootton Som 29 A
North Wraxall Wilts 44 B
North Wroughton
Swindon 45 A5
North Yorkshire Moors
Railway, Pickering
N Yorks 160 B
Northacre Norf 103 B
Northallerton N Yorks 158 B
Northam Devon 25 C
Northam Soton 32 D
Northampton Northants 83 A
Northaw Herts 68 C
Northbeck Lincs 116 A
Northborough P'boro 100 A
Northbourne Kent 53 D
Northbridge Street E Sus 37 D
Northchapel W Sus 34 D
Northchurch Herts 67 C
Northcott Devon 10 B
Northdown Kent 53 B
Northdyke Orkney 282 E
Northend Bath 44 C
Northend Bucks 66 D
Northend Warks 81 B
Northenden Gtr Man 137 D
Northfield Aberdeen 245 B
Northfield Borders 211 D
Northfield E Yorks 142 A
Northfield W Mid 96 D
Northfields Lincs 100 A
Northfleet Kent 50 B
Northgate Lincs 117 C
Northhouse Borders 186 B
Northiam E Sus 37 D
Northill Beds 84 C
Northington Hants 33 B
Northlands Lincs 134 D
Northlea Durham 179 D
Northleach Glos 64 B
Northleigh Devon 14 B
Northlew Devon 11 B
Northmoor Oxon 65 C
Northmoor Green or
Moorland Som 28 B

Northmuir Angus 232 C1
Northney Hants 19 A6
Northolt London 48 A4
Northop Flint 126 C2
Northop Hall Flint 126 C2
Northorpe Lincs 116 D3
Northorpe Lincs 117 B5
Northorpe Lincs 141 D6
Northover Som 29 B4
Northover Som 29 C5
Northowram W Yorks 139 A4
Northport Dorset 16 C3
Northpunds Shetland 285 L6
Northrepps Norf 120 B4
Northtown Orkney 283 H5
Northumbria Craft Centre, Morpeth Northumb 178 A3
Northway Glos 80 D2
Northwich Ches 127 B6
Northwick S Glos 43 A4
Northwold Norf 102 B3
Northwood Derbys 130 C2
Northwood London 67 D5
Northwood I o W 18 B3
Northwood Kent 53 C5
Northwood Shrops 110 B3
Northwood Green Glos 62 B3
Norton E Sus 22 B2
Norton Glos 63 A4
Norton Halton 127 A5
Norton Herts 84 D4
Norton I o W 18 C2
Norton Mon 61 B6
Norton Notts 131 B5
Norton Northants 82 A3
Norton Powys 77 A7
Norton Shrops 94 C2
Norton Shrops 94 A3
Norton Shrops 95 A5
Norton Stockton 168 C2
Norton Suff 87 A5
Norton S Yorks 140 B3
Norton Wilts 44 A2
Norton Worcs 80 B1
Norton Worcs 80 C3
Norton W Sus 20 C1
Norton W Sus 20 B2
Norton Bavant Wilts 30 A3
Norton Bridge Staffs 112 B2
Norton Canes Staffs 96 A3
Norton Canon Hereford 78 C1
Norton Corner Norf 120 C2
Norton Disney Lincs 132 D3
Norton East Staffs 96 A3
Norton Ferris Wilts 30 B1
Norton Fitzwarren Som 28 C1
Norton Green I o W 18 C2
Norton Hawkfield Bath 43 C4
Norton Heath Essex 69 C6
Norton in Hales Shrops 111 B6
Norton-in-the-Moors Stoke 128 D3
Norton-Juxta-Twycross Leics 97 A6
Norton-le-Clay N Yorks 158 D3
Norton Lindsey Warks 81 A5
Norton Malreward Bath 43 C5
Norton Mandeville Essex 69 C5
Norton-on-Derwent N Yorks 159 D6
Norton St Philip Som 43 D6
Norton sub Hamdon Som 29 D4
Norton Woodseats S Yorks 130 A3
Norwell Notts 132 C2
Norwell Woodhouse Notts 132 C2
Norwich Norf 104 A3
Norwich Castle Museum Norf 104 A3
Norwich Cathedral Norf 104 A3
Norwich International Airport Norf 120 D4
Norwick Shetland 284 B8
Norwood Derbys 131 A4
Norwood Hill Sur 35 B5
Norwoodside Cambs 101 B6
Noseley Leics 99 B4
Noss Mayo Devon 7 C4
Nosterfield N Yorks 157 C6
Nostie Highld 249 D5
Notgrove Glos 64 A2
Nothe Fort, Weymouth Dorset 15 D6
Nottage Bridgend 40 D3

Nottingham Nottingham 114 B3
Nottingham Castle Museum Nottingham 114 B3
Nottingham East Midlands Airport Leics 114 C2
Nottingham Racecourse Nottingham 114 B3
Nottington Dorset 15 C6
Notton Wilts 44 C3
Notton W Yorks 139 B6
Nounsley Essex 70 B1
Noutard's Green Worcs 79 A5
Novar House Highld 264 D2
Nox Shrops 110 D3
Nuffield Oxon 47 A4
Nun Hills Lancs 138 A1
Nun Monkton N Yorks 148 B4
Nunburnholme E Yorks 150 C1
Nuncargate Notts 131 D5
Nuneaton Warks 97 B6
Nuneham Courtenay Oxon 65 D6
Nunney Som 30 A1
Nunnington N Yorks 159 D5
Nunnykirk Northumb 188 D3
Nunsthorpe NE Lincs 143 C4
Nunthorpe M'bro 168 D3
Nunthorpe York 149 B5
Nunton Wilts 31 C5
Nunwick N Yorks 157 D7
Nupend Glos 62 C3
Nursling Hants 32 D2
Nursted Hants 33 C6
Nutbourne W Sus 20 A3
Nutbourne W Sus 19 A6
Nutfield Sur 35 A6
Nuthall Notts 114 A3
Nuthampstead Herts 85 D6
Nuthurst W Sus 35 D4
Nutley E Sus 36 D2
Nutley Hants 33 A5
Nutwell S Yorks 140 C4
Nybster Highld 281 B5
Nyetimber W Sus 20 C1
Nyewood W Sus 33 C7
Nymans Garden, Crawley W Sus 35 D5
Nymet Rowland Devon 12 A2
Nymet Tracey Devon 12 A2
Nympsfield Glos 63 C4
Nynehead Som 27 C6
Nyton W Sus 20 B2

O

Oad Street Kent 51 C5
Oadby Leics 98 A3
Oak Cross Devon 11 B6
Oakamoor Staffs 113 A4
Oakbank W Loth 208 D3
Oakdale Caerph 41 B6
Oake Som 27 C6
Oaken Staffs 95 A6
Oakenclough Lancs 145 C5
Oakengates Telford 111 D6
Oakenholt Flint 126 B2
Oakenshaw Durham 167 B5
Oakenshaw W Yorks 139 A4
Oakerthorpe Derbys 130 D3
Oakes W Yorks 139 B4
Oakfield Torf 61 D5
Oakford Ceredig 74 C3
Oakford Devon 27 C4
Oakfordbridge Devon 27 C4
Oakgrove Ches 129 C4
Oakham Rutland 99 A5
Oakhanger Hants 33 B6
Oakhill Som 29 A6
Oakhurst Kent 36 A3
Oakington Cambs 85 A6
Oaklands Herts 68 B2
Oaklands Powys 76 B4
Oakle Street Glos 62 B3
Oakley Beds 84 B2
Oakley Bucks 66 B1
Oakley Fife 208 B3
Oakley Hants 46 D3
Oakley Oxon 66 C2
Oakley Poole 17 B4
Oakley Suff 104 D2
Oakley Green Windsor 48 B2
Oakley Park Powys 92 C3
Oakmere Ches 127 C5
Oakridge Glos 63 C5
Oakridge Hants 47 D4
Oaks Shrops 94 A2
Oaks Green Derbys 113 B5
Oaksey Wilts 63 D5

Oakthorpe Leics 113 D7
Oakwood Adventure Park, Narberth Pembs 55 C6
Oakwoodhill Sur 35 C4
Oakworth W Yorks 147 D4
Oape Highld 272 D2
Oare Kent 52 C2
Oare Som 26 A3
Oare W Berks 46 B3
Oare Wilts 45 C5
Oasby Lincs 116 B3
Oathlaw Angus 232 C2
Oatlands N Yorks 148 B2
Oban Argyll 226 D3
Oban Argyll 238 D2
Oborne Dorset 29 D6
Obthorpe Lincs 116 D3
Occlestone Green Ches 128 C1
Occold Suff 104 D2
Ocean Beach Amusement Park, Rhyl Denb 125 A4
Ochiltree E Ayrs 193 C5
Ochtermuthill Perth 218 C3
Ochtertyre Perth 218 B3
Ockbrook Derbys 114 B2
Ockham Sur 34 A3
Ockle Highld 235 C4
Ockley Sur 35 C4
Ocle Pychard Hereford 78 C3
Octon E Yorks 150 A3
Octon Cross Roads E Yorks 150 A3
Odcombe Som 29 D5
Odd Down Bath 43 C6
Oddendale Cumb 164 D3
Odder Lincs 133 B4
Oddingley Worcs 80 B2
Oddington Glos 64 A3
Oddington Oxon 65 B6
Odell Beds 83 B6
Odie Orkney 282 E7
Odiham Hants 47 D5
Odstock Wilts 31 C5
Odstone Leics 97 A6
Offchurch Warks 81 A6
Offenham Worcs 80 C3
Offham E Sus 22 A1
Offham Kent 37 A4
Offham W Sus 20 B3
Offord Cluny Cambs 84 A4
Offord Darcy Cambs 84 A4
Offton Suff 87 C6
Offwell Devon 14 B1
Ogbourne Maizey Wilts 45 B5
Ogbourne St Andrew Wilts 45 B5
Ogbourne St George Wilts 45 B6
Ogil Angus 232 B2
Ogle Northumb 178 B3
Ogmore V Glam 40 D3
Ogmore-by-Sea V Glam 40 D3
Ogmore Vale Bridgend 40 B4
Okeford Fitzpaine Dorset 30 D2
Okehampton Devon 11 B6
Okehampton Camp Devon 11 B6
Okraquoy Shetland 285 K6
Old Northants 99 D4
Old Aberdeen Aberdeen 245 B6
Old Alresford Hants 33 B4
Old Arley Warks 97 B5
Old Basford Nottingham 114 A3
Old Basing Hants 47 D4
Old Bewick Northumb 188 A3
Old Blacksmith's Shop Centre, Gretna Green Dumfries 175 B6
Old Bolingbroke Lincs 134 C3
Old Bramhope W Yorks 147 C6
Old Brampton Derbys 130 B3
Old Bridge of Tilt Perth 230 B2
Old Bridge of Urr Dumfries 173 B5
Old Buckenham Norf 103 B6
Old Burghclere Hants 46 D2
Old Byland N Yorks 159 C4
Old Cassop Durham 167 B6
Old Castleton Borders 186 D4
Old Catton Norf 120 D4
Old Clee NE Lincs 143 C4
Old Cleeve Som 27 A5
Old Clipstone Notts 131 C6
Old Colwyn Conwy 124 B3
Old Coulsdon London 35 A6
Old Crombie Aberds 267 D6
Old Dailly S Ayrs 181 B4
Old Dalby Leics 115 C4
Old Deer Aberds 257 B4
Old Denaby S Yorks 140 D2

Old Edlington S Yorks 140 D3
Old Eldon Durham 167 C5
Old Ellerby E Yorks 151 D4
Old Felixstowe Suff 88 D1
Old Fletton P'boro 100 B3
Old Glossop Derbys 138 D3
Old Goole E Yorks 141 A5
Old Hall Powys 91 D7
Old Heath Essex 71 A4
Old Heathfield E Sus 36 D3
Old Hill W Mid 96 C2
Old House, Rochford Essex 70 D2
Old Hunstanton Norf 118 A3
Old Hurst Cambs 101 D4
Old Hutton Cumb 155 C4
Old Kea Corn 4 C3
Old Kilpatrick W Dunb 205 A4
Old Kinnernie Aberds 245 B4
Old Knebworth Herts 68 A2
Old Langho Lancs 145 D7
Old Laxey I o M 152 C4
Old Leake Lincs 135 D4
Old Malton N Yorks 159 D6
Old Micklefield W Yorks 148 D3
Old Milton Hants 17 B6
Old Milverton Warks 81 A5
Old Monkland N Lnrk 207 D5
Old Netley Hants 18 A3
Old Philpstoun W Loth 208 C3
Old Quarrington Durham 167 B6
Old Radnor Powys 77 B6
Old Rattray Aberds 269 D5
Old Rayne Aberds 256 D1
Old Romney Kent 38 C2
Old Sarum, Salisbury Wilts 31 B5
Old Sodbury S Glos 43 A6
Old Somerby Lincs 116 B2
Old Stratford Northants 83 C4
Old Thirsk N Yorks 158 C3
Old Town Cumb 164 A2
Old Town Cumb 155 C4
Old Town Northumb 188 D1
Old Town Scilly 2 E4
Old Trafford Gtr Man 137 D7
Old Tupton Derbys 130 C3
Old Warden Beds 84 C3
Old Weston Cambs 100 D2
Old Whittington Derbys 130 B3
Old Wick Highld 281 C5
Old Windsor Windsor 48 B2
Old Wives Lees Kent 52 D2
Old Woking Sur 34 A3
Old Woodhall Lincs 134 C2
Oldany Highld 270 A4
Oldberrow Warks 80 A4
Oldborough Devon 12 A2
Oldbury Shrops 95 B5
Oldbury Warks 97 B6
Oldbury W Mid 96 C2
Oldbury-on-Severn S Glos 62 D2
Oldbury on the Hill Glos 44 A2
Oldcastle Bridgend 40 D4
Oldcastle Mon 61 A5
Oldcotes Notts 131 A5
Oldfallow Staffs 112 D3
Oldfield Worcs 79 A6
Oldford Som 44 D1
Oldham Gtr Man 138 C2
Oldhamstocks E Loth 211 C4
Oldland S Glos 43 B5
Oldmeldrum Aberds 256 D3
Oldshore Beg Highld 276 C2
Oldshoremore Highld 276 C3
Oldstead N Yorks 158 C4
Oldtown Aberds 255 D6
Oldtown of Ord Aberds 267 D7
Oldway Swansea 57 D5
Oldways End Devon 26 C3
Oldwhat Aberds 268 D3
Olgrinmore Highld 280 C2
Oliver's Battery Hants 32 C3
Ollaberry Shetland 284 E5
Ollerton Ches 128 B2
Ollerton Notts 131 C6
Ollerton Shrops 111 C5
Olmarch Ceredig 75 C5
Olney M Keynes 83 B5
Olrig Ho. Highld 280 B3
Olton W Mid 96 C4
Olveston S Glos 43 A5
Olwen Ceredig 75 D4
Ombersley Worcs 79 A6
Ompton Notts 132 C1
Onchan I o M 152 D3
Onecote Staffs 129 D5
Onen Mon 61 B6

Ongar Hill Norf 118 C2
Ongar Street Hereford 78 A1
Onibury Shrops 94 D2
Onich Highld 237 C4
Onllwyn Neath 59 D5
Onneley Staffs 111 A6
Onslow Village Sur 34 B2
Onthank E Ayrs 205 D4
Openwoodgate Derbys 114 A1
Opinan Highld 261 A5
Opinan Highld 261 C4
Orange Lane Borders 198 B1
Orange Row Norf 118 C2
Orasaigh W Isles 288 F4
Orbliston Moray 266 D4
Orbost Highld 258 D2
Orby Lincs 135 C4
Orchard Hill Devon 25 C5
Orchard Portman Som 28 C2
Orcheston Wilts 31 A4
Orcop Hereford 61 A6
Orcop Hill Hereford 61 A6
Ord Highld 247 C5
Ordhead Aberds 244 A3
Ordie Aberds 244 B1
Ordiequish Moray 266 D4
Ordsall Notts 132 A1
Ore E Sus 23 A6
Oreton Shrops 95 C4
Orford Suff 89 C5
Orford Warr 137 D5
Orgreave Staffs 113 D5
Orlestone Kent 38 B1
Orleton Hereford 78 A2
Orleton Worcs 79 A4
Orlingbury Northants 99 D5
Ormesby Redcar 168 D3
Ormesby St Margaret Norf 121 D6
Ormesby St Michael Norf 121 D6
Ormiclate Castle W Isles 286 C3
Ormiscaig Highld 261 A5
Ormiston E Loth 209 D7
Ormsaigbeg Highld 234 D3
Ormsaigmore Highld 234 D3
Ormsary Argyll 202 A2
Ormsgill Cumb 153 C2
Ormskirk Lancs 136 C3
Orpington London 50 C1
Orrell Gtr Man 136 C4
Orrell Mers 136 D2
Orrisdale I o M 152 B3
Orroland Dumfries 173 D5
Orsett Thurrock 50 A3
Orslow Staffs 112 D2
Orston Notts 115 A5
Orthwaite Cumb 163 A5
Ortner Lancs 145 B5
Orton Cumb 155 A5
Orton Northants 99 D5
Orton Longueville P'boro 100 B3
Orton-on-the-Hill Leics 97 A6
Orton Waterville P'boro 100 B3
Orwell Cambs 85 B5
Osbaldeston Lancs 145 D6
Osbaldwick York 149 B5
Osbaston Shrops 110 C2
Osborne House I o W 18 B4
Osbournby Lincs 116 B3
Oscroft Ches 127 C5
Ose Highld 258 D3
Osgathorpe Leics 114 D2
Osgodby Lincs 142 D2
Osgodby N Yorks 149 D5
Osgodby N Yorks 161 C4
Oskaig Highld 248 C2
Oskamull Argyll 224 B3
Osmaston Derbys 113 A6
Osmaston Derby 114 B1
Osmington Dorset 16 C1
Osmington Mills Dorset 16 C1
Osmotherley N Yorks 158 B3
Ospisdale Highld 264 B3
Ospringe Kent 52 C2
Ossett W Yorks 139 A5
Ossington Notts 132 C2
Ostend Essex 70 D3
Oswaldkirk N Yorks 159 D5
Oswaldtwistle Lancs 137 A6
Oswestry Shrops 110 C1
Otford Kent 36 A3
Otham Kent 37 A5
Othery Som 28 B3
Otley Suff 88 B3

Otley W Yorks 147 C6
Otter Ferry Argyll 214 D2
Otterbourne Hants 32 C3
Otterburn Northumb 188 D1
Otterburn N Yorks 146 B2
Otterburn Camp
  Northumb 188 D1
Otterham Corn 10 B2
Otterhampton Som 28 A2
Ottershaw Sur 48 C3
Otterswick Shetland 284 E7
Otterton Devon 13 C5
Ottery St Mary Devon 13 B6
Ottinge Kent 38 A3
Ottringham E Yorks 143 A4
Oughterby Cumb 175 C5
Oughtershaw N Yorks 156 C2
Oughterside Cumb 174 D4
Oughtibridge S Yorks 139 D6
Oughtrington Warr 128 A1
Oulston N Yorks 158 D4
Oulton Cumb 175 C5
Oulton Norf 120 C3
Oulton Staffs 112 B3
Oulton Suff 105 B6
Oulton W Yorks 139 A6
Oulton Broad Suff 105 B6
Oulton Park Motor
  Racing Circuit Ches 127 C5
Oulton Street Norf 120 C3
Oundle Northants 100 C2
Ousby Cumb 165 B4
Ousdale Highld 275 B4
Ousden Suff 86 B3
Ousefleet E Yorks 141 A6
Ouston Durham 179 D4
Ouston Northumb 178 B2
Out Newton E Yorks 143 A5
Out Rawcliffe Lancs 144 C4
Outertown Orkney 282 F3
Outgate Cumb 154 B2
Outhgill Cumb 155 A6
Outlane W Yorks 138 B3
Outwell Norf 101 A7
Outwick Hants 31 D5
Outwood Sur 35 B6
Outwood W Yorks 139 A6
Outwoods Staffs 112 D1
Ovenden W Yorks 138 A3
Ovenscloss Borders 196 C3
Over Cambs 101 D5
Over Ches 127 C6
Over S Glos 43 A4
Over Compton Dorset 29 D5
Over Green W Mid 97 B4
Over Haddon Derbys 130 C2
Over Hulton Gtr Man 137 C5
Over Kellet Lancs 154 D4
Over Kiddington Oxon 65 A5
Over Knutsford Ches 128 B2
Over Monnow Mon 61 B7
Over Norton Oxon 64 A4
Over Peover Ches 128 B2
Over Silton N Yorks 158 B3
Over Stowey Som 28 B1
Over Stratton Som 28 D4
Over Tabley Ches 128 A2
Over Wallop Hants 32 B1
Over Whitacre Warks 97 B5
Over Worton Oxon 65 A5
Overbister Orkney 282 C7
Overbury Worcs 80 D2
Overcombe Dorset 15 C6
Overgreen Derbys 130 B3
Overleigh Som 29 B4
Overley Green Warks 80 B3
Overpool Ches 126 B3
Overscaig Hotel Highld 271 B7
Overseal Derbys 113 D6
Oversland Kent 52 D2
Overstone Northants 83 A5
Overstrand Norf 120 A4
Overthorpe Northants 82 C1
Overton Aberds 245 A5
Overton Ches 127 B5
Overton Dumfries 174 B2
Overton Hants 32 A4
Overton Lancs 144 B4
Overton N Yorks 149 B4
Overton Shrops 94 D3
Overton Swansea 57 D4
Overton W Yorks 139 B5
Overton = Owrtyn Wrex 110 A2
Overton Bridge Wrex 110 A2

Overtown N Lnrk 194 A3
Oving Bucks 66 A2
Oving W Sus 20 B2
Ovingdean Brighton 21 B6
Ovingham Northumb 178 C2
Ovington Durham 166 D4
Ovington Essex 86 C3
Ovington Hants 33 B4
Ovington Norf 103 A5
Ovington Northumb 178 C2
Ower Hants 32 D2
Owermoigne Dorset 16 C1
Owlbury Shrops 93 B7
Owler Bar Derbys 130 B2
Owlerton S Yorks 130 A3
Owl's Green Suff 88 A3
Owlswick Bucks 66 C2
Owmby Lincs 142 C2
Owmby-by-Spital Lincs 133 A5
Owrtyn = Overton Wrex 110 A2
Owslebury Hants 32 C4
Owston Leics 99 A4
Owston S Yorks 140 B3
Owston Ferry N Lincs 141 C6
Owstwick E Yorks 151 D5
Owthorne E Yorks 143 A5
Owthorpe Notts 115 B4
Oxborough Norf 102 A3
Oxburgh Hall Norf 102 A3
Oxcombe Lincs 134 B3
Oxen Park Cumb 154 C2
Oxenholme Cumb 154 C4
Oxenhope W Yorks 147 D4
Oxenton Glos 80 D2
Oxenwood Wilts 45 D7
Oxford Oxon 65 C6
Oxford University Botanic
  Garden Oxon 65 C6
Oxhey Herts 67 D6
Oxhill Warks 81 C6
Oxley W Mid 96 A2
Oxley Green Essex 70 B3
Oxley's Green E Sus 37 D4
Oxnam Borders 187 B6
Oxshott Sur 48 C4
Oxspring S Yorks 139 C5
Oxted Sur 36 A1
Oxton Borders 196 A3
Oxton Notts 131 D6
Oxwich Swansea 57 D4
Oxwick Norf 119 C6
Oykel Bridge Highld 271 D6
Oyne Aberds 256 D1

P

Pabail Iarach W Isles 288 D6
Pabail Uarach W Isles 288 D6
Pace Gate N Yorks 147 B5
Packington Leics 114 D1
Padanaram Angus 232 C2
Padbury Bucks 83 D4
Paddington London 49 A5
Paddlesworth Kent 38 B3
Paddock Wood Kent 37 B4
Paddockhaugh Moray 266 D3
Paddockhole Dumfries 185 D5
Padfield Derbys 138 D3
Padiham Lancs 146 D1
Padog Conwy 124 D3
Padside N Yorks 147 B5
Padstow Corn 9 D5
Padworth W Berks 47 C4
Page Bank Durham 167 B5
Pagelsham Eastend Essex 70 D3
Pagham W Sus 20 C1
Paglesham Churchend
  Essex 70 D3
Paibeil W Isles 287 H2
Paible W Isles 287 E5
Paignton Torbay 8 A2
Paignton & Dartmouth
  Steam Railway Devon 8 A2
Paignton Zoo Devon 8 B2
Pailton Warks 98 C1
Painscastle Powys 77 C5
Painshawfield Northumb 178 C2
Painsthorpe E Yorks 149 B7
Painswick Glos 63 C4
Pairc Shiaboist W Isles 288 C3
Paisley Renfs 205 B4
Pakefield Suff 105 B6
Pakenham Suff 87 A5
Palace House, Beaulieu
  Hants 18 A2
Palace of Holyroodhouse
  Edin 209 C5

Pale Gwyn 109 B4
Palestine Hants 31 A6
Paley Street Windsor 47 B6
Palfrey W Mid 96 B3
Palgowan Dumfries 181 C5
Palgrave Suff 104 D2
Pallion T & W 179 D5
Palmarsh Kent 38 B3
Palnackie Dumfries 173 C6
Palnure Dumfries 171 A6
Palterton Derbys 131 C4
Pamber End Hants 47 D4
Pamber Green Hants 47 D4
Pamber Heath Hants 47 C4
Pamphill Dorset 16 A3
Pampisford Cambs 85 C6
Pan Orkney 283 H4
Panbride Angus 221 A5
Pancrasweek Devon 10 A3
Pandy Gwyn 90 B4
Pandy Mon 61 A5
Pandy Powys 91 B7
Pandy Wrex 109 B6
Pandy Tudur Conwy 124 C3
Panfield Essex 70 A1
Pangbourne W Berks 47 B4
Pannal N Yorks 148 B2
Panshanger Herts 68 B2
Pant Shrops 110 C1
Pant-glas Carms 58 C2
Pant-glas Gwyn 107 B4
Pant-glâs Powys 91 C5
Pant-glas Shrops 110 B1
Pant gwyn Carms 58 C2
Pant Mawr Powys 91 D6
Pant-teg Carms 58 C1
Pant-y-Caws Carms 73 D4
Pant-y-dwr Powys 92 D3
Pant-y-ffridd Powys 93 A5
Pant-y-Wacco Flint 125 B6
Pant-yr-awel Bridgend 40 C4
Pantgwyn Ceredig 73 B5
Pantlasau Swansea 57 C6
Panton Lincs 134 B1
Pantperthog Gwyn 91 B5
Pantyffynnon Carms 57 A6
Pantymwyn Flint 126 C1
Panxworth Norf 121 D5
Papa Westray Airport
  Orkney 282 B5
Papcastle Cumb 163 A4
Papigoe Highld 281 C5
Papil Shetland 285 K5
Papley Orkney 283 H5
Papple E Loth 210 C2
Papplewick Notts 131 D5
Papworth Everard Cambs 85 A4
Papworth St Agnes Cambs 85 A4
Par Corn 5 B5
Paradise Wildlife Park,
  Broxbourne Herts 68 C3
Parbold Lancs 136 B3
Parbrook Som 29 B5
Parbrook W Sus 34 D3
Parc Gwyn 108 B3
Parc-Seymour Newport 61 D6
Parc-y-rhôs Carms 75 D4
Parcllyn Ceredig 73 A5
Pardshaw Cumb 162 B3
Parham Suff 88 A4
Park Dumfries 183 C7
Park Corner Oxon 47 A4
Park Corner Windsor 47 A6
Park End M'bro 168 D3
Park End Northumb 177 B6
Park Gate Hants 18 A4
Park Hill Notts 132 D1
Park Hill N Yorks 148 A2
Park Rose Pottery and
  Leisure Park,
  Bridlington E Yorks 151 A4
Park Street W Sus 35 C4
Parkend Glos 62 C2
Parkeston Essex 88 D3
Parkgate Ches 126 B2
Parkgate Dumfries 184 D3
Parkgate Kent 37 C6
Parkgate Sur 35 B5
Parkham Devon 25 C4
Parkham Ash Devon 25 C4
Parkhill Ho. Aberds 245 A5
Parkhouse Mon 61 C6
Parkhouse Green Derbys 131 C4
Parkhurst I o W 18 B3
Parkmill Swansea 57 D5
Parkneuk Aberds 233 A5
Parkstone Poole 17 B4

Parley Cross Dorset 17 B4
Parracombe Devon 26 A1
Parrog Pembs 72 C3
Parsley Hay Derbys 129 C6
Parson Cross S Yorks 139 D6
Parson Drove Cambs 101 A5
Parsonage Green Essex 69 C7
Parsonby Cumb 163 A4
Parson's Heath Essex 71 A4
Partick Glasgow 205 B5
Partington Gtr Man 137 D6
Partney Lincs 135 C4
Parton Cumb 162 B2
Parton Dumfries 173 A4
Parton Glos 63 A4
Partridge Green W Sus 21 A4
Parwich Derbys 130 D1
Passenham Northants 83 D4
Paston Norf 121 B5
Patchacott Devon 11 B5
Patcham Brighton 21 B6
Patching W Sus 20 B3
Patchole Devon 25 A7
Pathway S Glos 43 A5
Pateley Bridge N Yorks 147 A5
Paternoster Heath Essex 70 B3
Path of Condie Perth 219 C5
Pathe Som 28 B3
Pathhead Aberds 233 B5
Pathhead E Ayrs 182 A4
Pathhead Fife 209 A5
Pathhead Midloth 209 D6
Pathstruie Perth 219 C5
Patmore Heath Herts 68 A4
Patna E Ayrs 182 A2
Patney Wilts 45 D4
Patrick I o M 152 C2
Patrick Brompton N Yorks 157 B6
Patrington E Yorks 143 A5
Patrixbourne Kent 52 D3
Patterdale Cumb 164 D1
Pattingham Staffs 95 B6
Pattishall Northants 82 B3
Pattiswick Green Essex 70 A2
Patton Bridge Cumb 155 B4
Paul Corn 2 C2
Paulerspury Northants 83 C4
Paull E Yorks 142 A3
Paulton Bath 43 D5
Paultons Park, Totton
  Hants 32 D2
Pavenham Beds 84 B1
Pawlett Som 28 A3
Pawston Northumb 198 C2
Paxford Glos 81 D4
Paxton Borders 198 A3
Payhembury Devon 13 A5
Paythorne Lancs 146 B2
Peacehaven E Sus 22 B2
Peak Dale Derbys 129 B5
Peak Forest Derbys 129 B6
Peakirk P'boro 100 A3
Pearsie Angus 232 C1
Pease Pottage W Sus 35 C5
Peasedown St John Bath 43 D6
Peasemore W Berks 46 B2
Peasenhall Suff 89 A4
Peaslake Sur 34 B3
Peasley Cross Mers 136 D4
Peasmarsh E Sus 37 D6
Peaston E Loth 210 D1
Peastonbank E Loth 210 D1
Peat Inn Fife 221 D4
Peathill Aberds 269 C4
Peatling Magna Leics 98 B2
Peatling Parva Leics 98 C2
Peaton Shrops 94 C3
Peats Corner Suff 88 A2
Pebmarsh Essex 87 D4
Pebworth Worcs 80 C4
Pecket Well W Yorks 138 A2
Peckforton Ches 127 D5
Peckham London 49 B6
Peckleton Leics 98 A1
Pedlinge Kent 38 B3
Pedmore W Mid 96 C2
Pedwell Som 28 B4
Peebles Borders 196 B1
Peel I o M 152 C2
Peel Common Hants 19 A4
Peel Park S Lnrk 205 C6
Peening Quarter Kent 37 D6
Pegsdon Beds 84 D3
Pegswood Northumb 179 A4
Pegwell Kent 53 C5
Peinchorran Highld 247 A4
Peinlich Highld 259 C4

Pelaw T & W 179 C4
Pelcomb Bridge Pembs 55 C5
Pelcomb Cross Pembs 55 C5
Peldon Essex 70 B3
Pellon W Yorks 138 A3
Pelsall W Mid 96 A3
Pelton Durham 179 D4
Pelutho Cumb 174 D4
Pelynt Corn 5 B7
Pemberton Gtr Man 137 C4
Pembrey Carms 57 B4
Pembrey Motor Racing
  Circuit Carms 57 B4
Pembridge Hereford 78 B1
Pembroke = Penfro
  Pembs 55 D5
Pembroke Castle Pembs 55 D5
Pembroke Dock = Doc
  Penfro Pembs 55 D5
Pembury Kent 36 B4
Pen-bont Rhydybeddau
  Ceredig 91 D4
Pen-clawdd Swansea 57 C5
Pen-ffordd Pembs 55 B6
Pen-groes-oped Mon 61 C5
Pen-llyn Anglesey 122 B3
Pen-lon Anglesey 123 D4
Pen-sarn Gwyn 107 B4
Pen-sarn Gwyn 107 D5
Pen-twyn Mon 61 C7
Pen-y-banc Carms 58 C3
Pen-y-bont Carms 73 D5
Pen-y-bont Gwyn 91 B5
Pen-y-bont Gwyn 107 C5
Pen-y-bont Powys 109 C2
Pen-y-bont ar Ogwr =
  Bridgend Bridgend 40 D4
Pen-y-bryn Gwyn 91 A4
Pen-y-bryn Pembs 73 B5
Pen-y-cae Powys 59 D5
Pen-y-cae-mawr Mon 61 D6
Pen-y-cefn Flint 125 B6
Pen-y-clawdd Mon 61 C6
Pen-y-coedcae Rhondda 41 C5
Pen-y-fai Bridgend 40 C3
Pen-y-garn Ceredig 90 D4
Pen-y-garn Carms 58 B2
Pen-y-garnedd Anglesey 123 C5
Pen-y-gop Conwy 108 A4
Pen-y-graig Gwyn 106 C1
Pen-y-groes Carms 57 A5
Pen-y-groeslon Gwyn 106 C2
Pen-y-Gwryd Hotel Gwyn 107 A6
Pen-y-stryt Denb 126 D1
Pen-yr-heol Mon 61 C6
Pen-yr-Heolgerrig M Tydf 60 C2
Penallt Mon 61 C7
Penally Pembs 55 E7
Penalt Hereford 62 A1
Penare Corn 5 C4
Penarlâg = Hawarden
  Flint 126 C3
Penarth V Glam 41 D6
Penbryn Ceredig 73 A5
Pencader Carms 58 B1
Pencaenewydd Gwyn 107 B4
Pencaitland E Loth 210 D1
Pencarnisiog Anglesey 122 C3
Pencarreg Carms 75 D5
Pencelli Powys 60 A2
Pencoed Bridgend 41 C4
Pencombe Hereford 78 B3
Pencoyd Hereford 61 A7
Pencraig Hereford 62 A1
Pencraig Powys 109 C6
Pendeen Corn 2 C2
Pendennis Castle Corn 4 D3
Penderyn Rhondda 59 D6
Pendine Carms 56 A2
Pendlebury Gtr Man 137 C6
Pendleton Lancs 146 D1
Pendock Worcs 79 D5
Pendoggett Corn 9 D6
Pendomer Som 29 D5
Pendoylan V Glam 41 D5
Pendre Bridgend 40 C4
Penegoes Powys 91 B5
Penfro = Pembroke
  Pembs 55 D5
Pengam Caerph 41 B6
Penge London 49 B6
Pengenffordd Powys 77 D5
Pengorffwysfa Anglesey 123 A4
Pengover Green Corn 5 A7
Penhale Corn 3 D4
Penhale Corn 5 C5
Penhalvaen Corn 4 D2

Penhill Thamesdown	45 A5
Penhow Newport	61 D6
Penhurst E Sus	23 A4
Peniarth Gwyn	90 B4
Penicuik Midloth	209 D5
Peniel Carms	58 C1
Peniel Denb	125 C5
Penifiler Highld	259 D4
Peninver Argyll	190 C3
Penjsarwaun Gwyn	123 D5
Penistone S Yorks	139 C5
Penjerrick Corn	4 D2
Penketh Warr	127 A5
Penkill S Ayrs	181 B4
Penkridge Staffs	112 D3
Penley Wrex	110 B3
Penllergaer Swansea	57 C6
Penllyn V Glam	41 D4
Penmachno Conwy	124 D2
Penmaen Swansea	57 D5
Penmaenan Conwy	124 B2
Penmaenmawr Conwy	124 B2
Penmaenpool Gwyn	91 A4
Penmark V Glam	41 E5
Penmarth Corn	4 D2
Penmon Anglesey	123 B6
Penmore Mill Argyll	224 A3
Penmorfa Ceredig	73 A6
Penmorfa Gwyn	107 B5
Penmynydd Anglesey	123 C5
Penn Bucks	67 D4
Penn W Mid	96 B1
Penn Street Bucks	67 D4
Pennal Gwyn	91 B5
Pennan Aberds	268 C3
Pennant Ceredig	75 B4
Pennant Denb	109 B5
Pennant Denb	125 D5
Pennant Powys	91 C6
Pennant Melangell Powys	109 C5
Pennar Pembs	55 D5
Pennard Swansea	57 D5
Pennerley Shrops	94 B1
Pennington Cumb	153 C3
Pennington Gtr Man	137 D5
Pennington Hants	18 B2
Penny Bridge Cumb	154 C2
Pennycross Argyll	225 D4
Pennygate Norf	121 C5
Pennygown Argyll	225 B4
Pennymoor Devon	26 D3
Pennywell T & W	179 D5
Penparc Ceredig	73 B5
Penparc Pembs	55 A4
Penparcau Ceredig	90 D3
Penperlleni Mon	61 C5
Penpillick Corn	5 B5
Penpol Corn	4 D3
Penpoll Corn	5 B6
Penpont Dumfries	183 C6
Penpont Powys	59 C6
Penrherber Carms	73 C5
Penrhiw goch Carms	57 A5
Penrhiw-llan Ceredig	73 B6
Penrhiw-pâl Ceredig	73 B6
Penrhiwceiber Rhondda	41 B5
Penrhos Gwyn	106 C3
Penrhos Mon	61 B6
Penrhos Powys	59 D4
Penrhosfeilw Anglesey	122 B2
Penrhyn Bay Conwy	124 A3
Penrhyn Castle Gwyn	123 C6
Penrhyn-coch Ceredig	90 D4
Penrhyndeudraeth Gwyn	107 C6
Penrhynside Conwy	124 A3
Penrice Swansea	57 D4
Penrith Cumb	164 B3
Penrose Corn	9 D4
Penruddock Cumb	164 C2
Penryn Corn	4 D2
Pensarn Carms	57 A4
Pensarn Conwy	125 B4
Pensax Worcs	79 A5
Pensby Mers	126 A2
Penselwood Som	30 B1
Pensford Bath	43 C5
Penshaw T & W	179 D5
Penshurst Kent	36 B3
Pensilva Corn	6 A1
Penston E Loth	210 C1
Pentewan Corn	5 C5
Pentir Gwyn	123 D5
Pentire Corn	4 A2
Pentlow Essex	87 C4
Pentney Norf	119 D4
Penton Mewsey Hants	32 A2
Pentraeth Anglesey	123 C5
Pentre Carms	57 A5
Pentre Powys	93 C4
Pentre Powys	93 B6
Pentre Rhondda	41 B4
Pentre Shrops	110 D2
Pentre Wrex	110 A1
Pentre Wrex	109 B6
Pentre-bâch Ceredig	75 D4
Pentre-bach Powys	59 B6
Pentre Berw Anglesey	123 C4
Pentre-bont Conwy	124 D2
Pentre-celyn Denb	125 D6
Pentre-Celyn Powys	91 B6
Pentre-chwyth Swansea	57 C6
Pentre-cwrt Carms	73 C6
Pentre Dolau-Honddu Powys	76 C3
Pentre-dwr Swansea	40 B1
Pentre-galar Pembs	73 C4
Pentre-Gwenlais Carms	57 A6
Pentre Gwynfryn Gwyn	107 D5
Pentre Halkyn Flint	126 B2
Pentre-Isaf Conwy	124 C3
Pentre Llanrhaeadr Denb	125 C5
Pentre-llwyn-llŵyd Powys	76 B3
Pentre-llyn Ceredig	75 A5
Pentre-llyn cymmer Conwy	125 D4
Pentre Meyrick V Glam	41 D4
Pentre-poeth Newport	42 A1
Pentre-rhew Ceredig	75 C5
Pentre-tafarn-y-fedw Conwy	124 C3
Pentre-ty-gwyn Carms	59 B5
Pentrebach M Tydf	41 A5
Pentrebach Swansea	57 B6
Pentrebeirdd Powys	109 D6
Pentrecagal Carms	73 B6
Pentredwr Denb	109 A6
Pentrefelin Ceredig	75 D5
Pentrefelin Carms	58 C2
Pentrefelin Conwy	124 B3
Pentrefelin Gwyn	107 C5
Pentrefoelas Conwy	124 D3
Pentregat Ceredig	73 A6
Pentreheyling Shrops	93 B6
Pentre'r Felin Conwy	124 C3
Pentre'r-felin Powys	59 B6
Pentrich Derbys	130 D3
Pentridge Dorset	31 D4
Pentyrch Cardiff	41 C6
Penuchadre V Glam	40 D3
Penuwch Ceredig	75 B4
Penwithick Corn	5 B5
Penwyllt Powys	59 D5
Penybanc Carms	57 A6
Penybont Powys	77 A5
Penybontfawr Powys	109 C5
Penycae Wrex	110 A1
Penycwm Pembs	54 B4
Penyffordd Flint	126 C3
Penyffridd Gwyn	107 A5
Penygarnedd Powys	109 C6
Penygraig Rhondda	41 B4
Penygroes Gwyn	107 A4
Penygroes Pembs	73 C4
Penyrheol Caerph	41 C6
Penysarn Anglesey	123 A4
Penywaun Rhondda	41 A4
Penzance Corn	2 B2
Penzance Heliport Corn	2 B2
People's Palace Glasgow	205 B6
Peopleton Worcs	80 B2
Peover Heath Ches	128 B2
Peper Harow Sur	34 B2
Perceton N Ayrs	204 D3
Percie Aberds	244 C2
Percyhorner Aberds	269 C4
Periton Som	27 A4
Perivale London	49 A4
Perkinsville Durham	179 D4
Perlethorpe Notts	131 B6
Perranarworthal Corn	4 D2
Perranporth Corn	4 B2
Perranuthnoe Corn	2 C3
Perranzabuloe Corn	4 B2
Perry Barr W Mid	96 B3
Perry Green Herts	68 B4
Perry Green Wilts	44 A3
Perry Street Kent	50 B3
Perryfoot Derbys	129 A6
Pershall Staffs	112 B2
Pershore Worcs	80 C2
Pert Angus	233 B4
Pertenhall Beds	84 A2
Perth Perth	219 B6
Perth Racecourse Perth	219 B6
Perthy Shrops	110 B2
Perton Staffs	95 B6
Pertwood Wilts	30 B2
Peter Tavy Devon	11 D6
Peterborough P'boro	100 B3
Peterborough Cathedral P'boro	100 B3
Peterburn Highld	261 B4
Peterchurch Hereford	78 D1
Peterculter Aberdeen	245 B3
Peterhead Aberds	257 B6
Peterlee Durham	168 A2
Peter's Green Herts	67 B6
Peters Marland Devon	25 D5
Petersfield Hants	33 C6
Peterston super-Ely V Glam	41 D5
Peterstone Wentlooge Newport	42 A1
Peterstow Hereford	62 A1
Petertown Orkney	283 G4
Petham Kent	52 D3
Petrockstow Devon	11 A6
Pett E Sus	23 A6
Pettaugh Suff	88 B2
Petteridge Kent	37 B4
Pettinain S Lnrk	195 B4
Pettistree Suff	88 B3
Petton Devon	27 C5
Petton Shrops	110 C3
Petts Wood London	50 C1
Petty Aberds	256 C2
Pettycur Fife	209 B5
Pettymuick Aberds	257 D4
Petworth W Sus	34 D2
Petworth House W Sus	34 D2
Pevensey E Sus	22 B4
Pevensey Bay E Sus	23 B4
Pewsey Wilts	45 C5
Philham Devon	24 C3
Philiphaugh Borders	186 A3
Phillack Corn	2 B3
Philleigh Corn	4 D3
Philpstoun W Loth	208 C3
Phocle Green Hereford	62 A2
Phoenix Green Hants	47 D5
Piccotts End Herts	67 C5
Pickering N Yorks	159 C6
Picket Piece Hants	32 A2
Picket Post Hants	17 A5
Pickhill N Yorks	158 C2
Picklescott Shrops	94 B2
Pickletillem Fife	220 B4
Pickmere Ches	128 B1
Pickney Som	28 C1
Pickstock Telford	111 C6
Pickwell Devon	25 A5
Pickwell Leics	115 D5
Pickworth Lincs	116 B3
Pickworth Rutland	116 D2
Picton Ches	127 B4
Picton Flint	125 A6
Picton N Yorks	158 A3
Piddinghoe E Sus	22 B2
Piddington Northants	83 B5
Piddington Oxon	66 B1
Piddlehinton Dorset	15 B7
Piddletrenthide Dorset	15 B7
Pidley Cambs	101 D5
Piece Hall Art Gallery, Halifax W Yorks	138 A3
Piercebridge Darl	167 D5
Pierowall Orkney	282 C5
Pigdon Northumb	178 A3
Pikehall Derbys	130 D1
Pilgrims Hatch Essex	69 D5
Pilham Lincs	141 D6
Pill N Som	43 B4
Pillaton Corn	6 A2
Pillerton Hersey Warks	81 C6
Pillerton Priors Warks	81 C5
Pilleth Powys	77 A6
Pilley Hants	18 B2
Pilley S Yorks	139 C6
Pilling Lancs	144 C4
Pilling Lane Lancs	144 C3
Pillowell Glos	62 C2
Pillwell Dorset	30 D1
Pilning S Glos	43 A4
Pilsbury Derbys	129 C6
Pilsdon Dorset	14 B4
Pilsgate P'boro	100 A2
Pilsley Derbys	130 B2
Pilsley Derbys	131 C4
Pilton Devon	25 B6
Pilton Northants	100 C2
Pilton Rutland	99 A6
Pilton Som	29 A5
Pilton Green Swansea	57 D4
Pimperne Dorset	16 A3
Pinchbeck Lincs	117 C5
Pinchbeck Bars Lincs	117 C4
Pinchbeck West Lincs	117 C5
Pincheon Green S Yorks	141 B4
Pinehurst Thamesdown	45 A5
Pinged Carms	57 B4
Pinhoe Devon	13 B4
Pinkneys Green Windsor	47 A6
Pinley W Mid	97 D6
Pinmill Suff	88 D3
Pinminnoch S Ayrs	180 B3
Pinmore S Ayrs	181 B4
Pinmore Mains S Ayrs	181 B4
Pinner London	48 A4
Pinvin Worcs	80 C2
Pinwherry S Ayrs	180 C3
Pinxton Derbys	131 D4
Pipe and Lyde Hereford	78 C3
Pipe Gate Shrops	111 A6
Piperhill Highld	253 A4
Piper's Pool Corn	10 C3
Pipewell Northants	99 C5
Pippacott Devon	25 B6
Pipton Powys	77 D5
Pirbright Sur	34 A2
Pirnmill N Ayrs	202 D3
Pirton Herts	84 D3
Pirton Worcs	80 C1
Pisgah Ceredig	75 A5
Pisgah Stirl	218 D2
Pishill Oxon	47 A5
Pistyll Gwyn	106 B3
Pitagowan Perth	230 B2
Pitblae Aberds	269 C4
Pitcairngreen Perth	219 B5
Pitcalnie Highld	265 C4
Pitcaple Aberds	256 D2
Pitch Green Bucks	66 C2
Pitch Place Sur	34 A2
Pitchcombe Glos	63 C4
Pitchcott Bucks	66 A2
Pitchford Shrops	94 A3
Pitcombe Som	29 B6
Pitcorthie Fife	221 D5
Pitcox E Loth	210 C3
Pitcur Perth	220 A2
Pitfichie Aberds	244 A3
Pitforthie Aberds	233 A6
Pitgrudy Highld	264 A3
Pitkennedy Angus	232 C3
Pitkevy Fife	220 D2
Pitkierie Fife	221 D5
Pitlessie Fife	220 D3
Pitlochry Perth	230 C3
Pitmachie Aberds	256 D1
Pitmain Highld	241 B5
Pitmedden Aberds	256 D3
Pitminster Som	28 D2
Pitmuies Angus	232 D3
Pitmunie Aberds	244 A3
Pitney Som	29 C4
Pitscottie Fife	220 C4
Pitsea Essex	51 A4
Pitsford Northants	83 A4
Pitsmoor S Yorks	130 A3
Pitstone Bucks	67 B4
Pitstone Green Bucks	67 B4
Pitt Rivers Museum (See University Museum) Oxon	65 C6
Pittendreich Moray	266 C2
Pittentrail Highld	273 D5
Pittenweem Fife	221 D5
Pittington Durham	167 A6
Pittodrie Aberds	256 D1
Pitton Wilts	31 B6
Pittswood Kent	36 B4
Pittulie Aberds	269 C4
Pity Me Durham	167 A5
Pityme Corn	9 D5
Pityoulish Highld	242 A2
Pixey Green Suff	104 D3
Pixham Sur	35 A4
Pixley Hereford	79 D4
Place Newton N Yorks	160 D2
Plaidy Aberds	268 D2
Plains N Lnrk	207 D5
Plaish Shrops	94 B3
Plaistow W Sus	34 C3
Plaitford Hants	32 D1
Plank Lane Gtr Man	137 D5
Plâs Carms	58 C1
Plas-canol Gwyn	90 A3
Plas Gogerddan Ceredig	90 D4
Plas Llwyngwern Powys	91 B5
Plas Mawr, Conwy Conwy	124 B2
Plas Nantyr Wrex	109 B6
Plas-yn-Cefn Denb	125 B5
Plastow Green Hants	46 C3
Platt Kent	36 A4
Platt Bridge Gtr Man	137 C5
Platts Common S Yorks	139 C6
Plawsworth Durham	167 A5
Plaxtol Kent	36 A4
Play Hatch Oxon	47 B5
Playden E Sus	37 D7
Playford Suff	88 C3
Playing Place Corn	4 C3
Playley Green Glos	79 D5
Plealey Shrops	94 A2
Plean Stirl	207 B6
Pleasington Blkburn	137 A5
Pleasley Derbys	131 C5
Pleasure Island Theme Park NE Lincs	143 C5
Pleasureland Mers	136 B2
Pleckgate Blkburn	145 D6
Plenmeller Northumb	177 C5
Pleshey Essex	69 B6
Plockton Highld	249 C5
Plocrapol W Isles	288 H2
Ploughfield Hereford	78 C1
Plowden Shrops	94 C1
Ploxgreen Shrops	94 A1
Pluckley Kent	38 A1
Pluckley Thorne Kent	37 B7
Plumbland Cumb	163 A4
Plumley Ches	128 B2
Plumpton Cumb	164 B2
Plumpton E Sus	21 A6
Plumpton Green E Sus	21 A6
Plumpton Head Cumb	164 B3
Plumpton Racecourse E Sus	21 A6
Plumstead London	50 B1
Plumstead Norf	120 B3
Plumtree Notts	115 B4
Plungar Leics	115 B5
Plush Dorset	15 A7
Plwmp Ceredig	73 A6
Plymouth Plym	6 B3
Plymouth City Airport Plym	7 A4
Plympton Plym	7 B4
Plymstock Plym	7 B4
Plymtree Devon	13 A5
Pockley N Yorks	159 C5
Pocklington E Yorks	149 C7
Pode Hole Lincs	117 C5
Podimore Som	29 C5
Podington Beds	83 A6
Podmore Staffs	112 B1
Point Clear Essex	71 B4
Pointon Lincs	116 B4
Pokesdown Bmouth	17 B5
Pol a Charra W Isles	286 E3
Polbae Dumfries	181 D4
Polbain Highld	270 C2
Polbathic Corn	6 B2
Polbeth W Loth	208 D3
Polchar Highld	242 B1
Pole Elm Worcs	79 C6
Polebrook Northants	100 C2
Polegate E Sus	22 B3
Poles Highld	264 A3
Polesden Lacey, Dorking Sur	35 A4
Polesworth Warks	97 A5
Polgigga Corn	2 C1
Polglass Highld	270 D3
Polgooth Corn	5 B4
Poling W Sus	20 B3
Polkerris Corn	5 B5
Polla Highld	277 C4
Pollington E Yorks	140 B4
Polloch Highld	236 C1
Pollok Glasgow	205 B5
Pollok House Glasgow	205 B5
Pollokshields Glasgow	205 B5
Polmassick Corn	5 C4
Polmont Falk	208 C2
Polnessan E Ayrs	182 A2
Polnish Highld	235 B6
Polperro Corn	5 B7
Polruan Corn	5 B6
Polsham Som	29 A5

Polstead Suff 87 D5
Poltalloch Argyll 213 C6
Poltimore Devon 13 B4
Polton Midloth 209 D5
Polwarth Borders 197 A6
Polyphant Corn 10 C3
Polzeath Corn 9 D5
Ponders End London 68 D3
Pondersbridge Cambs 101 B4
Pondtail Hants 34 A1
Ponsanooth Corn 4 D2
Ponsworthy Devon 12 D2
Pont Aber Carms 59 C4
Pont Aber-Geirw Gwyn 108 C2
Pont-ar-gothi Carms 58 C2
Pont ar Hydfer Powys 59 C5
Pont-ar-llechau Carms 59 C4
Pont Cwm Pydew Denb 109 B5
Pont Cyfyng Conwy 124 D2
Pont Cysyllte Wrex 110 A1
Pont Dolydd Prysor Gwyn 108 B2
Pont-faen Pembs 76 D3
Pont Fronwydd Gwyn 108 C3
Pont-gareg Pembs 72 B4
Pont-Henri Carms 57 B4
Pont-Llogel Powys 109 D5
Pont Pen-y-benglog Gwyn 123 D6
Pont Rhyd-goch Conwy 124 C1
Pont-Rhyd-sarn Gwyn 108 C3
Pont Rhyd-y-cyff Bridgend 40 C3
Pont-rhyd-y-groes Ceredig 75 A6
Pont-rug Gwyn 123 D5
Pont Senni = Sennybridge Powys 59 C6
Pont-siân Ceredig 74 D3
Pont-y-gwaith Rhondda 41 B5
Pont-y-pant Conwy 124 D2
Pont y Pennant Gwyn 108 C4
Pont-y-Pŵl = Pontypool Torf 61 C4
Pont yclun Rhondda 41 C5
Pont yr Afon-Gam Gwyn 108 A2
Pont-yr-hafod Pembs 55 B5
Pontamman Carms 57 A6
Pontardawe Neath 40 A2
Pontarddulais Swansea 57 B5
Pontarsais Carms 58 C1
Pontblyddyn Flint 126 C2
Pontbren Araeth Carms 58 C3
Pontbren Llwyd Rhondda 59 E6
Pontefract W Yorks 140 A2
Pontefract Racecourse W Yorks 140 A2
Ponteland Northumb 178 B3
Ponterwyd Ceredig 91 D5
Pontesbury Shrops 94 A1
Pontfadog Wrex 110 B1
Pontfaen Pembs 55 A6
Pontgarreg Ceredig 73 A6
Ponthir Torf 61 D5
Ponthirwaun Ceredig 73 B5
Pontllanfraith Caerph 41 B6
Pontlliw Swansea 57 B6
Pontllyfni Gwyn 107 A4
Pontlottyn Caerph 60 C3
Pontneddfechan Powys 59 E6
Pontnewydd Torf 61 D4
Pontrhydfendigaid Ceredig 75 B6
Pontrhydyfen Neath 40 B2
Pontrilas Hereford 61 A5
Pontrobert Powys 109 D6
Ponts Green E Sus 23 A4
Pontshill Hereford 62 A2
Pontsticill M Tydf 60 B2
Pontwgan Conwy 124 B2
Pontyates Carms 57 B4
Pontyberem Carms 57 A5
Pontycymer Bridgend 40 B4
Pontyglasier Pembs 72 C4
Pontypool = Pont-y-Pŵl Torf 61 C4
Pontypridd Rhondda 41 C5
Pontywaun Caerph 41 B7
Pooksgreen Hants 32 D2
Pool Corn 3 A4
Pool W Yorks 147 C6
Pool o'Muckhart Clack 219 D5
Pool Quay Powys 110 D1
Poole Poole 17 B4
Poole Keynes Glos 63 D5
Poolend Staffs 129 D4

Poolewe Highld 261 B5
Pooley Bridge Cumb 164 C2
Poolfold Staffs 128 D3
Poolhill Glos 62 A3
Poolsbrook Derbys 131 B4
Pootings Kent 36 B2
Pope Hill Pembs 55 C5
Popeswood Brack 47 C6
Popham Hants 33 A4
Poplar London 49 A6
Popley Hants 47 D4
Porchester Notts 114 A3
Porchfield I o W 18 B3
Porin Highld 251 A5
Poringland Norf 104 A3
Porkellis Corn 3 B4
Porlock Som 26 A3
Porlock Weir Som 26 A3
Port Ann Argyll 214 D2
Port Appin Argyll 226 B4
Port Arthur Shetland 285 K5
Port Askaig Argyll 201 B4
Port Bannatyne Argyll 203 B5
Port Carlisle Cumb 175 B5
Port Charlotte Argyll 200 C2
Port Clarence Stockton 168 C2
Port Driseach Argyll 203 A4
Port e Vullen I o M 152 B4
Port Ellen Argyll 200 D2
Port Elphinstone Aberds 256 E2
Port Erin I o M 152 E1
Port Erroll Aberds 257 C5
Port-Eynon Swansea 57 D4
Port Gaverne Corn 9 C6
Port Glasgow Invclyd 204 A3
Port Henderson Highld 261 C4
Port Isaac Corn 9 C5
Port Lamont Argyll 203 A5
Port Lion Pembs 55 D5
Port Logan Dumfries 170 C2
Port Mholair W Isles 288 D6
Port Mor Highld 234 C3
Port Mulgrave N Yorks 169 D5
Port Nan Giùran W Isles 288 D6
Port nan Long W Isles 287 G3
Port Nis W Isles 288 A6
Port of Menteith Stirl 217 D5
Port Quin Corn 9 C5
Port Ramsay Argyll 226 B3
Port St Mary I o M 152 E2
Port Sunlight Mers 126 A3
Port Talbot Neath 40 B2
Port Tennant Swansea 57 C6
Port Wemyss Argyll 200 C1
Port William Dumfries 171 C5
Portachoillan Argyll 202 C2
Portavadie Argyll 203 B4
Portbury N Som 43 B4
Portchester Hants 19 A5
Portclair Highld 240 A2
Portencalzie Dumfries 180 D2
Portencross N Ayrs 204 D1
Portesham Dorset 15 C6
Portessie Moray 267 C5
Portfield Gate Pembs 55 C5
Portgate Devon 11 C5
Portgordon Moray 267 C4
Portgower Highld 274 C4
Porth Corn 4 A3
Porth Navas Corn 3 C5
Porth Tywyn = Burry Port Carms 57 B4
Porth-y-waen Shrops 110 C1
Porthaethwy = Menai Bridge Anglesey 123 C5
Porthallow Corn 3 C5
Porthallow Corn 6 B1
Porthcawl Bridgend 40 D3
Porthcothan Corn 9 D4
Porthcurno Corn 2 C1
Porthgain Pembs 54 A4
Porthill Shrops 110 D3
Porthkerry V Glam 41 E5
Porthleven Corn 3 C4
Porthllechog Anglesey 123 A4
Porthmadog Gwyn 107 C5
Porthmeor Corn 2 B2
Portholland Corn 5 C4
Porthoustock Corn 3 C6
Porthpean Corn 5 B5
Porthtowan Corn 3 A4
Porthyrhyd Carms 57 A5
Porthyrhyd Carms 59 B4
Portincaple Argyll 215 C5
Portington E Yorks 149 D6
Portinnisherrich Argyll 214 A2

Portinscale Cumb 163 B5
Portishead N Som 42 B3
Portkil Argyll 215 D5
Portknockie Moray 267 C5
Portlethen Aberds 245 C6
Portling Dumfries 173 C6
Portloe Corn 4 D4
Portmahomack Highld 265 B5
Portmeirion Gwyn 107 C5
Portmeirion Village Gwyn 107 C5
Portmellon Corn 5 C5
Portmore Hants 18 B2
Portnacroish Argyll 226 B4
Portnahaven Argyll 200 C1
Portnalong Highld 246 A2
Portnaluchaig Highld 235 B5
Portnancon Highld 277 B5
Portnellan Stirl 216 B4
Portobello Edin 209 C6
Porton Wilts 31 B5
Portpatrick Dumfries 170 B2
Portreath Corn 3 A4
Portree Highld 259 D4
Portscatho Corn 4 D3
Portsea Ptsmth 19 A5
Portskerra Highld 279 B4
Portskewett Mon 43 A4
Portslade Brighton 21 B5
Portslade-by-Sea Brighton 21 B5
Portsmouth Ptsmth 19 A5
Portsmouth W Yorks 138 A2
Portsmouth Sea Life Centre Ptsmth 19 B5
Portsonachan Argyll 227 D5
Portsoy Aberds 267 C6
Portswood Soton 32 D3
Portuairk Highld 234 D3
Portway Hereford 78 D2
Portway Worcs 96 D3
Portwrinkle Corn 6 B2
Poslingford Suff 86 C3
Postbridge Devon 12 D1
Postcombe Oxon 66 D2
Postling Kent 38 B3
Postwick Norf 104 A3
Potholm Dumfries 185 D6
Potsgrove Beds 67 A4
Pott Row Norf 119 C4
Pott Shrigley Ches 129 B4
Potten End Herts 67 C5
Potter Brompton N Yorks 160 D3
Potter Heigham Norf 121 D6
Potter Street Essex 69 C4
Potterhanworth Lincs 133 C5
Potterhanworth Booths Lincs 133 C5
Potteries Museum & Art Gallery, Stoke-on-Trent Stoke 112 A2
Potterne Wilts 44 D3
Potterne Wick Wilts 44 D3
Potternewton W Yorks 148 D2
Potters Bar Herts 68 C2
Potter's Cross Staffs 95 C6
Potterspury Northants 83 C4
Potterton Aberds 245 A6
Potterton W Yorks 148 D3
Potto N Yorks 158 A3
Potton Beds 84 C4
Poughill Corn 10 A3
Poughill Devon 12 A3
Poulshot Wilts 44 D3
Poulton Glos 64 C2
Poulton Mers 136 D2
Poulton-le-Fylde Lancs 144 D3
Pound Bank Worcs 95 D5
Pound Green E Sus 36 D3
Pound Green I o W 18 C2
Pound Green Worcs 95 D5
Pound Hill W Sus 35 C5
Poundfield E Sus 36 C3
Poundland S Ayrs 180 C3
Poundon Bucks 66 A1
Poundsgate Devon 12 D2
Poundstock Corn 10 B3
Powburn Northumb 188 B3
Powderham Devon 13 C4
Powderham Castle Devon 13 C4
Powerstock Dorset 15 B5
Powfoot Dumfries 174 B4
Powick Worcs 79 B6
Powmill Perth 208 A3
Poxwell Dorset 16 C1
Poyle Slough 48 B3

Poynings W Sus 21 A5
Poyntington Dorset 29 D6
Poynton Ches 129 A4
Poynton Green Telford 111 D4
Poystreet Green Suff 87 B5
Praa Sands Corn 2 C3
Pratt's Bottom London 50 C1
Praze Corn 2 B3
Praze-an-Beeble Corn 3 B4
Predannack Wollas Corn 3 D4
Prees Shrops 111 B4
Prees Green Shrops 111 B4
Prees Heath Shrops 111 B4
Prees Higher Heath Shrops 111 B4
Prees Lower Heath Shrops 111 B4
Preesall Lancs 144 C3
Preesgweene Shrops 110 B1
Prenderguest Borders 198 A3
Prendwick Northumb 188 B3
Prengwyn Ceredig 73 B7
Prenteg Gwyn 107 B5
Prenton Mers 126 A3
Prescot Mers 136 D3
Prescott Shrops 110 C3
Pressen Northumb 198 C2
Prestatyn Denb 125 A5
Prestbury Ches 129 B4
Prestbury Glos 63 A5
Presteigne = Llanandras Powys 77 A7
Presthope Shrops 94 B3
Prestleigh Som 29 A6
Preston Borders 198 A1
Preston Devon 12 D3
Preston Dorset 15 C7
Preston E Loth 210 C2
Preston E Yorks 151 D4
Preston Glos 63 C6
Preston Glos 79 D4
Preston Herts 68 A1
Preston Kent 52 C2
Preston Kent 53 C4
Preston Lancs 136 A4
Preston Northumb 189 A4
Preston Rutland 99 A5
Preston Shrops 111 D4
Preston Suff 87 B5
Preston Wilts 44 B4
Preston Wilts 45 B6
Preston Bagot Warks 81 A4
Preston Bissett Bucks 66 A1
Preston Bowyer Som 27 C6
Preston Brockhurst Shrops 111 C4
Preston Brook Halton 127 A5
Preston Candover Hants 33 A5
Preston Capes Northants 82 B2
Preston Crowmarsh Oxon 65 D7
Preston Gubbals Shrops 110 D3
Preston Hall Museum, Stockton-on-Tees Stockton 167 D6
Preston on Stour Warks 81 C5
Preston on the Hill Halton 127 A5
Preston on Wye Hereford 78 C1
Preston Plucknett Som 29 D5
Preston-under-Scar N Yorks 157 B4
Preston upon the Weald Moors Telford 111 D5
Preston Wynne Hereford 78 C3
Prestonmill Dumfries 174 C2
Prestonpans E Loth 209 C6
Prestwich Gtr Man 137 C7
Prestwick Northumb 178 B3
Prestwick S Ayrs 192 C3
Prestwood Bucks 66 C3
Price Town Bridgend 40 B4
Prickwillow Cambs 102 C1
Priddy Som 43 D4
Priest Hutton Lancs 154 D4
Priest Weston Shrops 93 B6
Priesthaugh Borders 186 C3
Primethorpe Leics 98 B2
Primrose Green Norf 120 D2
Primrose Valley N Yorks 161 D5
Primrosehill Herts 67 C5
Princes Gate Pembs 56 A1
Princes Risborough Bucks 66 C3
Princethorpe Warks 97 D7
Princetown Caerph 60 B3
Princetown Devon 11 D6
Prinknash Abbey, Gloucester Glos 63 B4

Prion Denb 125 C5
Prior Muir Fife 221 C5
Prior Park Northumb 198 A3
Priors Frome Hereford 78 D3
Priors Hardwick Warks 82 B1
Priors Marston Warks 82 B1
Priorslee Telford 111 D6
Priory Church, Lancs 145 A4
Priory Wood Hereford 77 C6
Priston Bath 43 C5
Pristow Green Norf 104 C2
Prittlewell Sthend 51 A5
Privett Hants 33 C5
Prixford Devon 25 B6
Probus Corn 4 C3
Proncy Highld 264 A3
Prospect Cumb 174 D4
Prudhoe Northumb 178 C2
Ptarmigan Lodge Stirl 215 B6
Pubil Perth 228 D3
Puckeridge Herts 68 A3
Puckington Som 28 D3
Pucklechurch S Glos 43 B5
Pucknall Hants 32 C2
Puckrup Glos 80 D1
Puddinglake Ches 128 C2
Puddington Ches 126 B2
Puddington Devon 26 D2
Puddledock Norf 103 B6
Puddletown Dorset 16 B1
Pudleston Hereford 78 B3
Pudsey W Yorks 147 D6
Pulborough W Sus 20 A3
Puleston Telford 111 C6
Pulford Ches 126 D3
Pulham Dorset 15 A7
Pulham Market Norf 104 C2
Pulham St Mary Norf 104 C3
Pulloxhill Beds 84 D2
Pumpherston W Loth 208 D3
Pumsaint Carms 58 A3
Puncheston Pembs 55 B5
Puncknowle Dorset 15 C5
Punnett's Town E Sus 36 D4
Purbrook Hants 19 A5
Purewell Dorset 17 B5
Purfleet Thurrock 50 B2
Puriton Som 28 A3
Purleigh Essex 70 C2
Purley London 49 C6
Purley W Berks 47 B4
Purlogue Shrops 93 B6
Purls Bridge Cambs 101 C6
Purse Caundle Dorset 29 D6
Purslow Shrops 94 C1
Purston Jaglin W Yorks 140 B2
Purton Glos 62 C2
Purton Glos 62 C2
Purton Wilts 45 A4
Purton Stoke Wilts 64 D5
Pury End Northants 83 C4
Pusey Oxon 65 D4
Putley Hereford 79 D4
Putney London 49 B5
Putsborough Devon 25 A4
Puttenham Herts 66 B3
Puttenham Sur 34 B2
Puxton N Som 42 C3
Pwll Carms 57 B4
Pwll-glas Denb 125 D5
Pwll-Meyric Mon 61 D7
Pwll-trap Carms 56 A2
Pwll-y-glaw Neath 40 B2
Pwllcrochan Pembs 55 D5
Pwllgloyw Powys 76 D4
Pwllheli Gwyn 106 C3
Pye Corner Newport 42 A2
Pye Green Staffs 112 D3
Pyecombe W Sus 21 A5
Pyewipe NE Lincs 143 B4
Pyle I o W 18 D3
Pyle = Y Pîl Bridgend 40 C3
Pylle Som 29 B5
Pymoor Cambs 101 C6
Pyrford Sur 34 A3
Pyrton Oxon 66 D1
Pytchley Northants 99 D5
Pyworthy Devon 10 A4

Q

Quabbs Shrops 93
Quadring Lincs 117
Quainton Bucks 66
Quarley Hants 31
Quarndon Derbys 114
Quarrier's Homes Invclyd 20

rrington Lincs 116 A3
rrington Hill Durham 167 B6
rry Bank W Mid 96 C2
rry Bank Mill, London 49 A5
ilmslow Ches 128 A3
rryford E Loth 210 D2
rryhill Highld 264 B3
rrywood Moray 266 C2
rter S Lnrk 194 A2
tford Shrops 95 B5
tt Shrops 95 C5
bec Durham 167 A4
dgeley Glos 63 B4
en Adelaide Cambs 102 C1
en Camel Som 29 C5
en Charlton Bath 43 C5
en Dart Devon 26 D3
en Oak Dorset 30 B1
en Street Kent 37 B4
en Street Wilts 44 A4
enborough Kent 51 B6
enhill Worcs 79 D6
en's Head Shrops 110 C2
en's Park Beds 84 C2
en's Park Northants 83 A4
en's View Centre,
ch Tummel Perth 230 C2
ensbury W Yorks 147 D5
ensferry Edin 208 C4
ensferry Flint 126 C3
enstown Blkpool 144 D3
enzieburn N Lnrk 207 C4
merford Wilts 44 C4
ndale Shetland 285 M5
ndon Essex 85 D7
niborough Leics 115 D4
nington Glos 64 C2
rnmore Lancs 145 B5
thiock Corn 6 A2
olm Orkney 282 F3
cks Green W Berks 46 B3
denham Norf 103 C6
dhampton Hants 46 D3
dhampton Wilts 31 B5
quox Aberds 257 C4
dry Orkney 283 H5
ton Northants 83 B4
ton W Mid 96 C2
trell Downs Corn 4 A3
khill Staffs 113 A5
ditch Devon 11 B5
ig Perth 218 B3
rndon Leics 114 D3
thquan S Lnrk 195 C4
yloo Orkney 282 E3
yness Orkney 283 G3
ys Shetland 284 B8
ys Shetland 285 G6

say Ho. Highld 248 C2
bit's Cross Kent 37 B5
y Mers 126 B3
han Mill Borders 195 C6
hub Gwyn 123 D6
kenford Devon 26 D3
kham W Sus 20 A3
kheath Norf 121 D4
ks Dumfries 174 A3
kwick Orkney 283 H3
kwick Orkney 282 C5
bourne Derbys 113 B6
cliffe Gtr Man 137 C6
cliffe Northumb 189 C5
cliffe on Trent Notts 115 B4
clive Bucks 82 D3
cot Oxon 64 D3
dery Highld 252 A3
ernie Fife 221 D4
ford Semele Warks 81 A6
ipole Dorset 15 C6
lett Herts 67 D6
ley Oxon 65 D6
manthwaite Notts 131 C5
moor Shrops 111 C5
ore Green Ches 127 D5
nage Bucks 66 D2
stock Bath 43 D5
stone Northants 82 C2
way Warks 81 C6
way Green Ches 128 D2
well Beds 84 B2
well Herts 84 D4
winter Essex 86 D2
yr Cardiff 41 C6

RAF Museum, Cosford Shrops 95 A5
RAF Museum, Hendon London 49 A5
Rafford Moray 253 A6
Ragdale Leics 115 D4
Raglan Mon 61 C6
Ragley Hall Warks 80 B3
Ragnall Notts 132 B3
Rahane Argyll 215 D5
Rainford Mers 136 L3
Rainford Junction Mers 136 C3
Rainham London 50 A2
Rainham Medway 51 C5
Rainhill Mers 136 D3
Rainhill Stoops Mers 136 D4
Rainow Ches 129 B4
Rainton N Yorks 158 D2
Rainworth Notts 131 D5
Raisbeck Cumb 155 A5
Raise Cumb 165 A5
Rait Perth 220 B2
Raithby Lincs 134 A3
Raithby Lincs 134 C3
Rake W Sus 33 C7
Rakewood Gtr Man 138 B2
Ram Carms 75 D4
Ram Lane Kent 38 A1
Ramasaig Highld 258 D1
Rame Corn 4 D2
Rame Corn 6 C3
Rameldry Mill Bank Fife 220 D3
Ramnageo Shetland 284 C8
Rampisham Dorset 15 A5
Rampside Cumb 153 D3
Rampton Cambs 85 A6
Rampton Notts 132 B2
Ramsbottom Gtr Man 137 B6
Ramsbury Wilts 45 B6
Ramscraigs Highld 275 B5
Ramsdean Hants 33 C6
Ramsdell Hants 46 D3
Ramsden Oxon 65 B4
Ramsden Bellhouse Essex 69 D7
Ramsden Heath Essex 69 D7
Ramsey Cambs 101 C4
Ramsey Essex 88 D3
Ramsey I o M 152 B4
Ramsey Forty Foot Cambs 101 C5
Ramsey Heights Cambs 101 C4
Ramsey Island Essex 70 C3
Ramsey Mereside Cambs 101 C4
Ramsey St Mary's Cambs 101 C4
Ramseycleuch Borders 185 A5
Ramsgate Kent 53 C5
Ramsgill N Yorks 157 D5
Ramshorn Staffs 113 A4
Ramsnest Common Sur 34 C2
Ranais W Isles 288 E5
Ranby Lincs 134 B2
Ranby Notts 131 A6
Rand Lincs 133 B6
Randwick Glos 63 C4
Ranfurly Renfs 204 B3
Rangag Highld 280 D3
Rangemore Staffs 113 C5
Rangeworthy S Glos 43 A5
Rankinston E Ayrs 182 A2
Ranmoor S Yorks 130 A3
Ranmore Common Sur 35 A4
Rannerdale Cumb 163 C4
Rannoch Station Perth 228 C3
Ranochan Highld 238 D2
Ranskill Notts 131 A6
Ranton Staffs 112 C2
Ranworth Norf 121 D5
Raploch Stirl 207 A5
Rapness Orkney 282 C6
Rascal Moor E Yorks 149 D7
Rascarrel Dumfries 173 D5
Rashiereive Aberds 257 D4
Raskelf N Yorks 158 D3
Rassau Bl Gwent 60 B3
Rastrick W Yorks 139 A4
Ratagan Highld 238 A3
Ratby Leics 98 A2
Ratcliffe Culey Leics 97 B6
Ratcliffe on Soar Leics 114 C2
Ratcliffe on the Wreake Leics 115 D4
Rathen Aberds 269 C5
Rathillet Fife 220 B3
Rathmell N Yorks 146 B2
Ratho Edin 208 C4
Ratho Station Edin 208 C4
Rathven Moray 267 C5

Ratley Warks 81 C6
Ratlinghope Shrops 94 B2
Rattar Highld 281 A4
Ratten Row Lancs 144 C4
Rattery Devon 7 A6
Rattlesden Suff 87 B5
Rattray Perth 231 D5
Raughton Head Cumb 164 A1
Raunds Northants 100 D1
Ravenfield S Yorks 140 D2
Ravenglass Cumb 153 A1
Ravenglass and Eskdale Railway & Museum Cumb 153 A1
Raveningham Norf 105 B4
Ravenscar N Yorks 160 A3
Ravenscraig Invclyd 204 A2
Ravensdale I o M 152 B3
Ravensden Beds 84 B2
Ravenseat N Yorks 156 A2
Ravenshead Notts 131 D5
Ravensmoor Ches 127 D6
Ravensthorpe Northants 98 D3
Ravensthorpe W Yorks 139 A5
Ravenstone Leics 114 D2
Ravenstone M Keynes 83 B5
Ravenstonedale Cumb 155 A6
Ravenstown Cumb 154 D2
Ravenstruther S Lnrk 194 B4
Ravensworth N Yorks 157 A5
Raw N Yorks 160 A3
Rawcliffe E Yorks 141 A4
Rawcliffe York 149 B4
Rawcliffe Bridge E Yorks 141 A4
Rawdon W Yorks 147 D6
Rawmarsh S Yorks 140 D2
Rawreth Essex 70 D1
Rawridge Devon 14 A2
Rawtenstall Lancs 137 A7
Raxton Aberds 256 C3
Raydon Suff 87 D6
Raylees Northumb 188 D2
Rayleigh Essex 70 D2
Rayne Essex 70 A1
Rayners Lane London 48 A4
Raynes Park London 49 C5
Reach Cambs 86 A1
Read Lancs 146 D1
Reading Reading 47 B5
Reading Street Kent 37 C7
Reagill Cumb 165 D4
Rearquhar Highld 264 A3
Rearsby Leics 115 D4
Reaster Highld 281 B4
Reawick Shetland 285 J5
Reay Highld 279 B5
Rechullin Highld 249 A5
Reculver Kent 53 C4
Red Dial Cumb 175 D5
Red Hill Worcs 79 B6
Red House Glass Cone, Wordsley W Mid 96 C1
Red Houses Jersey 6
Red Lodge Suff 102 D2
Red Rail Hereford 62 A1
Red Rock Gtr Man 137 C4
Red Roses Carms 56 A2
Red Row Northumb 189 D5
Red Street Staffs 128 D3
Red Wharf Bay Anglesey 123 B5
Redberth Pembs 55 D6
Redbourn Herts 67 B6
Redbourne N Lincs 142 D1
Redbrook Glos 62 B1
Redbrook Wrex 111 A4
Redburn Highld 264 D1
Redburn Highld 253 B5
Redburn Northumb 177 C5
Redcar Redcar 168 C4
Redcar Racecourse Redcar 168 C4
Redcastle Angus 233 C4
Redcastle Highld 252 B1
Redcliff Bay N Som 42 B3
Redding Falk 208 C2
Reddingmuirhead Falk 208 C2
Reddish Gtr Man 138 D1
Redditch Worcs 80 A3
Rede Suff 87 B4
Redenhall Norf 104 C3
Redesdale Camp Northumb 187 D7
Redesmouth Northumb 177 A6
Redford Aberds 233 A5
Redford Angus 232 D3
Redford Durham 166 B3
Redfordgreen Borders 185 A6

Redgorton Perth 219 B5
Redgrave Suff 103 D6
Redhill Aberds 256 C1
Redhill Aberds 245 B4
Redhill N Som 42 C3
Redhill Sur 35 A5
Redhouse Argyll 202 B3
Redhouses Argyll 200 B3
Redisham Suff 105 C5
Redland Bristol 43 B4
Redland Orkney 282 E4
Redlingfield Suff 104 D2
Redlynch Som 29 B7
Redlynch Wilts 31 C6
Redmarley D'Abitot Glos 79 D5
Redmarshall Stockton 167 C6
Redmile Leics 115 B5
Redmire N Yorks 156 B4
Redmoor Corn 5 A5
Rednal Shrops 110 C2
Redpath Borders 197 C4
Redpoint Highld 261 D4
Redruth Corn 3 A4
Redvales Gtr Man 137 C7
Redwick Newport 42 A3
Redwick S Glos 43 A4
Redworth Darl 167 C5
Reed Herts 85 D5
Reedham Norf 105 A5
Reedness E Yorks 141 A5
Reeds Beck Lincs 134 C2
Reepham Lincs 133 B5
Reepham Norf 120 C2
Reeth N Yorks 156 B4
Regaby I o M 152 B4
Regoul Highld 253 A4
Reiff Highld 270 C2
Reigate Sur 35 A5
Reighton N Yorks 161 D5
Reighton Gap N Yorks 161 D5
Reinigeadal W Isles 288 G3
Reiss Highld 281 C5
Rejerrah Corn 4 B2
Releath Corn 3 B4
Relubbus Corn 2 B3
Relugas Moray 253 B5
Remenham Wokingham 47 A5
Remenham Hill Wokingham 47 A5
Remony Perth 229 D6
Rempstone Notts 114 C3
Rendcomb Glos 63 C6
Rendham Suff 88 A4
Rendlesham Suff 88 B4
Renfrew Renfs 205 B5
Renhold Beds 84 B2
Renishaw Derbys 131 B4
Rennington Northumb 189 B5
Renton W Dunb 206 C1
Renwick Cumb 164 A3
Repps Norf 121 D6
Repton Derbys 113 C7
Reraig Highld 249 D5
Rescobie Angus 232 C3
Resipole Highld 235 D6
Resolis Highld 264 D2
Resolven Neath 40 A3
Reston Borders 211 D5
Reswallie Angus 232 C3
Retew Corn 4 B4
Retford Notts 132 A2
Rettendon Essex 70 D1
Rettendon Place Essex 70 D1
Revesby Lincs 134 C2
Revesby Bridge Lincs 134 C3
Rew Street I o W 18 B3
Rewe Devon 13 B4
Reydon Suff 105 D5
Reydon Smear Suff 105 D5
Reymerston Norf 103 A6
Reynalton Pembs 55 D6
Reynoldston Swansea 57 C4
Rezare Corn 11 D4
Rhaeadr Gwy = Rhayader Powys 76 A3
Rhandirmwyn Carms 59 A4
Rhayader = Rhaeadr Gwy Powys 76 A3
Rhedyn Gwyn 106 C2
Rhemore Highld 225 A4
Rhencullen I o M 152 B3
Rhes-y-cae Flint 126 B1
Rhewl Denb 125 C6
Rhewl Denb 109 A6
Rhian Highld 272 C3
Rhicarn Highld 270 B3
Rhiconich Highld 276 C3
Rhicullen Highld 264 C2

Rhidorroch Ho. Highld 262 A3
Rhifail Highld 278 D3
Rhigos Rhondda 59 E6
Rhilochan Highld 273 D5
Rhiroy Highld 262 B3
Rhisga = Risca Caerph 60 D4
Rhiw Gwyn 106 D2
Rhiwabon = Ruabon Wrex 110 A2
Rhiwbina Cardiff 41 C6
Rhiwbryfdir Gwyn 107 B6
Rhiwderin Newport 42 A1
Rhiwlas Gwyn 123 D5
Rhiwlas Gwyn 108 B4
Rhiwlas Powys 109 B6
Rhodes Gtr Man 138 C1
Rhodes Minnis Kent 38 A3
Rhodesia Notts 131 B5
Rhodiad Pembs 54 B3
Rhondda Rhondda 41 B4
Rhonehouse or Kelton Hill Dumfries 173 C5
Rhoose = Y Rhws V Glam 41 E5
Rhôs Carms 73 C6
Rhôs Neath 40 A2
Rhos-fawr Gwyn 106 C3
Rhos-hill Pembs 73 B4
Rhos-on-Sea Conwy 124 A3
Rhos-y-brithdir Powys 109 C6
Rhos-y-garth Ceredig 75 A5
Rhos-y-gwaliau Gwyn 108 B4
Rhos-y-llan Gwyn 106 C2
Rhos-y-Madoc Wrex 110 A2
Rhos-y-meirch Powys 77 A6
Rhosaman Carms 59 D4
Rhosbeirio Anglesey 122 A3
Rhoscefnhir Anglesey 123 C5
Rhoscolyn Anglesey 122 C2
Rhoscrowther Pembs 55 D5
Rhosesmor Flint 126 C2
Rhosgadfan Gwyn 107 A5
Rhosgoch Anglesey 123 B4
Rhosgoch Powys 77 C5
Rhoshirwaun Gwyn 106 D1
Rhoslan Gwyn 107 B4
Rhoslefain Gwyn 90 B3
Rhosllanerchrugog Wrex 110 A1
Rhosmaen Carms 58 C3
Rhosmeirch Anglesey 123 C4
Rhosneigr Anglesey 122 C3
Rhosnesni Wrex 126 D3
Rhosrobin Wrex 126 D3
Rhossili Swansea 57 D4
Rhosson Pembs 54 B3
Rhostryfan Gwyn 107 A4
Rhostyllen Wrex 110 A2
Rhosybol Anglesey 123 B4
RHS Garden, Wisley Sur 34 A3
Rhu Argyll 215 D5
Rhu Argyll 202 B3
Rhuallt Denb 125 B5
Rhuddall Heath Ches 127 C5
Rhuddlan Ceredig 58 A1
Rhuddlan Denb 125 B5
Rhue Highld 262 A2
Rhulen Powys 77 B5
Rhunahaorine Argyll 202 D2
Rhuthun = Ruthin Denb 125 D6
Rhyd Gwyn 107 B6
Rhyd Powys 92 A3
Rhyd-Ddu Gwyn 107 A5
Rhyd-moel-ddu Powys 93 D4
Rhyd-Rosser Ceredig 75 B4
Rhyd-uchaf Gwyn 108 B4
Rhyd-wen Gwyn 91 A5
Rhyd-y-clafdy Gwyn 106 C3
Rhŷd-y-foel Conwy 125 B4
Rhyd-y-fro Neath 59 E4
Rhyd-y-gwin Swansea 57 B5
Rhyd-y-meirch Mon 61 C5
Rhyd-y-meudwy Denb 125 D6
Rhyd-y-pandy Swansea 57 B6
Rhyd-yr-onen Gwyn 90 B4
Rhydaman = Ammanford Carms 57 A6
Rhydargaeau Carms 58 C1
Rhydcymerau Carms 58 B2
Rhydd Worcs 79 C6
Rhydding Neath 40 B2
Rhydfudr Ceredig 75 B4
Rhydlewis Ceredig 73 B6
Rhydlios Gwyn 106 C1
Rhydlydan Conwy 124 D3

Rhydnest Powys 77 C5
Rhydowen Ceredig 74 D3
Rhydspence Hereford 77 C6
Rhydtalog Flint 126 D2
Rhydwyn Anglesey 122 B3
Rhydycroesau Shrops 110 B1
Rhydyfelin Ceredig 75 A4
Rhydyfelin Rhondda 41 C5
Rhydymain Gwyn 108 C3
Rhydymwyn Flint 126 C2
Rhyl = Y Rhyl Denb 125 A5
Rhymney = Rhymni
  Caerph 60 C3
Rhymni = Rhymney
  Caerph 60 C3
Rhynd Fife 221 B4
Rhynd Perth 219 B6
Rhynie Aberds 255 D5
Rhynie Highld 265 C4
Ribbesford Worcs 95 D5
Ribblehead N Yorks 155 D6
Ribbleton Lancs 145 D5
Ribchester Lancs 145 D6
Ribigill Highld 277 C6
Riby Lincs 142 C3
Riby Cross Roads Lincs 142 C3
Riccall N Yorks 149 D5
Riccarton E Ayrs 193 B4
Richards Castle Hereford 78 A2
Richings Park Bucks 48 B3
Richmond London 49 B4
Richmond N Yorks 157 A5
Rickarton Aberds 245 D5
Rickinghall Suff 103 D6
Rickleton T & W 179 D4
Rickling Essex 85 D6
Rickmansworth Herts 67 D5
Riddings Cumb 175 A7
Riddings Derbys 131 D4
Riddlecombe Devon 25 D7
Riddlesden W Yorks 147 C4
Riddrie Glasgow 205 B6
Ridge Dorset 16 C3
Ridge Hants 32 D2
Ridge Wilts 30 B3
Ridge Green Sur 35 B6
Ridge Lane Warks 97 B5
Ridgebourne Powys 77 A4
Ridgehill N Som 43 C4
Ridgeway Cross Hereford 79 C5
Ridgewell Essex 86 C3
Ridgewood E Sus 22 A2
Ridgmont Beds 84 D1
Riding Mill Northumb 178 C2
Ridleywood Wrex 127 D4
Ridlington Norf 121 B5
Ridlington Rutland 99 A5
Ridsdale Northumb 177 A7
Riechip Perth 231 D4
Riemore Perth 230 D4
Rienachait Highld 270 A3
Rievaulx N Yorks 159 C4
Rievaulx Abbey N Yorks 159 C4
Rift House Hrtlpl 168 B2
Rigg Dumfries 175 B5
Riggend N Lnrk 207 C5
Rigsby Lincs 135 B4
Rigside S Lnrk 194 C3
Riley Green Lancs 137 A5
Rileyhill Staffs 113 D5
Rilla Mill Corn 10 D3
Rillington N Yorks 160 D2
Rimington Lancs 146 C2
Rimpton Som 29 C6
Rimswell E Yorks 143 A5
Rinaston Pembs 55 B5
Ringasta Shetland 285 M5
Ringford Dumfries 173 C4
Ringinglow S Yorks 130 A2
Ringland Norf 120 D3
Ringles Cross E Sus 36 D2
Ringmer E Sus 22 A2
Ringmore Devon 7 C5
Ringorm Moray 254 B3
Ring's End Cambs 101 A5
Ringsfield Suff 105 C5
Ringsfield Corner Suff 105 C5
Ringshall Herts 67 B4
Ringshall Suff 87 B6
Ringshall Stocks Suff 87 B6
Ringstead Norf 119 A4
Ringstead Northants 100 D1
Ringwood Hants 17 A5
Ringwould Kent 39 A5

Rinmore Aberds 243 A7
Rinnigill Orkney 283 H4
Rinsey Corn 2 C3
Riof W Isles 288 D2
Ripe E Sus 22 A3
Ripley Derbys 130 D3
Ripley Hants 17 B5
Ripley N Yorks 148 A1
Ripley Sur 34 A3
Riplingham E Yorks 150 D2
Ripon N Yorks 157 D7
Ripon Cathedral N Yorks 157 D7
Ripon Racecourse
  N Yorks 148 A2
Rippingale Lincs 116 C3
Ripple Kent 39 A5
Ripple Worcs 79 D6
Ripponden W Yorks 138 B3
Rireavach Highld 262 A2
Risabus Argyll 200 D3
Risbury Hereford 78 B3
Risby Suff 86 A3
Risca = Rhisga Caerph 60 D4
Rise E Yorks 151 C4
Riseden E Sus 36 C4
Risegate Lincs 117 C5
Riseholme Lincs 133 B4
Riseley Beds 84 A2
Riseley Wokingham 47 C5
Rishangles Suff 88 A2
Rishton Lancs 146 D1
Rishworth W Yorks 138 B3
Rising Bridge Lancs 137 A6
Risley Derbys 114 B2
Risley Warr 137 D5
Risplith N Yorks 147 A6
Rispond Highld 277 B5
Rivar Wilts 45 C7
Rivenhall End Essex 70 B2
River Bank Cambs 86 A1
Riverhead Kent 36 A3
Rivington Lancs 137 B5
Roa Island Cumb 153 D3
Roachill Devon 26 C3
Road Green Norf 104 B3
Roade Northants 83 B4
Roadhead Cumb 176 B3
Roadmeetings S Lnrk 194 B3
Roadside Highld 280 B3
Roadside of Catterline
  Aberds 233 A6
Roadside of Kinneff
  Aberds 233 A6
Roadwater Som 27 B5
Roag Highld 258 D2
Rob Roy and Trossachs
  Visitor Centre,
  Callander Stirl 217 D6
Robert Burns Centre,
  Dumfries Dumfries 174 A2
Roberton Borders 186 B3
Roberton S Lnrk 194 D4
Robertsbridge E Sus 37 D5
Roberttown W Yorks 139 A4
Robeston Cross Pembs 55 D4
Robeston Wathen Pembs 55 C6
Robin Hood W Yorks 139 A6
Robin Hood Doncaster
  Sheffield Airport
  S Yorks 141 D4
Robin Hood's Bay N Yorks 160 A3
Roborough Devon 25 D6
Roborough Devon 7 A4
Roby Mers 136 D3
Roby Mill Lancs 136 C4
Rocester Staffs 113 B5
Roch Pembs 55 B4
Roch Gate Pembs 55 B4
Rochdale Gtr Man 138 B1
Roche Corn 5 A4
Rochester Medway 51 C4
Rochester Northumb 188 D1
Rochester Castle Medway 51 C4
Rochester Cathedral
  Medway 51 C4
Rochford Essex 70 D2
Rock Corn 9 D5
Rock Northumb 189 A5
Rock Worcs 95 D5
Rock W Yorks 21 A4
Rock Ferry Mers 126 A3
Rockbeare Devon 13 B5
Rockbourne Hants 31 D5
Rockcliffe Cumb 175 B6
Rockcliffe Dumfries 173 C6
Rockfield Highld 265 B5

Rockfield Mon 61 B6
Rockford Hants 17 A5
Rockhampton S Glos 62 D2
Rockingham Northants 99 B5
Rockingham Motor
  Speedway Northants 99 B6
Rockland All Saints Norf 103 B5
Rockland St Mary Norf 104 A4
Rockland St Peter Norf 103 B5
Rockley Wilts 45 B5
Rockwell End Bucks 47 A5
Rockwell Green Som 27 C6
Rodborough Glos 63 C4
Rodbourne Thamesdown 45 A5
Rodbourne Wilts 44 A3
Rodbourne Cheney
  Thamesdown 45 A5
Rodd Hereford 77 A7
Roddam Northumb 188 A3
Rodden Dorset 15 C6
Rode Som 44 D2
Rode Heath Ches 128 D3
Rodeheath Ches 128 C3
Roden Telford 111 D4
Rodhuish Som 27 B5
Rodington Telford 111 D4
Rodley Glos 62 B3
Rodley W Yorks 147 D6
Rodmarton Glos 63 D5
Rodmell E Sus 22 B2
Rodmersham Kent 51 C6
Rodney Stoke Som 42 D3
Rodsley Derbys 113 A6
Rodway Som 28 B2
Rodwell Dorset 15 D6
Roe Green Herts 85 D5
Roecliffe N Yorks 148 A2
Roehampton London 49 B5
Roesound Shetland 284 G5
Roffey W Sus 35 C4
Rogart Highld 273 D5
Rogart Station Highld 273 D5
Rogate W Sus 33 C7
Rogerstone Newport 42 A1
Roghadal W Isles 287 F5
Rogiet Mon 42 A3
Rogue's Alley Cambs 101 A5
Roke Oxon 66 D1
Roker T & W 179 D6
Rollesby Norf 121 D6
Rolleston Leics 99 A4
Rolleston Notts 132 D2
Rolleston-on-Dove Staffs 113 C6
Rolston E Yorks 151 C5
Rolvenden Kent 37 C6
Rolvenden Layne Kent 37 C6
Romaldkirk Durham 166 C2
Roman Baths & Pump
  Room, Bath Bath 43 C6
Romanby N Yorks 158 B2
Romannobridge Borders 195 B6
Romansleigh Devon 26 C2
Romford London 50 A2
Romiley Gtr Man 138 D2
Romney, Hythe and
  Dymchurch Light
  Railway Kent 38 B3
Romsey Hants 32 C2
Romsey Town Cambs 85 B6
Romsley Shrops 95 C5
Romsley Worcs 96 D2
Ronague I o M 152 D2
Rookhope Durham 166 A2
Rookley I o W 18 C4
Rooks Bridge Som 42 D2
Roos E Yorks 151 D5
Roosebeck Cumb 153 D3
Rootham's Green Beds 84 B3
Rootpark S Lnrk 195 A4
Ropley Hants 33 B5
Ropley Dean Hants 33 B5
Ropsley Lincs 116 B2
Rora Aberds 269 D5
Rorandle Aberds 244 A3
Rorrington Shrops 93 A7
Roscroggan Corn 3 A4
Rose Corn 4 B2
Rose Ash Devon 26 C2
Rose Green W Sus 20 C2
Rose Grove Lancs 146 D2
Rose Hill E Sus 22 A2
Rose Hill Lancs 146 D2
Rose Hill Suff 88 C2
Roseacre Kent 37 A5
Roseacre Lancs 144 D4
Rosebank S Lnrk 194 B3
Rosebrough Northumb 189 A4

Rosebush Pembs 55 B6
Rosecare Corn 10 B2
Rosedale Abbey N Yorks 159 B6
Roseden Northumb 188 A3
Rosefield Highld 253 A4
Rosehall Highld 272 D2
Rosehaugh Mains Highld 252 A2
Rosehearty Aberds 269 C4
Rosehill Shrops 111 B5
Roseisle Moray 266 C2
Roselands E Sus 22 B4
Rosemarket Pembs 55 D5
Rosemarkie Highld 252 A3
Rosemary Lane Devon 27 D6
Rosemount Perth 231 D5
Rosenannon Corn 5 A4
Rosewell Midloth 209 D5
Roseworth Stockton 168 C2
Roseworthy Corn 3 B4
Rosgill Cumb 164 D3
Roshven Highld 235 C6
Roskhill Highld 258 D2
Roskill House Highld 252 A2
Rosley Cumb 175 D6
Roslin Midloth 209 D5
Rosliston Derbys 113 D6
Rosneath Argyll 215 D5
Ross Dumfries 172 D4
Ross Northumb 199 C5
Ross Perth 218 B2
Ross-on-Wye Hereford 62 A2
Rossett Wrex 126 D3
Rossett Green N Yorks 148 B2
Rossie Ochill Perth 219 C5
Rossie Priory Perth 220 A2
Rossington S Yorks 140 D4
Rosskeen Highld 264 D2
Rossland Renfs 205 A4
Roster Highld 281 E4
Rosthern Ches 128 A2
Rosthwaite Cumb 163 C5
Roston Derbys 113 A5
Rosyth Fife 208 B4
Rothbury Northumb 188 C3
Rotherby Leics 115 D4
Rotherfield E Sus 36 D3
Rotherfield Greys Oxon 47 A5
Rotherfield Peppard Oxon 47 A5
Rotherham S Yorks 140 D2
Rotherthorpe Northants 83 B4
Rotherwick Hants 47 D5
Rothes Moray 254 B3
Rothesay Argyll 203 B5
Rothiebrisbane Aberds 256 C2
Rothiemurchus Estate
  Visitor Centre Highld 242 A2
Rothienorman Aberds 256 C2
Rothiesholm Orkney 282 E7
Rothley Leics 114 D3
Rothley Northumb 178 A2
Rothley Shield East
  Northumb 188 D3
Rothmaise Aberds 256 C1
Rothwell Lincs 142 D3
Rothwell Northants 99 C5
Rothwell W Yorks 139 A6
Rothwell Haigh W Yorks 139 A6
Rotsea E Yorks 150 B3
Rottal Angus 232 B1
Rotten End Suff 89 A4
Rottingdean Brighton 21 B6
Rottington Cumb 162 C2
Roud I o W 18 C4
Rough Close Staffs 112 B3
Rough Common Kent 52 D3
Rougham Norf 119 C5
Rougham Suff 87 A5
Rougham Green Suff 87 A5
Roughburn Highld 240 D1
Roughlee Lancs 146 C2
Roughley W Mid 96 B4
Roughsike Cumb 176 B3
Roughton Lincs 134 C2
Roughton Norf 120 B4
Roughton Shrops 95 B5
Roughton Moor Lincs 134 C2
Roundhay W Yorks 148 D2
Roundstonefoot Dumfries 185 B4
Roundstreet Common
  W Sus 34 D3
Roundway Wilts 44 C4
Rous Lench Worcs 80 B3
Rousdon Devon 14 B2
Routenburn N Ayrs 204 B1
Routh E Yorks 150 C3
Row Corn 10 D1

Row Cumb 154 C3
Row Heath Essex 71 B5
Rowanburn Dumfries 175 A7
Rowardennan Stirl 206 A1
Rowde Wilts 44 C3
Rowen Conwy 124 B2
Rowfoot Northumb 177 C4
Rowhedge Essex 71 A4
Rowhook W Sus 35 C4
Rowington Warks 81 A5
Rowland Derbys 130 B2
Rowlands Castle Hants 33 D6
Rowlands Gill T & W 178 D3
Rowledge Sur 33 A7
Rowley E Yorks 150 D2
Rowley Shrops 93 A7
Rowley Hill W Yorks 139 B4
Rowley Regis W Mid 96 C2
Rowlstone Hereford 61 A5
Rowly Sur 34 B3
Rowney Green Worcs 96 D3
Rownhams Hants 32 D2
Rowrah Cumb 162 C3
Rowsham Bucks 66 B3
Rowsley Derbys 130 C3
Rowstock Oxon 46 A2
Rowston Lincs 133 D5
Rowton Ches 127 C4
Rowton Shrops 110 D3
Rowton Telford 111 D5
Roxburgh Borders 197 C5
Roxby N Lincs 141 B8
Roxby N Yorks 169 D5
Roxton Beds 84 B3
Roxwell Essex 69 C6
Royal Botanic Gardens
  Edin 209 C5
Royal Leamington Spa
  Warks 81 A6
Royal Museum of
  Scotland Edin 209 C5
Royal Oak Darl 167 C5
Royal Oak Lancs 136 C3
Royal Pavilion, Brighton
  Brighton 21 B6
Royal Tunbridge Wells
  Kent 36 C3
Royal Welch Fusiliers
  Regimental Museum
  (See Caernarfon
  Castle) Gwyn 123 D5
Royal Worcester
  Porcelain, Worcester
  Worcs 79 B6
Roybridge Highld 239 D6
Roydhouse W Yorks 139 B5
Roydon Essex 68 C4
Roydon Norf 119 C4
Roydon Norf 104 C1
Roydon Hamlet Essex 68 C4
Royston Herts 85 C5
Royston S Yorks 139 B6
Royton Gtr Man 138 C2
Rozel Jersey
Ruabon = Rhiwabon
  Wrex 110 A2
Ruaig Argyll 222 C3
Ruan Lanihorne Corn 4 C3
Ruan Minor Corn 3 D5
Ruarach Highld 249 D6
Ruardean Glos 62 B2
Ruardean Woodside Glos 62 B2
Rubery Worcs 96 D3
Ruckcroft Cumb 164 A3
Ruckhall Common
  Hereford 78 D2
Ruckinge Kent 38 B2
Ruckland Lincs 134 B3
Ruckley Shrops 94 A3
Rudbaxton Pembs 55 B5
Rudby N Yorks 158 A3
Ruddington Notts 114 B3
Rudford Glos 62 A3
Rudge Som 44 D2
Rudgeway S Glos 43 A5
Rudgwick W Sus 34 C3
Rudhall Hereford 62 A2
Rudheath Ches 128 B1
Rudley Green Essex 70 C2
Rudry Caerph 41 C6
Rudston E Yorks 150 A3
Rudyard Staffs 129 D4
Rufford Lancs 136 B3
Rufforth York 148 B4
Rugby Warks 98 D2
Rugeley Staffs 112 D4

...uglen S Ayrs 181 A4
...uilick Highld 251 B7
...uishton Som 28 C2
...uisigcarraidh W Isles 287 F4
...uislip London 48 A3
...uislip Common London 48 A3
...umbling Bridge Perth 208 A3
...umburgh Suff 104 C4
...umford Corn 9 D4
...umney Cardiff 41 D7
...uncun Halton 127 A3
...uncton W Sus 20 B1
...uncton Holme Norf 102 A2
...undlestone Devon 11 D6
...unfold Sur 34 B1
...unhall Norf 103 A6
...inham Norf 105 A6
...inham Norf 121 D6
...innington Som 27 C6
...insell Green Essex 70 C1
...inswick Bay N Yorks 169 D6
...inwell Essex 70 D1
...iscombe Wokingham 47 B5
...ish Green London 50 A2
...ish-head Aberds 256 B3
...ishall Hereford 79 D4
...ishall Norf 104 C2
...ishall Wilts 45 D5
...ishall W Mid 96 A3
...ishbrooke Suff 87 A4
...ishbury Shrops 94 B3
...ishden Herts 85 D5
...ishden Northants 83 A6
...ishenden Kent 51 B6
...ishford Norf 103 C5
...ishlake Green E Sus 22 A4
...ishmere Suff 105 C5
...ishmere St Andrew Suff 88 C3
...ishmoor Sur 34 B1
...ishock Worcs 96 D1
...isholme Gtr Man 138 D1
...ishton Ches 127 C5
...ishton Northants 99 C5
...ishton Shrops 95 A4
...ishton Spencer Staffs 129 C4
...ishwick Worcs 79 B6
...ishyford Durham 167 C5
...iskie Stirl 217 D6
...iskington Lincs 133 D5
...island Cumb 154 C2
...isper W Sus 35 C5
...ispidge Glos 62 B2
...issell's Water Oxon 47 A5
...issel's Green Suff 104 D3
...isthall Kent 36 C3
...istington W Sus 20 B3
...iston N Yorks 160 C3
...iston Parva E Yorks 150 A3
...iswarp N Yorks 160 A2
...istherford Borders 197 C5
...istherglen S Lnrk 205 B6
...isthernbridge Corn 5 A5
...isthin = Rhuthun Denb 125 D6
...isthin Craft Centre Denb 125 D6
...isthrieston Aberdeen 245 B6
...isaven Aberds 255 B6
...isaven Angus 231 D6
...isaven Highld 253 C4
...isaven Highld 241 C5
...isaven House Angus 231 D7
...isuvoes Corn 4 A4
...isuwell Dumfries 175 A5
...ison-XI-Towns Shrops 110 C2
...isthumb 178 B2
...isthFold Blkburn 137 A5
...is Dorset 14 B4
...ish Kent 37 A4
...isl Cumb 154 A2
...is I o W 19 B4
...is Sus 37 D7
...isForeign E Sus 37 D6
...isHarbour E Sus 38 D1
...isPark Herts 68 B3
...isStreet Worcs 79 D5
...isroft Gate Staffs 129 C4
...isill E Yorks 143 A4
...isl Rutland 116 D3
...isW Yorks 140 B1
...ispe T & W 179 D6
...isone N Yorks 146 B3
...is Intrinseca Dorset 29 D3
...isr N Yorks 149 D4
...is Glos 79 D5
...isN Yorks 159 D6
...isShrops 95 A5
...isT & W 178 C3
...is-on-Dunsmore
...iks 97 D6

S

Sabden Lancs 146 D1
Sacombe Herts 68 B3
Sacriston Durham 167 A5
Sadberge Darl 167 D6
Saddell Argyll 190 B3
Saddington Leics 98 B3
Saddle Bow Norf 118 D3
Saddlescombe W Sus 21 A5
Sadgill Cumb 154 A3
Saffron Walden Essex 86 D1
Sageston Pembs 55 D6
Saham Hills Norf 103 A5
Saham Toney Norf 103 A5
Saighdinis W Isles 287 H3
Saighton Ches 127 C4
St Abbs Borders 211 D6
St Abb's Haven Borders 211 D6
St Agnes Corn 4 B2
St Agnes Scilly 2 F3
St Albans Herts 67 C6
St Alban's Abbey Herts 67 C6
St Allen Corn 4 B3
St Andrews Fife 221 C5
St Andrew's Major V Glam 41 D6
St Anne Ald 7
St Annes Lancs 136 A2
St Ann's Dumfries 184 C3
St Ann's Chapel Corn 11 D5
St Ann's Chapel Devon 7 C5
St Anthony Corn 3 C5
St Anthony's Hill E Sus 22 B4
St Arvans Mon 61 D7
St Asaph = Llanelwy Denb 125 B5
St Athan V Glam 41 E5
St Aubin Jersey 6
St Austell Corn 5 B5
St Blazey Corn 5 B5
St Boswells Borders 197 C4
St Brelade Jersey 6
St Breock Corn 9 D5
St Breward Corn 10 D1
St Briavels Glos 62 C1
St Bride's Pembs 54 C4
St Bride's Major V Glam 40 D3
St Bride's Netherwent Mon 42 A3
St Brides super Ely V Glam 41 D5
St Brides Wentlooge Newport 42 A1
St Budeaux Plym 6 B3
St Buryan Corn 2 C2
St Catherine Bath 44 B1
St Catherine's Argyll 215 B4
St Clears = Sanclêr Carms 56 A2
St Cleer Corn 6 A1
St Clement Corn 4 C3
St Clements Jersey 6
St Clement's Caves, Hastings E Sus 23 A6
St Clether Corn 10 C3
St Colmac Argyll 203 B5
St Columb Major Corn 4 A4
St Columb Minor Corn 4 A3
St Columb Road Corn 4 B4
St Combs Aberds 269 C5
St Cross South Elmham Suff 104 C3
St Cyrus Aberds 233 B5
St David's Perth 218 B4
St David's = Tyddewi Pembs 54 B3
St Day Corn 4 C2
St Dennis Corn 4 B4
St Devereux Hereford 78 D2
St Dogmaels Pembs 73 B4
St Dogwells Pembs 55 B5
St Dominick Corn 6 A3
St Donat's V Glam 40 E4
St Edith's Wilts 44 C3
St Endellion Corn 9 D5
St Enoder Corn 4 B3
St Erme Corn 4 B3
St Erney Corn 6 B2
St Erth Corn 2 B3
St Ervan Corn 9 D4
St Eval Corn 4 A3
St Ewe Corn 5 C4
St Fagans Cardiff 41 D6
St Fagans Museum of Welsh Life Cardiff 41 D6
St Fergus Aberds 269 D5
St Fillans Perth 217 B6
St Florence Pembs 55 D6

St Genny's Corn 10 B2
St George Conwy 125 B4
St George's V Glam 41 D5
St Germans Corn 6 B2
St Giles Lincs 133 B4
St Giles Cathedral Edin 209 C5
St Giles in the Wood Devon 25 D6
St Giles on the Heath Devon 11 B4
St Harmon Powys 76 B4
St Helen Auckland Durham 167 C4
St Helena Warks 97 A5
St Helen's E Sus 23 A6
St Helens I o W 19 C5
St Helens Mers 136 D4
St Helier London 49 C5
St Helier Jersey 6
St Hilary Corn 2 B3
St Hilary V Glam 41 D5
Saint Hill W Sus 36 C1
St Illtyd Bl Gwent 41 A7
St Ippollitts Herts 68 A1
St Ishmael's Pembs 54 D4
St Issey Corn 9 D5
St Ive Corn 6 A2
St Ives Cambs 101 D5
St Ives Corn 2 A3
St Ives Dorset 17 A5
St James South Elmham Suff 104 C4
St Jidgey Corn 9 E5
St John Corn 6 B3
St John's I o M 152 C2
St John's Jersey 6
St John's Sur 34 A2
St John's Worcs 79 B6
St John's Chapel Durham 166 B1
St John's Fen End Norf 118 D2
St John's Highway Norf 118 D2
St John's Town of Dalry Dumfries 182 D4
St Judes I o M 152 B3
St Just I o M 2 B1
St Just in Penwith Corn 4 D3
St Just In Roseland Corn 4 D3
St Katherine's Aberds 256 C2
St Keverne Corn 3 C5
St Kew Corn 9 D6
St Kew Highway Corn 9 D6
St Keyne Corn 6 A1
St Lawrence Corn 5 A5
St Lawrence Essex 70 C3
St Lawrence I o W 18 D4
St Leonard's Bucks 67 C4
St Leonards Dorset 17 A5
St Leonards E Sus 23 B5
Saint Leonards S Lnrk 205 C6
St Levan Corn 2 C1
St Lythans V Glam 41 D6
St Mabyn Corn 9 D6
St Madoes Perth 219 B6
St Margaret South Elmham Suff 104 C4
St Margaret's Hereford 78 D1
St Margarets Herts 68 B3
St Margaret's at Cliffe Kent 39 A5
St Margaret's Hope Orkney 283 H5
St Mark's I o M 152 D2
St Martin Corn 6 B1
St Martins Corn 3 C5
St Martin's Jersey 6
St Martins Perth 219 A6
St Martin's Shrops 110 B2
St Mary Bourne Hants 46 D2
St Mary Church V Glam 41 D5
St Mary Cray London 50 C1
St Mary Hill V Glam 41 D4
St Mary Hoo Medway 51 B5
St Mary in the Marsh Kent 38 C2
St Mary's Jersey 6
St Mary's Orkney 283 G5
St Mary's Bay Kent 38 C2
St Mary's Church Warks 81 A5
St Maughans Mon 61 B6
St Mawes Corn 4 C3
St Mawgan Corn 4 A3
St Mellion Corn 6 A2
St Mellons Cardiff 42 A1
St Merryn Corn 9 D4
St Mewan Corn 5 B4
St Michael Caerhays Corn 5 C4
St Michael Penkevil Corn 4 C3
St Michael South Elmham Suff 104 C4

St Michael's Kent 37 C6
St Michaels Worcs 78 A3
St Michael's Mount, Penzance Corn 2 C3
St Michael's on Wyre Lancs 145 C4
St Minver Corn 9 D5
St Monans Fife 221 D5
St Neot Corn 5 A6
St Neots Cambs 84 A3
St Nicholas Pembs 72 C1
St Nicholas V Glam 41 D5
St Nicholas at Wade Kent 53 C4
St Ninians Stirl 207 A5
St Osyth Essex 71 B5
St Osyth Heath Essex 71 B5
St Owens Cross Hereford 62 A1
St Paul's Cathedral London 49 A6
St Paul's Cray London 50 C1
St Paul's Walden Herts 68 A1
St Peter Port Guern 6
St Peter's Jersey 6
St Peter's Kent 53 C5
St Petrox Pembs 55 E5
St Pinnock Corn 5 A7
St Quivox S Ayrs 192 C3
St Ruan Corn 3 D5
St Sampson Guern 6
St Stephen Corn 4 B4
St Stephen's Corn 10 C4
St Stephens Corn 6 B3
St Stephens Herts 67 C6
St Teath Corn 9 C6
St Thomas Devon 13 B4
St Tudy Corn 9 D6
St Twynnells Pembs 55 E5
St Veep Corn 5 B6
St Vigeans Angus 233 D4
St Wenn Corn 5 A4
St Weonards Hereford 61 A6
Saintbury Glos 80 D4
Salcombe Devon 7 D6
Salcombe Regis Devon 13 C6
Salcott Essex 70 B3
Sale Gtr Man 137 D6
Sale Green Worcs 80 B2
Saleby Lincs 135 B4
Salehurst E Sus 37 D5
Salem Ceredig 91 D4
Salem Carms 58 C3
Salen Argyll 225 B4
Salen Highld 235 D5
Salesbury Lancs 145 D6
Salford Beds 83 D6
Salford Gtr Man 137 D7
Salford Oxon 64 A3
Salford Priors Warks 80 B3
Salfords Sur 35 B5
Salhouse Norf 121 D5
Saline Fife 208 A3
Salisbury Wilts 31 C5
Salisbury Cathedral Wilts 31 C5
Salisbury Racecourse Wilts 31 C4
Sallachan Highld 236 C3
Sallachy Highld 249 C6
Sallachy Highld 272 D3
Salle Norf 120 C3
Salmonby Lincs 134 B3
Salmond's Muir Angus 221 A5
Salperton Glos 64 A1
Salph End Beds 84 B2
Salsburgh N Lnrk 207 D6
Salt Staffs 112 C3
Salt End E Yorks 142 A3
Saltaire W Yorks 147 D5
Saltaire 1853 Gallery W Yorks 147 D5
Saltash Corn 6 B3
Saltburn Highld 264 D3
Saltburn-by-the-Sea Redcar 169 C4
Saltby Leics 115 C6
Saltcoats Cumb 153 A1
Saltcoats N Ayrs 204 D2
Saltdean Brighton 22 B1
Salter Lancs 145 A6
Salterforth Lancs 146 C2
Salterswall Ches 127 C6
Saltfleet Lincs 143 D6
Saltfleetby All Saints Lincs 143 D6
Saltfleetby St Clements Lincs 143 D6
Saltfleetby St Peter Lincs 135 A4

Saltford Bath 43 C5
Salthouse Norf 120 A2
Saltmarshe E Yorks 141 A5
Saltney Flint 126 C3
Salton N Yorks 159 D6
Saltwick Northumb 178 B3
Saltwood Kent 38 B3
Salum Argyll 222 C2
Salvington W Sus 21 B4
Salwarpe Worcs 80 A1
Salwayash Dorset 15 B4
Sambourne Warks 80 A3
Sambrook Telford 111 C6
Samhla W Isles 287 H2
Samlesbury Lancs 145 D5
Samlesbury Bottoms Lancs 137 A5
Sammy Miller's Motorcycle Museum Hants 17 B6
Sampford Arundel Som 27 C6
Sampford Brett Som 27 A5
Sampford Courtenay Devon 12 A1
Sampford Peverell Devon 27 D5
Sampford Spiney Devon 11 D6
Sampool Bridge Cumb 154 C3
Samuelston E Loth 210 C1
Sanachan Highld 249 B5
Sanaigmore Argyll 200 A2
Sanclêr = St Clears Carms 56 A2
Sancreed Corn 2 C2
Sancton E Yorks 150 D2
Sand Highld 261 A6
Sand Shetland 285 J5
Sand Hole E Yorks 149 D7
Sand Hutton N Yorks 149 B5
Sandaig Highld 247 D6
Sandal Magna W Yorks 139 B6
Sandale Cumb 175 D5
Sanday Airport Orkney 282 C7
Sandbach Ches 128 C2
Sandbank Argyll 215 D4
Sandbanks Poole 17 C4
Sandend Aberds 267 C6
Sanderstead London 49 C6
Sandfields Glos 63 A5
Sandford Cumb 165 D5
Sandford Devon 12 A3
Sandford Dorset 16 C3
Sandford I o W 18 C4
Sandford N Som 42 D3
Sandford Shrops 111 B4
Sandford S Lnrk 194 B2
Sandford on Thames Oxon 65 C6
Sandford Orcas Dorset 29 C6
Sandford St Martin Oxon 65 A5
Sandfordhill Aberds 257 B6
Sandgate Kent 38 B3
Sandgreen Dumfries 172 C3
Sandhaven Aberds 269 C4
Sandhead Dumfries 170 C2
Sandhills Sur 34 C2
Sandhoe Northumb 178 C1
Sandholme E Yorks 150 D1
Sandholme Lincs 117 B6
Sandhurst Brack 47 C6
Sandhurst Glos 63 A4
Sandhurst Kent 37 D5
Sandhurst Cross Kent 37 D5
Sandhutton N Yorks 158 C2
Sandiacre Derbys 114 B2
Sandilands Lincs 135 A5
Sandilands S Lnrk 194 C3
Sandiway Ches 127 B6
Sandleheath Hants 31 D5
Sandling Kent 37 A5
Sandlow Green Ches 128 C2
Sandness Shetland 285 H3
Sandon Essex 70 C1
Sandon Herts 85 D5
Sandon Staffs 112 B3
Sandown I o W 19 C4
Sandown Park Racecourse Sur 48 C4
Sandplace Corn 6 B1
Sandridge Herts 67 B6
Sandridge Wilts 44 C3
Sandringham Norf 118 C3
Sandsend N Yorks 169 D6
Sandside Ho. Highld 279 B5
Sandsound Shetland 285 J5
Sandtoft N Lincs 141 C5
Sandway Kent 37 A6

Sandwell W Mid 96 C3
Sandwich Kent 53 D5
Sandwick Cumb 164 D2
Sandwick Orkney 283 K5
Sandwick Shetland 285 L6
Sandwith Cumb 162 C2
Sandy Beds 84 C3
Sandy Carms 57 B4
Sandy Bank Lincs 134 D2
Sandy Haven Pembs 55 D4
Sandy Lane Wilts 44 C3
Sandy Lane Wrex 110 A2
Sandycroft Flint 126 C3
Sandyford Dumfries 185 C5
Sandyford Stoke 128 D3
Sandygate I o M 152 B3
Sandyhills Dumfries 173 C6
Sandylands Lancs 144 A4
Sandypark Devon 12 C2
Sandysike Cumb 175 B6
Sangobeg Highld 277 B5
Sangomore Highld 277 B5
Sanna Highld 234 D3
Sanndabhaig W Isles 288 D5
Sanndabhaig W Isles 286 B4
Sannox N Ayrs 203 D5
Sanquhar Dumfries 183 B5
Santa Pod Raceway Beds 83 A6
Santon N Lincs 142 B1
Santon Bridge Cumb 163 D4
Santon Downham Suff 103 C4
Sapcote Leics 98 B1
Sapey Common Hereford 79 A5
Sapiston Suff 103 D5
Sapley Cambs 100 D4
Sapperton Glos 63 C5
Sapperton Lincs 116 B3
Saracen's Head Lincs 117 C6
Sarclet Highld 281 D5
Sardis Carms 57 B5
Sarn Bridgend 40 C4
Sarn Powys 93 B6
Sarn Bach Gwyn 106 D3
Sarn Meyllteyrn Gwyn 106 C2
Sarnau Ceredig 73 A6
Sarnau Carms 56 A3
Sarnau Gwyn 109 B4
Sarnau Powys 76 D4
Sarnau Powys 110 D1
Sarnesfield Hereford 78 B1
Saron Carms 73 C6
Saron Carms 57 A6
Saron Denb 125 C5
Saron Gwyn 107 A4
Saron Gwyn 123 D5
Sarratt Herts 67 D5
Sarre Kent 53 C4
Sarsden Oxon 64 A3
Sarsgrum Highld 277 B4
Satley Durham 166 A4
Satron N Yorks 156 B3
Satterleigh Devon 26 C1
Satterthwaite Cumb 154 B2
Satwell Oxon 47 A5
Sauchen Aberds 244 A3
Saucher Perth 219 A6
Sauchie Clack 208 A1
Sauchieburn Aberds 233 B4
Saughall Ches 126 B3
Saughtree Borders 187 D4
Saul Glos 62 C3
Saundby Notts 132 A2
Saundersfoot Pembs 56 B1
Saunderton Bucks 66 C2
Saunton Devon 25 B5
Sausthorpe Lincs 134 C3
Saval Highld 272 D3
Savary Highld 225 B5
Savile Park W Yorks 138 A3
Sawbridge Warks 82 A2
Sawbridgeworth Herts 69 B4
Sawdon N Yorks 160 C3
Sawley Derbys 114 B2
Sawley Lancs 146 C1
Sawley N Yorks 147 A6
Sawston Cambs 85 C6
Sawtry Cambs 100 C3
Saxby Leics 115 D6
Saxby Lincs 133 A5
Saxby All Saints N Lincs 142 B1
Saxelbye Leics 115 C5
Saxham Street Suff 88 A1
Saxilby Lincs 132 B3
Saxlingham Norf 120 B2

Saxlingham Green Norf 104 B3
Saxlingham Nethergate Norf 104 B3
Saxlingham Thorpe Norf 104 B3
Saxmundham Suff 89 A4
Saxon Street Cambs 86 B2
Saxondale Notts 115 B4
Saxtead Suff 88 A3
Saxtead Green Suff 88 A3
Saxthorpe Norf 120 B3
Saxton N Yorks 148 D3
Sayers Common W Sus 21 A5
Scackleton N Yorks 159 D5
Scadabhagh W Isles 288 H2
Scaftworth Notts 141 D4
Scagglethorpe N Yorks 160 D2
Scaitcliffe Lancs 137 A6
Scalasaig Argyll 212 C1
Scalby E Yorks 141 A6
Scalby N Yorks 160 B4
Scaldwell Northants 99 D4
Scale Houses Cumb 164 A3
Scaleby Cumb 176 C2
Scaleby Hill Cumb 176 C2
Scales Cumb 153 C3
Scales Cumb 163 B6
Scales Lancs 145 D4
Scalford Leics 115 C5
Scaling N Yorks 169 D5
Scallastle Argyll 225 C5
Scalloway Shetland 285 K6
Scalpay W Isles 288 H3
Scalpay Ho. Highld 247 B5
Scalpsie Argyll 203 C5
Scamadale Highld 235 A6
Scamblesby Lincs 134 B2
Scamodale Highld 236 B2
Scampston N Yorks 160 D2
Scampton Lincs 133 B4
Scapa Orkney 283 G5
Scapegoat Hill W Yorks 138 B3
Scar Orkney 282 C7
Scarborough N Yorks 160 C4
Scarborough Sea Life Centre N Yorks 160 B4
Scarcliffe Derbys 131 C4
Scarcroft W Yorks 148 C2
Scarcroft Hill W Yorks 148 C2
Scardroy Highld 250 A4
Scarff Shetland 284 E4
Scarfskerry Highld 281 A4
Scargill Durham 166 D3
Scarinish Argyll 222 C3
Scarisbrick Lancs 136 B2
Scarning Norf 119 D6
Scarrington Notts 115 A5
Scartho NE Lincs 143 C4
Scarwell Orkney 282 E3
Scatness Shetland 285 M5
Scatraig Highld 252 C3
Scawby N Lincs 142 C1
Scawsby S Yorks 140 C3
Scawton N Yorks 158 C4
Scayne's Hill W Sus 35 D6
Scethrog Powys 60 A3
Scholar Green Ches 128 D3
Scholes W Yorks 139 C4
Scholes W Yorks 139 A4
Scholes W Yorks 148 D2
School Green Ches 127 C6
Science & Industry Museum, Manchester Gtr Man 138 D1
Science Centre Glasgow 205 B5
Science Museum London 49 B5
Scleddau Pembs 55 A5
Sco Ruston Norf 121 C4
Scofton Notts 131 A6
Scole Norf 104 D2
Scolpaig W Isles 287 G2
Scone Perth 219 B6
Scone Palace, Perth Perth 219 B6
Sconser Highld 247 A4
Scoonie Fife 220 D3
Scoor Argyll 224 E3
Scopwick Lincs 133 D5
Scoraig Highld 262 A2
Scorborough E Yorks 150 C3
Scorrier Corn 4 C2
Scorton Lancs 145 C5
Scorton N Yorks 157 A6
Scotbheinn W Isles 286 A4
Scotby Cumb 176 D2
Scotch Corner N Yorks 157 A6
Scotforth Lancs 145 B4
Scothern Lincs 133 B5

Scotland Gate Northumb 179 A4
Scotlandwell Perth 219 D6
Scotney Castle Garden Kent 37 C4
Scotsburn Highld 264 C3
Scotscalder Station Highld 280 C2
Scotscraig Fife 220 B4
Scots'Gap Northumb 178 A2
Scotston Aberds 233 A3
Scotston Perth 230 D3
Scotstoun Glasgow 205 B5
Scotstown Highld 236 C2
Scotswood T & W 178 C3
Scottas Highld 247 D6
Scotter Lincs 141 C6
Scotterthorpe Lincs 141 C6
Scottlethorpe Lincs 116 C3
Scotton Lincs 141 D6
Scotton N Yorks 157 B5
Scotton N Yorks 148 B2
Scottow Norf 121 C4
Scoughall E Loth 210 R3
Scoulag Argyll 203 C6
Scoulton Norf 103 A5
Scourie Highld 276 D2
Scourie More Highld 276 D2
Scousburgh Shetland 285 M5
Scrabster Highld 280 B2
Scrafield Lincs 134 C3
Scrainwood Northumb 188 C2
Scrane End Lincs 117 A6
Scraptoft Leics 98 A3
Scratby Norf 121 D7
Scrayingham N Yorks 149 A6
Scredington Lincs 116 A3
Scremby Lincs 135 C4
Scremerston Northumb 198 B4
Screveton Notts 115 A5
Scrivelsby Lincs 134 C2
Scriven N Yorks 148 B2
Scrooby Notts 141 D4
Scropton Derbys 113 B5
Scrub Hill Lincs 134 D2
Scruton N Yorks 157 B6
Sculcoates Hull 150 D3
Sculthorpe Norf 119 B5
Scunthorpe N Lincs 141 B6
Scurlage Swansea 57 D4
Sea Palling Norf 121 C6
Sea Zoo Anglesey 123 D4
Seaborough Dorset 14 A4
Seacombe Mers 136 D2
Seacroft Lincs 135 C5
Seacroft W Yorks 148 D2
Seadyke Lincs 117 B6
Seafield S Ayrs 192 C3
Seafield W Loth 208 D3
Seaford E Sus 22 C2
Seaforth Mers 136 D2
Seagrave Leics 115 D4
Seaham Durham 168 A2
Seahouses Northumb 199 C6
Seal Kent 36 A3
Sealand Flint 126 C3
Seale Sur 34 B1
Seamer N Yorks 168 D2
Seamer N Yorks 160 C4
Seamill N Ayrs 204 D2
Searby Lincs 142 C2
Seasalter Kent 52 C2
Seascale Cumb 162 D3
Seathorne Lincs 135 C5
Seathwaite Cumb 153 A3
Seathwaite Cumb 163 C5
Seatoller Cumb 163 C5
Seaton Corn 6 B2
Seaton Cumb 162 A3
Seaton Devon 14 C2
Seaton Durham 179 D5
Seaton E Yorks 151 C4
Seaton Northumb 179 B5
Seaton Rutland 99 B6
Seaton Burn T & W 179 B4
Seaton Carew Hrtlpl 168 C3
Seaton Delaval Northumb 179 B5
Seaton Ross E Yorks 149 C6
Seaton Sluice Northumb 179 B5
Seatown Aberds 267 C6
Seatown Dorset 14 B4
Seave Green N Yorks 159 A4
Seaview I o W 19 B5
Seaville Cumb 175 C4
Seavington St Mary Som 28 D3
Seavington St Michael Som 28 D4
Sebergham Cumb 164 A1

Seckington Warks 97 A5
Second Coast Highld 261 A6
Sedbergh Cumb 155 B5
Sedbury Glos 62 D1
Sedbusk N Yorks 156 B2
Sedgeberrow Worcs 80 D3
Sedgebrook Lincs 115 B6
Sedgefield Durham 167 C6
Sedgefield Racecourse Durham 167 C6
Sedgeford Norf 119 B4
Sedgehill Wilts 30 C2
Sedgley W Mid 96 B2
Sedgwick Cumb 154 C4
Sedlescombe E Sus 23 A5
Sedlescombe Street E Sus 23 A5
Seend Wilts 44 C3
Seend Cleeve Wilts 44 C3
Seer Green Bucks 67 D4
Seething Norf 104 B4
Sefton Mers 136 C2
Seghill Northumb 179 B4
Seifton Shrops 94 C2
Seighford Staffs 112 C2
Seilebost W Isles 287 E5
Seion Gwyn 123 D5
Seisdon Staffs 95 B6
Seisiadar W Isles 288 D6
Selattyn Shrops 110 B1
Selborne Hants 33 B6
Selby N Yorks 149 D5
Selham W Sus 34 D2
Selhurst London 49 C6
Selkirk Borders 186 A3
Selkirk Glass Borders 186 A3
Sellack Hereford 62 A1
Sellafirth Shetland 284 D7
Sellibister Orkney 282 C8
Sellindge Kent 38 B2
Sellindge Lees Kent 38 B3
Selling Kent 52 D2
Sells Green Wilts 44 C3
Selly Oak W Mid 96 C3
Selmeston E Sus 22 B3
Selsdon London 49 C6
Selsey W Sus 20 C1
Selsfield Common W Sus 35 C6
Selsted Kent 39 A4
Selston Notts 131 D4
Selworthy Som 27 A4
Semblister Shetland 285 H5
Semer Suff 87 C5
Semington Wilts 44 C2
Semley Wilts 30 C2
Send Sur 34 A3
Send Marsh Sur 34 A3
Senghenydd Caerph 41 B6
Sennen Corn 2 C1
Sennen Cove Corn 2 C1
Sennybridge = Pont Senni Powys 59 C6
Serlby Notts 131 A6
Sessay N Yorks 158 D3
Setchey Norf 118 D3
Setley Hants 18 A2
Setter Shetland 285 H5
Setter Shetland 284 E6
Setter Shetland 285 J7
Settiscarth Orkney 282 F4
Settle N Yorks 146 A2
Settrington N Yorks 160 D2
Seven Kings London 50 A1
Seven Sisters Neath 59 E5
Sevenhampton Glos 63 A6
Sevenoaks Kent 36 A3
Sevenoaks Weald Kent 36 A3
Severn Beach S Glos 43 A4
Severn Bridges Visitor Centre S Glos 43 A4
Severn Stoke Worcs 79 C6
Severn Valley Railway Worcs 95 D5
Severnhampton Thamesdown 64 D3
Sevington Kent 38 A2
Sewards End Essex 86 D1
Sewardstone Essex 68 D3
Sewardstonebury Essex 68 D3
Sewerby Hall and Gardens, Bridlington E Yorks 151 A4
Seworgan Corn 4 D2
Sewstern Leics 116 C1
Sezincote Glos 81 D4
Sgarasta Mhor W Isles 287 E5
Sgiogarstaigh W Isles 288 A6

Shabbington Bucks 66 C
Shackerstone Leics 97 A
Shackleford Sur 34 B
Shade W Yorks 138 A
Shadforth Durham 167 A
Shadingfield Suff 105 C
Shadoxhurst Kent 38 B
Shadsworth Blkburn 137 A
Shadwell Norf 103 C
Shadwell W Yorks 148 L
Shaftesbury Dorset 30 C
Shafton S Yorks 140 B
Shakespeare's Birthplace, Stratford-upon-Avon Warks 81 B
Shalbourne Wilts 45 C
Shalcombe I o W 18 C
Shalden Hants 33 A
Shaldon Devon 13 D
Shalfleet I o W 18 C
Shalford Essex 69 A
Shalford Sur 34 B
Shalford Green Essex 69 A
Shallowford Devon 26 A
Shalmsford Street Kent 52 D
Shalstone Bucks 82 D
Shamley Green Sur 34 B
Shandon Argyll 215
Shandwick Highld 265
Shangton Leics 99
Shankhouse Northumb 179
Shanklin I o W 19
Shanklin Chine I o W 19
Shanquhar Aberds 255
Shanzie Perth 231
Shap Cumb 164
Shapwick Dorset 16
Shapwick Som 28
Shardlow Derbys 114
Shareshill Staffs 96
Sharlston N Yorks 140
Sharlston Common W Yorks 140
Sharnbrook Beds 84
Sharnford Leics 98
Sharoe Green Lancs 145
Sharow N Yorks 158
Sharp Street Norf 121
Sharpenhoe Beds 84
Sharperton Northumb 188
Sharpness Glos 62
Sharpthorne W Sus 35
Sharrington Norf 120
Shatterford Worcs 95
Shaugh Prior Devon 7
Shavington Ches 128
Shaw Gtr Man 138
Shaw W Berks 46
Shaw Wilts 44
Shaw Green Lancs 136
Shaw Mills N Yorks 147
Shawbury Shrops 111
Shawdon Hall Northumb 188
Shawell Leics 98
Shawford Hants 32
Shawforth Lancs 138
Shawhead Dumfries 173
Shawhill Dumfries 175
Shawton S Lnrk 194
Shawtonhill S Lnrk 194
Shear Cross Wilts 30
Shearington Dumfries 174
Shearsby Leics 98
Shebbear Devon 11
Shebdon Staffs 111
Shebster Highld 279
Sheddens E Renf 205
Shedfield Hants 33
Sheen Staffs 129
Sheepscar W Yorks 148
Sheepscombe Glos 63
Sheepstor Devon 7
Sheepwash Devon 11
Sheepway N Som 42
Sheepy Magna Leics 97
Sheepy Parva Leics 97
Sheering Essex 69
Sheerness Kent 51
Sheet Hants 33
Sheffield S Yorks 130
Sheffield Bottom W Berks 47
Sheffield Green E Sus 36
Sheffield Park, Uckfield E Sus 36
Shefford Beds 84
Shefford Woodlands W Berks 46

Place	County	Ref
Sheigra	Highld	276 B2
Sheinton	Shrops	95 A4
Shelderton	Shrops	94 D2
Sheldon	Derbys	129 C6
Sheldon	Devon	13 A6
Sheldon	W Mid	97 C4
Sheldwich	Kent	52 D2
Shelf	W Yorks	139 A4
Shelfanger	Norf	104 C2
Shelfield	Warks	80 A4
Shelfield	W Mid	96 A3
Shelford	Notts	115 A4
Shellacres	Northumb	198 B2
Shelley	Essex	69 C5
Shelley	Suff	87 D6
Shelley	W Yorks	139 B5
Shellingford	Oxon	64 D4
Shellow Bowells	Essex	69 C6
Shelsley Beauchamp	Worcs	79 A5
Shelsley Walsh	Worcs	79 A5
Shelthorpe	Leics	114 D3
Shelton	Beds	84 A2
Shelton	Norf	104 B3
Shelton	Notts	115 A5
Shelton	Shrops	110 D3
Shelton Green	Norf	104 B3
Shelve	Shrops	94 B1
Shelwick	Hereford	78 C3
Shenfield	Essex	69 D6
Shenington	Oxon	81 C6
Shenley	Herts	68 C1
Shenley Brook End	M Keynes	83 D5
Shenley Church End	M Keynes	83 D5
Shenleybury	Herts	68 C1
Shenmore	Hereford	78 D1
Shennanton	Dumfries	171 A5
Shenstone	Staffs	96 A4
Shenstone	Worcs	95 D6
Shenton	Leics	97 A6
Shenval	Highld	251 D6
Shenval	Moray	254 D3
Shepeau Stow	Lincs	117 D6
Shephall	Herts	68 A2
Shepherd's Green	Oxon	47 A5
Shepherd's Port	Norf	118 B3
Shepherdswell	Kent	39 A4
Shepley	W Yorks	139 C4
Shepperdine	S Glos	62 D2
Shepperton	Sur	48 C3
Shepreth	Cambs	85 C5
Shepshed	Leics	114 D2
Shepton Beauchamp	Som	28 A4
Shepton Mallet	Som	29 A6
Shepton Montague	Som	29 B6
Shepway	Kent	37 A5
Sheraton	Durham	168 B2
Sherborne	Dorset	29 D6
Sherborne	Glos	64 B2
Sherborne St John	Hants	47 D4
Sherbourne	Warks	81 A5
Sherburn	Durham	167 A6
Sherburn	N Yorks	160 D3
Sherburn Hill	Durham	167 A6
Sherburn in Elmet	N Yorks	148 D3
Shere	Sur	34 B3
Shereford	Norf	119 C5
Sherfield English	Hants	32 C1
Sherfield on Loddon	Hants	47 D4
Sherford	Devon	8 C1
Sheriff Hutton	N Yorks	149 A5
Sheriffhales	Shrops	111 D6
Sheringham	Norf	120 A3
Sherington	M Keynes	83 C5
Shernal Green	Worcs	80 A2
Shernborne	Norf	119 B4
Sherrington	Wilts	30 B3
Sherston	Wilts	44 A2
Sherwood Green	Devon	25 C6
Shettleston	Glasgow	205 B6
Shevington	Gtr Man	136 C4
Shevington Moor	Gtr Man	136 B4
Shevington Vale	Gtr Man	136 C4
Sheviock	Corn	6 B2
Shide	I o W	18 C3
Shiel Bridge	Highld	238 A3
Shieldaig	Highld	249 A5
Shieldaig	Highld	261 C5
Shieldhill	Dumfries	184 D3
Shieldhill	Falk	208 C1
Shieldhill	S Lnrk	195 B5
Shielfoot	Highld	235 D5
Shielhill	Angus	232 C2
Shielhill	Invclyd	204 A2
Shifford	Oxon	65 C4
Shifnal	Shrops	95 A5
Shilbottle	Northumb	189 C4
Shildon	Durham	167 C5
Shillingford	Devon	27 C4
Shillingford	Oxon	65 D6
Shillingford St George	Devon	13 C4
Shillingstone	Dorset	30 D2
Shillington	Beds	84 D3
Shillmoor	Northumb	188 C1
Shilton	Oxon	64 C3
Shilton	Warks	97 C7
Shilvington	Northumb	178 A3
Shimpling	Norf	104 C2
Shimpling	Suff	87 B4
Shimpling Street	Suff	87 B4
Shincliffe	Durham	167 A5
Shiney Row	T & W	179 D5
Shinfield	Wokingham	47 C5
Shingham	Norf	102 A3
Shingle Street	Suff	89 C4
Shinner's Bridge	Devon	8 A1
Shinness	Highld	272 C3
Shipbourne	Kent	36 A3
Shipdham	Norf	103 A5
Shipham	Som	42 D3
Shiphay	Torbay	8 A2
Shiplake	Oxon	47 B5
Shipley	Derbys	114 A2
Shipley	Northumb	189 B4
Shipley	Shrops	95 B6
Shipley	W Sus	35 D4
Shipley	W Yorks	147 D5
Shipley Shiels	Northumb	187 D6
Shipmeadow	Suff	105 C4
Shippea Hill Station	Cambs	102 C2
Shippon	Oxon	65 D5
Shipston-on-Stour	Warks	81 C5
Shipton	Glos	63 B6
Shipton	N Yorks	149 B4
Shipton	Shrops	94 B3
Shipton Bellinger	Hants	31 A6
Shipton Gorge	Dorset	15 B4
Shipton Green	W Sus	19 A7
Shipton Moyne	Glos	44 A2
Shipton on Cherwell	Oxon	65 B5
Shipton Solers	Glos	63 B6
Shipton-under-Wychwood	Oxon	64 B3
Shiptonthorpe	E Yorks	150 C1
Shirburn	Oxon	66 D1
Shirdley Hill	Lancs	136 B2
Shire Horse Centre, Stratford-upon-Avon	Warks	81 B5
Shirebrook	Derbys	131 C5
Shiregreen	S Yorks	139 D6
Shirehampton	Bristol	43 B4
Shiremoor	T & W	179 B5
Shirenewton	Mon	61 D6
Shireoaks	Notts	131 A5
Shirkoak	Kent	38 B1
Shirl Heath	Hereford	78 B2
Shirland	Derbys	130 D3
Shirley	Derbys	113 A6
Shirley	London	49 C6
Shirley	Soton	32 D3
Shirley	W Mid	96 D4
Shirrell Heath	Hants	33 D4
Shirwell	Devon	25 B6
Shirwell Cross	Devon	25 B6
Shiskine	N Ayrs	191 C5
Shobdon	Hereford	78 A2
Shobnall	Staffs	113 C6
Shobrooke	Devon	12 A3
Shoby	Leics	115 D4
Shocklach	Ches	110 A3
Shoeburyness	Sthend	51 A6
Sholden	Kent	53 D5
Sholing	Soton	32 D3
Shoot Hill	Shrops	110 D3
Shop	Corn	24 D3
Shop	Corn	9 D4
Shop Corner	Suff	88 D3
Shore Mill	Highld	264 D3
Shoreditch	London	49 A6
Shoreham	Kent	50 C2
Shoreham Airport	W Sus	21 B5
Shoreham-By-Sea	W Sus	21 B5
Shoresdean	Northumb	198 B3
Shoreswood	Northumb	198 B3
Shoreton	Highld	264 D2
Shorncote	Glos	63 D6
Shorne	Kent	50 B3
Short Heath	W Mid	96 A2
Shortacombe	Devon	11 C6
Shortgate	E Sus	22 A2
Shortlanesend	Corn	4 C3
Shortlees	E Ayrs	193 B4
Shortstown	Beds	84 C2
Shorwell	I o W	18 C3
Shoscombe	Bath	43 D6
Shotatton	Shrops	110 C2
Shotesham	Norf	104 B3
Shotgate	Essex	70 D1
Shotley	Suff	88 D3
Shotley Bridge	Durham	178 D2
Shotley Gate	Suff	88 D3
Shotleyfield	Northumb	178 D2
Shottenden	Kent	52 D2
Shottermill	Sur	34 C1
Shottery	Warks	81 B4
Shotteswell	Warks	81 C7
Shottisham	Suff	88 C4
Shottle	Derbys	113 A7
Shottlegate	Derbys	113 A7
Shotton	Durham	168 B2
Shotton	Flint	126 C3
Shotton	Northumb	198 C2
Shotton Colliery	Durham	167 A6
Shotts	N Lnrk	207 D6
Shotwick	Ches	126 B3
Shouldham	Norf	102 A2
Shouldham Thorpe	Norf	102 A2
Shoulton	Worcs	79 B6
Shover's Green	E Sus	37 C4
Shrawardine	Shrops	110 D3
Shrawley	Worcs	79 A6
Shrewley Common	Warks	81 A5
Shrewsbury	Shrops	110 D3
Shrewton	Wilts	31 A4
Shripney	W Sus	20 B2
Shrivenham	Oxon	45 A6
Shropham	Norf	103 B5
Shrub End	Essex	70 A3
Shucknall	Hereford	78 C3
Shudy Camps	Cambs	86 C2
Shulishadermor	Highld	259 D4
Shurdington	Glos	63 B5
Shurlock Row	Windsor	47 B6
Shurrery	Highld	279 C6
Shurrery Lodge	Highld	279 C6
Shurton	Som	28 A2
Shustoke	Warks	97 B5
Shute	Devon	14 B2
Shute	Devon	12 A3
Shutford	Oxon	81 C6
Shuthonger	Glos	80 D1
Shutlanger	Northants	83 B4
Shuttington	Warks	97 A5
Shuttlewood	Derbys	131 B4
Siabost bho Dheas	W Isles	288 C3
Siabost bho Thuath	W Isles	288 C3
Siadar	W Isles	288 B5
Siadar Iarach	W Isles	288 B4
Siadar Uarach	W Isles	288 B4
Sibbaldbie	Dumfries	185 D4
Sibbertoft	Northants	98 C3
Sibdon Carwood	Shrops	94 C2
Sibford Ferris	Oxon	81 D6
Sibford Gower	Oxon	81 D6
Sible Hedingham	Essex	86 D3
Sibsey	Lincs	134 D3
Sibson	Cambs	100 B2
Sibson	Leics	97 A6
Sibthorpe	Notts	115 A5
Sibton	Suff	89 A4
Sibton Green	Suff	105 D4
Sicklesmere	Suff	87 A4
Sicklinghall	N Yorks	148 C2
Sid	Devon	13 C6
Sidbury	Devon	13 B6
Sidbury	Shrops	95 C4
Sidcot	N Som	42 D3
Sidcup	London	50 B1
Siddick	Cumb	162 A3
Siddington	Ches	128 B3
Siddington	Glos	63 D6
Sidemoor	Worcs	96 D2
Sidestrand	Norf	121 B4
Sidford	Devon	13 B6
Sidlesham	W Sus	20 C1
Sidley	E Sus	23 B5
Sidlow	Sur	35 B5
Sidmouth	Devon	13 C6
Sigford	Devon	12 D2
Sigglesthorne	E Yorks	151 C4
Sighthill	Edin	209 C4
Sigingstone	V Glam	41 D4
Signet	Oxon	64 B3
Silchester	Hants	47 C4
Sildinis	W Isles	288 F3
Sileby	Leics	114 D3
Silecroft	Cumb	153 B2
Silfield	Norf	104 B2
Silian	Ceredig	75 C4
Silk Willoughby	Lincs	116 A3
Silkstone	S Yorks	139 C5
Silkstone Common	S Yorks	139 C5
Silloth	Cumb	174 C4
Sills	Northumb	188 C1
Sillyearn	Moray	267 D6
Siloh	Carms	59 B4
Silpho	N Yorks	160 B3
Silsden	W Yorks	147 C4
Silsoe	Beds	84 D2
Silver End	Essex	70 B2
Silverburn	Midloth	209 D5
Silverdale	Lancs	154 D3
Silverdale	Staffs	112 A2
Silvergate	Norf	120 C3
Silverhill	E Sus	23 A5
Silverley's Green	Suff	104 D3
Silverstone	Northants	82 C3
Silverstone Motor Racing Circuit	Northants	82 C3
Silverton	Devon	13 A4
Silvington	Shrops	95 D4
Silwick	Shetland	285 J4
Simmondley	Derbys	138 D3
Simonburn	Northumb	177 B6
Simonsbath	Som	26 B2
Simonstone	Lancs	146 D1
Simprim	Borders	198 B2
Simpson	M Keynes	83 D5
Simpson Cross	Pembs	55 C4
Sinclair's Hill	Borders	198 A2
Sinclairston	E Ayrs	182 A2
Sinderby	N Yorks	158 C2
Sinderhope	Northumb	177 D6
Sindlesham	Wokingham	47 C5
Singdean	Borders	187 C4
Singleborough	Bucks	83 D4
Singleton	Lancs	144 D3
Singleton	W Sus	20 A1
Singlewell	Kent	50 B3
Sinkhurst Green	Kent	37 B6
Sinnahard	Aberds	244 A1
Sinnington	N Yorks	159 C6
Sinton Green	Worcs	79 A6
Sipson	London	48 B3
Sirhowy	Bl Gwent	60 B3
Sisland	Norf	104 B4
Sissinghurst	Kent	37 C5
Sissington, Cranbrook	Kent	37 C6
Sisterpath	Borders	197 B6
Siston	S Glos	43 B5
Sithney	Corn	3 C4
Sittingbourne	Kent	51 C5
Six Ashes	Staffs	95 C5
Six Hills	Leics	115 C4
Six Mile Bottom	Cambs	86 B1
Sixhills	Lincs	133 A6
Sixpenny Handley	Dorset	30 D3
Sizewell	Suff	89 A5
Skail	Highld	278 D3
Skaill	Orkney	282 F3
Skaill	Orkney	282 D5
Skaill	Orkney	283 G6
Skara Brae	Orkney	282 F3
Skares	E Ayrs	182 A3
Skateraw	E Loth	211 C4
Skaw	Shetland	284 G7
Skeabost	Highld	259 D4
Skeabrae	Orkney	282 E3
Skeeby	N Yorks	157 A6
Skeffington	Leics	99 A4
Skeffling	E Yorks	143 B5
Skegby	Notts	131 C4
Skegness	Lincs	135 C5
Skelberry	Shetland	285 M5
Skelbo	Highld	264 A3
Skelbrooke	S Yorks	140 B3
Skeldyke	Lincs	117 B6
Skellingthorpe	Lincs	133 B4
Skellister	Shetland	285 H6
Skellow	S Yorks	140 B3
Skelmanthorpe	W Yorks	139 B5
Skelmersdale	Lancs	136 C3
Skelmonae	Aberds	256 C3
Skelmorlie	N Ayrs	204 B1
Skelmuir	Aberds	257 B4
Skelpick	Highld	278 C3
Skelton	Cumb	164 B2
Skelton	E Yorks	141 A5
Skelton	N Yorks	157 A4
Skelton	Redcar	169 D4
Skelton	York	149 B4
Skelton-on-Ure	N Yorks	148 A2
Skelwick	Orkney	282 C5
Skelwith Bridge	Cumb	154 A2
Skendleby	Lincs	135 C4
Skene Ho.	Aberds	245 B4
Skenfrith	Mon	61 A6
Skerne	E Yorks	150 B3
Skeroblingarry	Argyll	190 C3
Skerray	Highld	278 B2
Skerton	Lancs	145 A4
Sketchley	Leics	98 B1
Sketty	Swansea	57 C6
Skewen	Neath	40 B2
Skewsby	N Yorks	159 D5
Skeyton	Norf	120 C4
Skiag Bridge	Highld	271 B5
Skibo Castle	Highld	264 B3
Skidbrooke	Lincs	143 D6
Skidbrooke North End	Lincs	143 D6
Skidby	E Yorks	150 D3
Skilgate	Som	27 C4
Skillington	Lincs	116 C1
Skinburness	Cumb	174 C4
Skinflats	Falk	208 B2
Skinidin	Highld	258 D2
Skinnet	Highld	277 B6
Skinningrove	Redcar	169 C5
Skipness	Argyll	202 C3
Skippool	Lancs	144 C3
Skipsea	E Yorks	151 B4
Skipsea Brough	E Yorks	151 B4
Skipton	N Yorks	146 B3
Skipton-on-Swale	N Yorks	158 D2
Skipwith	N Yorks	149 D5
Skirbeck	Lincs	117 A6
Skirbeck Quarter	Lincs	117 A6
Skirlaugh	E Yorks	151 D4
Skirling	Borders	195 C5
Skirmett	Bucks	47 A5
Skirpenbeck	E Yorks	149 B6
Skirwith	Cumb	165 B4
Skirza	Highld	281 B5
Skulamus	Highld	247 B5
Skullomie	Highld	277 B7
Skyborry Green	Shrops	93 D6
Skye of Curr	Highld	253 D5
Skyreholme	N Yorks	147 A4
Slackhall	Derbys	129 A5
Slackhead	Moray	267 C5
Slad	Glos	63 C4
Slade	Devon	25 A6
Slade	Pembs	55 C5
Slade Green	London	50 B2
Slaggyford	Northumb	177 D4
Slaidburn	Lancs	145 B7
Slaithwaite	W Yorks	138 B3
Slaley	Northumb	178 D1
Slamannan	Falk	207 C6
Slapton	Bucks	67 A4
Slapton	Devon	8 C2
Slapton	Northants	82 C3
Slatepit Dale	Derbys	130 C3
Slattocks	Gtr Man	138 C1
Slaugham	W Sus	35 D5
Slaughterford	Wilts	44 B2
Slawston	Leics	99 B4
Sleaford	Hants	33 B7
Sleaford	Lincs	116 A3
Sleagill	Cumb	164 D3
Sleapford	Telford	111 D5
Sledge Green	Worcs	79 D6
Sledmere	E Yorks	150 A2
Sleightholme	Durham	166 D2
Sleights	N Yorks	160 A2
Slepe	Dorset	16 B3
Slickly	Highld	281 B4
Sliddery	N Ayrs	191 C5
Sligachan Hotel	Highld	246 B3
Slimbridge	Glos	62 C3
Slimbridge Wildfowl & Wetlands Centre, Frampton on Severn	Glos	62 C3
Slindon	Staffs	112 B2
Slindon	W Sus	20 B2
Slinfold	W Sus	35 C4
Sling	Gwyn	123 D6
Slingsby	N Yorks	159 D5
Slioch	Aberds	255 C6

Slip End Beds 67 D5
Slip End Herts 85 D4
Slipton Northants 99 D6
Slitting Mill Staffs 112 D4
Slochd Highld 253 D4
Slockavullin Argyll 213 C6
Sloley Norf 121 C4
Sloothby Lincs 135 B4
Slough Slough 48 B2
Slough Green W Sus 35 D5
Sluggan Highld 253 D4
Slumbay Highld 249 C5
Slyfield Sur 34 A2
Slyne Lancs 145 A4
Smailholm Borders 197 C5
Small Dole W Sus 21 A5
Small Hythe Kent 37 C6
Smallbridge Gtr Man 138 B2
Smallburgh Norf 121 C5
Smallburn Aberds 257 B5
Smallburn E Ayrs 194 D1
Smalley Derbys 114 A2
Smallfield Sur 35 B6
Smallridge Devon 14 A3
Smannell Hants 32 A2
Smardale Cumb 155 A6
Smarden Kent 37 B6
Smarden Bell Kent 37 B6
Smeatharpe Devon 28 D1
Smeeth Kent 38 B2
Smeeton Westerby Leics 98 B3
Smercleit W Isles 286 E3
Smerral Highld 275 A5
Smethwick W Mid 96 C3
Smirisary Highld 235 C5
Smisby Derbys 114 D1
Smith Green Lancs 145 B4
Smithfield Cumb 176 C2
Smithincott Devon 27 D5
Smith's Green Essex 69 A5
Smithstown Highld 261 C4
Smithton Highld 252 B3
Smithy Green Ches 128 B2
Smockington Leics 98 C1
Smoogro Orkney 283 G4
Smythe's Green Essex 70 B3
Snaefell Mountain
  Railway I o M 152 C4
Snaigow House Perth 231 D4
Snailbeach Shrops 94 A1
Snailwell Cambs 86 A2
Snainton N Yorks 160 C3
Snaith E Yorks 140 A4
Snape N Yorks 157 C6
Snape Suff 89 B4
Snape Green Lancs 136 B2
Snarestone Leics 97 A6
Snarford Lincs 133 A5
Snargate Kent 38 C1
Snave Kent 38 C2
Snead Powys 93 B7
Sneath Common Norf 104 C2
Sneaton N Yorks 160 A2
Sneatonthorpe N Yorks 160 A3
Snelland Lincs 133 A5
Snelston Derbys 113 A5
Snetterton Motor Racing
  Circuit Norf 103 C6
Snettisham Norf 118 B3
Snibston Discovery Park,
  Coalville Leics 114 D2
Sniseabhal W Isles 286 C3
Snitter Northumb 188 C3
Snitterby Lincs 142 D1
Snitterfield Warks 81 B5
Snitton Shrops 94 D3
Snodhill Hereford 77 C7
Snodland Kent 51 C3
Snowden Hill S Yorks 139 C5
Snowdon Mountain
  Railway, Llanberis
  Gwyn 107 A6
Snowdown Kent 53 D4
Snowshill Glos 80 D3
Snowshill Manor Glos 80 D3
Snydale W Yorks 140 B2
Soar Anglesey 122 C3
Soar Carms 58 C3
Soar Devon 7 D6
Soar-y-Mynydd Ceredig 76 B1
Soberton Hants 33 D5
Soberton Heath Hants 33 D5
Sockbridge Cumb 164 C3
Sockburn Darl 158 A2

Soham Cambs 102 D1
Soham Cotes Cambs 102 D1
Solas W Isles 287 G3
Soldon Cross Devon 24 D4
Soldridge Hants 33 B5
Sole Street Kent 50 C3
Sole Street Kent 38 A2
Solihull W Mid 97 D4
Sollers Dilwyn Hereford 78 B2
Sollers Hope Hereford 79 D4
Sollom Lancs 136 B3
Solva Pembs 54 B3
Somerby Leics 115 D5
Somerby Lincs 142 C2
Somercotes Derbys 131 D4
Somerford Dorset 17 B5
Somerford Keynes Glos 63 D6
Somerley W Sus 19 B7
Somerleyton Suff 105 B5
Somersal Herbert Derbys 113 B5
Somersby Lincs 134 B3
Somersham Cambs 101 D5
Somersham Suff 88 C1
Somerton Oxon 65 A5
Somerton Som 29 C4
Sompting W Sus 21 B4
Sonning Wokingham 47 B5
Sonning Common Oxon 47 A5
Sonning Eye Oxon 47 B5
Sontley Wrex 110 A2
Sopley Hants 17 B5
Sopwell Herts 67 C6
Sopworth Wilts 44 A2
Sorbie Dumfries 171 C6
Sordale Highld 280 B3
Sorisdale Argyll 223 A5
Sorn E Ayrs 193 C5
Sornhill E Ayrs 193 B5
Sortat Highld 281 B4
Sotby Lincs 134 B2
Sots Hole Lincs 133 C6
Sotterley Suff 105 C5
Soudley Shrops 111 C6
Soughton Flint 126 C2
Soulbury Bucks 66 A3
Soulby Cumb 165 D5
Souldern Oxon 82 D2
Souldrop Beds 84 A1
Sound Ches 111 A5
Sound Shetland 285 H5
Sound Shetland 285 J6
Sound Heath Ches 111 A5
Soundwell S Glos 43 B5
Sourhope Borders 188 A1
Sourin Orkney 282 D5
Sourton Devon 11 B6
Soutergate Cumb 153 B3
South Acre Norf 119 D5
South Allington Devon 8 D1
South Alloa Falk 208 A1
South Ambersham W Sus 34 D2
South Anston S Yorks 131 A5
South Ascot Windsor 48 C2
South Ballachulish Highld 237 D4
South Balloch S Ayrs 181 B5
South Bank N Yorks 168 C3
South Barrow Som 29 C6
South Beach Gwyn 106 C3
South Benfleet Essex 51 A4
South Bersted W Sus 20 B2
South Brent Devon 7 F2
South Brewham Som 29 B7
South Broomhill
  Northumb 189 D5
South Burlingham Norf 105 A4
South Cadbury Som 29 C6
South Cairn Dumfries 170 A1
South Carlton Lincs 133 B4
South Cave E Yorks 150 D2
South Cerney Glos 63 D6
South Chard Som 14 A3
South Charlton Northumb 189 A4
South Cheriton Som 29 C6
South Cliffe E Yorks 150 D1
South Clifton Notts 132 B3
South Cockerington
  Lincs 134 A3
South Cornelly Bridgend 40 C3
South Cove Suff 105 C5
South Creagan Argyll 227 B4
South Creake Norf 119 B5
South Croxton Leics 115 D4
South Croydon London 49 C6
South Dalton E Yorks 150 C2
South Darenth Kent 50 C2
South Duffield N Yorks 149 D5
South Elkington Lincs 134 A2

South Elmsall W Yorks 140 B2
South End Bucks 66 A2
South End Cumb 153 D3
South End N Lincs 142 A3
South Erradale Highld 261 C4
South Fambridge Essex 70 D2
South Fawley W Berks 46 A1
South Ferriby N Lincs 142 A1
South Garth Shetland 284 D7
South Garvan Highld 236 B3
South Glendale W Isles 286 E3
South Godstone Sur 35 B6
South Gorley Hants 31 D5
South Green Essex 69 D6
South Green Kent 51 C5
South-haa Shetland 284 E5
South Ham Hants 47 D4
South Hanningfield Essex 70 D1
South Harting W Sus 33 D6
South Hatfield Herts 68 C2
South Hayling Hants 19 B6
South Hazelrigg
  Northumb 199 C4
South Heath Bucks 67 C4
South Heighton E Sus 22 B2
South Hetton Durham 167 A6
South Hiendley W Yorks 140 B1
South Hill Corn 10 D4
South Hinksey Oxon 65 C6
South Hole Devon 24 C3
South Holme N Yorks 159 D5
South Holmwood Sur 35 B4
South Hornchurch London 50 A2
South Hykeham Lincs 133 C4
South Hylton T & W 179 D5
South Kelsey Lincs 142 D2
South Kessock Highld 252 B2
South Killingholme
  N Lincs 142 B3
South Kilvington N Yorks 158 C3
South Kilworth Leics 98 C3
South Kirkby W Yorks 140 B2
South Kirkton Aberds 245 B4
South Kiscadale N Ayrs 191 C6
South Kyme Lincs 117 A4
South Lancing W Sus 21 B4
South Leigh Oxon 65 C4
South Leverton Notts 132 A2
South Littleton Worcs 80 C3
South Lopham Norf 103 C6
South Luffenham Rutland 99 A6
South Malling E Sus 22 A2
South Marston
  Thamesdown 45 A5
South Middleton
  Northumb 188 A2
South Milford N Yorks 148 D3
South Millbrex Aberds 256 B3
South Milton Devon 7 C6
South Mimms Herts 68 C2
South Molton Devon 26 C2
South Moreton Oxon 46 A3
South Mundham W Sus 20 B1
South Muskham Notts 132 D2
South Newbald E Yorks 150 D2
South Newington Oxon 81 D7
South Newton Wilts 31 B4
South Normanton Derbys 131 D4
South Norwood London 49 C6
South Nutfield Sur 35 B6
South Ockendon Thurrock 50 A2
South Ormsby Lincs 134 B3
South Otterington
  N Yorks 158 C2
South Owersby Lincs 142 D2
South Oxhey Herts 67 D6
South Perrott Dorset 15 A4
South Petherton Som 28 D4
South Petherwin Corn 10 C4
South Pickenham Norf 103 A4
South Pool Devon 7 C6
South Port Argyll 227 D5
South Radworthy Devon 26 B2
South Rauceby Lincs 116 A3
South Raynham Norf 119 C5
South Reston Lincs 135 A4
South Runcton Norf 102 A2
South Scarle Notts 132 C3
South Shian Argyll 226 B4
South Shields T & W 179 C5
South Shields Museum
  T & W 179 C5
South Shore Blkpool 144 D3
South Somercotes Lincs 143 D6
South Stainley N Yorks 148 A2
South Stainmore Cumb 165 D6
South Stifford Thurrock 50 B3

South Stoke Oxon 46 A3
South Stoke W Sus 20 B3
South Street E Sus 22 A1
South Street London 36 A2
South Street Kent 52 C3
South Street Kent 52 D2
South Tawton Devon 12 B1
South Thoresby Lincs 135 B4
South Tidworth Wilts 31 A6
South Town Hants 33 B5
South View Hants 47 D4
South Walsham Norf 121 D5
South Warnborough Hants 33 A6
South Weald Essex 69 D5
South Weston Oxon 66 D2
South Wheatley Corn 10 B3
South Wheatley Notts 132 A2
South Whiteness Shetland 285 J5
South Widcombe Bath 43 D4
South Wigston Leics 98 B2
South Willingham Lincs 134 A1
South Wingfield Derbys 130 D3
South Witham Lincs 116 D2
South Wonston Hants 32 B3
South Woodham Ferrers
  Essex 70 D2
South Wootton Norf 118 C3
South Wraxall Wilts 44 C2
South Zeal Devon 12 B1
Southall London 48 A4
Southam Glos 63 A5
Southam Warks 81 A7
Southampton Soton 32 D3
Southampton
  International Airport
  Hants 32 D3
Southborough Kent 36 B3
Southbourne Bmouth 17 B5
Southbourne W Sus 19 A6
Southburgh Norf 103 A5
Southburn E Yorks 150 B2
Southchurch Sthend 51 A6
Southcott Wilts 45 D5
Southcourt Bucks 66 B3
Southdean Borders 187 C5
Southdene Mers 136 D3
Southease E Sus 22 B2
Southend Argyll 190 E2
Southend W Berks 46 B3
Southend Oxon 45 B5
Southend Airport Essex 51 A5
Southend-on-Sea Sthend 51 A5
Southend Sea Life Centre
  Essex 51 A5
Southernden Kent 37 B6
Southerndown V Glam 40 D3
Southerness Dumfries 174 C2
Southery Norf 102 B2
Southfield Northumb 179 B4
Southfleet Kent 50 B3
Southgate Ceredig 75 A4
Southgate London 68 D2
Southgate Norf 120 C3
Southgate Swansea 57 D5
Southill Beds 84 C3
Southleigh Devon 14 B2
Southminster Essex 70 D3
Southmoor Oxon 65 D4
Southoe Cambs 84 A3
Southolt Suff 88 A2
Southorpe P'boro 100 A2
Southowram W Yorks 139 A4
Southport Mers 136 B2
Southpunds Shetland 285 L6
Southrepps Norf 121 B4
Southrey Lincs 133 C6
Southrop Glos 64 C2
Southrope Hants 33 A5
Southsea Ptsmth 19 B5
Southstoke Bath 43 C6
Southtown Norf 105 A6
Southtown Orkney 283 H5
Southwaite Cumb 164 A2
Southwark London 49 B6
Southwater W Sus 35 D4
Southwater Street W Sus 35 D4
Southway Som 29 A5
Southwell Dorset 15 D6
Southwell Notts 132 D1
Southwell Minster Notts 132 D1
Southwell Racecourse
  Notts 132 D2
Southwick Hants 19 A5
Southwick Northants 100 B2
Southwick T & W 179 D5
Southwick Wilts 44 D2
Southwick W Sus 21 B5

Southwold Suff 105 D6
Southwood Norf 105 A4
Southwood Som 29 B5
Soval Lodge W Isles 288 C4
Sowber Gate N Yorks 158 C2
Sowerby N Yorks 158 C3
Sowerby W Yorks 138 A3
Sowerby Bridge W Yorks 138 A3
Sowerby Row Cumb 164 B3
Sowood W Yorks 138 B3
Sowton Devon 13 B4
Soyal Highld 264 A1
Spa Common Norf 121 B4
Spacey Houses N Yorks 148 B2
Spadeadam Farm Cumb 176 B3
Spalding Lincs 117 C5
Spaldington E Yorks 149 D6
Spaldwick Cambs 100 D3
Spalford Notts 132 C3
Spanby Lincs 116 B3
Sparham Norf 120 D2
Spark Bridge Cumb 154 C2
Sparkford Som 29 C6
Sparkhill W Mid 96 C3
Sparkwell Devon 7 B4
Sparrow Green Norf 119 D6
Sparrowpit Derbys 129 A5
Sparsholt Hants 32 B3
Sparsholt Oxon 46 A1
Spartylea Northumb 165 A6
Spaunton N Yorks 159 C6
Spaxton Som 28 B1
Spean Bridge Highld 239 D6
Spear Hill W Sus 21 A4
Speen Bucks 66 D3
Speen W Berks 46 C2
Speeton N Yorks 161 D5
Speke Mers 127 A4
Speke Hall Mers 127 A4
Speldhurst Kent 36 B3
Spellbrook Herts 69 B4
Spelsbury Oxon 64 A4
Spelter Bridgend 40 B3
Spencers Wood
  Wokingham 47 C5
Spennithorne N Yorks 157 C5
Spennymoor Durham 167 B5
Spetchley Worcs 80 B1
Spetisbury Dorset 16 A3
Spexhall Suff 105 C4
Spey Bay Moray 267 C4
Speybridge Highld 253 D6
Speyview Moray 254 B3
Spilsby Lincs 135 C4
Spindlestone Northumb 199 C5
Spinkhill Derbys 131 B4
Spinningdale Highld 264 B2
Spirit of the West, St
  Columb Major Corn 4 B4
Spirthill Wilts 44 B3
Spital Hill S Yorks 140 D4
Spital in the Street Lincs 133 A4
Spitfire and Hurricane
  Memorial, Manston
  Kent 53 C5
Spithurst E Sus 22 A2
Spittal Dumfries 171 B5
Spittal E Loth 210 C1
Spittal Highld 280 C3
Spittal Northumb 198 A4
Spittal Pembs 55 B5
Spittal Stirl 206 B3
Spittal of Glenmuick
  Aberds 243 D5
Spittal of Glenshee Perth 231 A6
Spittalfield Perth 231 D5
Spixworth Norf 120 D4
Splayne's Green E Sus 36 D2
Spofforth N Yorks 148 B2
Spon End W Mid 97 D6
Spon Green Flint 126 C2
Spondon Derby 114 B2
Spooner Row Norf 104 B1
Sporle Norf 119 D5
Spott E Loth 210 C3
Spratton Northants 99 D4
Spreakley Sur 34 B1
Spreyton Devon 12 B1
Spridlington Lincs 133 A5
Spring Vale S Yorks 139 C5
Spring Valley I o M 152 D3
Springburn Glasgow 205 B6
Springfield Dumfries 175 B6
Springfield Essex 69 C7
Springfield Fife 220 C3
Springfield Moray 253 A6
Springfield W Mid 96 C3

Springhill Staffs 96 A2
Springholm Dumfries 173 B6
Springkell Dumfries 175 A5
Springside N Ayrs 192 B3
Springthorpe Lincs 132 A3
Springwell T & W 179 D4
Sproatley E Yorks 151 D4
Sproston Green Ches 128 C2
Sprotbrough S Yorks 140 C3
Sproughton Suff 88 C2
Sprouston Borders 197 C6
Sprowston Norf 120 D4
Sproxton Leics 115 C6
Sproxton N Yorks 159 C5
Spurstow Ches 127 D5
Spynie Moray 266 C3
Squires Gate Blkpool 144 D3
Srannda W Isles 287 F5
Sronphadruig Lodge Perth 229 A6
SS Great Britain Bristol 43 B4
Stableford Shrops 95 B5
Stableford Staffs 112 B2
Stacey Bank S Yorks 139 D5
Stackhouse N Yorks 146 A2
Stackpole Pembs 55 E5
Staddiscombe Devon 7 B4
Staddlethorpe E Yorks 141 A6
Stadhampton Oxon 65 D7
Stadhlaigearraidh W Isles 286 C3
Staffield Cumb 164 A3
Staffin Highld 259 B4
Stafford Staffs 112 C3
Stagsden Beds 84 C1
Stainburn Cumb 162 B3
Stainburn N Yorks 147 C6
Stainby Lincs 116 C2
Staincross S Yorks 139 B6
Staindrop Durham 166 C4
Staines Sur 48 B3
Stainfield Lincs 116 C3
Stainfield Lincs 133 B6
Stainforth N Yorks 146 A2
Stainforth S Yorks 140 B4
Staining Lancs 144 D3
Stainland W Yorks 138 B3
Stainsacre N Yorks 160 A3
Stainsby Derbys 131 C4
Stainton Cumb 154 C4
Stainton Cumb 164 C2
Stainton Durham 166 D3
Stainton M'bro 168 D2
Stainton N Yorks 157 B5
Stainton S Yorks 140 D3
Stainton by Langworth Lincs 133 B5
Stainton le Vale Lincs 142 D3
Stainton with Adgarley Cumb 153 C3
Staintondale N Yorks 160 B3
Stair Cumb 163 B5
Stair E Ayrs 193 C4
Stairhaven Dumfries 171 B4
Staithes N Yorks 169 D5
Stake Pool Lancs 144 C4
Stakeford Northumb 179 A4
Stalbridge Dorset 30 D1
Stalbridge Weston Dorset 29 D7
Stalham Norf 121 C5
Stalham Green Norf 121 C5
Stalisfield Green Kent 51 D6
Stalling Busk N Yorks 156 C3
Stallingborough NE Lincs 142 B3
Stalmine Lancs 144 C3
Stalybridge Gtr Man 138 D2
Stambourne Essex 86 D3
Stambourne Green Essex 86 D3
Stamford Lincs 100 A2
Stamford Bridge Ches 127 C4
Stamford Bridge E Yorks 149 B6
Stamfordham Northumb 178 B2
Stanah Cumb 163 C6
Stanborough Herts 68 B2
Stanbridge Beds 67 A4
Stanbridge Dorset 17 A4
Stanbrook Worcs 79 C6
Stanbury W Yorks 147 D4
Stand Gtr Man 137 C6
Stand N Lnrk 207 D5
Standburn Falk 208 C2
Standeford Staffs 96 A2
Standen Kent 37 B6
Standen, East Grinstead W Sus 36 C1
Standford Hants 33 B7
Standingstone Cumb 162 A3
Standish Gtr Man 137 B4
Standlake Oxon 65 C4
Standon Hants 32 C3
Standon Herts 68 A3
Standon Staffs 112 B2
Stane N Lnrk 194 A3
Stanfield Norf 119 C6
Stanford Beds 84 C3
Stanford Kent 38 B3
Stanford Bishop Hereford 79 B4
Stanford Bridge Worcs 79 A5
Stanford Dingley W Berks 46 B3
Stanford in the Vale Oxon 64 D4
Stanford-le-Hope Thurrock 50 A3
Stanford on Avon Northants 98 D2
Stanford on Soar Notts 114 C3
Stanford on Teme Worcs 79 A5
Stanford Rivers Essex 69 C5
Stanfree Derbys 131 B4
Stanghow Redcar 169 D4
Stanground P'boro 100 B4
Stanhoe Norf 119 B5
Stanhope Borders 195 D6
Stanhope Durham 166 B2
Stanion Northants 99 C6
Stanley Derbys 114 A2
Stanley Durham 178 D3
Stanley Lancs 136 C3
Stanley Perth 219 A6
Stanley Staffs 129 D4
Stanley W Yorks 139 A6
Stanley Common Derbys 114 A2
Stanley Gate Lancs 136 C3
Stanley Hill Hereford 79 C4
Stanlow Ches 127 B4
Stanmer Brighton 21 B6
Stanmore London 67 D6
Stanmore Hants 32 C3
Stanmore W Berks 46 B2
Stannergate Dundee 220 A4
Stanningley W Yorks 147 D6
Stannington Northumb 179 B4
Stannington S Yorks 130 A3
Stansbatch Hereford 78 A1
Stansfield Suff 86 B3
Stanstead Suff 87 C4
Stanstead Abbotts Herts 68 B3
Stansted Kent 50 C3
Stansted Airport Essex 69 A5
Stansted Mountfitchet Essex 69 A5
Stanton Glos 80 D3
Stanton Mon 61 A5
Stanton Northumb 178 A3
Stanton Staffs 113 A5
Stanton Suff 103 D5
Stanton by Bridge Derbys 114 C1
Stanton-by-Dale Derbys 114 B2
Stanton Drew Bath 43 C4
Stanton Fitzwarren Thamesdown 64 D2
Stanton Harcourt Oxon 65 C5
Stanton Hill Notts 131 C4
Stanton in Peak Derbys 130 C2
Stanton Lacy Shrops 94 D2
Stanton Long Shrops 94 B3
Stanton-on-the-Wolds Notts 115 B4
Stanton Prior Bath 43 C5
Stanton St Bernard Wilts 45 C4
Stanton St John Oxon 65 C6
Stanton St Quintin Wilts 44 B3
Stanton Street Suff 87 A5
Stanton under Bardon Leics 114 D2
Stanton upon Hine Heath Shrops 111 C4
Stanton Wick Bath 43 C5
Stanwardine in the Fields Shrops 110 C3
Stanwardine in the Wood Shrops 110 C3
Stanway Essex 70 A3
Stanway Glos 80 D3
Stanway Green Suff 104 D3
Stanwell Sur 48 B3
Stanwell Moor Sur 48 B3
Stanwick Northants 100 D1
Stanwick-St-John N Yorks 167 D4
Stanwix Cumb 175 C7
Stanydale Shetland 285 H4
Staoinebrig W Isles 286 C3
Stape N Yorks 159 B6
Stapehill Dorset 17 A4
Stapeley Ches 111 A5
Stapeley Water Gardens, Nantwich Ches 127 D6
Stapenhill Staffs 113 C6
Staple Kent 53 D4
Staple Som 27 A6
Staple Cross E Sus 37 D5
Staple Fitzpaine Som 28 D2
Staplefield W Sus 35 D5
Stapleford Cambs 85 B6
Stapleford Herts 68 B3
Stapleford Leics 115 D6
Stapleford Lincs 132 D3
Stapleford Notts 114 B2
Stapleford Wilts 31 B4
Stapleford Abbotts Essex 69 D5
Stapleford Tawney Essex 69 D5
Staplegrove Som 28 C2
Staplehay Som 28 C2
Staplehurst Kent 37 B5
Staplers I o W 18 C4
Stapleton Bristol 43 B5
Stapleton Cumb 176 B3
Stapleton Hereford 78 A1
Stapleton Leics 98 B1
Stapleton N Yorks 167 D5
Stapleton Shrops 94 A2
Stapleton Som 29 C4
Stapley Som 28 D1
Staploe Beds 84 A3
Staplow Hereford 79 C4
Star Fife 220 D3
Star Pembs 73 C5
Star Som 42 D3
Stara Orkney 282 E3
Starbeck N Yorks 148 B2
Starbotton N Yorks 156 D3
Starcross Devon 13 C4
Stareton Warks 97 D6
Starkholmes Derbys 130 D3
Starlings Green Essex 85 D6
Starston Norf 104 C3
Startforth Durham 166 D3
Startley Wilts 44 A3
Stathe Som 28 C3
Stathern Leics 115 B5
Station Town Durham 168 B2
Staughton Green Cambs 84 A3
Staughton Highway Cambs 84 A3
Staunton Glos 62 B1
Staunton Glos 62 A3
Staunton in the Vale Notts 115 A6
Staunton on Arrow Hereford 78 A1
Staunton on Wye Hereford 78 C1
Staveley Cumb 154 C2
Staveley Cumb 154 B3
Staveley Derbys 131 B4
Staveley N Yorks 148 A2
Staverton Devon 8 A1
Staverton Glos 63 A4
Staverton Northants 82 A2
Staverton Wilts 44 C2
Staverton Bridge Glos 63 A4
Stawell Som 28 B3
Staxigoe Highld 281 C5
Staxton N Yorks 160 D4
Staylittle Powys 91 C6
Staynall Lancs 144 C3
Staythorpe Notts 132 D2
Stean N Yorks 157 D4
Stearsby N Yorks 159 D5
Steart Som 28 A2
Stebbing Essex 69 A6
Stebbing Green Essex 69 A6
Stedham W Sus 34 D1
Steele Road Borders 186 D4
Steen's Bridge Hereford 78 B3
Steep Hants 33 C6
Steep Marsh Hants 33 C6
Steeple Dorset 16 C3
Steeple Essex 70 C3
Steeple Ashton Wilts 44 D3
Steeple Aston Oxon 65 A5
Steeple Barton Oxon 65 A5
Steeple Bumpstead Essex 86 C2
Steeple Claydon Bucks 66 A1
Steeple Gidding Cambs 100 C3
Steeple Langford Wilts 31 B4
Steeple Morden Cambs 85 C4
Steeton W Yorks 147 C4
Stein Highld 258 C2
Steinmanhill Aberds 256 B2
Stelling Minnis Kent 38 A3
Stemster Highld 280 B3
Stemster Ho. Highld 280 B3
Stenalees Corn 5 B5
Stenhousemuir Falk 207 B6
Stenigot Lincs 134 A2
Stenness Shetland 284 F4
Stenscholl Highld 259 B4
Stenso Orkney 282 E4
Stenson Derbys 114 C1
Stenton E Loth 210 C3
Stenton Fife 209 A5
Stenwith Lincs 115 B6
Stepaside Pembs 56 B1
Stepping Hill Gtr Man 129 A4
Steppingley Beds 84 D2
Stepps N Lnrk 205 B6
Sterndale Moor Derbys 129 C6
Sternfield Suff 89 A4
Sterridge Devon 25 A6
Stert Wilts 44 D4
Stetchworth Cambs 86 B2
Stevenage Herts 68 A2
Stevenston N Ayrs 204 D2
Steventon Hants 32 A4
Steventon Oxon 65 D5
Stevington Beds 84 B1
Stewartby Beds 84 C2
Stewarton Argyll 190 D2
Stewarton E Ayrs 205 D4
Stewkley Bucks 66 A3
Stewton Lincs 134 A3
Steyne Cross I o W 19 C5
Steyning W Sus 21 A4
Steynton Pembs 55 D5
Stibb Corn 24 D3
Stibb Cross Devon 25 D5
Stibb Green Wilts 45 C6
Stibbard Norf 120 C1
Stibbington Cambs 100 B2
Stichill Borders 197 C6
Sticker Corn 5 B4
Stickford Lincs 134 D3
Sticklepath Devon 12 B1
Stickney Lincs 134 D3
Stiffkey Norf 119 A6
Stifford's Bridge Hereford 79 C5
Stillingfleet N Yorks 149 C4
Stillington N Yorks 149 A4
Stillington Stockton 167 C6
Stilton Cambs 100 C3
Stinchcombe Glos 62 D3
Stinsford Dorset 15 B7
Stirchley Telford 95 A5
Stirkoke Ho. Highld 281 C5
Stirling Aberds 257 B6
Stirling Stirl 207 A5
Stirling Castle Stirl 207 A5
Stisted Essex 70 A1
Stithians Corn 4 D2
Stittenham Highld 264 C2
Stivichall W Mid 97 D6
Stixwould Lincs 134 C1
Stoak Ches 127 B4
Stobieside S Lnrk 193 B6
Stobo Borders 195 C6
Stoborough Dorset 16 C3
Stoborough Green Dorset 16 C3
Stobshiel E Loth 210 D1
Stobswood Northumb 189 D5
Stock Essex 69 D6
Stock Green Worcs 80 B2
Stock Wood Worcs 80 B3
Stockbridge Hants 32 B2
Stockbury Kent 51 C5
Stockcross W Berks 46 C2
Stockdalewath Cumb 164 A1
Stockerston Leics 99 B5
Stockheath Hants 19 A6
Stockiemuir Stirl 206 B3
Stocking Pelham Herts 69 A4
Stockingford Warks 97 B6
Stockland Devon 14 A2
Stockland Bristol Som 28 A2
Stockleigh English Devon 12 A3
Stockleigh Pomeroy Devon 12 A3
Stockley Wilts 44 C4
Stocklinch Som 28 D3
Stockport Gtr Man 138 D1
Stocksbridge S Yorks 139 D5
Stocksfield Northumb 178 C2
Stockton Hereford 78 A3
Stockton Norf 105 B4
Stockton Shrops 93 A6
Stockton Shrops 95 B5
Stockton Warks 82 A1
Stockton Wilts 30 B3
Stockton Heath Warr 127 A6
Stockton-on-Tees Stockton 168 D2
Stockton on Teme Worcs 79 A5
Stockton on the Forest York 149 B5
Stockwood Park Museum, Luton Luton 67 B5
Stodmarsh Kent 53 C4
Stody Norf 120 B2
Stoer Highld 270 B3
Stoford Som 29 D5
Stoford Wilts 31 B4
Stogumber Som 27 B5
Stogursey Som 28 A2
Stoke Devon 24 C3
Stoke Hants 46 D2
Stoke Hants 19 A6
Stoke Medway 51 B5
Stoke Suff 88 C2
Stoke Abbott Dorset 15 A4
Stoke Albany Northants 99 C5
Stoke Ash Suff 104 D2
Stoke Bardolph Notts 115 A4
Stoke Bliss Worcs 79 A4
Stoke Bruerne Northants 83 C4
Stoke by Clare Suff 86 C3
Stoke-by-Nayland Suff 87 D5
Stoke Canon Devon 13 B4
Stoke Charity Hants 32 B3
Stoke Climsland Corn 11 D4
Stoke D'Abernon Sur 35 A4
Stoke Doyle Northants 100 C2
Stoke Dry Rutland 99 B5
Stoke Farthing Wilts 31 C4
Stoke Ferry Norf 102 B3
Stoke Fleming Devon 8 C2
Stoke Gabriel Devon 8 B2
Stoke Gifford S Glos 43 B5
Stoke Golding Leics 97 B6
Stoke Goldington M Keynes 83 C5
Stoke Green Bucks 48 A2
Stoke Hammond Bucks 66 A3
Stoke Heath Shrops 111 C5
Stoke Holy Cross Norf 104 A3
Stoke Lacy Hereford 79 C4
Stoke Lyne Oxon 65 A6
Stoke Mandeville Bucks 66 B3
Stoke Newington London 49 A6
Stoke on Tern Shrops 111 C5
Stoke-on-Trent Stoke 112 A2
Stoke Orchard Glos 63 A5
Stoke Poges Bucks 48 A2
Stoke Prior Hereford 78 B3
Stoke Prior Worcs 80 A2
Stoke Rivers Devon 26 B1
Stoke Rochford Lincs 116 C2
Stoke Row Oxon 47 A4
Stoke St Gregory Som 28 C3
Stoke St Mary Som 28 C2
Stoke St Michael Som 29 A6
Stoke St Milborough Shrops 94 C3
Stoke sub Hamdon Som 29 D4
Stoke Talmage Oxon 66 D1
Stoke Trister Som 30 C1
Stoke Wake Dorset 16 A1
Stokeford Dorset 16 C2
Stokeham Notts 132 B2
Stokeinteignhead Devon 13 D4
Stokenchurch Bucks 66 D2
Stokenham Devon 8 C2
Stokesay Shrops 94 C2
Stokesby Norf 121 D6
Stokesley N Yorks 158 A4
Stolford Som 28 A2
Ston Easton Som 43 D5
Stondon Massey Essex 69 C5
Stone Bucks 66 B2
Stone Glos 62 D2
Stone Kent 38 C1
Stone Kent 50 B2
Stone Staffs 112 B3
Stone S Yorks 131 A5
Stone Worcs 95 D6
Stone Allerton Som 42 D3
Stone Bridge Corner P'boro 101 A4
Stone Chair W Yorks 139 A4
Stone Cross E Sus 22 B4
Stone Cross Kent 53 D5
Stone-edge Batch N Som 42 B3
Stone House Cumb 155 C6
Stone Street Kent 36 A3
Stone Street Suff 87 D5
Stone Street Suff 105 C4
Stonebroom Derbys 131 D4

Stoneferry Hull 131 D4
Stonefield S Lnrk 194 A1
Stonegate E Sus 37 D4
Stonegate N Yorks 159 A6
Stonegrave N Yorks 159 D5
Stonehaugh Northumb 177 B5
Stonehaven Aberds 245 D5
Stonehenge, Amesbury Wilts 31 A5
Stonehouse Glos 63 C4
Stonehouse Northumb 177 D4
Stonehouse S Lnrk 194 B2
Stoneleigh Warks 97 D6
Stonely Cambs 84 A3
Stoner Hill Hants 33 C6
Stone's Green Essex 71 A5
Stonesby Leics 115 C6
Stonesfield Oxon 65 B4
Stonethwaite Cumb 163 C5
Stoney Cross Hants 31 D6
Stoney Middleton Derbys 130 B2
Stoney Stanton Leics 98 B1
Stoney Stoke Som 29 B7
Stoney Stratton Som 29 B6
Stoney Stretton Shrops 94 A1
Stoneybreck Shetland 285 L3
Stoneyburn W Loth 208 D2
Stoneygate Aberds 257 C5
Stoneygate Leicester 98 A3
Stoneyhills Essex 70 D3
Stoneykirk Dumfries 170 B2
Stoneywood Aberdeen 245 A5
Stoneywood Falk 207 B5
Stonganess Shetland 284 C7
Stonham Aspal Suff 88 B2
Stonnall Staffs 96 A3
Stonor Oxon 47 A5
Stonton Wyville Leics 99 B4
Stony Cross Hereford 79 C5
Stony Stratford M Keynes 83 C4
Stonyfield Highld 264 C2
Stoodleigh Devon 27 D4
Stopes S Yorks 130 A2
Stopham W Sus 20 A3
Stopsley Luton 67 A6
Stores Corner Suff 89 C4
Storeton Mers 126 A3
Stornoway W Isles 288 D5
Stornoway Airport
    W Isles 288 D5
Storridge Hereford 79 C5
Storrington W Sus 20 A3
Storrs Cumb 154 B2
Storth Cumb 154 C3
Storwood E Yorks 149 C6
Stotfield Moray 266 B3
Stotfold Beds 84 D4
Stottesdon Shrops 95 C4
Stoughton Leics 98 A3
Stoughton Sur 34 A2
Stoughton W Sus 33 D7
Stoul Highld 235 A6
Stoulton Worcs 80 C2
Stour Provost Dorset 30 C1
Stour Row Dorset 30 C2
Stourbridge W Mid 96 C2
Stourhead Garden Wilts 30 B1
Stourpaine Dorset 16 A2
Stourport on Severn
    Worcs 95 D6
Stourton Staffs 95 C6
Stourton Warks 81 D5
Stourton Wilts 30 B1
Stourton Caundle Dorset 29 D7
Stove Orkney 282 D7
Stove Shetland 285 L6
Stoven Suff 105 C5
Stow Borders 196 B3
Stow Lincs 132 A3
Stow Lincs 116 B3
Stow Bardolph Norf 102 A2
Stow Bedon Norf 103 B5
Stow cum Quy Cambs 85 A7
Stow Longa Cambs 100 D3
Stow Maries Essex 70 D2
Stow-on-the-Wold Glos 64 A2
Stowbridge Norf 102 A2
Stowe Shrops 93 D7
Stowe-by-Chartley Staffs 112 C4
Stowe Green Glos 62 C1
Stowe House and
    Gardens, Buckingham
    Bucks 82 D3
Stowell Som 29 C6

Stowford Devon 11 C5
Stowlangtoft Suff 87 A5
Stowmarket Suff 87 B6
Stowting Kent 38 A3
Stowupland Suff 87 B6
Straad Argyll 203 B5
Strachan Aberds 244 C3
Stradbroke Suff 104 D3
Stradishall Suff 86 B3
Stradsett Norf 102 A2
Stragglethorpe Lincs 133 D4
Straid S Ayrs 180 B3
Straith Dumfries 183 D6
Straiton Edin 209 D5
Straiton S Ayrs 181 A5
Straloch Aberds 256 D3
Straloch Perth 230 B4
Stramshall Staffs 113 B4
Strang I o M 152 D3
Stranraer Dumfries 170 A2
Stratfield Mortimer
    W Berks 47 C4
Stratfield Saye Hants 47 C4
Stratfield Turgis Hants 47 C4
Stratford London 49 A6
Stratford Racecourse
    Warks 81 B4
Stratford St Andrew Suff 89 A4
Stratford St Mary Suff 87 D6
Stratford Sub Castle Wilts 31 B5
Stratford Tony Wilts 31 C4
Stratford-upon-Avon
    Warks 81 B4
Strath Highld 281 C4
Strath Highld 261 C4
Strathan Highld 238 C3
Strathan Highld 277 B6
Strathan Highld 270 B3
Strathaven S Lnrk 194 B2
Strathblane Stirl 205 A5
Strathcanaird Highld 271 D4
Strathcarron Highld 249 B6
Strathcoil Argyll 225 C5
Strathdon Aberds 243 A6
Strathellie Aberds 269 C5
Strathkinness Fife 221 C4
Strathmashie House
    Highld 240 C3
Strathmiglo Fife 220 C2
Strathmore Lodge Highld 280 D3
Strathpeffer Highld 251 A6
Strathrannoch Highld 263 C5
Strathtay Perth 230 C3
Strathvaich Lodge Highld 263 C5
Strathwhillan N Ayrs 191 B6
Strathy Highld 279 B4
Strathyre Stirl 217 C5
Stratton Corn 10 A3
Stratton Dorset 15 B6
Stratton Glos 63 C6
Stratton Audley Oxon 65 A7
Stratton on the Fosse Som 43 D5
Stratton St Margaret
    Thamesdown 45 A5
Stratton St Michael Norf 104 B3
Stratton Strawless Norf 120 C4
Stravithie Fife 221 C5
Streat E Sus 21 A6
Streatham London 49 B6
Streatley Beds 67 A5
Streatley W Berks 46 A3
Street Lancs 145 B5
Street N Yorks 159 A6
Street Som 29 B4
Street Dinas Shrops 110 B2
Street End Kent 52 D3
Street End W Sus 20 C1
Street Gate T & W 179 D4
Street Lydan Wrex 110 B3
Streethay Staffs 113 D5
Streetlam N Yorks 157 B7
Streetly W Mid 96 B3
Streetly End Cambs 86 C2
Strefford Shrops 94 C2
Strelley Notts 114 A3
Strensall York 149 A5
Stretcholt Som 28 A2
Strete Devon 8 C2
Stretford Gtr Man 137 D7
Strethall Essex 85 D6
Stretham Cambs 101 D7
Strettington W Sus 20 B1
Stretton Ches 127 D4
Stretton Derbys 130 C3
Stretton Rutland 116 D2
Stretton Staffs 112 D2
Stretton Staffs 113 C6

Stretton Warr 127 A6
Stretton Grandison
    Hereford 79 C4
Stretton-on-Dunsmore
    Warks 97 D7
Stretton-on-Fosse Warks 81 D5
Stretton Sugwas Hereford 78 C2
Stretton under Fosse
    Warks 98 C1
Stretton Westwood Shrops 94 B3
Strichen Aberds 269 D4
Strines Gtr Man 129 A4
Stringston Som 28 A1
Strixton Northants 83 A6
Stroat Glos 62 D1
Stromeferry Highld 249 C5
Stromemore Highld 249 C5
Stromness Orkney 283 G3
Stronaba Highld 239 D6
Stronachlachar Stirl 216 C4
Stronchreggan Highld 237 B4
Stronchrubie Highld 271 C5
Strone Argyll 215 D4
Strone Highld 252 D1
Strone Highld 239 D5
Strone Invclyd 204 A2
Stronmilchan Argyll 227 D6
Stronsay Airport Orkney 282 E7
Strontian Highld 236 C2
Strood Medway 51 C4
Strood Green Sur 35 B5
Strood Green W Sus 34 D3
Strood Green W Sus 35 C4
Stroud Glos 63 C4
Stroud Hants 33 C6
Stroud Green Essex 70 D2
Stroxton Lincs 116 B2
Struan Highld 246 A2
Struan Perth 230 B2
Strubby Lincs 135 A4
Strumpshaw Norf 104 A4
Strutherhill S Lnrk 194 B2
Struy Highld 251 C5
Stryt-issa Wrex 110 A1
Stuartfield Aberds 257 B4
Stub Place Cumb 153 A1
Stubbington Hants 19 A4
Stubbins Lancs 137 B6
Stubbs Cross Kent 38 B1
Stubb's Green Norf 104 B3
Stubbs Green Norf 105 B4
Stubhampton Dorset 30 D3
Stubton Lincs 115 A6
Stuckgowan Argyll 215 B6
Stuckton Hants 31 D5
Stud Green Windsor 48 B1
Studham Beds 67 B5
Studland Dorset 17 C4
Studley Warks 80 A3
Studley Wilts 44 B3
Studley Roger N Yorks 157 D6
Stump Cross Essex 85 C7
Stuntney Cambs 102 D1
Sturbridge Staffs 112 B2
Sturmer Essex 86 C2
Sturminster Marshall
    Dorset 16 A3
Sturminster Newton
    Dorset 30 D1
Sturry Kent 52 C3
Sturton N Lincs 142 C1
Sturton by Stow Lincs 132 A3
Sturton le Steeple Notts 132 A2
Stuston Suff 104 D2
Stutton N Yorks 148 C3
Stutton Suff 88 D2
Styal Ches 128 A3
Styrrup Notts 140 D4
Suainebost W Isles 288 A6
Suardail W Isles 288 D5
Succoth Aberds 255 C5
Succoth Argyll 215 B5
Suckley Worcs 79 B5
Suckquoy Orkney 283 K5
Sudborough Northants 99 C6
Sudbourne Suff 89 B5
Sudbrook Lincs 116 A2
Sudbrook Mon 43 A4
Sudbrooke Lincs 133 B5
Sudbury Derbys 113 B5
Sudbury London 49 A4
Sudbury Suff 87 C4
Suddie Highld 252 A2
Sudeley Castle and
    Gardens Glos 63 A6
Sudgrove Glos 63 C5
Suffield Norf 120 B4

Suffield N Yorks 160 B3
Sugnall Staffs 112 B1
Suladale Highld 258 C3
Sulaisiadar W Isles 288 D6
Sulby I o M 152 B3
Sulgrave Northants 82 C2
Sulham W Berks 47 B4
Sulhamstead W Berks 47 C4
Sulland Orkney 282 C6
Sullington W Sus 20 A3
Sullom Shetland 284 F5
Sullom Voe Oil Terminal
    Shetland 284 F5
Sully V Glam 41 E6
Sumburgh Shetland 285 N6
Sumburgh Airport
    Shetland 285 M5
Summer Bridge N Yorks 147 A6
Summer-house Darl 167 D5
Summercourt Corn 4 B3
Summerfield Norf 119 B4
Summergangs Hull 151 D4
Summerleaze Mon 42 A3
Summerlee Heritage
    Centre, Coatbridge
    N Lnrk 207 D5
Summersdale W Sus 20 B1
Summerseat Gtr Man 137 B6
Summertown Oxon 65 C6
Summit Gtr Man 138 C2
Sunbury-on-Thames Sur 48 C4
Sundaywell Dumfries 183 D6
Sunderland Argyll 200 B2
Sunderland Cumb 163 A4
Sunderland T & W 179 D5
Sunderland Bridge
    Durham 167 B5
Sundhope Borders 196 D2
Sundon Park Luton 67 A5
Sundown Kiddies
    Adventureland,
    Rampton Notts 132 B2
Sundridge Kent 36 A2
Sunipol Argyll 224 A2
Sunk Island E Yorks 143 B4
Sunningdale Windsor 48 C2
Sunninghill Windsor 48 C2
Sunningwell Oxon 65 C5
Sunniside Durham 166 B4
Sunniside T & W 179 D4
Sunnyhurst Blkburn 137 A5
Sunnylaw Stirl 207 A5
Sunnyside W Sus 36 C1
Sunton Wilts 45 D6
Surbiton London 49 C4
Surby I o M 152 D2
Surfleet Lincs 117 C5
Surfleet Seas End Lincs 117 C5
Surlingham Norf 104 A4
Sustead Norf 120 B3
Susworth Lincs 141 C6
Sutcombe Devon 24 D4
Suton Norf 104 B1
Sutors of Cromarty
    Highld 265 D4
Sutterby Lincs 134 B3
Sutterton Lincs 117 B5
Sutton Beds 84 C4
Sutton Cambs 101 D6
Sutton London 49 C5
Sutton Kent 39 A5
Sutton Mers 136 D4
Sutton Norf 121 C5
Sutton Notts 115 B5
Sutton Notts 132 A1
Sutton N Yorks 140 A2
Sutton Oxon 65 C5
Sutton P'boro 100 B2
Sutton Shrops 95 C5
Sutton Shrops 111 B5
Sutton Som 29 B6
Sutton Staffs 111 C6
Sutton Suff 88 C4
Sutton Sur 34 B4
Sutton S Yorks 140 B3
Sutton W Sus 20 A2
Sutton at Hone Kent 50 B2
Sutton Bassett Northants 99 B4
Sutton Benger Wilts 44 B3
Sutton Bonington Notts 114 C3
Sutton Bridge Lincs 118 C1
Sutton Cheney Leics 97 A7
Sutton Coldfield W Mid 96 B4
Sutton Courtenay Oxon 65 D6
Sutton Crosses Lincs 118 C1
Sutton Grange N Yorks 157 D6
Sutton Green Sur 34 A3

Sutton Howgrave N Yorks 157 B7
Sutton In Ashfield Notts 131 D4
Sutton in Craven
    N Yorks 147 C4
Sutton in the Elms Leics 98 B2
Sutton Ings Hull 151 D4
Sutton Lane Ends Ches 129 B4
Sutton Leach Mers 136 D4
Sutton Maddock Shrops 95 A5
Sutton Mallet Som 28 B3
Sutton Mandeville Wilts 30 C3
Sutton Manor Mers 136 D4
Sutton Montis Som 29 C6
Sutton on Hull Hull 151 D4
Sutton on Sea Lincs 135 A5
Sutton-on-the-Forest
    N Yorks 149 A5
Sutton on the Hill Derbys 113 B6
Sutton on Trent Notts 132 C2
Sutton St Edmund Lincs 117 D6
Sutton St James Lincs 117 D6
Sutton St Nicholas
    Hereford 78 C2
Sutton Scarsdale Derbys 131 C4
Sutton Scotney Hants 32 B3
Sutton under Brailes
    Warks 81 D6
Sutton-under-
    Whitestonecliffe
    N Yorks 158 C3
Sutton upon Derwent
    E Yorks 149 C6
Sutton Valence Kent 37 B6
Sutton Veny Wilts 30 A3
Sutton Waldron Dorset 30 D3
Sutton Weaver Ches 127 B5
Sutton Wick Bath 43 D5
Swaby Lincs 134 B3
Swadlincote Derbys 113 D7
Swaffham Norf 103 A4
Swaffham Bulbeck Cambs 86 A2
Swaffham Prior Cambs 86 A2
Swafield Norf 121 B5
Swainby N Yorks 158 A3
Swainshill Hereford 78 C2
Swainsthorpe Norf 104 A3
Swainswick Bath 43 C6
Swalcliffe Oxon 81 D6
Swalecliffe Kent 52 C3
Swallow Lincs 142 C3
Swallowcliffe Wilts 30 C3
Swallowfield Wokingham 47 C5
Swallownest S Yorks 131 A4
Swallows Cross Essex 69 D6
Swan Green Ches 128 B2
Swan Green Suff 104 D3
Swanage Dorset 17 D4
Swanage Railway Dorset 17 D4
Swanbister Orkney 283 G4
Swanbourne Bucks 66 A3
Swanland E Yorks 142 A1
Swanley Kent 50 C2
Swanley Village Kent 50 C2
Swanmore Hants 33 D4
Swannery, Abbotsbury
    Dorset 15 C6
Swannington Leics 114 D2
Swannington Norf 120 D3
Swanscombe Kent 50 B3
Swansea = Abertawe
    Swansea 57 C6
Swanton Abbot Norf 121 C4
Swanton Morley Norf 120 D2
Swanton Novers Norf 120 C2
Swanton Street Kent 37 A6
Swanwick Derbys 131 D4
Swanwick Hants 18 A4
Swarby Lincs 116 A3
Swardeston Norf 104 A3
Swarister Shetland 284 E7
Swarkestone Derbys 114 C1
Swarland Northumb 189 C4
Swarland Estate
    Northumb 189 C4
Swarthmoor Cumb 153 C3
Swathwick Derbys 130 C3
Swaton Lincs 116 B4
Swavesey Cambs 85 A5
Sway Hants 18 B1
Swayfield Lincs 116 C2
Swaythling Soton 32 D3
Sweet Green Worcs 79 A4
Sweetham Devon 10 E3
Sweethouse Corn 5 A5
Swefling Suff 89 A4
Swepstone Leics 114 D1
Swerford Oxon 81 D6

Swettenham Ches 128 C3
Swetton N Yorks 157 D5
Swffryd Bl Gwent 60 D4
Swiftsden E Sus 37 D5
Swilland Suff 88 B2
Swillington W Yorks 148 D2
Swimbridge Devon 25 C7
Swimbridge Newland
  Devon 25 B7
Swinbrook Oxon 64 B3
Swinderby Lincs 132 C3
Swindon Glos 63 A5
Swindon Staffs 95 B6
Swindon Thamesdown 45 A5
Swine E Yorks 151 D4
Swinefleet E Yorks 141 A5
Swineshead Beds 84 A2
Swineshead Lincs 117 A5
Swineshead Bridge Lincs 117 A5
Swiney Highld 275 A6
Swinford Leics 98 D2
Swinford Oxon 65 C5
Swingate Notts 114 A3
Swingfield Minnis Kent 39 A4
Swingfield St Kent 39 A4
Swinhoe Northumb 189 A5
Swinhope Lincs 143 D4
Swining Shetland 284 G6
Swinithwaite N Yorks 156 C4
Swinnow Moor W Yorks 147 D6
Swinscoe Staffs 113 A5
Swinside Hall Borders 187 B6
Swinstead Lincs 116 C3
Swinton Borders 198 B2
Swinton Gtr Man 137 C6
Swinton N Yorks 157 D6
Swinton N Yorks 159 D6
Swinton S Yorks 140 D2
Swintonmill Borders 198 B2
Swithland Leics 114 D3
Swordale Highld 264 D1
Swordland Highld 238 C1
Swordly Highld 278 B3
Sworton Heath Ches 128 B1
Swydd-ffynnon Ceredig 75 B5
Swynnerton Staffs 112 B2
Swyre Dorset 15 C5
Sychtyn Powys 92 A3
Syde Glos 63 B5
Sydenham London 49 B6
Sydenham Oxon 66 C2
Sydenham Damerel Devon 11 D5
Syderstone Norf 119 B5
Sydling St Nicholas Dorset 15 B6
Sydmonton Hants 46 D2
Syerston Notts 115 A5
Syke Gtr Man 138 B1
Sykehouse S Yorks 140 B4
Sykes Lancs 145 B6
Syleham Suff 104 D3
Sylen Carms 57 B5
Symbister Shetland 285 G7
Symington S Ayrs 192 B3
Symington S Lnrk 195 C4
Symonds Yat Hereford 62 B1
Symondsbury Dorset 14 B4
Synod Inn Ceredig 73 A7
Syon Park & House London 49 B4
Syre Highld 278 D2
Syreford Glos 63 A6
Syresham Northants 82 C3
Syston Leics 115 D4
Syston Lincs 116 A2
Sytchampton Worcs 79 A6
Sywell Northants 83 A5

...gan Highld 262 D2
...ost W Isles 288 A6
...ost W Isles 288 F4
...kley Oxon 65 A5
...leit W Isles 288 D2
...olneston Norf 104 B2
...caster N Yorks 148 C3
...dington Derbys 129 B6
...diport Devon 25 D5
...ley Hants 47 C4
...low Beds 85 C4
...marton Oxon 81 D6
...worth Sur 35 A5
...arn-y-gelyn Denb 126 C1
...rnau-bach Bl Gwent 60 B3
...'s Well Rhondda 41 C6
...lwern Powys 91 B6
...Conwy 124 C2
...bach Powys 109 C6

Tai-mawr Conwy 109 A4
Tai-Ucha Denb 125 D5
Taibach Neath 40 C2
Taigh a Ghearraidh
  W Isles 287 G2
Tain Highld 264 B3
Tain Highld 280 B4
Tainant Wrex 110 A1
Tainlon Gwyn 107 A4
Tai'r-Bull Powys 60 A1
Tairbeart = Tarbert
  W Isles 288 G2
Tairgwaith Neath 59 D4
Takeley Essex 69 A5
Takeley Street Essex 69 A5
Tal-sarn Ceredig 75 C4
Tal-y-bont Ceredig 91 D4
Tal-y-Bont Conwy 124 C2
Tal-y-bont Gwyn 123 C6
Tal-y-bont Gwyn 107 D5
Tal-y-cafn Conwy 124 B2
Tal-y-llyn Gwyn 91 B5
Tal-y-wern Powys 91 B6
Talachddu Powys 77 D4
Talacre Flint 125 A6
Talardd Gwyn 108 C3
Talaton Devon 13 B5
Talbenny Pembs 54 C4
Talbot Green Rhondda 41 C5
Talbot Village Poole 17 B4
Tale Devon 13 A5
Talerddig Powys 92 A3
Talgarreg Ceredig 74 C3
Talgarth Powys 77 D5
Talisker Highld 246 A2
Talke Staffs 128 D3
Talkin Cumb 176 D3
Talla Linnfoots Borders 195 B6
Talladale Highld 261 C6
Tallarn Green Wrex 110 A3
Tallentire Cumb 163 A4
Talley Carms 58 B3
Tallington Lincs 100 A2
Talmine Highld 277 B6
Talog Carms 73 D6
Talsarn Carms 59 C4
Talsarnau Gwyn 107 C6
Talskiddy Corn 4 A4
Talwrn Anglesey 123 C4
Talwrn Wrex 110 A1
Talybont-on-Usk Powys 60 A3
Talygarn Rhondda 41 C5
Talyllyn Powys 60 A3
Talysarn Gwyn 107 A4
Talywain Torf 61 C4
Tame Bridge N Yorks 158 A4
Tamerton Foliot Plym 6 A3
Tamworth Staffs 97 A5
Tan Hinon Powys 91 D6
Tan-lan Conwy 124 C2
Tan-lan Gwyn 107 B6
Tan-y-bwlch Gwyn 107 B6
Tan-y-fron Conwy 125 C4
Tan-y-graig Anglesey 123 C5
Tan-y-graig Gwyn 106 C3
Tan-y-groes Ceredig 73 B5
Tan-y-pistyll Powys 109 C5
Tan-yr-allt Gwyn 107 A4
Tandem W Yorks 139 B4
Tanden Kent 37 C7
Tandridge Sur 35 A6
Tanerdy Carms 73 D7
Tanfield Durham 178 D3
Tanfield Lea Durham 178 D3
Tangasdal W Isles 286 G2
Tangiers Pembs 55 C5
Tangley Hants 46 D1
Tanglwst Carms 73 C6
Tangmere W Sus 20 B2
Tangwick Shetland 284 F4
Tank Museum, Bovington
  Dorset 16 C2
Tankersley S Yorks 139 C6
Tankerton Kent 52 C3
Tannach Highld 281 D5
Tannachie Aberds 245 D4
Tannadice Angus 232 C2
Tannington Suff 88 A3
Tansley Derbys 130 C3
Tansley Knoll Derbys 130 C3
Tansor Northants 100 B2
Tantobie Durham 178 D3
Tanton N Yorks 168 D3
Tanworth-in-Arden Warks 96 D4
Tanygrisiau Gwyn 107 B6
Tanyrhydiau Ceredig 75 B6
Taobh a Chaolais W Isles 286 E3

Taobh a Thuath Loch
  Aineort W Isles 286 D3
Taobh a Tuath Loch
  Baghasdail W Isles 286 D3
Taobh a'Ghlinne W Isles 288 F4
Taobh Tuath W Isles 287 F4
Taplow Bucks 48 A2
Tapton Derbys 130 B3
Tarbert Argyll 213 D4
Tarbert Argyll 202 C1
Tarbert = Tairbeart
  W Isles 288 G2
Tarbet Argyll 215 B6
Tarbet Highld 276 D2
Tarbet Highld 238 C1
Tarbock Green Mers 127 A4
Tarbolton S Ayrs 193 C4
Tarbrax S Lnrk 195 A5
Tardebigge Worcs 80 A3
Tarfside Angus 232 A2
Tarland Aberds 244 B1
Tarleton Lancs 136 A3
Tarlogie Highld 264 B3
Tarlscough Lancs 136 B3
Tarlton Glos 63 D5
Tarnbrook Lancs 145 B5
Tarporley Ches 127 C5
Tarr Som 27 B6
Tarrant Crawford Dorset 16 A3
Tarrant Gunville Dorset 30 D3
Tarrant Hinton Dorset 30 D3
Tarrant Keyneston Dorset 16 A3
Tarrant Launceston Dorset 16 A3
Tarrant Monkton Dorset 16 A3
Tarrant Rawston Dorset 16 A3
Tarrant Rushton Dorset 16 A3
Tarrel Highld 265 B4
Tarring Neville E Sus 22 B2
Tarrington Hereford 79 C4
Tarsappie Perth 219 B6
Tarskavaig Highld 247 D4
Tarves Aberds 256 C3
Tarvie Highld 251 A6
Tarvie Perth 230 B4
Tarvin Ches 127 C4
Tasburgh Norf 104 B3
Tasley Shrops 95 B4
Taston Oxon 65 A4
Tate Gallery London 49 B5
Tate Gallery, Albert Dock
  Mers 126 A3
Tate Modern London 49 B6
Tate St Ives Corn 2 A3
Tatenhill Staffs 113 C6
Tathall End M Keynes 83 C5
Tatham Lancs 145 A6
Tathwell Lincs 134 A3
Tatling End Bucks 48 A3
Tatsfield Sur 36 A2
Tattenhall Ches 127 D4
Tattenhoe M Keynes 83 D5
Tatterford Norf 119 C5
Tattersett Norf 119 B5
Tattershall Lincs 134 D2
Tattershall Bridge Lincs 134 D1
Tattershall Thorpe Lincs 134 D2
Tattingstone Suff 88 D2
Tatton House, Knutsford
  Ches 128 A2
Tatworth Som 14 A3
Taunton Som 28 C2
Taunton Racecourse Som 28 C2
Taverham Norf 120 D3
Tavernspite Pembs 56 A1
Tavistock Devon 11 D5
Taw Green Devon 12 B1
Tawstock Devon 25 C6
Taxal Derbys 129 B5
Tay Bridge Dundee 220 B4
Tayinloan Argyll 202 D1
Taymouth Castle Perth 230 D1
Taynish Argyll 213 D5
Taynton Glos 62 A3
Taynton Oxon 64 B3
Taynuilt Argyll 227 C5
Tayport Fife 221 B4
Tayvallich Argyll 213 D5
Tealby Lincs 142 D3
Tealing Angus 220 A4
Teangue Highld 247 D5
Teanna Mhachair W Isles 287 H2
Tebay Cumb 155 A5
Tebworth Beds 67 A4
Tedburn St Mary Devon 12 B3
Teddington Glos 80 D2

Teddington London 49 B4
Tedstone Delamere
  Hereford 79 B4
Tedstone Wafre Hereford 79 B4
Teeton Northants 98 D3
Teffont Evias Wilts 30 B3
Teffont Magna Wilts 30 B3
Tegryn Pembs 73 C5
Teigh Rutland 115 D6
Teigncombe Devon 12 C1
Teigngrace Devon 12 D3
Teignmouth Devon 13 D4
Telford Telford 95 A4
Telham E Sus 23 A5
Tellisford Som 44 D2
Telscombe E Sus 22 B2
Telscombe Cliffs E Sus 22 B1
Templand Dumfries 184 D3
Temple Corn 10 D2
Temple Glasgow 205 B5
Temple Midloth 196 A2
Temple Balsall W Mid 97 D5
Temple Bar Ceredig 75 C4
Temple Bar Carms 57 A5
Temple Cloud Bath 43 D5
Temple Combe Som 29 C7
Temple Ewell Kent 39 A4
Temple Grafton Warks 80 B4
Temple Guiting Glos 64 A1
Temple Herdewyke Warks 81 B6
Temple Hirst N Yorks 140 A4
Temple Normanton
  Derbys 131 C4
Temple Sowerby Cumb 165 C4
Templehall Fife 209 A5
Templeton Devon 26 D3
Templeton Pembs 55 C7
Templeton Bridge Devon 26 D3
Templetown Durham 178 D3
Tempsford Beds 84 B3
Ten Mile Bank Norf 102 B2
Tenbury Wells Worcs 78 A3
Tenby = Dinbych-y-
  Pysgod Pembs 56 B1
Tendring Essex 71 A5
Tendring Green Essex 71 A5
Tenston Orkney 282 F3
Tenterden Kent 37 C6
Terling Essex 70 B1
Ternhill Shrops 111 B5
Terregles Banks Dumfries 174 A2
Terrick Bucks 66 C3
Terrington N Yorks 159 D5
Terrington St Clement
  Norf 118 D2
Terrington St John Norf 118 D2
Teston Kent 37 A5
Testwood Hants 32 D2
Tetbury Glos 63 D4
Tetbury Upton Glos 63 D4
Tetchill Shrops 110 B2
Tetcott Devon 10 B4
Tetford Lincs 134 B3
Tetney Lincs 143 C5
Tetney Lock Lincs 143 C5
Tetsworth Oxon 66 C1
Tettenhall W Mid 96 A1
Teuchan Aberds 257 C5
Teversal Notts 131 C4
Teversham Cambs 85 B6
Teviothead Borders 186 C3
Tewel Aberds 245 D5
Tewin Herts 68 B2
Tewkesbury Glos 80 D1
Tewkesbury Abbey Glos 80 D1
Teynham Kent 51 C6
Thackthwaite Cumb 163 B4
Thainston Aberds 233 A4
Thakeham W Sus 21 A4
Thame Oxon 66 C2
Thames Ditton Sur 49 C4
Thames Haven Thurrock 51 A4
Thamesmead London 50 A1
Thanington Kent 52 D3
Thankerton S Lnrk 195 C4
Tharston Norf 104 B2
Thatcham W Berks 46 C3
Thatto Heath Mers 136 D4
Thaxted Essex 86 D2
The Aird Highld 259 C4
The All England Jumping
  Course, Hickstead
  W Sus 21 A5
The Arms Norf 103 B4
The Bage Hereford 77 C6
The Balloch Perth 218 C3
The Barony Orkney 282 E3

The Bluebell Railway,
  Sheffield Park E Sus 36 D2
The Bog Shrops 94 B1
The Bourne Sur 33 A7
The Braes Highld 247 A4
The Broad Hereford 78 A2
The Burrell Collection
  Glasgow 205 B5
The Butts Som 30 A1
The Camp Glos 63 C5
The Camp Herts 67 C6
The Chequer Wrex 110 A3
The City Bucks 66 D2
The Common Wilts 31 B6
The Craigs Highld 263 A6
The Cronk I o M 152 B3
The Dell Suff 105 B5
The Den N Ayrs 204 C3
The Dinosaur Museum,
  Dorchester Dorset 15 B7
The Eals Northumb 177 A5
The Eaves Glos 62 C2
The Flatt Cumb 176 B3
The Four Alls Shrops 111 B5
The Friars, Aylesford Kent 37 A5
The Garths Shetland 284 B8
The Green Cumb 153 B2
The Green Wilts 30 B2
The Grove Dumfries 174 A2
The Hall Shetland 284 D8
The Haven W Sus 34 C3
The Heath Norf 120 C3
The Heath Suff 88 D2
The Hill Cumb 153 B2
The Howe Cumb 154 C3
The Howe I o M 152 E1
The Hundred Hereford 78 A3
The Lee Bucks 67 C4
The Lhen I o M 152 A3
The Living RainForest
  W Berks 46 B3
The Long Man of
  Wilmington E Sus 22 B3
The Lost Gardens of
  Heligan, Mevagissey Corn 5 C4
The Lowry, Salford
  Gtr Man 137 D7
The Marsh Powys 93 B7
The Marsh Wilts 45 A4
The Middles Durham 179 D4
The Moor Kent 37 D5
The Moors Centre, Danby
  N Yorks 159 A6
The Mumbles = Y
  Mwmbwls Swansea 57 D6
The Murray S Lnrk 205 C6
The National Archives,
  Kew London 49 B4
The National Tramway
  Museum, Crich Derbys 130 D3
The Needles Old Battery
  I o W 18 C1
The Neuk Aberds 245 C4
The Oval Bath 43 C6
The Oval Cricket Ground
  London 49 B6
The Oxford Story, Oxford
  Oxon 65 C6
The Pole of Itlaw Aberds 268 D1
The Quarry Glos 62 D3
The Rhos Pembs 55 C6
The Rock Telford 95 A4
The Ryde Herts 68 C2
The Sands Sur 34 B1
The Stocks Kent 37 D7
The Tales of Robin Hood
  Nottingham 114 B3
The Throat Wokingham 47 C6
The Tutankhamun
  Exhibition, Dorchester
  Dorset 15 B7
The Vauld Hereford 78 C3
The Vyne Hants 47 D4
The World of Beatrix
  Potter, Bowness-on-
  Windermere Cumb 154 B3
The Wyke Shrops 95 A5
Theakston N Yorks 157 C7
Thealby N Lincs 141 B6
Theale Som 29 A4
Theale W Berks 47 B4
Thearne E Yorks 150 D3
Theberton Suff 89 A5
Theddingworth Leics 98 C3

Theddlethorpe All Saints Lincs 135 A4
Theddlethorpe St Helen Lincs 135 A4
Thelbridge Barton Devon 26 D2
Thelnetham Suff 103 D6
Thelveton Norf 104 C2
Thelwall Warr 127 A6
Themelthorpe Norf 120 C2
Thenford Northants 82 C2
Therfield Herts 85 D5
Thetford Lincs 116 D4
Thetford Norf 103 C4
Theydon Bois Essex 68 C4
Thickwood Wilts 44 B2
Thimbleby Lincs 134 C2
Thimbleby N Yorks 158 B3
Thingwall Mers 126 A2
Thirdpart N Ayrs 204 D1
Thirlby N Yorks 158 C3
Thirlestane Borders 197 B4
Thirn N Yorks 157 C6
Thirsk N Yorks 158 C3
Thirsk Racecourse N Yorks 158 C3
Thirtleby E Yorks 151 D4
Thistleton Lancs 144 D4
Thistleton Rutland 116 D2
Thistley Green Suff 102 D2
Thixendale N Yorks 150 A1
Thockrington Northumb 178 B1
Tholomas Drove Cambs 101 A5
Tholthorpe N Yorks 148 A3
Thomas Chapel Pembs 55 D7
Thomas Close Cumb 164 A2
Thomastown Aberds 255 C6
Thompson Norf 103 B5
Thomshill Moray 266 D3
Thong Kent 50 B3
Thongsbridge W Yorks 139 C4
Thoralby N Yorks 156 C4
Thoresway Lincs 142 D3
Thorganby Lincs 143 D4
Thorganby N Yorks 149 C5
Thorgill N Yorks 159 B6
Thorington Suff 105 D5
Thorington Street Suff 87 D6
Thorlby N Yorks 146 B3
Thorley Herts 69 B4
Thorley Street Herts 69 B4
Thorley Street I o W 18 C2
Thormanby N Yorks 158 D3
Thornaby on Tees Stockton 168 D2
Thornage Norf 120 B2
Thornborough Bucks 83 D4
Thornborough N Yorks 157 D6
Thornbury Devon 11 A5
Thornbury Hereford 79 B4
Thornbury S Glos 62 D2
Thornby N Yorks 147 D5
Thornby Northants 98 D3
Thorncliffe Staffs 129 D5
Thorncombe Dorset 14 A3
Thorncombe Street Sur 34 B3
Thorncote Green Beds 84 C3
Thorncross I o W 18 C3
Thorndon Suff 88 A2
Thorndon Cross Devon 11 B6
Thorne S Yorks 141 B4
Thorne St Margaret Som 27 C5
Thorner W Yorks 148 C2
Thorney Notts 132 B3
Thorney P'boro 101 A4
Thorney Crofts E Yorks 143 A4
Thorney Green Suff 87 A6
Thorney Hill Hants 17 B5
Thorney Toll Cambs 101 A5
Thornfalcon Som 28 C2
Thornford Dorset 29 D6
Thorngumbald E Yorks 143 A4
Thornham Norf 119 A4
Thornham Magna Suff 104 D2
Thornham Parva Suff 104 D2
Thornhaugh P'boro 100 A2
Thornhill Caerph 41 C6
Thornhill Cumb 162 D3
Thornhill Derbys 130 A1
Thornhill Dumfries 183 C6
Thornhill Soton 32 D3
Thornhill Stirl 207 A4
Thornhill W Yorks 139 B5
Thornhill Edge W Yorks 139 B5

Thornhill Lees W Yorks 139 B5
Thornholme E Yorks 151 A4
Thornley Durham 166 B4
Thornley Durham 167 B6
Thornliebank E Renf 205 C5
Thorns Suff 86 B3
Thorns Green Ches 128 A2
Thornsett Derbys 129 A5
Thornthwaite Cumb 163 B5
Thornthwaite N Yorks 147 B5
Thornton Angus 232 D1
Thornton Bucks 83 D4
Thornton Bucks 149 C6
Thornton Fife 209 A5
Thornton Lancs 144 C3
Thornton Leics 98 A1
Thornton Lincs 134 C2
Thornton Mers 136 C2
Thornton M'bro 168 D2
Thornton Northumb 198 B3
Thornton Pembs 55 C5
Thornton W Yorks 147 D5
Thornton Curtis N Lincs 142 B2
Thornton Heath London 49 C6
Thornton Hough Mers 126 A3
Thornton in Craven N Yorks 146 C3
Thornton-le-Beans N Yorks 158 B2
Thornton-le-Clay N Yorks 149 A5
Thornton-le-Dale N Yorks 160 C2
Thornton le Moor Lincs 142 D2
Thornton-le-Moor N Yorks 158 C2
Thornton-le-Moors Ches 127 B4
Thornton-le-Street N Yorks 158 C3
Thornton Rust N Yorks 156 C3
Thornton Steward N Yorks 157 C5
Thornton Watlass N Yorks 157 C6
Thorntonhall S Lnrk 205 C5
Thorntonloch E Loth 211 C4
Thorntonpark Northumb 198 B3
Thornwood Common Essex 69 C4
Thornydykes Borders 197 B5
Thoroton Notts 115 A5
Thorp Arch W Yorks 148 C3
Thorpe Derbys 129 D6
Thorpe E Yorks 150 C2
Thorpe Lincs 135 A4
Thorpe Norf 105 B5
Thorpe Notts 115 A5
Thorpe N Yorks 147 A4
Thorpe Sur 48 C3
Thorpe Abbotts Norf 104 D2
Thorpe Acre Leics 114 C3
Thorpe Arnold Leics 115 C5
Thorpe Audlin W Yorks 140 B2
Thorpe Bassett N Yorks 160 D2
Thorpe Bay Sthend 51 A6
Thorpe by Water Rutland 99 B5
Thorpe Common Suff 88 D3
Thorpe Constantine Staffs 97 A5
Thorpe Culvert Lincs 135 C4
Thorpe End Norf 121 D4
Thorpe Fendykes Lincs 135 C4
Thorpe Green Essex 71 A5
Thorpe Green Suff 87 B5
Thorpe Hesley S Yorks 140 D1
Thorpe in Balne S Yorks 140 B3
Thorpe in the Fallows Lincs 133 A4
Thorpe Langton Leics 99 B4
Thorpe Larches Durham 167 C6
Thorpe-le-Soken Essex 71 A5
Thorpe le Street E Yorks 150 C1
Thorpe Malsor Northants 99 D5
Thorpe Mandeville Northants 82 C2
Thorpe Market Norf 121 B4
Thorpe Marriot Norf 120 D3
Thorpe Morieux Suff 87 B5
Thorpe on the Hill Lincs 133 C4
Thorpe Park, Chertsey Sur 48 C3
Thorpe St Andrew Norf 104 A3
Thorpe St Peter Lincs 135 C4
Thorpe Salvin S Yorks 131 A5
Thorpe Satchville Leics 115 D5
Thorpe Thewles Stockton 168 C2
Thorpe Tilney Lincs 133 D6
Thorpe Underwood N Yorks 148 B3
Thorpe Waterville Northants 100 C1

Thorpe Willoughby N Yorks 149 D4
Thorpeness Suff 89 B5
Thorrington Essex 71 A4
Thorverton Devon 13 A4
Thrandeston Suff 104 D2
Thrapston Northants 100 D1
Thrashbush N Lnrk 207 D5
Threapland Cumb 163 A4
Threapland N Yorks 146 A3
Threapwood Ches 110 A3
Threapwood Staffs 112 A4
Threave Gardens Dumfries 173 B5
Three Ashes Hereford 61 A7
Three Bridges W Sus 35 C5
Three Burrows Corn 4 C2
Three Chimneys Kent 37 C6
Three Cocks Powys 77 D5
Three Counties Showground, Malvern Worcs 79 C5
Three Crosses Swansea 57 C5
Three Cups Corner E Sus 36 D4
Three Holes Norf 101 A7
Three Leg Cross E Sus 37 C4
Three Legged Cross Dorset 17 A4
Three Oaks E Sus 23 A6
Threehammer Common Norf 121 D5
Threekingham Lincs 116 B3
Threemile Cross Wokingham 47 C5
Threemilestone Corn 4 C2
Threemiletown W Loth 208 C3
Threlkeld Cumb 163 B6
Threshfield N Yorks 146 A3
Thrigby Norf 121 D6
Thringarth Durham 166 C2
Thringstone Leics 114 D2
Thrintoft N Yorks 157 B7
Thriplow Cambs 85 C6
Throckenholt Lincs 101 A5
Throcking Herts 85 D5
Throckley T & W 178 C3
Throckmorton Worcs 80 C2
Throphill Northumb 178 A3
Thropton Northumb 188 C3
Throsk Stirl 207 A6
Throwleigh Devon 12 B1
Throwley Kent 52 D1
Thrumpton Notts 114 B3
Thrumster Highld 281 D5
Thrunton Northumb 188 B3
Thrupp Glos 63 C4
Thrupp Oxon 65 B5
Thrushelton Devon 11 C5
Thrussington Leics 115 D4
Thruxton Hants 32 A1
Thruxton Hereford 78 D2
Thruxton Motor Racing Circuit Hants 32 A1
Thrybergh S Yorks 140 D2
Thulston Derbys 114 B2
Thundersley Essex 51 A4
Thundridge Herts 68 B3
Thurcaston Leics 114 D3
Thurcroft S Yorks 131 A4
Thurgarton Norf 120 B3
Thurgarton Notts 115 A4
Thurgoland S Yorks 139 C5
Thurlaston Leics 98 B2
Thurlaston Warks 98 D1
Thurlbear Som 28 C2
Thurlby Lincs 116 D4
Thurlby Lincs 133 C4
Thurleigh Beds 84 B2
Thurlestone Devon 7 C5
Thurloxton Som 28 B2
Thurlstone S Yorks 139 C5
Thurlton Norf 105 B5
Thurlwood Ches 128 D3
Thurmaston Leics 98 A3
Thurnby Leics 98 A3
Thurne Norf 121 D6
Thurnham Kent 37 A6
Thurnham Lancs 145 B4
Thurning Norf 120 C2
Thurning Northants 100 C2
Thurnscoe S Yorks 140 C2
Thurnscoe East S Yorks 140 C2
Thursby Cumb 175 C6
Thursford Norf 120 B1
Thursford Collection, Fakenham Norf 120 B1

Thursley Sur 34 C2
Thurso Highld 280 B3
Thurso East Highld 280 B3
Thurstaston Mers 126 A2
Thurston Suff 87 A5
Thurstonfield Cumb 175 C6
Thurstonland W Yorks 139 B4
Thurton Norf 104 A4
Thurvaston Derbys 113 B6
Thuxton Norf 103 A6
Thwaite N Yorks 156 B2
Thwaite Suff 88 A2
Thwaite St Mary Norf 104 B4
Thwaites W Yorks 147 C4
Thwaites Brow W Yorks 147 C4
Thwing E Yorks 160 D4
Tibbermore Perth 219 B5
Tibberton Glos 62 A3
Tibberton Telford 111 C5
Tibberton Worcs 80 B2
Tibenham Norf 104 C2
Tibshelf Derbys 131 C4
Tibthorpe E Yorks 150 B2
Ticehurst E Sus 37 C4
Tichborne Hants 33 B4
Tickencote Rutland 100 A1
Tickenham N Som 42 B3
Tickhill S Yorks 140 D3
Ticklerton Shrops 94 B2
Ticknall Derbys 114 C1
Tickton E Yorks 150 C3
Tidcombe Wilts 45 D6
Tiddington Oxon 66 C1
Tiddington Warks 81 B5
Tidebrook E Sus 36 D4
Tideford Corn 6 B2
Tideford Cross Corn 6 A2
Tidenham Glos 62 D1
Tideswell Derbys 129 B6
Tidmarsh W Berks 47 B4
Tidmington Warks 81 D5
Tidpit Hants 31 D4
Tidworth Wilts 31 A6
Tiers Cross Pembs 55 C5
Tiffield Northants 82 B3
Tifty Aberds 256 B2
Tigerton Angus 232 B3
Tigh-na-Blair Perth 218 C2
Tighnabruaich Argyll 203 A4
Tighnafinle Highld 261 B5
Tigley Devon 7 A6
Tilbrook Cambs 84 A2
Tilbury Thurrock 50 B3
Tilbury Juxta Clare Essex 86 C3
Tile Cross W Mid 97 C4
Tile Hill W Mid 97 D5
Tilehurst Reading 47 B4
Tilford Sur 34 B1
Tilgate W Sus 35 C5
Tilgate Forest Row W Sus 35 C5
Tillathrowie Aberds 255 C5
Tilley Shrops 111 C4
Tillicoultry Clack 208 A2
Tillingham Essex 70 C3
Tillington Hereford 78 C2
Tillington W Sus 34 D2
Tillington Common Hereford 78 C2
Tillyarblet Angus 232 B3
Tillybirloch Aberds 244 B3
Tillycorthie Aberds 257 D4
Tillydrine Aberds 244 C3
Tillyfour Aberds 244 A2
Tillyfourie Aberds 244 A3
Tillygarmond Aberds 244 C3
Tillygreig Aberds 256 D3
Tillykerrie Aberds 256 D3
Tilmanstone Kent 53 D5
Tilney All Saints Norf 118 D2
Tilney High End Norf 118 D2
Tilney St Lawrence Norf 118 D2
Tilshead Wilts 31 A4
Tilstock Shrops 111 B4
Tilston Ches 127 D4
Tilstone Fearnall Ches 127 C5
Tilsworth Beds 67 A4
Tilton on the Hill Leics 99 A4
Timberland Lincs 133 D6
Timbersbrook Ches 128 C3
Timberscombe Som 27 A4
Timble N Yorks 147 B5
Timperley Gtr Man 128 A2
Timsbury Bath 43 D5
Timsbury Hants 32 C2
Timsgearraidh W Isles 287 A5
Timworth Green Suff 87 A4
Tincleton Dorset 16 B1

Tindale Cumb 176 D4
Tingewick Bucks 82 D3
Tingley W Yorks 139 A5
Tingrith Beds 84 D2
Tingwall Orkney 282 E4
Tinhay Devon 11 C4
Tinshill W Yorks 147 D5
Tinsley S Yorks 140 D2
Tintagel Corn 9 C6
Tintagel Castle Corn 9 C6
Tintern Abbey Mon 62 C7
Tintern Parva Mon 62 C1
Tintinhull Som 29 D5
Tintwistle Derbys 138 D3
Tinwald Dumfries 184 D2
Tinwell Rutland 100 A1
Tipperty Aberds 257 D4
Tipsend Norf 101 B6
Tipton W Mid 96 B2
Tipton St John Devon 13 B6
Tiptree Essex 70 B3
Tir-y-dail Carms 57 A4
Tirabad Powys 59 A4
Tiraghoil Argyll 224 D2
Tiree Airport Argyll 222 C3
Tirley Glos 63 A4
Tirphil Caerph 41 A4
Tirril Cumb 164 C3
Tisbury Wilts 30 C1
Tisman's Common W Sus 34 C2
Tissington Derbys 130 D1
Titchberry Devon 24 C3
Titchfield Hants 18 A4
Titchmarsh Northants 100 D1
Titchwell Norf 119 A4
Tithby Notts 115 B4
Titley Hereford 78 A1
Titlington Northumb 189 B4
Titsey Sur 36 A1
Tittensor Staffs 112 B2
Tittleshall Norf 119 C6
Tiverton Ches 127 C5
Tiverton Devon 27 D4
Tivetshall St Margaret Norf 104 C2
Tivetshall St Mary Norf 104 C2
Tividale W Mid 96 B2
Tivy Dale S Yorks 139 C5
Tixall Staffs 112 C3
Tixover Rutland 99 A5
Toab Orkney 283 G6
Toab Shetland 285 M5
Toadmoor Derbys 130 D3
Tobermory Argyll 225 A4
Toberonochy Argyll 213 A5
Tobha Mor W Isles 286 B3
Tobhtarol W Isles 288 D2
Tobson W Isles 288 D2
Tocher Aberds 256 C1
Tockenham Wilts 44 B4
Tockenham Wick Wilts 44 B4
Tockholes Blkburn 137 A5
Tockington S Glos 43 A5
Tockwith N Yorks 148 B3
Todber Dorset 30 C1
Todding Hereford 94 D2
Toddington Beds 67 A5
Toddington Glos 80 D3
Todenham Glos 81 D5
Todhills Cumb 175 B6
Todlachie Aberds 244 A3
Todmorden W Yorks 138 A2
Todrig Borders 186 B3
Todwick S Yorks 131 A4
Toft Cambs 85 B5
Toft Lincs 116 D3
Toft Hill Durham 167 C4
Toft Hill Lincs 134 C2
Toft Monks Norf 105 B5
Toft next Newton Lincs 133 A5
Toftrees Norf 119 C5
Tofts Highld 281 B5
Toftwood Norf 120 D1
Togston Northumb 189 C5
Tokavaig Highld 247 C5
Tokers Green Oxon 47 B5
Tolastadh a Chaolais W Isles 288 D2
Tolastadh bho Thuath W Isles 288 C6
Toll Bar S Yorks 140 C3
Toll End W Mid 96 B2
Toll of Birness Aberds 257 C5
Tolland Som 27 B6
Tollard Royal Wilts 30 D3
Tollbar End W Mid 97 D6
Toller Fratrum Dorset 15 B5

Toller Porcorum Dorset	15 B5	Torver Cumb	154 B1
Tollerton Notts	115 B4	Torwood Falk	207 B6
Tollerton N Yorks	148 A4	Torworth Notts	131 A6
Tollesbury Essex	70 B3	Tosberry Devon	24 C3
Tolleshunt D'Arcy Essex	70 B3	Toscaig Highld	249 C4
Tolleshunt Major Essex	70 B3	Toseland Cambs	84 A4
Tolm W Isles	288 D5	Tosside N Yorks	146 B1
Tolpuddle Dorset	16 B1	Tostock Suff	87 A5
Tolvah Highld	241 C6	Totaig Highld	258 C2
Tolworth London	49 C4	Totaig Highld	249 D5
Tomatin Highld	253 D4	Tote Highld	259 D4
Tombreck Highld	252 C2	Totegan Highld	279 B4
Tomchrasky Highld	239 A6	Tothill Lincs	135 A4
Tomdoun Highld	239 B5	Totland I o W	18 C2
Tomich Highld	251 D5	Totnes Devon	8 A2
Tomich Highld	264 C2	Toton Notts	114 B3
Tomich House Highld	252 B1	Totronald Argyll	223 B4
Tomintoul Aberds	242 C4	Totscore Highld	258 B3
Tomintoul Moray	243 A4	Tottenham London	68 D3
Tomnaven Moray	255 C5	Tottenhill Norf	118 D3
Tomnavoulin Moray	254 D3	Tottenhill Row Norf	118 D3
Ton-Pentre Rhondda	41 B4	Totteridge London	68 D2
Tonbridge Kent	36 B3	Totternhoe Beds	67 A4
Tondu Bridgend	40 C3	Tottington Gtr Man	137 B6
Tonfanau Gwyn	90 B3	Totton Hants	32 D2
Tong Shrops	95 A5	Touchen End Windsor	48 B1
Tong W Yorks	147 D6	Tournaig Highld	261 B5
Tong Norton Shrops	95 A5	Toux Aberds	269 D4
Tonge Leics	114 C2	Tovil Kent	37 A5
Tongham Sur	34 B1	Tow Law Durham	166 B4
Tongland Dumfries	173 C4	Toward Argyll	203 B6
Tongue Highld	277 C6	Towcester Northants	82 C3
Tongue End Lincs	117 D4	Towcester Racecourse Northants	83 C4
Tongwynlais Cardiff	41 C6	Towednack Corn	2 B2
Tonna Neath	40 B2	Tower End Norf	118 D3
Tonwell Herts	68 B3	Tower Knowe Visitor Centre, Kielder Water Northumb	177 A4
Tonypandy Rhondda	41 B4	Tower of London London	49 A6
Tonyrefail Rhondda	41 C5	Towersey Oxon	66 C2
Toot Baldon Oxon	65 C6	Towie Aberds	244 A1
Toot Hill Essex	69 C5	Towie Aberds	268 C3
Toothill Hants	32 D2	Towiemore Moray	255 B4
Top of Hebers Gtr Man	138 C1	Town End Cambs	101 B6
Topcliffe N Yorks	158 D3	Town End Cumb	154 C3
Topcroft Norf	104 B3	Town Row E Sus	36 C3
Topcroft Street Norf	104 B3	Town Yetholm Borders	187 A7
Toppesfield Essex	86 D3	Townend W Dunb	205 A4
Toppings Gtr Man	137 B6	Towngate Lincs	116 D4
Topsham Devon	13 C4	Townhead Cumb	164 B3
Torbay Torbay	8 B3	Townhead Dumfries	173 D4
Torbeg N Ayrs	191 C5	Townhead S Ayrs	181 A4
Torboll Farm Highld	264 A3	Townhead S Yorks	139 C4
Torbrex Stirl	207 A5	Townhead of Greenlaw Dumfries	173 B5
Torbryan Devon	8 A2	Townhill Fife	208 B4
Torcross Devon	8 C2	Townsend Bucks	66 C2
Tore Highld	252 A2	Townsend Herts	67 C6
Torinturk Argyll	202 B3	Townshend Corn	2 B3
Torksey Lincs	132 B3	Towthorpe York	149 B5
Torlum W Isles	286 A3	Towton N Yorks	148 D3
Torlundy Highld	237 B5	Towyn Conwy	125 B4
Tormarton S Glos	43 B6	Toxteth Mers	126 A3
Tormisdale Argyll	200 C1	Toynton All Saints Lincs	134 C3
Tormitchel S Ayrs	181 B4	Toynton Fen Side Lincs	134 C3
Tormore N Ayrs	191 B4	Toynton St Peter Lincs	135 C4
Tornagrain Highld	252 B3	Toy's Hill Kent	36 A2
Tornahaish Aberds	243 B5	Trabboch E Ayrs	193 C4
Tornaveen Aberds	244 B3	Traboe Corn	3 C5
Torness Highld	252 D1	Tradespark Highld	253 A4
Toronto Durham	167 B4	Tradespark Orkney	283 G5
Torpenhow Cumb	163 A5	Trafford Park Gtr Man	137 D6
Torphichen W Loth	208 C2	Trago Mills, Newton Abbot Devon	12 D3
Torphins Aberds	244 B3	Trallong Powys	59 C6
Torpoint Corn	6 B3	Tranent E Loth	209 C7
Torquay Torbay	8 A3	Tranmere Mers	126 A3
Torquhan Borders	196 B3	Trantlebeg Highld	279 C4
Torran Argyll	214 B1	Trantlemore Highld	279 C4
Torran Highld	248 B2	Tranwell Northumb	178 A3
Torran Highld	264 C3	Trapp Carms	57 A6
Torrance E Dunb	205 A6	Traprain E Loth	210 C2
Torrans Argyll	224 D3	Traquair Borders	196 C2
Torranyard N Ayrs	204 D3	Trawden Lancs	146 D3
Torre Torbay	8 A3	Trawsfynydd Gwyn	108 B2
Torridon Highld	249 A6	Tre-Gibbon Rhondda	60 C1
Torridon Ho. Highld	249 A5	Tre-Taliesin Ceredig	91 C4
Torrin Highld	247 B4	Tre-vaughan Carms	73 D7
Torrisdale Highld	278 B2	Tre-wyn Mon	61 A5
Torrisdale-Square Argyll	190 B3	Trealaw Rhondda	41 B5
Torrish Highld	274 C3	Treales Lancs	144 D4
Torrisholme Lancs	145 A4	Trearddur Anglesey	122 C2
Torroble Highld	272 D3	Treaslane Highld	258 C3
Torry Aberdeen	245 B6	Trebah Garden, Mawnan Smith Corn	3 C5
Torryburn Fife	208 B3	Trebanog Rhondda	41 B5
Torterston Aberds	257 B5		
Torthorwald Dumfries	174 A3		
Tortington W Sus	20 B3		
Tortworth S Glos	62 D3		
Torvaig Highld	259 D4		

Trebanos Neath	40 A2	Tremail Corn	10 C2
Trebartha Corn	10 D3	Tremain Ceredig	73 B5
Trebarwith Corn	9 C6	Tremaine Corn	10 C3
Trebetherick Corn	9 D5	Tremar Corn	6 A1
Treborough Som	27 B5	Trematon Corn	6 B2
Trebudannon Corn	4 A3	Tremeirchion Denb	125 B5
Trebullett Corn	10 D4	Trenance Corn	4 A3
Treburley Corn	10 D4	Trenarren Corn	5 C5
Trebyan Corn	5 A5	Trench Telford	111 D5
Trecastle Powys	59 C5	Treneglos Corn	10 C3
Trecenydd Caerph	41 C6	Trenewan Corn	5 B6
Trecwn Pembs	55 A5	Trent Dorset	29 D5
Trecynon Rhondda	41 A4	Trent Vale Stoke	112 A2
Tredavoe Corn	2 C2	Trentham Stoke	112 A2
Treddiog Pembs	55 B4	Trentham Gardens, Newcastle-under-Lyme Staffs	112 A2
Tredegar Bl Gwent	60 C3	Trentishoe Devon	26 A1
Tredegar Newydd = New Tredegar Caerph	41 A6	Treoes V Glam	40 D4
Tredington Glos	63 A5	Treorchy = Treorci Rhondda	41 B4
Tredington Warks	81 C5	Treorci = Treorchy Rhondda	41 B4
Tredinnick Corn	9 D5	Tre'r-ddôl Ceredig	91 C4
Tredomen Powys	77 D5	Trerule Foot Corn	6 B2
Tredunnock Mon	61 D5	Tresaith Ceredig	73 A5
Tredustan Powys	77 D5	Tresawle Corn	4 C3
Treen Corn	2 C1	Trescott Staffs	95 B6
Treeton S Yorks	131 A4	Trescowe Corn	2 B3
Tref-y-Clawdd = Knighton Powys	93 D6	Tresham Glos	62 D3
Trefaldwyn = Montgomery Powys	93 B6	Tresillian Corn	4 C3
Trefasser Pembs	72 C1	Tresinwen Pembs	72 B1
Trefdraeth Anglesey	123 C4	Treskinnick Cross Corn	10 B3
Trefdraeth = Newport Pembs	72 C3	Tresmeer Corn	10 C3
Trefecca Powys	77 D5	Tresparrett Corn	10 B2
Trefechan Ceredig	90 D3	Tresparrett Posts Corn	10 B2
Trefeglwys Powys	92 B3	Tressait Perth	230 B2
Trefenter Ceredig	75 B5	Tresta Shetland	285 H5
Treffgarne Pembs	55 B5	Tresta Shetland	284 D8
Treffynnon Pembs	54 B4	Treswell Notts	132 B2
Treffynnon = Holywell Flint	126 B1	Trethosa Corn	4 B4
Trefgarn Owen Pembs	55 B4	Trethurgy Corn	5 B5
Trefil Bl Gwent	60 B3	Tretio Pembs	54 B3
Trefilan Ceredig	75 C4	Tretire Hereford	62 A1
Trefin Pembs	54 A4	Tretower Powys	60 A3
Treflach Shrops	110 C1	Treuddyn Flint	126 D2
Trefnanney Powys	109 D7	Trevalga Corn	10 C1
Trefnant Denb	125 B5	Trevalyn Wrex	126 D3
Trefonen Shrops	110 C1	Trevanson Corn	9 D5
Trefor Anglesey	122 B3	Trevarren Corn	4 A4
Trefor Gwyn	106 B3	Trevarrian Corn	4 A3
Treforest Rhondda	41 C5	Trevarrick Corn	5 C4
Trefriw Conwy	124 C2	Trevaughan Carms	56 A1
Trefynwy = Monmouth Mon	61 B7	Treveighan Corn	9 D6
Tregadillett Corn	10 C3	Trevellas Corn	4 B2
Tregaian Anglesey	123 C4	Treverva Corn	4 D2
Tregare Mon	61 B6	Trevethin Torf	61 C4
Tregaron Ceredig	75 C5	Trevigro Corn	6 A2
Tregarth Gwyn	123 D6	Treviscoe Corn	4 B4
Tregeare Corn	10 C3	Trevone Corn	9 D4
Tregeiriog Wrex	109 B6	Trewarmett Corn	9 C6
Tregele Anglesey	122 A3	Trewassa Corn	10 C2
Tregidden Corn	3 C5	Trewellard Corn	2 B1
Treglemais Pembs	54 B4	Trewen Corn	10 C3
Tregole Corn	10 B2	Trewennack Corn	3 C4
Tregonetha Corn	5 A4	Trewern Powys	110 D1
Tregony Corn	4 C4	Trewethern Corn	9 D6
Tregoss Corn	5 A4	Trewidland Corn	6 B1
Tregoyd Powys	77 D6	Trewint Corn	10 C3
Tregroes Ceredig	73 B7	Trewint Corn	10 B2
Tregurrian Corn	4 A3	Trewithian Corn	4 D3
Tregynon Powys	93 B4	Trewoofe Corn	2 C2
Trehafod Rhondda	41 B5	Trewoon Corn	5 B4
Treharris M Tydf	41 B5	Treworga Corn	4 C3
Treherbert Rhondda	40 B4	Treworlas Corn	4 D3
Trekenner Corn	10 D4	Treyarnon Corn	9 D4
Treknow Corn	9 C6	Treyford W Sus	33 D7
Trelan Corn	3 D5	Trezaise Corn	5 B4
Trelash Corn	10 B2	Triangle W Yorks	138 A3
Trelassick Corn	4 B3	Trickett's Cross Dorset	17 A4
Trelawnyd Flint	125 B5	Triffleton Pembs	55 B5
Trelech Carms	73 C5	Trimdon Durham	167 B6
Treleddyd-fawr Pembs	54 B3	Trimdon Colliery Durham	167 B6
Trelewis M Tydf	41 B6	Trimdon Grange Durham	167 B6
Treligga Corn	9 C6	Trimingham Norf	121 B5
Trelights Corn	9 D5	Trimley Lower Street Suff	88 D3
Trelill Corn	9 D6	Trimley St Martin Suff	88 D3
Trelissick Corn	4 D3	Trimley St Mary Suff	88 D3
Trelissick Garden, Feock Corn	4 D3	Trimpley Worcs	95 D5
Trelleck Mon	61 C7	Trimsaran Carms	57 B4
Trelleck Grange Mon	61 C6	Trimstone Devon	25 A5
Trelogan Flint	125 A6	Trinafour Perth	229 B6
Trelystan Powys	93 A6	Trinant Caerph	41 A7
Tremadog Gwyn	107 B5	Tring Herts	67 B4
		Tring Wharf Herts	67 B4
		Trinity Angus	233 B4
		Trinity Jersey	6

Trisant Ceredig	75 A6
Trislaig Highld	237 B4
Trispen Corn	4 B3
Tritlington Northumb	189 D5
Trochry Perth	230 D3
Trodigal Argyll	190 C2
Troed rhiwdalar Powys	76 B3
Troedyraur Ceredig	73 B6
Troedyrhiw M Tydf	41 A5
Tromode I o M	152 D3
Trondavoe Shetland	284 F5
Troon Corn	3 B4
Troon S Ayrs	192 B3
Trosaraidh W Isles	286 E3
Trossachs Hotel Stirl	217 D5
Troston Suff	103 D4
Trottiscliffe Kent	50 C3
Trotton W Sus	34 D1
Troutbeck Cumb	154 A3
Troutbeck Cumb	164 C1
Troutbeck Bridge Cumb	154 A3
Trow Green Glos	62 C1
Trowbridge Wilts	44 D2
Trowell Notts	114 B2
Trowle Common Wilts	44 D2
Trowley Bottom Herts	67 B5
Trows Borders	197 C5
Trowse Newton Norf	104 A3
Trudoxhill Som	30 A1
Trull Som	28 C2
Trumaisgearraidh W Isles	287 G3
Trumpan Highld	258 B2
Trumpet Hereford	79 D4
Trumpington Cambs	85 B6
Trunch Norf	121 B4
Trunnah Lancs	144 C3
Truro Corn	4 C3
Truro Cathedral Corn	4 C3
Trusham Devon	12 C3
Trusley Derbys	113 B6
Trusthorpe Lincs	135 A5
Trysull Staffs	95 B6
Tubney Oxon	65 D5
Tuckenhay Devon	8 B2
Tuckhill Shrops	95 C5
Tuckingmill Corn	3 A4
Tuddenham Suff	102 D3
Tuddenham St Martin Suff	88 C2
Tudeley Kent	36 B4
Tudhoe Durham	167 B5
Tudorville Hereford	62 A1
Tudweiliog Gwyn	106 C2
Tuesley Sur	34 B2
Tuffley Glos	63 B4
Tufton Hants	32 A3
Tufton Pembs	55 B6
Tugby Leics	99 A4
Tugford Shrops	94 C3
Tullibardine Perth	218 C4
Tullibody Clack	207 A6
Tullich Argyll	214 A3
Tullich Highld	252 D2
Tullich Muir Highld	264 C3
Tullie House, Carlisle Cumb	175 D3
Tulliemet Perth	230 C3
Tulloch Aberds	233 A5
Tulloch Aberds	256 C3
Tulloch Perth	219 B5
Tulloch Castle Highld	264 D1
Tullochgorm Argyll	214 C2
Tulloes Angus	232 D3
Tullybannocher Perth	218 B2
Tullybelton Perth	219 A5
Tullyfergus Perth	231 D6
Tullymurdoch Perth	231 C5
Tullynessle Aberds	244 A2
Tumble Carms	57 A5
Tumby Woodside Lincs	134 D2
Tummel Bridge Perth	229 C6
Tunga W Isles	288 D5
Tunstall E Yorks	151 D6
Tunstall Kent	51 C5
Tunstall Lancs	155 D5
Tunstall Norf	105 A5
Tunstall N Yorks	157 B6
Tunstall Stoke	128 D3
Tunstall Suff	89 B4
Tunstall T & W	179 D5
Tunstead Derbys	129 B6
Tunstead Gtr Man	138 C3
Tunstead Norf	121 C4
Tunworth Hants	33 A5

Tupsley Hereford 78 C2
Tupton Derbys 130 C3
Tur Langton Leics 99 B4
Turgis Green Hants 47 D4
Turin Angus 232 C3
Turkdean Glos 64 B2
Turleigh Wilts 44 C2
Turn Lancs 137 B7
Turnastone Hereford 78 D1
Turnberry S Ayrs 192 E2
Turnditch Derbys 113 A6
Turners Hill W Sus 35 C6
Turners Puddle Dorset 16 B2
Turnford Herts 68 C3
Turnhouse Edin 209 C4
Turnworth Dorset 16 A2
Turriff Aberds 268 D2
Turton Bottoms Blkburn 137 B6
Turves Cambs 101 B5
Turvey Beds 83 B6
Turville Bucks 66 D2
Turville Heath Bucks 66 D2
Turweston Bucks 82 D3
Tushielaw Borders 185 A6
Tutbury Staffs 113 C6
Tutnall Worcs 96 D2
Tutshill Glos 62 D1
Tuttington Norf 120 C4
Tutts Clump W Berks 46 B3
Tuxford Notts 132 B2
Twatt Orkney 282 E3
Twatt Shetland 285 H5
Twechar E Dunb 207 C4
Tweedmouth Northumb 198 A3
Tweedsmuir Borders 195 D5
Twelve Heads Corn 4 C2
Twemlow Green Ches 128 C2
Twenty Lincs 117 C4
Twerton Bath 43 C6
Twickenham London 49 B4
Twickenham Stadium London 48 B4
Twigworth Glos 63 A4
Twineham W Sus 21 A5
Twinhoe Bath 43 D6
Twinstead Essex 87 D4
Twinstead Green Essex 87 D4
Twiss Green Warr 137 D5
Twiston Lancs 146 C2
Twitchen Devon 26 B2
Twitchen Shrops 94 D1
Two Bridges Devon 11 D7
Two Dales Derbys 130 C2
Two Mills Ches 126 B3
Twycross Leics 97 A6
Twycross Zoo, Ashby-de-la-Zouch Leics 97 A6
Twyford Bucks 66 A1
Twyford Derbys 114 C1
Twyford Hants 32 C3
Twyford Leics 115 D5
Twyford Lincs 116 C2
Twyford Norf 120 C2
Twyford Wokingham 47 B5
Twyford Common Hereford 78 D3
Twyn-y-Sheriff Mon 61 C6
Twynholm Dumfries 173 C4
Twyning Glos 80 D1
Twyning Green Glos 80 D2
Twynllanan Carms 59 C4
Twynmynydd Carms 57 A6
Twywell Northants 99 D6
Ty-draw Conwy 124 C2
Ty-hen Carms 73 D6
Ty-hen Gwyn 106 C1
Ty-mawr Anglesey 123 B4
Ty Mawr Carms 58 A2
Ty Mawr Conwy Conwy 108 A4
Ty-nant Conwy 109 A4
Ty-nant Gwyn 108 C4
Ty-uchaf Powys 109 C5
Tyberton Hereford 78 D1
Tyburn W Mid 96 B4
Tycroes Carms 57 A6
Tycrwyn Powys 109 D6
Tydd Gote Lincs 118 D1
Tydd St Giles Cambs 118 D1
Tydd St Mary Lincs 118 D1
Tyddewi = St David's Pembs 54 B3
Tyddyn-mawr Gwyn 107 B5
Tye Green Essex 86 D1
Tye Green Essex 70 A1
Tye Green Essex 69 C4

Tyldesley Gtr Man 137 C5
Tyler Hill Kent 52 C3
Tylers Green Bucks 67 D4
Tylorstown Rhondda 41 B5
Tylwch Powys 92 C3
Tyn-y-celyn Wrex 109 B6
Tyn-y-coed Shrops 110 C1
Tyn-y-fedwen Powys 109 B6
Tyn-y-ffridd Powys 109 B6
Tyn-y-graig Powys 76 B4
Ty'n-y-groes Conwy 124 B2
Ty'n-y-maes Gwyn 123 D6
Ty'n-y-pwll Anglesey 123 B4
Ty'n-yr-eithin Ceredig 75 B5
Tyncelyn Ceredig 75 B5
Tyndrum Stirl 216 A3
Tyne Tunnel T & W 179 C5
Tyneham Dorset 16 C2
Tynehead Midloth 196 A2
Tynemouth T & W 179 C5
Tynemouth Sea Life Centre T & W 179 B5
Tynewydd Rhondda 40 B4
Tyninghame E Loth 210 C3
Tynron Dumfries 183 C6
Tynygongl Anglesey 123 B5
Tynygraig Ceredig 75 B5
Tŷ'r-felin-isaf Conwy 124 C3
Tyrie Aberds 269 C4
Tyringham M Keynes 83 C5
Tythecott Devon 25 D5
Tythegston Bridgend 40 D3
Tytherington Ches 129 B4
Tytherington S Glos 43 A5
Tytherington Som 30 A1
Tytherington Wilts 30 A3
Tytherleigh Devon 14 A3
Tywardreath Corn 5 B5
Tywyn Conwy 124 B2
Tywyn Gwyn 90 B3

U

Uachdar W Isles 286 A3
Uags Highld 249 C4
Ubbeston Green Suff 104 D4
Ubley Bath 43 D4
Uckerby N Yorks 157 A6
Uckfield E Sus 36 D2
Uckington Glos 63 A5
Uddingston S Lnrk 207 D4
Uddington S Lnrk 194 C3
Udimore E Sus 23 A6
Udny Green Aberds 256 D3
Udny Station Aberds 257 D4
Udston S Lnrk 194 A1
Udstonhead S Lnrk 194 B2
Uffcott Wilts 45 B5
Uffculme Devon 27 D5
Uffington Lincs 100 A2
Uffington Oxon 45 A7
Uffington Shrops 111 D4
Ufford P'boro 100 A2
Ufford Suff 88 B3
Ufton Warks 81 A6
Ufton Nervet W Berks 47 C4
Ugadale Argyll 190 C3
Ugborough Devon 7 B5
Uggeshall Suff 105 C5
Ugglebarnby N Yorks 160 A2
Ughill S Yorks 139 D5
Ugley Essex 69 A5
Ugley Green Essex 69 A5
Ugthorpe N Yorks 169 D5
Uidh W Isles 286 G2
Uig Argyll 215 D4
Uig Highld 258 B3
Uig Highld 258 C1
Uigen W Isles 287 A5
Uigshader Highld 259 D4
Uisken Argyll 224 E2
Ulbster Highld 281 D5
Ulceby Lincs 135 B4
Ulceby N Lincs 142 B3
Ulceby Skitter N Lincs 142 B3
Ulcombe Kent 37 B6
Uldale Cumb 163 A5
Uley Glos 62 D3
Ulgham Northumb 189 D5
Ullapool Highld 262 A3
Ullenhall Warks 80 A4
Ullenwood Glos 63 B5
Ulleskelf N Yorks 148 C4
Ullesthorpe Leics 98 C2
Ulley S Yorks 131 A4
Ullingswick Hereford 78 C3
Ullinish Highld 246 A2
Ullock Cumb 162 B3

Ulnes Walton Lancs 136 B4
Ulpha Cumb 153 A2
Ulrome E Yorks 151 B4
Ulsta Shetland 284 E6
Ulva House Argyll 224 C3
Ulverston Cumb 154 D1
Ulwell Dorset 17 C4
Umberleigh Devon 25 C7
Unapool Highld 271 A5
Unasary W Isles 286 D3
Underbarrow Cumb 154 B3
Undercliffe W Yorks 147 D5
Underhoull Shetland 284 C7
Underriver Kent 36 A3
Underwood Notts 131 D4
Undy Mon 42 A3
Unifirth Shetland 285 H4
Union Cottage Aberds 245 C5
Union Mills I o M 152 D3
Union Street E Sus 37 C5
University Museum, Oxford Oxon 65 C6
Unst Airport Shetland 284 C8
Unstone Derbys 130 B3
Unstone Green Derbys 130 B3
Unthank Cumb 164 B2
Unthank Cumb 165 A4
Unthank End Cumb 164 B2
Up Cerne Dorset 15 A6
Up Exe Devon 13 A4
Up Hatherley Glos 63 A5
Up Holland Lancs 136 C4
Up Marden W Sus 33 D6
Up Nately Hants 47 D4
Up Somborne Hants 32 B2
Up Sydling Dorset 15 A6
Upavon Wilts 45 D5
Upchurch Kent 51 C5
Upcott Hereford 78 B1
Upend Cambs 86 B2
Upgate Norf 120 D3
Uphall W Loth 208 C3
Uphall Station W Loth 208 C3
Upham Devon 12 A3
Upham Hants 32 C4
Uphampton Worcs 79 A6
Uphill N Som 42 D2
Uplawmoor E Renf 205 C4
Upleadon Glos 62 A3
Upleatham Redcar 168 D4
Uplees Kent 52 C1
Uploders Dorset 15 B5
Uplowman Devon 27 D5
Uplyme Devon 14 B3
Upminster London 50 A2
Upnor Medway 51 B4
Upottery Devon 14 A2
Uppark, Petersfield Hants 33 D6
Upper Affcot Shrops 94 C2
Upper Ardchronie Highld 264 B2
Upper Arley Worcs 95 C5
Upper Arncott Oxon 65 B7
Upper Astrop Northants 82 D2
Upper Badcall Highld 276 D2
Upper Basildon W Berks 46 B3
Upper Beeding W Sus 21 A4
Upper Benefield Northants 100 C1
Upper Bighouse Highld 279 C4
Upper Boddington Northants 82 B1
Upper Borth Ceredig 90 D4
Upper Boyndlie Aberds 269 C4
Upper Brailes Warks 81 D6
Upper Breakish Highld 247 B5
Upper Breinton Hereford 78 C2
Upper Broadheath Worcs 79 B6
Upper Broughton Notts 115 C4
Upper Bucklebury W Berks 46 C3
Upper Burnhaugh Aberds 245 C5
Upper Caldecote Beds 84 C3
Upper Catesby Northants 82 B2
Upper Chapel Powys 76 C4
Upper Church Village Rhondda 41 C5
Upper Chute Wilts 45 D6
Upper Clatford Hants 32 A2
Upper Clynnog Gwyn 107 B4
Upper Cumberworth W Yorks 139 C5
Upper Cwm-twrch Powys 59 D4
Upper Cwmbran Torf 61 D4
Upper Dallachy Moray 267 C4
Upper Dean Beds 84 A2
Upper Denby W Yorks 139 C5
Upper Denton Cumb 176 C4
Upper Derraid Highld 253 C6
Upper Dicker E Sus 22 B3

Upper Dovercourt Essex 88 D3
Upper Druimfin Argyll 225 A4
Upper Dunsforth N Yorks 148 A3
Upper Eathie Highld 264 D3
Upper Elkstone Staffs 129 D5
Upper End Derbys 129 B5
Upper Farringdon Hants 33 B6
Upper Framilode Glos 62 B3
Upper Glenfintaig Highld 239 D6
Upper Gornal W Mid 96 B2
Upper Gravenhurst Beds 84 D3
Upper Green Mon 61 B5
Upper Green W Berks 46 C1
Upper Grove Common Hereford 62 A1
Upper Hackney Derbys 130 C2
Upper Hale Sur 34 B1
Upper Halistra Highld 258 C2
Upper Halling Medway 50 C3
Upper Hambleton Rutland 99 A5
Upper Hardres Court Kent 52 D3
Upper Hartfield E Sus 36 C2
Upper Haugh S Yorks 140 D2
Upper Heath Shrops 94 C3
Upper Hellesdon Norf 120 D4
Upper Helmsley N Yorks 149 B5
Upper Hergest Hereford 77 B6
Upper Heyford Northants 82 B3
Upper Heyford Oxon 65 A5
Upper Hill Hereford 78 B2
Upper Hopton W Yorks 139 B4
Upper Horsebridge E Sus 22 A3
Upper Hulme Staffs 129 C5
Upper Inglesham Thamesdown 64 D3
Upper Inverbrough Highld 253 C4
Upper Killay Swansea 57 C5
Upper Knockando Moray 254 B2
Upper Lambourn W Berks 45 A7
Upper Leigh Staffs 112 B4
Upper Lenie Highld 251 D7
Upper Lochton Aberds 244 C3
Upper Longdon Staffs 113 D4
Upper Lybster Highld 275 A6
Upper Lydbrook Glos 62 B2
Upper Maes-coed Hereford 78 D1
Upper Midway Derbys 113 C6
Upper Milovaig Highld 258 D1
Upper Minety Wilts 63 D6
Upper Mitton Worcs 95 D6
Upper North Dean Bucks 66 D3
Upper Obney Perth 219 A5
Upper Ollach Highld 247 A4
Upper Padley Derbys 130 B2
Upper Pollicott Bucks 66 B2
Upper Poppleton York 149 B4
Upper Quinton Warks 81 C4
Upper Ratley Hants 32 C2
Upper Rissington Glos 64 B3
Upper Rochford Worcs 79 A4
Upper Sandaig Highld 238 A1
Upper Sanday Orkney 283 G6
Upper Sapey Hereford 79 A4
Upper Seagry Wilts 44 A3
Upper Shelton Beds 84 C1
Upper Sheringham Norf 120 A3
Upper Skelmorlie N Ayrs 204 B2
Upper Slaughter Glos 64 A2
Upper Soudley Glos 62 B2
Upper Stondon Beds 84 D3
Upper Stowe Northants 82 B3
Upper Stratton Thamesdown 45 A5
Upper Street Norf 31 D5
Upper Street Norf 121 D5
Upper Street Norf 121 D5
Upper Street Suff 88 D2
Upper Strensham Worcs 80 D2
Upper Sundon Beds 67 A5
Upper Swell Glos 64 A2
Upper Tean Staffs 112 B4
Upper Tillyrie Perth 219 D6
Upper Tooting London 49 B5
Upper Tote Highld 259 C5
Upper Town N Som 43 C4
Upper Treverward Shrops 93 D6
Upper Tysoe Warks 81 C6
Upper Upham Wilts 45 B6
Upper Wardington Oxon 82 C1
Upper Weald M Keynes 83 D4
Upper Weedon Northants 82 B3
Upper Wield Hants 33 B5
Upper Winchendon Bucks 66 B2
Upper Witton W Mid 96 B3
Upper Woodend Aberds 244 A3
Upper Woodford Wilts 31 B5

Upper Wootton Hants 46 D3
Upper Wyche Worcs 79 C5
Upperby Cumb 175 C2
Uppermill Gtr Man 138 C2
Uppersound Shetland 285 J6
Upperthong W Yorks 139 C4
Upperthorpe N Lincs 141 C5
Upperton W Sus 34 D2
Uppertown Derbys 130 C3
Uppertown Highld 281 A5
Uppertown Orkney 283 H5
Uppingham Rutland 99 B5
Uppington Shrops 95 A4
Upsall N Yorks 158 C3
Upshire Essex 68 C4
Upstreet Kent 53 C4
Upthorpe Suff 103 D5
Upton Cambs 100 D3
Upton Ches 127 C4
Upton Corn 10 A4
Upton Dorset 16 C4
Upton Dorset 16 B1
Upton Hants 32 D2
Upton Hants 46 D2
Upton Leics 97 B6
Upton Lincs 132 A3
Upton Mers 126 A2
Upton Norf 121 D5
Upton Notts 132 C2
Upton Notts 132 B2
Upton Northants 83 A4
Upton Oxon 46 A3
Upton P'boro 100 A3
Upton Slough 48 B2
Upton Som 27 C4
Upton W Yorks 140 B2
Upton Bishop Hereford 62 A2
Upton Cheyney S Glos 43 C5
Upton Cressett Shrops 95 B4
Upton Cross Corn 10 D3
Upton Grey Hants 33 A5
Upton Hellions Devon 12 A3
Upton House Warks 81 C6
Upton Lovell Wilts 30 B3
Upton Magna Shrops 111 D4
Upton Noble Som 29 B7
Upton Pyne Devon 13 B4
Upton St Leonard's Glos 63 B4
Upton Scudamore Wilts 30 A2
Upton Snodsbury Worcs 80 B2
Upton upon Severn Worcs 79 C6
Upton Warren Worcs 80 A2
Upwaltham W Sus 20 A2
Upware Cambs 102 D1
Upwell Norf 101 A6
Upwey Dorset 15 C6
Upwood Cambs 101 C4
Uradale Shetland 285
Urafirth Shetland 284
Urchfont Wilts 44
Urdimarsh Hereford 78
Ure Shetland 284
Ure Bank N Yorks 157
Urgha W Isles 288
Urishay Common Hereford 77
Urlay Nook Stockton 167
Urmston Gtr Man 137
Urpeth Durham 179
Urquhart Highld 252
Urquhart Moray 266
Urquhart Castle, Drumnadrochit Highld 252
Urra N Yorks 159
Urray Highld 251
Ushaw Moor Durham 167
Usk = Brynbuga Mon 61
Usselby Lincs 142
Usworth T & W 179
Utkinton Ches 127
Utley W Yorks 147
Uton Devon 12
Utterby Lincs 143
Uttoxeter Staffs 113
Uttoxeter Racecourse Staffs 113
Uwchmynydd Gwyn 106
Uxbridge London 48
Uyeasound Shetland 284
Uzmaston Pembs 55

V

Valley Anglesey 122
Valley Truckle Corn 10
Valleyfield Dumfries 173
Valsgarth Shetland 284
Valtos Highld 259
Van Powys 92

ange Essex 51 A4
arteg Torf 61 C4
atten Highld 258 D2
aul Argyll 222 C3
aynor M Tydf 60 B2
eensgarth Shetland 285 A6
elindre Powys 77 D5
ellow Som 27 B5
eness Orkney 282 E6
nn Green Devon 25 D4
nn Ottery Devon 13 B5
ennington Shrops 94 A1
enny Tedburn Devon 12 B3
entnor I o W 19 D4
entnor Botanic Garden
I o W 19 D4
rnham Dean Hants 46 D1
rnham Street Hants 46 D1
rnolds Common Shrops 94 C2
rwood Dorset 17 A4
ryan Corn 4 D4
carage Devon 14 C2
ckerstown Cumb 153 D2
ctoria Corn 5 A4
ctoria S Yorks 139 C4
ctoria and Albert
Museum London 49 B5
e Shetland 284 G6
ewpark N Lnrk 207 D5
go Village Kent 50 C3
nehall Street S Sus 37 D5
ne's Cross E Sus 22 A3
ey Hill Glos 62 C2
ginia Water Sur 48 C3
ginstow Devon 11 B4
bster Som 29 A7
e Shetland 285 G6
e Shetland 284 E5
wchurch Hereford 78 D1
xter Shetland 284 F5
y Orkney 282 F3

ckerfield Durham 167 C4
cton Norf 104 B2
dbister Shetland 285 J6
dborough Worcs 80 C2
ddesdon Bucks 66 B2
ddesdon Manor,
ylesbury Bucks 66 B2
ddingham Lincs 142 D1
ddington Lancs 146 C1
ddington Lincs 133 C4
debridge Corn 9 D5
deford Som 28 D3
denhoe Northants 100 C2
desmill Herts 68 B3
dhurst E Sus 36 C4
dshelf Derbys 130 B3
dsley S Yorks 139 D6
dsley Bridge S Yorks 139 C6
dworth S Yorks 140 D3
en Denb 125 C6
en Denb 125 C4
en Fach Powys 109 D7
en Goleugoed Denb 125 B5
g Highld 274 B4
nfleet All Saints Lincs 135 D4
nfleet Bank Lincs 135 D4
nfleet St Mary Lincs 135 D5
nfleet Tofts Lincs 135 D4
nhouse Corner Corn 10 B2
nscott Medway 51 B4
nstalls W Yorks 138 A3
by Cumb 155 A6
he Lincs 143 C4
e Lady Green N Yorks 159 B5
efield W Yorks 139 A6
ehurst Place Garden,
awley W Sus 35 C6
erley Northants 99 B6
es Colne Essex 70 A2
erswick Suff 105 D5
erton W Sus 20 B2
ottle T & W 178 C3
ot Lincs 116 B3
ot N Lincs 141 A6
ot Shrops 94 C1
ot Telford 111 D4
ot Thamesdown 45 A5
ot Green Norf 104 C2
ote Leics 98 C2
ote Warks 80 B4
ott Lincs 133 D6
ott Norf 121 B5
en N Yorks 156 C4

Walden Head N Yorks 156 C3
Walden Stubbs N Yorks 140 B3
Waldersey Cambs 101 A6
Walderslade Medway 51 C4
Walderton W Sus 33 D6
Walditch Dorset 15 B4
Waldley Derbys 113 B5
Waldridge Durham 179 D4
Waldringfield Suff 88 C3
Waldringfield Heath Suff 88 C3
Waldron E Sus 22 A3
Wales S Yorks 131 A4
Walesby Lincs 142 D3
Walesby Notts 132 B1
Walford Hereford 94 D1
Walford Hereford 62 A1
Walford Shrops 110 C3
Walford Heath Shrops 110 D3
Walgherton Ches 111 A5
Walgrave Northants 99 D5
Walhampton Hants 18 B2
Walk Mill Lancs 146 D2
Walkden Gtr Man 137 C6
Walker T & W 179 C4
Walker Art Gallery Mers 136 D2
Walker Barn Ches 129 B4
Walker Fold Lancs 145 C6
Walkerburn Borders 196 C2
Walkeringham Notts 141 D5
Walkerith Lincs 141 D5
Walkern Herts 68 A2
Walker's Green Hereford 78 C3
Walkerville N Yorks 157 B6
Walkford Dorset 17 B6
Walkhampton Devon 7 A4
Walkington E Yorks 150 D2
Walkley S Yorks 130 A3
Walkley Clogs, Hebden
Bridge W Yorks 138 A3
Wall Northumb 177 C7
Wall Staffs 96 A4
Wall Bank Shrops 94 B3
Wall Heath W Mid 96 C1
Wall under Heywood
Shrops 94 B3
Wallaceton Dumfries 183 D6
Wallacetown S Ayrs 181 A4
Wallacetown S Ayrs 192 C3
Wallands Park E Sus 22 A2
Wallasey Mers 136 D2
Wallcrouch E Sus 37 C4
Wallingford Oxon 47 A4
Wallington London 49 C5
Wallington Hants 19 A4
Wallington Herts 85 D4
Wallington House,
Ponteland Northumb 178 A2
Wallis Pembs 55 B6
Walliswood Sur 35 C4
Walls Shetland 285 J4
Wallsend T & W 179 C4
Wallston V Glam 41 D6
Wallyford E Loth 209 C6
Walmer Kent 53 D5
Walmer Bridge Lancs 136 A3
Walmersley Gtr Man 137 B7
Walmley W Mid 96 B4
Walney Island Airport
Cumb 153 C2
Walpole Suff 105 D4
Walpole Cross Keys Norf 118 D2
Walpole Highway Norf 118 D2
Walpole Marsh Norf 118 D1
Walpole St Andrew Norf 118 D2
Walpole St Peter Norf 118 D2
Walsall W Mid 96 B3
Walsall Arboretum W Mid 96 B3
Walsall Wood W Mid 96 A3
Walsden W Yorks 138 A2
Walsgrave on Sowe W Mid 97 C6
Walsham le Willows Suff 103 D5
Walshaw Gtr Man 137 B6
Walshford N Yorks 148 B3
Walsoken Cambs 118 D1
Walston S Lnrk 195 B5
Walsworth Herts 84 D4
Walters Ash Bucks 66 D3
Walterston V Glam 41 D5
Walterstone Hereford 78 A3
Waltham Kent 38 A3
Waltham NE Lincs 143 C4
Waltham Abbey Essex 68 C3
Waltham Chase Hants 33 D4
Waltham Cross Herts 68 C3
Waltham on the Wolds
Leics 115 C6
Waltham St Lawrence
Windsor 47 B6

Walthamstow London 49 A6
Walton Cumb 176 C3
Walton Derbys 130 C3
Walton Leics 98 C2
Walton Mers 136 D2
Walton M Keynes 83 D5
Walton P'boro 100 A3
Walton Powys 77 B6
Walton Som 29 B4
Walton Staffs 112 B2
Walton Suff 88 D3
Walton Telford 111 D4
Walton Warks 81 B5
Walton W Yorks 139 B6
Walton W Yorks 148 C3
Walton Cardiff Glos 80 D2
Walton East Pembs 55 B6
Walton Hall Warr 127 A6
Walton-in-Gordano N Som 42 B3
Walton-le-Dale Lancs 137 A4
Walton-on-Thames Sur 48 C4
Walton on the Hill Staffs 112 C3
Walton on the Hill Sur 35 A5
Walton-on-the-Naze
Essex 71 A6
Walton on the Wolds
Leics 114 D3
Walton-on-Trent Derbys 113 D6
Walton West Pembs 55 C4
Walwen Flint 126 B2
Walwick Northumb 177 B7
Walworth Darl 167 D5
Walworth Gate Darl 167 C5
Walwyn's Castle Pembs 55 C4
Wambrook Som 14 A2
Wanborough Sur 34 B2
Wanborough Thamesdown 45 A6
Wandsworth London 49 B5
Wangford Suff 105 D5
Wanlockhead Dumfries 183 A6
Wansford E Yorks 150 B3
Wansford P'boro 100 B2
Wanstead London 49 A7
Wanstrow Som 29 A7
Wanswell Glos 62 C2
Wantage Oxon 46 A1
Wapley S Glos 43 B6
Wappenbury Warks 81 A6
Wappenham Northants 82 C3
Warbleton E Sus 22 A4
Warblington Hants 19 A6
Warborough Oxon 65 D6
Warboys Cambs 101 C5
Warbreck Blkpool 144 D3
Warbstow Corn 10 B3
Warburton Gtr Man 128 A2
Warcop Cumb 165 D5
Ward End W Mid 96 C4
Ward Green Suff 87 A6
Warden Kent 52 B2
Warden Northumb 177 C7
Wardhill Orkney 282 E7
Wardington Oxon 82 C1
Wardlaw Borders 185 A5
Wardle Ches 127 D6
Wardle Gtr Man 138 B2
Wardley Rutland 99 A5
Wardlow Derbys 130 B1
Wardy Hill Cambs 101 C6
Ware Herts 68 B3
Ware Kent 53 C4
Wareham Dorset 16 C3
Warehorne Kent 38 B1
Waren Mill Northumb 199 C5
Warenford Northumb 189 A4
Warenton Northumb 199 C5
Wareside Herts 68 B3
Waresley Cambs 84 B4
Waresley Worcs 95 D6
Warfield Brack 48 B1
Warfleet Devon 8 B2
Wargrave Wokingham 47 B5
Warham Norf 119 A6
Warhill Gtr Man 138 D2
Wark Northumb 177 B6
Wark Northumb 198 C2
Warkleigh Devon 26 C1
Warkton Northants 99 D5
Warkworth Northants 82 C1
Warkworth Northumb 189 C5
Warlaby N Yorks 158 B2
Warland W Yorks 138 A2
Warleggan Corn 5 A6
Warlingham Sur 35 A6
Warmfield W Yorks 140 A1
Warmingham Ches 128 C2
Warmington Northants 100 B2

Warmington Warks 81 C7
Warminster Wilts 30 A2
Warmlake Kent 37 A6
Warmley S Glos 43 B5
Warmley Tower S Glos 43 B5
Warmonds Hill Northants 83 A6
Warmsworth S Yorks 140 C3
Warmwell Dorset 16 C1
Warndon Worcs 80 B1
Warnford Hants 33 C5
Warnham W Sus 35 C4
Warningcamp W Sus 20 B3
Warninglid W Sus 35 D5
Warren Ches 128 B3
Warren Pembs 55 E5
Warren Heath Suff 88 C3
Warren Row Windsor 47 A6
Warren Street Kent 51 D6
Warrington M Keynes 83 B5
Warrington Warr 127 A6
Warsash Hants 18 A3
Warslow Staffs 129 D5
Warter E Yorks 150 B1
Warthermarske N Yorks 157 D6
Warthill N Yorks 149 B5
Wartling E Sus 23 B4
Wartnaby Leics 115 C5
Warton Lancs 136 A3
Warton Lancs 154 D3
Warton Northumb 188 C3
Warton Warks 97 A5
Warwick Warks 81 A5
Warwick Bridge Cumb 176 D2
Warwick Castle Warks 81 A5
Warwick on Eden Cumb 176 D2
Warwick Racecourse
Warks 81 A5
Wasbister Orkney 282 D4
Wasdale Head Cumb 163 D4
Wash Common W Berks 46 C2
Washaway Corn 5 A5
Washbourne Devon 8 B1
Washfield Devon 27 D4
Washfold N Yorks 157 A4
Washford Som 27 A5
Washford Pyne Devon 26 D3
Washingborough Lincs 133 B5
Washington T & W 179 D5
Washington W Sus 21 A4
Wasing W Berks 46 C3
Waskerley Durham 166 A3
Wasperton Warks 81 B5
Wasps Nest Lincs 133 C5
Wass N Yorks 159 D4
Watchet Som 27 A5
Watchfield Oxon 64 D3
Watchfield Som 28 A3
Watchgate Cumb 154 B4
Watchhill Cumb 175 D4
Watcombe Torbay 8 A3
Watendlath Cumb 163 C5
Water Devon 12 C2
Water Lancs 138 A1
Water End E Yorks 149 D6
Water End Herts 67 B5
Water End Herts 68 C2
Water Newton Cambs 100 B3
Water Orton Warks 97 B4
Water Stratford Bucks 82 D3
Water Yeat Cumb 154 C1
Waterbeach Cambs 85 A6
Waterbeck Dumfries 175 A5
Waterden Norf 119 B5
Waterfall Staffs 129 D5
Waterfoot E Renf 205 C5
Waterfoot Lancs 138 A1
Waterford Herts 68 B3
Waterhead Cumb 154 A2
Waterhead Dumfries 185 C4
Waterheads Borders 196 A1
Waterhouses Durham 167 A4
Waterhouses Staffs 129 D5
Wateringbury Kent 37 A4
Waterloo Gtr Man 138 C2
Waterloo Highld 247 B5
Waterloo Mers 136 D2
Waterloo N Lnrk 194 A3
Waterloo Norf 120 D4
Waterloo Perth 219 A5
Waterloo Poole 17 B4
Waterloo Shrops 111 B4
Waterloo Port Gwyn 123 D4
Waterlooville Hants 19 A5
Watermeetings S Lnrk 184 A2

Watermillock Cumb 164 C2
Watermouth Castle,
Ilfracombe Devon 25 A6
Waterperry Oxon 66 C1
Waterrow Som 27 C5
Water's Nook Gtr Man 137 C5
Waters Upton Telford 111 D5
Watersfield W Sus 20 A3
Watershed Mill Visitor
Centre, Settle N Yorks 146 A2
Waterside Aberds 257 D5
Waterside Blkburn 137 A6
Waterside Cumb 175 D5
Waterside E Ayrs 182 B2
Waterside E Ayrs 205 A4
Waterside E Dunb 207 C4
Waterside E Renf 205 C5
Waterstock Oxon 66 C1
Waterston Pembs 55 D5
Watford Herts 67 D6
Watford Northants 82 A3
Watford Gap W Mid 96 A4
Wath N Yorks 147 A5
Wath N Yorks 157 D7
Wath N Yorks 159 D5
Wath Brow Cumb 162 C3
Wath upon Dearne
S Yorks 140 C2
Watley's End S Glos 43 A5
Watlington Norf 118 D3
Watlington Oxon 66 D1
Watnall Notts 114 A3
Watten Highld 280 C4
Wattisfield Suff 103 D6
Wattisham Suff 87 B6
Wattlesborough Heath
Shrops 110 D2
Watton E Yorks 150 B3
Watton Norf 103 A5
Watton at Stone Herts 68 B3
Wattston N Lnrk 207 C5
Wattstown Rhondda 41 B5
Wauchan Highld 238 D3
Waulkmill Lodge Orkney 283 G4
Waun Powys 91 B6
Waun-y-clyn Carms 57 B4
Waunarlwydd Swansea 57 C6
Waunclunda Carms 58 B3
Waunfawr Gwyn 107 A5
Waungron Swansea 57 B5
Waunlwyd Bl Gwent 60 C3
Wavendon M Keynes 83 D6
Waverbridge Cumb 175 D5
Waverton Ches 127 C4
Waverton Cumb 175 D5
Wavertree Mers 126 A3
Wawne E Yorks 150 D3
Waxham Norf 121 C6
Waxholme E Yorks 143 A5
Way Kent 53 C5
Way Village Devon 26 D3
Wayfield Medway 51 C4
Wayford Som 14 A4
Waymills Shrops 111 A4
Wayne Green Mon 61 B6
Wdig = Goodwick Pembs 72 C2
Weachyburn Aberds 268 D1
Weald Oxon 64 C4
Weald and Downland
Open Air Museum,
Chichester W Sus 20 A1
Wealdstone London 49 A4
Weardley W Yorks 148 C1
Weare Som 42 D3
Weare Giffard Devon 25 C5
Wearhead Durham 165 B6
Weasdale Cumb 155 A5
Weasenham All Saints
Norf 119 C5
Weasenham St Peter
Norf 119 C5
Weatherhill Sur 35 B6
Weaverham Ches 127 B6
Weaverthorpe N Yorks 160 D3
Webheath Worcs 80 A3
Wedderlairs Aberds 256 C3
Wedderlie Borders 197 A5
Weddington Warks 97 B6
Wedgwood Visitor
Centre, Barlaston
Staffs 112 B2
Wedhampton Wilts 45 D4
Wedmore Som 28 A4
Wednesbury W Mid 96 B2

Wednesfield W Mid 96 A2
Weedon Bucks 66 B3
Weedon Bec Northants 82 B3
Weedon Lois Northants 82 C3
Weeford Staffs 96 A4
Week Devon 26 D2
Week St Mary Corn 10 D3
Weeke Hants 32 B3
Weekley Northants 99 C5
Weel E Yorks 150 D3
Weeley Essex 71 A5
Weeley Heath Essex 71 A5
Weem Perth 230 D2
Weeping Cross Staffs 112 C3
Weethley Gate Warks 80 B3
Weeting Norf 102 C3
Weeting Heath NNR Norf 102 C3
Weeton E Yorks 143 A5
Weeton Lancs 144 D3
Weeton N Yorks 148 C1
Weetwood Hall Northumb 188 A3
Weir Lancs 138 A1
Weir Quay Devon 6 A3
Welborne Norf 120 E2
Welbourn Lincs 133 D4
Welburn N Yorks 149 A6
Welburn N Yorks 159 C5
Welbury N Yorks 158 A2
Welby Lincs 116 B2
Welches Dam Cambs 101 C6
Welcombe Devon 24 D3
Weld Bank Lancs 137 B4
Weldon Northumb 189 D4
Welford Northants 98 C3
Welford W Berks 46 B2
Welford-on-Avon Warks 81 B4
Welham Leics 99 B4
Welham Notts 132 A2
Welham Green Herts 68 C2
Well Hants 33 A6
Well Lincs 135 B4
Well N Yorks 157 C6
Well End Bucks 48 A1
Well Heads W Yorks 147 D4
Well Hill Kent 50 C1
Well Town Devon 13 A4
Welland Worcs 79 C5
Wellbank Angus 221 A4
Welldale Dumfries 175 B4
Wellesbourne Warks 81 B5
Welling London 50 B1
Wellingborough Northants 83 A5
Wellingham Norf 119 C5
Wellingore Lincs 133 D4
Wellington Cumb 162 D3
Wellington Hereford 78 C2
Wellington Som 27 C6
Wellington Telford 111 D5
Wellington Heath Hereford 79 C5
Wellington Hill W Yorks 148 D2
Wellow Bath 43 D6
Wellow I o W 18 C2
Wellow Notts 131 C6
Wellpond Green Herts 68 A4
Wells Som 29 A5
Wells Cathedral Som 29 A5
Wells Green Ches 128 D1
Wells-next-the-Sea Norf 119 A6
Wellsborough Leics 97 A6
Wellswood Torbay 8 A3
Wellwood Fife 208 B3
Welney Norf 102 B1
Welsh Bicknor Hereford 62 B1
Welsh End Shrops 111 B4
Welsh Frankton Shrops 110 B2
Welsh Highland Railway, Caernarfon Gwyn 123 D4
Welsh Highland Railway, Porthmadog Gwyn 107 C5
Welsh Hook Pembs 55 B5
Welsh National Velodrome Newport 42 A2
Welsh Newton Hereford 61 B6
Welsh St Donats V Glam 41 D5
Welshampton Shrops 110 B3
Welshpool = Y Trallwng Powys 93 A6
Welton Cumb 164 A1
Welton E Yorks 142 A1
Welton Lincs 133 B5
Welton Northants 82 A2
Welton Hill Lincs 133 A5
Welton le Marsh Lincs 135 C4
Welton le Wold Lincs 134 A2

Welwick E Yorks 143 A5
Welwyn Herts 68 B2
Welwyn Garden City Herts 68 B2
Wem Shrops 111 C4
Wembdon Som 28 B2
Wembley London 49 A4
Wembley Stadium London 49 A4
Wembury Devon 7 C4
Wembworthy Devon 12 A1
Wemyss Bay Invclyd 204 B1
Wenallt Ceredig 75 A5
Wenallt Gwyn 109 A4
Wendens Ambo Essex 85 D7
Wendlebury Oxon 65 B6
Wendling Norf 119 D6
Wendover Bucks 66 C3
Wendron Corn 3 B4
Wendy Cambs 85 C5
Wenfordbridge Corn 10 D1
Wenhaston Suff 105 D5
Wennington Cambs 100 D4
Wennington London 50 A2
Wennington Lancs 155 D5
Wensley Derbys 130 C2
Wensley N Yorks 157 C4
Wentbridge W Yorks 140 B2
Wentnor Shrops 94 B1
Wentworth Cambs 101 D6
Wentworth S Yorks 140 D1
Wenvoe V Glam 41 D6
Weobley Hereford 78 B2
Weobley Marsh Hereford 78 B2
Wereham Norf 102 A2
Wergs W Mid 95 A6
Wern Powys 109 D4
Wern Powys 110 D1
Wernffrwd Swansea 57 C5
Wernyrheolydd Mon 61 B5
Werrington Corn 10 C4
Werrington P'boro 100 A3
Werrington Staffs 112 A3
Wervin Ches 127 B4
Wesham Lancs 144 D4
Wessington Derbys 130 D3
West Acre Norf 119 D4
West Adderbury Oxon 82 D1
West Allerdean Northumb 198 B3
West Alvington Devon 7 C6
West Amesbury Wilts 31 A5
West Anstey Devon 26 C3
West Ashby Lincs 134 B2
West Ashling W Sus 19 A7
West Ashton Wilts 44 D2
West Auckland Durham 167 C4
West Ayton N Yorks 160 C3
West Bagborough Som 27 B6
West Barkwith Lincs 133 A6
West Barnby N Yorks 169 D6
West Barns E Loth 210 C3
West Barsham Norf 119 B6
West Bay Dorset 15 B4
West Beckham Norf 120 B3
West Bedfont Sur 48 B3
West Benhar N Lnrk 208 D1
West Bergholt Essex 70 A3
West Bexington Dorset 15 C5
West Bilney Norf 119 D4
West Blatchington Brighton 21 B5
West Bowling W Yorks 147 D5
West Bradford Lancs 146 C1
West Bradley Som 29 B5
West Bretton W Yorks 139 B5
West Bridgford Notts 114 B3
West Bromwich W Mid 96 B3
West Buckland Devon 26 B1
West Buckland Som 28 C1
West Burrafirth Shetland 285 H4
West Burton N Yorks 156 C4
West Burton W Sus 20 A2
West Butterwick N Lincs 141 C6
West Byfleet Sur 48 C3
West Caister Norf 121 D7
West Calder W Loth 208 D3
West Camel Som 29 C5
West Challow Oxon 46 A1
West Chelborough Dorset 15 A5
West Chevington Northumb 189 D5
West Chiltington W Sus 20 A3
West Chinnock Som 29 D4
West Chisenbury Wilts 45 D5
West Clandon Sur 34 A3
West Cliffe Kent 39 A5
West Clyne Highld 274 D2
West Clyth Highld 275 A6
West Coker Som 29 D5
West Compton Dorset 15 B5

West Compton Som 29 A5
West Cowick E Yorks 140 A4
West Cranmore Som 29 A6
West Cross Swansea 57 D6
West Cullery Aberds 245 B4
West Curry Corn 10 B3
West Curthwaite Cumb 175 D6
West Darlochan Argyll 190 C2
West Dean Wilts 31 C6
West Dean W Sus 20 A1
West Deeping Lincs 100 A3
West Derby Mers 136 D2
West Dereham Norf 102 A2
West Didsbury Gtr Man 138 D1
West Ditchburn Northumb 189 A4
West Down Devon 25 A6
West Drayton London 48 B3
West Drayton Notts 132 B2
West Ella E Yorks 142 A2
West End Beds 84 B1
West End E Yorks 150 D2
West End E Yorks 151 D4
West End Hants 32 D3
West End Lancs 137 A6
West End Norf 103 A5
West End Norf 121 D7
West End N Som 42 C3
West End N Yorks 147 B5
West End Oxon 65 C5
West End S Lnrk 195 B4
West End Suff 105 C5
West End Sur 48 C2
West End S Yorks 141 C4
West End Wilts 30 C3
West End W Berks 44 B3
West End W Sus 21 A5
West End Green Hants 47 C4
West Farleigh Kent 37 A5
West Felton Shrops 110 C2
West Fenton E Loth 210 B1
West Ferry Dundee 221 A4
West Firle E Sus 22 B2
West Ginge Oxon 46 A2
West Grafton Wilts 45 C6
West Green Hants 47 D5
West Greenskares Aberds 268 C2
West Grimstead Wilts 31 C6
West Grinstead W Sus 35 D4
West Haddlesey N Yorks 140 A3
West Haddon Northants 98 D3
West Hagbourne Oxon 46 A3
West Hagley Worcs 96 C2
West Hall Cumb 176 C3
West Hallam Derbys 114 A2
West Halton N Lincs 141 A7
West Ham London 49 A7
West Handley Derbys 130 B3
West Hanney Oxon 65 D5
West Hanningfield Essex 70 D1
West Hardwick W Yorks 140 B2
West Harnham Wilts 31 C5
West Harptree Bath 43 D4
West Hatch Som 28 C2
West Head Norf 102 A1
West Heath Ches 128 C3
West Heath Hants 34 A1
West Heath Hants 46 D3
West Helmsdale Highld 274 C4
West Hendred Oxon 46 A2
West Heslerton N Yorks 160 D3
West Hill Devon 13 B5
West Hill E Yorks 151 A4
West Hill N Som 42 B3
West Hoathly W Sus 35 C6
West Holme Dorset 16 C1
West Horndon Essex 50 A3
West Horrington Som 29 A5
West Horsley Sur 34 A3
West Horton Northumb 198 C4
West Hougham Kent 39 A4
West Houlland Shetland 285 H4
West-houses Derbys 131 D4
West Huntington York 149 B5
West Hythe Kent 38 B3
West Ilsley W Berks 46 A2
West Itchenor W Sus 19 A6
West Keal Lincs 134 C3
West Kennett Wilts 45 C5
West Kilbride N Ayrs 204 D2
West Kingsdown Kent 50 C3
West Kington Wilts 44 B2
West Kinharrachie Aberds 257 C4
West Kirby Mers 126 A2
West Knapton N Yorks 160 D2
West Knighton Dorset 16 C1
West Knoyle Wilts 30 B2

West Kyloe Northumb 199 B4
West Lambrook Som 28 D4
West Langdon Kent 39 A5
West Langwell Highld 273 D4
West Lavington Wilts 44 D4
West Lavington W Sus 34 D1
West Layton N Yorks 157 A5
West Lea Durham 168 A2
West Leake Notts 114 C3
West Learmouth Northumb 198 C2
West Leigh Devon 12 A1
West Lexham Norf 119 D5
West Lilling N Yorks 149 A5
West Linton Borders 195 A6
West Liss Hants 33 C6
West Littleton S Glos 43 B6
West Looe Corn 6 B1
West Luccombe Som 26 A3
West Lulworth Dorset 16 C2
West Lutton N Yorks 150 A2
West Lydford Som 29 B5
West Lyng Som 28 C3
West Lynn Norf 118 C3
West Malling Kent 37 A4
West Malvern Worcs 79 C5
West Marden W Sus 33 D6
West Marina E Sus 23 B5
West Markham Notts 132 B2
West Marsh NE Lincs 143 B4
West Marton N Yorks 146 B2
West Meon Hants 33 C5
West Mersea Essex 71 B4
West Midlands Safari Park, Kidderminster Worcs 95 D6
West Milton Dorset 15 B5
West Minster Kent 51 B6
West Molesey Sur 48 C4
West Monkton Som 28 C2
West Moors Dorset 17 A4
West Morriston Borders 197 B5
West Muir Angus 232 B3
West Ness N Yorks 159 D5
West Newham Northumb 178 B2
West Newton E Yorks 151 D4
West Newton Norf 118 C3
West Norwood London 49 B6
West Ogwell Devon 12 D3
West Orchard Dorset 30 D2
West Overton Wilts 45 C5
West Park Hrtlpl 168 B2
West Parley Dorset 17 B4
West Peckham Kent 36 A4
West Pelton Durham 179 D4
West Pennard Som 29 B5
West Pentire Corn 4 A2
West Perry Cambs 84 A3
West Putford Devon 25 D4
West Quantoxhead Som 27 A6
West Rainton Durham 167 A6
West Rasen Lincs 133 A5
West Raynham Norf 119 C5
West Retford Notts 132 A1
West Rounton N Yorks 158 A3
West Row Suff 102 D2
West Rudham Norf 119 C5
West Runton Norf 120 A3
West Saltoun E Loth 210 D1
West Sandwick Shetland 284 E6
West Scrafton N Yorks 157 C4
West Sleekburn Northumb 179 A4
West Somerset Railway, Minehead Som 27 A4
West Somerton Norf 121 D6
West Stafford Dorset 16 C1
West Stockwith Notts 141 D5
West Stoke W Sus 20 B1
West Stonesdale N Yorks 156 A2
West Stoughton Som 28 A4
West Stour Dorset 30 C1
West Stourmouth Kent 53 C4
West Stow Suff 103 D4
West Stowell Wilts 45 C5
West Strathan Highld 277 B6
West Stratton Hants 32 A4
West Street Kent 37 A7
West Tanfield N Yorks 157 D6
West Taphouse Corn 5 A6
West Tarbert Argyll 202 B3
West Thirston Northumb 189 D4
West Thorney W Sus 19 A6
West Thurrock Thurrock 50 B2
West Tilbury Thurrock 50 B3
West Tisted Hants 33 C5
West Tofts Norf 103 B4
West Tofts Perth 219 A6

West Torrington Lincs 133 A
West Town Hants 19 B
West Town N Som 42 C
West Tytherley Hants 32 C
West Tytherton Wilts 44 B
West Walton Norf 118 D
West Walton Highway Norf 118 D
West Wellow Hants 32 D
West Wemyss Fife 209 A
West Wick N Som 42 C
West Wickham Cambs 86 C
West Wickham London 49 C
West Williamston Pembs 55 C
West Willoughby Lincs 116 A
West Winch Norf 118 C
West Winterslow Wilts 31 B
West Wittering W Sus 19 B
West Witton N Yorks 157 C
West Woodburn Northumb 177 A
West Woodhay W Berks 46 C
West Woodlands Som 30
West Worldham Hants 33
West Worlington Devon 26
West Worthing W Sus 21
West Wratting Cambs 86
West Wycombe Bucks 66 B
West Wylam Northumb 178
West Yell Shetland 284
Westacott Devon 25
Westbere Kent 52
Westborough Lincs 115
Westbourne Bmouth 17
Westbourne Suff 88
Westbourne W Sus 19
Westbrook W Berks 46
Westbury Bucks 82
Westbury Shrops 94
Westbury Wilts 44
Westbury Leigh Wilts 44
Westbury-on-Severn Glos 62
Westbury on Trym Bristol 43
Westbury-sub-Mendip Som 29
Westby Lancs 144
Westcliff-on-Sea Sthend 51
Westcombe Som 29
Westcote Glos 64
Westcott Bucks 66
Westcott Devon 13
Westcott Sur 35
Westcott Barton Oxon 65
Westdean E Sus 22
Westdene Brighton 21
Wester Aberchalder Highld 252
Wester Balgedie Perth 219
Wester Culbeuchly Aberds 268
Wester Dechmont W Loth 208
Wester Denoon Angus 232
Wester Fintray Aberds 245
Wester Gruinards Highld 264
Wester Lealty Highld 264
Wester Milton Highld 253
Wester Newburn Fife 220
Wester Quarff Shetland 285
Wester Skeld Shetland 285
Westerdale Highld 280
Westerdale N Yorks 159
Westerfield Shetland 285
Westerfield Suff 88
Westergate W Sus 20
Westerham Kent 36
Westerhope T & W 178
Westerleigh S Glos 43
Westerton Angus 233
Westerton Durham 167
Westerton W Sus 20
Westerwick Shetland 285
Westfield Cumb 162
Westfield E Sus 23
Westfield Hereford 79
Westfield Highld 279
Westfield N Lnrk 207
Westfield Norf 103
Westfield W Loth 208
Westfields Dorset 16
Westfields of Rattray Perth 231
Westgate Durham 166
Westgate N Lincs 141
Westgate Norf 119
Westgate on Sea Kent 53
Westhall Aberds 256
Westhall Suff 105

Westham Dorset 15 D6
Westham E Sus 22 B4
Westham Som 28 A4
Westhampnett W Sus 20 B1
Westhay Som 28 A4
Westhead Lancs 136 C3
Westhide Hereford 78 C3
Westhill Aberds 245 B5
Westhill Highld 252 B3
Westhope Hereford 78 B2
Westhope Shrops 94 C2
Westhorpe Lincs 117 B5
Westhorpe Suff 87 A6
Westhoughton Gtr Man 137 C5
Westhouse N Yorks 155 D5
Westhumble Sur 35 A4
Westing Shetland 284 C7
Westlake Devon 7 B5
Westleigh Devon 25 C5
Westleigh Devon 27 D5
Westleigh Gtr Man 137 C5
Westleton Suff 89 A5
Westley Shrops 94 A1
Westley Suff 87 A4
Westley Waterless Cambs 86 B3
Westlington Bucks 66 B2
Westlinton Cumb 175 B6
Westmarsh Kent 53 C4
Westmeston E Sus 21 A6
Westmill Herts 68 A3
Westminster London 49 B6
Westminster Cathedral, London 49 B5
Westmuir Angus 232 C1
Westness Orkney 282 E4
Westnewton Cumb 174 D4
Westnewton Northumb 198 C3
Westoe T & W 179 C5
Weston Bath 43 C6
Weston Ches 128 D2
Weston Devon 13 C6
Weston Dorset 15 D6
Weston Halton 127 A5
Weston Hants 33 C6
Weston Herts 85 D4
Weston Lincs 117 C5
Weston Notts 132 C2
Weston Northants 82 C2
Weston N Yorks 147 C5
Weston Shrops 94 B3
Weston Shrops 111 C4
Weston Staffs 112 C3
Weston W Berks 46 B1
Weston Beggard Hereford 78 C3
Weston by Welland Northants 99 B4
Weston Colville Cambs 86 B3
Weston Coyney Stoke 112 A3
Weston Favell Northants 83 A4
Weston Green Cambs 86 B2
Weston Green Norf 120 D3
Weston Heath Shrops 112 D1
Weston Hills Lincs 117 C5
Weston-in-Gordano Som 42 B3
Weston Jones Staffs 111 C6
Weston Longville Norf 120 D3
Weston Lullingfields Shrops 110 C3
Weston-on-the-Green Oxon 65 B6
Weston-on-Trent Derbys 114 C2
Weston Park Staffs 112 D2
Weston Patrick Hants 33 A5
Weston Rhyn Shrops 110 B1
Weston-Sub-Edge Glos 80 C4
Weston-super-Mare Som 42 C2
Weston Turville Bucks 66 B3
Weston under Lizard Staffs 112 D2
Weston under Penyard Hereford 62 A2
Weston under Wetherley Warks 81 A6
Weston Underwood Derbys 113 A6
Weston Underwood M Keynes 83 B5
Westonbirt Glos 44 A2
Westonbirt Arboretum, Tetbury Glos 44 A2
Westoncommon Shrops 110 C3
Westoning Beds 84 D2
Westonzoyland Som 28 B3
Westow N Yorks 149 A6
Westport Argyll 190 C2

Westport Som 28 D3
Westray Airport Orkney 282 B5
Westrigg W Loth 208 D2
Westruther Borders 197 B5
Westry Cambs 101 B5
Westville Notts 114 A3
Westward Cumb 175 D5
Westward Ho! Devon 25 C5
Westwell Kent 38 A1
Westwell Oxon 64 C3
Westwell Leacon Kent 38 A1
Westwick Cambs 85 A6
Westwick Durham 166 D3
Westwick Norf 121 C4
Westwood Devon 13 B5
Westwood Wilts 44 D2
Westwoodside N Lincs 141 D5
Wetheral Cumb 176 D2
Wetherby W Yorks 148 C3
Wetherby Racecourse W Yorks 148 C3
Wetherden Suff 87 A6
Wetheringsett Suff 88 A2
Wethersfield Essex 86 D3
Wethersta Shetland 284 G5
Wetherup Street Suff 88 A2
Wetley Rocks Staffs 112 A3
Wettenhall Ches 127 C6
Wetton Staffs 129 D6
Wetwang E Yorks 150 B2
Wetwood Staffs 111 B6
Wexcombe Wilts 45 D6
Wexham Street Bucks 48 A2
Weybourne Norf 120 A3
Weybread Suff 104 C3
Weybridge Sur 48 C3
Weycroft Devon 14 B3
Weydale Highld 280 B3
Weyhill Hants 32 A2
Weymouth Dorset 15 D6
Weymouth Sea Life Park Dorset 15 C6
Whaddon Bucks 83 D5
Whaddon Cambs 85 C5
Whaddon Glos 63 B4
Whaddon Wilts 31 C5
Whale Cumb 164 C3
Whaley Derbys 131 B5
Whaley Bridge Derbys 129 A5
Whaley Thorns Derbys 131 B5
Whaligoe Highld 281 D5
Whalley Lancs 146 D1
Whalsay Airport Shetland 284 G7
Whalton Northumb 178 A3
Wham N Yorks 146 A1
Whaplode Lincs 117 C6
Whaplode Drove Lincs 117 D6
Whaplode St Catherine Lincs 117 C6
Wharfe N Yorks 146 A1
Wharles Lancs 144 D4
Wharncliffe Side S Yorks 139 D5
Wharram le Street N Yorks 150 A1
Wharton Ches 127 C6
Wharton Green Ches 127 C6
Whashton N Yorks 157 A5
Whatcombe Dorset 16 A2
Whatcote Warks 81 C6
Whatfield Suff 87 C6
Whatley Som 14 A3
Whatley Som 30 A1
Whatlington E Sus 23 A5
Whatstandwell Derbys 130 D3
Whatton Notts 115 B5
Whauphill Dumfries 171 C6
Whaw N Yorks 156 A3
Wheatacre Norf 105 B5
Wheatcroft Derbys 130 D3
Wheathampstead Herts 68 B1
Wheathill Shrops 95 C4
Wheatley Devon 13 B4
Wheatley Hants 33 A6
Wheatley Oxon 65 C6
Wheatley S Yorks 140 C3
Wheatley W Yorks 138 A3
Wheatley Hill Durham 167 B6
Wheaton Aston Staffs 112 D2
Wheddon Cross Som 27 B4
Wheedlemont Aberds 255 D5
Wheelerstreet Sur 34 B2
Wheelock Ches 128 D2
Wheelock Heath Ches 128 D2
Wheelton Lancs 137 A5
Wheen Angus 232 A1
Wheldrake York 149 C5
Whelford Glos 64 D2

Whelpley Hill Bucks 67 C4
Whempstead Herts 68 A3
Whenby N Yorks 149 A5
Whepstead Suff 87 B4
Wherstead Suff 88 C2
Wherwell Hants 32 A2
Wheston Derbys 129 B6
Whetsted Kent 37 B4
Whetstone Leics 98 B2
Whicham Cumb 153 B2
Whichford Warks 81 D6
Whickham T & W 179 C4
Whiddon Down Devon 12 B1
Whigstreet Angus 232 D2
Whilton Northants 82 A3
Whim Farm Borders 195 A7
Whimble Devon 11 A4
Whimple Devon 13 B5
Whimpwell Green Norf 121 C5
Whinburgh Norf 103 A6
Whinnieliggate Dumfries 173 C5
Whinnyfold Aberds 257 C5
Whippingham I o W 18 B4
Whipsnade Beds 67 B5
Whipsnade Wild Animal Park, Dunstable Beds 67 B5
Whipton Devon 13 B4
Whirlow S Yorks 130 A3
Whisby Lincs 133 C4
Whissendine Rutland 115 D6
Whissonsett Norf 119 C6
Whistlefield Argyll 215 C4
Whistlefield Argyll 215 C5
Whistley Green Wokingham 47 B5
Whiston Mers 136 D3
Whiston Northants 83 A5
Whiston Staffs 112 D2
Whiston Staffs 112 A4
Whiston S Yorks 131 A4
Whitbeck Cumb 153 B2
Whitbourne Hereford 79 B5
Whitbread Hop Farm, Beltring Kent 37 B4
Whitburn T & W 179 C6
Whitburn W Loth 208 D2
Whitburn Colliery T & W 179 C6
Whitby Ches 126 B3
Whitby N Yorks 169 D6
Whitby Abbey N Yorks 169 D7
Whitbyheath Ches 126 B3
Whitchurch Bucks 66 A2
Whitchurch Cardiff 41 C6
Whitchurch Devon 11 D5
Whitchurch Hants 32 A3
Whitchurch Hereford 62 B1
Whitchurch Oxon 47 B4
Whitchurch Pembs 54 B3
Whitchurch Shrops 111 A4
Whitchurch Canonicorum Dorset 14 B3
Whitchurch Hill Oxon 47 B4
Whitcombe Dorset 15 C7
Whitcott Keysett Shrops 93 C6
White Coppice Lancs 137 B5
White Lackington Dorset 15 B7
White Ladies Aston Worcs 80 B2
White Lund Lancs 144 A4
White Mill Carms 58 C1
White Ness Shetland 285 J5
White Notley Essex 70 B1
White Pit Lincs 134 B3
White Post Notts 131 D6
White Post Farm Centre, Farnsfield Notts 131 D6
White Rocks Hereford 61 A6
White Roding Essex 69 B5
White Waltham Windsor 47 B6
Whiteacen Moray 254 B3
Whiteacre Heath Warks 97 B5
Whitebridge Highld 240 A2
Whitebrook Mon 62 C1
Whiteburn Borders 197 B4
Whitecairn Dumfries 171 B4
Whitecairns Aberds 245 A6
Whitecastle S Lnrk 195 B5
Whitechapel Lancs 145 C5
Whitecleat Orkney 283 G6
Whitecraig E Loth 209 C6
Whitecroft Glos 62 C2
Whitecross Corn 9 D5
Whitecross Falk 208 C2
Whitecross Staffs 112 C2
Whiteface Highld 264 B3
Whitefarland N Ayrs 202 D3
Whitefaulds S Ayrs 192 E2
Whitefield Gtr Man 137 C7

Whitefield Perth 219 A6
Whiteford Aberds 256 D2
Whitegate Ches 127 C6
Whitehall Blkburn 137 A5
Whitehall W Sus 35 D4
Whitehall Village Orkney 282 E7
Whitehaven Cumb 162 C2
Whitehill Hants 33 B6
Whitehills Aberds 268 C1
Whitehills S Lnrk 205 C6
Whitehouse Aberds 244 A3
Whitehouse Argyll 202 B3
Whiteinch Glasgow 205 B5
Whitekirk E Loth 210 B2
Whitelaw S Lnrk 205 D6
Whiteleas T & W 179 C5
Whiteley Bank I o W 19 C4
Whiteley Green Ches 129 B4
Whiteley Village Sur 48 C3
Whitemans Green W Sus 35 D6
Whitemire Moray 253 A5
Whitemoor Corn 5 B4
Whitemore Staffs 128 C3
Whitenap Hants 32 C2
Whiteoak Green Oxon 64 B4
Whiteparish Wilts 31 C6
Whiterashes Aberds 256 D3
Whiterow Highld 281 D5
Whiteshill Glos 63 C4
Whiteside Northumb 177 C5
Whiteside W Loth 208 D2
Whitesmith E Sus 22 A3
Whitestaunton Som 28 D2
Whitestone Devon 12 B3
Whitestone Devon 25 A5
Whitestone Warks 97 C6
Whitestones Aberds 268 D3
Whitestreet Green Suff 87 D5
Whitewall Corner N Yorks 159 D6
Whiteway Glos 63 D4
Whiteway Glos 63 B5
Whitewell Aberds 269 C4
Whitewell Lancs 145 C6
Whitewell Bottom Lancs 138 A1
Whiteworks Devon 11 D7
Whitfield Kent 39 A5
Whitfield Northants 82 D3
Whitfield Northumb 177 D5
Whitfield S Glos 62 D2
Whitford Devon 14 B2
Whitford Flint 125 B6
Whitgift E Yorks 141 A6
Whitgreave Staffs 112 C2
Whithorn Dumfries 171 C6
Whiting Bay N Ayrs 191 C6
Whitington Norf 102 B3
Whitkirk W Yorks 148 D2
Whitland Carms 56 A1
Whitletts S Ayrs 192 C3
Whitley N Yorks 140 A3
Whitley Reading 47 B5
Whitley Wilts 44 C2
Whitley Bay T & W 179 B5
Whitley Chapel Northumb 178 D1
Whitley Lower W Yorks 139 B5
Whitley Row Kent 36 A2
Whitlock's End W Mid 96 D4
Whitminster Glos 62 C3
Whitmore Staffs 112 A2
Whitnage Devon 27 D5
Whitnash Warks 81 A6
Whitney Hereford 77 C6
Whitrigg Cumb 163 A5
Whitrigg Cumb 175 C5
Whitsbury Hants 31 D5
Whitsome Borders 198 A2
Whitson Newport 42 A2
Whitstable Kent 52 C3
Whitstone Corn 10 B3
Whittingham Northumb 188 B3
Whittingslow Shrops 94 C2
Whittington Glos 63 A6
Whittington Lancs 155 D5
Whittington Shrops 110 B2
Whittington Staffs 95 C6
Whittington Staffs 97 A4
Whittington Worcs 80 B1
Whittle-le-Woods Lancs 137 A4
Whittlebury Northants 82 C3
Whittlesey Cambs 101 B4
Whittlesford Cambs 85 C6
Whittlestone Head Blkburn 137 B6
Whitton Borders 187 A6
Whitton N Lincs 141 A7
Whitton Northumb 188 C3

Whitton Powys 77 A6
Whitton Shrops 94 D3
Whitton Stockton 167 C6
Whitton Suff 88 C2
Whittonditch Wilts 45 B6
Whittonstall Northumb 178 D2
Whitway Hants 46 D2
Whitwell Derbys 131 B5
Whitwell Herts 68 A1
Whitwell I o W 18 D4
Whitwell N Yorks 157 B6
Whitwell Rutland 99 A6
Whitwell-on-the-Hill N Yorks 149 A6
Whitwell Street Norf 120 C3
Whitwick Leics 114 D2
Whitwood W Yorks 140 A2
Whitworth Lancs 138 B1
Whixall Shrops 111 B4
Whixley N Yorks 148 B3
Whoberley W Mid 97 D6
Whorlton Durham 166 D4
Whorlton N Yorks 158 A3
Whygate Northumb 177 B5
Whyle Hereford 78 A3
Whyteleafe Sur 35 A6
Wibdon Glos 62 D1
Wibsey W Yorks 147 D5
Wibtoft Leics 98 C1
Wichenford Worcs 79 A5
Wichling Kent 37 A7
Wick Bmouth 17 B5
Wick Devon 25 A5
Wick Highld 281 C5
Wick S Glos 43 B6
Wick Shetland 285 K6
Wick V Glam 40 D4
Wick Wilts 31 C5
Wick Worcs 80 C2
Wick W Sus 20 B3
Wick Airport Highld 281 C5
Wick Hill Wokingham 47 C5
Wick St Lawrence N Som 42 C2
Wicken Cambs 102 D1
Wicken Northants 83 D4
Wicken Bonhunt Essex 85 D6
Wicken Green Village Norf 119 B5
Wickenby Lincs 133 A5
Wickersley S Yorks 140 D2
Wickford Essex 70 D1
Wickham Hants 33 D4
Wickham W Berks 46 B1
Wickham Bishops Essex 70 B2
Wickham Market Suff 88 B4
Wickham St Paul Essex 87 D4
Wickham Skeith Suff 88 A1
Wickham Street Suff 86 B3
Wickham Street Suff 88 A1
Wickhambreux Kent 53 D4
Wickhambrook Suff 86 B3
Wickhamford Worcs 80 C3
Wickhampton Norf 105 A5
Wicklewood Norf 104 A1
Wickmere Norf 120 B3
Wicksteed Park, Kettering Northants 99 D5
Wickwar S Glos 43 A6
Widdington Essex 86 D1
Widdrington Northumb 189 D5
Widdrington Station Northumb 189 D5
Wide Open T & W 179 B4
Widecombe in the Moor Devon 12 D2
Widegates Corn 6 B1
Widemouth Bay Corn 10 A3
Widewall Orkney 283 H5
Widford Essex 69 C6
Widford Herts 68 B4
Widham Wilts 45 A4
Widmer End Bucks 66 D3
Widmerpool Notts 115 C4
Widnes Halton 127 A5
Wigan Gtr Man 137 C4
Wigan Pier Gtr Man 137 C4
Wiggaton Devon 13 B6
Wiggenhall St Germans Norf 118 D2
Wiggenhall St Mary Magdalen Norf 118 D2
Wiggenhall St Mary the Virgin Norf 118 D2
Wigginton Herts 67 B4

Wigginton Oxon 81 D6	Wilmington E Sus 22 B3	Winkburn Notts 132 D2	Wistanswick Shrops 111 C5
Wigginton Staffs 97 A5	Wilmington Kent 50 B2	Winkfield Brack 48 B2	Wistaston Ches 128 D1
Wigginton York 149 B4	Wilmstone Devon 11 D5	Winkfield Row Brack 48 B1	Wistaston Green Ches 128 D1
Wigglesworth N Yorks 146 B2	Wilmslow Ches 128 A3	Winkhill Staffs 129 D5	Wiston Pembs 55 C6
Wiggonby Cumb 175 C5	Wilnecote Staffs 97 A5	Winklebury Hants 47 D4	Wiston S Lnrk 195 C4
Wiggonholt W Sus 20 A3	Wilpshire Lancs 145 D6	Winkleigh Devon 12 A1	Wiston W Sus 21 A4
Wighill N Yorks 148 C3	Wilsden W Yorks 147 D4	Winksley N Yorks 157 D6	Wistow Cambs 101 C4
Wighton Norf 119 B6	Wilsford Lincs 116 A3	Winkton Dorset 17 B5	Wistow N Yorks 149 D4
Wigley Hants 32 D2	Wilsford Wilts 45 D5	Winlaton T & W 178 C3	Wiswell Lancs 146 D1
Wigmore Hereford 78 A2	Wilsford Wilts 31 B5	Winless Highld 281 C5	Witcham Cambs 101 C6
Wigmore Medway 51 C5	Wilsill N Yorks 147 A5	Winmarleigh Lancs 145 C4	Witchampton Dorset 16 A3
Wigsley Notts 132 B3	Wilsley Pound Kent 37 C5	Winnal Hereford 78 D2	Witchford Cambs 101 D7
Wigsthorpe Northants 100 C2	Wilsom Hants 33 B6	Winnall Hants 32 C3	Witham Essex 70 B2
Wigston Leics 98 B3	Wilson Leics 114 C2	Winnersh Wokingham 47 B5	Witham Friary Som 30 A1
Wigthorpe Notts 131 A5	Wilsontown S Lnrk 195 A4	Winscales Cumb 162 B3	Witham on the Hill Lincs 116 D3
Wigtoft Lincs 117 B5	Wilstead Beds 84 C2	Winscombe N Som 42 D3	Withcall Lincs 134 A2
Wigton Cumb 175 D5	Wilsthorpe Lincs 116 D3	Winsford Ches 127 C6	Withdean Brighton 21 B6
Wigtown Dumfries 171 B6	Wilstone Herts 67 B4	Winsford Som 27 B4	Witherenden Hill E Sus 36 D4
Wigtwizzle S Yorks 139 D5	Wilton Borders 186 B3	Winsham Som 14 A3	Witheridge Devon 26 D3
Wike W Yorks 148 C2	Wilton Cumb 162 C3	Winshill Staffs 113 C6	Witherley Leics 97 B6
Wike Well End S Yorks 141 B4	Wilton N Yorks 160 C2	Winskill Cumb 164 B3	Withern Lincs 135 A4
Wilbarston Northants 99 C5	Wilton Redcar 168 D3	Winslade Hants 33 A5	Withernsea E Yorks 143 A5
Wilberfoss E Yorks 149 B6	Wilton Wilts 31 B4	Winsley Wilts 44 C2	Withernwick E Yorks 151 C4
Wilberlee W Yorks 138 B3	Wilton Wilts 45 C6	Winslow Bucks 66 A2	Withersdale Street Suff 104 C3
Wilburton Cambs 101 D6	Wilton House, Salisbury Wilts 31 B5	Winson Glos 64 C1	Withersfield Suff 86 C2
Wilby Norf 103 C6	Wimbish Essex 86 D1	Winson Green W Mid 96 C3	Witherslack Cumb 154 C3
Wilby Northants 83 A5	Wimbish Green Essex 86 D2	Winsor Hants 32 D2	Withiel Corn 5 A4
Wilby Suff 104 D3	Wimblebury Staffs 112 D4	Winster Cumb 154 B3	Withiel Florey Som 27 B4
Wilcot Wilts 45 C5	Wimbledon London 49 B5	Winster Derbys 130 C2	Withington Glos 63 B6
Wilcott Shrops 110 D2	Wimbledon All England Tennis Club London 49 B5	Winston Durham 166 D4	Withington Gtr Man 138 D1
Wilcrick Newport 42 A3	Wimblington Cambs 101 B6	Winston Suff 88 A2	Withington Hereford 78 C3
Wilday Green Derbys 130 B3	Wimborne Minster Dorset 17 B4	Winston Green Suff 88 A2	Withington Shrops 111 D4
Wildboarclough Ches 129 C4	Wimborne Minster Dorset 17 B4	Winstone Glos 63 C5	Withington Staffs 112 B4
Wilden Beds 84 B2	Wimborne St Giles Dorset 31 D4	Winswell Devon 25 D5	Withington Green Ches 128 B3
Wilden Worcs 95 D6	Wimbotsham Norf 102 A2	Winter Gardens Essex 51 A4	Withleigh Devon 27 D4
Wildfowl and Wetland Centre, Martin Mere Lancs 136 B3	Wimpole Hall and Home Farm, Royston Cambs 85 B5	Winterborne Bassett Wilts 45 B5	Withnell Lancs 137 A5
Wildhern Hants 46 D1	Wimpstone Warks 81 C5	Winterborne Clenston Dorset 16 A2	Withybrook Warks 98 C1
Wildhill Herts 68 C2	Wincanton Som 29 C7	Winterborne Herringston Dorset 15 C6	Withycombe Som 27 A5
Wildlife & Dinosaur Park, Combe Martin Devon 25 A6	Wincanton Racecourse Som 29 C7	Winterborne Houghton Dorset 16 A2	Withycombe Raleigh Devon 13 C5
Wildmoor Worcs 96 D2	Wincham Ches 128 B1	Winterborne Kingston Dorset 16 B2	Withyham E Sus 36 C2
Wildsworth Lincs 141 D6	Winchburgh W Loth 208 C3	Winterborne Monkton Dorset 15 C6	Withypool Som 26 B3
Wilford Notts 114 B3	Winchcombe Glos 63 A6	Winterborne Monkton Wilts 45 B5	Witley Sur 34 C2
Wilkesley Ches 111 A5	Winchelsea E Sus 23 A7	Winterborne Stickland Dorset 16 A2	Witnesham Suff 88 B2
Wilkhaven Highld 265 B5	Winchelsea Beach E Sus 23 A7	Winterborne Whitechurch Dorset 16 A2	Witney Oxon 65 B4
Wilkieston W Loth 208 D4	Winchester Hants 32 C3	Winterborne Zelston Dorset 16 B2	Wittering P'boro 100 A2
Willand Devon 27 D5	Winchester Cathedral Hants 32 C3	Winterbourne S Glos 43 A5	Wittersham Kent 37 D6
Willaston Ches 126 B3	Winchet Hill Kent 37 B5	Winterbourne W Berks 46 B2	Witton Angus 232 A3
Willaston Ches 128 D1	Winchfield Hants 47 D5	Winterbourne Abbas Dorset 15 B6	Witton Worcs 80 A1
Willen M Keynes 83 C5	Winchmore Hill Bucks 67 D4	Winterbourne Dauntsey Wilts 31 B5	Witton Bridge Norf 121 B5
Willenhall W Mid 97 D6	Winchmore Hill London 68 D3	Winterbourne Down S Glos 43 B5	Witton Gilbert Durham 167 A5
Willenhall W Mid 96 B2	Wincle Ches 129 C4	Winterbourne Earls Wilts 31 B5	Witton-le-Wear Durham 166 B4
Willerby E Yorks 150 D3	Wincobank S Yorks 140 D1	Winterbourne Gunner Wilts 31 B5	Witton Park Durham 167 B4
Willerby N Yorks 160 D4	Windermere Cumb 154 B3	Winterbourne Steepleton Dorset 15 C6	Wiveliscombe Som 27 C5
Willersey Glos 80 D4	Winderton Warks 81 C6	Winterbourne Stoke Wilts 31 A4	Wivelrod Hants 33 B5
Willersley Hereford 77 C7	Windhill Highld 252 B1	Winterburn N Yorks 146 B3	Wivelsfield E Sus 35 D6
Willesborough Kent 38 A2	Windhouse Shetland 284 D6	Winteringham N Lincs 142 A1	Wivelsfield Green E Sus 35 D6
Willesborough Lees Kent 38 A2	Windlehurst Gtr Man 129 A4	Winterley Ches 128 D2	Wivenhoe Essex 71 A4
Willesden London 49 A5	Windlesham Sur 48 C2	Wintersett W Yorks 140 B1	Wivenhoe Cross Essex 71 A4
Willett Som 27 B6	Windley Derbys 113 A7	Wintershill Hants 32 D4	Wiveton Norf 120 A2
Willey Shrops 95 B4	Windmill Hill E Sus 22 A4	Winterton N Lincs 142 A1	Wix Essex 71 A5
Willey Warks 98 C1	Windmill Hill Som 28 D3	Winterton-on-Sea Norf 121 D6	Wixford Warks 80 B3
Willey Green Sur 34 A2	Windrush Glos 64 B2	Winthorpe Lincs 135 C5	Wixhill Shrops 111 C4
Williamscott Oxon 82 C1	Windsor N Lincs 141 B5	Winthorpe Notts 132 D3	Wixoe Suff 86 C3
Willian Herts 84 D4	Windsor Windsor 48 B2	Winton Bmouth 17 B4	Woburn Beds 83 D6
Willingale Essex 69 C5	Windsor Castle Windsor 48 B2	Winton Cumb 165 D5	Woburn Abbey, Woburn Beds 83 D6
Willingdon E Sus 22 B3	Windsor Racecourse Windsor 48 B2	Winton N Yorks 158 B3	Woburn Sands M Keynes 83 D6
Willingham Cambs 101 D6	Windsoredge Glos 63 C4	Wintringham N Yorks 160 D2	Woburn Wild Animal Kingdom Beds 83 D6
Willingham by Stow Lincs 132 A3	Windygates Fife 220 D3	Winwick Cambs 100 C3	Wokefield Park W Berks 47 C4
Willington Beds 84 C3	Windyknowe W Loth 208 D2	Winwick Northants 98 D3	Woking Sur 34 A3
Willington Derbys 113 C6	Windywalls Borders 197 C6	Winwick Warr 137 D5	Wokingham Wokingham 47 C6
Willington Durham 167 B4	Wineham W Sus 35 D5	Wirksworth Derbys 130 D2	Wolborough Devon 12 D3
Willington T & W 179 C5	Winestead E Yorks 143 A4	Wirksworth Moor Derbys 130 D3	Wold Newton E Yorks 160 D4
Willington Warks 81 D5	Winewall Lancs 146 C3	Wirswall Ches 111 A4	Wold Newton NE Lincs 143 D4
Willington Corner Ches 127 C5	Winfarthing Norf 104 C2	Wisbech Cambs 101 A6	Woldingham Sur 35 A6
Willisham Tye Suff 87 B6	Winford I o W 19 C4	Wisbech St Mary Cambs 101 A6	Wolfclyde S Lnrk 195 C5
Willitoft E Yorks 149 D6	Winford N Som 43 C4	Wisborough Green W Sus 34 D3	Wolferton Norf 118 C3
Williton Som 27 A5	Winforton Hereford 77 C6	Wiseton Notts 132 A2	Wolfhill Perth 219 A6
Willoughbridge Staffs 111 A6	Winfrith Newburgh Dorset 16 C2	Wishaw N Lnrk 194 A2	Wolf's Castle Pembs 55 B5
Willoughby Lincs 135 B4	Wing Bucks 66 A3	Wishaw Warks 97 B4	Wolfsdale Pembs 55 B5
Willoughby Warks 82 A2	Wing Rutland 99 A5	Wisley Sur 34 A3	Woll Borders 186 A3
Willoughby-on-the-Wolds Notts 115 C4	Wingate Durham 168 B2	Wispington Lincs 134 B2	Wollaston Northants 83 A6
Willoughby Waterleys Leics 98 B2	Wingates Gtr Man 137 C5	Wissenden Kent 37 B7	Wollaston Shrops 110 D2
Willoughton Lincs 142 D1	Wingates Northumb 189 D4	Wissett Suff 105 D4	Wollaton Nottingham 114 B3
Willows Green Essex 69 B7	Wingerworth Derbys 130 C3	Wistanstow Shrops 94 C2	Wollaton Hall Nottingham 114 B3
Willsbridge S Glos 43 B5	Wingfield Beds 67 A5	Wistanstow Shrops 94 C2	Wollerton Shrops 111 B5
Willsworthy Devon 11 C6	Wingfield Suff 104 D3		Wollescote W Mid 96 C2
Wilmcote Warks 81 B4	Wingfield Wilts 44 D2		Wolsingham Durham 166 B3
Wilmington Devon 14 B2	Wingham Kent 53 D4		Wolstanton Staffs 112 A2
	Wingmore Kent 38 A3		Wolston Warks 97 D7
	Wingrave Bucks 66 B3		Wolvercote Oxon 65 C5
			Wolverhampton W Mid 96 B2
			Wolverhampton Racecourse W Mid 96 A2
			Wolverley Shrops 110 B3

Wolverley Worcs 95 D
Wolverton Hants 46 D1
Wolverton M Keynes 83 C
Wolverton Common Hants 46 D1
Wolverton Warks 81 A
Wolvesnewton Mon 61 D
Wolvey Warks 98
Wolviston Stockton 168 C
Wombleton N Yorks 159
Wombourne Staffs 95
Wombwell S Yorks 140
Womenswold Kent 53
Womersley N Yorks 140
Wonastow Mon 61
Wonersh Sur 34
Wonson Devon 12
Wonston Hants 32
Wooburn Bucks 48
Wooburn Green Bucks 48
Wood Dalling Norf 120
Wood End Herts 68
Wood End Warks 96
Wood End Warks 97
Wood Enderby Lincs 134
Wood Field Sur 35
Wood Green London 68
Wood Green Animal Shelter, Godmanchester Cambs 85
Wood Hayes W Mid 96
Wood Lanes Ches 129
Wood Norton Norf 120
Wood Street Norf 121
Wood Street Sur 34
Wood Walton Cambs 100
Woodacott Devon 11
Woodale N Yorks 156
Woodbank Argyll 190
Woodbastwick Norf 121
Woodbeck Notts 132
Woodborough Notts 115
Woodborough Wilts 45
Woodbridge Dorset 29
Woodbridge Suff 88
Woodbury Devon 13
Woodbury Salterton Devon 13
Woodchester Glos 63
Woodchurch Kent 38
Woodchurch Mers 126
Woodcombe Som 27
Woodcote Oxon 47
Woodcott Hants 46
Woodcroft Glos 62
Woodcutts Dorset 30
Woodditton Cambs 86
Woodeaton Oxon 65
Woodend Cumb 153
Woodend Northants 82
Woodend W Sus 19
Woodend Northants 82
Woodfalls Wilts 31
Woodfield Oxon 65
Woodfield S Ayrs 192
Woodford Corn 24
Woodford Devon 7
Woodford Glos 62
Woodford London 68
Woodford Gtr Man 128
Woodford Northants 99
Woodford Bridge London 68
Woodford Halse Northants 82
Woodgate Norf 120
Woodgate W Mid 96
Woodgate Worcs 80
Woodgate W Sus 20
Woodgreen Hants 31
Woodhall Herts 68
Woodhall Invclyd 204
Woodhall N Yorks 156
Woodhall Spa Lincs 134
Woodham Sur 48
Woodham Ferrers Essex 70
Woodham Mortimer Essex 70
Woodham Walter Essex 70
Woodhaven Fife 220
Woodhead Aberds 256
Woodhey Gtr Man 137
Woodhill Shrops 95
Woodhorn Northumb 179
Woodhouse Leics 114
Woodhouse N Lincs 141
Woodhouse S Yorks 131
Woodhouse W Yorks 148
Woodhouse W Yorks 147
Woodhouse Eaves Leics 114
Woodhouse Park Gtr Man 128
Woodhouselee Midloth 209

oodhouselees Dumfries 175 A6
oodhouses Staffs 113 D5
oodhurst Cambs 101 D5
oodingdean Brighton 21 B6
oodkirk W Yorks 139 A5
oodland Devon 8 A1
oodland Durham 166 C3
oodland Leisure Park,
  Dartmouth Devon 8 B2
oodlands Aberds 245 C4
oodlands Dorset 17 A4
oodlands Hants 32 D2
oodlands Highld 264 D1
oodlands S Yorks 148 B2
oodlands Park Windsor 47 B6
oodlands St Mary
  W Berks 46 B1
oodlane Staffs 113 C5
oodleigh Devon 7 C6
oodlesford W Yorks 139 A6
oodley Gtr Man 138 D2
oodley Wokingham 47 B5
oodmancote Glos 62 D3
oodmancote Glos 63 C6
oodmancote Glos 63 A5
oodmancote W Sus 19 A6
oodmancote W Sus 21 A5
oodmancott Hants 33 A4
oodmansey E Yorks 150 D3
oodmansterne Sur 35 A5
oodminton Wilts 31 C4
oodnesborough Kent 53 D5
oodnewton Northants 100 B2
oodplumpton Lancs 145 D5
oodrising Norf 103 A5
ood's Green E Sus 36 C4
oodseaves Shrops 111 B5
oodseaves Staffs 112 C1
oodsend Wilts 45 B6
oodsetts S Yorks 131 A5
oodsford Dorset 16 B1
oodside Aberdeen 245 B6
oodside Aberds 257 B5
oodside Brack 48 B2
oodside Fife 220 D4
oodside Hants 18 B2
oodside Herts 68 C2
oodside Perth 220 A2
oodside Farm &
  Wildfowl Park, Luton
  Beds 67 B5
oodside of Arbeadie
  Aberds 245 C4
oodstock Oxon 65 B5
oodstock Pembs 55 B6
oodthorpe Derbys 131 B4
oodthorpe Leics 114 D3
oodthorpe Lincs 135 A4
oodthorpe York 149 C4
odton Norf 104 B3
odtown Devon 25 C5
odtown Devon 25 C5
odvale Mers 136 B2
odville Derbys 113 D7
odyates Dorset 31 D4
offerton Shrops 78 A3
okey Som 29 A5
okey Hole Som 29 A5
okey Hole Caves &
  apermill, Wells Som 29 A5
ol Dorset 16 C2
olacombe Devon 25 A5
olage Green Kent 39 A4
olaston Glos 62 D1
olavington Som 28 A3
olbeding W Sus 34 D1
oldale W Yorks 139 C4
oler Northumb 188 A2
olfardisworthy Devon 24 C4
olfardisworthy Devon 12 A3
olfords Cottages
  nrk 195 A5
ghampton W Berks 46 C3
lhope Hereford 79 D4
lhope Cockshoot
  reford 79 D4
land Dorset 16 A1
laton Devon 25 D5
lley Bath 43 C6
lley Cambs 100 D3
ley Corn 24 D3
ley Derbys 130 C3
ley W Yorks 139 B6
mer Green Herts 68 B2
mere Green Worcs 80 A2
pit Suff 87 A5

Woolscott Warks 82 A1
Woolsington T & W 178 C3
Woolstanwood Ches 128 D1
Woolstaston Shrops 94 B2
Woolsthorpe Lincs 115 B6
Woolsthorpe Lincs 116 C2
Woolston Devon 7 C6
Woolston Shrops 94 C2
Woolston Shrops 110 C2
Woolston Soton 32 D3
Woolston Warr 127 A0
Woolstone M Keynes 83 D5
Woolstone Oxon 45 A6
Woolton Mers 127 A4
Woolton Hill Hants 46 C2
Woolverstone Suff 88 D2
Woolverton Som 44 D1
Woolwich London 50 B1
Woolwich Ferry London 50 B1
Woonton Hereford 78 B1
Wooperton Northumb 188 A3
Woore Shrops 111 A6
Wootton Beds 84 C2
Wootton Hants 17 B6
Wootton Hereford 78 B1
Wootton Kent 39 A4
Wootton N Lincs 142 B2
Wootton Northants 83 B4
Wootton Oxon 65 B5
Wootton Oxon 65 C5
Wootton Shrops 94 D2
Wootton Shrops 110 C2
Wootton Staffs 112 C2
Wootton Staffs 113 A5
Wootton Bassett Wilts 45 A4
Wootton Bridge I o W 18 B4
Wootton Common I o W 18 B4
Wootton Courtenay Som 27 A4
Wootton Fitzpaine Dorset 14 B3
Wootton Rivers Wilts 45 C5
Wootton St Lawrence
  Hants 46 D3
Wootton Wawen Warks 81 A4
Worcester Worcs 79 B6
Worcester Cathedral
  Worcs 79 B6
Worcester Park London 49 C5
Worcester Racecourse
  Worcs 79 B6
Wordsley W Mid 96 C1
Worfield Shrops 95 B5
Work Orkney 282 F5
Workington Cumb 162 B2
Worksop Notts 131 B5
Worlaby N Lincs 142 B2
World of James Herriot
  N Yorks 158 C3
World's End W Berks 46 B2
Worle N Som 42 C2
Worleston Ches 127 D6
Worlingham Suff 105 C5
Worlington Suff 102 D2
Worlingworth Suff 88 A3
Wormald Green N Yorks 148 A2
Wormbridge Hereford 78 D2
Wormegay Norf 118 D3
Wormelow Tump Hereford 78 D2
Wormhill Derbys 129 B6
Wormingford Essex 87 D5
Worminghall Bucks 66 C1
Wormington Glos 80 D3
Worminster Som 29 A5
Wormit Fife 220 B3
Wormleighton Warks 82 B1
Wormley Herts 68 C3
Wormley Sur 34 C2
Wormley West End Herts 68 C3
Wormshill Kent 37 A6
Wormsley Hereford 78 C2
Worplesdon Sur 34 A2
Worrall S Yorks 139 D6
Worsbrough S Yorks 139 C6
Worsbrough Common
  S Yorks 139 C6
Worsley Gtr Man 137 C6
Worstead Norf 121 C5
Worsthorne Lancs 146 D2
Worston Lancs 146 C1
Worswell Devon 7 C4
Worth Kent 53 D5
Worth W Sus 35 C6
Worth Matravers Dorset 16 D3
Wortham Suff 104 D1
Worthen Shrops 94 A1
Worthenbury Wrex 110 A3
Worthing Norf 120 D1

Worthing W Sus 21 B4
Worthington Leics 114 C2
Worting Hants 47 D4
Wortley S Yorks 139 D6
Wortley W Yorks 147 D6
Worton N Yorks 156 B3
Worton Wilts 44 D3
Wortwell Norf 104 C3
Wotherton Shrops 93 A6
Wotter Devon 7 A4
Wotton Sur 35 B4
Wotton-under-Edge Glos 62 D3
Wotton Underwood Bucks 66 B1
Woughton on the Green
  M Keynes 83 D5
Wouldham Kent 51 C4
Wrabness Essex 88 D2
Wrafton Devon 25 B5
Wragby Lincs 133 B6
Wragby W Yorks 140 B2
Wragholme Lincs 143 D5
Wramplingham Norf 104 A2
Wrangbrook W Yorks 140 B2
Wrangham Aberds 256 C1
Wrangle Lincs 135 D4
Wrangle Bank Lincs 135 D4
Wrangle Lowgate Lincs 135 D4
Wrangway Som 27 D6
Wrantage Som 28 C3
Wrawby N Lincs 142 C2
Wraxall Dorset 15 A5
Wraxall N Som 42 B3
Wraxall Som 29 B6
Wray Lancs 145 A6
Wraysbury Windsor 48 B3
Wrayton Lancs 155 D5
Wrea Green Lancs 144 D3
Wreay Cumb 164 C2
Wreay Cumb 164 A2
Wrecclesham Sur 34 B1
Wrecsam = Wrexham
  Wrex 126 D3
Wrekenton T & W 179 D4
Wrelton N Yorks 159 C6
Wrenbury Ches 111 A4
Wrench Green N Yorks 160 C3
Wreningham Norf 104 B2
Wrentham Suff 105 C5
Wrenthorpe W Yorks 139 A6
Wrentnall Shrops 94 A2
Wressle E Yorks 149 D6
Wressle N Lincs 142 C1
Wrestlingworth Beds 85 C4
Wretham Norf 103 C5
Wretton Norf 102 B2
Wrexham = Wrecsam
  Wrex 126 D3
Wrexham Industrial
  Estate Wrex 110 A2
Wribbenhall Worcs 95 D5
Wrightington Bar Lancs 136 B4
Wrinehill Staffs 111 A6
Wrington N Som 42 C3
Writhlington Bath 43 D6
Writtle Essex 69 C6
Wrockwardine Telford 111 D5
Wroot N Lincs 141 C5
Wrotham Kent 36 A4
Wrotham Heath Kent 36 A4
Wroughton Thamesdown 45 A5
Wroxall I o W 19 D4
Wroxall Warks 97 D5
Wroxeter Shrops 94 A3
Wroxham Norf 121 D5
Wroxham Barns, Hoveton
  Norf 121 C5
Wroxton Oxon 81 C7
Wyaston Derbys 113 A5
Wyberton Lincs 117 A6
Wyboston Beds 84 B3
Wybunbury Ches 111 A6
Wych Cross E Sus 36 C2
Wychbold Worcs 80 A2
Wyck Hants 33 B6
Wyck Rissington Glos 64 A2
Wycoller Lancs 146 D3
Wycomb Leics 115 C5
Wycombe Marsh Bucks 66 B3
Wyddial Herts 85 D5
Wye Kent 38 A2
Wyesham Mon 61 B7
Wyfordby Leics 115 D5
Wyke Dorset 30 C1
Wyke Shrops 95 A4
Wyke Sur 34 A2
Wyke W Yorks 139 A4
Wyke Regis Dorset 15 D6

Wykeham N Yorks 160 C3
Wykeham N Yorks 159 D7
Wyken W Mid 97 C6
Wykey Shrops 110 C2
Wylam Northumb 178 C3
Wylde Green W Mid 96 B4
Wyllie Caerph 41 B6
Wylye Wilts 31 B4
Wymering Ptsmth 19 A5
Wymeswold Leics 115 C4
Wymington Beds 83 A6
Wymondham Leics 115 D6
Wymondham Norf 104 A2
Wyndham Bridgend 40 B4
Wynford Eagle Dorset 15 B5
Wyng Orkney 283 H4
Wynyard Village Stockton 168 C2
Wyre Piddle Worcs 80 C2
Wysall Notts 115 C4
Wythall Worcs 96 D3
Wytham Oxon 65 C5
Wythburn Cumb 163 C6
Wythenshawe Gtr Man 128 A3
Wythop Mill Cumb 163 B4
Wyton Cambs 101 D4
Wyverstone Suff 87 A6
Wyverstone Street Suff 87 A6
Wyville Lincs 116 C1
Wyvis Lodge Highld 263 C6

Y

Y Bala = Bala Gwyn 108 B4
Y Barri = Barry V Glam 41 E6
Y Bont-Faen =
  Cowbridge V Glam 41 D4
Y Drenewydd =
  Newtown Powys 93 B5
Y Felinheli Gwyn 123 D5
Y Fenni = Abergavenny
  Mon 61 B4
Y Fflint = Flint Flint 126 B2
Y Ffôr Gwyn 106 C3
Y-Ffrith Denb 125 A5
Y Gelli Gandryll =
  Hay-on-Wye Powys 77 C6
Y Mwmbwls = The
  Mumbles Swansea 57 D6
Y Pil = Pyle Bridgend 40 C3
Y Rhws = Rhoose V Glam 41 E5
Y Rhyl = Rhyl Denb 125 A5
Y Trallwng = Welshpool
  Powys 93 A6
Y Waun = Chirk Wrex 110 B1
Yaddlethorpe N Lincs 141 C6
Yafford I o W 18 C3
Yafforth N Yorks 158 B2
Yalding Kent 37 A4
Yanworth Glos 63 B6
Yapham E Yorks 149 B6
Yapton W Sus 20 B2
Yarburgh Lincs 143 D5
Yarcombe Devon 14 A2
Yard Som 27 B5
Yardley W Mid 96 C4
Yardley Gobion Northants 83 C4
Yardley Hastings Northants 83 B5
Yardro Powys 77 B6
Yarkhill Hereford 79 C4
Yarlet Staffs 112 C3
Yarlington Som 29 C6
Yarlside Cumb 153 D3
Yarm Stockton 168 D2
Yarmouth I o W 18 C2
Yarmouth Racecourse
  Norf 121 D7
Yarnbrook Wilts 44 D2
Yarnfield Staffs 112 B2
Yarnscombe Devon 25 C6
Yarnton Oxon 65 B5
Yarpole Hereford 78 A2
Yarrow Borders 196 D2
Yarrow Feus Borders 196 D2
Yarsop Hereford 78 C2
Yarwell Northants 100 B2
Yate S Glos 43 A6
Yateley Hants 47 C5
Yatesbury Wilts 45 B4
Yattendon W Berks 46 B3
Yatton Hereford 78 A2
Yatton Hereford 79 D4
Yatton N Som 42 C3
Yatton Keynell Wilts 44 B2
Yaverland I o W 19 C5

Yeading London 48 A4
Yeadon W Yorks 147 C6
Yealand Conyers Lancs 154 D4
Yealand Redmayne Lancs 154 D4
Yealmpton Devon 7 B4
Yearby Redcar 168 C4
Yearsley N Yorks 159 D4
Yeaton Shrops 110 D3
Yeaveley Derbys 113 A5
Yedingham N Yorks 160 D2
Yeldon Beds 84 A2
Yelford Oxon 65 C4
Yelland Devon 25 B5
Yelling Cambs 85 A4
Yelvertoft Northants 98 D2
Yelverton Devon 7 A4
Yelverton Norf 104 A3
Yenston Som 29 C7
Yeo Mill Devon 26 C3
Yeoford Devon 10 A4
Yeolmbridge Corn 10 C4
Yeovil Som 29 D5
Yeovil Marsh Som 29 D5
Yeovilton Som 29 C5
Yerbeston Pembs 55 D6
Yesnaby Orkney 282 F3
Yetlington Northumb 188 C3
Yetminster Dorset 29 D5
Yettington Devon 13 C5
Yetts o'Muckhart Clack 219 D5
Yieldshields S Lnrk 194 A3
Yiewsley London 48 A3
Ynys-meudwy Neath 59 E4
Ynysboeth Rhondda 41 B5
Ynysddu Caerph 41 B6
Ynysgyfflog Gwyn 90 A4
Ynyshir Rhondda 41 B5
Ynyslas Ceredig 90 C4
Ynystawe Swansea 40 A1
Ynysybwl Rhondda 41 B5
Yockenthwaite N Yorks 156 D3
Yockleton Shrops 110 D2
Yokefleet E Yorks 141 A6
Yoker Glasgow 205 B5
Yonder Bognie Aberds 255 B6
York York 149 B4
York Castle Museum
  York 149 B4
York Minster York 149 B5
York Racecourse York 149 B4
York Town Sur 47 C6
Yorkletts Kent 52 C2
Yorkley Glos 62 C2
Yorkshire Museum York 149 B4
Yorkshire Sculpture
  Park, Wakefield
  W Yorks 139 B5
Yorton Shrops 111 C4
Youlgreave Derbys 130 C2
Youlstone Devon 24 D3
Youlthorpe E Yorks 149 B6
Youlton N Yorks 148 A3
Young Wood Lincs 133 B6
Young's End Essex 70 B1
Yoxall Staffs 113 D5
Yoxford Suff 89 A4
Yr Hôb = Hope Flint 126 D3
Yr Wyddgrug = Mold
  Flint 126 C2
Ysbyty-Cynfyn Ceredig 75 A6
Ysbyty Ifan Conwy 108 A3
Ysbyty Ystwyth Ceredig 75 A6
Ysceifiog Flint 125 B6
Yspitty Carms 57 C5
Ystalyfera Neath 59 E4
Ystrad Rhondda 41 B4
Ystrad Aeron Ceredig 75 C4
Ystrad-mynach Caerph 41 B6
Ystradfellte Powys 59 D6
Ystradffin Carms 76 C1
Ystradgynlais Powys 59 D4
Ystradmeurig Ceredig 75 B6
Ystradowen Carms 59 D4
Ystradowen V Glam 41 D5
Ystumtuen Ceredig 75 A6
Ythanbank Aberds 257 C4
Ythanwells Aberds 256 C1
Ythsie Aberds 256 C3

Z

Zeal Monachorum Devon 12 A2
Zeals Wilts 30 B1
Zelah Corn 4 B3
Zennor Corn 2 B2

PHILIP'S MAPS
the Gold Standard for drivers

◆ **Philip's street atlases cover every county
in England, Wales and much of Scotland**

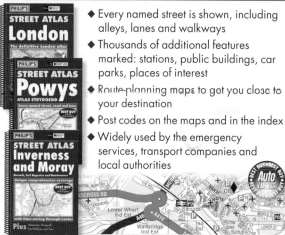

- ◆ Every named street is shown, including alleys, lanes and walkways
- ◆ Thousands of additional features marked: stations, public buildings, car parks, places of interest
- ◆ Route-planning maps to got you close to your destination
- ◆ Post codes on the maps and in the index
- ◆ Widely used by the emergency services, transport companies and local authorities

How to order
Philip's maps and atlases are available from bookshops, motorway services and petrol stations. You can order direct from the publisher by phoning **01903 828503** or online at **www.philips-maps.co.uk** For bulk orders only, phone 020 7644 6940

Street atlases currently available

England		Scotland
Bedfordshire	Greater Manchester	Ceredigion and South Gwynedd
Berkshire	Merseyside	Denbighshire, Flintshire, Wrexham
Birmingham and West Midlands	Norfolk	Herefordshire Monmouthshire
Bristol and Bath	Northamptonshire	Powys
Buckinghamshire	Northumberland	
Cambridgeshire	Nottinghamshire	**Scotland**
Cheshire	Oxfordshire	Aberdeenshire
Cornwall	Shropshire	Ayrshire
Cumbria	Somerset	Dumfries and Galloway
Derbyshire	Staffordshire	Edinburgh & East Central Scotland
Devon	Suffolk	Fife and Tayside
Dorset	Surrey	Glasgow West Central Scotland
County Durham and Teesside	East Sussex	Inverness & Moray
Essex	West Sussex	Lanarkshire
North Essex	Tyne and Wear	Scottish Borders
South Essex	Warwickshire	
Gloucestershire	Birmingham and West Midlands	**Northern Ireland***
Hampshire	Wiltshire and Swindon	County Armagh and County Down
North Hampshire	Worcestershire	Belfast
South Hampshire	East Yorkshire	County Londonderry and County Antrim
Herefordshire Monmouthshire	Northern Lincolnshire	County Tyrone and County Fermanagh
Hertfordshire	North Yorkshire	*Publishing autumn 2006
Isle of Wight	South Yorkshire	
Kent	West Yorkshire	
East Kent		
West Kent	**Wales**	
Lancashire	Anglesey, Conwy and Gwynedd	
Leicestershire and Rutland	Cardiff, Swansea and The Valleys	
Lincolnshire	Carmarthenshire, Pembrokeshire and Swansea	
London		

A Skill for Life
An estimated 11,000 car drivers will be killed or seriously injured this year. Don't be one of them.

By raising your driving skills to the standard of the Advanced Test, you will be better equipped to help safeguard the lives of yourself, your family and friends, and even people you have never met.

The IAM is a nationwide charity providing an advanced driving course for just £85.

visit **www.iam.org.uk**
or call **020 8996 9600**